Corporate Information Systems Management
Text and Cases

Corporate Information Systems Management

Text and Cases

James I. Cash, Jr.
F. Warren McFarlan
James L. McKenney
Lynda M. Applegate

All of the
Graduate School of Business Administration
Harvard University

Third Edition

IRWIN

Burr Ridge, Illinois
Boston, Massachusetts
Sydney, Australia

This symbol indicates that the paper in this book is made from recycled paper. Its fiber content exceeds the recommended minimum of 50% waste paper fibers as specified by the EPA.

Senior sponsoring editor: Larry E. Alexander
Project editor: Karen Murphy
Production manager: Bob Lange
Designer: Larry J. Cope
Compositor: Carlisle Communications, Ltd.
Typeface: 10/12 Century Schoolbook
Printer: R.R. Donnelley & Sons Company

Library of Congress Cataloging-in-Publication Data

Corporate information systems management : text and cases / James

I. Cash, Jr. . . . [et al.].—3rd ed.

   p.   cm.

  Includes index.

  ISBN 0-256-08705-9

  1. Management information systems. I. Cash, James I.

T58.6.C674 1992

658.4′ 038 —dc20   91–44242

Printed in the United States of America
5 6 7 8 9 0 DOC 9 8 7 6 5 4

To Clemmie, Karen, Mary, Paul, and Christopher

Preface

Corporate Information Systems Management, Text and Cases, Third Edition, is written for students and managers who desire an overview of contemporary information systems technology (IT)—computer, telecommunications, and office systems—management. It explains the relevant issues of effective management of information services activities and highlights the areas of greatest potential application of the technology. No assumptions are made concerning the reader's experience in IT technology, but it is assumed that the reader has some course work or work experience in administration or management.

Our purpose is to provide perspective on the business management implications of the information explosion—as evidenced by the doubling of the number of volumes in the Library of Congress between 1933 and 1966, another doubling between 1967 and 1979, and yet another doubling by 1987. Huge leaps in the growth of scientific knowledge have stimulated a dramatic increase in the number of new products based on new information technologies. Ranging from the sophisticated super computer to the humble, ubiquitous facsimile machine, these products have impacted the very heart of a corporation's operations and will continue to do so. In many cases, the firm's competitiveness and its very survival are at stake. This growth, coupled with the increasing international nature of business, puts an enormous burden on the individual and the organization to keep abreast of events and to make intelligent decisions and plans. The broad objective of this book is to help individuals and their organizations to better adapt new technologies to their circumstances and thus to compete in their industry segments more effectively.

Since the first and second editions of this book appeared in 1983 and 1988, IT has continued to evolve. This Third Edition addresses this evolution by giving particular attention to the technology-enabled changes in corporation organization, control, response times, and costs. Its treatment of organizational issues as they relate to the development of IT resources has also been modified to deal with the new challenges posed by technologies. This book will help present and future managers to recognize and implement effective information services management.

Corporate Information Systems Management, Third Edition, is organized around a management audit of the information services activity. This management audit details all the questions that should be asked in identifying whether a firm is appropriately using and controlling IT. The book's text, examples, tables, and figures convey and illustrate key conceptual frameworks. Chapter 1 presents an overview of the key questions to ask in assessing the effectiveness of an IT activity. Chapter 2 then presents frameworks we have found useful for analyzing and structuring problems in the field. Subsequent chapters show how information technology can best be applied and how the IT activity can best be organized, planned, and controlled.

The material in this book is the outgrowth of directed field-based research we have conducted at the Harvard Business School since the early 1970s. We thank Dean John H. McArthur for making the time available for this work.

We are particularly indebted to the many firms and government organizations that provided us with much time and insight during the course of our research. All of the examples and concepts in this book are based on observation of actual practice. Without the cooperation of these organizations, it would have been impossible to prepare this Third Edition.

We are especially grateful for the many valuable suggestions and insights provided us by our Harvard Business School colleagues Donna Stoddard, Nancy Balaguer, Bill Bruns, Benn Konsynski, Jane Linder, John Sviokla, and Shoshana Zuboff as well as Associate Professor Eric Clemens of the Wharton School. In addition, we acknowledge the valuable work of doctoral students Jim McGee, Poppy McLeod, Charley Osborn, Keri Ostrofski, Jeff Smith, Arthur Warbelow, and Kathleen Curley. Lynn Salerno and Bernard Avishai, in their editorial capacity at the *Harvard Business Review,* provided valuable assistance. We would also like to express our appreciation to Judith Tully, Maureen Donovan, and Nancy Hayes, who typed and edited numerous versions of the work.

James I. Cash, Jr.
F. Warren McFarlan
James L. McKenney
Lynda M. Applegate

Contents

Corporate Information Systems Management
Text and Cases

Chapter 1

The Challenge of Information Systems Technology

INTRODUCTION TO IT MANAGEMENT

Over the past 30 years, a major set of managerial challenges has been created by the rapid evolution and spread of information systems technology (IT), which in this book is defined to include the technologies of computers, telecommunications, and office automation. To deal with these challenges, new departments have been created, massive recruiting of new types of staff has occurred, major investments have been made in computer hardware and software, and systems have been installed that have profoundly affected how firms operate and compete. IT's impact has not been confined to large corporations; in its current form, it influences mid-size and very small (that is, under $1 million in sales) firms as well. Further, its influence in large corporations has been pervasive, reaching into the smallest departments and into managerial decision-making processes to an extent not even visualized 10 years ago.

Dealing with these challenges is complex because many members of corporate senior management received their education and early work experience before the wide-scale introduction of computer technology or in environments where the capabilities of information technologies were widely different from what they are today. Consequently, many of these people feel somewhat uneasy about the subject (legitimately so) and lack sufficient grasp of the issues to provide appropriate managerial direction. Many IT managers face similar problems, since their initial and technical experience was with technologies so different from those of the 1990s that their early experience is of little practical value. Understanding the programming challenges caused by the rotational delay of the drum on an IBM 650 (a popular machine in the late 1950s) has no value in dealing with the challenges posed by the sophisticated computer operating systems, local area networks, computer-assisted software-engineering tools, and other technologies of the 1990s.

Further, the identification of what makes effective management practice in the IT field has changed dramatically since 1976, when the personal computer first appeared and AT&T was reorganized. Virtually all major, currently accepted conceptual frameworks for theories of management in this field have been developed since 1976. Therefore, a special burden has been placed on IT management, not just for meeting day-to-day operating problems and new technologies but for assimilating and implementing quite different methods for managing the activity. IT managers who are not committed to continuing self-renewal very quickly become obsolete.

This book is aimed at two quite different corporate audiences. The first is corporate general managers who are collectively responsible for providing general guidance for all activities, including IT. For these readers, this book offers frameworks for evaluating the IT activity in their firm, defines policies that must be executed, and provides insights on the specific challenges of execution. It will help them to integrate IT and its management challenge with the overall activities of the firm.

The book's second audience is senior IT management. For these readers, this book provides an integrated view of the totality of IT management issues for the 1990s. Key patterns that organize and make sense out of a bewildering cluster of operational detail are identified. The focus for these senior managers is to move from analysis of "bark composition" of individual "trees" to an overall perspective of the IT "forest" and its management challenge. The book thus integrates the needs of two quite different—though operationally interdependent—audiences and provides them with a set of common perspectives and a language system for communicating with each other.

It would be a serious mistake, of course, to think of the problems of IT management as totally different from those found in other management settings. While the authors freely admit to having spent most of their professional lives dealing with IT technical and managerial issues, their thinking has been shaped by literature dealing with general business. The issues of IT organization, for example, are best thought of as special applications of the work on integration and differentiation begun by the behaviorists Paul Lawrence and Jay Lorsch. Issues of IT strategy formulation are influenced on the one hand by the work of Michael Porter and Alfred Chandler in business policy and on the other hand by that of Kirby Warren and Richard Vancil in the area of planning. Notions of budgeting, zero-based budgeting, transfer pricing, profit centers, and so forth, from the general field of management control are relevant here. The work of Richard Rosenbloom, Robert Hayes, Kim Clark, and Steve Wheelwright in the areas of management of technology has shed light on how the computer operations function can be better managed.

Concepts of IT Management

Many individual aspects of IT management challenges thus are not unique. What *is* unique is the peculiar *confluence* of these challenges, which must be resolved if an organization is to be effectively supported by IT in the long term. In thinking about this, the authors have sometimes found it useful to regard IT as a business within a business. Integrating the IT "business" into the rest of the firm poses many organizational and strategy-formulating challenges. Four concepts that permeate this book relate to how this kind of integrated IT business can be better managed. They are explained here.

Strategic Relevance.   The strategic impact of the IT activity varies among industries and firms and, over time, within an individual firm. Further, it is more significant to some operating units and functions within a company than to others. This notion of differing strategic relevance is critical in understanding the wide diversity of potential practices that can be used to manage and integrate IT within a firm.

Corporate Culture.   *Within a business* corporate culture is a phrase that must be stressed when attempting to identify how the IT business should be managed. The values of a firm's senior management, the firm's approach to corporate planning, its philosophy of control, and the speed of technological change in its core products all influence how the IT business should be managed. Of course, there are also generic tools such as databases, management systems for example, that should permeate all environments. Combining these generic tools with the values, culture, and processes of a particular firm is the art of management. A combination that works in one corporate environment can fail abysmally in another.

Contingency.   IT management in the 1990s is much more influenced by notions of contingency than it was in the 1970s and 1980s. In the 1970s IT management systems were implemented in settings where sheer chaos had existed. Consequently, simplistic and mechanistic approaches to work organization, management control, and planning were a great improvement over what was there before. As these new approaches and tools were assimilated into the firm, the initial surge of value from their introduction gave way to frustration in many cases because of their inherent rigidity. They answered some types of challenges very well and others not at all. For example, the emergence of PCs in the 1980s freed up constraints by permitting new types of networking possibilities, which in turn posed challenges to previously installed tools and structures. These factors combined to require more complexity and flexibility in the management approaches and tools to enable them to better fit the needs of a complex, changing environment. As we face the challenge of managing the diffusion, particularly of intelligent terminals with mainframe power, the situation will become more important.

Technology Transfer.   The diffusion of information technology can and must be managed. If it is poorly managed, IT will evolve not into a well-functioning system but, instead, into a collection of disjointed islands of technology that pass data between each other only with great difficulty. Since IT can now change the very infrastructure of how an organization functions, the implementation problems are very difficult. Success only comes when people are able to change their old habits and thinking processes. Hence we must think of IT as an "intellectual technology." Without concomitant change in thinking when a new system is installed, technical success is likely to be accompanied by administrative failure.

CHALLENGES IN IT MANAGEMENT

A number of other factors make the assimilation of IT a particularly challenging task. An understanding of these factors is essential if a sensible IT management strategy is to be developed. The more important of these factors are enumerated here.

A Young Technology

At least in its modern form (with high-speed computers), IT has had a very short life; its earliest commercial application occurred in 1952. Forty years is a very short time for the distilled outline of a new management profession to develop. Fields like management policy, accounting, finance, and production had thriving bodies of literature and know-how in place by 1930. Incredible amounts of knowledge and changes in thinking have occurred in these fields in this century, but they could be assimilated within an organized field of thought. Evolution, not revolution, has been the challenge in these fields. The challenge in IT, conversely, has been that of developing from a zero base during a period when its applications have grown from narrow and specialized to broad and integrated—with budgets and staffs that have been exploding in size.

Not surprisingly, the half-life of administrative knowledge in this environment has been quite short. No framework or avenue of thinking in this book predates 1973 in a published form, and most currently useful theories were developed in the late 1970s or later. Indeed, this Third Edition differs markedly from its predecessor, which was published only four years earlier. (The authors are under no illusion that this edition will be the last word on the subject and hope to contribute to better insights through further research.)

Technological Growth

Another source of administrative challenge lies in the fact that the field has undergone sustained and dramatic growth in the cost performance of its technologies. Over a billionfold improvement in processing and storage capacity has occurred since 1953, and the rate of change is expected to continue through the 1990s and early 21st century. (As with all technologies, a point of maturity will be reached, but we are not yet there.) Further complicating this, some core technologies—such as CPU size and speed—have grown explosively, while others such as software development tools have grown much more slowly.

This technical explosion has continuously cast up new families of profitable applications and permitted old ones to be done in new ways. One painful aspect of this has been that yesterday's strategic coup (a dramatic set of new customer service tools) may be today's high-overhead, inefficient liability (outperformed by those that followed and improved on the design). The natural tendency to utilize a particular approach too long has been exacerbated by the prevailing accounting practice of writing off software expense as it is incurred, rather than capitalizing it and amortizing it over a period of years. These practices conceal two facts: (1) that the organization has an asset, and (2) that it is an aging and often very inefficient asset.

IT—User Coordination

The complexities associated with developing IT systems have forced the creation of departments filled with specialists that continue to persist although many of the reasons for their existence have disappeared. Today data center consolidation, distributing development staff, and out-sourcing dominate debate on the organization of IT resources. Very often these specialist departments with their specialized vocabularies have created strained relationships with the users of their service. This has been an enduring headache from the start of IT. While the proliferation of desktop PCs, local area networks, and departmental minicomputers has changed the nature of the dialogue, there is probably no better example of C. P. Snow's technocrat-versus-generalist problem in the 1990s than the relationship between IT staff and general management.

IT has specialized in order to harness the various technical skills necessary for accomplishing its tasks, and not surprisingly, the specialists have developed their own language systems. To communicate among each other, they use words such as *bits, bytes, DOS, CICS,* and so on, which are totally opaque to general managers. General managers, conversely, have a quite different language that includes such terms as *sales growth, return on investment,* and *productivity,* terms that are opaque to the IT specialists. While it is clear that some of the newer technologies (such as object-oriented programming languages and spreadsheet programming languages) have helped IT specialist–user communication, substantial problems remain. A long-term need will exist for continually developing new integrating devices within firms to help handle the problem.

For numerous reasons, education will continue to address the technical versus generalist gap only partially. The experiences college and high-school students have in writing one-time, problem-solving programs and using PC-based word-processing packages, while useful and confidence expanding, develop a very different set of skills than those skills necessary to generate programs for processing business transactions reliably on a day-in, day-out basis. Similarly, experience in preparing spreadsheet programs as a staff analyst or in working with a word-processing package do not provide necessary perspective on the issues involved in large-transaction processing and data-base management systems. Unfortunately, education often fails to acknowledge these differences and produces graduates who are ill-trained for these tasks, do not know they are ill-trained, and thus have excessive self-confidence. Another educational issue is that some general managers are cognitively better equipped to deal with information technology issues than others. One of our colleagues describes the world's people as being equally divided into "poets" and "engineers." This split seems to prevail in general management as well.

Specialization

The increased complexity of contemporary technology has created a number of subspecialties. This explosion of skills needed for staffing IT has posed a fourth major managerial challenge. As IT has evolved, it has proliferated languages, data-base management systems, tele-communications issues, and operating systems support staff. All of this has increased the complexity of staff coordination within the organization.

Shift in Focus

A fifth challenge is the significant shift in the types of applications being developed. Early applications were heavily focused on highly structured problems, such as transaction processing for payroll and order processing, in which one could be quite precise about the potential stream of benefits and the nature of the end outputs. These applications automated clerical and operational control functions, such as inventory management, airline seat reservations, and credit extension. In the case of airline seat reservations, the shift led to a level of structure and decision rules not previously present and it sharply increased customer service.

Increasingly, today's applications are providing new types of decision support information for both management control and strategic planning. Evaluation of the payout of these expenditures on an objective basis before, during, or after they are expended is extraordinarily difficult and judgmental. Individuals may have opinions about these values, but meaningful quantification is very elusive.

Additionally, the development of these decision support applications differs from that of the transaction-driven systems. The detailed systems study, with its documentation and controls prior to programming, is often too rigid and fails to build the end-user commitment necessary for success. For these decision support systems, prototyping or doing it "rough and dirty" is proving to be the best approach. In short, new applications are forcing shifts in the ways projects are evaluated and in the ways they are developed. This is not an argument for a more permissive approach to system design and evaluation but, rather, a cry to be tough-minded in a positive way.

In combination, these factors create a very complex and challenging managerial environment. They form the backdrop for the discussions of specific managerial approaches in the succeeding chapters.

QUESTIONS FROM SENIOR MANAGEMENT

In viewing the health of an organization's IT activity, our research indicated that six critical questions repeatedly emerge in senior management's minds. We will not argue at this stage that these are the questions that *should* be raised but, rather, note that they are the questions that *are* raised. Four of these questions are essentially diagnostic in nature, whereas the remaining two are clearly action oriented.

1. Is my firm being affected *competitively* either by omissions in IT work being done or by poor execution of this work? Am I missing bets that, if properly executed, would give me a competitive edge? Conversely, maybe I am not doing so well in IT, but I don't have to do well in IT in my industry to be a success. Failure to do well in a competitively important area is a significant problem. Failure to perform well in a nonstrategic area is something that should be dealt with more calmly.

2. Is my development portfolio *effective*? Am I spending the right amount of money, and is it focused at the appropriate applications? This question is one that is often inappropriately raised. Scenario: An industry survey calculating IT expenditures as a percent of something or other for 15 industry competitors is circulated among the firm's senior management. On one dimension or another, it is observed that their firm is distinctly different from the others, which causes great excitement (normally, when their firm's figures are on the high side). After much investigation, one of two findings often emerges: (a) Our company uses a different accounting system for IT than our competitors use, and therefore the numbers are not directly comparable, or (b) Our company has a different strategy, geographical location, and/or mix of management strengths and weaknesses than our competitors, and therefore, what competitors are or are not doing with IT is not directly comparable.

   Raising the question of effectiveness is appropriate, in our judgment, but attempting to answer it simplistically through industry surveys of competitors' expenditures is not. Similarly, rules of thumb on expenditure levels a decade ago are virtually useless in today's environment, where very different technology labor cost tradeoffs are possible. For example, a fast-food chain is now exploring a set of technologies that would eliminate the need for up to 90 percent of its staff in a store. The approach was not viable even three years ago.

3. Is my firm spending *efficiently*? Maybe I have the right expenditure level, but am I getting the productivity out of my hardware and staff resources that I should get? This is a particularly relevant question in the 1990s, a decade that will be dominated both by extreme levels of professional staff shortages and by intensified international competition.

4. Is my firm's IT activity sufficiently insulated against the *risks* of a major *operational disaster*? There is no general-purpose answer as

to what an appropriate level of protection is. Rather, it varies by organization, relating to the current dependence on the smooth operation of existing systems. In general, however, firms are *much* more operationally dependent on IT's smooth performance than their general managers believe.

5. Is the *leadership* of IT activity being exercised appropriately for the role it now plays in our organization and for the special challenges it now faces? Historically, senior general management has used change of IT management as its main tool in dealing with frustrating IT performance shortfalls. (This high turnover has continued unabated into the 1990s.) One key reason for this is that it represents the quickest and apparently easiest step for senior management when it is uneasy about departmental performance. Also, as we note in Chapter 2, the nature of the job and its requisite skills tend to evolve over time, and the set of leadership skills and perspectives for one point in time may not be appropriate for another. Further, in many situations the problem is compounded by a lack of suitable explicit performance-measurement standards (metrics) and data for assessing performance objectively. As will be discussed in subsequent chapters, we believe the development and installation of these metrics is absolutely vital. In the absence of these metrics a 50 percent improvement in the firm's ability to meet service schedules, for example, may be totally overlooked by the end users. Their articulated concerns about remaining problems are simply amplified, so the managerial situation is judged not to have changed.

6. Are the IT resources *appropriately* placed in the firm? Organizational issues such as where the IT resource should report, how development and hardware resources should be distributed within the company, what activities, if any, should be out-sourced, and the existence and potential role of an executive steering committee are examples of topics of intense interest to senior management. Easily actionable, they are similar in breadth to decisions made by general managers in other aspects of the firm's operations.

These questions are intuitive from the viewpoint of general managers and flow naturally from their perspective and experience in dealing with other areas of the firm. We have not found them, as stated, to be easily researchable or answerable in specific situations and have consequently neither selected them as the basic framework for this book nor attempted to describe specifically how each can be answered. Rather, we selected a complementary set of questions that form the outline for the book and whose answers will give insight into these six questions. The next section briefly summarizes these questions and relates them to the content of this book.

ISSUES IN INFORMATION TECHNOLOGY

The IT Environment

Chapters 2, 3, 4, 5, and 6 define a role for IT in the 1990s that is very different from its uses in the 1970s. One way of describing this new role is illustrated in the chart in Figure 1–1. The chart explains the changing environment by focusing on three items: the administrative framework for facilitating and controlling the assimilation of information technology, the primary target of IT applications, and the way IT applications have been justified.

Era I.   From the 1950s to the early 1970s the manager of data processing was the single source of computing cycles and technology expertise. To use an industrial analogy, IT operated as a "regulated monopoly." If someone wanted access to computing cycles and technology expertise, he or she had to go to the data processing manager. There was no alternative. The primary focus of applications was organization-wide (payroll, accounting, production scheduling, order entry). New applications were justified on either a cost-elimination or cost-displacement basis. We call this IT management environment *ERA I.*

Era II.   Era II began with the introduction of minicomputers and time-sharing in the early 1970s. It was dramatically accelerated in the late 1970s by the personal computer. Suddenly a wide range of new channels was introduced for users to acquire technology expertise, processing cycles, and software. This introduced a "free market" (at least, relatively; users no longer had to go to the IT manager to gain access to computer and communications technology). Today's M.B.A. graduates often enter a company bringing with them a computer that has 20 times the capability of an early computer at 0.5 percent the price. In Era II's free-market arena, the rigid top-down controls developed and implemented in Era I were no longer applicable. At this point for many applications, the individual was the primary decision maker and had sufficient discretionary resources to reinforce that independence, and not deal with the central IT function unless they wanted to.

During this period a dramatic shift occurred in project justification. Individual and corporate *effectiveness* became the key justification measure. Era-I applications and their administrative systems could not and did not disappear. Rather, the IT management environment was made more complex with the additional challenge of managing easily accessible, individually exploited technology concurrently with Era-I technology.

Era III.   In what we designate the third era of information technology, management again did not preempt prior applications, although it

FIGURE 1–1   The IT Environment

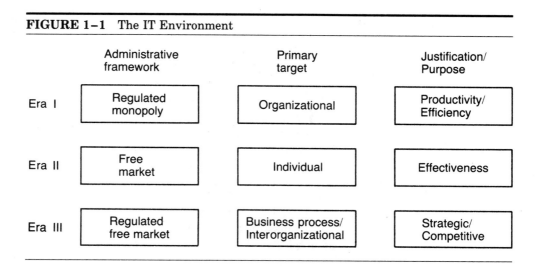

forced important changes in administrative processes. Era III is best distinguished on the basis of the justification/purpose column in Figure 1–1. A growing number of companies have used IT to cause significant shifts in market share, competitive positioning, and organizational restructuring. As we examine the administrative framework for these companies, it becomes clear they are not at one end of the regulated versus free-market spectrum or the other. They have attempted to create a "regulated free-market environment" where the primary objective is exploiting the awareness, knowledge, and expertise generated during Era II to innovate and create dramatically different approaches to the conduct of business based on the capability of IT. Frequently these uses of technology transcend traditional company or industry boundaries and/or facilitate restructuring internal organizations and functions. Dealing with these issues makes IT strategy, on balance, much more important than it was a decade ago.

Organization

Chapters 7 and 8 are most closely aligned to the senior management questions 5 and 6 listed earlier in this chapter relating to the leadership and organization of the IT activity. Several main themes are addressed in those chapters. First and foremost, what is an appropriate way to think about the architecture of the distribution of hardware networks, software development resources, and data bases within the corporation? The issues of patterns of distributed resources have been well studied, and appropriate ways of thinking about them continue to be developed as new technology capabilities emerge. These issues go well beyond the technology itself and are heavily contingent on such influences as corporate organization, corporate culture, leadership style of the chief executive officer (CEO), importance of IT to achievement of corporate goals, and current sophistication of IT management. Surrounding the selected architecture of distributed and networked resources, there is need for central administrative policies to ensure that suitable overall direction is being maintained. The nature, intensity, and criticality of this direction varies widely among settings.

A second theme is ensuring that IT is broadly enough defined and that the converging and increasingly integrated technologies of computing, telecommunications, and word processing are in fact being adequately integrated. International coordination issues are much more complicated than those in the domestic arena. **Chapter 12** is devoted to discussing the coordination issues posed by different national infrastructures: staff availability, level of telecommunications sophistication, specific vendor support, great geographic distance, different spoken languages, transborder data flows, national culture and sensitivity, and so forth.

Finally, issues of organization reporting chains, level of reporting, IT leadership style, and other coordinating processes are also of concern. We believe there are better ways to think about these issues in the 1990s than there were a decade ago. Although common questions and methods of analysis exist, very different answers will emerge in different organizational settings.

Appropriate controls over daily IT operations as described in **Chapter 11** ensure that both cost efficiency and operations reliability are being achieved. The IT operations activity represents a very specialized form of manufacturing environment with some unique problems. First, operations have moved from primarily a batch, job-shop style to a continuous-process manufacturing or utility style. Not only has this changed the way these tasks can best be organized, but it has dramatically altered the types of controls that are appropriate. Second, in a number of firms, the IT activity has embedded itself so deeply in the heart of the firm's operations that unevenness in its performance causes immediate operating problems. These firms need significantly greater controls and back-up arrangements than firms with less dependence on IT.

The performance of operations can be measured on a number of dimensions. Cost control, ability to meet batch report deadlines, peak-load response time, and speed of response to complaints or unexpected requests are examples of these dimensions. To optimize all of these simultaneously is impossible. Each firm needs a clear identification and prioritization of these items before it can come up with a coherent operations strategy. Different firms will have quite different priorities; hence, a search for a universal IT operations strategy and set of management tools represents a fruitless quest.

Management Control

The questions of efficiency and, to a lesser degree, those of effectiveness are best addressed by ensuring that an appropriate IT management-control structure and process, as discussed in **Chapter 9**, are in place. Planning's role is to ensure that long-term direction is spelled out and that steps are taken to acquire the necessary hardware/staff resources to implement it. The role of management control is to ensure that the appropriate short-term resource-allocation decisions are made and that acquired resources are being utilized efficiently. The key issues in this field include the following:

1. Establishing an appropriate balance between user and IT responsibility for costs. Establishment of IT as a managed cost center, profit center, and so on, is a critical strategic decision for an organization, as is the election of an appropriate IT transfer-pricing policy to go along with it. Again, not only does this policy appropriately change over time, but it varies by type of organization as well.
2. Identification of an appropriate budgeting policy for IT. While many components of the IT budget are either fixed or transaction-driven, others are discretionary. These discretionary components need to be examined to ensure both that they are still being allocated to essential missions and that an appropriate balance is struck between the needs of many legitimate end users. This balance is necessary in a world where financial resources for projects are limited and where project benefits in many cases are not easily quantifiable.
3. A need for a regular weekly and monthly performance reporting. Reporting should reflect performance against goals and also against objective standards wherever possible. Unfortunately, the move of IT operations from primarily a batch activity to an on-line or networked activity not only reduces the territory for objective standard setting, but has made many of the older approaches obsolete.

Project Management

The questions of efficiency and effectiveness are also addressed through analysis of the project management process in **Chapter 10**. The 1980s generated a plethora of so-called project management processes and methodologies that have helped to rationalize a formerly very diverse area. The installation of these methodologies, an obvious improvement, has created a new set of opportunities.

The first opportunity lies in the area of implementation risk. The advocates of these methodologies have implied that by utilizing their approach, implementation risk will be eliminated. A careful examination of the long list of partial and major project fiascoes in the past decade suggests clearly that this is not the case. As described in Chapter 10, our contention is that project implementation risk not only exists but can be measured, and a decision can be made regarding its acceptability long before the majority of funds must be committed to a project development effort. In the same vein, it is possible and appropriate to talk about the aggregate-implementation-risk profile of the development and maintenance portfolio of projects. Not only does implementation-risk information provide a better language between general management, user management, and IT management during the project planning phase (where many options can be considered), but it provides a firmer and more valid context for after-the-fact performance assessment.

The second opportunity exists in the recognition that different types of projects are best attacked by quite different management methodologies. A single methodology is usually an improvement over the anarchy and chaos that often precede its introduction. Several years of its use, however, can create a straitjacket environment. A single approach may fit one kind of project very well and others considerably less well. Organization structure within a project team, types of user interfaces, leadership skill, and planning and control approaches legitimately differ by type of project. Today it is clear that the most appropriate management approach for any project should flow out of the project's innate characteristics. (That is, tell me something about the project, and then we can select an appropriate management approach.)

IT Strategy

"Is my firm competitive and effectively focused on the right questions?" We believe this question is best answered by looking carefully at the IT strategy formulation process covered in **Chapter 13**. The design and evolution of this process has turned out to be much more complicated than anticipated in the early 1980s, when some fairly prescriptive ways of dealing with it were identified. Elements creating this complexity can be classified in three general categories.

1. The first is an increased recognition that, at any time, IT plays very different strategic roles in different companies. These strategic roles significantly influence both the structure of the planning process (who should be involved, the level of time and financial resources to be devoted to it, and so on) and its interconnection to the corporate strategy and formulation processes. Where new developments are critical to the introduction of new products and to achievement of major operating efficiencies or speeded-up compet-

itive response times, firms must devote significantly more senior management time to this direction setting than in firms where this is not the case.

2. The second category of issues relates to IT and user familiarity with the nuances of the specific technologies being examined. Applications of technologies with which both IT and user staffs have extensive experience can be planned in considerable detail and with great confidence. To IT and/or the users, the newer technologies pose very different problems, both as to why planning is being done and how it can best be done. In any given year, a company will be dealing with a mix of older and newer technologies that complicates the strategy formulation task tremendously.

3. The third category of issues relates to the matter of the specific corporate culture. The nature of the corporate planning process, formality versus informality of organizational decision making and planning, and geographic and organizational distance of IT management from senior management all influence how IT planning can best be done. These issues suggest that, as important as IT planning is, it must be evolutionary and highly individualistic to fit the specific corporation.

The IT Business

Chapter 14, the last chapter, integrates this discussion by considering the challenge of managing IT development and diffusion from the perspective of a business within a business. In that chapter, we emphasize the present marketing posture of the IT business.

We see the early years of IT as unavoidably captured by the term *R&D:* "Can it work, and can we learn to make it work?" Subsequent years were characterized by start-up production: "Can large projects be managed in a way that will create useful, reliable services in a period of rapid growth when technology is new and changing?" We learned to manage a service organization with a rapidly evolving technology, and applications proliferated. Today's environment is characterized by focused marketing. The challenge is to blend, in a thoughtful manner, new product opportunities posed by new technologies with new customers.

CONCLUSION

This chapter has identified, from a managerial viewpoint, the key forces shaping the IT environment, senior management's most frequent questions in assessing the activity, and the questions that we think are most useful in diagnosing the situation and taking corrective action. In this final section, we would like to leave you with a set of questions that we believe both IT management and general management should ask on a periodic basis—every six months or so. They are a distillation of the previous analysis and, we believe, a useful managerial shorthand.

1. Do the perspective and skills of my IT and general management team fit the firm's changing applications thrust, operations challenges, user environment, and often shift in strategic relevance? There are no absolute, for-all-time answers to these questions, only transitional ones.
2. Is the firm organized to identify, evaluate, and assimilate new information technologies? In this fast-moving field an internally focused, low-quality staff can generate severe problems. Unprofitable, unwitting obsolescence (from which it is hard to recover) is terribly easy here. There is no need for a firm to adopt leading-edge technology (indeed, many are ill equipped to do so), but it is inexcusable not to be aware of what the possibilities are.
3. Are the three main management systems for integrating the IT environment to the firm as a whole in place and implemented? These are the strategic planning system, the management control system, and the project management system.
4. Are the security, priority-setting, manufacturing-procedure, and change-control systems in the IT operations function appropriate for the role it now plays in my firm?
5. Are organization structures and linking mechanisms in place that will ensure informed senior-management guidance of IT-informed user innovation and appropriate insertion of IT realities?

To help you answer these questions, this book presents a framework for analysis that encompasses four organizing concepts: strategic relevance, corporate culture, contingent action planning, and managed IT technology transfer. In each of the areas of organization—strategic planning, management control, project management, and operations—we will be examining the concepts' implications for action. Realistically, we are moving today in a complicated milieu of people, differing organization strategies, different cultures, and changing technologies. We have taken up the task of identifying a sequence of frameworks that can allow better analysis of the problems and issues facing organizations in relation to IT. We rely upon readers to apply this discussion to their own business situations in formulating realistic action plans.

Case 1-1

XEROX CORPORATION: LEADERSHIP OF THE INFORMATION TECHNOLOGY FUNCTION (A)

Patricia (Tosh) Barron became director of Corporate Information Management (CIM), a corporate staff function that reported to Vice Chairman Bill Glavin, on June 1, 1987. "Our mission," said Barron of her organization,

> is to develop the information technology strategy for Xerox and ensure that the strategy is implemented in all of the business units. The CIM organization is small. At the end of 1987 there were approximately 25 people in the group. Of those, there are four managers who report directly to me. Our annual budget is approximately $4 million, derived from chargebacks to our internal customers.

Xerox executives viewed information technology as critical to their business. Xerox not only marketed information technology-based products, but also relied on information technology to enable management to reorganize the company and simplify critical business processes. According to Xerox CEO David Kearns,

> IS was once an independent slice of overhead, seemingly out of control, growing at 40 percent per year while the rest of the company grew at 20 percent. Today it is an integral part of Xerox's corporate strategy. The IS budget, about $500 million for people and hardware, now grows at 20 percent per year, with every penny of that growth offset by productivity increases.

By the end of January 1988, Barron and the CIM management team had reevaluated CIM's roles and responsibilities. A new CIM mission and responsibility statement was to be presented to Xerox President Paul Allaire on March 1. As she reviewed what had been put together, Barron wondered whether the new direction for CIM would provide the information technology leadership the corporation needed.

Company Background

Xerox was a multinational company that competed in the business products and systems and financial services markets. Its business products and systems segment developed, manufactured, marketed, and serviced a complete range of document-processing products and systems designed to make offices more productive. Its financial services businesses provided financial products and services primarily on a wholesale basis. They included a property and casualty insurer, a specialized investment banking firm, and a commercial and industrial financing unit. Exhibit 1 presents the organization of Xerox Corporation at the end of 1987, Exhibit 2 the company's financial statistics.

Research Associate Donna B. Stoddard prepared this case under the supervision of Professor Lynda M. Applegate as the basis for class discussion rather than to illustrate either effective or ineffective handling of an administrative situation.

EXHIBIT 1 Xerox Corporation: Leadership of the Information Technology Function (A) —
Corporate Organization

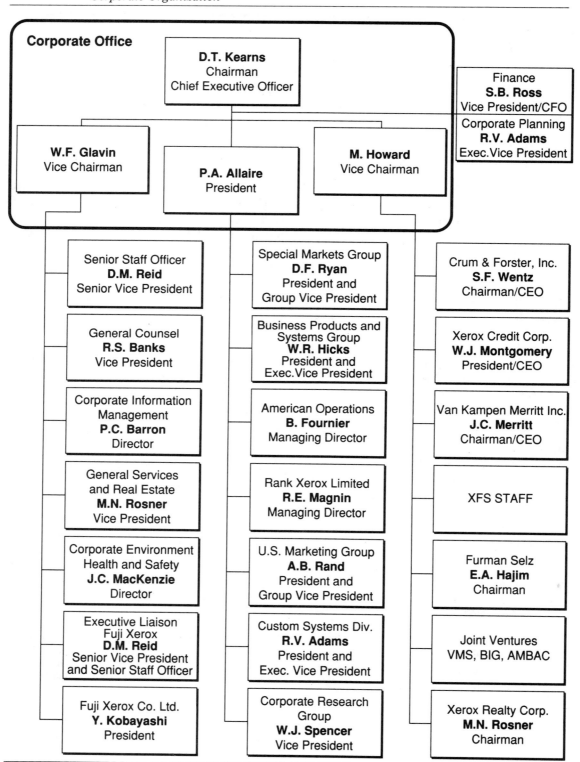

EXHIBIT 2 Xerox Corporation: Financial Highlights

Operations (millions)	1987	1986	1985	1984	1983	1982	1981	1980	1975	1970	1960
Operating revenues (rentals, sales, service)	10,320	9,355	8,676	8,374	8,464	8,456	8,510	8,037	4,140	1,690	40
Equity in net income of financial services	342	278	76	74	197	39	25	3	—	—	—
Research and development expenses	722	650	597	555	555	565	526	430	198	87	3
Income from continuing operations	578	488	381	362	466	368	572	553	346	210	
Income (loss) from discontinued operations		−65	94	−71	—	56	26	12	−98	−18	
Net income	578	465	475	291	466	424	598	565	248	192	3
Financial position (millions)											
Current assets	4,459	3,973	3,901	3,739	3,655	3,814	3,616	3,560	1,741	842	15
Rental equipment and related inventories	2,597	2,951	3,401	3,799	3,987	4,196	4,621	4,845	2,592	1,328	6
Investment in financial services businesses, at equity	2,667	2,530	2,121	2,175	2,017	225	161	79	—	—	—
Total assets	11,598	10,608	9,817	9,537	9,297	7,668	7,674	7,514	4,765	1,929	56
Current liabilities	2,850	2,206	2,215	2,451	2,306	2,175	2,081	2,085	1,172	510	11
Long-term debt	1,539	1,730	1,583	1,614	1,461	850	870	898	1,317	382	5
Shareholders equity	5,105	4,687	4,386	4,101	4,222	3,724	3,728	3,630	1,947	918	29
Per share											
Net income per common share	$5.35	$4.52	$3.47	$3.28	$4.50	$4.06	$7.08	$6.69	$2.98	$2.33	$0.13
Dividends per common share	$3.00	$3.00	$3.00	$3.00	$3.00	$3.00	$3.00	$2.80	$1.00	$0.65	$0.05
Employees at year-end	99,032	100,367	101,636	100,146	97,778	103,275	117,930	117,247	96,632	59,267	2,973

Results for 1986 include $42 million ($0.43 per common share) for the cumulative effect on prior years of change in accounting for pension costs. Financial results before 1983 are shown prior to restatement.

Source: Xerox Annual Reports.

19

Xerox's business priorities were simple: customer satisfaction, improved return on assets, and increased market share. (See Exhibit 3.) Said Kearns, "A commitment to quality must be our most basic value. And when I speak of quality I mean giving our customers, both internal and external, what they want and what they expect."[1]

Business Products and Systems

Business Products and Systems, considered Xerox's mainstay, employed a direct sales force and a growing network of dealers and distributors to market copiers, duplicators, electronic printers and typewriters, workstations, related products, software, and

---

EXHIBIT 3   Xerox Corporation: Corporate Philosophy and Guidelines

---

Corporate Philosophy

- We succeed through satisfied customers.
- We value our employees.
- We aspire to deliver excellence in all we do.
- We require premium return on assets.
- We use technology to develop product leadership.
- We behave responsibly as a corporate citizen.

Corporate Guidelines

- Every Xerox person will use the tools and processes of Leadership Through Quality to satisfy the requirements of our customers.
- We must do what's right for the customer and what's right for Xerox. In that order.
- We serve Xerox only if we serve the customer.
- Only by meeting the requirements of our customers can we improve ROA and market share.
- We depend on satisfied employees to produce satisfied customers.

---

supplies in more than 130 countries. In 1986, this segment accounted for revenue of $9.4 billion (72 percent of Xerox's total revenue), $7 billion of which was attributed to copier/duplicator sales and service.

Xerox literally invented the copier industry in 1959 with the announcement of its first product, the 914 copier. The 914 was a milestone in communications history, enabling people to share information inexpensively and easily. In the mid-1950s, 20 million copies were made annually in the United States using the elementary equipment of the day, primarily carbon paper and the Kodak Verifax process. In 1965, 9.5 billion copies were made. By 1985, more than 700 billion copies were being made annually, worldwide.[2]

The 1960s were boom years for Xerox. Just two years after the introduction of the 914, the company made the *Fortune 500* for the first time, ranking 423 in 1962. In 1963, it climbed to 295, and reached 32 in 1986. Xerox held the record for reaching $1 billion in sales faster than any company in American history. A Xerox executive was quoted as saying, "We were able to sell almost everything we made at whatever price we wanted to charge for it."[3]

With the expiration of key patents in 1970, Xerox finally had to face competition. IBM's introduction of its first office copying machine was followed, in 1975, by Kodak's first plain-paper copier. The Japanese also entered the U.S. copier market in the 1970s. But it wasn't until 1980 that Xerox finally realized just how good its Japanese competitors were. Senior management was horrified to learn that Japanese firms were selling their small machines for what it cost Xerox to manufacture its own. In the early

---

[1]Gary Jacobson and John Hillkirk, *Xerox American Samurai* (New York: Collier Books, 1986), p. 67.

[2]Ibid.
[3]Ibid., p. 8.

1980s, Xerox management began to work diligently to improve the company's competitive position.

Financial Services

Xerox entered the financial services arena in 1979 with the founding of Xerox Credit Corporation, whose major business was to provide financing for customers who wanted to buy Xerox office and systems products. Since its founding, Xerox Credit Corporation had become a full-service leasing and finance company.

Xerox acquired Crum and Forster, a property and casualty insurance company, in 1983, and Van Kampen Merritt, a specialized investment banking firm, in 1984. By the end of 1986, Van Kampen Merritt had become one of the nation's largest sponsors of insured unit investment trusts and one of the fastest growing mutual fund managers.

Xerox Financial Services was becoming an increasingly important part of Xerox Corporation. Though in 1986 it contributed only 28 percent of Xerox's total revenue, income from continuing operations generated by Xerox Financial Services topped $278 million, surpassing for the first time the $240 million profits generated by Business Products and Systems.[4]

Corporate Information Management

Corporate Information Management was established in the early 1970s to provide overall information technology leadership for the corporation.

Essentially, CIM had two sets of customers: Xerox corporate managers, and managers in the Business Products and Systems business units. (Because its systems did not need to be tightly integrated with those of

---

[4]Phillip Zweig, "A Pale Copy," *Financial World,* October 20, 1987, p. 20.

Business Products and Systems, Xerox management determined that Financial Services should only receive consulting services from CIM.)

Serving two sets of customers led CIM sometimes to feel that it was being pulled in two directions. "We [the CIM management team] often feel that we are walking a tightrope," explained Barron.

> Senior management expects CIM to *ensure* that the $500 million information technology budget is well spent. That implies an audit function which the business unit managers see as unnecessary.
>
> The CIM managers and I feel that the important role that we can play is that of advocate for information technology projects that the business units want funded. Also, we believe that it is important to ensure that the successful information technology projects get visibility in the corporation, both with senior management and with other business units. To fulfill our role effectively as information technology advocate, we must have the support and confidence of the business unit managers. We cannot be viewed as an adversary.

Senior management's expectations of CIM were summed up by Vice Chairman Bill Glavin. "We expect CIM to provide the overall information technology leadership to the company," said Glavin.

> We believe that information technology is a critical resource that can help us simplify our business processes and further streamline our organization. We believe that IT can help us gain competitive advantage.

The 25-person organization Barron inherited, shown in Exhibit 4, was committed to (1) supporting the business unit IT organizations by defining an overall IT architecture for Xerox and providing technical support when needed, and (2) providing IT support for corporate officers and their staffs.

EXHIBIT 4   Xerox Corporation: Existing CIM Organization

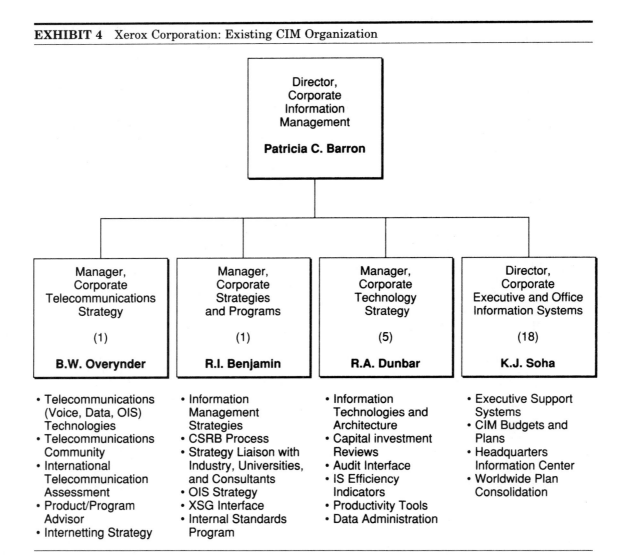

Four managers reported directly to Barron: Bob Benjamin, who had responsibility for strategic issues; Dick Dunbar, whose group was responsible for technology architecture and provided technical assistance to business units; Bernard Overynder, who was responsible for telecommunications; and Ken Soha, whose group provided applications development and end-user support for corporate officers and their staffs.

Strategies and Programs

Benjamin, the chief strategist in the group, worked with business units to identify critical issues that needed CIM's resources. He also worked with industry groups and with Xerox's Palo Alto Research Center (PARC), the company's research and development lab, to identify and ensure that Xerox exploited the capabilities of emerging technologies. One of Benjamin's key projects in

1987, the development of a Xerox strategy for planning, developing, and implementing knowledge-based systems, led to the approval of funding for a knowledge-based systems competency center.

Technology Strategy

The Technology Strategy group, under Dick Dunbar, was responsible for setting overall corporate technical strategy. Having been an IT manager in one of the business units before joining CIM in the early 1980s, Dunbar had credibility with the business unit IT managers. The Technology Strategy group worked successfully with the IT managers in the business units to define an information technology architecture that would protect Xerox's investment in software, allow for portability of applications on a multinational basis, facilitate the integration of business processes, and develop a critical mass of common skills. The technology architecture, adopted in the mid-1980s, provided standards for three levels of information processing.

- *General data processing* described the environment used for major business data processing applications. This type of environment supported multiple function, high-volume processing with integrated databases.
- *Distributed processing* environments were smaller, multi-use systems that provided dedicated processing for a specific business application or departmental work group.
- *Workstations and office information systems* provided local, single-user computing, document processing, input/output services, and related tasks.

Exhibit 5 describes the technology strategy for these levels of processing and for the network. Business requirements that called for systems that did not fit this architecture were reviewed by Dunbar's group.

Telecommunications Strategy

In carrying out his responsibility for defining the telecommunications architecture and standards for Xerox Corporation, Bernard Overynder worked closely with the telecommunications managers in the business units and foreign subsidiaries to ensure that resources, needed to facilitate communication among groups within Xerox and between Xerox and its customers and suppliers, were in place.

Executive and Office Information Systems

Ken Soha, as director of Corporate Executive and Office Information Systems, headed the one function under Barron that had the characteristics of a line organization. One of the major initiatives of this group, which provided application development support to corporate functions, was the development and operation of the executive support system (ESS), a combination of new management processes and electronic technology. ESS was the brainchild of Xerox President Paul Allaire, who began laying the groundwork for the system when he was chief staff officer.

"We wanted to change the way we ran the business, to make meetings more efficient, to ensure that our planning process was getting at the real issues and that we were making timely decisions based on the best available data," Allaire had said in *Benchmark,* an internal Xerox publication.

> Like a lot of other companies, we asked, "Are there any technological tools that can help us improve our way of operating?" We designed the ESS to provide those tools.

ESS was very easy to use, allowing executives to access critical information, mail it to other executives, or print it out on a network-linked Xerox laser printer with a few clicks of a mouse. Enhancements to ESS

EXHIBIT 5   Xerox Corporation: Technology Architecture

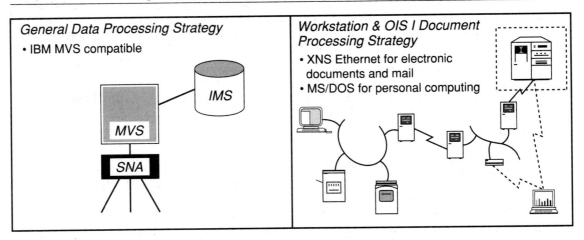

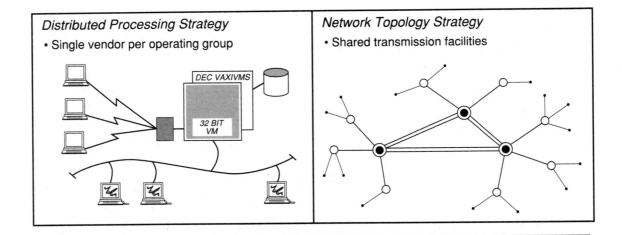

were a critical activity for Soha's group during 1988.

CIM extended its influence and capabilities within the business units through a number of task forces (see Exhibit 6), and CIM managers participated on business unit project teams that focused on critical business issues.

Don Stephenson, manager, computer integrated engineering and manufacturing systems within BPSG, commented on the role of CIM:

> Tosh and her group have the opportunity to make a significant contribution to the IS community in Xerox. Many of the strategic systems that we have identified cut across boundaries that exist within the company. A group like CIM can enable the development of these systems by defining the overall IS strategy and architecture and ensuring that

EXHIBIT 6   Xerox Corporation: CIM Task Forces

Task Force	Management Level	Charter
CISB (Corporate Information Systems Board)	Top management	Provide overall management guidance for information management function Approve strategies and policies Assess successful implementation of strategies
KBS (Knowledge-based Systems)	Senior management	Coordinate use of knowledge-based systems within Xerox Set strategies and policies Act as board of directors for KBS competency center
BIMC (Business Information Management Committee)	Senior IC management	Coordinate information management activities within function Develop joint programs Review strategies, architectures, standards, and policies
TNSC (Telecommunications Network Strategy Committee)	Technical management	Develop strategies and secure agreement on overall telecommunications issues Supported by several operational committees: Internet, Video Conferencing, Voice Messaging, SNA
DMC (Data Management Committee)	Technical management	Set policies for the use of the primary data elements in the corporation (key codes) Secure agreement on code definitions and operation group implementation

the needed commitment from senior management exists to facilitate development and implementation.

General Services Division

A separate group, the General Services Division, was responsible for major data centers and network management. GSD operated two large data centers, one at corporate headquarters in Webster, New York, and one in California. It was responsible for the U.S. telecommunications network and for providing links to key international locations. GSD employed 650 systems professionals, and all of its more than $150 million in annual IT expenditures were charged back to users.

Xerox Business Unit IT Organizations

IT groups within each of Xerox's business units were responsible for applications development and departmental systems. (Shared services, such as host processing and telecommunications, were provided by the General Services Division.) Exhibit 7 contains a list of the major applications in production and under development in each business unit. A few of these are described below.

Business Products and Systems Group

The Business Products and Systems Group (BPSG) employed a staff of more than 400 in product development, product planning, and

EXHIBIT 7   Xerox Corporation: Business-Unit Major Applications

Operational Systems	*In Process/Planned*

Business Products and Systems Group (BPSG)

Engineering:
  CAD/CAM—design delivery
  Engineers tool kit—admin. systems
  Product delivery system
  Unit manufacturing cost tracking
  Early supplier involvement systems

Engineering:
  Computer-integrated manufacturing
  Artificial intelligence for product engineering
  Spare parts planning
  Repair strategy implementation

Manufacturing:
  Material requirement planning
  Commodity management
  Materials logistics—warehousing
  Material control systems
  Materials management systems
  Shopfloor systems
  Free zone trade
  Flexible manufacturing cells

Manufacturing:
  Just-in-time
  Multinational ordering
  Electronics data interchange
  Robotics
  Plastics FMS

Marketing Operating Groups (USMG, SMG, International)

Distribution:
  Warehouse control
  Parts planning
  Multinational ordering
  In-transit tracking

Distribution:
  Global planning
  Visibility tech rep inventories
  Single system for equipment and parts inventories (Europe only)
  Integration of supplier and demander systems
  Repair strategy implementation

Service:
  Tech rep dispatch
  Level of service reporting

Service:
  Hand-held computers for call completion
  Remote diagnostics

Marketing-Customer Administration:
  Order entry
  Telemarketing
  Equipment management
  Equipment scheduling

Marketing–Customer Administration:
  Single customer order-entry interface
  Customer administration system strategy
  Telemarketing
  Order entry
  Equipment management
  Intelligent assistant
  Automated sales process

Finance:
  End-user services—distributed processing
  Common ledger
  Business resource investment management
  Operating budget reviews
  Financial analysis
  Database for strategic business operations

manufacturing. Its annual expenditures for IT in 1986 exceeded $100 million.

BPSG's business objectives were concerned largely with product quality, product design, and manufacturing flexibility. Part of the group's charter was to be able to "design anywhere, build anywhere, and service everywhere." BPSG focused its IT resources on applications that would increase the productivity of engineering and manufacturing processes, promote portability of manufacturing processes, and facilitate connectivity among manufacturing locations.

By late 1987, many of BPSG's development teams had begun to utilize CAD/CAM technology in their product development activities. Consequently, BPSG, in 1988, undertook a major technology initiative—development and implementation of a common product delivery architecture for all development projects. The architecture was to include productivity tools for professional staff and standardized management reports that would facilitate tracking of product cost relative to product or market maturity, and tracking of problems during design and manufacturing.

To enable the development of common manufacturing systems, the IT reporting structure in the manufacturing area was changed in the fall of 1987. Previously, manufacturing IT managers had reported to the management of the plants they supported. With the change, all plant IT managers reported to a manager of manufacturing systems (Butch Milliman), who reported directly to the manufacturing organization.

Dunbar, whose technical managers had effectively supported BPSG IT managers in the areas of technology assessment and defining and implementing standards for internal communication, wished that his group could be more actively involved in specific projects, such as the development of the product delivery system. "We would like to play a more active role on many of the

project teams on which we participate, but we have limited technical resources," he observed. "We have to be careful. Any one project could consume all of our technical talent."

U.S. Marketing Group

The U.S. Marketing Group (USMG), with a staff of some 1,000 systems professionals, was by far Xerox's largest user of information technology. USMG's 1986 expenditures for IT exceeded $195 million.

One of the major challenges the group faced was merging the many administrative systems and databases that had resulted from several sales reorganizations in the late 1970s and early 1980s. These multiple, nonintegrated systems impeded USMG's ability to provide timely responses to customer inquiries and to process customer orders quickly and accurately.

Two of the major IT projects under way in USMG at the end of 1987 were targeted at the sales administration area. One was the development of an application, called the intelligent assistant, that would provide a single interface to the multiple administrative systems. The goal of the other project, termed the Automated Sales Process (ASP), was to enable sales representatives to quickly prepare complex proposals for customers.

International

The International Group was similar in many ways to USMG. Its applications focus was similar, and its staff included more than 1,000 systems professionals. International's 1986 IT expenditures exceeded $100 million.

One of the issues facing Xerox's International Group, Rank Xerox Limited (RXL), was that each of its business units (e.g., country or region) had its own systems. Although in many instances separate systems were needed to support local reporting requirements and decision making, efficiencies stood to be realized from the ability to connect the disparate systems.

One of International's major IT projects at the end of 1987 involved spare parts inventory management. RXL was developing a single logistical process that would enable it to track spare parts inventory throughout Europe.

Special Markets Group

The Special Markets Group (SMG) focused on products not sold by the USMG sales force (e.g., toner or Xerox reproduction centers). SMG's 1986 IT expenditures exceeded $20 million and it employed a systems staff of more than 100.

The number and diversity of businesses handled by SMG made it difficult to identify common business processes. Because it had inherited some of its businesses and product lines from USMG, SMG found itself in the position of having to purchase some of its IT resources from USMG. In some cases, the cost of services purchased from USMG was greater than would have been the cost of purchasing an equivalent system for SMG. Yet, from a corporate perspective, there were advantages to having SMG and USMG share systems, since they sold to many of the same customers. (Barron noted that her group would likely be involved in evaluating any proposals to either decouple or better integrate USMG and SMG systems.)

SMG's projects included a major outbound telemarketing facility that implemented hardware and software geared to enhance the productivity of telemarketing operators. In 1986, this system generated sales in excess of $400 million.

The New CIM Leader

Before coming to Xerox in 1978, Barron had spent six years with a leading general management consulting firm. She had earned an MBA from a well-known eastern business school in the early 1970s.

Barron's understanding of Xerox's business derived from having held a number of key posts in the company, including manager of multinational projects, manager of future products integration, director of the China Project, and region sales manager for the Mid-Atlantic Region. Just prior to her appointment to the position of director of CIM, Barron had held the position of vice president and region manager of the Eastern Region.

Allaire explained why Barron had been chosen for the position. "We had a very difficult time finding someone to fill the CIM director position," he recalled.

> We wanted someone with both a knowledge of our business *and* information systems. No one within Xerox with a systems background had the needed business perspective for the position, so we looked to the outside. We were unable to attract the *one* candidate that had both the necessary business and information systems background. We then sought someone from within the organization who had a solid grasp of our business and who had credibility with our senior executives.

Of her decision to accept the position, Barron remarked:

> When I evaluate career opportunities there are several criteria that are important to me: my ability to add value to the organization; my ability to be heard by senior management; and how the position will affect my future career options.
>
> I felt strongly that in this position I could make a significant difference, that senior management would be accessible to me, and that this kind of experience would be invaluable to a future general manager.

"During my first few months as the director of CIM," Barron recalled,

> I focused on two objectives, educating myself on managing information technology and the role of a corporate information technology group, and understanding the IT needs of Xerox's business units.

To accomplish the first objective, I spent three months visiting other corporate IS departments around the country, networked at IS conferences, and attended a seminar for information systems executives at a leading business school. I also attended executive briefings offered by major computer vendors. To accomplish the second objective, I spent quite a bit of time in meetings with my staff and with business and IT managers throughout the company.

A New Role for CIM

From these meetings, Barron recognized that her first priority would have to be improving people, not improving computers. She also observed that, as might be expected, there were no clear definitions of the responsibilities of the centralized CIM group and the decentralized business unit IS groups.

"In the past," Barron explained,

there were always debates about what functions should be centralized and what should be decentralized. I think these discussions miss the point. We have to find the right balance of accountability for our shared responsibilities. We can appoint accountability at a given level of the organization, but in the end we have to cooperate to get the job done. In this company we have a common set of business objectives and values that must cascade down throughout the organization. We need to keep reminding ourselves that our competition is outside, not inside, the company.

Working with the business unit IT managers, corporate and business unit executives, and her staff, Barron developed a mission statement for CIM and a statement of responsibility that she would share with Allaire on March 1, 1988. (See Exhibit 8 and Exhibit 9.)

EXHIBIT 8   Xerox Corporation: CIM Mission

CIM Mission

- Transformation of the I.M. function for 1990s in partnership with the I.M. community.

- Develop I.M. leadership strategy and ensure implementation in all units.

- Define Xerox technology infrastructure, architecture, policies and standards, and ensure adherence in all units.

- Identify requirements and ensure systems development for common business processes.

- Provide executive support systems for corporate senior management and staffs.

- Develop partnership with SBUs and OP units to support Xerox product and marketing strategies.

- Provide a center of excellence for knowledge-based systems.

EXHIBIT 9   Xerox Corporation: I.M. Leadership Roles and Responsibilities

I.M. Leadership Objectives	*CIM*	*Operating Units/Utilities*
Business strategy/process	Ensure I.M. focus and adequate support for business strategy and processes within and across groups	Identify opportunities and implement applications to support new and improved business strategies and processes
Strategic applications	Ensure a continual flow of strategic applications to support critical business processes	Identify and implement strategic applications
Customer and field	Ensure support to marketing for external customer	Provide support to marketing for external customer
Technology infrastructure, standards, and architecture	Define Xerox I.M. technology infrastructure, architecture, policies and standards	Provide input to and implement agreed directions
Product support/internal users	Ensure I.M. supports internal customer requirements throughout Xerox and provide input to product strategies	Ensure I.M. direction supports business unit customer requirements and provide input to product strategies
Advocacy for I.M. community	Ensure capabilities and requirements of I.M. community well understood throughout corporation	Ensure capabilities and requirements of I.M. organization well understood throughout the unit
Emerging technologies	Ensure timely identification and participation in key technologies that can provide substantial benefit to the company	Ensure timely piloting and implementation of key technologies that can provide substantial benefit to the unit
Human resource development	Ensure a quality supply of I.M. talent to meet the specialized needs of the Xerox I.M. community and serve as a feeder for product and marketing organizations	Source, develop, and train I.M. professionals consistent with I.M. strategy
Management processes	Ensure appropriate processes are in place to implement I.M. leadership strategy utilizing the "Leadership Through Quality" principles and tools	Ensure appropriate processes are in place to implement I.M. leadership strategy utilizing the "Leadership Through Quality" principles and tools

Barron knew that Allaire would expect her to be prepared to discuss these documents at the forthcoming meeting. As she prepared for her meeting with Allaire, Barron reflected on her first few months at the helm of CIM. How could she position the organization to provide leadership to the Xerox IT community? How should she evaluate the effectiveness of CIM and communicate its mission and accomplishments throughout the organization? What was the appropriate structure for the organization, and how large should it be to accomplish its mission? How could CIM balance an advocacy and accountability function? Finally, should it remain strictly a staff function, or should it develop line responsibilities (and, if so, what should those line responsibilities be)?

Barron wondered what new initiatives she should undertake. She was aware that Allaire had targeted human resource management as a key focus for the organization. This fit well with her assessment of the need to develop formal mechanisms for preparing future IT leaders well-versed in both business and IS for all levels of the company. Another critical concern was how to develop formal mechanisms for identifying and assimilating technology innovations.

Chapter 2

Manageable Trends

UNDERLYING THEMES

In the first chapter, we identified key issues that make the assimilation of information technology (IT) challenging. We then discussed four implications of these issues for management practice. This book is designed to provide a comprehensive treatment of these key issues. (An analysis of these areas for a firm, complete with appropriate recommendations, is referred to as an *IT management audit.*) Underlying our treatment of each issue are six themes that reflect current insight into management practice and guidance for administrative action. This chapter discusses the nature and implications of each theme. These themes also provide the organizational basis for the chapters that follow, because they represent what we believe to be the most useful ways to think about the forces that are driving transition in the use and management of IT in the mid-1990s. Our expectation, as mentioned in Chapter 1, is that additional experience, research, and evolving technology will inevitably produce new formulation of these and other themes in subsequent years.

1. IT impacts different industries and firms within them in different ways strategically. In many settings this has great strategic importance. The thrust of the impact strongly influences which IT management tools and approaches are appropriate for a firm.
2. Office technology, telecommunications technology, and information-processing technologies are evolving and will continue to evolve dramatically. This evolution will continue to destabilize existing systems and offer new types of IT application opportunities.
3. Organizational learning about IT is a dominant fact of life and limits the practical speed of change. The type of management ap-

proaches appropriate for assimilating a specific technology must change sharply as the organization gains familiarity with it.

4. External industry pressures have shifted the balance of make-or-buy IT decisions in the direction of buy. Managing this is complex.
5. While all the elements of the system life cycle remain, the new technologies allow them to be executed in dramatically different ways for different types of applications in various settings.
6. Effective IT policy and control involve a partnership between general management, IT management, and user management. Managing the long-term evolution of this partnership is crucial as technologies and opportunities change.

THEME 1: STRATEGIC IMPACT

Increasingly, it is clear that different industries are being affected in fundamentally different ways by information technology. In many industries, IT has enabled massive transformation of the various operational aspects of the value chain. Embedding technology in the product, computer-aided design and manufacturing (CAD/CAM), automation of factories and inbound logistics, increased quality, and massive cost shocks have all profoundly changed many industries' standards of competition in producing goods and services, and industry leaders have put great pressure on competitors to meet new standards. Many of these changes have linked independent functions into integrated systems that allow ever faster delivery of new and more complex products.

In other industries, the new technology has more strongly affected marketing, sales, distribution, and service to meet ever more focused and differentiated markets. New channels of distribution have been set up, prior methods outmoded, new customer service features introduced, and new promotion and market research methods developed. In such areas as product formulation and service response time, both operational and marketing impacts have been achieved; this separation between operational and marketing impact permits us to make a useful distinction between the role of technology in different industry settings.

Table 2–1 presents a series of questions for managers who are trying to place their firm and industry in the marketing axis. If the answers to most of the questions are no, IT probably would play a rather limited role in transforming the marketing function. Conversely, if the answers to most are yes, technology has played or will play a major role in transforming the firm's marketing organization. Table 2–2 provides a similar series of questions for managers trying to place firms on the operational axis.

TABLE 2–1   Marketing Questions for Managers

- Does the business require a large number of routine interactions each day with vendors for ordering or requesting information?
- Is product choice complex?
- Do customers need to compare competitors' product/service/price configurations simultaneously?
- Is a quick customer decision necessary?
- Is accurate, quick customer confirmation essential?
- Would an increase in multiple ordering or service sites provide value to the customer?
- Are consumer tastes potentially volatile?
- Do significant possibilities exist for product customization?
- Is pricing volatile (can/should salesperson set price at point of sale)?
- Is the business heavily regulated?
- Can the product be surrounded by value-added information to the customer?
- Is the real customer two or more levels removed from the manufacturer?

TABLE 2–2   Production Questions for Managers

- Is there large geographic dispersion in sourcing?
- Is high technology embedded in the product?
- Does the product require a long, complex design process?
- Is the process of administering quality control standards complex?
- Is the design integration between customer and supplier across company boundaries complex?
- Are there large buffer inventories in the manufacturing process?
- Does the product require complex manufacturing schedule integration?
- Are time and cost savings possible?
- Is there potential for major inventories reductions?
- Are direct and indirect labor levels high?

Figure 2–1 shows how leaders in several industries have competitively used IT very differently. In the airline industry, for example, the reservation system, which heavily controls the travel agencies, has given leading developers American Airlines and United Airlines major marketing and operations advantages. It has been the foundation for better aircraft utilization and new services such as "frequent flyer" programs and has also allowed the development of joint incentive programs with hotels and car rental agencies. The ongoing operations of seat allocation, crew scheduling, maintenance, and so on, have also

FIGURE 2–1 IT Impact: Current Position of Industry Leaders

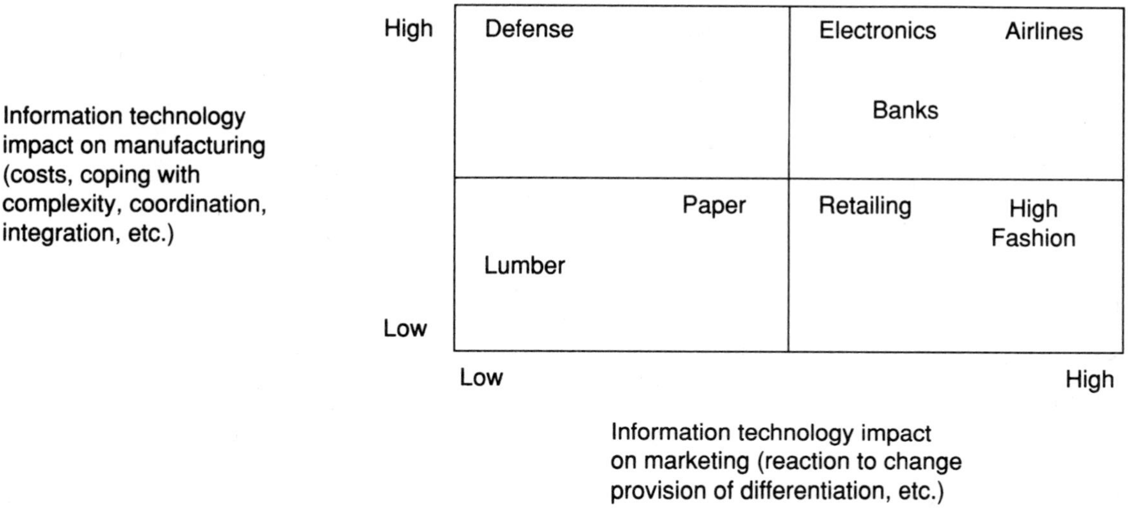

Information technology
impact on manufacturing
(costs, coping with
complexity, coordination,
integration, etc.)

High	Defense	Electronics	Airlines
		Banks	
		Retailing	High Fashion
	Paper		
	Lumber		
Low			

Low   High

Information technology impact
on marketing (reaction to change
provision of differentiation, etc.)

been profoundly impacted. When one of these systems fails, the overall operations of the airline are unfavorably affected almost immediately. As Figure 2–2 illustrates, however, second-tier airlines have invested much less and consequently have paid a significant penalty in terms of their ability to differentiate their services in the eyes of the buying public (marketing) and in their ability to coordinate and cost-effectively transform the delivery of their product (manufacturing). Indeed it has been cited as a leading cause for several failures.

A similar analysis of the banking industry shows, for example, that Bank-1, Citibank, and Chemical Bank have moved aggressively to distinguish their products and services through effective use of information technology. Other banks, however, have used it primarily to transform the back office and have been unable to significantly change the front office (to ultimate competitive disadvantage). The competitive problem is further complicated because some large players in industries such as banking and airlines have made major (and successful) investments that have created very high entry barriers for their successors, who are smaller and who find such investments prohibitive.

Figure 2–1 shows the impact of information technology for the leader in several other industries. Defense, for example, with CAD/ CAM robotics and embedded technology has been deeply affected by this technology on the manufacturing side. The marketing impact on defense, however, has been markedly less significant, partly because of the much lower transaction rate, but also because the much higher value

FIGURE 2–2   IT Impact: Position of Key Players in Airlines and Banks

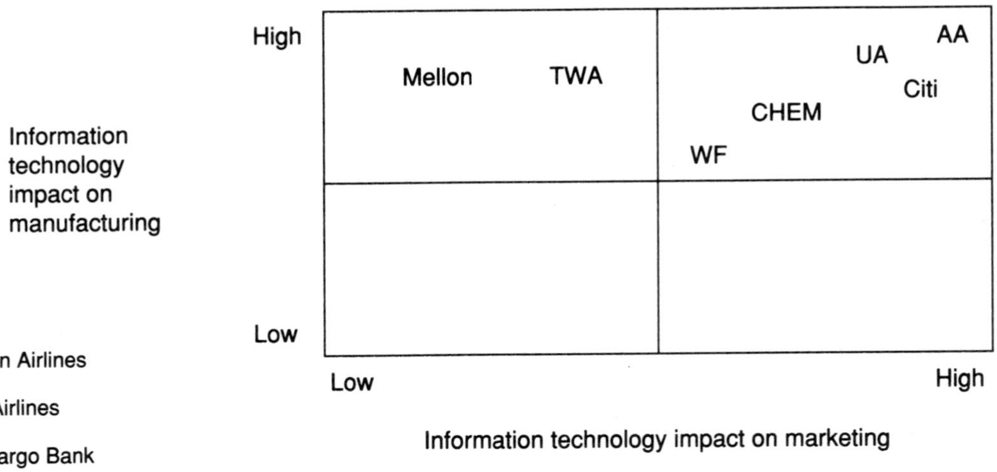

Information technology impact on manufacturing

High

Mellon   TWA

CHEM

WF

UA   AA

Citi

Low

Low   High

Information technology impact on marketing

Key:

AA—American Airlines

UA—United Airlines

WF—Wells Fargo Bank

Citi—First National Citibank

CHEM—Chemical Bank of New York

TWA—TransWorld Airlines

Mellon—Mellon Bank

of transactions brings into play a very different set of marketing forces that are less sensitive to the technology's impact.

By comparison, retailing operations have been significantly altered by the technology (but not to the same extent as for the leading airlines or banks) through just-in-time ordering and cost-reduction programs. Similarly, display management, computer-assisted cosmetics analysis, and point-of-sale terminals have made important marketing contributions (but again, not in the same life-and-death fashion as in other industries).

Interestingly enough, significant impact for retailing operations has come from the effective use of IT by suppliers as they fight for space on the retailers' shelves. Twenty-four-hour delivery on key items, on-premise order entry, and other important features are now being demanded by retailers from their suppliers.

In the lumber and cement industries, on the other hand, the manufacturing and the marketing impacts of the technology have been relatively limited except for impacts on office work and order handling. Although there was great technology change in their production process control systems in the 1970s, their products remain commodities, which are purchased primarily on cost and timely delivery. Further, their core administration processes have been automated to a point that overhead is an insignificant aspect of cost due to links to customers, automatic ordering, and sophisticated production control processes. Consequently, the opportunity to use systems to change the nature of competition appears low for many firms in these industries.

Different IT Challenges

Figure 2–3 identifies the competitive investment selections facing players in industries in which IT gives major transforming advantage in marketing, operations, or both. First are those firms that have already made dramatic transformations in the marketing and operations areas and are positioned strongly relative to the competition. They have normally been facilitated by leadership and structure. (At Bank 1 the CEO chairs the IT planning committee and is responsible for this technology; at Sears, Roebuck and Co. the chief information officer (CIO) sits on the company's executive committee.) The challenge is to *maintain advantage,* and current management approaches are usually adequate.

Another group of firms is in settings where the marketing component is relatively unimportant but where major investments are

FIGURE 2–3   Competitive Investment Selection: Task as compared with Industry Leader

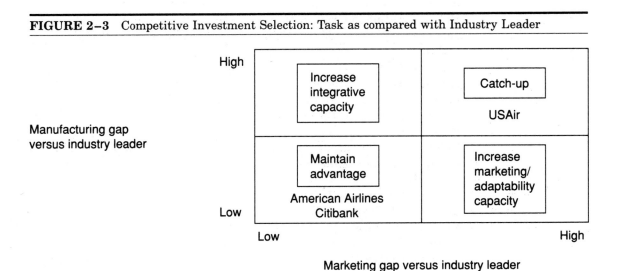

needed in operations to increase integration and to control costs and catch up with the industry leaders. Firms in industries such as aerospace, manufacturing, and petroleum often require work that cuts across many organizational boundaries and that cannot be easily implemented by a highly decentralized IT organization. Strong IT and senior-management linkage is needed to *increase the firm's integrative capacity.*

A third group of firms faces a primary challenge of catching up with industry leaders through better differentiating their products and services to meet the needs of ever more focused markets. Many of these firms need investments in IT research and development and new marketing analysis infrastructures for tracking trends and revising marketing strategies to meet competition. Items such as capturing point-of-sale (POS) data in order to analyze individual buyer habits and providing capacity for responding quickly to competitors' prices and product moves are often key. Similarly, the ability to use data and networks to move aspects of product decision making downward in the organization can increase responsiveness to local needs; the new systems at Frito-Lay illustrate this.

Finally, some firms are in a deep *catch-up* situation, having been outmaneuvered on both dimensions vis-à-vis the industry leader. Strong, coordinated efforts are needed by both the CEO and IT management of these firms to enable organizational adaptation to the new environment. The combination of being outmaneuvered by competitors in ways that really matter, the long lead times required to develop a competitive response, and the high capital investment costs of a new response has in some cases created a situation so serious that the survival of the corporation is at stake. (This is felt by many to be the primary cause of the demise of People's Express and Frontier Airlines.)

In short, information technology plays very different roles in various industry settings. In some industries it has played a predominantly operational role, while in others its impact has been primarily on marketing. In many of these settings, industry leaders have been so aggressive that they have transformed the rules of competition and put followers under great pressure. Leadership, structure, and other changes, as mentioned in the previous chapter, are all part of this adaptation.

Given this industry context, it is increasingly clear that good management of IT varies widely in different settings. For some organizations, IT activities have great strategic importance; for other organizations, they play and, appropriately, will continue to play a role that is cost-effective and useful but distinctly supportive in nature. Organizations of this latter type require less senior-management strategic thinking to be devoted to their IT organization.

FIGURE 2–4   Categories of Strategic Relevance and Impact

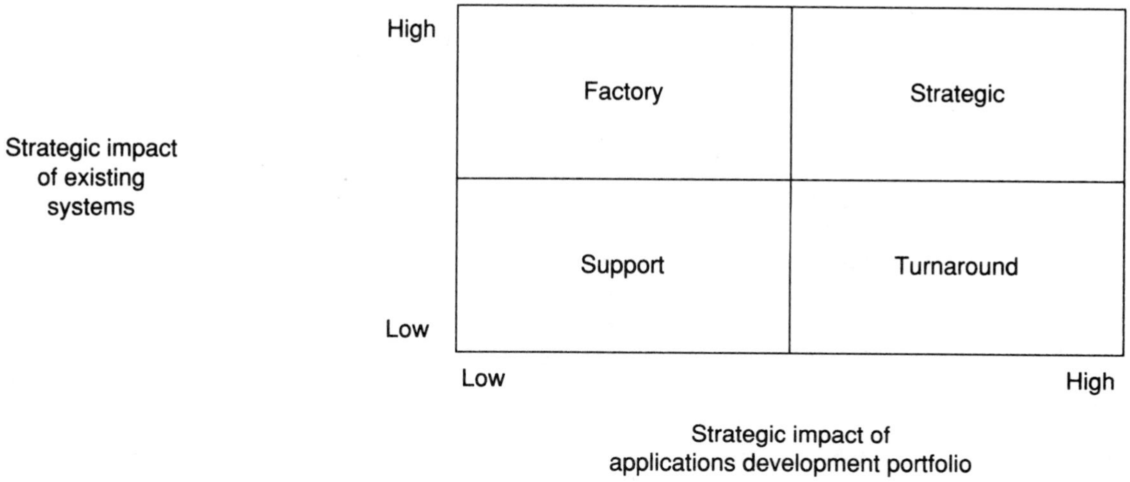

IT Environments

As an individual firm approaches the management of IT, two aspects embedded in the previous discussion have profound importance. The first is that for some firms, the second-by-second, utterly reliable, zero-defect quality of its IT operations is crucial to its very survival. Even small interruptions in service or disruptions in quality may have profound impact. In other firms, significant disturbances in IT operations would have to occur over an extended period before the firm's overall operations would be severely impacted. The second aspect, discussed earlier, is that whereas new IT development initiatives are of great strategic importance for some firms, for other firms, what is under development is useful but not a matter of life or death. Understanding an organization's position on these two aspects is critical in trying to develop an appropriate IT management strategy. Figure 2–4 summarizes these points by identifying four quite different IT environments.

Strategic.   For some companies, smooth functioning of the IT activity is critical to their daily operation and applications under development are critical for their future competitive success. The IT strategy is the backbone of such firms' competitive success and receives considerable attention. Banks, insurance companies, and heavy-equipment manufacturing companies exemplify firms that frequently fall into this category. Appropriately managed, these firms require considerable IT planning, and the organizational relationship between IT and senior management is very close. In fact, in some of these firms the head of the IT function, broadly defined, sits on the board of directors.

Turnaround.   Some firms may receive considerable amounts of IT operational support, but the company is not absolutely dependent on the uninterrupted cost-effective functioning of this support in order to achieve its short-term or long-term objectives. The applications under development, however, are absolutely vital if the firm is to reach its strategic objectives. A good example of this is a manufacturing firm that was undergoing rapid growth. The information technology embedded in its factories and accounting processes, though important, was not absolutely vital to their effectiveness. However, the rapid growth of the firm's domestic and international installations in number of products, number of sites, number of staff, and so on, severely strained its management control systems and made their improvement of critical strategic interest to the company. Steps the company took to resolve the situation included enhanced IT leadership, new organizational placement of IT, and increased commitment to planning.

Another firm got into this quadrant by systematically stunting the IT development function over a period of years until the existing systems became dangerously obsolete. In fact, they were running on unique hardware platforms that their vendor was about to decommit on. Retrieving this situation through a crash systems rebuilding effort became a matter of high corporate priority.

Factory.   For smooth operations, some firms are heavily dependent on cost-effective, totally reliable IT operational support. Their applications portfolios, however, are dominated by maintenance work and applications that, though profitable and important in their own right, are not fundamental to the firm's ability to compete. Some manufacturing, service, and retailing firms fit into this category very nicely. In these organizations, even a one-hour disruption in service from existing systems has severe operational consequences on the performance of the business unit. In the 1990 AT&T long-distance collapse, one telemarketing firm had to send its 500 telephone representatives home, and that day's sales were irretrievably lost.

Support.   Some firms, some of them with very large IT budgets, are not fundamentally operationally dependent on the smooth functioning of the IT activity, nor are their applications portfolios critical to achieving strategic revenue and profit goals. For example, a large professional services firm is spending nearly $30 million per year on IT activities that involve more than 200 employees. Without a doubt, this sum is being well spent, and the firm is getting a good return on its investment. Nonetheless, the firm could operate, albeit unevenly, in the event of major operational difficulties, and the strategic impact of the application portfolio under development, viewed realistically, is quite limited. Consequently, their attention to the development and maintenance of an IT strategy is modest, although they keep abreast of new software products. (Their competitors are in much the same position.) IT appropriately is positioned at a significantly lower organizational level in this firm than in other settings, and the commitment to linking IT to business planning activities particularly at the senior-management level is essentially nonexistent. Our research has uncovered a surprisingly large number of companies still in this category, although over time the number has diminished somewhat.

In attempting to diagnose where a firm or business unit should be on the dimension of strategic impact of the applications development portfolio, careful analysis of the impact of IT on each part of the value chain is essential (as described in Chapter 3). In addition, competitors' use of IT must be analyzed periodically to ensure that major opportunities have not been missed. For example, ten years ago the retailing industry was considered to be *support*. Few competitors paid attention to what Wal-Mart was doing, and now most of them are trying to play catch-up in what is emerging as an industry in which IT is a strategic force. Subsequent chapters describe several widely used frameworks of competitive analysis and suggest how they can facilitate the identification of strategic IT applications when used effectively.

THEME 2: CHANGING TECHNOLOGIES

At the heart of the challenges lies the dramatic, sustained, long-term evolution of the cost performance of this technology. This means that applications undoable in 1985 would be state of the art by 1990 and distinctly unimaginative and obsolete by 1995. This theme above all has contributed to the complexity of managerial endeavor in this field.

The 1980s produced development of increasing electronic and storage capacities, which in turn supported an explosion of new types of software. As we enter the era of increasing chip density—jumps in excess of one million logic gates—new capabilities will exceed the installed base by several orders of magnitude. These changes will continue well on into the next century. The 64-million-bit chip is in development, and the next size is already in the research laboratory. This capacity will quickly add full-motion digital video, voice attachment to spreadsheets, new development procedures, and a cost of text communication approaching zero. Additionally, management of data processing or computing has long since ceased to be a useful concept around which to organize a program of management focus. Rather, the technologies of computing (DP), telecommunications (TP), and office support (OS) must be thought of as an intertwined cluster around which policies and management focus must be developed. When we refer to information technology departments or policies, we include all three technologies under this umbrella. At present, the coordination and, indeed, integrated management of these technologies have been accomplished in most firms, although the performance of these technologies continues to accelerate dramatically.

For at least two major reasons, the three technologies are viewed and managed (at least at a policy level) as a totality. The first reason is that an enormous number of physical interconnections must occur among the three. On-line inquiry systems, electronic mail, and end-user programming terminals exemplify the types of applications requiring the physical integration of two or more of the technologies. The second major reason is that, today, execution of all projects utilizing one or more of these technologies pose very similar management problems. Each technology involves large coordinated projects in terms of expenditures, rapidly changing technology, substantial disruptions to people's work styles, and often the development of complex computer programs.

Integration has been complicated by the facts that until about 1976 these technologies were not integrated and that they come from vastly different managerial traditions. The three technologies must be thought of as a totality at a policy-setting level and, in many settings, must have common line management, at least over architectural issues.

Since 1980 this integration has advanced from a largely speculative idea to one that is overwhelmingly embedded in management practice. Consequently, we will spend little time defending it and will focus rather on the managerial implications of this ongoing integration in a world of sustained rapid changes in the technology. Particularly we will attempt to distinguish between decisions that must be guided by central policies and decisions that are better left to end users.

THEME 3: ORGANIZATION LEARNING

Implementing a portfolio of IT systems projects built around continually evolving technologies is an extraordinarily complex endeavor. However, a range of concepts exists to assist the manager in managing technological diffusion. Key to most of these is early involvement of the users whose lives will be impacted by the design and adoption of the technology in their daily activities. Successful implementation of IT requires that individuals learn new ways of performing intellectual tasks. This learning process involves unscrambling old procedures and attitudes, moving to a new pattern, and then cementing this new process into the procedures of the individuals and groups. From a broader perspective, success demands that users be heavily involved in deciding how the systems can be designed to meet their needs and then in ensuring that the new system is actually assimilated into the key staff and managers' work routines instead of becoming an idle, expensive appendage.

Throughout the development of IT there has been an ongoing effort to understand the managerial issues associated with implementing and evolving automated systems in an organization. Starting with Thomas Whisler and Harold Leavitt's article[1] on the demise of middle management and going on to Dick Nolan and Cyrus Gibson's stages[2] and Chris Argyris's[3] espoused theory versus theories in actions, a range of concepts has been advanced for dealing with the problem of getting individuals to use automated systems appropriately. After field studies (many of them longitudinal) on 28 organizations over a decade, we have concluded that the managerial situation can be best framed as one of managing technological diffusion. Successful implementation of a technology requires that individuals learn new ways of performing intellectual tasks. As this learning takes place, changes occur in information flows as well as in individual roles. Often this has resulted in organization changes substantiating Leavitt and Whisler's conjecture and reinforcing Nolan and Gibson's original four stages.

We consider this process to be closely akin to the problems of organizational change identified by Kurt Lewin[4] and described in action form by Ed Schein[5] as unfreezing, moving, and then refreezing again. The process can best be summarized by rephrasing Nolan and Gibson's original four stages (called *phases* here) and considering the process as ongoing, with a new start for each new technology—be it database, local area networks, or new CAD workstations. This approach usefully emphasizes the continual tension between efficiency and effectiveness in the use of IT. At one time it is necessary to relax and let the organization search for effectiveness; at another it is necessary to focus on efficiency in order to control costs.

---

[1]Thomas L. Whisler and Harold J. Leavitt, "Management in the 1980s," *Harvard Business Review,* November–December 1958.

[2]Cyrus F. Gibson and Richard L. Nolan, "Managing the Four Stages of EDP Growth," *Harvard Business Review,* January–February 1974.

[3]Chris Argyris, "Double-Loop Learning on Organizations," *Harvard Business Review,* September–October 1977, p. 115.

[4]Kurt Lewin, "Group Decision and Social Change," in *Readings in Social Psychology,* ed. G. E. Swanson, T. M. Newcomb, and E. L. Hartley (New York: Holt Reinhart & Winston, 1952).

[5]Ed Schein, "Management Development as a Process of Influence," *Industrial Management Review,* Second Issue (1961), pp. 59–77.

Phase 1. Technology Identification and Investment

The first phase involves identifying a technology of potential interest to the company and funding a pilot project, which may be considered akin to R&D. An alternative approach is to identify promising applications in the corporate strategic plan that seem amenable to systems innovations and then to provide funds for investigating whether this potential in fact exists. This approach is designed to attract product champions for systems innovations. The key outputs of the project should be seen as expertise on technical problems involved in using the technology and a first cut at identifying the types of applications where it might be most useful. It is generally inappropriate to demand any hard profit-and-loss payoff identification either before or after the implementation of this pilot project.

An important role of strategic planning is to encourage ongoing scanning for potentially relevant new technologies and to foster careful experimentation. In the past these were more often initiated by IT, but in recent time the user community is launching more pilot programs. For example, a major chemicals company recently authorized funds to investigate how to link overseas plants more closely. One pilot program connected similar U.S. plants to their European counterpart with a radio communications link and found they could quickly exchange process control innovations. This has led to an entirely new concept of distributing process control enhancements throughout the organization.

Phase 2. Technological Learning and Adaptation

The objective during the second phase is to take the newly identified technology of interest where a first level of technical expertise has been developed and to encourage user-oriented experimentation with it through a series of pilot projects. The primary purpose of these pilot projects is to develop user-oriented insights into the potential profitable applications of the technology and to stimulate user awareness of the existence of the technology. In the past, what key IT staff thought were going to be the practical implications of a technology have repeatedly turned out to be quite different in reality. As is true of Phase 1, there is a strong effectiveness thrust to Phase 2.

Phase 3. Rationalization/Management Control

Phase-3 technologies are those whose end applications are reasonably understood by both IT personnel and key user personnel. The basic challenge in this phase is to develop appropriate support systems and controls to ensure that the technologies are utilized efficiently as they spread across the organization. In earlier phases, basic concerns revolve around stimulating awareness and experimentation. In this phase, the primary attention turns to developing standards and controls to ensure that the applications are done economically and can be maintained over a long period of time. Formal standards for development and documentation, cost-benefit studies, and user charge-out mechanisms are all appropriate for technologies in this phase.

Phase 4. Maturity/Widespread Technology Transfer

Technologies in the fourth phase have essentially passed through the gauntlet of organizational learning with technological skills, user awareness, and management controls in place. A common pitfall in this phase is for the initiating staff to become bored because they want to move on to new technologies and to spend little energy transferring their expertise. If not managed, this phenomenon may sharply slow the process of adaption of the new technology.

This product life cycle of innovation, learning, rationalization, and maturity is now clearly understood within most well-managed firms. The framework is a useful base around which to develop a strategic view of diffusion of technology throughout the firm. As the experiments with a specific technology spread new by-product innovations should be encouraged in an organized fashion. Knowledgeable managers have proven to be better sources of new application ideas than either technology experts or single-minded product champions.

The key decision is how much to allocate to exploiting Phase-2 and Phase-3 technologies versus how much to allocate for Phase-1 technologies. There is no hard and fast guideline for making this decision, although clearly *strategic*-quadrant firms must do much more Phase-1 technology investment than *support*-quadrant firms.

The general theory on fostering innovation suggests waiting for a product champion to emerge and only then funding the product. Our thesis, however, is that an aggressively funded Phase-1 technology effort is a key precondition for generating these entrepreneurial product champions, who have been so important to successful IT innovation.

Technologies in all four phases exist simultaneously in an organization at any point in time. The art of management in the 1990s is to bring the appropriate perspectives to bear on each technology simultaneously; that is, support IT Phase-1 research, IT Phase-2 aggressive selling to the end user, and intensive IT Phase-3 generation of controls. This calls for a subtlety and flexibility from IT management and general management that too often they do not possess or see the need for. A monolithic IT management approach, however, will not do the job. This will be discussed further in Chapters 6 and 7.

THEME 4: SOURCING POLICIES FOR THE IT VALUE CHAIN

An issue of great tension and repositioning of IT in the 1980s was the acceleration of pressures pushing firms toward greater reliance on external sources for software and computing support. Outsourcing is one of the genuinely hot topics today. Escalating costs of large-system development, limited staff, availability of proprietary industry databases, and a dramatic increase in the number of potential applications have been some of the factors driving the trend to buy from outside sources rather than make systems internally. Increasingly, firms are also asking, "Do I really need to develop competence in running large computing centers, or can I delegate it to professionals and focus my energy more effectively on areas where I can get a real strategic edge?" These pressures will dramatically accelerate in the 1990s.

Make.   Key factors that favor the "make" decision include the following:

1.   Potential for the firm to develop a customized product that is totally responsive to its very specific needs. This is true for initial development as well as for necessary system enhancements and maintenance throughout its life. Further, one has the psychological comfort gained by having key elements of one's firm under one's supervision (the corollary of "not invented here").

2.   Ability to maintain confidentiality about data and type of business practices being implemented. This is particularly important in situations where IT services are at the core of how the firm chooses to compete.

3.   Ability to avoid vulnerability to the fluctuating business fortunes of outside software or data services suppliers.

4.   Increased ease in developing systems due to the growth of user-oriented programming languages, database management systems, on-line debugging aids, computer-assisted software engineering, and other user-oriented software. (It should be noted that the development and adoption of these tools has been slow.)

5.   Ease of adapting made software to rapidly changing business needs without having to coordinate the requirement with other firms.

6.   Developing leading-edge competence that puts extraordinary pressure on competitors who do not have this competence. American Airlines and Wal-Mart are examples of firms that have excelled in this area.

Buy.   Key factors that favor the "buy" decision include the following:

1.   Ability to gain access to specialized skills that cannot be retained or for which there is insufficient need to have continuously available. These include skills in end-use applications, programming and system construction, system operation, and system maintenance.

Demographic trends (reduced work-force entrants) and increased end-use specialization needs are making this factor more important.

2. Cost. The ability to leverage a portion of the development cost over a number of firms can drive the costs down for everyone and make the in-house development alternative unattractive. This is particularly significant for standard accounting applications and database systems.

3. Staff utilization. Scarce in-house resources can be reserved for applications that are company-specific or so confidential that they cannot safely be subcontracted. Reserving these resources may involve buying into a set of systems specifications for the common applications that are less than optimal.

4. Ability to make a short-term commitment for IT processing support instead of having to make a major investment in staff recruitment and training.

5. Immediate access to the high standards of internal control and security offered by the large, well-run service organization. (A fee is charged for this of course.)

6. Proliferation in the types of information services that can be bought. Key categories include:

- Programmers (contract programmers, etc.)
- Proprietary databases.
- Service-bureau computer processing.
- Large-scale facilities-management firms.

The change in balance of these pressures in favor of the buy alternative has significantly impacted IT management practice as internally supplied services lose market share. Care must be taken to ensure that adequate management procedures are in place so that an appropriate balance exists. For example, the management control system must be checked to ensure that it is not, through excess charges, tilting the balance too much in favor of buy. Another example is that as software development is being outsourced, clear audit procedures must be developed to ensure that the suppliers have project-management systems that will enable them to deliver on their commitments. Implementation risk on a fixed-price contract is strongly related to vendor viability. A "good" price is not good if the supplier goes under before completing the project. For operational outsourcing this is critical, since 10 years is the normal length of these contracts.

THEME 5: APPLICATIONS DEVELOPMENT PROCESS

Traditionally, the activities necessary to produce and deliver a specific information service have been characterized as a series of steps:

1. Design.
2. Construct.
3. Implement.
4. Operate.
5. Maintain.

Since the First Edition of this book was published, the practical shape of this process has been dramatically impacted by the emergence of very different types of projects. At one extreme are the traditional projects that were once the mainstay of the industry. These projects are noted for being large, requiring extensive development periods (often well in excess of 18 months), changing the nature of work in several departments, being functionally complex, and involving at the outset unknown data structures and processing procedures. Production scheduling, airline reservation systems, and demand-deposit accounting systems are examples of projects that lie in this area. The traditional system life cycle described here continues to be appropriate for these projects, although one or more pieces may be done in parallel or overlapped in ways that make the old processes unrecognizable.

At the other extreme are projects that may involve the construction of a decision support system (DSS) on a department minicomputer or personal computer, perhaps using data from a central database. Here a heuristic approach (repeatedly cycling through the design and construction activities) using prototyping and other tools is most appropriate; the rigid sequencing of steps implied in the traditional development cycle is simply inappropriate. Further, a significant amount of software is often purchased for these types of projects. As a practical matter, the majority of firms' development dollars today are associated with this type of project. For all projects, however, design and implementation are essential.

The following paragraphs define the traditional components of the life cycle of the traditional project and also identify those aspects most likely to be mismanaged today in the development of decision support systems. A test of the appropriateness of an IT organization and its project management policies is how successful they are in encouraging and controlling each of the steps below for multiple large projects. While changing technology and improved managerial insights have significantly altered the way each of these steps can be implemented, their functions have remained relatively unchanged for a considerable period. With the increasing shift to buy (versus make) decisions, however, significant changes are needed in many of these steps, and IT management in many cases is becoming more like a broker.

Design

The objective of the design step is to produce a definition of the information service desired. This includes identification of the users, the initial tasks to be implemented, and the long-run service and support to be provided. Traditionally, the first step has been either a user request or a joint IT department–user proposal based on the IT plan. More and more, however, it is being initiated by a user request. The design step is a critical activity that demands careful attention to short- and long-term information service requirements as well as to ensuring the delivery of reliable service. Implementation of this step was traditionally dominated by the IT staff but is more and more being assumed by the user.

Design normally begins with an analysis to determine the feasibility and potential costs and benefits of the proposed system. If the results of the analysis are favorable, an explicit decision to proceed is made. This is followed by substantive collaborative work by the potential user and an IT professional to develop a working approach to a systems design. Depending on the systems scope, these design efforts may range from formal systematic analysis to informal discussions.

The end product of design is a definition of the desired service accompanied by an identification of the means (including in-house or purchased) for providing it. Prototyping is proving to be an indispensable tool today for speeding up the design process, improving the quality of the design, and reducing the possibility of major misunderstandings.

Construction

A highly specialized activity, construction involves the structuring of automatic procedures for performing a timely, errorless information service. IT combines art and logic. Professional judgment is needed in the areas of:

1. Selection of brand of equipment, firm, and/or service bureau.
2. Selection of programming system, database system, and so on.
3. Documentation of operating procedures and content of software.
4. Identification and implementation of appropriate testing procedures.
5. Review of adequacy or long-term viability of purchased software service.

Very technical in content, this work depends on good professional skills and good IT management skills. In the past it was very dependent upon good organization linkage to the users to ensure that design needs did not change. As more services are purchased, this phase is being eliminated entirely for many projects, although a portion often remains that involves modifying a standard system to the specific details of the situation. This phase, the design phase, and the implementation phase are often inextricably intertwined in the development of decision support systems.

Implementation

Implementation involves extensive user–IT coordination as the transition is made from the predominantly technical, IT-driven tasks of the construction step to its completed installation and operation in the user environment. Whether the system is bought or made, the implementation phase is very much a joint effort. Establishment and testing of necessary communication links between staff and departments, bringing new skills to the firm, and managing an assortment of intrusions into the normal habits of the organization are critical.

Operation

In most settings the operation of systems has received the least amount of attention during the systems development process. Consequently, enormous frustration and ill will have frequently occurred when a system is installed. Further, as more users become operators, the subtleties of operations shortfalls become familiar to all managers. A significant amount of the difficulty, as will be discussed later, stems from inadequate attention to clearly defining the critical performance specifications to be met by the new system and from failure to recognize the often inherent conflicts between specific service goals.

A part of the design phase is identification of the specific procedures that will be used to test the services. These usually include a formal procedure for approval by operations personnel, which serves to clearly separate responsibility for a service's construction from responsibility for its operation. This role separation is particularly important when the same department (or individual) is responsible for both constructing and operating a system. In addition, operations approval procedures are needed for system enhancements and maintenance.

After the system is built and installed, measures must be developed to assess the actual delivery of the service and its quality. This is a point of weakness in many user-designed decision support systems. Many of them are so idiosyncratically designed that they cannot easily be transferred to another user when the initial user is promoted or easily be linked into the firm's networks and databases.

Maintenance

Ongoing design, construction, and implementation activities on existing services are components of maintenance. (The word *maintenance* is a complete misnomer because it implies an element of deferrability that does not exist in many situations. *Modernization* is a better term.)

Much of the maintenance requirement stems from real-world changes in tax laws, organization shifts such as new offices or unit mergers, business changes such as new product line creation or elimination, acquisition of new technology, and so on. It can be as simple as changing a number in a database of depreciation rates or as complex as rewriting the tax portion of the payroll. Effective maintenance faces two serious problems:

1. Most professionals consider it to be dull and noncreative, because it involves working on systems created by someone else. Consequently, the work may be done by individuals of lesser talent.
2. Maintenance can be very complex, particularly for older systems. It requires highly competent professionals to safely perform necessary changes in a way that does not bring the system (or the firm) to its knees.

Newer systems permit users to develop their own adaptations by including report writers or editors. Because these complex systems require more CPU cycles, however, a cost accompanies the benefit. Managing maintenance continues to be a troublesome problem, but organization, planning, and management control all provide critical context to ensure that these issues are resolved appropriately. For the user-designed decision-support applications, this has been an area of particular concern.

Summary

This description of the systems life cycle helps to show the complexity of IT management. At any time an organization may have hundreds of systems, each at a different position along this life-cycle line. Of necessity, the IT department in the overwhelming majority of cases must be organized by IT functions (user programming, operations, etc.), rather than by a specific application system. This inevitably creates significant friction, because the IT organization forces the passing of responsibility for an application system from one unit to another as it passes through these steps. The user is often the only link (although changes often occur here also) as responsibility for the system is passed from one group of technical specialists to another.

To further complicate the situation, the execution of the life-cycle process (as well as the dividing line between the steps) varies widely from one type of application system to another. For example, a structured, transaction-oriented system requires an intensive, up-front design effort to arrive at firm specifications that can then be programmed. A decision support system as described in the last section, however, may involve a process of user learning. An appropriate methodology here may begin with a crude design followed by a simple program. Use of the program by the user leads to successively different and more comprehensive designs as its performance is analyzed and then to a series of new programs. This interactive sequence cycles through a number of times. Such a design process (pragmatically useful) flies in the face of many generally held nostrums about good development practices.

In Chapter 11 we deal with the issues of operations management and the impact of buy decisions on the systems life cycle.

THEME 6: PARTNERSHIP OF THREE CONSTITUENCIES

Much of the complexity of IT management problems stems from managing the conflicting pressures of three different and vitally concerned constituencies: IT management, user management, and the general management of the organization. The relationships between these groups around IT users quite appropriately varies over time as the organization's familiarity with different technologies evolves, as the strategic impact of IT shifts, and as the company's overall IT management skills grow. Chapters 7 through 11 are largely devoted to identifying the various aspects of managing this relationship.

IT Management

A number of forces have driven the creation of an IT department and ensured its existence. The IT department provides a pool of technical skills that can be developed and deployed to resolve complex problems facing the firm. Appropriately staffed, an important part of the department's mission is to scan leading-edge technologies and make sure that the organization is aware of their existence. The department is responsible for conveying knowledge of the existence of a technology, and of how to use it, to appropriate clusters of potential users. By virtue of its central location, IT can help identify where potential interconnection between the needs of different user groups exists and facilitate the development of the interconnection. In a world of changing and merging technologies, this unit is under continued pressure to modernize in order to remain relevant. Basically, the reason the unit exists is that its specialization permits the identification of new opportunities and the cost-efficient implementation of tasks, which often cross departmental boundaries.

As information technology has evolved, the problem has become more complex because IT staff members themselves have become important users of the system (to test and develop new systems, etc.). Further complicating the situation is the growing availability of user-friendly systems and experienced users who do not feel the need to call on IT for help. Unfortunately, inadequate involvement of IT skills in the development of new systems often comes at the peril of the organization. Great fiascoes can occur when user vision and excitement overlooks the realities of implementation and the ongoing operation of a system.

User Management

Specialization of the IT function has taken place at a cost: it has transferred some detailed operational tasks from the users to the IT department without relieving the users of the responsibility for ensuring that ultimately the tasks are well done. Obviously, this is a source of friction. Additionally, in the past, the often mysterious requirements of the technology appeared to disenfranchise users from some aspects of the design of services. These frictions, when coupled with a complicated charge-out system, further estranged the user from IT.

Also complicating matters is the aggressively marketed availability of outside services that go directly to the user. (The IT department is no longer the sole source provider.)

The term *user* often implies a narrower definition than exists in a real situation: the user may be many individuals at different levels scattered across several departments. Particularly in the early stages of a technology, the user is a specialist in living with the problem and not a specialist in the technologies that can be brought to solve the problem. As the user has become more sophisticated through experience with the older IT technologies, and as the newer technologies become more user friendly, some (not all) of the reasons for having a specialized IT organization disappear. User management, through increased experience with personal computing, is gaining more confidence (sometimes unwarranted) in its ability to manage all aspects of information systems development. (The same is true of general management; see the next discussion.) Appropriately, the division of service functions between the IT specialist department and the user is being reappraised continuously.

General Management

The task of general management is to ensure that the appropriate structure and management processes are in place for monitoring the balance between the user and IT to fulfill the overall needs of the organization. (This task is complicated for executive decision-support systems when general management becomes the user.) The ability and enthusiasm of executives for playing this role vary widely. This is both a function of their comfort with IT and their perception of its strategic importance to the firm as a whole. Since many have reached their positions with little exposure to IT issues early in their careers or with exposure to radically different types of IT issues, discomfort is often extreme. Much of this book is aimed at helping this group to feel more comfortable with this activity. It should be noted, however, that over the past decade general management has become more comfortable with this technology. Experience with personal computing and earlier encounters with different (now obsolete) IT technologies have generated confidence (often misplaced) in their ability to handle the policy issues implicit in information systems technology.

In brief, each group's perspective and confidence is evolving. Although these changes are solving some problems, they are also creating new ones.

SUMMARY

In this chapter we have identified the manageable trends that are intimate to all aspects of managing information services in the 1990s. Figure 2–5 maps the remaining chapters and identifies each chapter's emphasis in relation to these six organizing themes.

Chapter 3 describes how IT is changing the way companies compete. It provides a set of five diagnostic questions that can reveal the likely impact of technology in a firm. It then introduces value-chain analysis and shows how each element of the chain is permeated by information opportunities in different settings. The chapter concludes by identifying some strategic risks posed by this technology. Chapter 4 describes the types of strategic alliances that IT has enabled. Chapter 5 focuses on the role of interorganizational IT systems and how they have changed the boundaries of firms and industries. Chapter 6 identifies how IT is changing organization structure, management controls, and other aspects of the firm's infrastructure.

Chapter 7 describes the assimilation of new technology as an organizational learning problem that requires a series of contingent actions for managing the diffusion of technology effectively. It then proposes a new organizational unit for focusing on this need. Chapter 8 describes in depth the special management issues posed by the new, fast-moving evolution in technology and some essential modifications in the IT organization structure.

Chapter 9 explains the influence of corporate cultures on managerial roles and describes various management controls that

FIGURE 2–5 Map of Chapters and Themes

	Strategic Impact	DP/TP/OA	Organization Learning	Make/Buy Decisions	Life Cycle	Power Balance
Manageable Trends **Chapter 2**						
Effects of IT on Competition **Chapter 3**	●	●				
Interorganizational Systems **Chapter 4**	●	●				●
Organization and Control **Chapter 5**	●	●				●
Information-Enabled Alliances **Chapter 6**	●	●				●
IT Architectural Alternatives **Chapter 7**		●	●			●
IT Organizational Issues **Chapter 8**	●		●	●		●
IT Management Control **Chapter 9**	●		●	●		●
A Portfolio Approach to IT Development **Chapter 10**	●				●	●
Operations Management **Chapter 11**	●			●	●	●
Transnational IT Issues **Chapter 12**		●				●
IT Planning—A Contingent Focus **Chapter 13**	●		●			●
The IT Business **Chapter 14**	●		●	●		●

can be used to integrate the IT services into the firm. Chapter 10, on project management, focuses on developing a set of contingent actions for IT, users, and general management for different types of projects and the inherent risks of different types of projects. Chapter 11 focuses on the special issues and challenges of delivering reliable day-to-day service. Chapter 12 extends the culture concept to include the range of complexities present in international situations. The planning discussion in Chapter 13 focuses on how planning is influenced by the strategic relevance of IT and on its potential impact on the organization. This includes both corporate culture and the type of contingent actions needed to assimilate the technology. Chapter 14 uses the marketing mix model to synthesize the overall issues in order to interface IT activity with the company as a whole.

Case 2–1

BURLINGTON NORTHERN: THE ARES DECISION (A)

ARES will give Operations better control over its assets. We will schedule locomotives and cars more precisely, and get more efficiency and utilization of locomotives and tracks. ARES will also enable us to service our customers better by offering more reliable and predictable deliveries.

Joe Galassi, *executive vice president, Operations*

In July 1990, Burlington Northern's senior executives were deciding whether to invest in ARES (Advanced Railroad Electronics System), an automated railroad control system. ARES, expected to cost $350 million, would radically change how railroad operations were planned and controlled. The potential implications of this investment were so extensive that they affected virtually all parts of the BN organization. Nine years had passed since BN managers had begun to consider whether automated control technology could be applied to the railroad. Yet managers were still divided about whether the ARES project should be continued.

Company Background

Burlington Northern Railroad was formed in 1970, by the merger of four different railroads. In addition to a vast rail system, the merged company owned substantial natural resources including extensive land grant holdings containing minerals, timber, and oil and gas. In 1989, up to 800 trains per day ran on BN routes (see Exhibit 1) generating revenues of $4,606 million and net income of $242 million. Total assets equaled $6,146 million, and 1989 capital expenditures were $465 million (see Exhibit 2 for recent financial data).

BN's diverse operations and staffs were headquartered in three cities (see Exhibit 3 for an organization chart). The firm's CEO, COO, and corporate functions such as finance, stragetic planning, marketing, and labor relations were located in Fort Worth, Texas. The Operations Department, headquartered in Overland Park, Kansas, was the largest department in BN. It oversaw operating divisions comprising train dispatchers, operators, and their supervisors, and managed support functions such as research and development, engineering, and maintenance. Additional corporate staff functions, such as Information System Services, were located in St. Paul, Minnesota.

Products, Markets, Competitors, and the Effects of Deregulation

BN's revenues came from seven primary segments: coal, agricultural commodities, industrial products, intermodal, forest products, food and consumer products, and auto-

Professors Julie H. Hertenstein and Robert S. Kaplan prepared this case as the basis for class discussion rather than to illustrate either effective or ineffective handling of an administrative situation.

EXHIBIT 1   Burlington Northern Route System

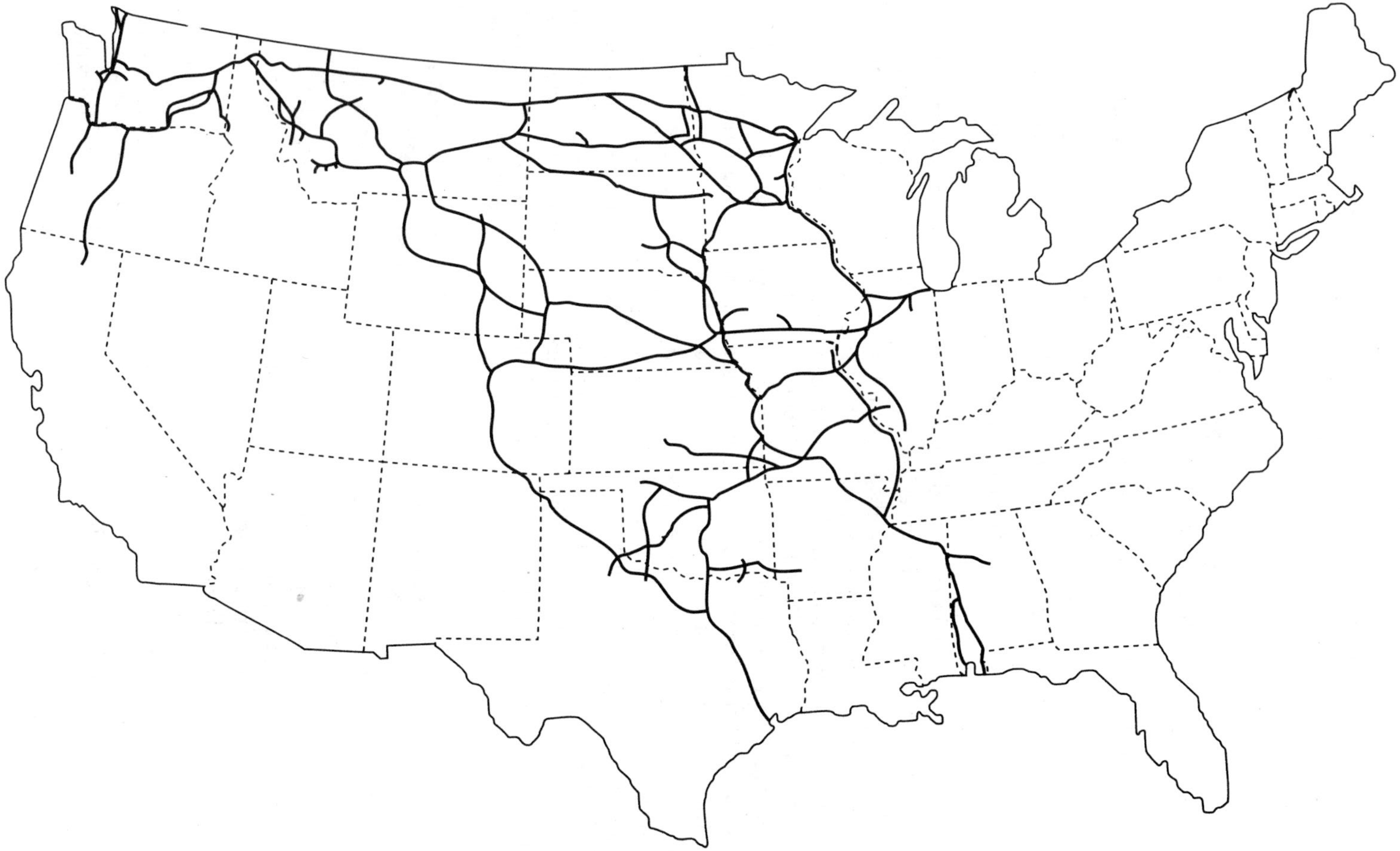

Source: Company documents.

EXHIBIT 2   Recent Financial Data ($000)

Income Statements	Year Ended December 31	
	1989	1988 Restated
Revenues		
Railroad	$4,606,286	$4,541,001
Corporate and nonrail operations	—	158,516
Total revenues	**$4,606,286**	**$4,699,517**
Costs and Expenses		
Compensation and benefits	1,701,146	1,630,283
Fuel	327,606	288,477
Material	319,497	341,126
Equipment rents	343,436	320,900
Purchased services	524,845	531,555
Depreciation	309,206	350,948
Other	410,266	406,459
Corporate and nonrail operations	13,748	150,869
Total costs and expenses	**$3,949,750**	**$4,020,617**
Operating income	656,536	678,900
Interest expense on long-term debt	270,272	292,050
Litigation settlement	—	(175,000)
Other income (expense)—net	4,397	(32,655)
Income from continuing operations before income taxes	**390,661**	**179,195**
Provision for income taxes	147,670	80,493
Income from continuing operations	**$242,991**	**$98,702**
Income from discontinued operations		
Net of income taxes	—	57,048
Net income	**$242,991**	**$155,750**

EXHIBIT 2   (*continued*)

	Year Ended December	
Balance Sheets ($000)	*1989*	*1988 Restated*
Assets		
Current assets:		
Cash and cash equivalents	$ 82,627	$ 83,620
Accounts receivable—net	430,355	685,018
Material and supplies	133,286	157,954
Current portion of deferred		
income taxes	119,589	98,339
Other current assets	31,137	39,740
Total current assets	**$ 796,994**	**$1,064,671**
Property and equipment—net	5,154,532	5,078,262
Other assets	196,254	187,401
Total assets	**$6,147,780**	**$6,330,334**
Liabilities and Stockholders' Equity		
Total current liabilities	$1,287,966	$1,218,757
Long-term debt	2,219,619	2,722,625
Other liabilities	268,721	270,702
Deferred income taxes	1,277,715	1,186,124
Total liabilities	**$5,054,021**	**$5,398,208**
Preferred stock—redeemable	13,512	14,101
Common stockholders' equity:		
Common stock	967,528	992,405
Retained earnings (deficit)	131,544	(20,624)
Cost of treasury stock	(18,825)	(53,756)
Total common stockholders' equity	**$1,080,247**	**$ 918,025**
Total liabilities and stockholders' equity	**$6,147,780**	**$6,330,334**

	Year Ended December 31	
Capital Expenditures ($000,000)	*1989*	*1988 Restated*
Roadway	$297	$305
Equipment	154	155
Other	14	14
Total	**$465**	**$474**

Source: *1989 Annual Report.*

EXHIBIT 3   Burlington Northern Organization Chart

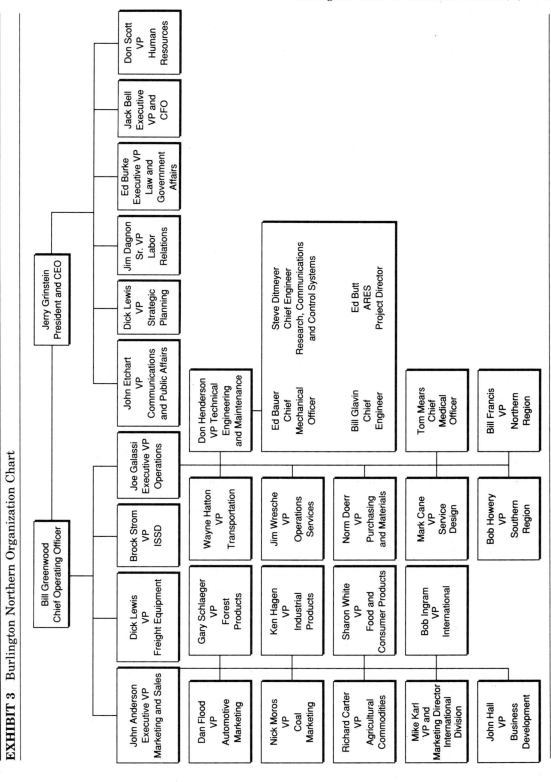

motive products (Exhibit 4 contains segment information).

Coal was BN's largest source of revenue, representing about one-third of total revenue. Over 90 percent of the coal carried by BN originated in the Powder River Basin of Montana and Wyoming. BN had invested heavily in the 1970s to build lines to serve the Powder River Basin. If the U.S. government enacted the anticipated acid rain legislation, demand for the Powder River Basin's low-sulphur coal was expected to increase substantially. Managers also believed that Powder River coal had promising export potential to Japan and other Pacific Rim nations from the West Coast ports served by BN.

Coal was carried in unit trains or "sets" (108 cars, each holding 102 tons of coal, powered by 3 to 6 engines). Virtually all the unit coal traffic was under long-term contract with fewer than two dozen customers. To ensure good asset utilization, cycle time was important. A reduction in the average cycle time reduced the number of sets required to carry a given amount of coal, and hence, reduced the capital investment in coal cars, most of which were owned by customers. Thus, unit coal trains never stopped, and the coal business was almost totally predictable. Although sensitive to cycle time, the coal business was not sensitive to arrival time precision, as coal could be dumped on the ground without waiting for special unloading facilities or warehouse space. Even electric utilities, however, were becoming aware of just-in-time delivery benefits.

BN's major competition in coal was other railroads, especially the Union Pacific (UP). UP had made substantial investments in heavy-duty double track and in new-technology, fuel-efficient engines for carrying coal. BN management believed UP had excess capacity whereas BN, with its single track lines, was running close to capacity on its coal lines.

Agricultural commodities, primarily grain, were BN's second largest segment. Strategically located to serve the Midwest and Great Plains grain-producing regions, BN was the number one hauler of spring wheat, and the number two hauler of corn. Although grain and coal were both bulk commodity businesses with little competition from trucks, the grain business differed substantially from coal. Demand for grain deliveries was more random since the time of harvest varied from year to year, and export demand for grain also fluctuated with the highly variable market price of grain. Grain traders dealt for the best prices, and long-term arrangements were uncommon. BN managers expected that with the change in economic policies in Eastern Europe (and possibly the Soviet Union), the standard of living in these countries would rise, leading to an increased demand for grain. With its ability to serve both the grain-producing regions and West Coast and Gulf ports, BN expected this segment of its business to grow significantly in future years.

During the late 1980s, BN changed the marketing of grain transportation through its Certificates of Transportation (COT) program. Under this program, BN sold contracts containing commitments to move carloads of grain within a three-day interval, six months in the future. The COT was helping to eliminate some of the randomness in grain shipments and pricing. BN, though, now had to have cars available reliably for the contracted shipment, or else incur a large penalty for failure to perform. The COT program had been a successful innovation but it put a premium on BN to coordinate and plan its grain operations.

EXHIBIT 4 Burlington Northern's Seven Business Segments

Segment	Description	Revenue (in millions)		Revenue Ton Miles (in millions)		Revenue per Revenue Ton Mile (in cents)	
		1989	1988	1989	1988	1989	1988
Coal	90% originates in Powder River Basin	$1,504	$1,500	111,087	107,202	1.35	1.40
Agricultural	Primarily grain; also food and other products	718	743	37,443	38,167	1.92	1.95
Industrial Products	44 major commodities, including chemicals and allied products, primary metal products	682	626	26,511	23,289	2.57	2.69
Intermodal	Highway trailers and marine containers moved on specially designed flatcars or double stack cars	649	615	21,505	20,222	3.02	3.04
Forest Products	Lumber and wood products; pulp paper and allied products	480	490	18,956	18,593	2.53	2.64
Food and Consumer	Food and parts for various finished products industries	413	403	15,202	14,436	2.72	2.79
Automotive	Shipment of finished automobiles; evenly divided between domestic and import traffic originating principally from Pacific Northwest ports	154	145	1,823	1,649	8.45	8.79

Source: *1989 Annual Report.*

John Anderson, executive vice president for Marketing and Sales, believed that BN's five other commodity businesses had many similarities:

> Although the customers differ, these five businesses all have significant flat or boxcar movements. They have random movement and demand, and are strongly service-sensitive. Customers make tradeoffs between price and quality, and these businesses all put us into severe competition with trucks.
>
> Think of a continuum of commodities. At one end of the continuum are commodities that should go by train such as coal or grain. These commodities are heavy and low-cost, have low time sensitivity, and come in large lots. At the other end are commodities that should go by truck, such as strawberries, electronics, and garments. These are light and high-cost, have extremely high time sensitivity, and come in small lots. In between these two extremes are many commodities where trucks and trains compete vigorously on price and service.

Historically, trucks had taken over the transportation of more and more of the contested commodities. At the end of World War II, about 70 percent of intercity freight had been shipped by rail. In the post-WW II era, rail's share of intercity shipments was lost, primarily to trucking, and especially in the service-sensitive segments. Ed Butt, ARES project director, highlighted the reasons for trucking's inroads:

> Trucks charge as much as two to three times what it would cost for rail service. But trucks go door-to-door, and people will pay for that level of service.

Recent trends in manufacturing, such as just-in-time production systems and cycle-time reduction were making trucking's service time advantages even more valuable. Railroads were using their intermodal trailer/container-on-flatcar service to offer door-to-door delivery but still could not offer the reliability of delivery that trucks could obtain on a highway system where drivers could often make up for unexpected delays. As Butt explained:

> We may have peaked at 75 percent on-time delivery for our general merchandise, and 80 percent for intermodal. But 75 to 80 percent is not good enough for just-in-time service. Trucks are 90 to 95 percent, and we need to get into that range to attract the just-in-time customers, who are enormously sensitive to consistent, reliable deliveries.

Effects of Deregulation

The deregulation of both the trucking and railroad industries in 1980 had changed both the railroads' and the truckers' competitive environment. The Motor Carrier Act of 1980 gave truckers much greater freedom in setting rates and entering markets. The Staggers Rail Act of 1980 gave railroads similar freedom in setting their own rates; it also included provisions allowing railroads to own other forms of transportation.

Following deregulation, BN modernized its railroad operations. Richard Bressler, the chairman in 1980, established a research and development department in Operations and hired Steve Ditmeyer to head the group. Numerous new technologies and innovations were considered and, where appropriate, were applied to railroad operations. During the 1980s, railroad productivity increased dramatically: the number of employees declined by 50 percent while revenue ton miles increased by over two-thirds.

But trucking rates fell significantly after deregulation, putting pressure on the railroads' chief advantage: the low-cost transportation of freight. In 1990, additional regulatory changes permitting trucks to be longer and heavier were under consideration. These changes would enable trucks to further reduce their costs. Dick Lewis, vice president of Strategic Planning, however, recognized:

In our recent analysis we've been surprised to find that railroads and not trucks are some of our major competition. Since deregulation, intra-railroad competition is increasing and driving down prices at a fearsome rate. [See Exhibit 5.] Trucks have carved off their own segments fairly solidly. Railroads want to compete in these segments, but they don't, and trucks are pretty secure in them.

Existing Operations

In 1990, each day up to 800 trains traveled approximately 200,000 train-miles on the 23,356 miles of track on BN routes. The 5,000 junctions created 25 million possible distinct routings, or origin-destination pairs, for the cars that made up BN trains. Meets and passes—two trains "meeting" on a single track with one of them directed off to a siding so that the other can "pass"—were carefully managed by the railroad's dispatchers. BN managers believed that thousands of meets and passes occurred each day, but were unsure about the precise number; some believed the actual number was as high as 10,000 per day.

A train running off schedule could potentially affect many other trains because of the limited number of tracks—often only one— and sidings in any area. Thus, controlling train operations meant controlling an extensive, complex network of dynamic, interdependent train and car movements.

Trains were controlled by dispatchers, each responsible for a distinct territory. Dispatchers still utilized technology developed around 1920, and little had changed since then. A dispatcher was responsible for the 20 or 30 trains operating on his or her shift in his or her territory. Operations personnel, however, estimated that a good dispatcher could really only focus on and expedite five to seven trains. The remainder were inevitably treated with less attention and lower priority. At present, dispatcher priority went to scheduling competitive segments like in-

termodal and merchandise traffic; unit trains carrying coal and grain were not scheduled. Dispatchers had little basis for trading off delaying an intermodal train versus reducing the cycle time for a coal train.

Dispatchers saw information only about their own territories, and not others. Thus, if a delayed train entered a dispatcher's territory, he would be unaware that enough slack existed farther down the line to make up all the lost time, and that he should not jeopardize the schedules of his other trains by trying to catch the delayed train up to its schedule. Typically, trains were directed to run as fast as they could and then halted to wait at sidings.

Dispatchers also scheduled maintenance-of-way (MOW) crews. MOW crews would travel to a section of track that needed maintenance and repair. But the crews were not allowed to initiate work on the track until the dispatcher was confident that no train would run down the track during the crew's work period. At present, train arrivals at MOW work sites could be predicted within a 30- to 45-minute window, but for safety reasons, the work crews were cleared off the track much sooner than the beginning of this window.

Dispatchers spent considerable time establishing communications with trains and MOW vehicles. Dispatchers had to search various radio frequencies to establish contact with trains; MOW vehicles often reported long waits until they were able to get through to the dispatcher for permission to get onto the track. In fact, on some occasions, the MOW crew traveled to the maintenance site but was unable to get through to the dispatcher before the maintenance window closed and another train was scheduled to arrive, hence wasting the trip.

Current information about railroad operations was difficult to obtain. For example, to know how much fuel was available, an engineer had to stop the train, get out, and

EXHIBIT 5 Railroad Rates and Ton-Mile Revenue

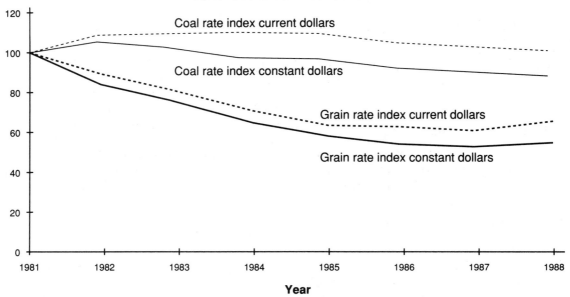

**Grain and Coal Rate Index
Current Dollars and Constant Dollars**

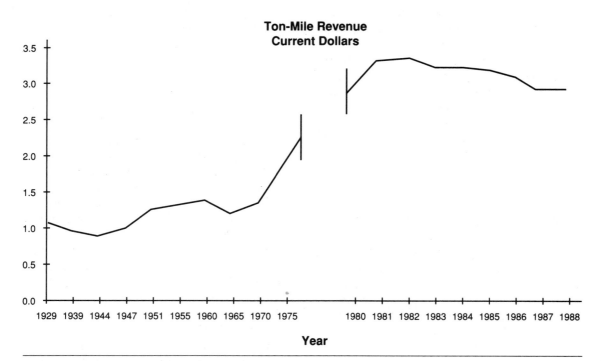

**Ton-Mile Revenue
Current Dollars**

Source: Association of American Railroads.

look at the gauge on the tank at the back of the locomotive. Trains refueled nearly every time they passed a fueling station, even if the added fuel was not necessary for the next part of the trip. Further, despite daily maintenance checks of critical components such as brakes, lights, and bells, and scheduled periodic maintenance every 92 days, the only evidence of a locomotive performing poorly came from reports filed by the crew about observable failures or breakdowns. Except for the newest locomotives, no gauges or recording systems monitored conditions that could foreshadow failures such as oil pressure or temperature changes.

Information about the location of cars and trains was also subject to delay and error. Conductors were given instructions about which cars to set out and pick up at each location. Following completion of a set-out or pick-up, the conductor made a written notation. When the train arrived at the next terminal (conceivably hours later), the paper was given to a clerk who entered the data via keyboard to update management data files. Arrivals of trains at stations were recorded by clerks who, if busy, might not observe the actual arrival, thus recording a 12:00 train as 12:15, and then entering this fact at 1:00 to the management data files.

Some executives were exploring the application of modern management science philosophy to improve railroad scheduling. According to Mark Cane, vice president, Service Design:

> There are many potentially useful operations research and artificial intelligence techniques that are not yet being used by the railroad. Decision support technology has made a quantum leap forward, and we are trying to take advantage of it.

Dick Lewis illustrated the contrast between the BN and another highly scheduled transportation company:

A benchmark company in this area is UPS. UPS has 1,200 industrial engineers working for them; BN has only half a dozen.

One view, integrated network management, was being discussed among BN's senior managers. Using this approach, scientifically designed schedules would be generated and broken down into "standards" for each task, plus the appropriate education and incentives would be provided for local operations personnel to cause them to run the railroad to schedule. One operating manager voiced the concerns of many about this approach to railroad train scheduling:

> BN has talked a lot about running a scheduled railroad. However, the real challenge is how to manage the unscheduled, for example, a broken air hose or a broken rail. The problem is that problems do not happen on schedule.

By mid-1980, BN's service design organization had begun to institute a reporting system called the service measurement system. Bands of acceptable performance were established for scheduled trains and compared with actual results. On-time scheduled performance measures became part of the bonus incentive system for nonunion operating personnel. Following the institution of the reporting scheme, service showed definite and steady improvement. The percentage of scheduled cars arriving within targeted performance bands jumped from 25 percent in January 1990 to 58 percent in June. This suggested to BN managers that service performance could be improved simply by better collection and reporting of performance measures.

Strategic View of Operations

In late 1989, BN executives undertook a major strategic review to help shape the future. Gerald Grinstein, the chief executive officer of BN, focused the review on answering questions like, "What kind of railroad should we be?" Executives formed eight teams to examine in depth the following areas: operating strategies, customer behavior, information technology, labor, business economics, organizational performance, industry restructuring, and competitive analysis.

Dick Lewis, explained the conclusions reached by this strategic directions project:

This company, and the railroad industry, face two major challenges: service and capital intensity. We must improve our ability to deliver service. We must reform and reconstitute our service offerings, especially in highly service-sensitive segments. Since World War II, railroads have retrenched from service-sensitive segments. For example, they have stopped carrying passengers and less-than-carload shipments.

If we improve service, the first opportunity created is to increase volume, at the expense of other rail carriers. The second opportunity is to raise prices, but this is more questionable. To be able to raise price requires a *radical* service change, not a marginal one. The change must be radical enough to be perceived by a customer, who says, "Wow! That's different!" For example, in our chemical business we recently made such a change. We reduced the average delivery time by more than half, and we also reduced the variability of the delivery time. The shipper found he could get rid of 100 rail cars. That had a measurable value significant enough for the customer to perceive the service improvement. We have subsequently been able to structure an agreement with the shipper to provide financial incentives to BN to further improve the service.

The other side of this equation is that BN must improve utilization of assets. We have high capital intensity, poor utilization of rolling stock, and low asset turnover ratios. Actually, BN is good for the industry, but the industry itself has very poor ratios. Not only are the ratios poor, but the capital require-

ments for the 1990s are daunting. Just the traditional investments in locomotives, freight cars, and track replacements are daunting. If we can improve utilization of these assets, then we can reduce the capital investment required during the 1990s.

The ARES Project: The Origins

Steve Ditmeyer, chief engineer, Research, Communications and Control Systems, reached deep into his desk and withdrew a slip of paper with a handwritten note: "Any application to locomotives?" BN's chairman, Bressler, had written that note in 1981 shortly after Ditmeyer had joined the company, and attached the note to an article on new aircraft instrumentation that promised lowered costs by improving fuel and other operating efficiencies. The note and article eventually filtered down to numerous railroad staffs.

In 1982, BN's R&D department contacted the Collins Air Transport Division of Rockwell International to learn whether aircraft technology could be applied to the rail industry. The two companies agreed to work together to identify workable solutions. By the end of 1983 they discovered that the technology existed to integrate control, communications, and information. An electronics unit, placed in each locomotive, could receive signals from the Department of Defense's Global Positioning System (GPS) satellites, and calculate the train's position to within ± 100 feet, a significant improvement over the existing $\pm 10-15$ mile resolution from existing systems. By calculating the train's location every second, the train's speed could also be estimated accurately. A communications network could then be developed to carry information back and forth between the train and a control center.

The R&D department managed the early stages of the ARES project, with oversight by the R&D Steering Committee comprising senior officers of Transportation, Engineering, Mechanical, Operations Services, Marketing and Information Systems. The Board of Directors in July 1985 viewed a demonstration of the proposed technology installed on two locomotives. In August 1985 BN's senior executives agreed to fund a prototype system: equipping 17 locomotives on BN's Minnesota Iron Range, putting the data segment in place in the Iron Range, and building those elements of the control segment that would permit BN to communicate with and control the locomotives from the Minneapolis control center. The Iron Range was chosen because it was a closed-loop segment of BN's network with a variety of train control systems, and was served by a limited set of equipment.

By 1986 the ARES project had grown too large to be carried out by the small R&D staff, and Don Henderson was chosen to oversee the formation of a separate ARES team to manage the project's development. Henderson ensured that team members represented various Operations departments that would potentially be affected by ARES: dispatching, mechanical, maintenance-of-way, control systems and communications, freight car management, and information system services. The team members worked with their respective departments and with others such as general managers and operating vice presidents to ensure a system that met operational needs and worked in the railroad environment. Operations managers saw ARES as a means to accomplish key goals of service improvements, operating efficiencies and improved capital utilization. Operations incorporated ARES into the strategic plans it prepared and presented to corporate.

The ARES prototype was installed on the Iron Range in 1987. The ARES team, BN field personnel, and system developer Rockwell spent the next several years testing, evaluating, and improving the ARES system.

Under Henderson's guidance, the ARES concept evolved to a full command, control, communications, and information system that would enable BN to gain additional control over its operations. ARES, using high-speed computing, digital communications, and state-of-the-art electronics, could generate efficient traffic plans, convert those plans into movement instructions for individual trains and MOW units, and display those instructions to engine crews. By knowing the position and speed of trains and other equipment on the tracks, ARES could automatically detect deviations from plan or potential problems and communicate these exceptions to control center dispatchers. Dispatchers could determine the corrective action required and use ARES to send and confirm new movement instructions to trains. In many ways, ARES could be considered analogous to the Air Traffic Control system that controlled the aviation industry. ARES eventually came to consist of three segments: Control, Data, and Vehicle.

The Control segment received information on train position and speed to produce schedules and to check that vehicles followed proper operating procedures. It warned dispatchers of violations to limits of authority and speed, and produced authorities and checked them for conflict. The Control segment also helped to schedule the MOW crews to get much higher utilization of MOW equipment and labor time. The Control segment displayed for dispatchers the activity in their territories, and supplied information about consists, crews, and work orders for any train.

The Data segment communicated data back and forth between the Control segment and locomotives, MOW vehicles, and track monitoring and control equipment. It made use of BN's existing microwave and VHF radio network.

The Vehicle segment on board each locomotive or MOW vehicle included a display (CRT) to provide information from the Control segment, a keypad to communicate back to the dispatcher, an on-board computer to monitor various aspects of locomotive performance, and a throttle-brake interface that the dispatcher or the on-board computer could activate to stop the train if the crew became disabled, if the train violated its movement authorities, or if communication was lost with the ARES system. This segment included a receiver for satellite signals to calculate train position and speed, which were then communicated to the Control segment.

The Vehicle segment incorporated an Energy Management System that received information on track profile and conditions, speed limits, power, and car weight to determine a recommended train speed that met service requirements, while minimizing fuel consumption and providing good train-handling characteristics.

The Vehicle segment also included the Locomotive Analysis and Reporting System (LARS). LARS used a number of sensors and discrete signals to monitor the health and efficiency of locomotives and provide early warning signals about potential failures. LARS was expected to permit problematic locomotives to be pulled out of service for maintenance before they failed unexpectedly in a remote region and to provide a database that maintenance people could analyze to prevent future malfunctions.

The ARES Project: Current Status

By 1989, BN had spent approximately $15 million, cumulatively, on the ARES project. BN managers estimated that Rockwell had spent three times this amount. "Concept validation" had been accomplished through the Iron Range test, which had proven that the technology could locate trains under real operating conditions and could communicate back and forth between the control center and the locomotive. Rolling stock hardware

had been tested for robustness and reliability. The Iron Range prototype system was demonstrated not only to numerous groups of BN executives and operating personnel but also to customers, representatives of other railroads, and numerous industry and governmental groups. By late 1989, testing of the prototype was completed. (See Exhibit 6 for a summary of the development process and Exhibit 7 for details of further development required for full implementation.)

The ARES team had seen enough from the Iron Range testing to believe that it would enable BN to provide better service, improve asset utilization, and reduce costs. The ARES project that senior executives were evaluating and deciding whether to authorize in 1990 was an integrated command, control, communication, and information (C^3-I) system for controlling train movements with, according to the ARES staff, "unprecedented safety, precision, and efficiency." According to a document prepared by R&D and project staff members:

> ARES will allow BN to run a scheduled railroad with smaller staffs and more modest [capital] investments than current signaling systems. It will maintain accurate, timely information about train consists and locations. The results will be improved service, with higher revenue potential, and cost reductions. Another important benefit will be the elimination of train accidents caused by violations of movement authority.

The ARES team now requested authorization for the expenditures needed to complete the development of the full operational system and to roll out implementation through the railroad. The ARES team, and its sponsors Don Henderson, vice president, Technology, Engineering, and Maintenance, and Joe Galassi, executive vice president, Operations, faced several important considerations as they prepared to present this investment for authorization.

EXHIBIT 6 BN Personnel Involvement in ARES Design and Implementation

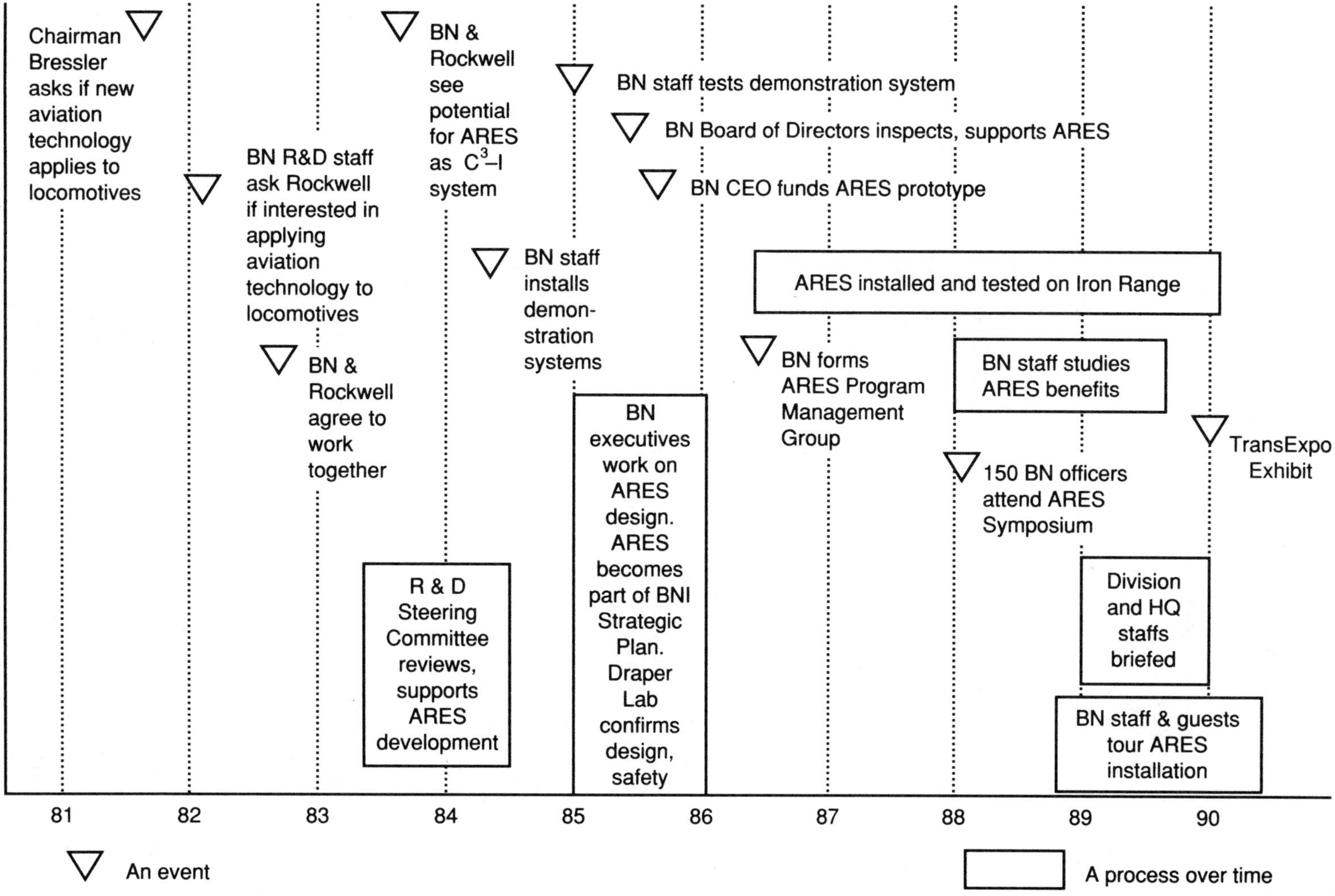

A timeline chart spanning years 81 through 90, showing "A process over time."

- **81** — Chairman Bressler asks if new aviation technology applies to locomotives (An event)
- **82** — BN R&D staff ask Rockwell if interested in applying aviation technology to locomotives
- **83** — BN & Rockwell agree to work together
- **84** — BN & Rockwell see potential for ARES as C³–I system
- **85** — BN staff installs demonstration systems; BN staff tests demonstration system
- **84–86** — R & D Steering Committee reviews, supports ARES development
- **85–86** — BN executives work on ARES design. ARES becomes part of BNI Strategic Plan. Draper Lab confirms design, safety
- **86** — BN Board of Directors inspects, supports ARES; BN CEO funds ARES prototype
- **87** — BN forms ARES Program Management Group
- **87–90** — ARES installed and tested on Iron Range
- **88** — 150 BN officers attend ARES Symposium
- **88–89** — BN staff studies ARES benefits
- **90** — TransExpo Exhibit
- **89** — Division and HQ staffs briefed
- **89–90** — BN staff & guests tour ARES installation

Source: Company documents.

71

EXHIBIT 7   Development Required to Implement ARES as of Early 1990

Scheduling Programs

Train scheduling programs comprised two modules: the Strategic Traffic Planner (STP) and the Tactical Traffic (or Meet and Pass) Planner. The STP viewed railroad operations globally, for example, determining optimal schedules for the entire railroad system. It could determine whether a late train should be caught up in the current dispatcher's territory, or a subsequent one with more slack. BN had contracted to have STP specifications written, but no computer programs had been written.

The Meet and Pass Planner functioned at a local level. STP schedules were passed to the Meet and Pass Planner. Treating STP schedulers as constraints, the Meet and Pass Planner produced a meet and pass schedule for a dispatcher's shift; the dispatcher revised this schedule, if necessary, and authorized it. Authorized meets and passes were communicated through ARES to the trains as operating instructions, which the engineers carried out. Prototype Meet and Pass Planner computer programs had been written; ARES staff members had tested their functionality and had used them in simulation to evaluate ARES benefits. However, the Meet and Pass Planner had not been tested in the Iron Range nor had it actually controlled trains. ARES staff had identified prototype bugs requiring resolution; they were also concerned whether the meet and pass planning algorithms were the most efficient.

Energy Management System

The ARES staff considered Rockwell's original Energy Management System prototype unacceptable; it was not used to provide control input to trains in the Iron Range. Rockwell was reworking the Energy Management System, but it was not yet complete nor was it ready for testing.

Locomotive Analysis and Reporting System (LARS)

The data gathering aspect of LARS had been tested in the Iron Range. However, BN had little experience analyzing these data. It could not evaluate the nature and magnitude of potential savings, due in part to the Iron Range's unique closed-loop where locomotives passed a maintenance station daily instead of every several days as on other portions of the railroad.

Existing Iron Range Software

The software used in Iron Range tests was considered prototype software. While it was designed as efficiently as possible, the prototype testing had revealed that greater efficiencies were possible. The production software would further have to be designed to gain greater efficiencies when regulatory restrictions were lifted in the future. Thus, the Iron Range prototype software required redesign before it could be implemented as efficient production software.

First, corporate management was significantly changed from the management that had authorized earlier phases. Four CEOs, including the current executive, Gerald Grinstein, had held office since the 1981 inception of the project. None of the vice presidents who were on the R&D steering committee in 1982 and 1983 was still with the railroad. Of the board members who saw the ARES demonstration in July 1985, only one, the current chairman, remained. Thus, although ARES had undergone a lengthy development process within BN, many who must now support and authorize it were unfamiliar with the choices that had guided its development.

Second, there was a question of whether to propose a full-blown implementation of the ARES project or just an initial phase or two. Presenting the full-blown project would inform top management of the potential range of ARES features and would give them the bottom line for fully installing ARES for the entire railroad: about $350 million. (See Ex-

---

EXHIBIT 8　ARES Cost Breakdown

Major Cost Categories	*Cost*	*Comments*
Control Center	≅ $80 million	Software development is a major component of this cost.
Data link (wayside communications)	≅ $80 million	BN planned to replace much of its existing pole line communication network with an ARES-compatible data link regardless of the decision on ARES. However, this conversion had barely begun.
On-board equipment	≅ $200 million	Roughly $100,000 per road locomotive; less for switch locomotives and MOW vehicles. Of this, LARS = $16,000/locomotive with total costs (including software development) expected to be less than $35 million. Although not expected to exceed LARS, Energy Management System costs had not been estimated in detail.

LARS and the Energy Management System were generally considered modules separable from the rest of ARES. Beyond these two, however, it was difficult to identify ARES modules that could be implemented independently. For example, sending a movement authority to a train required the control segment to check conflicts with other vehicles' authorities, the data link to communicate the authority to the train, and the on-board equipment to enable the engineer to receive and confirm the authority. Thus, each of these three segments had to be implemented for ARES to operate in any given region. Although not every locomotive had to be equipped, as fewer locomotives in a region were equipped the overall system became less effective since ARES could no longer confirm the location of—and spacing between—all trains. Limiting ARES to a geographic region within BN reduced data link and on-board equipment costs commensurate with track and vehicle reductions, and reduced Control Center costs somewhat.

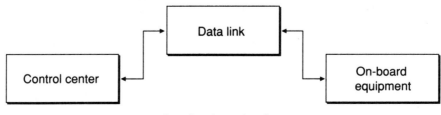

Source: Case writer's estimate, based on interview data.

hibit 8 for cost breakdown.) Even for a company of the size of BN, this investment was a large amount. And ARES was a complex project, different from typical railroad investments in modern locomotives, cars, track, and ties. According to Henderson:

> We may not do the entire railroad; early implementation at least would inevitably be limited to specific geographic areas. Further, we may or may not implement all of the ARES features; the LARS system and the energy management system are clearly very separable pieces.

Galassi explained the rationale for proposing the entire project:

> We figured that top management would want to have a picture of the total project, rather than being fed a piece at a time for incremental decisions and wondering where the end of the line was.

Finally, there was the issue of how to communicate the ARES benefits and credibly measure their value. Some of the benefits that the ARES team had identified were either difficult to measure because the values were unknown—how much more would a customer be willing to pay for a 1 percent improvement in service?—or because the railroad did not record and track certain data—how much time was lost by trains waiting for meets and passes? The team firmly believed that if they implemented this innovative technology, they would experience benefits they had not yet even anticipated.

To help measure the variety of benefits from a full-blown implementation of ARES, the team economist, Michael Smith, contracted with a half-dozen outside consultants, each of whom focused on a specific area such as measurement of market elasticity, measurement of LARS effects, measurement of meet/pass efficiency, and improved safety. (See Exhibit 9 for a summary of each benefit study.) Some benefits could be measured only partially in financial terms; for example, improved safety would reduce damaged equipment and freight by perhaps $20 million per year, although its value in human and political terms was even more significant. According to Steve Ditmeyer:

> ARES reduces the probability of a collision by two orders of magnitude because, in contrast with our existing railroad control system where one failure or a mistake by one person can cause an accident, with ARES no single person or piece of equipment can cause an accident; two must fail simultaneously.

The Strategic Decisions Group (SDG) was hired to help the ARES team integrate the results of the individual consulting studies with other BN data into a single, coherent analysis of benefits. The analysis was conducted using three strategic scenarios supplied by BN's planning and evaluation department: base, focused, and expansion. Using probability distributions of key uncertainties supplied by BN managers, a set of computer models was built to calculate the probability distributions of the net present value of ARES under each of the strategic scenarios.[1] Exhibit 11 illustrates a representative annual and cumulative after-tax cash flow for the ARES project. The SDG report concluded:

> The potential benefit of ARES is large but highly uncertain. Using the best information currently available, we estimated the gross benefit in the range of $400 million to $900 million, with an expected present value of about $600 million. This benefit should be weighed against a cost of approximately $220 million (present value). . . . The benefits depend greatly on implementation success: The system design must be sound, a strong imple-

---

[1]The cumulative probability distributions of the net present value of ARES benefits under each of the strategic scenarios are shown in Exhibit 10.

EXHIBIT 9 Consultants' Studies of ARES Benefits

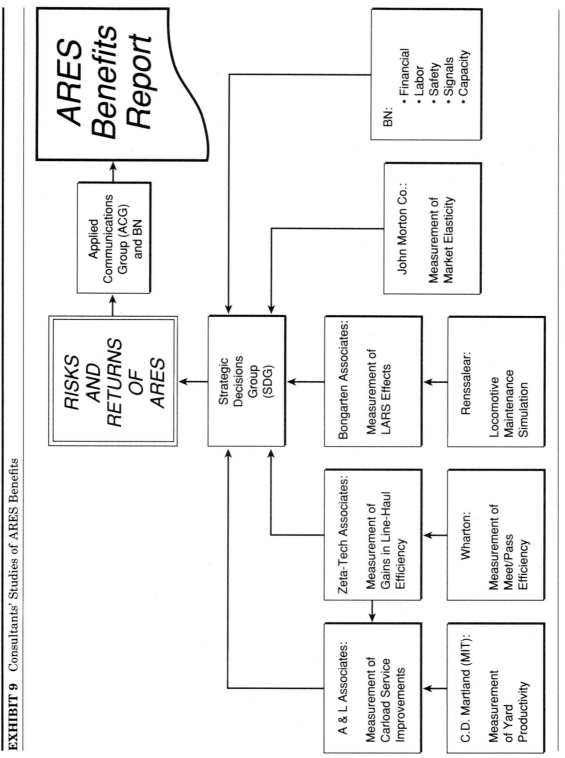

Source: Company documents.

EXHIBIT 9 (continued)

Consultant	Purpose	Approach	Results
A & L Associates	Measure effect of ARES improvements in terminal and line-haul performance on carload service.	Service improvements were modeled for a representative BN section using the Service Planning Model with inputs on existing conditions and expected changes in performance supplied by C.D. Martland, Wharton, and Zeta-Tech.	Reductions in line-haul times and increased terminal performance will decrease total trip times by 7–8% even if scheduled connections and blocking strategies are unchanged.
John Morton Company	Measure the increase in traffic expected with an increase in the level of service offered customers in given market/commodity areas.	Questionnaires were distributed to decision makers who routinely select modes/carriers for shipping commodities in or across BN territories. A demand elasticity model was constructed using conjoint analysis. The model was calibrated, tested, and sensitivity analyses were conducted to generate demand elasticities for each service attribute.	Perceived performance differences between truck and rail are most dramatic with respect to transit time, reliability, equipment usability, and level of effort. Improving reliability offers greatest leverage for increasing BN's revenues. A 1% improvement in reliability, if, and only if, fully implemented and perceived in the marketplace, could yield a 5% increase in revenues; a 5% improvement in reliability could yield a 20% increase in prices.
Bongarten Associates	Evaluate the Locomotive Analysis and Reporting System (LARS).	A simulation using actual BN data on train information, trouble reports, and repairs tested LARS in four modes: (1) inspection of units committed to shops; (2) examining component status during on-road failures; (3) using prospective diagnostics to schedule additional repairs when locomotive is already committed to the shop; (4) using prospective diagnostics to bring the unit into the shop before a failure occurs.	The two LARS modes which offer the greatest promise are modes 2 and 3; mode 3 offers higher savings but requires development of a prospective diagnostics system. Savings of 3% to 5% were calculated in five areas: departure delay, on-line delay, time off-line, maintenance manhours, and reduced severity of repair due to early detection.
Charles Stark Draper Laboratory	Analyze how safe ARES would be, compared to BN's existing train control systems.	Modeling using Markov analysis.	The probability of a train control system-related accident would be reduced by a factor of 100 when ARES is in place. The primary reason for this improvement is that ARES' integrated system architecture provides highly reliable checks and balances that limit the impact and propagation of human errors.

EXHIBIT 9 (concluded)

Consultant	Purpose	Approach	Results
Zeta-Tech Associates	Measure gains in line-haul efficiency from Energy Management System (EMS) module and Meet/Pass Planning module.	Recorded actual operating data on 846 trains (55 were selected for detailed analysis) from 16 "lanes" chosen to represent BN's full range of operating conditions, control systems, traffic volumes, and mixes. Modeled actual operation to establish baseline fuel consumption and running time; then modeled fuel consumption and running time using (1) EMS module and (2) Meet/Pass Planner.	EMS module produced only 2% net fuel savings and large increases in running times for some trains. Z-T argued this was due to software flaws in algorithm and priorities. Meet/Pass Planner reduced running time for all 846 trains by an average of 21%. For the 55 selected trains, travel time decreased 17% and fuel consumption decreased 2.5%. Reliability increased; the travel-time standard deviation also decreased.
Wharton	Measure Meet/Pass efficiency and feasibility.	Modeled fuel consumption and running time using various Meet/Pass dispatching algorithms on selected study trains in the 16 lanes evaluated.	ARES can produce meet/pass plans consistent with operating policies which yield travel time and fuel savings in 30 seconds or less; a pacing algorithm produces further fuel savings.
C.D. Martland (MIT)	Measurement of yard productivity.	Collected detailed data from several BN yards. Modeled effect of improved reliability of train operations on (1) yard efficiency through improved interface between line-haul, terminal operations, and crew assignments and enhanced capabilities for communications with and supervision of crews; (2) yard processing times; and (3) train connection reliability.	Train performance was variable enough to allow considerable room for increased reliability, reducing average yard times about one hour. Modest improvements in terminal efficiency and train connection performance could be achieved through better utilization of terminal crews. Overall ARES could reduce average yard time 0.5 to 2 hours at major terminals and reduce missed connections by 15 to 17%.

EXHIBIT 10   Cumulative Probability Distributions of ARES Benefits Under Three Scenarios

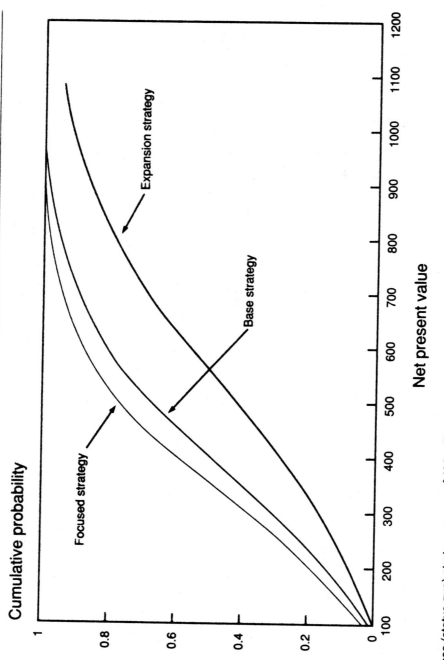

Base (status quo) strategy mean = $406 million
Focused strategy mean = $360 million
Expansion strategy mean = $576 million

Source: Company documents.

Burlington Northern: The ARES Decision (A) 79

EXHIBIT 11 ARES Projected Annual and Cumulative After-Tax Cash Flow

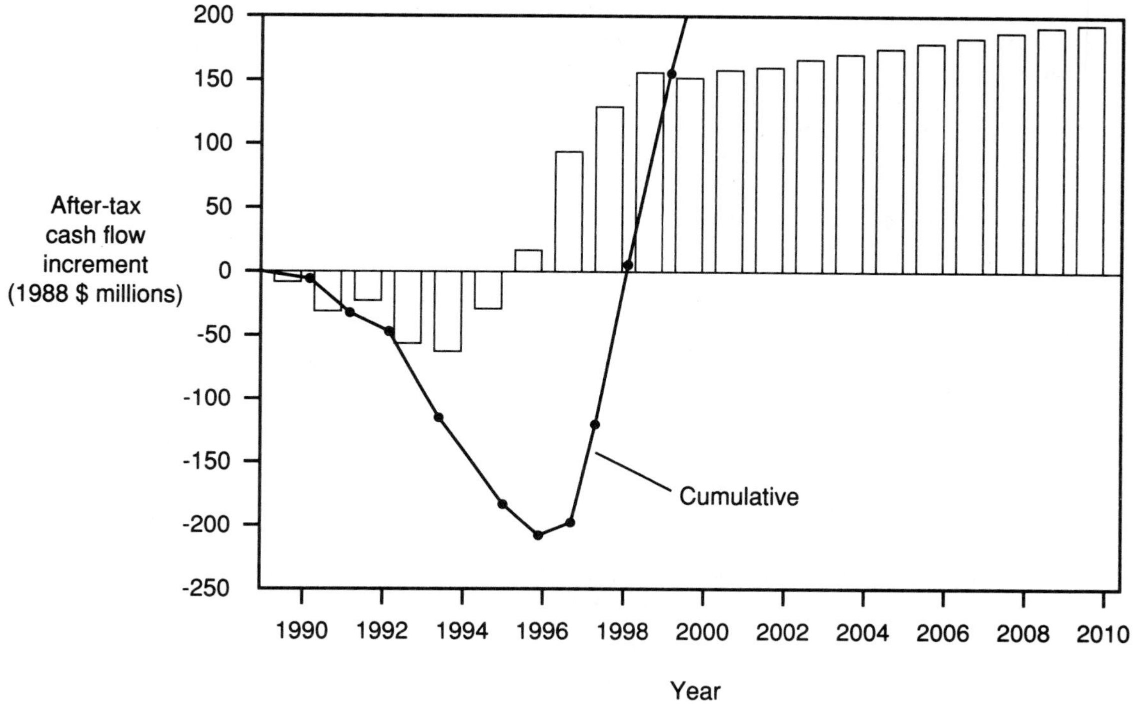

Source: Company documents.

mentation plan must be developed, and functional groups across the BN system must be committed to using it to full advantage.

The ARES team concluded that the primary known benefits of ARES (see Exhibit 12) were to be measured in reduced expendi-tures on fuel, equipment, labor, and track-side equipment; damage prevention; and enhanced revenues. The largest component, revenue enhancements, however, had the most uncertain estimates (see Exhibit 13).

EXHIBIT 12 Primary ARES Benefits

ARES offers many benefits which enable BN to reach its goals of safe and profitable rail operations. Following is a summary of those benefits.

- Increased rail operations safety results from constant monitoring of wayside signal and detector equipment, train movement, and locomotive health.
- Greater operating efficiency and improved customer service come from operating trains to schedule and handling trains that deviate from schedule, the results of improved traffic planning.
- Improved safety and increased customer service come from real-time position, speed, and ETAs for all trains, computed continuously and automatically provided to MOW crews and other BN users through existing BN computer systems.
- Improved dispatcher productivity results from automating routine dispatching activities such as threat monitoring, warrant generation, traffic planning, and train sheet documentation.
- Higher effective line capacity is provided by accurate vehicle position information and automatic train movement authorization.
- Improved MOW productivity results from improved traffic planning.
- Improved business management is possible with accurate, current information about the status and performance of operations and equipment.

Key Points

The study examines benefits in the following areas and estimates the present value of those benefits:

- Fuel $ 52 million
- Equipment $ 81 million
- Labor $190 million
- Trackside equipment and damage prevention $ 96 million
- Enhanced revenues $199 million

Total $618 million

To account for uncertainty in these estimates, the study calculated ranges of values for them and probabilities of achieving values within the ranges.

The factors with the largest potential for delivering benefits are also the most uncertain:

- ARES' ability to improve transit time and
- The amount customers are willing to pay for better service.

Accounting for ranges and probabilities, ARES will make the following mean contribution to net present value for each corporate strategy:

- Focused strategy $360 million
- Base strategy $406 million
- Expansion strategy $576 million

The probability of ARES earning less than 9% real after-tax rate of return is extremely small.

Source: Company documents.

EXHIBIT 13 Price Gain Versus Increased Service Reliability

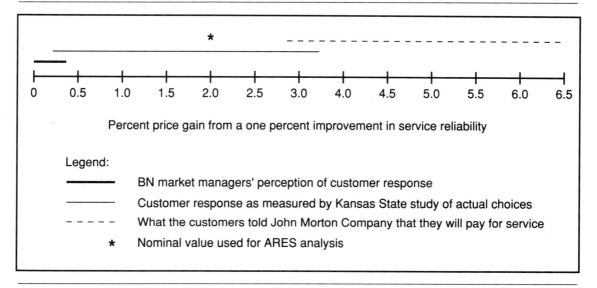

Percent price gain from a one percent improvement in service reliability

Legend:

──────── BN market managers' perception of customer response

──────── Customer response as measured by Kansas State study of actual choices

─ ─ ─ ─ ─ What the customers told John Morton Company that they will pay for service

* Nominal value used for ARES analysis

Source: Company documents.

Case 2–2

BURLINGTON NORTHERN: THE ARES DECISION (B)

ARES seems to be a technology in search of a problem. The projected benefits from ARES have been derived from a bottom-up approach, not from a top-level strategic planning process.

Dick Lewis, *vice president of Strategic Planning*

ARES has the aura of an R & D–driven project. It was never subjected to the company's long-term resource allocation financing process or to a ranking among strategic priorities.

Jack Bell, *chief financial officer*

Ed Butt, ARES project director, and Don Henderson, vice president, Technology, Engineering and Maintenance, had presented ARES benefits to senior executives.[1] While the executives found the benefits "fairly convincing," according to CEO Grinstein, they still had questions: "Do we need those benefits? Will there be a return on the $350 million? Is there a cheaper way to get them?" Senior executives had a nagging feeling that BN might be able to obtain 80 percent of the benefits for only 20 percent of the costs. Jack Bell articulated these concerns:

> ARES is a very large, complex project. It has many bells and whistles. We need to figure out what is the most important aspect of the project. If it is meet and pass planning, then we should assess the most cost-effective way of doing meet and pass planning. "Unbundling," however, is not the favorite activity of project teams, especially late in the development process.

Managers were also worried that the ARES team had become over-committed to their project and had lost their objectivity for analysis. Some referred to ARES team members as "zealots." It seemed that whenever senior managers identified a problem, ARES was offered as the solution; this confused some executives about exactly what ARES benefits were.

Executives also did not fully believe all aspects of the ARES benefits analysis, particularly the service-price elasticities. The marketing department considered the estimates overstated (see Exhibit 1) and wondered why its people had not been more involved in developing this analysis beyond providing suggestions on market research firms, research sites, and questionnaire content.

Others worried about the magnitude of the investment itself. A $350 million investment was not the largest BN had made, es-

---

[1]The ARES project was described in "Burlington Northern: The ARES Decision (A)," HBS Case No. 191-122.

Professors Julie H. Hertenstein and Robert S. Kaplan prepared this case as the basis for class discussion rather than to illustrate either effective or ineffective handling of an administrative situation.

EXHIBIT 1 Price Gain Versus Increased Service Reliability.

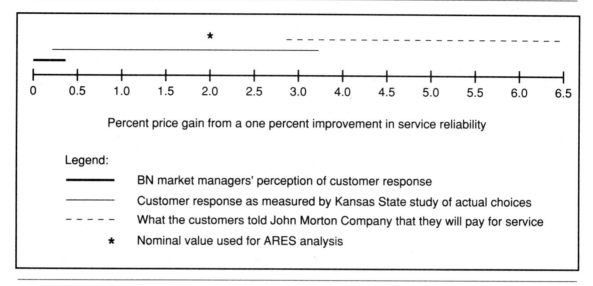

Percent price gain from a one percent improvement in service reliability

Legend:

▬▬▬	BN market managers' perception of customer response
———	Customer response as measured by Kansas State study of actual choices
- - - -	What the customers told John Morton Company that they will pay for service
*	Nominal value used for ARES analysis

Source: Company documents.

pecially considering that the investment would be made over a several-year period. However, some were concerned that the actual investment would turn out to be much larger. According to Bill Greenwood, chief operating officer:

> Many things may be incomplete in the ARES system. Therefore, I don't know if the $350 million represents a bottom-line price tag, or if the actual cost to design, program, implement, and debug ARES will be a considerably larger number. The technology—vehicle identification, radio and satellite communication, and locomotive monitoring—is almost the least of our concerns. The technology alone does not deliver the benefits. We need to change our underlying business processes, which are not only large in number, but intensely interrelated. And the roles and responsibilities of many of our operating positions must be redesigned in order to achieve the objectives and benefits of ARES. This kind of planning process was not undertaken

in the piloting of ARES, but it will be vital to successful, widespread adoption.

The significance of the required organizational changes concerned other managers as well. Observers noted that this investment would catapult the organization from the Iron Age into the Electronic Age. According to Dick Lewis:

> We wanted to increase our confidence in how the railroad's traditional, hierarchical organization with its deeply rooted, hundred-year-old history would handle the major organization changes that would be necessary.

Financial Operations and Restructuring

Even if ARES were justified, did BN have adequate funds to undertake it? During the late 1970s railroad industry financial performance had been generally poor. The industry was capital intensive, return on assets was low, and some railroads had been forced into bankruptcy.

Concurrently, concerns developed among some of BN's most senior managers that the firm was not doing enough to exploit its extensive land grant and natural resource holdings. They also believed that BN's stock price did not adequately reflect the value of its railroad operations and its natural resource holdings. This belief was made more tangible when T. Boone Pickens started to purchase Burlington Northern shares in 1987. BN management decided to restructure the company. Burlington Resources Inc. (BR) was created in May 1988 as a holding company for BN's natural resource operations. In July 1988, BR completed an initial public offering of its stock and in December, BN distributed its shares of BR common stock to BN's common stock holders, thus spinning BR off from BN, and leaving BN with one principal subsidiary: Burlington Northern Railroad Company. All previous debt was retained by BN; following the spin-off of BR, BN was left with a debt-to-total-capital ratio of 76 percent, a level considered high for the industry.

In his 1988 letter to shareholders, CEO Gerald Grinstein stated:

> We must manage the substantial debt load remaining after the spin-off of Burlington Resources Inc. This will require a clear strategic focus so that we can maximize the cash flows available for capital improvements while reducing the outstanding debt.

Jack Bell soon noticed the investment community's enthusiasm for debt repayment.

> Following the recapitalization, the investment community estimated BN's earnings per share at $3.20 and its share price at $22, a 7× P/E multiple. We queried analysts about why the multiple was so low, and they told us about their concern with the level of debt for a company in a cyclical industry. To convince the investment community that BN had a viable program to pay down the debt and still invest in the railroad, we announced an accelerated debt repayment program that would repay more than the amount required in the debt covenants. Subsequently, we supported this program with progress reports of BN's cash flows and debt paydown in 1989 ($500 million as of year end) and a projection of 1990 cash flows (excluding net income). [See Exhibit 2.] BN's stock price rose significantly in the months following this report.

BN planned to continue to accelerate paydown. Grinstein's 1989 letter to shareholders said:

> One of our top priorities has been to improve our financial structure. We have undertaken a major improvement program and made significant first-year progress, retiring over $500 million in debt [debt-to-total-capital ratio: 68 percent]. . . . Our goal is to achieve a total debt level of 50 percent of total capitalization by 1994, paying down debt at an average rate of $200 million per year.

To emphasize the urgency of debt repayment, BN instituted a bonus plan in 1989 for all 3,000 of its salaried employees. The average percent bonus in any year depended on the company's earnings per share, net income, and debt paid down. Individual performance could make individual bonuses somewhat higher or lower than average. Salaried employees below the level of vice president were divided into three groups whose bonuses could range up to 10 percent, 20 percent, or 40 percent of their annual salary respectively. Bonuses for employees at or above vice president level were administered separately.

In an era of accelerated debt paydown, funds for investment were tight, and there were many competing demands for available funds. Normal aging of equipment would require heavy expenditures to replace locomotives, freight cars, and track. Recently ac-

EXHIBIT 2   Post-Spin-Off Cash Flows ($ in millions)

1989 Cash Flow		*1990 Cash Flow Planning Assumptions*		
Sources of Cash		**Sources of Cash**		
Net income	$ 243	Net income	$?	
Depreciation	310	Depreciation	350	
Deferred taxes	69	Deferred taxes	30	
Lease financing	100	Lease financing	100	
Cash balance drawdown	1	Cash balance drawdown	40	
Accounts receivable sale	250	Other	50	
Working capital change	124	**Total**	**$570**	**+ Net income**
Asset sales net	19			
Total	**$1,116**			
Uses of Cash		**Uses of Cash**		
Capital expenditures	$ 473	Capital expenditures	$537	
Dividends	109	Dividends	92	
Debt service	505	Required debt service	115	
—Required	112	ETSI	25	
—Optional	393	Other	1	
ETSI	25	**Total**	**$770**	**+ Discretionary**
Other	4			**debt paydown**
Total	**$1,116**			

Source: Company documents.

quired concrete ties had already demonstrated benefits beyond those originally projected, leading to proposals to make further investments in them as well. The growth in export potential caused some BN managers to consider whether additional railroad acquisitions with good access to West Coast ports should be sought. Brock Strom, vice president, Information System Services, believed that the new strategies resulting from the firm's strategic review would require additional MIS investments to support them. The strategies were still emerging so no specific demands were defined, though his "unsubstantiated guess" was that $100–200 million would be required. Jim Dagnon, senior vice president, Labor Relations, suggested that if the current round of labor negotiations produced an agreement that train crew sizes could be reduced, an investment of $100–

200 million to "buy out" the excess crew would have an 18-month payback.

Technology Concerns

Apart from financial considerations, some managers were concerned that BN was considering adopting an automated train control technology that differed from the Advanced Train Control System (ATCS) being developed by members of the Association of American Railroads (AAR). ATCS controlled trains; ARES controlled the entire railroad operation. By 1990, when BN had already tested the ARES prototype, the AAR was still developing specifications for ATCS. Some believed that the ARES system was as many as five years ahead of ATCS in development.

Other managers pondered whether BN should be first in the industry with an automated train control technology. According to Joe Galassi:

> If the investment is unique for some period and represents a competitive advantage, then BN should be the first mover and get the additional business. However, if the technology does not offer a big marketplace advantage, then it is not best to be first. If other competitors implement it first, BN has the advantage of watching them and avoiding their mistakes.

Many believed that the development of the control center represented another notable risk. Software development was a key element of the $80 million control center cost. Much of the complex set of control center software had yet to be developed and integrated, although some algorithms had already been tested. Forecasts of development costs, or of development time, might be exceeded. Brock Strom suggested that some prior computer applications had not always gone exactly as planned. For example, the computerized track warrant system that one division got from the Canadian Pacific Railroad was supposed to take one year to implement; it actually took four. However, the remaining ARES software resembled existing software applications such as the FAA's air traffic control system. According to Brock Strom:

> The technology risks are not that significant. The hardware technologies have been used in other industries; therefore the issue is not developing a brand new technology but transitioning an existing technology to the railroad. ARES is a major software development effort with all the normal problems, but the programming effort is quite feasible and should be able to be implemented.

Gerald Grinstein believed:

> For the industry to succeed, it will inevitably have to get into some kind of new technology. I don't want BN to be the sole ARES advocate. I've invited other railroads to come and

observe the prototype system in the Iron Range. If BN goes with ARES, it will probably drive the rest of the industry this way. The others have to stay competitive, and ATCS is not realistically available now, so ARES is the only operating solution at the current time.

The ARES decision is caught up in another process, shaping BN's future. Major questions to be answered are, "What kind of railroad should we be?" If we deliver a much greater, more reliable level of service, can we profit from that?

Joe Galassi stated:

> There are really two reasons to do ARES. The first is better service. The second is that we will be better able to control assets by scheduling locomotives and cars more precisely and getting better productivity out of the assets. However, the real heart of the matter is service to the customer.

Mark Cane, vice president, Service Design, concurred:

> ARES could bring higher reliability to the railroad. It could improve the mechanical quality of the railroad, through fewer engine breakdowns. It could improve reliability in terms of consistent arrival time through dispatching and schedule discipline. It could also increase the capacity of the physical plant by tightening the spacing between trains, thus allowing more trains to travel on the existing track. If ARES cost $50 million, we might have already begun it, but $350 million is a problem in light of competing demands for capital.

Jim Dagnon also found that ARES offered significant advantages from his perspective:

> The union leadership has toured the ARES prototype facilities. They loved it. The work force is as ready to adopt ARES as any work force I've ever seen. A significant aspect of ARES for all labor is safety; safety is extremely important, and they see ARES as increasing safety. They see ARES as making their job easier and more important, espe-

cially the engineers. Conductors are a little less enthusiastic; it may reduce their job responsibilities. Ultimately, ARES has the potential to schedule the crews' work; this would lead to a higher quality of life compared with today's unscheduled, on-call environment in which crews don't know whether or when they will be called to work.

As BN's executives pondered whether or not to proceed with ARES, they still were not fully comfortable with whether the assessment of ARES benefits was realistic or optimistic. They also struggled with whether the benefits, or many of them, could be attained at a lower cost: Were technologies cheaper than the one prototyped with Rockwell available to support the ARES project? Could the benefits be unbundled? For example, the recent experience with the service measurement system suggested to some executives that improved discipline and reporting could enhance service without the large capital investment required by ARES. Yet, in contrast to JIT experiences which had taught manufacturing firms to fix their manufacturing processes before automating them, at BN, without automation—that is, ARES—managers lacked information on operations needed to fix the process. Could BN have the cake without the icing?

Before proceeding with a decision, BN's senior executives decided to conduct an outside audit of the ARES proposal. SRI International (formerly Stanford Research Institute) was engaged to audit the benefits analysis, to investigate the possibility of unbundling the benefits, and to study whether alternative, less expensive technologies were feasible.

Chapter 3

Effects of IT on Competition

To solve customer service problems, a major distributor installed an on-line network to its key customers so that they could enter orders into its computer directly. The computer was intended to cut order-entry costs, to speed processing time, and to provide more flexibility to customers in the order submission process. Although the company's expectations for the system were very modest initially, it yielded a large competitive advantage, adding value for customers and generating a substantial rise in the distributor's sales. Over a period of years new features were added, and the resulting increase in the company's market share forced a primary competitor into corporate reorganization and a massive systems-development effort to contain the damage, but these corrective actions were only partially successful. Only when the distributor stopped innovating because of internal cost pressures did its advantage deteriorate.

A regional airline testified before Congress that it had been badly hurt by the reservation system of a national carrier. It claimed that the larger airline, through access to the reservation levels on every one of the smaller line's flights, could pinpoint all mutually competitive routes where the regional was performing well and take competitive pricing and service action. Since the regional airline lacked access to the bigger carrier's data, it alleged, it was at a decided competitive disadvantage. Partly because of this, the airline ultimately failed.

A large aerospace company required major suppliers to acquire CAD (computer-aided design) equipment to link directly to its CAD installation. The company claims this has dramatically reduced the total cost and time of design changes, parts acquisition, and inventory, which has made it more competitive.

These examples capture the changing face of the IT applications world. With great speed the sharp reduction in the cost of information systems technology (IT) has allowed computer systems to move from back-office support to applications that offer significant competitive advantage. Particularly outstanding are systems that link customer and supplier (discussed at length in Chapter 4). As this chapter will explain, the evolution of such systems is usually extraordinarily expensive and extends over a number of years. The very competitive airline reservations systems, for example, have evolved over 30 years and they continue to evolve. To use a track analogy, the investment decisions in this area are more akin to the marathon than to the one-hundred-meter dash.

Though such initiatives offer an opportunity for a competitive edge, they also bring a risk of strategic vulnerability. In the case of the aerospace manufacturer, operating procedures have shown much improvement, but it has been at the cost of vastly greater dependence, since it is now much harder for the manufacturer to change suppliers.

In many cases the new technology has opened up new opportunities for a company to redeploy its assets and rethink its strategy. This gives the organization the potential for forging sharp new tools that can produce lasting gains in market share. Of course, such opportunities vary widely from one company to another, just as the intensity and the rules of competition vary widely from one industry to another. Similarly, a company's location, size, and basic product technology also shape potential IT applications. These opportunities are not restricted to the large firms; they affect even the smallest companies. Further, in different situations, a company may appropriately attempt to be either a leader or an alert follower. In many settings, what is a strategic advantage for the first investor becomes a necessity for the other firms in the industry as the rules of competition shift. The stakes can be so high, however, that this must be an explicit, well-planned decision.

ANALYZING IMPACT

Forces that Shape Strategy

The variety of potential competitive and strategic uses of IT is as broad and complex as the industries within which the uses have evolved. To facilitate planning for these uses, general managers need a comprehensive framework. This framework must view use of computer and communications technology from a strategic rather than a tactical perspective. Michael Porter's industry and competitive analysis (ICA) framework,[1] augmented with potential technological uses, has proven very effective in this respect.

Porter's work was directed at strategic business planners and general managers. He argued that many of the contemporary strategic

---

[1]Michael E. Porter, *Competitive Strategy: Techniques for Analyzing Industries and Competitors* (New York: The Free Press, 1980).

planning frameworks viewed competition too narrowly and pessimistically because they were primarily based on projections of market share and market growth. He asserted that the economic and competitive forces in an industry segment were the result of a broader range of factors than the strengths and weaknesses of established combatants in a particular industry. According to him, the state of competition in an industry depends on five basic forces: (1) bargaining power of suppliers, (2) bargaining power of buyers, (3) threat of new entrants into the industry segment, (4) threat of substitute products or services, and (5) positioning of traditional intraindustry rivals. Figure 3–1 shows the five competitive forces and illustrates the ICA framework.

Although Porter's initial work did not include information systems as part of the company's resource pool for ICA, it has proven very useful in considering the business and industry impact of IT. Table 3–1 puts the basic ICA model in the context of implications for industry and potential technology impact.

Column 1 lists the key competitive forces that shape competition in a given industry segment. In a specific industry, not all forces are of equal importance (Figure 3–2). Some industries are dominated by suppliers (for example, the impact of OPEC on the petroleum industry), while other industries are preoccupied with the threat of new entrants and/or substitute products (such as the banking and insurance industries).

Column 2 of Table 3–1 lists key implications of each competitive force. For example, when new entrants move into an established industry segment, they generally introduce significant additional capacity. They frequently have allocated substantial resources in order to establish a beachhead in the industry. The result of new entrants typically is reduced product prices or increased costs for incumbents.

FIGURE 3–1   Competitive Forces

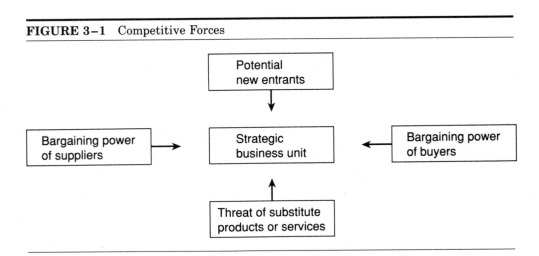

TABLE 3-1 Impact of Competitive Forces

Force	Implication	Potential Uses of IT to Combat Force
Threat of new entrants	New capacity Substantial resources Reduced prices or inflation of incumbents' costs	Provide entry barriers: Economies of scale Switching costs Product differentiation Access to distribution channels
Buyers' bargaining power	Prices forced down High quality More services Competition encouraged	Buyer selection Switching costs Differentiation Entry barriers
Suppliers' bargaining power	Prices raised Reduced quality and services (labor)	Selection Threat of backward integration
Threat of substitute products or services	Potential returns limited Ceiling on prices	Improve price/performance Redefine products and services
Traditional intraindustry rivals	Competition: Price Product Distribution and service	Cost-effectiveness Market access Differentiation: Product Services Firm

Column 3 lists some examples of how IT can be used to combat the implications of the given competitive force. For example, the establishment of entry barriers can be implemented with IT that generates significant economies of scale, builds in switching costs that reduce the ability of suppliers and buyers to move to new entrants, differentiates product or company, or limits access to key markets or distribution channels.

Two basic types of competitive advantage, combined with the scope of activities for a firm seeking to achieve them, make for three *generic strategies* for achieving above-average performance in an industry: cost leadership, differentiation, and focus. (See Figure 3–3.) The focus strategy has two variants: cost advantage and differentiation.

Each generic strategy involves a fundamentally different route to competitive advantage, combining a choice about the type of competitive advantage sought with the scope of the strategic target in which

FIGURE 3–2 Elements of Industry Structure

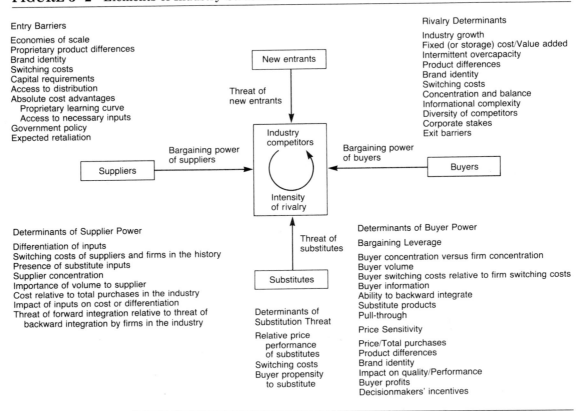

Entry Barriers

Economies of scale
Proprietary product differences
Brand identity
Switching costs
Capital requirements
Access to distribution
Absolute cost advantages
  Proprietary learning curve
  Access to necessary inputs
Government policy
Expected retaliation

Rivalry Determinants

Industry growth
Fixed (or storage) cost/Value added
Intermittent overcapacity
Product differences
Brand identity
Switching costs
Concentration and balance
Informational complexity
Diversity of competitors
Corporate stakes
Exit barriers

Determinants of Supplier Power

Differentiation of inputs
Switching costs of suppliers and firms in the history
Presence of substitute inputs
Supplier concentration
Importance of volume to supplier
Cost relative to total purchases in the industry
Impact of inputs on cost or differentiation
Threat of forward integration relative to threat of
  backward integration by firms in the industry

Determinants of
Substitution Threat

Relative price
  performance
  of substitutes
Switching costs
Buyer propensity
  to substitute

Determinants of Buyer Power

Bargaining Leverage

Buyer concentration versus firm concentration
Buyer volume
Buyer switching costs relative to firm switching costs
Buyer information
Ability to backward integrate
Substitute products
Pull-through

Price Sensitivity

Price/Total purchases
Product differences
Brand identity
Impact on quality/Performance
Buyer profits
Decisionmakers' incentives

competitive advantage is to be achieved. The cost leadership and differentiation strategies seek competitive advantage in a broad range of industry segments, while focus strategies aim at cost advantage (cost focus) or differentiation (differentiation focus) in a narrow segment. The specific actions required to implement each generic strategy vary widely from industry to industry, as do feasible generic strategies in a particular industry. Selecting and implementing the appropriate generic strategy is very difficult, but it lies at the heart of what a firm must do if it is to achieve long-term competitive advantage in an industry.

At the core of the concept of generic strategies are the notions that competitive advantage is the goal of any strategy and that to achieve competitive advantage a firm must define the type of competitive advantage it seeks to attain and the scope within which it will attain it. Being "all things to all people" is a recipe for strategic mediocrity and below-average performance, because it often means that a firm has no competitive advantage at all.

FIGURE 3–3   Three Generic Strategies Related to Competitive Advantage and Scope

Competitive Advantage

		Lower Cost	Differentiation
Competitive Scope	Broad Target	Cost leadership	Differentiation
	Narrow Target	Cost focus	Differentiation focus

Search for Opportunity

To assess the ultimate impact of IT for planning purposes, companies should begin by addressing five questions. If the answer to one or more of these questions is yes, IT may be a strategic resource that requires attention at the highest level. These questions "operationalize" the competitive IT analysis implicit in the previous discussion.

Can IT Build Barriers to Entry?   In an example early in the chapter, a distributor was able to open up a new electronic channel to its customers. The move was highly successful for the company, and other companies found it very hard to replicate. Customers did not want devices from different vendors on their premises; for space, training, and ease of use purposes, they wanted one device from one supplier.

A successful entry barrier not only offers a new service that appeals to customers; it also offers features that keep the customers "hooked." The harder the service is to emulate, the higher the barrier is for the competition. An example of such a defensible barrier is the development of a complex software package that adds value and is capable of evolution and refinement. A large financial service firm used this approach to launch a different and highly attractive financial product that depended on sophisticated software. Because of the complexity of the concept and its software, it took competitors several years to develop similar features, which gave the firm valuable time to establish market position. Further, the firm did not sit on its laurels; it enhanced its original product significantly, thus making itself a moving target.

The payoff from value-added features that increase both sales and market share is particularly noteworthy for industries in which there are great economies of scale and where price is important to the customer. By being the first to move onto the learning curve, a company can gain a cost advantage that enables it to put great pressure on its competitors. In the airline industry, for example, where the software costs have run into the hundreds of millions of dollars, this has been particularly significant.

Electronic tools that increase the scope and speed of price quotes for salespeople represent another kind of barrier. The sophisticated financial-planning packages with embedded expert systems that are being used by sales forces of major insurance companies around the globe are building similar barriers, because they have raised the standards of service.

Conversely, while many of these projects require large capital investments, they also have uncertain ultimate benefits, which poses real risks. Further, in difficult economic times, investment in these electronic systems may create both serious cost rigidity and barriers against an orderly exit from the industry. It is difficult, for example, for a large airline to scale down its computing activity sharply in order to deal with reduced operations or great cost pressures.

Can IT Build in Switching Costs?   Are there ways to encourage customer reliance on the supplier's electronic support, to build it into their operations so that increased operational dependence and normal human inertia make switching to a competitor unattractive? Ideally, the electronic support system is simple for the customer to adopt and contains a series of increasingly complex and useful procedures that gradually insinuate themselves into the customer's daily routines. Thus the customer will become so dependent on these value-added procedures that it will be reluctant to change suppliers. Electronic home banking is a good example of this. It is hoped that once customers have learned to use the system and have coded all their monthly creditors for the system, they will be very reluctant to change banks.

A manufacturer of heavy machines provides another example of electronic services and features that add value to and support a company's basic product line while increasing the switching cost. The company has attached electronic devices to its major machine installed on customer premises. In case of mechanical failure, the device signals over the telecom network to a computer program at corporate headquarters. The program analyzes the data, diagnoses the problem, and either suggests changes in the machine's control settings or pinpoints the cause of the failure and identifies the defective parts and, when appropriate, triggers the dispatching of a mechanic. Now installed around the globe, the system has dramatically improved service levels and significantly cemented customer loyalty. Attrition on service contracts has shrunk dramatically.

Can IT Change the Basis of Competition?   In some industries dominated by cost-based competition, IT has permitted development of product features that are so different that they cause the basis of competition to change radically. For example, in the mid-1970s, a major distributor of magazines to newsstands and stores was in an industry segment that was dominated by cost-based competition. For years it had used electronic technology to drive costs down by developing cheaper methods of sorting and distributing magazines. Using less staff and lower inventory, it had achieved the position of low-cost producer.

In 1977 the distributor decided to build on the fact that its customers were small, unsophisticated, and unaware of their profit structures. By using its records of weekly shipments and returns from a newsstand, the distributor could identify what was selling on the newsstand. It developed programs that calculated profit per square foot for every magazine and compared these data with information from newsstands operating in economically and ethnically similar neighborhoods with varying mixes of merchandise. The distributor could thus tell each newsstand every month how it could improve the product mix. In addition to distributing magazines, the company used technology to offer a valuable inventory-management feature that changed the basis of competition from cost- to service-based differentiation, while raising its prices substantially.

Dramatic cost reduction can significantly alter the old ground rules of competition. In a cost-competitive environment, companies should look for a strategic IT opportunity. There may be an opportunity for sharp cost reduction, such as through staff reduction or the ability to grow without hiring staff, improved material use, increased machine efficiency through better scheduling or more cost-effective maintenance, or inventory reduction. Alternatively, there may be an opportunity to add value to the product that will permit the company to compete on the basis of product differentiation.

A large insurance carrier recently identified systems development as its biggest bottleneck in the introduction of new insurance products. It is, therefore, investing heavily in software packages and outside staff to complement its large (500-person) development organization. A cost-cutting activity in the 1960s and 1970s, the carrier's IT organization became vital to the implementation of a product-differentiation strategy in the 1980s. Though the company is cutting staff and financial expenditures overall, it is increasing IT expenditures and staff as a strategic investment.

Understanding when to move on these issues is particularly difficult and troublesome. For example, few people doubt that videotext and cable services will eventually become important in retailing, particularly in upscale markets, but *when* that will happen and in what *form* it will come remain very murky. In many cases, however, these changes could in a short time dramatically alter old processes and structures, to the extent that today's forms will be unrecognizable. No example is more striking than the situation confronting libraries. They have a 1,000-year-plus tradition of storing books made of parchment and wood pulp. Soaring materials costs, the advent of cheap microfiche and microfilm, expansion of computer databases, CD-ROM (compact disk read-only memory), and electronic links between libraries will make the research facility of the year 2000 utterly unrecognizable from that of today. The period of transition will be short, and the discontinuity with the past sharp. Those libraries that persist in spending 65 percent of their budget to keep aged wood pulp warm (and cool) will be irrelevant to the needs of their users.

Though in the early stages it is difficult to distinguish the intriguing (but ephemeral) from an important structural innovation, the consequences can be devastating if managers misread the issues in either direction.

Can IT Change the Balance of Power in Supplier Relationships?
The development of interorganizational systems has been a powerful asset in many settings for dealing with suppliers. For example, just-in-time delivery systems have drastically reduced inventory levels in the automotive and other industries, thus permitting big cost savings in holding costs, warehouse expenses, and so on. Since companies in these industries are uncertain about what they will need downstream or when they will be cut off from their suppliers, they used to keep enormous safety stocks of components and ready-to-ship subassemblies. Increasingly, they are taking up slack by using electronic links between suppliers and dealers; in essence, substituting information for surplus inventory, capital, and production facilities.

Similarly, electronic CAD links from one organization to another permit faster response, smaller inventory, and better service to the final consumer. In one case, a large retailer has linked its materials-ordering system electronically to its suppliers' order-entry systems. If 100 sofas are needed for a particular region, the retailer's computer automatically checks the order-entry systems of its primary sofa suppliers, and the one with the lowest cost gets the order.

Equally important, the retailer's computer continually monitors its suppliers' finished-goods inventories, factory scheduling, and commitments against its schedule to make sure enough inventory will be available to meet unexpected demand. If a supplier's inventories are inadequate, the retailer alerts the supplier. If any suppliers are unwilling to go along with this system, they may find their overall share of business dropping until they are replaced by others.

A major manufacturer proposed CAD/CAD links with a $100 million/year in sales pressed-powder metal parts manufacturer. Within 18 months this system shrunk what had been an eight-month product design cycle down to three months.

Such interorganizational systems can redistribute power between buyer and supplier. In the case of the aerospace manufacturer, the CAD/CAD systems increased dependence on an individual supplier, making it hard for the company to replace the supplier and leaving it vulnerable to major price increases. The retailer, on the other hand, was in a much stronger position to dictate the terms of its relationship with its suppliers.

Can IT Technology Generate New Products? As described earlier, IT can lead to products that are of higher quality, can be delivered faster, or are cheaper. Similarly, at little extra cost, existing products can be tailored with special features to customers' needs. Some companies may be able to combine one or more of these advantages. They should ask themselves if they can attach an electronic support service to a product to increase the value of the total package in the consumer's eyes. This can often be done at little additional cost, as in the case of the on-line diagnostic system for machine failure described earlier.

In another example, credit card companies are voracious consumers of delinquent account receivable data from other firms. Indeed, there is a whole industry dedicated to the collection and organization of these data. Similarly, nonproprietary research data files often have significant value to third parties.

In some cases, a whole new industry has emerged. POS data in supermarkets is a case in point. The first firm in the industry began by purchasing data from a large supermarket chain. The chain was under great cost pressure (like most U.S. chains) and could not profitably use the data; the cost of developing a market research system for itself would have been too great. Consequently, they sold the data for cash and future access to it. These data have been organized by ZIP code into a research tool for retail chains, food suppliers, and others interested in consumer activity.

ANALYZING THE VALUE CHAIN FOR IT OPPORTUNITIES

An effective formal way to organize a search for effective IT opportunities is through a systematic analysis of a company's value chain—the series of interdependent activities that brings a product or service to the customer. Figure 3–4 shows a typical value chain, drawn from Michael Porter's analysis, and briefly defines the meaning of each of the company's activities. In different settings, IT can profoundly affect one or more of these activities, sometimes simply by improving effec-

FIGURE 3–4 The Value Chain

Support activities	Corporate infrastructure						
	Human resource management						
	Technology development						
	Procurement						
		Inbound logistics	Operations	Outbound logistics	Marketing and sales	Service	
		Primary activities					Margin

Activity	*Definition**
Inbound logistics	Materials receiving, storing, and distribution to manufacturing premises.
Operations	Transforming inputs into finished products.
Outbound logistics	Storing and distributing products.
Marketing and sales	Promotion and sales force.
Service	Service to maintain or enhance product value.
Corporate infrastructure	Support of entire value chain, such as general management, planning, finance, accounting, legal services, government affairs, and quality management.
Human resource management	Recruiting, hiring, training, and development.
Technology development	Improving product and manufacturing process.
Procurement	Function or purchasing input.

*Abstracted from Michael E. Porter, *Competitive Advantage* (New York: Free Press, 1985), pp. 39–43.

Source: Michael E. Porter and Victor E. Millar, "How Information Gives You Competitive Advantage," *Harvard Business Review,* July–August 1985, p. 151.

tiveness, sometimes by fundamentally changing the activity, and sometimes by altering the relationship between activities. In the process, what a firm does may have a significant effect on the value chains of key customers and suppliers as well.

Inbound Logistics

As can be seen from the earlier examples, in many settings, IT has already had an important impact on expediting materials to the point of manufacture. One major distribution company, for example, has installed hundreds of terminals on supplier premises to permit implementation of just-in-time, on-line ordering. The company requires its suppliers to keep adequate inventory and to make their figures on available stock accessible to its computerized purchasing system.

This system has cut down on warehousing needs for incoming materials and has reduced disruptions due to inventory shortfalls. The need to maintain inventory safety stocks and the associated holding costs have been passed along to the suppliers. The purchaser's computer can also rapidly scan several suppliers' databases and order from the one offering the lowest price. This new efficiency has sharply eroded suppliers' margins. Because this distribution company has great purchasing power, it has reaped most of the system's benefits. Changing vendors, however, has become more difficult for the distributor.

A large department store chain is linked directly to several of its textile suppliers. This hookup has not only improved delivery and permitted inventory reduction; it has also provided the chain the flexibility to meet changing demand almost immediately. This in turn has offset price differentials by making it easier to deal with domestic suppliers than with remote foreign suppliers. In this cost-sensitive environment, this has been enormously important to U.S. textile manufacturers.

Operations and Product Structure

Information systems technologies affect a manufacturer's operations and its product offerings. In 1989 a manufacturer of thin transparent film completed a $30 million investment in new computer-controlled manufacturing facilities for one of its major product lines. This change slashed order response time from 10 weeks to 2 days and improved quality levels significantly.

When one financial services firm decided to go after more small private investors (with portfolios of about $25,000), it introduced a flexible financial instrument. It gave investors immediate on-line ability to move their funds among stocks or out of stocks, and it provided money market rates on idle funds as well as liquidity equal to that of a checking account. The company was the first to introduce this service and captured a huge initial market share. Continued product enhancement has ensured that investors have no incentive to switch services. In the first two years, this original provider achieved six times the volume of its nearest competitor. Five years later it still retained a 70 percent share of the market.

A videotext service company reconceptualized its business as essentially a bit-moving operation—that is, getting data from one place to another. This concept led it to offer a new line of financial services, such as instantaneous financial information (up-to-the-second foreign exchange rates, for example), and was the key to development of other new services. The company had to make no important changes in its technology, and its sales and profits soared.

A major insurance company thought of its business as a provider of diversified financial services and as a bit-moving company. It improved its services to policyholders by allowing them immediate on-line checking of status for claims and claims processing. The company also provided on-line access to new services and products. These included modeling packages that enabled corporate benefits officers to determine the costs of various benefit packages so as to tailor them to costs and employee requests. It further responded to clients' needs by selling either software for claims processing or claims-processing services to corporate clients who elect to self-insure. The company credits these information technology–enabled product initiatives with keeping it firmly in place at the top of its industry despite tremendous competition from other diversified financial services companies.

Outbound Logistics

IT has had a great impact on the way services and products are delivered to customers. As mentioned earlier, the reservations-system links to travel agents, provided chiefly by United Airlines and American Airlines, have affected their business relationships so profoundly that the smaller airlines that do not furnish this service have found it difficult to match. Indeed, in December 1984 the prominent placement on the screen of their flights, versus those of competition, was believed to so strongly influence purchasing behavior that the Civil Aeronautics Board issued a cease-and-desist order against the practice. Automatic teller machines allow cash and services to be rapidly and reliably delivered to outlying locations. Theater-ticket and airline-ticket machines are other examples. Obviously, each example just cited of inbound logistics for one company represents outbound logistics for the other partner.

Marketing and Sales

A large pharmaceutical company offers on-line order-entry services to pharmacies for itself and a consortium of allied, noncompeting companies. This service has increased its market share and derived sizable added revenues from its consortium partners. Some companies excluded from the bundle have threatened legal action because of damage to their market shares.

In the industrial air-conditioning industry a major corporation built a microcomputer-based modeling system to help architects model the heating and cooling system requirements for commercial properties, measurably reducing their design time. The system leads many architects to consider this company's products more favorably than others. A competing corporation subsequently made a similar model available to remote users via communications links, providing rapid support and allowing the architect to get detailed costs and parts listings quickly to complete the design. Because the system is on-line, this company was able to neutralize the damage produced by the competitor's earlier product.

An agricultural chemicals company has obtained similar results through a sophisticated on-line crop-planning service for its chief agricultural customers. From a personal computer, using a standard telephone connection, farmers can call up agricultural databases containing prices of various crops, necessary growing conditions, and the costs of various chemicals. They can then call up various models and decision support systems and tailor them to their fields' requirements, after which they can experiment with the models and examine the implications of various crop rotations and timing for planting. The model then helps the farmers to select fertilizer and chemical applications and to group their purchases to achieve maximum discounts. Finally, farmers can place orders for future delivery by hitting a few keys. Similar services have been offered by a major seed company and at least one state's Agricultural Extension Service.

Along a different vein, a major bank that is trying to strengthen its marketing of agricultural loans has offered a similar crop-planning service. Two previously noncompetitive companies are now competing in the same software arena. Marketing, the functional area most often bypassed in the first three decades of IT, is now the area of highest impact in a number of firms, and they are arming their sales forces with a wide array of handheld and laptop computers.

Over the past five years a major food company has assembled a national database that keeps track of daily sales of each of its products in each of the 300,000 stores they service. This database is now totally accessible through a wide-area network to market planners in their 21 regional districts. Combined with comparative data from market research companies, it has brought another order of precision and sophistication to their market research activities.

After-Sale Service

On its new line of elevators, an elevator company has installed flight-recording devices similar to those used by the airlines. It has done so because customers often place service calls without indicating how their elevators have malfunctioned. The service representative connects the recording device to the elevator company's computer, discovers the cause of the malfunction of two hours before, and then makes the necessary repairs on the spot. This reduces repair costs and increases customer satisfaction because the proper repairs are made on the first service call.

A large manufacturer of industrial machinery has installed an expert maintenance system in its home-office computer. When a machine failure occurs on a customer's premises, the machine is connected over a telephone line to the manufacturer's computer, which performs a fault analysis and issues instructions to the machine operator. Direct service visits are down by 50 percent, and customer satisfaction is up markedly.

Corporate Infrastructure

A large travel agency uses an on-line link to provide support to small, outlying offices. Because the travel industry still needs to deliver paper documents—passports, visas, tickets, itineraries—satellite or remote offices near big corporate customers are highly useful for pickup and delivery. These offices must have the full support capabilities of the home office. The on-line links have changed the organizational structure from that of one large, central office to many small, full-service offices. This change appears to have produced a 27 percent growth in sales. Chapter 6 will examine these organizational ramifications in far greater detail.

Management Control.   A major financial services firm used to pay a sales commission on each product sold by its sales force. The result was that the sales force had maximum incentive to make the initial sale of a product and no incentive to make sure the customer was happy and did not take his money elsewhere (a matter of intense concern to the management of the financial services firm). With its new integrated customer database in place, the company has reduced the commissions it pays on initial sales of products and pays a new commission for maintaining and expanding the customer assets managed by the financial services firm. This approach, made possible by new technology, has aligned the company strategy and its sales incentive system much more effectively.

In some instances IT has dramatically enhanced coordination through fairly simple but powerful tools such as voice mail, electronic mail, videotext to update instructions to sales personnel in the field, and so on. These tools have dramatically accelerated the depth and breadth of communication. Other means of increasing coordination may involve much more extensive use of modern technologies including wide-area networks, local area networks, executive information packages, image processing, and so on. These tools, as discussed in greater detail in Chapter 6, both reduce staff costs and enhance effectiveness.

For example, at least one U.S. air carrier uses a network to monitor the location of all its aircraft. By knowing its airplanes' locations and passenger lists, the passengers' planned connections, and the connection schedules, it can instantaneously make decisions about speeding up late flights or delaying connecting departures. The opportunities for controlling fuel costs and preventing revenue loss (because many passengers must continue on competitors' flights if they miss their connections) amounts to tens of millions of dollars a year. Trucking companies and railroads use similar methods to track cargoes and optimize schedules.

Human Resources

The sophistication of human resources management has turned inside out. For example, an oil company has given desk terminals to all its corporate management committee members. Through these machines the committee has full on-line access to the detailed personnel files of the 400 most senior members in the corporation, complete with such data as five-year performance appraisals, photographs, and lists of positions each person is backing up. The company believes this capability has facilitated its important personnel decisions. Special government compliance reports, which used to take months to complete, can now be done in hours.

Technology Development

On-line access to large computing facilities inside and outside the company has allowed a heavy industrial manufacturer to increase technical productivity by more than half. Senior technical management now would not want to operate without this support.

To guide its drilling decisions, a large oil company processes large amounts of infrared data gathered from an overhead satellite. The company believes this information, which is used in all aspects of the search for petroleum deposits, is essential to its operations, from deciding on which tracts to bid to determining where to drill. Similarly, CAD/CAM (computer-aided design and manufacturing) technology has fundamentally changed the quality and speed with which the company can manufacture its drilling platforms.

A seed company notes its single most important technology expenditure is computer support for research. Modern genetic planning involving hundreds of thousands of plant variations and molecular simulation models—the keys to their future—are not possible without large-scale computing capacity. Their detailed data files repeatedly have allowed them to find appropriate germ plasms thousands of miles away to solve a problem in an Iowa cornfield.

Procurement

Procurement activities are also being transformed. For example, with a series of on-line electronic bulletin boards that make the latest spot prices instantly available around the country, a manufacturing company directs its nationwide purchasing effort. The boards have led to a tremendous improvement in purchasing price effectiveness, both in discovering and implementing new quantity pricing discount data as well as ensuring that the lowest prices are being achieved.

A retailer, by virtue of its large size, has succeeded in its demand for on-line access to the inventory files and production schedules of its suppliers. This access has permitted the company to manage its inventories more tightly than before and to pressure suppliers on price and product availability. This is another dimension of the earlier cited inbound logistics example.

In short, we have found systematic examination of a company's value chain to be an effective way to search for profitable IT applications. This analysis requires keen administrative insight, awareness of industry structure, and familiarity with the rules of competition in the particular setting. Companies need to understand their own value chains as well as those of key customers and suppliers in order to uncover potential new service areas. Similarly, understanding competitors' value chains provides insight on likely sources of competitive attack. Careful thought is needed in order to identify potential new entrants to an industry. These are companies whose value chains make expansion into a particular area attractive.

THE RISKS OF INFORMATION SYSTEMS SUCCESS[2]

A real and complex danger for developers of would-be strategic information systems is that they will succeed in the narrow technical sense but generate disastrous organizational and competitive consequences.

---

[2]Some of the material in this section has been adapted from Michael R. Vitale, "The Growing Risks of Information Systems Success," *MIS Quarterly,* December 1986.

Problems and Evaluations

This section discusses nine problems of information systems "success" and identifies management policies and procedures that help to ensure that potentially high-risk projects are appropriately evaluated. These risks focus on strategic vulnerabilities as opposed to the more-defined implementation issues covered in Chapter 10.

Systems that Change the Basis of Competition to a Company's Disadvantage.   Once information systems are used to gain competitive advantage in a given industry, in some settings their use not only may become obligatory for continued competitive viability, but significant additional resources may have to be expended to keep them viable. An organization that is not prepared to stay the course with continued investments in information systems may be better off not firing the first salvo.

This lesson was learned, through experience, by a U.S. manufacturer of commercial appliances. The company's products were typically purchased and installed by building contractors who worked from a set of technical specifications for size, capacity, and so on. Historically the company had offered contractors a mail-in consulting service that could translate specifications into products and instructions for the wiring, plumbing, and other site preparation work required.

The company initially built this consulting expertise into programs for a mainframe and an early-model microcomputer. Contractors could continue to send specifications by mail; the company would feed the requirements through the mainframe and mail back a neatly printed list of products and instructions. (As would be expected, most of the products were manufactured by the company itself.) The relatively few contractors who at that time owned that particular microcomputer could, using company-supplied software, enter their specifications onto a diskette and mail that instead of written data. The micro itself was not powerful enough to analyze the specifications, although it could check them for completeness and consistency.

Over time the appliance market evolved, as did the microcomputer industry. Having achieved success with its initial development, the company reaped a harvest of increased market share but carried out no further development. One of its competitors—larger, older, and equipped with a larger, more progressive information systems staff—developed a similar system. This system, however, ran on the more powerful and more readily available IBM personal computer. Software was provided to contractors at no charge, as were electronic connections to the company's mainframe. Analysis could be performed immediately, and the required products made almost exclusively by that system's owner could be ordered at the push of a key. As IBM began to dominate the business microcomputer market, the second company recaptured its lost market share and more.

By introducing customers and competitors to the use of information systems and then failing to track or adapt to changes in the technology, the first company turned an initial IT success into a competitive failure.

The moral: Once you have entered the game it is very hard to disengage.

Systems that Lower Entry Barriers. As described earlier, information technology can be used to raise and/or maintain barriers to entry in many industries. In some situations an extensive investment in hardware and software has become necessary for all participants, increasing the investment required for entry. In other circumstances information systems have been used to capture distribution channels, again increasing the cost and difficulty of entrance.

On the other hand, by making information systems the major vehicle for producing, selling, distributing, or servicing its product, a company may in fact be encouraging competitors that have greater IT resources.

A major seller of health and casualty insurance faced this type of decision. The company does the majority of its business on a payroll-deduction basis with very small employers who do not offer insurance as a fringe benefit. These employers often do their payrolls by hand, making bookkeepers a major target for the insurer's sales force. The primary competition is not so much from other insurers as from the bookkeepers' lack of time and willingness to handle additional deductions.

To help overcome this obstacle, the insurer considered offering a computerized payroll preparation package for small companies. The development of such software was considered to be well within the capabilities of its IT group, and its sales force was already in contact with many potential customers for the new service. Pricing was designed to provide some profit, but the main intent was to create tighter links to small customers.

Before much work had been done on the new payroll system, the vice president for IT recognized a danger. Although it might well be possible to convince customers to do their payrolls by computer, he could see there was a risk that the business would go not to the insurer but to one of the large, experienced firms that dominate the payroll business. Any of these organizations could, if they chose, offer health and casualty insurance as well through a relationship with another insurer. The link to customers might well be tighter, but it was not clear who would be at the other end! The company postponed the idea of offering payroll service until such time as their customers began to show some interest in doing their payroll by computer. To continue the project would, in the company's opinion, have risked opening its primary line of business to new competitors.

Systems that Bring on Litigation or Regulation. These systems are in the category of things that work too well for their own good. They achieve their initial objectives and then continue to grow in size and effectiveness, eventually giving rise to claims of unfair competition and cries for government regulation. Other possible outcomes are forced divestiture of the system and an agreement to share the system with competitors.

The airline reservations systems used by travel agents are a clear example of this danger. The United and American reservation systems control the offices of nearly 80 percent of U.S. travel agents. Some of the two carriers' competitors have claimed that this level of penetration allows the two big airlines to effectively control the industry's channels of distribution. Examples of such alleged domination include biased display of data, close monitoring and control of travel agents, and inaccurate data on competitors' flights.

After a lengthy investigation of these claims, the Civil Aeronautics Board (CAB) ordered changes in the operation and pricing of computer reservations systems. Nevertheless, United and American were sued by 11 competitors, who demanded that the two carriers spin off their reservations systems into separate subsidiaries. United and American opposed the suit but did agree, along with TWA, to provide unbiased displays. As this book is being produced, the lawsuit is in abeyance because of financial stresses unrelated to the issues in the lawsuit, but its central themes that there is such a thing as an unfair "information monopoly" and that control of electronic channels of distribution may be unacceptable to the public cast a shadow over the 1990s. A similar set of lawsuits and challenges has been engendered around ATMs.

Although they deny unfair practices, United and American have never denied using their reservations systems to gain competitive advantage. Indeed, the two airlines claim that the systems are not economically viable on the basis of usage fee income alone—they were *intended* to generate increased sales. United and American may in fact already have recovered their investments in the reservation systems. The precedent of government intervention suggests, however, that future developers of competitively effective systems may find their returns limited by law or regulation.

Systems that Increase Customers' or Suppliers' Power to the Detriment of the Innovator. Strengthening relationships with customers and suppliers is an area in which information systems have been used most effectively. In some circumstances, however, companies appear to give their customers or suppliers the tools and expertise to get along without them. This change may be inevitable over the long run, but there is no reason to hasten its onset.

An overnight delivery company, for example, instituted very fast delivery of electronically transmitted messages between its offices. The original was picked up from the sender and put through a facsimile machine at a nearby office; the transmitted image was received at an office near the recipient and delivered by hand.

As fax technology grew, the delivery company announced that it would place facsimile machines on its customers' premises and act as a switch among the installed machines. Delivery promised to be even quicker, since there would be no need to take the original copy to the sending office or to deliver the received copy. The value the delivery company was able to add to off-the-shelf facsimile technology was questionable. Little existed to prevent its customers from installing similar equipment directly; indeed, the manufacturer of the facsimile machines advertised its products prominently as the ones supporting the delivery company's system. The firm soon abandoned this line of business.

A somewhat similar risk is created by systems that unintentionally lower switching costs in an attempt to make the customer's life easier. The American Hospital Supply Corporation (now a division of Baxter Travenol) provides an interesting example of steps taken to avoid this danger. American's "ASAP" system, installed in more than 3,000 U.S. hospitals, allows on-line ordering of medical and surgical supplies from American's extensive product line. Substitutes are suggested for out-of-stock items, and the hospital can specify several options for delivery time, depending on how urgently each item is needed. ASAP is generally felt to have contributed heavily to the steady growth that made American the largest company in its field by the mid-1980s.

Some of American's competitors developed similar systems of their own but found it difficult to overcome American's lead. (Hospitals, like travel agents, were generally reluctant to install more than one on-line system.) The extensive use of computerized order-entry systems, however, offered another potential competitive opportunity. Why not develop a "master system" that would take data from hospitals and pass it to suppliers' systems? The hospitals could retain the advantages of a single system and might get lower prices as well, since the master system could "shop" among suppliers for the best price.

As long as American continued to develop and enhance ASAP, this danger was manageable. During its successful life, in fact, the company had taken the system well beyond the order-entry stage. Later versions of ASAP allowed the hospital to order on the basis of its own stock numbers as well as American's, to create and store files of frequently ordered items, and to "personalize" ASAP to its own environment in other ways. After American's acquisition by Baxter Travenol, in a well-meaning effort to control costs, all development expenditures were frozen. Over a two-year period ASAP's competitors caught up.

Baxter finally responded by developing an industry system for all competitors aided by a public accountant to ensure that all players would be treated equitably. Although costly to develop, the new system promises to stabilize the situation. A once formidable technological advantage disappeared, and ASAP now competes primarily through the breadth of its product line and its ability to execute fast delivery.

Bad Timing.   A delicate analysis balances cost and culture in determining the time to make a bold move. Get there too early with an expensive, clumsy technology in an unreceptive customer environment, as Chemical Bank did with its electronic home banking product in the early 1980s, and you can create a real fiasco. (They lost $100 million on the venture.) Get there too late, as the regional airlines and hundreds of drug wholesalers did, and you may lose your life. Behind the technology issues lie very real marketing and business policy issues.

Investments that Turn Out to Be Indefensible and Fail to Produce Lasting Advantages.   There are numerous reasons an investment can turn out to be indefensible. In general, interorganization systems with high potential daily transaction rates with the other party have turned out to be very successful. Where low daily transaction rates exist (one to two per day or less), they have often turned into strategic liabilities with end users getting lost in the procedural details. In another vein, features that have great value to end users but that are easily replicable by the firm's competitors are of much less value than those that, because of size and/or peculiar reinforcing linkage with the firm's products, are hard to replicate. Similarly, systems where the firm can start simple and continue to add new features and services as technology and industry conditions change are much more effective than one-time moves, which then stand as fixed targets for competitors to shoot at.

Systems that Pose an Immediate Threat to Large, Established Competitors.   Several organizations in the hotel industry have recognized that they cannot by themselves develop a link to travel agencies because they would risk being crushed by the airline systems anxious to prevent erosion of their franchise. By putting together a group of hotels as an association, they have combined sufficient market power and purchasing power to make this viable.

Inadequate Understanding of Buying Dynamics across Market Segments.   It is very easy to apply inappropriately a set of concepts that works in one set of market niches to another set. For example, airline reservations systems have been widely cited as an example of effective IT use. Over the past decade, however, two of the most consistently profitable routes in the United States have been Washington National to New York La Guardia and New York La Guardia to Boston Logan. A passenger cannot get a reservation on these routes; rather, each route is served by an every-half-hour shuttle concept. Different market niches may have very different dynamics, and you can get into great trouble by ignoring these differences.

Cultural Lag and Perceived Transfer of Power.   Some systems are beyond the customers' technical comfort level. This was clearly the case with the earlier mentioned electronic home banking failure. It is the great imponderable issue in the early 1990s as one considers the massive joint venture between IBM and Sears that is targeted at bringing hundreds of electronic databases into U.S. homes using a menu-driven architecture. It has worked in the very different environment in France. Whether it will work here is a matter of heated debate. A second related issue is the concern by one party in an interorganization system (IOS) that it may be manipulated by another party and that it may not be able to resist the pressure without losing the business relationship. Not all IOS's are win–win situations.

These are hard but very important questions to address. Quite separate are the areas of technical project management addressed in Chapter 10. Chapter 10 focuses primarily on the real problems of implementation, while this chapter is focused on failures of conceptualization.

Assessing Competitor Risk

Understanding competitive risks is the first step in managing them. Understanding, in turn, is a two-phase process: (1) describing in advance and in detail the industry-level changes that may be brought about by development and implementation of particular information technologies, and (2) determining the potential impact of these changes on the company. Such views of the future, sadly, are very cloudy, and their probabilities are only rough estimates. But together with estimates of project costs and benefits, they must be analyzed before a decision is made on whether to proceed.

Increasing use of information systems is often naively viewed as inevitable. Certainly, situations occur where firms must invest in and adapt to IT in order to remain viable, even if the increase in technological intensity causes a complete reevaluation and reformulation of the firm's strategy. Yet some technological "advances" have remained in an embryonic stage for years. Electronic home banking and home shopping, as noted earlier, are two examples. Sometimes these developments are stalled for reasons of cost, IT capability, or consumer acceptance. Others are held back by lack of support from established industry participants. Rather than uniformly criticizing these firms for technological backwardness, it is more appropriate to entertain the possibility that they understand the technology completely and are prepared to utilize it when it becomes necessary but are unwilling to precipitate a potentially unfavorable change in their competitive environment.

An appropriate place to start in considering the potential impact of a new strategic use of information systems is with the motivation for the new system. As noted earlier, potential justifications include raising entry barriers, increasing switching costs, reducing the power of buyers or suppliers, deterring substitute products, lowering costs, and increasing differentiation. Inevitably, if the initiative is successful, the outcome over time will be a change in the competitive forces affecting the industry. It is tempting but dangerous and shortsighted to consider these forces as impacting only current industry participants— suppliers, buyers, and competitors. As some of the examples indicate, certain IT uses can open up an industry to new and potentially dominant players in a way so threatening to a firm that it is an entirely prudent reason to delay offensive moves.

Equally practical as a firm considers new investments in strategic information systems, it must candidly assess whether it will obtain any sustainable competitive advantage or if a more likely outcome is an extension of the current competitive situation at an increased level of cost. Additional caveats in this area include recognizing that IT software purchased from a nonexclusive source is unlikely to confer lasting advantage. Also, the mobility of skilled IT personnel between firms often results in the rapid proliferation of key ideas, leaving the pioneering firm relatively no better off than before. In the absence of strong, first-mover advantages, some investments in information systems, regardless of their short-term glitz and appeal, may simply not pay off competitively over the long run.

As will be discussed later, the long-term commitment of top management must be obtained before firing the first shot on the IT battlefield. Before starting an IT effort a clear view must exist of the company's long-range strategy and how this move fits into it. Further, the resources and capabilities of competitors, both current and potential, should be considered carefully.

Most crucial is the assessment of the likely long-term consequences of a new system. Initial development cost and benefit may not be an accurate indicator of the potential effects. A positive control is the "impact statement" that lays out the competitive changes expected to result from a new information system. Substantial benefits accruing from an improved competitive situation should alert the organization to consider the risks as well. Consideration of the positive impacts of the new system on competition forces broad-gauge thinking on potential negative impacts as well.

Over time the key to managing these sorts of risks will be the organization's ability to learn from its experience so that it can continue to roll out strategic IT applications as and when appropriate. There must be a common understanding among general managers and senior IT executives about which pieces of software should be considered "directional"—that is, likely to have a major effect on the organization's future competitive position. A thorough review of the potential impacts should be carried out before such systems are developed and again before they are implemented.

THE CHALLENGE

Achieving these advantages while avoiding the pitfalls requires broad IT management–user dialogue plus imagination. The process is complicated by the fact that, while many IT products are strategic, the potential benefits are very subjective and not easily verified. Often a strict return-on-investment (ROI) focus by senior management may turn attention toward narrow, well-defined targets rather than to broader, strategic opportunities that are harder to analyze.

Visualizing their systems in terms of the strategic grid (see Figure 2–4), senior and IT managements in a number of organizations have concluded that their company or business unit is located in either the "support" or the "factory" quadrant and have set up staffing, organization, and planning activities accordingly. Because of the sharp change in IT performance and the evolution of competitive conditions, this categorization may be wrong as one looks to the future. For the new conditions, for example, the competitor of the distributor described in this chapter's opening paragraph was complacent about its position in the support quadrant. The company did not realize what was happening until it was too late. Playing catch-up can be difficult and expensive in the IT area.

A number of companies and industry groups will appropriately remain in the support and factory quadrants. Technical changes, however, have been so sudden in the past several years that the role of a company's IT function needs reexamination to ensure its placement is still appropriate.

A NEW POINT OF VIEW

To address the issues raised here, management will need to change the way it operates.

Planning Issues

The CEO must insist that the end products of IT planning clearly communicate the true competitive impact of the expenditures involved. Figure 3–5 provides a framework for thinking about how to accomplish this by identifying priorities for the allocation of financial and staff resources.

In this connection, managers should realize that an extraordinarily large amount of the systems development effort is often devoted to repairing worn-out systems and to maintaining them in order to meet changed business conditions (over 50 percent in many settings). Also, a vital but often unrecognized need exists for research and development to keep up with the technology and to ensure that the company can know the full range of possibilities. (This idea is developed in depth in Chapter 13.) Distinctly separate are the areas where a company spends money to obtain pure competitive advantage (very exciting) or to regain or maintain competitive parity (not so exciting, because the company is trying to recover from its shortsightedness). Finally, projects where the investment is defined for pure measurable return on investment (ROI) are also separate.

The aim of the ranking process is to allocate resources to areas with the most growth potential. Each company should have an IT plan summary, about three pages long, that vividly communicates to the CEO the data derived from Figure 3–5, explains why IT expenditures are allocated as they are, and enumerates explicitly the types of competitive benefits the company might expect from its IT expenditures. Few companies do this today.

Confidentiality and Competition

Until recently it has been the industry norm for organizations and individuals to share data about information systems technology and plans, on the grounds that no lasting competitive advantage would emerge from IT and that collaboration would allow all firms to reduce administrative headaches. Managers today, however, must take appropriate steps to ensure the confidentiality of strategic IT plans and thinking. Great care should be taken in determining who will attend industry meetings, what they may talk about, and what information they may share with vendors and competitors.

Evaluating Expenditures

Executives should not permit use of simplistic rules to calculate desirable IT expense levels. Judging an IT budget as a percentage of something, such as sales, has always been an easy way to compare the

---

FIGURE 3–5   Identifying Resource Allocation Priorities by Strategic
Business Unit

Goal of IT expenditure	Growing, highly competitive industry	Relatively stable industry, known ground rules	Static or declining industry
Rehabilitate and maintain system	1	1	1
Experiment with new technology	2	3	3
Attain competitive advantage	2	2	3*
Maintain or regain competitive parity	2	3	4
Defined return on investment †	3	3	4

*Assuming the change is not so dramatic as to revolution- ize the industry's overall performance

†In an intensely cost- competitive environment, defined ROI is the same as gaining competitive advantage

Note:
Numbers indicate relative attractiveness or importance of the investment, with 1 having the highest priority.

*Assuming the change is not so dramatic as to revolutionize the industry's overall performance.
†In an intensely cost-competitive environment, defined ROI is the same as gaining competitive advantage.
Note: Numbers indicate relative attractiveness or importance of the investment, with 1 denoting the highest priority.

performance of different companies. In today's more volatile competitive arena, such comparisons are very dangerous. We have observed some companies that are spending 6 percent of their total sales in this area and that are clearly underinvesting. We have seen others spending 1 percent of their sales volume that are overspending.

The IT–Management Partnership

To make full use of the opportunities that IT presents, managers need close partnership with technical experts. Bridging the gap between IT specialists and general management for purposes of strategic planning is, however, an enduring problem. Often uncomfortable with technology, many general managers are unaware of new options IT provides and the ways in which it can support strategy. For their part, IT professionals are often not attuned to the complexities and subtleties of strategy formulation. They are generally not part of the strategy development process (discussed further in Chapter 13).

Partnership is necessary. IT experts understand the economies of the technology and know its limits. They can also help move the organization toward the potential of tomorrow's technology. A change that is clumsy and inefficient in today's technology might eliminate the need for architecture redesign in the next generation. For example, very rich, interrelated databases today may be so slow to access as to present serious cost (and possibly response-time) problems. Tomorrow's technology, conversely, may remove the speed and cost problems and highlight the usefulness of the data.

General managers bring insight to overall business priorities. They have detailed knowledge of the various value chains and their potential in the real world and can help identify the paths of least staff resistance in implementation. Synthesis of the two worlds is essential.

Opening Questions

Finally, as a way of starting the process, establishing joint task forces to address the following questions has proved valuable.

1. What business are we really in? To answer that question, the task force may ask: What value do we provide to our customer? Do widespread, cheap, high-volume data communications and computer technology change this? Are we an insurance company, or should we think of ourselves as a provider of diversified financial services? A videotext service, or a mover of electronic bits? A provider of spare parts, or of parts and parts status reporting?

2. *Who are our biggest competitors? What new competitors will this technology make possible in the future? Who else does, or can, provide the same products or services?* If we see ourselves in the future as an insurance company, our competitors will be companies such as Aetna and Travelers. If we see ourselves as a financial services company, our competitors will be firms such as American Express/Shearson Lehman, Merrill Lynch, Sears Financial Services, and Citicorp.

3. *Can we integrate our clients' operations with our own through telecommunications and offer clients faster, easier, or cheaper service? In particular, how can we lock them in? Can we introduce significant switching costs?*

4. *Can we permanently lock competitors out through aggressive use of telecommunications or other electronic services?*

5. *Has our operating environment been changed by deregulation of our industry? Can technology help us compete for marketing, scheduling, control, and coordination in this new setting?*

6. *Has our environment changed due to deregulation of a related industry? Again, can technology help us compete? How can we add new products and services to retain our existing customer base?*

7. *Can we get there first? Should we attempt to make this move?* These two questions may be the most difficult of all. They require anticipating what's going to happen in the marketplace and in relationships with clients, customers, competitors, and regulators. Also, the company must determine which innovations will provide sustainable advantage versus which competitors can readily copy—adding to the costs of all industry participants or shaving all margins.

A Final Thought

At resource allocation time, the difference between an effective strategic initiative and a harebrained scheme is razor-thin. Only after the passage of money and time is the outcome obvious.

Case 3–1

MRS. FIELDS' COOKIES

Creating something new, given the old and familiar, is an art rather than a science. The late, latter-day Da Vinci, Buckminster Fuller, has been credited with this ability. "Part of Fuller's genius," wrote Tom Richman,[1] "was his capacity to transform a technology from the merely new to the truly useful by creating a new form to take advantage of its characteristics." What Fuller's geodesic designs had done for plastic, observed Richman, the administrative management processes Debbi and Randy Fields developed for Mrs. Fields' Cookies did for information technology.

Fuller, who once suggested that a particularly awkward application of a new technology to an old process would be "like putting an outboard motor on a skyscraper," would very likely have approved of the Fields' creation— "*a* shape if not *the* shape, of business organizations to come," according to Richman.

> [Information technology] gives top management a dimension of personal control over dispersed operations that small companies otherwise find impossible to achieve. It projects a founder's vision into parts of a company that have long ago outgrown his or her ability to reach in person.
>
> In the [Fields'] structure . . . computers don't just speed up old administrative processes. They alter the process. Management . . . becomes less administration and more inspiration. The management hierarchy of the company *feels* almost flat.

Debbi Fields had created the business. Randy had devised a corporate structure fit to be wed to an information system. They believed theirs was a case of putting an outboard motor, not on a skyscraper, but on a boat.

The Company

In 1988, Debbi Sivyer Fields, as president of Mrs. Fields' Inc. and Mrs. Fields' Cookies, controlled over 416 Mrs. Fields' Cookie outlets, 122 La Petite Boulangerie Stores, 129 Jessica's Cookies and Famous Chocolate units, 2 Jenessa's retail gift stores, Jenny's Swingset (a children's casual clothing store in Park City, Utah), Mrs. Fields' Dessert Store (a Los Angeles store that sold ice cream, cookies, cakes, and pies), Mrs. Fields' Candy Factory (in Park City), Mrs. Fields' Cookie College (for training store managers and assistant managers), and a macadamia nut processing plant in Hawaii. Mrs. Fields' Cookies operated 370 cookie stores in the United States, 10 in Canada, 6 in Hong Kong (through 50 percent ownership of Mrs. Field's Cookies Far East Ltd., a joint venture with a local company, Dairy Farm Ltd.), 7 in Japan, 6 in the United Kingdom, and 17 in Australia. The company employed 8,000 people, 140 in staff positions at the Park City corporate offices.

Mrs. Fields' Cookies, like many of Buckminster Fuller's designs, achieved elegance of function by marrying what might at first seem to be incongruous elements. Customers knew Mrs. Fields' Cookies as the upscale

---

[1] Tom Richman, "Mrs. Fields' Secret Ingredient," *Inc.* (October 1987): 67–72.

Keri Ostrofsky prepared this case under the supervision of Professor James I. Cash as the basis for class discussion rather than to illustrate either effective or ineffective handling of an administrative situation.

brown, red, and white retail outlets that dispensed hot, fresh, chewy cookies like Grandmother used to bake. Few were aware that by 6:00 A.M. Utah time, a computer in Park City, high in the Uinta Mountains, would know of their purchase and every other purchase made at the more than 500 Mrs. Fields' Cookie stores in 25 states and five countries on four continents.

The cookies, of course, came first. Debbi Sivyer began baking cookies as a teenager. "Chocolate chip cookies were an easy project . . . just the thing to keep you busy on a rainy afternoon. . . . The Sivyer clan was always delighted to discover a plateful of chocolate chip cookies, and they weren't expensive to make."[2] Debbi perfected her recipe while a teenager, working first for the Oakland A's baseball club (retrieving foul balls on the third base line) and later for a local department store. These experiences fueled her enthusiasm and drive, and were a source of the fundamental philosophies she would later bring to the management of Mrs. Fields' Cookies.

At 19, Debbi married economist and Stanford University graduate Randy Fields, then 29. Finding her expertise in demand by her husband's clients, who often asked that she bake for their visits, Debbi convinced Randy that she should go into the cookie business. The couple borrowed $50,000 and, in August 1977, within a year of being married, Debbi opened her first store, Mrs. Fields' Chocolate Chippery, in Palo Alto, California. Debbi sold $50 worth of cookies on her first day in business, and $75 worth on her second day, thereby winning a friendly bet made between Debbi and Randy regarding the total sales she would make each day.

More than a year passed before Debbi opened a second store in a high-traffic tourist area of San Francisco. "With the first store, I had what I wanted," Debbi recalled. "As Randy had his thing to do every day, I had mine. When the people at Pier 39 shopping mall called and asked me to open a store there, I was immensely flattered . . . thanked the leasing agent profusely, and turned him down. . . . What I saw as a store, he perceived as a business—a business that could grow. The point wasn't to make money, the point was to bake great cookies, and we sacrificed for that principle." Her employees' desire for growth and greater opportunity finally convinced Debbi to open the second store.

Explosive Growth

The San Francisco store was followed by several others in northern California and, in 1980, by an outlet in Honolulu, Hawaii. Mrs. Fields' next expanded east to Salt Lake City, Utah. By 1981, the company had 14 stores. Seeking further opportunities for expansion, the Fields tried to attract shopping mall managers at a 1982 trade show in Las Vegas, but drew a lukewarm response. At the same trade show a year later, Debbi handed out cookie samples to conventioneers from a booth arranged as a working prototype of a store, complete with oven and mixer. This brought her to the attention of the landlords, some of whom not only let Mrs. Fields' into their existing malls, but asked that stores be opened in future locations, as well. The cookie company's East Coast debut also came in 1983—Bloomingdale's invitation to open a Mrs. Fields' store in its New York location was considered a major milestone by Debbi and Randy.

International Expansion

In 1982, Chuck Borash, a vice president at Mrs. Fields', suggested that international expansion be the next project. The challenge was irresistible, and, after some preliminary research, the company formed Mrs. Fields'

---

[2]Several quotations in this case are taken from Debbi Fields, *One Smart Cookie* (New York: Simon and Schuster, 1987).

International and targeted Japan, Hong Kong, and Australia.

The Fields searched for a Japanese partner, which they were told was a prerequisite to doing business in Japan. Prospective partners warned Debbi and Randy that the cookies would have to be changed to appeal to the Japanese palate, specifically, that the spices and physical scale of the cookies were wrong. When Debbi, Randy, and several other executives visited a potential partner in Japan, Debbi brought along ingredients to make cookies according to her recipe, a company trade secret. "Agreement was universal that these cookies were all wrong for the Japanese taste," Debbi recalled, "and yet in less than a minute, there wasn't a crumb to be seen." Although that was the end of the partnership, the actions of these executives convinced the Fields that they could sell cookies in Japan, and they opened several stores without a partner.

Adjustments were necessary in some countries, however. For example, it was decided that the practice of encouraging sampling when business was slow should be continued in the international stores. The store manager in Hong Kong, however, was unable to interest people in sampling cookies. When Debbi visited the store and tried offering samples herself, she encountered the same reaction. Observing that neighboring store window displays were very neatly organized, in contrast to her piled samples, Debbi rearranged the tray so that people could take one piece without touching the others, and the passersby became willing to sample. Overall, Mrs. Fields International looked to be a promising avenue for expansion.

Products and Competition

Mrs. Fields' cookies came in 14 varieties. An early move into brownies and muffins was followed, in 1988, by expansion into candies and ice cream. All baked products were made on premises in the individual stores and were to be sold within a specified time. Cookies not sold within two hours, for example, were discarded (usually given to the local Red Cross or other charity).

Mrs. Fields' Cookies was part of the sweet snack industry, which included the packaged snacks segment (e.g., Frito-Lay's Grandma's Cookies; Nabisco's Fig Newtons, Vanilla Wafers, Chips Ahoy, and Oreos; and Keebler's Soft Batch). Competitors for impulse snack dollars included New York's David's Cookies, Atlanta's Original Great American Chocolate Chip Cookie Company, and the Nestlé Company's Original Cookie Co.

Specialty stores selling chocolates, ice cream, cinnamon rolls, and croissants constituted another segment of the sweet snack food industry. Shopping malls represented the largest source of spontaneous business for specialty stores, and some 80 percent of Mrs. Fields' outlets were in malls. Competition for the most favorable mall locations, which were typically next to large apparel stores rather than in areas with other foods stores, was fierce. "Customers," noted one industry observer, "are too busy filling up on traditional 'main meal' fare to think seriously about any edible specialty items. Even if they decide afterward to have them as a dessert, they won't have the patience to stand in line once again."[3] As most malls had few such locations, developers were selective about the stores they allowed outside the "food courts." Said one New York leasing director, "We can only accept operations with some sort of proven production record."[4]

Management Philosophy

The second Mrs. Fields' store raised a host of new issues for Debbi, who recognized that she could not be in two places at one time, yet historically had resisted delegating authority.

---

[3]*Chain Store Age Executive,* September 1986, p. 66.
[4]Ibid., p. 62.

Management theory claims that it is wrong not to delegate authority to those who work for you. Okay, I'm wrong, but in my own defense, I have to say that my error came from caring too much. If that's a sin, it's surely a small one. Eventually, I was forced, kicking and screaming, to delegate authority because that was the only way the business could grow.

Debbi Fields had no formal business school training. She attributed her success to learning by doing, and imparted her standards to her employees through example. Whenever possible, she visited her stores and sold cookies behind the counter. On a visit to one store in early 1988, she and a data processing employee with no retail experience generated an additional $600 in sales.

Debbi believed in having fun. "We combine intense work with spontaneous wackiness that keeps everybody loose and relaxed in the middle of tension," she observed. She also believed in treating employees as though they were customers. "For all the things we say to be effective, the people in the stores have to believe in what they're doing. . . . If we can sell them on quality and caring, they will sell the customers. . . . If we make them understand how important they are—by deeds, not just words—they will make their customers feel important in turn."

Store designs were closely controlled. Each store was made to look as inviting and accessible as possible, with products displayed so customers could see exactly what was available. Most stores had their ovens directly behind the sales counter so the aroma of baking cookies would fill the store. Each of the store elements was designed to impart to customers a "feel good" feeling.

The Fields had consistently refused to franchise their stores. The notion went against their ideals, as expressed by Debbi.

This business—every business—works in its own quirky ways, and Mrs. Fields' Cookies was not created specifically to make a profit. I can't imagine a franchisee buying into it for any other reason. And once the profit motive worked its way to a dominant position, it would be downhill. It's a feel-good product. It has to be sold in a feel-good way.

Franchises typically controlled standards by specifying actions and quantifying details for the franchisees to follow. Because Debbi regarded each outlet as an extension of her original Palo Alto store, where each sale reflected her own personal philosophy of making the customer happy, she viewed franchising as a loss of control over the end product and loss of touch with the customer.

Even in partly owned stores, such as those in Hong Kong, Debbi and Randy played a major role. For example, Mrs. Fields' provided product and technical knowledge for the Hong Kong stores, for which Dairy Farms Ltd. provided real estate and on-site management.

Financing Strategy

Although the Fields had always managed to find bank financing when they needed it, each experience had been more unpleasant than the last. Consequently, when expansion pressed them to find additional capital, Debbi and Randy decided to go public, pay off the banks, and use the rest of the money to finance growth. Their initial offering, made on the London Exchange in 1986, was not very successful. English institutional buyers did not know the company (there was only one store in London) and doubted that growth could be sustained without franchising. The stock settled, and then began to rise slowly. In 1987, Randy announced that future growth would be funded by cash flow and debt, not by further public offerings.

Accounting was straightforward. Expenses incurred in a store were charged to the store. Conversely, no corporate expenses were allocated to stores. "When you do that," explained Randy, "you lose track of what corporate is doing." Each store operated as a profit center, with average store revenue of $250,000 per year.

In 1987, Mrs. Fields' Inc. had after-tax profits of $17.6 million on revenue of $113.9 million, a 34 percent increase from 1986 revenue, and a 9.3 percent increase from 1986 net income (see Exhibit 1). In 1988, a write-off of $19.9 million on revenues of $133.1 million for store and plant closings left Mrs. Fields' with an after-tax loss of $18.5 million.

Organization

The Fields believed that "the less hierarchy, the better. . . . that with hierarchy, the larger an organization, the more managers turn to managing people and less to managing key business processes." Thus, employees had titles and job responsibilities, but there was no official organization chart. Communication took place between people as needed, regardless of title or position.

Staff. Field sales staff included store clerks, store management, and district and regional managers. At year end 1987, 105 district sales managers (DSMs) reported to 17 regional directors of operations (RDOs), who reported to four senior regional directors.

One regional director described her job and the company's management philosophy as follows:

> I manage six district managers, each of whom manages six stores. I also manage a store myself, so I know what my district managers need to know. To do this, I print out about 300 pages of reports a day. My district managers get about 50 pages a day. Daily, I work with my controller in Park City to discuss any accounting differences in my stores.
>
> My store managers are on average 20 to 25 years old and have one to two years of college

education. I believe we are split 50/50 between males and females. The turnover of store managers is about 100 percent per year, although many work in that job 12 to 14 months. When they leave, they usually return to college. I think our turnover is above average for this kind of business, however.

> My store managers are compensated in two ways. First, they receive a salary which is competitive with other retail food store managers in this area. Second, they are eligible for a monthly bonus if they meet their sales forecasts. They receive 1.25 percent of sales, and if they exceed their quota, they receive 10 percent of all revenue above the goal. The company does not limit the amount of bonus, in fact, one store manager made an additional 90 percent of his salary, I believe.

Quotas, which determined the amount of bonus a store manager could make, were set by the district sales manager. They were based on year-to-year trends. The DSM considered each store separately, looking at past trends, the maturity of the market served by the store, and future projections of how the store could grow. The DSMs then forecast how much or how little additional sales could be made at that store and set the quota. They were set on volumes.

Mrs. Fields' "promote from within" policy reflected the high value the company placed on loyalty. Rewarding loyalty extended even to suppliers. In 1987, Mrs. Fields' purchased approximately $6.6 million worth of chocolate from the same supplier it had used on its first day of business, when a company salesman had treated Debbi as if she were his only customer.

The financial side of the stores' business was handled at headquarters. Local marketing decisions were made by the regional and district managers. The average number of stores under the supervision of a DSM decreased from 5.3 to 4.2 in 1987.

Corporate. At corporate headquarters, responsibility for store management fell to

EXHIBIT 1   Mrs. Fields' Cookies

Financial Information
(U.S. $000)

Statement of Operations	1988	1987	1986	1985
Revenues	$133,143	$113,908	$84,751	$72,562
Cost of goods sold	42,049	32,739	19,961	19,165
Selling, G&A costs	74,525	50,643	39,442	38,477
Depreciation and amortization	9,133	5,903	4,505	3,498
Losses from closed stores	19,900	5,397	1,375	577
Income (loss) before interest and taxation	$(12,464)	$ 19,226	$19,468	$10,845
Net interest	6,039	1,540	2,333	4,088
Taxation	0	0	1,000	347
Net income (loss)	$(18,503)	$ 17,686	$16,135	$ 6,410
Dividends paid	0	10,453	4,500	0
Earnings (net loss) retained by company	$(18,503)	$ 7,233	$11,635	$ 6,410

Consolidated Balance Sheet

Assets	1988	1987	1986	1985
Property and equipment at cost less depreciation	82,827	82,033	51,496	37,838
Leasehold developments at cost less depreciation	10,672	11,429	5,529	2,809
Other[a]	1,273	863		
Current assets				
Inventories	6,640	7,779	4,406	3,198
Accounts receivable	3,816	3,585	3,222	1,522
Prepaid expenses and miscellaneous	8,937	9,363	4,761	2,105
Due from affiliates	5,000	0	740	0
Cash	3,971	6,059	1,543	2,257
	$123,136	$121,111	$71,697	$49,729

Liabilities and Shareholders' Equity

	1988	1987	1986	1985
Current liabilities				
Accounts payable, due to affiliates and accrued expenses	18,762	24,963	11,295	7,006
Income taxes	550	184	514	63
Long-term debt	69,732	42,734	13,187	20,100
Shareholders' equity and retained earnings	34,092	53,230	46,701	22,560
	$123,136	$121,111	$71,697	$49,729

[a]Other assets include costs of developing computer software for sale or license to third parties.

store controllers, who reported to Debbi through a vice president of operations. The controllers, each of whom managed between 35 and 75 stores, reviewed daily computer reports summarizing sales overall and by product type for each store; monitored unusual conditions, problems, and trends, as well as cash underages and overages; and contacted field managers for explanations. Within 24 hours of the store controllers' review, Debbi saw the same reports at an aggregate level.

MIS. The objective of being able to run each store essentially as Debbi ran the original Palo Alto store guided the implementation of information technology at Mrs. Fields'. The strategic goal of the MIS area, according to Randy Fields, was "to put as much decision making and intelligence into the store level PC as is necessary to free the manager to do those things that uniquely people do." Randy believed that it was "demeaning for people to do what machines can do." Store managers, he felt had better things to do than paperwork—such as selling cookies.

Director of MIS Paul Quinn reported directly to Randy Fields and was responsible for implementing his vision. Quinn's 11-person organization was responsible for development, support, and operations for the store personal computers and financial and sales systems, and for managing the firm's telecommunications equipment, a Rolm Private Branch Exchange (PBX), and a voice-mail system. The MIS organization chart is shown in Exhibit 2.

With respect to systems development at Mrs. Fields', Quinn explained:

> Anyone can come to me or any of my people and ask for anything. We do an ad hoc cost/benefit analysis and justify a system on one of three criteria:
>
> • Potential payback (will it cut costs and/or save money?).

> • Drive sales (will it generate new sales?).
> • Strategic importance (will it put the company in a position to take advantage of something it could not otherwise do, like the interview system?).
>
> "Strategic" in our industry means promoting sales and controlling labor and food costs. If you can do that you will be successful. I am in an enviable position as the MIS director here, because this company has more information than people can act upon. When someone wants a new report, I have usually already collected the information; it's just a matter of massaging and formatting.

Randy believed that keeping the staff small kept employees solving business problems rather than managing layers of people. He believed this kept jobs interesting and, moreover, that smaller groups of people make decisions faster and better. Randy felt that in order to avoid large groups, a company had to either limit business growth or leverage its people.

Randy saw information systems as a way to accommodate growth without expanding staff. He consistently encouraged the people working with the technology to think up new, creative applications. "Suppose you could not have any people working for you," he would say. "What must the computer do for you then? Don't be limited by what you think the computer can do." An accounts payable clerk, who routinely paid invoices that were regular and consistent, had wondered whether this redundant activity might be automated. This employee's initiative gave rise to the development of an expert system, which was designed to not only automate the routine elements of the activity, but also learn how to respond to exceptions by prompting the manager for input each time an exception was encountered. As the system learned, the exceptions became routine, and the system was able to respond to them automatically without further input from the manager.

EXHIBIT 2 Mrs. Fields' Cookies—MIS Organization

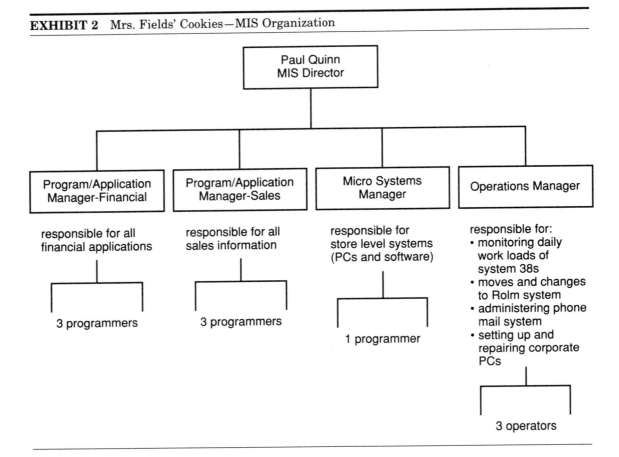

Cookie Store Operations

Mrs. Fields' cookie stores were typically divided into two areas (see Exhibit 3). The ovens faced the retail area, fronted by an island of counter space used to fill and unload cookie sheets. Customers were drawn into the store by the openness of the design, and by the aroma of hot cookies fresh from the ovens plainly in view under the Lucite-covered display. The back room contained the mixers, a work space, a small office area with a personal computer, and sufficient storage space for ingredients. This was Mrs. Fields' at the level of the friendly, inviting retail outlets located in high-density shopping areas around the world.

But there was another level to Mrs. Fields'—the level of the sophisticated management information system that tracked the financial performance of each company-owned outlet and provided comprehensive scheduling of activities within stores, including marketing support, hourly sales projections, and even candidate interviewing for prospective employees.

Each store's personal computer accessed a sophisticated store management system designed by Randy and the MIS organization (see *Appendix A*). Menu-driven applications included day planning, time clocks, store accounting and inventory, interview scheduling, skill testing, and electronic mail (see *Appendix B*). One application dialed the

EXHIBIT 3 Typical Mrs. Fields' Store Floorplan*

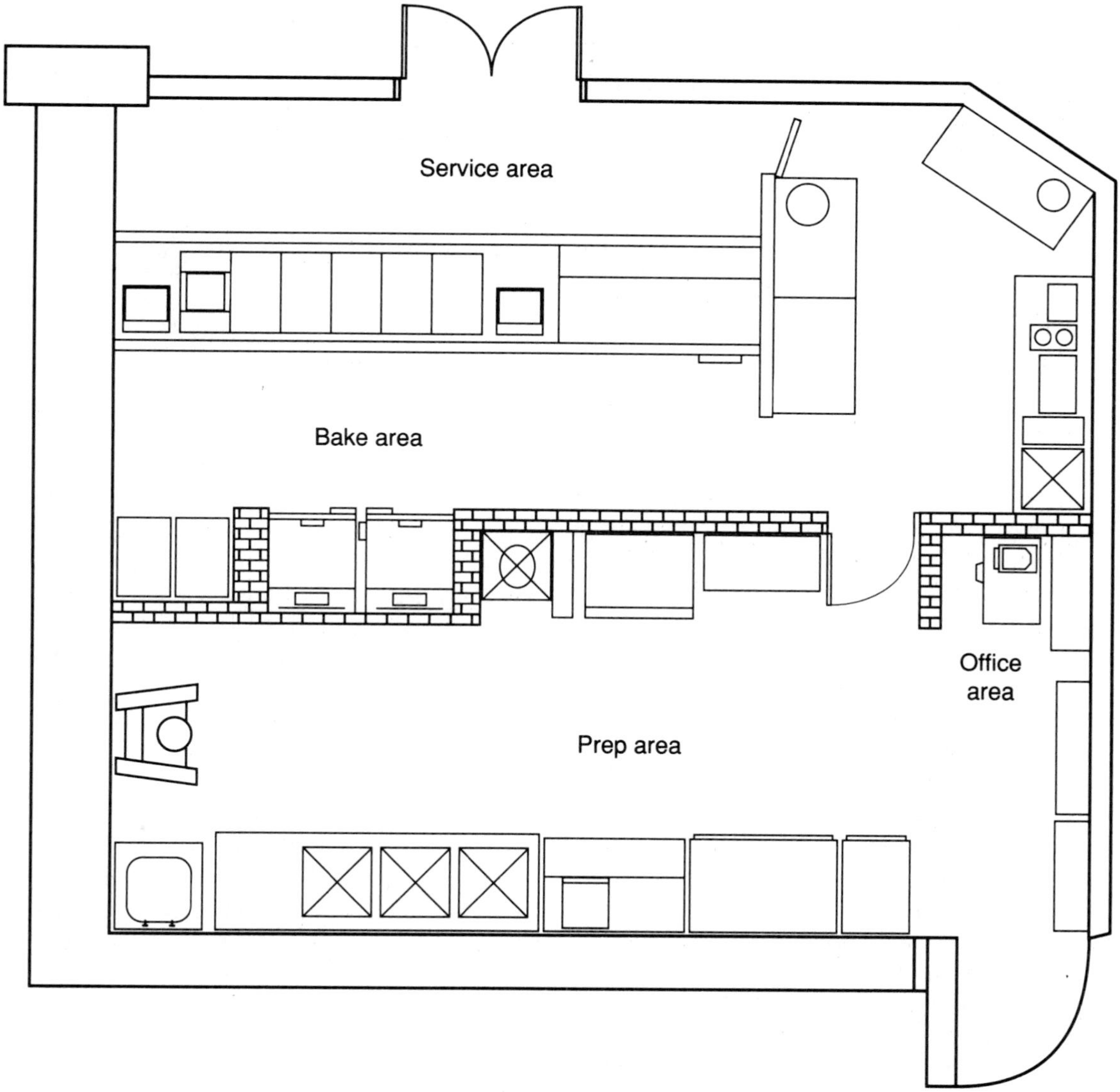

Service area

Bake area

Office area

Prep area

*This floorplan is approximately 600 sq. ft. Stores ranged from 400 sq. ft. to 1,250 sq. ft.

headquarters' computer, deposited the day's transactions, and retrieved any mail for store employees.

A store manager's day began in the back room at the personal computer. After entering workday characteristics, such as day of the week, school day or holiday, weather conditions, etc., the manager answered a series of questions that caused the system to access a specific mathematical model for computing the day's schedule. The manager was subsequently advised how many cookies to bake per hour and the projected sales per hour. The manager would enter the types of cookies to be made that day and the system would respond with the number of batches to mix and when to mix them. For example, the following mixing information

When to Mix	Length of Time	Number of Batches to Mix
8 a.m.	10 a.m.–3 p.m.	31
1 p.m.	3 p.m.–6 p.m.	7

would tell the manager: "At 8 a.m. mix 31 batches of cookies. Use the dough from 10 a.m. to 3 p.m. At that time the dough is no longer up to our standards, so discard any remaining dough. At 1 p.m. mix 7 batches of dough for use from 3 p.m. to 6 p.m."

As store sales were periodically entered throughout the day, either manually by the manager or by an automated cash register, the system would revise its projections and offer recommendations. For example, if the customer count was down, the system might suggest doing some sampling. If, on the other hand, the customer count was acceptable, but average sales were down, the system might recommend that more suggestive selling be done. Store managers could follow or disregard these suggestions.

From sales and inventory information stored in the computer, the information system computed projections, and prepared and (after being checked by the store manager) generated orders for supplies. A single corporate database tracked sales in each store and produced reports that were reviewed daily. Headquarters thus learned immediately when a store was not meeting its objectives and was able to respond quickly. Exhibit 4 shows a schematic diagram of the overall information system.

The information system had been explicitly designed to reflect the manager's perspective to foster the kind of symbiotic relationship described above, according to Debbi. "Asking store managers making salaries of $20,000 to $25,000 annually to meet an annual quota of a half-million dollars," she explained,

is like asking them to fly to the moon. They cannot really relate to those big numbers. But if you break it down to $50 or $60 an hour, the quotas become easy goals. Even if an hourly quota is missed by $5 or $6, our employees feel they can easily make it up the next hour.

The most efficient way for managers to communicate was via electronic mail, but they also called their phone mailbox in Park City for audio messages on a daily basis. Debbi, who had from the outset promised to respond within 48 hours to electronic and voice mail directed to her, sent messages through this network several times a week. Thus, the manager did not simply read memos from the president, but often personally heard her voice.

The information system helped Debbi maintain a degree of personal involvement with each store manager. "Even when she isn't there, she's there," wrote Richman, "in the standards built into the scheduling program, in the hourly goals, in the sampling and suggestive selling, on the phone. The technology has 'leveraged' Debbi's ability to project her influence into more stores than she could ever reach effectively without it."[5]

The information system also helped the manager make hiring decisions. After conducting initial interviews, the manager entered information from the handwritten applications into the computer, which compared it with stored information on pre-

---

[5]"Mrs. Fields' Secret Ingredient," p. 67.

EXHIBIT 4   Mrs. Fields' Information Systems Diagram

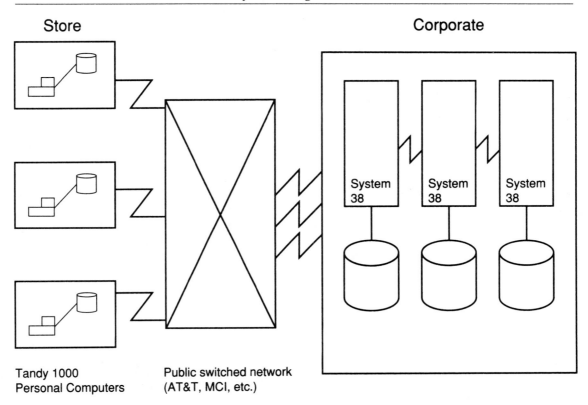

Store   Corporate

Tandy 1000   Public switched network
Personal Computers   (AT&T, MCI, etc.)

Applications

Electronic mail
Day planner
Skills test
Interview
Time clock
Labor scheduler

Applications

Personal records management
Sales management
Electronic mail
Accounting
Property management system
Systems development

vious applicants who had been hired. The system thus helped the manager to narrow the field to applicants who were "Mrs. Fields' kind of people," people who possessed attributes the company valued highly—e.g., honesty, values, punctuality, availability, education, experience, salesmanship, knowl-

edge, and attitude—and hence would fit into the corporate culture. Promising applicants were recalled for an interview conducted interactively with the computer. The applicants' answers were compared with those of existing employees and became part of the personnel database. The manager could override the system's final recommendation on hiring by going to the personnel department. The manager could do this, or go anywhere else within Mrs. Fields' for that matter, electronically.

Diversification

In April 1987, Mrs. Fields' Holdings Inc. acquired from Pepsico a 119 store French bakery/sandwich chain, La Petite Boulangerie (LPB). In the month following the acquisition, Randy reduced the subsidiary's administrative staff from 53 to 3, explaining: "We absorbed many of the overhead functions into our existing organization including accounting, finance, personnel, human resources, training, and development. We left two people in operations and one in R&D."

This was not Mrs. Fields' first acquisition. The company had acquired another retail cookie chain, the Famous Chocolate Chip Company, in 1984. The forerunner of Mrs. Fields' current MIS system had been designed to incorporate that chain's cookie stores into the Mrs. Fields' fold. But the LPB acquisition was different, primarily because of the size of the company, which Randy estimated would add $45 million in revenue in 1987. LPB stores baked (from frozen dough) and served croissants, breads, and other baked goods as well as hot soups and sandwiches. "It was," according to Randy, "a logical extension for the bakery aspect of Mrs. Fields' Cookies."

The focus of the company's "expanded store" strategy was Mrs. Fields' Bakeries. "These," explained Randy, "are destination outlets combining full lines of both cookies and bakery products." La Petite Boulangerie provided the real estate and Mrs. Fields' the "feel good" element for these upscale, sit-down cafes. This was not mere expansion; this was a new concept for Mrs. Fields'. Debbi was involved with designing the new combination stores, and planned to have existing senior managers work in them for a month or two in order to become familiar with their operation.

Randy was excited about the combination store approach. It presented an opportunity to carve out a niche in a highly fractionalized market, and the size of the operation constituted an investment barrier to competition. The Mrs. Fields' name was demographically well established, and Randy believed whatever they put it on would sell. Furthermore, a recent market analysis had suggested that enormous, demographically driven growth in the popularity of quality baked goods would not be significantly affected by fluctuations in the economy.

Randy wanted to pay for future expansion with profits, and he was convinced that the greater profits generated by the combination stores would enable them to open more new stores.

> As you will see from the financial results, our strategy required a comprehensive rationalization of our real estate portfolio, including consolidating and closing a number of stores that either did not complement the bakery store concept or were performing poorly. This necessitated a real estate write-down of $19.9 million, which we consider R&D expense related to opening our new combination stores. This program is now completed, with the cost fully provided for in the 1988 accounts. This has enabled us to establish both a broader and more solid base with greatly enhanced potential for generating future profits.

Corporate direction was clear. "Our bakery strategy," Randy explained,

> is long-term, and is based on our operational experience and extensive market and consumer research. But it will take some time for the company to reach its full potential due to the significant expenditures inherent in the bakery store program and the sheer size of the market we intend to dominate.

These changes caught the attention of the financial press, which suggested that Mrs. Fields' faced the characteristic management dilemmas of a growing business. Its expansion, both domestically and abroad, had precipitated changes in organizational and financial structure. The company was in a state of flux. It was attempting to diversify, some claimed belatedly, into combination stores. Earlier it had begun to sell its proprietary information system. Finally, what Randy viewed as record revenues were reported by the press as record losses in 1988 (see Exhibit 1).

Future Growth

What was a cookie company to do? Just a year earlier, explaining what he meant by "having a consistent vision," Randy Fields had said that he could have described as far back as 1978, when he first began to create it, the system that exists today. But he doesn't mean the machines or how they're wired together. "MIS in this company," he says,

has always had to serve two masters. First, control.Rapid growth without control equals disaster. We needed to keep improving control over our stores. And second, information that leads to control also leads to better decision making. To the extent that the information is then provided to the stores and field management level, the decisions that are made there are better, and they are more easily made.[6]

Had Mrs. Fields' lost control? Just a year earlier, the MIS director had remarked that he had more information available than people could act upon. Was the information system still that cornucopia? The Fields had accommodated past expansion by modifying their information system. Was that what was needed now Randy Fields wondered as he walked purposefully through corporate headquarters, one floor below the Main Street shopping mall in Park City.

---

[6]Ibid., p. 72.

Appendix A

Mrs. Fields' Information Systems—Hardware

Mrs. Fields' standard personal computer configuration was a Tandy 1000 (an MS-DOS system with 8086-based CPU) with one floppy disk drive, a 20-megabyte hard disk, and an internal 1200-bps modem used for communication with the Utah data center. Tandy computers were chosen because of a favorable service arrangement. Mrs. Fields' maintained a 24-hour service contract with Tandy, but most managers simply contacted the nearest Radio Shack if they had problems.

Software was the responsibility of the Micro Systems manager in Park City. The data center in Park City utilized three IBM System 38s, each equipped with six 9335 hard disks. Chosen for their database strengths, the System 38s were dedicated, one to sales systems, one to financial systems, and one to applications development.

With all significant corporate data residing in one database, disaster planning was of critical importance. The company had experienced several system failures and had a simple disaster plan: if one of the System 38s failed, one of the remaining two would back it up for critical functions. Store PCs that had not transmitted their daily work would store the information locally and transmit later. If data had already been transmitted, but the nightly backup tapes had not been run, the information would be lost. Such problems hadn't occurred, though there had been recoverable disk failures.

Appendix B

Mrs. Fields' Information Systems—Applications

Randy Fields' notion of having "a vision of what you want to accomplish with the technology" was reflected in the applications he had developed. The most frequently used applications are described below.

Form Mail, the menu-driven electronic mail application, was used mainly for brief messages between managers and staff. Managers decided when mail was transmitted to headquarters—whether immediately or when their daily paperwork was sent.

Day Planner was the first application a store manager used each morning. It produced a schedule for the day based on the minimum sales target (in dollars), the day of the week, and type of day (holiday, school day, etc.). This schedule was updated every time hourly sales information was entered into the system. (Manual entry by the manager was to be eliminated by cash registers custom designed to automatically feed the hourly sales into the personal computer.)

Labor Scheduler was an expert system that, given requirements for a specific day, scheduled staff to run a store.

Skill Tests was a set of computer-based multiple choice tests any employee could take to be considered for raises and promotions. The system indicated how many questions were answered correctly and provided tutorial sessions for questions answered incorrectly. Scores were sent to the personnel database when other information was transmitted to the corporate offices.

Interview helped store managers make hiring decisions. Managers entered information from applications filled out by candidates into the program, which made recommendations based on the historical demographics of people who had previously interviewed and worked for Mrs. Fields'. Prospective employees were called back to the store for an interactive interview with the computer application, which made a final recommendation for hiring.

Time Clock was a planned application that would enable employees to punch in and out via the Tandy computers. The automatic time card maintained by the system would facilitate the payroll process.

Case 3–2

FRONTIER AIRLINES, INC. (A)

"I am not a programmer, and in fact I've never written a line of code in my life." Lowell R. Shirley, senior director of information services at Frontier Airlines, was discussing his background with a visitor in mid-1983.

> My previous experience was designing aircraft, and later I was involved in project management in a rocket manufacturing company and a large construction firm. I've always been a user of information services, of course, but before I joined Frontier two years ago my only direct responsibility for DP [data processing] had been twelve years earlier. Ironically, at that time I was helping Frontier's management dismantle their in-house data processing operation.

Shirley's initial mandate from the airline's president was to develop the tools necessary for competing more effectively in the newly deregulated and rapidly changing airline industry. In the next two years following deregulation, Frontier spent over $10 million on new computer hardware and the facilities to house it. The information services (I/S) staff grew from 9 to 55 technicians, with an annual operating budget of $11 million. In July 1983, I/S personnel and equipment moved into a remodeled building (following the only new construction that Frontier had done in many years).

Company Background

Founded in 1946 and later expanded through mergers with two local carriers operating DC-3s to Rocky Mountain communities, Frontier added steadily to its route structure and equipment as the Denver area

developed. In 1964 RKO General, a subsidiary of General Tire & Rubber Company, purchased a controlling interest in the airline (see Exhibit 1 for General Tire's organizational divisions). Frontier's growth was accelerated by a 1967 merger with Texas-based Central Airlines. By the mid-1970s Frontier served almost 100 cities—more than any other carrier in the country. Under the federal regulations then in effect, airlines required government permission to begin or end service on a given route. To maintain minimum essential services, carriers flying to certain small cities were paid a government subsidy. Thirteen of Frontier's 100 cities accounted for 70 percent of the airline's profits; the 55 subsidy-eligible cities generated 8 percent (see Exhibit 2 for overall revenues and income). Frontier's stops included almost 30 Rocky Mountain ski resorts, and the airline promoted itself heavily to vacationers. Its jet flights offered one-class service, with the rows of seats separated by as much space as was ordinarily found in first class. Frontier also had a reputation for superior food service.

Frontier had often been a technical leader; it was an early user of Boeing 727 and 737 aircraft and was one of the first airlines to computerize its passenger reservations. Financial returns, however, did not improve as

Assistant Professor Michael R. Vitale prepared this case as a basis for class discussion rather than to illustrate either effective or ineffective handling of an administrative situation.

EXHIBIT 1   General Tire & Rubber: Corporate Organization

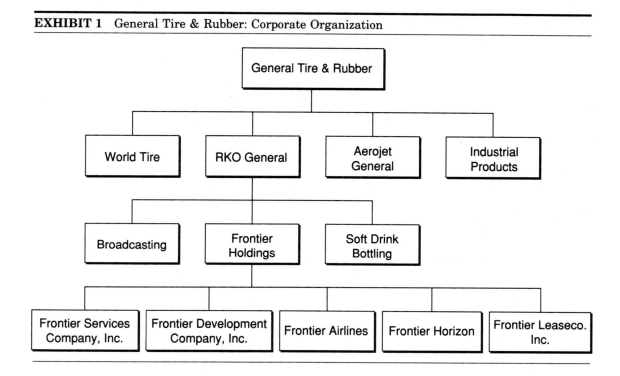

fast as the airline's use of technology (see Exhibit 3), and in 1971 Frontier's parent company installed new management from Aerojet General, another subsidiary of General Tire & Rubber. The team included Alvin Lindbergh Feldman, president and chief executive officer, and Glen L. Ryland, vice president of finance.

The new managers instituted *management by commitment,* a system developed at Aerojet General. The chief executive officer announced a set of goals—profits, return on investment, market share, and so forth— every fall. Each division, and then each organization within a division, put together its plan for meeting one or more of the goals; for example, marketing might target a certain load factor, catering a maximum number of complaints per 10,000 meals, and so on. The process, which extended down to the individual level, resulted in formal *commitments* against which performance would be measured. Commitments were expected to be met exactly: there was no reward for overachievement (since the rest of the organization was typically not prepared to take full advantage of it) and missing by a small amount was still regarded as failure. For 1983 Lowell Shirley drew up five commitments for I/S: reducing maintenance of some old applications from five person-years to three; reducing the cost of Frontier's voice communications network by $30,000 per month; relocating data entry to user departments; relocating hardware to the new facility; and completing a set of new applications. These commitments were supported by more detailed commitments from each of the four I/S directors who also received commitments from their staffs. The commitments, in turn, supported the annual I/S budget.

EXHIBIT 2 General Tire & Rubber and Subsidiaries: 1982 Revenue and Income ($ thousands)

General Tire & Rubber

Segment	Revenue	Operating Income	
World Tire	$ 999,246	$ 39,167	
Industrial Products	498,247	18,033	
Aerojet General	564,166	51,525	
Total	$2,061,659	$108,725	
Loss before tax and income of RKO General			$ (1,931)
Income before taxes of RKO General			6,507
RKO General net income			$20,929
Income from continuing operations			27,436
Loss on disposal of discontinued operations			(8,000)
Net income			$19,436

RKO General

Segment	Revenue	Operating Income	
Broadcasting	$ 164,030	$ 14,607	
Soft Drink Bottling	117,800	14,781	
Other	9,988	1,047	
Total	$ 291,818	$ 30,435	
Net income after tax from continuing operations			$ 8,097
Equity in net income of Frontier Holdings, Inc.			12,832
Net income after tax			$20,929

Frontier Holdings, Inc.

Revenue	$ 548,846	
Net income after tax	$ 24,140	

Source: 1982 Annual Report.

One goal of the commitment system was to refocus managers on the areas for which they were directly responsible. The environment created by this policy was described within the airline as one in which operating divisions were surrounded by *brick walls*. Implementation of I/S applications tended to put *windows* in those brick walls through the use of common systems, data, and equipment.

The Airline Deregulation Act of 1978 allowed air carriers to change routes simply by giving a 90-day notice. Between 1978 and early 1982, Frontier dropped 39 cities, added 29 others, and expanded operations at its Denver hub. In March 1978 Frontier served 490 city-pairs; by March 1983, 231, including only 90 of those served five years earlier. In Denver Frontier had seven new competi-

EXHIBIT 3   Frontier Airlines: General Statistics

Year	RPM[a]	ASM[b]	Load Factor[c] (%)	Operating Expenses (in cents) Per RPM	Per ASM	Yield[d]
1982	3,571	5,852	61.0%	14.87¢	9.07¢	13.71¢
1981	3,502	5,642	62.1	15.03	9.33	14.78
1980	2,972	5,009	59.3	14.55	8.63	13.91
1979	3,012	4,944	60.9	11.86	7.23	11.32
1978	2,398	3,771	63.6	11.34	7.21	10.52
1977	1,902	3,235	58.8	11.00	6.46	10.66
1976	1,690	2,951	57.3	10.75	6.16	10.27
1975	1,460	2,617	55.8	10.67	5.96	9.76
1974	1,392	2,491	55.9	9.87	5.52	9.16
1973	1,308	2,473	52.9	9.04	4.78	8.00
1972	1,102	2,123	51.9	8.96	4.65	7.88
1971	1,066	2,306	46.2	4.65	4.16	7.65
1970	1,075	2,427	44.3	8.52	3.77	7.38
1969	988	2,179	45.3	8.32	3.77	7.26
1968	910	2,052	44.3	8.11	3.61	6.55
1967	658	1,512	43.6	8.37	3.64	6.84
1966	466	1,042	44.7	8.89	3.97	7.10
1965	310	776	39.9	11.03	4.40	7.58
1964	274	674	40.6	11.43	4.64	7.16
1963	233	597	39.0%	12.22¢	4.76¢	7.08¢

a. Revenue passenger miles, in millions. One revenue-paying passenger flown one mile generates one RPM.
b. Available seat miles, in millions. One seat available for passengers flown one mile on scheduled service generates one ASM.
c. Load factor = RPM divided by ASM, expressed as a percentage.
d. Passenger revenue per RPM, in cents (scheduled service only).

tors, including American, Eastern, Northwest, Piedmont, and Southwest. Both of its traditional competitors, United and Continental, added flights to Denver: United had 145 daily flights by early 1983 and Continental had 108. Frontier, which started, ended, or connected each of its flights through Denver (see Exhibit 4), offered 114. The airline, operating more than 50 aircraft, served 84 cities in Canada, Mexico, and 27 states in the United States. Its passengers were almost evenly divided between business and pleasure travelers. Frontier competed with United on 34 routes, up from 8 at the time of deregulation. "I assume United will survive in Denver, and I assume there will be room for one other major carrier," Frontier's president commented.

In May 1982 Frontier Airlines became a subsidiary of the newly formed Frontier Holdings, Inc. Another subsidiary of Frontier Holdings, Frontier Services, offered training, maintenance, ground handling, and ground transportation in Denver and other cities. Glen Ryland, by then chairman and president of the airline, assumed those posts at the holding company as well (see Exhibit 5 for partial organization chart). In

EXHIBIT 3   (continued)

Operating Results ($ millions)

| Year | Operating Revenues | | | Operating Expenses | | Income | |
	Passenger	Subsidy	Total	Depreciation	Total	Operating	Net
1982	$489.6	$ 9.9	$539.8	$30.7	$530.9	$ 9.0	$ 17.2
1981	517.6	22.8	577.4	24.1	526.5	50.9	32.0
1980	413.4	18.0	468.9	20.9	432.5	36.4	23.2
1979	340.9	20.8	389.7	18.2	357.3	32.3	21.1
1978	251.9	17.1	290.8	14.3	271.9	18.9	16.2
1977	202.6	11.5	234.3	11.4	209.1	25.2	12.7
1976	173.5	11.1	201.0	11.3	181.7	19.3	9.9
1975	142.5	11.8	168.8	9.4	155.9	12.9	6.7
1974	127.5	11.4	153.0	8.8	137.4	15.7	10.6
1973	104.7	11.8	129.1	8.8	118.3	10.8	7.2
1972	86.6	14.3	108.9	6.6	98.7	10.1	7.1
1971	79.6	9.6	97.4	6.6	96.0	1.3	(2.5)
1970	75.5	6.6	91.8	6.7	91.5	0.3	(3.6)
1969	66.8	6.7	82.7	6.8	82.2	0.5	(11.9)
1968	56.8	7.6	71.8	7.1	74.0	(2.2)	(6.1)
1967	41.7	8.7	57.0	4.6	55.1	1.9	1.6
1966	31.9	9.6	45.6	2.6	41.4	4.2	2.0
1965	23.4	9.6	35.4	1.2	34.1	1.3	0.5
1964	19.5	11.0	32.6	1.2	31.3	1.3	0.6
1963	$ 16.1	$12.3	$ 30.4	$ 1.1	$ 28.4	$ 1.9	$ 0.9

Source: Company reports.

August 1983 Ryland announced the formation of a second airline subsidiary, Frontier Horizon, scheduled to begin flight operations in December. Frontier Horizon was to be a separate company operated by its own management as a low-cost carrier. Its initial schedule of 10 round-trip flights per day included service to New York, Chicago, Washington, and San Francisco. This schedule was integrated with Frontier Airlines', and the two carriers shared gate space, ground equipment, and other facilities, based upon arm's-length negotiations with Frontier.

In late 1982 the Civil Aeronautics Board (CAB) and the Department of Justice began a joint investigation of possible antitrust violations by airline reservations systems. The investigation had been ordered by the Senate Appropriations Committee, which requested a report by early 1983. In a document (reproduced in the *Appendix*) filed in connection with the investigation, Frontier Airlines charged that United Airlines unfairly restricted competition by using its Apollo computerized reservations system. United made no formal response to Frontier's charges; it and other reservations system operators generally claimed that their systems were developed independently as part of long-range strategies to sell tickets through travel agents. Other airlines could participate in these systems for a fee.

EXHIBIT 4 Route System in Mid-1983

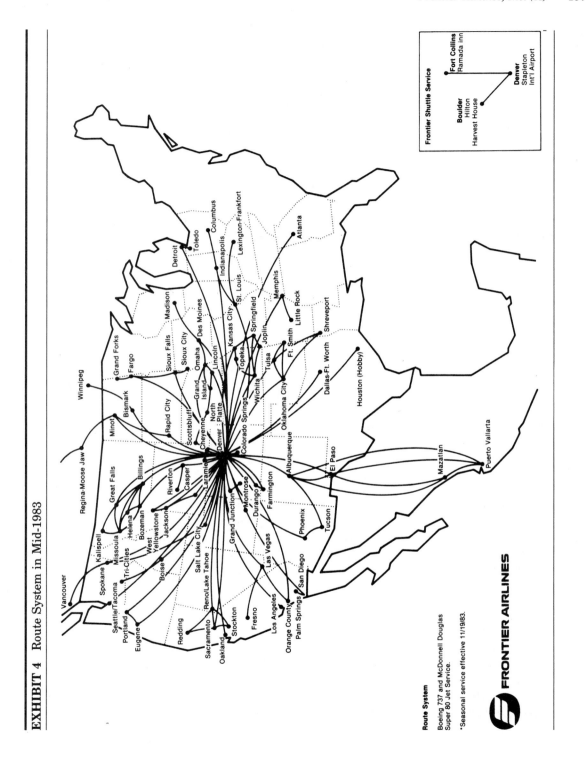

Frontier Shuttle Service

Fort Collins Ramada Inn

Boulder Hilton Harvest House

Denver Stapleton Int'l Airport

Route System

Boeing 737 and McDonnell Douglas Super 80 Jet Service.

*Seasonal service effective 11/19/83.

FRONTIER AIRLINES

EXHIBIT 5   Frontier Airlines: Partial Organization Chart, August 1983

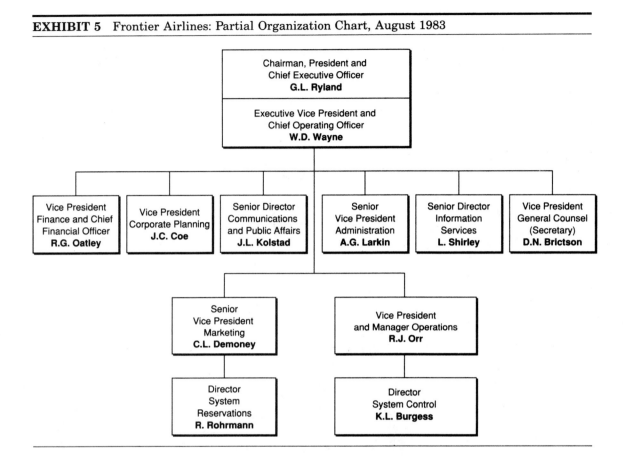

Information Systems

Frontier was an early user of data processing, having automated its accounting systems by 1965 and its passenger reservations system a few years later. The new management group from Aerojet General believed that some Frontier managers paid closer attention to printouts than to operations, and they were determined to de-emphasize data processing: in the words of one veteran, "They fired the computers." It was in this context that Shirley, who had worked for Ryland at Aerojet General, was brought briefly to Frontier to, along with other assignments, study the dismantling of its in-house data processing. The DP staff was reduced to nine programmers, and applications programs were run at service bureaus. In September 1972, after a brief experiment with a manual system, Frontier decided to purchase computerized reservations services from Greenwich Data Systems, a subsidiary of Planning Research Corporation. And then in 1974 Frontier's reservations software was moved onto hardware operated by Control Data Corporation; finally, in 1976 Frontier began purchasing reservations services from Continental Airlines. Shirley remarked that this decision was the most important one Frontier had ever made regarding information systems.

At most airlines, the res[ervations] system drives the information systems strategy. Frontier decided that it made economic sense to share the overhead of a res system. Supposedly there are some marketing advantages to owning your res system, but those advantages had never happened in Frontier's experience.

With all of Frontier's centrally maintained information systems running in batch mode on a variety of outside computers, I/S users were (in one manager's words) "surly but not rebellious." Nevertheless, in 1978 a number of them obtained stand-alone minicomputers for marketing, crew scheduling, and other applications. One manager described their impact on the airline.

Each minicomputer application was an uphill battle, but each represented a significant stride as well. In aircraft scheduling, for example, turnaround dropped from two days with the batch system to a few minutes with the minicomputer. We were not concerned about a uniform data base—we wanted to maintain the manager's ability to innovate.

The use of outside time-sharing had also increased. President Ryland, feeling he did not have adequate decision-support tools, hired outside consultants to evaluate Frontier's information systems. The consultants found a large backlog of desired applications, many of which had never been proposed formally. They recommended that Frontier consolidate its data processing and telecommunications within a single in-house organization, using IBM mainframes and purchased software. "The most important impact of the study," Shirley noted, "was probably the message that the airline had to do *something*." In the summer of 1981, shortly after receiving the consultant's report, Frontier recruited Shirley from a major engineering and construction company.

Hardware

Shirley made a survey of Frontier's data needs and formulated some basic policies for hardware and information systems management.

My first decision was that we would not ever run a res system. Then I started to address everything else. When I first spoke to users, they all said they needed "real-time data." It turned out, though, that they really meant "yesterday's data." Compared to the batch environment, yesterday was "real time"! I estimated that only 5 percent of the applications—for example, flight dispatching—really required real-time data.

I next asked how much data sharing was required. About 90 percent of our data is used within a single division—only about 10 percent is ever shared. Finally, I investigated the source of our data. About 5 percent comes from the Official Airline Guide, the Airline Tariff Publishing Company, the weather bureau, and other outside organizations. The great majority, however, is generated inside Frontier.

Based on this survey of our data needs, I thought about what hardware would be most suitable. At my previous employer I had seen tremendous gains in programmer productivity when a mainframe computer was replaced with several super-minicomputers. You don't save a lot on hardware by buying multiple small machines instead of one big one, but overall, system reliability is higher and overhead—for example, systems programmers and facilities—is lower. Another advantage of using smaller boxes is that you can start small and grow.

There were some disadvantages to the super-mini approach, of course. At the time there were no good systems for integrating several machines, so each application had to fit entirely on one super-mini. There was little packaged software available—in evaluating the super-mini alternative, I assumed that we would not be able to buy anything from the outside. And using a distributed system instead of a central mainframe was a unique approach in the airline industry.

I was familiar with the IBM System 38, and I believed that IBM would continue to expand and develop that line. I liked the System 38 architecture, particularly the built-in database features, and our largest application would just fit on the biggest System 38 available at the time. I therefore decided to use the 38, and our first machine was delivered in November 1981. By February of 1982 we had our initial applications up and running.

By mid-1983 Frontier was using three System 38s, with a fourth due in early 1984; one machine was used for production, one for software development, and one for remote job entry to those applications still running outside. A task force on station computing had recommended IBM Series 1s to handle remote computing and communications routing on Frontier's distributed network, and the first such machine had been installed. The network itself, which would eventually link all of Frontier's outlying stations to Denver, was designed to use the X.25 packet-switching protocol. X.25 was widely used by public and private data networks, but it was unusual in the airline industry, which, almost universally, relied on a protocol designed in the early days of computer reservations systems. X.25 had a somewhat slower response time but it was far more reliable.

Frontier's use of distributed processing was also unusual for the industry, but it fit in with the airline's super-mini choice. "Trying to do all the processing in Denver would have buried the System 38s," Shirley commented. In addition, there were a number of applications—aircraft weight and balance, air cargo tracing, cash drawer reconciliation, and so forth—that affected only a single station; by doing them locally, network traffic was reduced. The Series 1 was capable of controlling ticket and boarding pass printers, credit card readers, and other devices in addition to terminals, and it was good at message routing. Like the System 38, the Series 1 was modular and could be expanded to meet growth.

Several Frontier managers had become interested in microcomputers, and Shirley felt that the introduction of micros was an important issue. "I decided to initiate the move to micros, not fight it," he said. Under Frontier policy all purchases of computer hardware had to be approved by Shirley, and he had elected to standardize on the IBM Personal Computer. Once a division was allowed to obtain a PC, all applications had to be approved by a technical specialist in Shirley's group; only BASIC, a single spreadsheet analysis package, and qualified third-party applications were permitted, and only divisional data could be used. It was possible to draw data from one of the System 38s, but data could not be sent in the opposite direction; violators risked losing their machines. One of the first divisions to acquire a PC was marketing, which used the micro to keep track of expenditures. Other micro applications in Denver included budgeting, maintaining personnel records, and domiciling flight attendants.

Software

The largest single application under development at Frontier was revenue accounting, which was being converted from a largely manual system. Frontier handled about 600,000 ticket coupons a month; each had to be scanned, microfilmed, and sorted to determine whether the coupon represented an asset or a liability. Increasing complexity and the rate of change in airline fares had made the job more difficult. "Without adequate controls, only bad things can happen; you underbill, overpay, or both," said Robert G. Oatley, Frontier's vice president of finance and chief financial officer. The automated system, justified on the basis of manpower replacement and revenue recovery, was expected to pay back its development costs in less than 18 months. The current accounting system produced some reports on yield, fare usage, and so on, and they were supplemented by manual reports. "We really should correlate revenue accounting with ticket lift data," Oatley said, "but it's better to take the information from revenue accounting and feed it to other systems than to try to keep one big database. We're aiming for compatibility, not integration."

Oatley believed that Frontier needed several additional applications in the accounting area; for example, accounts payable and general ledger were both automated, but they were not linked. The airline's computerized payroll system also needed to be replaced. "The question," Oatley said, "is what to do first. None of these accounting systems are critical to our daily operations, and it's more important to give the operating guys their data first."

Although Oatley noted that Frontier users were generally unsophisticated (and sometimes impatient), he felt that their general attitude toward information systems was healthy. "They had to learn that they were responsible for specifying their own systems," he said, "and they had to commit manpower and time to the job." When a new project was approved, a technical specialist was made project manager and assigned a team of programmer/analysts. The team worked in a matrix arrangement with its own department and the user; it was expected that each team member would understand the user's job well enough to perform it. The user organization paid the technical specialists' salaries during project development.

Shortly after arriving at Frontier, Shirley agreed with top management on the number of people required to complete certain critical applications within a given time. Frontier then hired more than 30 technical personnel, only two of whom had previous airline experience. Shirley noted that, "Airline people would have wanted to use airline methods. It's key that our technical specialists establish with the user that they both understand the user's problem and can help solve it." Thereafter, users who wanted new

applications proposed them to their vice president; it was that vice president's job to sell each new project to Shirley's boss and to persuade him to obtain the additional people and equipment needed. The general basis for project approval was an evaluation of information systems costs versus benefits to the user.

Shirley noted that in his two years at Frontier he had not seen a proposal for a project with a payback of more than 18 months; despite efforts by Shirley, Ryland, and others to convince users that there were other reasons for proposing a project, most users apparently felt that direct cost savings were the only allowable justification. "We could double our staff and still work only on systems with a payback of less than two years," Shirley commented. "I want to focus on the high-leverage items."

Frontier used a structured development methodology to generate requirements, external specifications, and internal technical specifications. All software development was done in-house. Frontier built new applications on-line, using a database approach and a heuristic design philosophy. Bob Oatley noted:

> *Heuristic* does not mean *freewheeling;* we have specifications, including screen designs and reports, at the outset. It does mean that we don't consider an application finished when it's first released. In fact, if it's any good it will continue to be changed.

Frontier estimated that its programmers were able to complete an application in about half the time required in other development environments. The System 38 included a query facility that allowed users to create their own one-time reports, but users were not permitted to change their programs.

Frontier departments were charged for terminals and other hardware and for the cost of running their applications. Time on the System 38 was billed at $5 a terminal hour, and paper reports cost 50¢ a page. The hourly rate was intended to recover the out-of-pocket cost of operating the in-house machines. There was no charge for any software maintenance needed to bring an application up to specifications, but users had to pay for enhancements. "I want to draw attention to the fact that fixing old things also uses resources," Shirley said. Large, interdepartmental projects and telecommunications were funded from corporate resources. Shirley explained the billing philosophy:

> In the service bureau environment, everything was billed back. The attitude was, "This must be worth something, because someone is willing to pay for it." We're moving toward allocating less and less cost to the user—we charge only when the act of charging accomplishes some goal.

Fares and Reservations

Chuck Demoney, Frontier's senior vice president for marketing, observed that deregulation had changed the airline's need for timely information.

> Under regulation, we had very little latitude. The CAB required us to keep certain data, and timeliness was not very important. In the new, changing environment, it's vital to be able to take rapid advantage of opportunities. Our planning cycle has gone from four or five years to four or five weeks, and our previous knowledge of our competition has been replaced by vast uncertainty.

One of the first applications for the System 38 was a database of some 70,000 fares.

The database was used to monitor competitors' fares and to maintain Frontier's own fare data. Fare data were exchanged with the Airline Tariff Publishing Company, with Frontier's reservation and ticketing system, and with a pricing model run on an outside time-sharing system.

Frontier's reservation system had been enhanced to include advance seat selection and assignment and boarding pass production. The airline also became part of American Airlines' frequent-flyer program, AAdvantage (see Exhibit 6); American maintained a separate database on these Frontier passengers, but Demoney noted that it was "nearly impossible" to manipulate the data in any useful way. Frontier used its own System 38 data base for analysis purposes.

Of all the I/S-related issues facing Frontier, Demoney felt that travel agency use of reservations systems was the most important:

> We have mounted a vocal campaign to let the CAB, the Department of Justice, and others know about biases in these systems, and we believe we may have seen some softening recently. It's a very critical issue, but maybe not one on which our in-house information systems can help much.

At one time Frontier had marketed its reservations system, SENTRY, to travel agents, but had not been able to compete with the large carriers (United and American) for travel agent acceptance.

EXHIBIT 6   Ad for Frontier's Appeal to Frequent Fliers

Frequent fliers. . .

don't forget, Frontier has the American Airlines A̤Advantage® Program that can earn you Travel Awards to over 150 cities in more than a dozen countries!*

Ask your Ticket Agent how you can qualify.

*AAdvantage rules, regulations and special offers are subject to change without notice.

A̤A AmericanAirlines

Appendix

Before the Civil Aeronautics Board—Washington, D.C.

Report to Congress on Computer: Reservations Systems

Docket 41207

Comments of Frontier Airlines, Inc.

At the present time about 80% of the nation's travel agencies have automated reservations systems.[1] Computerized agencies tend to be the high-volume operators, with mostly the smaller (often rural) agencies remaining unautomated. In 1981, computerized agencies accounted for $24.5 *billion* of airline ticket sales! (*supra*). Sales through travel agencies are critically important to Frontier's business since they account for 65% of our total sales volume.

While American Airlines' SABRE system and United Airlines' Apollo system are the largest in use throughout the nation, Frontier's comments focus primarily on United's Apollo system because of its impact upon Frontier and the Denver hub. Frontier is United's chief competitor at Denver, with United enplaning 3.6 million passengers versus 2.5 million by Frontier in 1982. United and Frontier now compete head to head on 34 routes out of Denver, versus only 8 when the Deregulation Act of 1978 was implemented. United's January 1983 Denver departures are 145 a day, up 40% from one year ago.

The combined effect of United's leverage through the Apollo system and its other extraordinary measures at Denver have had a serious impact on the competitive airline picture at this important hub:[2]

- United enplaned 1,013,975 passengers at Denver in the fourth quarter of 1982, a 40.2% increase over the fourth quarter of 1981. This translates into a 36.9% share of Denver enplanements for United at the end of 1982 versus 26.8% for the fourth quarter of 1981.
- The growth of United's domination at Denver is more clearly reflected by comparing quarterly increases during 1982 with one year earlier. United's percentage share of enplaned Denver passengers increased 1.5%, 4.6%, 17.6% and 28.1% during each of the four quarters of 1982 over the same periods in 1981, while Frontier's quarterly share of enplaned Denver passengers *decreased* 9.2%, 6.5%, 8.3% and 9.8% versus the same periods last year.

The ability of United to significantly affect the Denver hub through its Apollo system is shown by the following section.

1. United Dominates the Computerized Reservations System Market at the Denver Hub

At Denver, the dominance of United's Apollo system among agencies is particularly strong:

- 148 out of 198 (75%) automated travel agencies in the Denver area subscribe to Apollo.
- Apollo has automated four times more travel agencies in the Denver area than its next largest competitor.

---

[1] This is Frontier's current best estimate. According to *Travel Weekly*'s Louis Harris Study (May 1982, p. 46), 68% of the travel agencies were automated in 1981, and Frontier knows the growth has continued since then.

[2] Based on preliminary fourth quarter 1982 data.

• Apollo travel agencies in the Denver area account for about $250 million in airline revenues, or about 82% of total airline revenues generated by Denver's automated agencies.[3]

Frontier believes that United has used its control over one market, i.e., the Denver travel agents' automated reservations systems, as an unfair and anticompetitive means to further United's goals in another market, i.e., that sale of air transportation, where it competes with Frontier and other carriers.

2. *Normal Market Forces Have Not Disciplined the Travel Agency Computer Reservation Systems Market.*

Normally, competition between United's Apollo system, American's SABRE system, TWA's PARS system and other lesser competitors for placement of computer reservation systems at travel agencies would discipline this market. However, this has not been the case as demonstrated by abuses which have occurred. Set forth below are examples of past practices, as well as future prospects, of the anticompetitive impact of United's control of the Apollo system.

3. *United Uses Apollo in an Unfair and Uncompetitive Manner.*

(a) *United has discriminatorily excluded carriers from Apollo.*

For over two years United refused to allow Frontier to become an Apollo co-host for "competitive" reasons. Although Frontier was finally allowed to become a co-host in July of 1982, our prior efforts to join Apollo

[3]As of March 1982: Apollo 148; SABRE 37; PARS 12; EA 1. Denver metro area includes Boulder, Longmont, Loveland and several other front-range communities. Estimated annual revenues of $1.8 million per agency, which was the average annual revenue figure of 47 Denver Apollo travel agencies as of June 1981.

were stalled by United's claim that its Apollo system did not have the capacity to handle Frontier. However, during the same time period at least three other major carriers were granted co-host status. After repeated inquiries, Frontier was finally told in August of 1981 by a United Vice President that it was to be excluded for "competitive" reasons. Further entreaties by Frontier were similarly rebuffed, until soon after the Department of Justice and the CAB began their investigative efforts into anticompetitive aspects of automated reservation systems.

Frontier also understands that Midway Airlines' complete schedules—direct and connecting—were expunged from Apollo for a period of time. (During the period Frontier was denied co-host status, its direct flights remained in the Apollo system). United therefore has the power to completely eliminate smaller carriers' schedules from Apollo unless a fee is paid, regardless of the impact on the carrier, the public or travel agents. Air California now pays such a fee for inclusion of its direct flights, and had Frontier not become a co-host, United threatened complete expulsion of all our flights from Apollo unless a fee were paid.

(b) *"Tying" arrangements under Apollo.*

In order to become a co-host under United's Apollo system, Frontier was forced to also agree on a "net ticketing arrangement" with United. Under the "net ticketing arrangement," Frontier pays United a dollar amount for tickets written by United on Frontier, and United pays Frontier a dollar amount for tickets written by Frontier on United. However, Frontier did not want this agreement, since United writes more tickets on Frontier, and we asked that separate negotiations be held on this subject. United refused, saying it was a package deal. Frontier estimates that the ticketing "tying" arrangement will cost the company about

$350,000 in 1983. Thus, United used its power in the "tying" product—co-host status in the Apollo system—to impose its will with respect to a separate agreement—net ticketing. Interestingly, in Frontier's negotiations with TWA, a similar package deal was presented to Frontier, i.e., membership in PARS coupled with net ticketing, but TWA agreed to sever the two products and negotiate each separately.

(c) Bias problems continue even after achieving co-host status.

Even after Frontier achieved co-host status under Apollo, and during Frontier's long-standing co-host status under SABRE, bias problems continue to exist which give host carriers such as United and American an unfair competitive advantage.

Host carriers continue to maintain a super-bias which displays their schedules in a superior manner to that afforded co-host carriers. For example, when a travel agent requests flight information from Apollo, the system will display schedules of co-hosts from the desired time *forward,* while United alone will display backwards in time (about two hours) in addition to displaying schedules after the desired time. More comprehensive and complicated rules are employed to display connecting schedules—always designed to give United a leg up on its co-hosts.

In addition to the super-bias enjoyed by United as a host carrier, some co-hosts are more equal than other co-hosts in the tradition of Orwell's *Animal Farm.* Thus, Delta is accorded a special display on Apollo. Host carriers also retain the right to create new categories of co-hosts such as that United has accorded to Delta and thereby create new echelons of bias among co-hosts for which differentiated (and higher) rates can be charged.

To date, host carriers have concentrated on biasing schedule displays in their travel agent systems, but Frontier expects that bias will play a greater role in reservation systems' *fare* displays in the future. Even now the fare categorization/classification program employed by United in the Apollo system can result in a competitively inferior display for a carrier desiring to improvise with new fares. A host carrier such as United also enjoys a competitive advantage in institution of a new fare, since United can plan and control the display of its new fares in Apollo, whereas Frontier and other co-hosts must hope that the display accorded the new fare in Apollo is a good one (or a co-host must conform its new fare within existing fare display formats, which is not always possible or desirable). If such a new and innovative fare by a co-host does not receive a favorable Apollo display, its acceptance by travel agents can be drastically affected.

(d) Host carriers have an unfair advantage by their computerized access to confidential information of the competitors.

United and American have *exclusive* and *immediate* access on their respective Apollo and SABRE systems to highly sensitive sales data which they can use to their competitive advantage. United, for example, generates reports for each Apollo travel agency identifying by market the total number of passengers carried in the period, and the amount and percentage of traffic carried by each competitive carrier in the market. This information is not available to co-hosts such as Frontier. The only information United will give Frontier is the total number of passengers carried by Frontier, and currently even this limited information (which does not indicate Frontier's share of the total market, or other carriers' shares) is available about one month in arrears.

Access to this information gives United/American a tremendous and unfair competitive advantage. United sales representatives have immediate knowledge whether United and its competitors are losing/gaining market share, and United can promptly take measures (e.g., bonus incentives, lower fares, more schedules) to rectify the developing situation. The *immediate* access of United sales representatives to this data allows United sales representatives to contact travel agents long before Frontier knows of market changes. At several travel agencies where Frontier has made inroads into United market shares, the agents have mentioned "pressure" from United sales representatives to increase United market shares, as reflected in a recent article appearing in *Travel Agent:*

> Agents are also becoming accustomed to receiving printouts of their reservation histories with little comments, sometimes nasty at that, asking why some other carrier was used instead of them. (October 11, 1982, p. 19.)

(e) United coerces agents into exclusive use of Apollo.

While Frontier has finally attained cohost status in Apollo, United still maintains its schedule bias over Frontier in the system, and Frontier's schedules enjoy a superior display vis-a-vis United in American's SABRE system. Therefore United's efforts to maintain exclusivity with travel agents using Apollo—particularly in the crucial Denver market—harms Frontier (not to mention travel agencies and the public). United uses several means to preclude competition by SABRE and other automated systems.

> *The 95% Rule.* Over the last year, United has added a clause to its Apollo contract requiring the travel agent to ". . . process 95% of its tickets containing at least one United segment through the Apollo equipment." To assure compliance, United has the right to audit the agency's books and records without notice. The admitted purpose of this provi-

sion, according to United's Senior Vice President in charge of marketing (John Zeeman), is to prevent agencies from maintaining two systems:

> He agreed that this section would have the effect of forcing agents to make a choice between two or more systems, but he said the written document is only a manifestation of a continuing policy of pushing agents to make such choices. *** It is clear that any agency with two airline systems could not possibly satisfy the 95% rule, but Zeeman said United would not let such an agency have the option of signing the contract anyway. The agency would be asked to choose between Apollo and the second system. (*Travel Weekly,* November 15, 1982.)

The December issue of *Frequent Flyer* speaks of the same subject:

> But to American and United, second automated res systems are pure anathema. Reportedly, both carriers have threatened to pull their computer terminals out of agencies that install a competitor's hardware.

> United admits that it discourages Apollo users from using another system, particularly SABRE: "We feel that it is not an effective way to do business," says Zeeman. ("New Reservations about Airlines Computers," pp. 45 and 49.)

Other Coercive Efforts. The September 13, 1982, issue of the *Aviation Daily* contains another example of United pressure to preclude a Colorado Springs travel agency from using two systems:

> Myers originally wanted two systems in order to get boarding passes and last-seat availability for both carriers. He said a succession of meetings between Ambassador Travel and each airline made it clear that United prefers an exclusive arrangement so that it can look at any agency's business and determine if it is delivering to United a share of business that reflects the carrier's market share in the area.

(f) The pending "Boarding Pass" enhancement to Apollo.

United is currently seeking to add a new feature to Apollo which would allow travel agencies to automatically issue boarding passes to United passengers. This feature, we understand, will not be allowed for Frontier passengers, nor will United permit SABRE users to issue United boarding passes, whether manually or otherwise. This seems to be yet another means to be used by United to enhance its airline market position, by way of its control over the Apollo system.

(g) Host carriers can also control the content of data reaching travel agents.

Host carriers have the ability to control the content of information reaching travel agencies. This control has adverse competitive implications to Frontier and other outsiders. For example, Frontier recently instituted a $99 one-way fare in many markets on its system. While United did insert the Frontier fare information into Apollo, United used the same system to undermine Frontier in the eyes of the travel agents using Apollo. Thus, United inserted a "sales message" to agents informing them that it was matching Frontier fares, but gratuitously added that "Because these fares are *nongenerative,* we have planned a 3/3/83 travel expiration date *to try to minimize dilution of your commission.*" (Wednesday, 1/12/83 message to Apollo users.)

The clear message by United to the travel agents was that Frontier's new fares would not produce any new passengers, and that all they would do was reduce travel agents' commissions. Standing alone, this may not seem earthshaking, but how many other messages have been sent which Frontier has not seen?

Other examples of potential anticompetitive effects of hosts' control of information in their automated systems include:

- The Host carrier alone knows the intricate details of the bias system program. The Host also controls when changes are made, as well as variations to bias that are implemented from time to time in "special" markets, where a Host may perceive a lower usage of its service or an opportunity to improve market penetration. Despite continuous efforts, Frontier has not been able to effectively monitor its schedules in the Apollo and SABRE systems.

- At times, Frontier schedules are "dropped" from Apollo/SABRE, or fares are delayed in their entry. Frontier's monitoring catches some of these problems, but not all of them. The host always explains these problems as attributable to a computer mistake or other vagary of the system, and Frontier is in no position to contest these explanations. However, with a prime competitor controlling the system, a co-host's doubts are never really satisfied.

- From time to time, Frontier receives reports from travel agents that Apollo/SABRE reflects Frontier flights as being fully booked, whereas, in fact, seats remain to be sold. Again, these occurrences may be unintentional breakdowns, but a co-host never really knows.

(h) Other means host carriers use to maintain exclusivity or to proselytize travel agents.

- According to the October 1982 *Michigan Travel Bulletin,* a tour wholesaler in the Detroit area was told by United that its Winter Hawaii Program was in jeopardy ostensibly because of unavailability of aircraft. In an open letter to United, the publication asked:

  "Why no airplanes? They don't happen to use Apollo computers. We're told that you (United) advised this wholesaler, in so many words, switch to Apollo or else."

  "Has it really come to this?"

- United discriminates against non-Apollo agencies by withholding information. For example, we understand United has informed travel agents that only Apollo users will be able to sell special "last-minute" fares based on seat availability, and that these fares will be denied to SABRE travel agencies. In a similar vein, United has threatened to steer commercial accounts to/from travel agencies depending upon their usage of the Apollo system.

- Large bonuses paid to travel agencies to switch automated systems, e.g.,:
- The July 29, 1982, issue of *The Travel Agent* refers to an allegation that "one Midwestern travel agent was offered $100,000 to switch reservation systems."
- Another periodical claims that ". . . United has agreed to provide Apollo free of charge if they drop SABRE . . . United has even gone a step further, offering not only cash payments to some agencies of as much as $500,000 to make such a switch, but also to override commissions . . . and installation givebacks." ("New Reservations about Airline Computers," *Frequent Flyer,* December 1982, pp. 45, 46.)
- *Business Week* of August 23, 1982, confirms these practices:

   "To compete, United this spring began offering what one agent calls 'convenience money' as well as bonuses on increases in United sales, contract buyouts, and free installation to tempt agencies—and not just SABRE users—to take Apollo." (p. 68)

   "Some agents resent United's pressure tactics, says one: Using power and money to buy market share may be a wise move for United from an airline point of view. But its insistence on getting rid of other airline systems, and *the thinly veiled threat that it will give us rotten service if we don't,* has dire implications for an agent's independence." (supra, p. 69)

(i) Concerns about charges.

Exclusion from either Apollo or SABRE can have devastating results because of the number of agencies they serve, and this is particularly true with respect to hub-and-spoke carriers who rely heavily on a favorable display of connecting flights. In this context, a host carrier can charge just about all it pleases. Since Frontier initially negotiated to become an Apollo co-host, segment charges imposed by United have increased 5

to 10 times the originally quoted rates. Frontier is very concerned that United's leverage on the Apollo system will enable it to extract excessive fees in the future.

Conclusion

Frontier and the other smaller airlines are not the only ones hurt by the giant host carriers' control over this distribution system. The travel agent industry and the public at large are also ill-served by the current situation.

The American Society of Travel Agents (ASTA) has passed a resolution warning carriers that "any attempt, either subtle or blatant, to pervert or undermine the impartiality of travel agent system subscribers will henceforth be resisted whenever possible, and that the 'deliberate suppression' of computerized information on competing carriers' schedules is 'not in the best interest' of either the public or the agency community" (Vol. XIII, No. 158, *Travel Management Daily,* August 18, 1982). An official of the Travel Agent's Computer Society has likewise stated:

   Most agents see themselves as professionals—able to present unbiased information to clients. They resent a "dealership" relationship. They feel it would jeopardize their integrity. ("Bias, Dealerships' Top Concerns," *The Travel Agent,* October 11, 1982, p. 94.)

So also the members of Associated Travel Nationwide (ATN) issued a press release on August 2, 1982, proclaiming:

   As responsible travel agents, ATN members recognize their primary obligations to the consumer, and in order to meet their needs, full and complete unprejudiced information about air transportation must be available at all times.

The initial adverse effects of giant carriers' control of this distribution system upon their smaller competitors, upon travel agencies, and upon the public has already been felt. The future impact augurs to be even more pervasive. Smaller carriers such as Frontier, even with the help of the travel agencies, have not been able to avoid the consequences of the current situation. Frontier strongly believes that legislative relief is necessary, as suggested below.

Frontier's Proposed Remedy

Frontier recommends that the CAB and the DOJ recommend to Congress that legislation be enacted to remedy the anticompetitive evils resulting from host airlines controlling these automated reservations systems. The law should require nondiscriminatory treatment of all airlines, including hosts and co-hosts, and schedules, fares and other information should be displayed on the basis of objective standards. There should be no host or co-host levels, and all airlines should have access to the systems on an impartial basis and for a fee, graduated according to their relative inputs into the system. Each airline owner of a computer display system should also be required to form a separate subsidiary which would operate the computerized display and reservation systems independently of the airline parent.

Respectfully submitted.

FRONTIER AIRLINES, INC.

By /s/DAVID N. BRICTSON

David N. Brictson
Vice President-General Counsel

Chapter 4

Interorganizational Systems

In a 1966 *Harvard Business Review* article, Felix Kaufman implored general managers to think beyond their own organizational boundaries to the possibilities of extracorporate system.[1] His was a visionary argument about newly introduced computer time-sharing and networking capabilities. Since that article was written, as noted in Chapter 3, developments in information technology (IT) have made feasible many new applications of strategic importance.

Today many of the most dramatic and potentially powerful uses of IT involve networks that transcend company boundaries. These interorganizational systems (IOS's)—defined as automated information systems shared by two or more companies—will significantly contribute to enhanced productivity, flexibility, and competitiveness for many companies. However, current examples illustrate that some IOS's will radically change the balance of power in buyer–supplier relationships, provide entry and exit barriers in industry segments, and in most instances shift the competitive position of intraindustry competitors.

For example, a major automotive manufacturer has established computer-to-computer communication with its primary suppliers to implement just-in-time inventory systems. As an extension, the automotive manufacturer could add instructions to scan the computers of its primary suppliers and place an order with the company whose computer contained the lowest bid or price for the desired product (assuming that other things such as product quality are equal).

Such an expansion of the system would encourage competition among the vendors, and this rivalry could enhance the manufacturer's

---

[1]Felix Kaufman, "Data Systems that Cross Company Boundaries," *Harvard Business Review,* January–February 1966, p. 141.

bargaining power with them. Unfortunately, many companies make decisions about participating in these systems and the terms of participating without an appreciation for the broader strategic implications of the system. In some cases, in fact, such decisions have been made at the production-clerk level. Approximately half the time, under the guise of faster information flow and greater data integrity, the new system suddenly shifts inventory holding costs and business risk to a supplier. Such an imbalance would clearly far outweigh any advantages that the more efficient information system might bring to the supplier.

Some IOS's already have 10- to 15-year histories that clearly illustrate the economic impact and the social and public policy implications of such systems. The most dramatic and best-documented example is the airline industry's reservation systems, a class of IOS shared by intra-industry competitors and organizations that have a buyer–supplier relationship, as noted in Chapter 3 and the Frontier Airlines case. In testimony before the Civil Aeronautics Board (CAB), Frontier Airlines alleged that United Airlines, developer-owner of the widely used APOLLO reservation system, was enjoying unfair competitive advantage by monitoring loading factors of competitors and then using the system to either lower prices or broadcast special messages to travel agents. Since two major carriers, American and United, own reservation systems that provide the primary market access for almost two thirds of the travelers who make reservations through U.S. travel agents, this issue generated a great deal of public interest.

The CAB's airline reservation system inquiry showed the necessity for participants to anticipate the effects of an IOS. Further, it illustrated a need for social, regulatory, and strategic business perspectives in this rapidly evolving area. Given the rapid diffusion of computer and communications technology into most organizations, the potential is great for similar IOS growth and impact in a broad range of industries. In the following discussion we will describe the trends contributing to IOS development, show what an IOS is and how it works, describe frameworks for analyzing the impact of an IOS on business and industry, and suggest a way to consider alternative forms of participation in these systems.

IOS DEVELOPMENT

The growth of interorganizational systems is due to various technological, economic, and organizational changes:

The Need for Fast, Reliable Information Exchange in Response to Rapidly Changing Markets, Products, and Services.   This trend is mainly based on increasing international competition, shrinking geographic separation, and deregulation with more open competition.

The shift in world economics is shown by the change in the world aggregate GNPs. Shortly after World War II the U.S. GNP was about half the world GNP; by 1986 it was about one fourth. This shift has greatly stepped up international competition.

The new international competitors often have different cost structures (for example, the relative labor component of total costs), production processes, and so on. In many industries the injection of these new competitors has changed fundamental characteristics of products (cars, for example), reduced the time span of product life cycles, and added much new productive capacity (which generally limits prices and margins and/or increases costs).

Increased deregulation in industries ranging from trucking to petroleum, to airline and financial services has accompanied the shifts already mentioned. Together these changes foster redefinition of products, of the relationships between buyers and suppliers in a product-service delivery chain, and of ancillary services to the end consumer. Some industry segments that are still heavily regulated, such as the insurance industry, are also affected by this trend.

The Evolution of Guidelines, Standards, and Protocols. As a response to the need for better and faster information exchange, interest has grown in developing standard definitions, protocols, and product encoding. Historically, government regulation was the primary impetus for establishing standards. Now, however, industry associations, industry groups, and the like, also are introducing standards. Two examples are the universal product code (UPC) in the grocery industry and magnetic ink character (MICR) sets and magnetic strips on credit cards and cards for automatic teller machines (ATM). By forcing consistency of message content and product form, such standards make it much easier for firms to establish and participate in interorganizational systems.

Penetration of Information Technology into Internal Business Processes. The combination of decreasing IT costs and increasing capability has resulted in a broader range of internal computer applications. As more and more data are stored in computers, the logical next step is to transmit these data in machine-readable form to wherever they are needed. This avoids redundant encoding of data, makes information readily accessible, and ensures higher quality of data by eliminating multiple keying of the same item. The money and time savings easily justify such data and resource sharing. With more internal company data on computers, developed standards for intercompany exchange of information, and clear economic justification, participation in interorganizational systems is very attractive.

Technical Quality and Capability of Information Technology. As IT has become increasingly reliable, companies are able to use

IOS's in business-sensitive areas, such as in dealing with customers. For example, a customer's perception of his or her bank's service is tested at each use of an ATM. Too frequent problems may cause users to change banks.

Favorable experience with internal computer and communications systems has led companies to explore external applications of these technologies.

Use of IT to Distinguish Product and/or Company. An example of such use is a large construction company that developed for its own internal use a program for more efficient project management. Eventually the company gave "dumb" terminals (those with no independent processing ability) to its clients so that they could track progress of the project, analyze changes in specifications, and forecast maintenance schedules and costs. In this second step, the company sought to distinguish itself from its competitors, who lacked such computer backup.

Later the company gave "intelligent" terminals to customers to use primarily for special maintenance management programs that originate with the construction company's computer. In competitive bidding, this IT service distinguishes the construction company from its competitors. Further, it links the customer in a manner that encourages a continuing relationship with the company after the project is completed.

IOS VERSUS DDP

In the broadest terms, an IOS consists of a computer and communication infrastructure that permits the sharing of an application, such as programs for making reservations or ordering supplies. The players in a system are either participants or facilitators.[2] An IOS *participant* is an organization that develops, operates, or utilizes an IOS to exchange information that supports a primary business process. Participants can be competitors, organizations in the buyer–supplier chain, or a combination of these. An IOS *facilitator* is an organization that aids in the development, operation, or use of such a network for exchange of information among participants. The supporting products or services are a part of the primary business of the facilitator.

Although some larger companies have well-established IOS's, many executives barely understand the concept of such systems. The most

---

[2]The definitions in this section are partially based on S. Barrett and Benn R. Konsynski, "Inter-Organizational Information Sharing Systems," *MIS Quarterly,* special issue, Fall 1982, p. 93.

frequent response to a general description of an interorganizational system is "What's different about it? Isn't it a special form of distributed data processing (DDP)?"

IOS differs from distributed data processing in four important ways:

1. Whereas DDP is under the control of a single company, an IOS crosses company boundaries. Thus one company's employee can directly allocate resources and initiate business processes in another company. This capability introduces very different challenges for a company's internal control, planning, and resource allocation systems. As a result, most companies must revise these management control systems to permit the requisite coordination across organization boundaries for IOS.

2. With an IOS, in contrast to DDP, the question of government regulation arises as a result of the information exchange across the boundaries of separate organizations and hence of separate legal entities. Among the numerous potential issues are questions of legal liability. For example, when does the electronic message passing over communication lines in an IOS actually become an order? When an IOS involves competitors, as illustrated by airline reservation systems, what constitutes unfair business practice? When an IOS involves participants engaged in interstate commerce, are current regulations sufficient to protect consumer interests?

3. The IOS facilitator is a player that does not exist in DDP. Although intermediaries are not new in most industry segments, their role in interorganizational electronic communication is new. An example of an IOS facilitator is the CIRRUS nationwide network of ATMs. CIRRUS, which is not a bank, permits subscribing banks to give their customers 24-hour, coast-to-coast access to their ATM system. The home banking system network offered by CompuServe is another example of an IOS facilitator.

4. An IOS frequently has a broader and more significant potential competitive impact than the traditional internal uses of IT. For example, a major bank has developed an application it calls the treasury decision support system (TDSS). TDSS is a microcomputer-based system that the bank makes available to its largest corporate customers for use by their company treasurers. The system communicates with the bank's host computer and accepts input from a range of other systems. TDSS permits a treasurer to track, report, analyze, and perform simple manipulation of data concerning the company's funds. Data for TDSS can be transferred from several sources, including the company's computer or computers owned by competitive banks. The company may ask other banks or repositories to transfer data on company funds under their control to TDSS in machine-readable form. Currently, the bank that developed TDSS is the only organization, in addition to the (customer) company, that can examine all the data in the microcomputer. This examination would yield a complete profile of the company's funds management and would (the bank hopes) provide an excellent basis for developing a new (and tailored) product offering for the customer. Implementation of an IOS is not guaranteed to demonstrably improve return on investment, productivity, or operational efficiency. The impact of such systems may be more subtle.

IOS AND GENERIC STRATEGY

As part of strategic planning, IOS's potential impact on the competitive environment and on the implementation of competitive strategy should be considered. Following are examples of how a company can use an IOS to implement competitive strategy.

Overall Cost Leadership

Interorganizational systems can improve efficiency and scale in production and distribution. A number of these systems have reduced costs through electronic purchasing and ordering. The fashionable just-in-time delivery systems are examples of such electronic links among organizations. In one plant, General Motors has experimentally tied its CAD/CAM (computer-aided design and manufacturing) and order-entry systems to its suppliers' production systems. A supplier's computer communicates directly with GM's robot-based assembly line to provide "flexible" manufacturing.

Differentiation

In support of a differentiation strategy, an IOS can be used to add value to products and services. It may be coupled with a special service that distinguishes the product or company. For example, a company that manufactures maintenance chemicals gave its largest customers microcomputers linked to its host computers. Customers could thus use an application that helped them make decisions on product mix, order frequency, and maintenance schedules (as well as the obligatory direct order-entry capability). Over time, the chemical company changed the basis of competition from price alone to a range of services. And once its customers had accepted the microcomputers, they were unwilling to accept similar systems from the chemical company's competitors.

An IOS may serve as a means of differentiation by a radical modification of access and distribution channels. American Airlines' SABRE and United's APOLLO reservation systems, developed from the late

1960s to 1991, illustrate interorganizational links that control market access in their industry. Travel agencies that use automated reservations systems, on average, use one of these two systems for 65 percent of the reservations they make.[3]

Focus

This strategy usually combines low cost and differentiation. In addition, the business entity chooses to address a particular niche of one industry. An example of this strategy is a consortium of small stockbrokerage and investment firms with various specialties. They are sponsoring the development of an application similar to Merrill Lynch's Cash Management Account. Access to the system will be by a home banking network offered by a major West Coast bank. The target customer for this product is the investor with a portfolio of $40,000 or more. The consortium will attempt to offer a flexible range of integrated services at a much lower cost than its competitors.

ORGANIZATIONAL IMPACT

Interorganizational systems can have a range of impacts on the informal organizational structures of the participants. The amount of internal change triggered by an IOS appears to vary depending on whether an organization is reacting to an IOS implemented by another company or whether it is the initiator or implementer of the IOS.

A company's general management frequently does not participate in the decision to join an IOS proposed by another organization, and it may neither explicitly plan nor consider the change implications of the system. These changes will occur in business process (first-order impact), skills and staff requirements (second-order impact), and then organization structure and business strategy (third-order impacts).

Initial changes generally occur in business processes. The particular process (such as order entry and production) must change to conform with the standards of the IOS, as designed by the facilitator, or to take into account various procedures in internal control, report formats, planning systems, and communication patterns. This shift in the underlying business process and communication pattern brings about changes in the skills needed by employees, and in some cases new employee categories.

---

[3]*Report to Congress on Airlines Computer Reservation Systems* and addendum to the report, prepared by the Civil Aeronautics Board in consultation with the Department of Justice, Spring 1983.

Examples of this include independent insurance agencies that now illustrate products through a computer network and do their back-office accounting through links to the home offices of large insurance companies. This has enabled insurance brokers to become "estate planners" and to sell more complex, customized products than were feasible before. Similarly, customer service representatives in large travel agencies have evolved from clerks who simply flipped pages in airline guidebooks to sophisticated computer users who can access numerous databases on hotels and car rental agencies. When an IOS is used for a key business function such as market-access systems (for example, shared ATMs in retail banking), the IOS may force changes not only in business processes, required skills, and organization structure, but even in business strategy.

The order of these impacts differs in organizations that initiate or implement an IOS, due primarily to the heavy planning and financial commitment for the system, which must be done by the facilitator. The IOS is the enabling vehicle for changes in organization structure and strategy. Skill and staff-level changes are next, and changes in the business process occur last.

IOS PARTICIPATION PROFILES

Managers reacting to or contemplating the implementation of an IOS should also understand the range of involvement alternatives and their financial and strategic implications. Technologically, participation in IOS's falls into three levels:

1. Information entry and receipt.
2. Software development and maintenance.
3. Network and processing management.

As the level of involvement increases, there are also increases in responsibility, cost commitment, and organizational and technical complexity.

Information Entry and Receipt

At the first level, the IOS participant performs no application processing and merely acts as an information entry-receipt node. The user generally has access only through restricted protocols. The IOS simply provides standard messages, such as when an independent travel agency uses one of the major airline reservation systems without additional in-house processing capability. Most current IOS participants are operating at this entry level. Employees using these systems include shipping clerks, order clerks, salespersons, and fund and credit managers — all of whom are involved in information retrieval, authorization, and validations activities.

At this first level of participation, higher-level participants determine the standards and procedures and retain control of the application. In the airline reservation system, for example, the travel agent must follow the policies and procedures embedded in the computer programs written and maintained by the major carrier. At this stage, interconnections exist only at the basic data-exchange level, and the switching cost (for example, the cost of moving from one automated reservation or home banking system to another if simple inquiry is the only use) is low.

Compatibility requirements generally exist, but exact protocols are rarely needed initially. In some situations, the higher-level participant will increase the dependence of lower-level participants. (Some home banking systems, for example, permit automatic payment systems after the customer keys in a large amount of data, which dramatically increases the cost of changing to another system.) The first-level participant can become increasingly dependent on the higher-level participant as tasks or processes require more coordination across organizational boundaries. Although first-level participation is not complex, the relationships established with other organizations over time can help restructure the industrial marketplace in which the participant operates. This restructuring is driven by the provider of the IOS.

For example, IOS brokerage networks have permitted savings and loan (S&L) organizations to offer discount brokerage services. This innovation has given the larger S&Ls a new customer segment, and the resulting increased transaction volume has forced improvements in their software and communications systems. This improvement in turn has had the effect of bringing about economies of scale, driving unit costs down, and introducing other products and services (such as insurance). This chain of events illustrates why the distinctions among brokerage houses, insurance agencies, and banks have become blurred from a consumer perspective and how structural change in one element of an industry can cause industry or marketplace changes. Changes are not isolated; a change in one element brings about changes in other elements.

Software Development and Maintenance

Companies participating at the second level develop and maintain software used by other IOS participants. Usually, the developer of the IOS absorbs development and maintenance costs in order to gain exclusive control over decisions on access, price, and design of the application and the network. The expenses and investment associated with the development and operation of such a system can be truly extraordinary; in the airline case, it is hundreds of millions of dollars. In the airline reservation system examples already mentioned, American and United are second-level participants; they are primarily responsible for developing their SABRE and APOLLO systems, respectively. Data Resources, Inc., an economic modeling and information resource firm that permits customers to access its data and applications, is another example.

Administrative overhead is very significant for second-level participants, as they must initiate and manage the coordination across organizational boundaries. For example, planning the system requires detail inputs (such as estimates of transaction volume for capacity planning) from other participant or facilitator organizations, which increases the time required to develop the plan.

Network and Processing Management

The third-level participant serves as a utility and usually owns or manages all the network facilities as well as the computer processing resources. Examples include public information networks such as the Bell operating companies, The Source, and CompuServe. Costs increase dramatically at this level.

In addition to network development and maintenance costs, the third-level participant accepts considerable internal control responsibility for the integrity of the information exchanged. For example, the CIRRUS network that permits ATM transactions nationwide accepts a great deal of responsibility for the reliability, availability, integrity, security, and privacy of its system.

SUMMARY

In considering IOS's as a strategic possibility, managers must weigh internal and industry aspects, participation issues, and social impact and public policy.

The key internal issue is the organization's readiness to deal with changes in business process, personnel, and structure that it may face as a result of IOS participation. It must also have the ability to adapt to the competitive pressures that may arise.

The industry issues involve the strategy and repositioning of the firm in its market. Companies must also determine the appropriate level of investment and the level of control they expect to exert over an IOS. When an organization becomes a participant in a new entity, new problems as well as opportunities are presented.

The social impact and public policy issues, though not always obvious, are critical. How might continued rapid introduction of IOS systems in the buyer–supplier chain affect the large portion of the work force involved in direct sales, for example? At what point will the consumer have to pay such an inappropriate price because of biases built into dominant systems (such as those in the airline industry) that regulatory or legislative relief is necessary?

Case 4–1

BAXTER HEALTHCARE CORPORATION: ASAP EXPRESS

In late 1987 the Hospital Systems Division of Baxter Healthcare Corporation (Baxter) and three hospitals of the Premier Hospitals Alliance began a pilot test of the ASAP Express computerized order entry system. The new system would allow orders to be placed with all participating vendors in a standard format, from the same terminal, and with a single telephone call. An outgrowth of the fabled ASAP system, ASAP Express offered a "level playing field" that gave no advantage to any one vendor.

"As a single-vendor purchasing order entry system, ASAP had given American Hospital Supply Corporation, and now Baxter, a distinct competitive advantage," said Michael Hudson, president of the Hospital Systems Division. "By now, most of the major medical-surgical and laboratory suppliers have developed order entry systems of their own. Some of these are on a par with our system, and it is not uncommon to find hospitals using multiple-order entry systems. Each system requires a separate phone call and user protocol. This increases the amount of time it takes to place orders, and has resulted in customer demands for consolidated systems where supplies from all vendors can be ordered. The once strong product pull through effect of electronic order entry systems has lessened in recent years, due to the proliferation of systems. ASAP Express opens a new era of electronic order entry in which suppliers must compete in other areas such as product line breadth, distribution capabilities, and value-added services. This is where Baxter truly excels."

Baxter Healthcare

After the merger with American Hospital Supply Company in 1985, Baxter developed, manufactured, or distributed more than 120,000 products for use in hospitals, laboratories, blood and dialysis centers, nursing homes, physicians' offices, and at home. The company could provide about 70 percent of a hospital's supply needs and nearly 100 percent of a blood or dialysis center's. Computerized systems for ordering, tracking, and managing supplies, both internally and at customer sites, were a significant company strength.

Changes in the Health Care Industry

Following World War II, the government began to increase support for health care, regularly increasing funding for the National Institutes of Health, supporting community hospitals, and increasing the doctor pool. In 1965, Medicare came into being as one of the highest priorities of the Great Society initiatives. The practice developed to reimburse hospitals for costs rather than contracted rates, with the government retaining little control over the program or its costs. In the 1970s, government policy shifted from redis-

Prepared by Professor Benn Konsynski and Associate Professor Michael Vitale as the basis for class discussion rather than to illustrate either effective or ineffective handling of an administrative situation.

tribution to regulation as costs rose out of control. In 1970 health care costs were 7.2 percent of GNP. Soon, Certificate of Need programs developed to curtail hospital construction, and local agencies were mandated by the government to monitor and control resource utilization.

By 1980, health-care costs accounted for 9.4 percent of GNP. In 1982, Medicare reimbursement changed to a scheme based on diagnostic related groups, or DRGs. The result was a reduction in the rate of cost increase. In 1984, doctors shifted to a national fee schedule for Medicare work. After some slowdown in cost increase, health-care costs continued to rise, representing over 11 percent of GNP by 1988.

By the middle of the 1980s, the health-care industry was in the midst of dramatic change, with hospitals feeling extraordinary pressures. Fixed-rate reimbursement from the government-sponsored Medicare program, which paid for 40 percent of all hospital patient days, had made hospitals much more cost-conscious. Businesses and insurers also were exerting pressure to cut health-care expenditures. Hospital admissions were declining, and the average hospital stay had shortened to less than seven days. The total number of hospitals had declined from a peak in 1980, although the number of beds had increased slightly.

Aggregate demand for health care would likely increase, but more slowly than in the past, and customers would exert more choice. More and more care would be moved outside of hospitals to alternative sites, such as doctor's offices and walk-in emergency and surgical centers, and health maintenance organizations (HMOs) would continue to proliferate. At the same time, hospitals would enter into less traditional markets, such as occupational health care and "wellness" programs, sometimes in partnership with physicians, nurses, and other providers. The fragmented supplies market participants focused on reducing their operating expenses and increasing sales. Margins were particularly attractive on products that the suppliers manufactured in-house.

In the past, and in many hospitals today, in each hospital there might be as many as 10 different buyers—the pharmacy, food service, anesthesiology, and so on—and even in hospitals that had adopted centralized purchasing, individual department heads and physicians often remained powerful buying influences. The price of each item was negotiated by the customer and the sales representative, making billing a complex process.

Supplies in hospitals were receiving more attention than in the past. They made up an estimated 10–15 percent of hospital costs, while the logistical expenses associated with supplies made up another 20–30 percent. Many hospitals were centralizing their purchasing functions and creating a more "professional" purchasing and materials handling function. The suppliers, many with their own sales force, often tried to establish direct linkages with the hospitals buyers, threatening the distributor's role. Hospitals sought to create buyer groups and leverage the trend in hospital consolidation to increase their power.

Although there were hundreds of competitors, and the barriers to entry in the hospital supplies industry were low, there were only a few distributors of any significant size. They competed on price, delivery, inventory, quality, and relationships with the buyer representatives. The distributors were well aware that consolidation of hospitals would continue and that cost-containment programs would grow in importance.

The Beginnings

"The Computer is at the heart of our success," said Karl D. Bays, chairman and chief executive officer of American Hospital Supply Corporation (AHSC) in early 1985, describing the importance of information systems to the company. Traditionally, AHSC's products had been sold by its field salespeople, who worked from their homes and called directly on hospitals and other organizations. Until 1964, orders were generally taken in person by the salesperson, who would then mail the orders to company headquarters. Bays, who joined AHSC in 1958 as a salesperson, recalled that upon arrival in a town he would immediately find out when the last mail of the day went out." When I had made my calls," Bays continued, "I would rush back to my hotel room and write out all my orders and customer inquiries and get to the post office in time to make the last mail. That was an imperative." The paperwork could be formidable: an 800-bed hospital might easily stock 30,000 items and generate 50,000 purchase orders per year—at an estimated preparation cost of $25–30 each.

In 1957 AHSC had begun to automate its order entry and billing procedures by installing IBM 632 tab-card billing machines in its distribution centers. Orders received at the centers would be keypunched, and the cards were fed through the billing machines. A packing list for the warehouse was produced, as was a summary card for the accounts receivable system. The line-item cards from the order were sent on to the home office for sales analysis.

In the early 1960s one of AHSC's West Coast offices began having difficulty servicing a large hospital customer. Orders were frequently delivered late and incomplete, creating problems for both the customer and AHSC. The West Coast office manager put an IBM 1001 Dataphone in the hospital's purchasing department and attached an IBM 026 card punch in the AHSC distribution center to a phone line. The hospital was given a box of prepunched cards—one for each item purchased from AHSC. The cards were physically placed on the shelves of the hospital's stockroom, each card stuck between boxes of supplies at the point where more stock should be ordered. When the box above the card was taken from the stockroom, the prepunched card was added to the pile of items to be ordered. On a regular schedule the hospital connected the 1001 Dataphone to the 026 card punch via telephone. Each card was fed through the Dataphone, causing a duplicate to be punched by the 026 at the AHSC distribution center. The result was a duplicate deck representing the hospital's order. This deck was fed through the 632 billing machine, and the order process continued as usual. The hospital was able to speed up communications and thus could reduce its inventory. Orders were more accurate and more timely. AHSC benefited as well, and decided to offer the 1001 Dataphone-based service to other customers. More than 200 agreed immediately and the system, named Tel-American, was extended to other West Coast customers, then to Chicago, and then to other areas. A similar service, Telephone American, worked in somewhat the same way but without the 1001 Dataphone. Instead, the prepunched cards were kept in a box at the AHSC office, and customers called in their orders. The cards were taken from the box manually by the telephone order entry clerk.

Tel-American was well in place by 1969, when Gary Nei was hired as product manager for systems marketing and asked to identify additional customer benefits of the system. "The 1001 was the nucleus but not magic," Nei said later. "The customers could just as easily phone in their orders, and many did. The question was how to bundle additional services." Nei read the relatively small amount of material then available on materials management and wrote a document translating the general theory to the hospital environment. He began to advocate a "prime vendor" approach, in which hospitals would contract to obtain a major portion of their supplies from AHSC. In return, the hospital would accrue the benefits of lower inventory, reduced paper handling, lower "shrinkage" due to loss, spoilage, and theft, fewer purchase orders and deliveries to handle, and guaranteed service. Tel-American was promoted as part of an overall hospital materials management system. Nei worked with the field sales force to educate and bring home to hospitals the benefits of materials management and to obtain commitments to implement the required disciplines and procedures. In some cases Nei and his staff swept stockroom floors and physically rearranged inventory in order to get a customer started. Later, as rising interest rates made holding inventory more expensive and as hospital purchasing agents began to understand their ability to become more professional through the use of modern techniques, the concepts promoted by AHSC became widely adopted. "We changed the industry," Nei noted, "we really did."

By the mid-1970s some of the novelty of Tel-American had worn off, and IBM had decided to drop support for the 1001 Dataphone. In response, AHSC's laboratory manufacturing division, TekPro, designed and built a much faster device to read and transmit data from cards. By this time, AHSC had installed a mainframe computer system that kept track of orders and inventory, and the TekPro device was attached to this system rather than to a reproducing card punch. The TekPro unit also allowed the hospital to enter some data—for example, order quantities—by hand; more important, it acknowledged that each line of data had

been received correctly. The new order entry system, with mainframe computer support, was called Analytic Systems Automatic Purchasing (ASAP).

The ASAP System
Both the Tel-American system and its successor, ASAP, were essentially one way linkages; although special inventories were reserved to Tel-American and TekPro users, the customer could find out for certain when the ordered items would be delivered and in what quantity only by phoning the AHSC office or by waiting until the AHSC truck arrived. The TekPro unit was highly reliable—some were still in use in 1985—but customers' needs for a printed response led to the adoption of the Bell 43 terminal as a standard input and output device in 1977.

The printing device and steady improvements in its central computer software gave AHSC the ability to respond to customer orders by verifying the item number and showing the availability and price of each item. Items could be ordered using AHSC's catalog numbers or those of its competitors, and orders could be edited for accuracy and completeness before they were transmitted. For items that were not currently in stock, the system could often recommend a substitute but did not make any substitutions automatically. The enhanced system, called ASAP 2, also allowed messages to be transmitted electronically among AHSC, the sales representatives, and customers. As with earlier systems, customers who used ASAP 2 paid for the terminal themselves; AHSC paid the telephone line charges.

In 1980 AHSC announced ASAP 3, which allowed customers to enter orders using the hospital's own internal stock numbers. Customers could also build electronic files for standing orders and for repetitive orders. These files shortened the customer's order entry time and improved ordering accuracy.

ASAP 3 produced output to customer specifications as well, including inventory lists, purchase orders, and requisition forms. The customer could inquire on-line into pending back orders, prices, and delivery dates. Like its predecessors, ASAP 3 was intended to be used as part of an overall materials management program. The system did not, however, actually manage the hospital's inventory. An enhancement, ASAP 3 PLUS, incorporated bar code scanning of shelf labels, requisition forms, or a catalog to facilitate order entry. Over the next few years, teletypes, CRTs, and other "dumb" terminals were added to the list of devices supported by ASAP.

ASAP 4, a computer-to-computer order entry system, was released in 1983. It simplified the hospital's purchasing process by eliminating all the manual steps except actual approval. The customer's internal computer system produced recommended orders that, once approved, were automatically transmitted through a high-speed phone connection to AHSC's mainframe. Order confirmations were sent directly to the customer's computer system to update the hospital's files. Hospital size did not always correlate with information systems capability: some small hospitals were relatively sophisticated, while some very big hospitals relied almost totally on manual systems. Nevertheless, it was expected that ASAP 4 would be used initially by the major multi-hospital groups that had corporate agreements with AHSC.

Each hospital placed its ASAP 4 orders at prearranged times of the day; the system was not designed for emergency orders. Customers did not pay for the use of ASAP or for any necessary software customization, which could take up to eight hours of work.

ASAP 5, which went into pilot use in December 1984, promised to extend the capabilities of ASAP 3 by using an IBM Personal Computer (PC) as the customer's input and output device. Customers could build and edit order files on the PC instead of on-line, thus reducing telephone expenses. The PC was equipped with extensive tutorial software, allowing a new user to learn how to enter ASAP orders in about 15 minutes. The new system would be menu-driven and would include a HELP facility that could be accessed while entering an order. As in the past, the hardware would be supplied by the customer.

By late 1984, ASAP and a few AHSC financial applications were running on five Burroughs mainframes. About 50 percent of AHSC's hospital orders came through ASAP. The ASAP software, which had been written totally by AHSC, was in a mixture of ALGOL and COBOL. A program to convert ASAP to IBM hardware had been under way for a year and had another 18 months to go. Looking back, AHSC estimated that it had spent about $30 million to build ASAP. Ongoing maintenance required six to nine full-time people. Annual operating costs for the 9,000-terminal system were about $3 million.

AHSC had also implemented VIP, a "reverse ASAP" that linked the company to its suppliers. Purchase orders were transmitted to suppliers electronically, as were messages about inventory levels, pricing information, and so on. VIP was not mandatory, but the benefits of faster communications were sufficient to convince most suppliers to use the system.

Merger

The first quarter of 1985 was a difficult period for AHSC, by now the country's largest seller of medical supplies. The increasingly competitive health-care industry was watching costs more closely than ever, and AHSC's sales fell 4 percent from the first quarter of 1984, while net income declined by 16 percent.

On March 31, 1985, AHSC stunned the health-care industry by announcing plans to merge with Hospital Corporation of America

(HCA), the largest U.S. hospital management company. With 1984 revenues of $4.2 billion and earnings of $297 million, HCA owned 420 for-profit hospitals and planned to spend $1.2 billion in 1985 to build and acquire more. The merger was intended to guarantee HCA supplies at the best price available while offering AHSC an opportunity to diversify. The combined company planned to acquire nursing homes and clinics, and to develop out-of-hospital medical care programs.

While little difficulty was expected in gaining the approval of the Federal Trade Commission, serious objections were voiced by some of AHSC's customers, who competed directly with HCA, and by the AHSC sales representatives who served those customers. In the months following the announcement of the AHSC-HCA merger, the share prices of both firms declined, and AHSC lost business as some customers that competed with HCA took their business to other supply firms. On June 20, Baxter Travenol Laboratories, Inc. (Baxter), a medical products company with annual sales of about $1.8 billion, made an unexpected bid for American Hospital Supply.

Baxter offered $50 a share for half of AHSC's shares and debt securities of equal value for the other half. The merger of AHSC and HCA would have brought AHSC shareholders stock valued at about $36.50. AHSC's directors rejected the Baxter proposal, citing fears of antitrust violations. Baxter agreed to sell some $500 million of assets that would overlap and continued to press its offer. AHSC's stockholders, particularly institutional investors, made known their preference for the higher bid. After three weeks of often-bitter wrangling, AHSC's board accepted a $51-per-share offer, in cash for up to 53 percent of the company's shares and in securities for the remainder. "Baxter Healthcare Corporation" was the name adopted in mid-1987.

Prior to the merger, Baxter Travenol had been primarily in the intravenous therapy business. Its product line of some 7,000 items was shipped from 25 distribution centers. American Hospital Supply distributed 150,000 items—none of them manufactured by Baxter Travenol—from 150 centers. Baxter cited AHSC's strengths in distribution, corporate sales programs, and information systems as significant factors leading to the merger. In the face of strong competition and continued cost pressures in the health-care industry, Baxter's earnings had fallen somewhat and the company had instituted cost-cutting measures, including by mid-1987 the reduction of some 3,000 overlapping positions from the immediate post-merger workforce of 62,100.

In addition to differences in product line and size—AHSC's sales had been almost twice as large as Baxter's—the two companies differed in culture and structure. Like AHSC, Baxter had a relatively large number of MBAs, including president Vernon R. Loucks, Jr., who became the chief executive officer of Baxter Healthcare. AHSC's management, including president Karl D. Bays, were generally described as somewhat more sales-oriented, entrepreneurial, and willing to take risks. "At AHSC we used experience and good gut feel," one vice president noted, "while Baxter used analysis. The merger married the two strengths."

Baxter had generally been more centralized than the more diverse AHSC, and the structural differences extended to information systems as well. Carl Steiner, who had been vice president for information resources planning and administration at AHSC and held the same title at post-merger Baxter, recalled that Bays had once told the head of AHSC's data processing department, "Do whatever you want to do as long as it's right—and I'll tell you if it's not right. If you can sell what you develop to the divisions, fine; if they don't want what you have, they can build their own." At the time of the merger, one-third of AHSC's information systems resources were distributed to the operating divisions; the central information resources (IR) division controlled the remainder. A decentralization strategy was adopted in 1987. As Heschel put it, "When there's no synergy," he asked rhetorically, "why do it centrally?"

ASAP EXPRESS

Baxter Senior Vice President Richard B. Egen, who had been in charge of the merger integration team, noted that ASAP was one of the benefits in Baxter's consideration of AHSC. "There was probably a bit of the 'grass is greener' syndrome," Egen noted later, "and in fact Baxter already had TOPS, a fine system for entering and tracking orders taken over the telephone. But the merger allowed us to stop a $2 million project to make TOPS available to customers through terminals." In part to demonstrate that the two companies were really coming together, ASAP was linked to TOPS within four months of the merger, allowing customers to order Baxter products as well as those distributed by AHSC.

By 1986, AHSC's competitors had systems that were fully competitive with, and sometimes technically superior to ASAP. Utilization of ASAP had leveled off at about 55 percent of orders. Management changes, a conversion from Burroughs mainframes to IBM, and the relatively small size of the ASAP development staff had virtually stopped enhancements for about two years. Michael Hudson believed that 70–80 percent of orders was a reasonable goal for ASAP utilization. "ASAP saves Baxter about $11 million per year now by automating the customer service function," Hudson noted, "and there is another $4 to $5 million available in realistic incremental savings through increased penetration and system utilization. In addition, there re-

mains some product pull-through effect." A consulting study recommended adding some features to ASAP to meet or surpass the competition; creating one entity to be responsible for the system; encouraging use of the system by all divisions; and gathering additional information on system utilization. A second phase of the study resulted in the development of ASAP Express.

The consultants noted significant customer interest in all-vendor systems, which were considerably more convenient than separate systems with individual formats, passwords, and reports. Hospitals incurred nearly $2 in logistics costs for every $1 they spent on supplies. About 5 percent of the logistics costs were due to ordering itself, and an all-vendor system might reduce this directly by only 10 percent, but there was also significant value in the consolidated data that could be produced by an all-vendor system.

ASAP Express used the facilities of both Baxter and the General Electric Information Services (GEIS). The latter provided a worldwide telecommunications network and a clearinghouse that dispatched orders into electronic mailboxes that could be accessed only by the vendors to which they were assigned. ASAP Express would allow hospitals to enter, in ANSI X.12 format, orders for all participating vendors. Baxter orders would be handled through ASAP, while orders for other vendors would be passed to GEIS's electronic clearing house to be distributed to other participating vendors. Price and product availability information would be initially available only for items distributed by Baxter. Vendor-specific features, such as electronic catalogs, could be added to ASAP Express, and, as a result, vendors offering such features might achieve some advantage over their rivals.

ASAP market manager Sharon Hacker noted that ASAP Express could be an advantage to vendors who had not yet automated their order entry systems, or who had built customized systems that did not conform to the standard format used by ASAP Express. Although the first outside vendor actually using ASAP Express sold office supplies, two of Baxter's smaller competitors had asked to join the pilot project, and Baxter executives had held discussions with their counterparts at several very large health-care supply companies. All of these potential participants in ASAP Express already had their own computerized order entry systems.

Security of data entered into ASAP Express was a concern for all participants, but especially for the other health-care supply companies that were considering participation. Both Baxter and GEIS had hired "Big Eight" public accounting firms to audit the integrity of ASAP Express, and both firms had issued positive reports. Customers and vendors alike could send in their own auditors on 24 hours' notice to examine the security of the system. Passwords, authorizations, and audit trails formed an electronic security scheme, and data encryption was an available option. In the minds of many at Baxter, however, the real guarantee of data security was a legal environment and corporate culture that strongly discouraged the illicit use of data in any form. "We're not looking for lawsuits," Sharon Hacker said, while vice president Terry Mulligan noted, "We wouldn't look at anyone else's data—that would be stupid and a real job-loser around here."

Richard Egen believed that, for Baxter's hospital customers, the ultimate potential of ASAP Express was "the total automation of hospital logistics, virtually eliminating the clerical aspects of purchasing. This is very consistent with our total approach of creating a strong partnership relation with those hospital functions that have a major influence on supplies purchases. There will be fewer people in purchasing, but they will be more professional—all this software has to

be managed by someone. Conceptually, how much more can you do with automated order entry beyond adding all vendors?"

There would, of course, be benefits for Baxter as well. Although pricing for ASAP Express had yet to be determined, there would be some revenue from participating vendors. Asked about vendors' potential concern about high transaction costs, Sharon Hacker said, "I can understand the fear of exorbitant rates, but we would not do that—our hospital customers wouldn't let us. Six or eight years from now we may make money on ASAP Express, but we designed the system as a service to our customers, not as a way to make money." Beyond the direct revenue, ASAP Express would bring Baxter additional control over the customer contact point. Of the 5,500 hospitals using ASAP, almost 3,500 accessed the system from a teletype or other terminal; competitors' systems were almost exclusively PC-based. "Customer recognition that computerized order entry can lower their costs is growing constantly," vice president Brien Laing noted. "More systems have been installed in the past four years than in the preceding ten. If somebody else gets their system into a hospital, it's two or three times as hard to get ours in as if we get there first." A third benefit of ASAP Express, thought by some at Baxter to be the most significant, came from additional product sales similar to those that had resulted from the installation of ASAP and other Baxter systems.

American Impact

Product "pull-through" had long been a goal, and an assumed outcome, of the installation of value-added systems from American Hospital Supply. In fact, analysis had consistently shown that hospitals with ASAP bought more items on each order, and more supplies per bed from American overall, than hospitals that did not use ASAP. There was always some question, however, about cause and effect: did hospitals order more because they had ASAP, or did they have ASAP because they ordered more?

As one method of combining the profit center style and the product pull-through focus, AHSC developed, and Baxter later adopted, the American Impact program. "Initially, our turn-key systems were sold or leased to hospitals. In 1986 we started an alternative financing program called Impact," Mike Hudson said. "This program allowed hospitals to pay for their information systems through increased purchases of Baxter supplies. The program has been very successful for Baxter and our customers." By making a three-year commitment for additional purchases from Baxter, hospitals that sign up for the Impact program were able to get, without charge, software and hardware costing as much as $200,000. "Prices for supplies purchased under the Impact program are the same as always," Paul Goldberg, director of systems and programming for hospital services, noted. "The name of the game is incremental sales." Mike Hudson commented, "There is a tremendous need in the health care industry for systems—our customers are screaming for help. The real problem has been availability of funds. We show them opportunities; it's a real win/win situation." By mid-1987 more than 100 hospitals had used Impact to obtain software and hardware, the latter including IBM and Texas Instrument minicomputers as well as personal computers. Although other health-care suppliers had added software to their product lines by buying into software companies, hospitals liked both Baxter's products themselves and the fact that they gained additional leverage over the software supplier by virtue of their product purchases.

Ownership, Authority, and Profits

Historically, AHSC's Hospital Supply Division (HSD) had had its own information

technology group, originally to do financial reporting and other relatively low-level tasks. Over time, ASAP and other value-added software became the responsibility of the Hospital Systems Division, which was established as a profit center with its own development and marketing resources. Paul Goldberg noted, "We run as a profit center not so much to make money as to keep from losing too much. Our real reason for being is to pull through product." Terry Mulligan agreed, saying, "We run Hospital Systems on a profit and loss basis to keep score; if it were only a cost center then we would get people inordinately tapping in. But it is not our expectation that the division will become a big business."

Paul Goldberg described what he saw as some of the pros and cons of having a separate group for development and support of systems like ASAP:

My staff loves being close to the business. And I feel very strongly that the key is to have programmers, support people, salespeople, and so on acting like a small business that has a common goal. All of these people need the contact and the experience with customers. On the other hand, because my bosses have always been nontechnical, they could not necessarily tell if I was making technical mistakes. In ten years, I have never been asked about backups. If I were incompetent, we would be at tremendous risk. But if they ever called up my boss and told him they wanted to do a technical audit, I'd be delighted—I would come out looking very good.

Considering the organizational history of support for ASAP, Brien Laing commented,

There comes a time when, in order to gain attention, it is justifiable to keep things decentralized—for example, keeping ASAP out of the central IS group. I've started special divisions for supply products whose sales were way down, and the focused attention brought increases. ASAP had in fact suffered from a lack of attention, so perhaps it does deserve its separate division. But it was easier to have separate divisions when the industry was growing at a double-digit rate. I led the charge to get ASAP taken over as a corporate function. Now I believe that the central IS group should take care of the technical aspects of ASAP, with marketing of the system done by a separate sales force. Moreover, I don't think the corporation should continue to charge the divisions for their customers' use of ASAP. In the pre-merger AHSC, we had such an elaborate cross-charging system that divisions were assessed for the use of the company auditorium. We need to be smart enough as a corporation to handle that sort of thing without hiring ten accountants.

Views from the Field

Laura Nozewski, the corporate systems manager for ASAP in New England, joined Baxter in January 1987, after working in sales positions for Hershey and MCI. Nozewski was one of nine systems representatives hired to expand Hospital Systems' field sales force from 5 to 14. After receiving classroom training in ASAP, the new reps were assigned to locations around the country. Upon arriving in Boston, Nozewski found herself besieged with requests for ASAP support. "My predecessor, who was based in New Jersey, covered the five New England states plus Connecticut, Pennsylvania, New Jersey, and New York," Nozewski said, "so she was stretched too thin to provide complete support. Customers can always call the hot line in Illinois, but sometimes they prefer to talk face to face."

Nozewski's responsibilities included the sale and installation of ASAP as well as training and support. In her first nine months with Baxter, she had worked with some 60 hospitals, dividing her time about equally between sales and service. "For hospitals that have no system," Nozewski said, "it's basically a concept sell. I promote the time and labor savings that ASAP can provide, along with flexibility in building or-

ders, the ability to retrieve historical data, and the priority inventory position that ASAP orders receive. In hospitals that already have a competitor's system, I push ASAP features and capabilities—pricing and availability information, requisition lists, and customized order files and print-back formats. My first goal is to move business that's already being placed with Baxter to ASAP. Secondarily, I aim to get hospitals with ASAP to shift business to Baxter. The system is simple and friendly, and many hospitals just don't want to bother with another system." Nozewski used a list of hospitals in her region, showing the savings that Baxter would obtain if the hospital shifted all of its ordering to ASAP, to develop her sales plan. Nozewski noted that her customers were already asking about ASAP Express, even though the system had not been released. "Customers *want* standardization," she said, "and even some hospitals who are not large Baxter customers are interested in ASAP Express."

At Portsmouth Regional Hospital in Portsmouth, New Hampshire, materials manager Richard Pedrick oversaw the ordering of some $100,000 of supplies monthly. About 75 percent of these supplies were purchased from Baxter, 80 percent under a long-term contract that had been negotiated with Baxter by Hospital Corporation of America, which had owned Portsmouth Regional since early 1984. The hospital had used ASAP for seven years, moving from punch cards to a Bell 43 terminal to an IBM AT. "As part of our contract with Baxter," Pedrick said, "they supply the computer equipment. But we could easily have justified the purchase of the gear on the basis of doing our job more quickly and efficiently. ASAP is worth whatever it takes to get it working. For one thing, the alternative of using the telephone is dreadful. But in a positive sense we have reduced invoice discrepancies and enjoy the flexibility that ASAP provides." Portsmouth had tried to use COACT, an electronic order entry system sold by Johnson & Johnson, but their volume of orders did not justify devoting much time to the system. "We were having some hardware problems a few weeks ago," Pedrick said, "and while trying to fix them we accidentally erased COACT from the AT's hard disk. It hasn't been worth it to put the software back on the disk."

At Emerson Hospital in Concord, Massachusetts, a suburb of Boston, materials manager Coco Richmond was considering a move away from ASAP. Emerson was a member of Voluntary Hospitals of America (VHA), a very large buying association of nonprofit hospitals. After an abortive attempt by American to merge with HCA, VHA had decided to form a supply company of its own, and had signed a contract with a competitor for its order entry and materials management systems. "Potentially," Richmond said, "this is the end of ASAP at Emerson. We would return the Bell 43 terminal and install a PC. I want to be sure that I can get features that AHSC provided from a new system as well. Also, I refuse to regress to an exclusive system that would only let us order from one vendor. So although we have a group purchasing agreement through VHA for this other system, I will be looking at it quite carefully to be sure that it compares with ASAP." In mid-November 1987, Richmond and her staff met with representatives of the competitor's company. Richmond found that the alternative system duplicated some of ASAP, but was less informative and slower. She therefore decided to stay with the Baxter system for the immediate future.

Chapter 5

Organization and Control

Imaginative companies are not just using the technology to support existing organization structure and control systems; they are creatively applying the speed and flexibility of low-cost computer and communications systems to transform the control function and the organization structure. Managers once stymied by the slow flow of information from the work force or customers can now grab data from the most remote corners of their companies in an instant. This offers the possibility of moving decision making from the field to corporate headquarters, thus bringing more consistency to decisions. Other firms are using the technology to distribute large amounts of data to the desks of decentralized managers, thus facilitating decentralized decision making. The key point of this chapter is that technology encourages neither centralized structures and controls nor decentralized structures and controls but offers new possibilities.

For example, Wal-Mart, the nation's largest retailer, is now using IT to *centralize* control, whereas Frito-Lay, the largest snack food supplier, is using IT to *decentralize* control. In a way not well understood until recently, existing structures and controls have been heavily influenced by "the art of the possible" in information handling. The technology of the 1990s allows us to readdress some long-dormant issues.

CONTROL AND THE CHANGING ENVIRONMENT

The obvious benefit of this fast, flexible, reasonably priced information management technology is that it can revitalize the three traditional purposes that control systems serve. It can help managers use resources more effectively, better align disparate parts of the organization with companywide goals, and improve the collection of data for strategic and operating decisions.

But information technology—PCs, spreadsheets, networks, and data- base systems—has done more than just enhance existing processes. It has created a whole new set of options for gathering, organizing, and using information. Those who have selected wisely from the new options have seen their control systems and structures transformed. They have found ways to channel the power of information to the muscles of their corporations. As a result, they have boosted their efficiency and overall competitive position.

So far, only the most progressive companies have fully utilized the new technology, perhaps because only they could bridge the gap between the financial systems group and the IT group and effectively engage the enormous change in management issues. We believe the success of these efforts is stimulating many other companies to address these issues. The following examples show the kinds of benefits a business can obtain when it uses information technology to overhaul its control processes. Each of the enterprises described below has capitalized on the technology by organizing information in one of three ways: by consolidating it, by centralizing it, or by decentralizing it.

Consolidating Data to Transform Retail Banking Relationships. The new technology speed and lower costs permit managers to get information more quickly and to shape data files into new forms as needed. This means that if the rules of the game change, managers can reshuffle material into whatever forms are needed in order to analyze it and meet the challenge. By consolidating reports and raw numbers, companies in essence create new information from old, and new data can stimulate solutions to nagging problems or point to unexploited opportunities.

A prominent bank recently spent millions of dollars to consolidate and reorganize its computer files by customer and by product. The old system of data files meshed with the company's long-standing incentive system, which focused on individual products and product-oriented organizations. Relationship managers had no easy way to identify the full set of relationships each customer had with the bank. Consequently, they were frequently embarrassed when making individual calls and tended to avoid cross-selling opportunities. They lacked a mechanism for reviewing a customer's total holdings regularly and seeking an appropriate mix of products for the customer. Compounding the problem was people's names appearing in several variations on purchase records—sometimes two initials, sometimes the full name, and so on. Even if salespeople had wanted to plow through mountains of product files for customer information, it is doubtful they could have caught all of the listings for every customers.

The new system enables the organization to regularly review a customer's entire product portfolio. They can use this information for suggesting replacement of outdated financial products and additions where appropriate. The company thus helps to forestall customers' switching to other financial institutions and continually generates new business. A new incentive system has been instituted that pays commissions to customer-oriented managers who develop comprehensive long-term relationships with customers, thereby aligning the manager's goals with company goals. Simultaneously, management is also able to measure performance by product line.

Many of the company's competitors are now scrambling to install similar systems but they face two or more years of costly systems programming to reorder their large, inflexible data files. This type of capability is becoming a requirement for retail and wholesale banks that want to stay in business.

Centralizing Data to Improve the Elevator Service Call.   Corporate headquarters can now promptly gather information from branch offices at low cost. This allows close performance tracking and timely corrective action when needed.

A passenger elevator company used information technology to replace its decentralized service system with a centralized one by which customer trouble calls bypass field service offices and come directly to corporate headquarters. Since service contracts are highly profitable in the elevator business and customers' switching costs are low, competition for such contracts is intense. Sustained high service levels are critical for staying in business. For this reason, providing excellent service and dealing with customer problems immediately are primary corporate goals.

Under the old system more than 100 branches fielded customer calls, serviced them, recorded the results, and sent monthly reports to headquarters summarizing their activity. Many important customer complaints and product-line service problems did not reach top management, because the write-ups filtered up through four reporting levels. In fact, company executives suspected that some troubled branches regularly underreported complaints and problems in an attempt to avoid the spotlight. This system was the only possible way of operating until recently.

The new system, in contrast, pumps out weekly service reports from a massive, centralized database and allows management to zero in on trouble spots at once. The database keeps track of *all* service activity on every elevator they have serviced. The system identifies troubled customers, troubled product lines, low-volume service branches, and incompetent mechanics in a way that facilitates appropriate management action. For instance, after several months' data had come in, top management discovered that certain elevators had been breaking down between 18 and 30 times each quarter. The problem had existed for years but had been buried in files at field offices. Focused action on these data initiated a sweeping reorganization that included training in use of systems and adapting the system to the field organization. Elevator service problems have decreased to 50 percent of their previous level.

Whether such old difficulties stem from the inattention of service personnel or product design weaknesses, field managers can now respond with quick action. Further analysis of recurring problems now leads executives to adjust staff levels, retrain service representatives, or send a product back to the engineering department to resolve a design problem. It has also opened the opportunity to remove one level from the organization structure—referred to as "flattening" it.

Additionally, the new system has improved the quality of each service call. The database at headquarters contains the history of every elevator the company has installed. Before headquarters dispatches a service representative by beeper to answer a complaint about an elevator, he or she is briefed on its service history. The service person learns whether the elevator is due for any preventive maintenance, which can save a trip later. The service rep is also given information that permits quicker identification of an emerging pattern of service difficulties on an elevator. Under the old system, the company had to rely on the service rep's memory and often incomplete branch files.

The improved system has increased the company's market share in service while cutting service costs. Needless to say, however, there were enormous implementation challenges as the firm evolved from an independent field system with bottom-up reporting to a totally linked reporting system that challenged 40 years of operating history.

Decentralizing Data to Target Supermarket Inventory.   In other settings the transmission of important data from headquarters to the work force through new control systems gives decentralized staff the information they need for doing their jobs well. It also allows the creation of incentive programs that provide additional motivation for them to do so. Whether funneling new price information to the personal computer in a salesperson's briefcase, providing data to regional market planners, or monitoring customer buying patterns in retail outlets, companies are using IT to leverage effectiveness.

For example, many supermarket chains have applied the speed and flexibility of the new technology to their decentralized inventory monitoring system. The old setup demanded that employees count stock and then translate the numbers into buying and merchandising plans. If sales of an item surged, store managers often learned about it too late. Furthermore, because suppliers had the only up-to-date facts on what was selling where, they acted as consultants and sometimes prodded stores to overstock slow-moving products. This consulting relationship also increased suppliers' bargaining power in price setting.

With the new system, scanners at checkout counters log every item that leaves the store. The scanners post inventory records instantly and far more accurately than earlier methods. As a result, store managers have been able to lower inventory levels, weed out slow-moving items, boost turnover, and match product mixes to their consumers' changing tastes. Managers are better able to offer special promotions or merchandise items in a timely way. Moreover, because they now possess the best information, their bargaining power with suppliers is greater. The system has sharply improved the performance of decentralized managers. In each of these cases the firm's structure and control systems were sharply impacted, albeit in very different ways.

REDESIGN, NOT JUST REPAIR

Traditional control systems often fall short of serving their intended purposes. Failure can usually be blamed on one of three reasons: people do not understand the corporate goals, they understand them but lack the resources to meet them, or they simply are not motivated to fulfill them.

Sometimes people do not know what is expected of them because the corporate plan has changed and dissemination of the new message is lagging. For instance, a cash-flow crisis may cause the vice president of finance to cut budgets. In a huge conglomerate that relies on old technology, management can take weeks to rework budgets and get new spending guidelines out to operating units. In the meantime, large amounts of cash may be drained away. (As noted elsewhere, IT-enabled time compression can be a very significant competitive advantage.)

Even after a message has made the long trip from headquarters to dispersed units, the work force may lack the information to act on it. For example, recall the bank that directed its relationship managers to manage each customer's total relationship. Had the bank not given the managers customer-oriented data files, they would not have had the information they needed in order to meet the company goal. When performance is not measured accurately or promptly it's more difficult to maintain motivation, and bad work habits may evolve. Sales reps whose bonuses are tallied only once a year have no way of knowing where they stand six months into a new year. They may not realize until too late that their techniques are off the mark and need redirection.

Control systems made possible by new technologies arm managers with the tools to solve problems. More importantly, however, they enable managers to step back and rethink what they want a control system to do and to make meaningful adjustments. Some of the new options are discussed here.

Meaningful Budgets

Because budgets identify individual and unit tasks in detail, managers use them to tell people what is expected of them. When individuals help to develop the budgets, however, those individuals tend to become bound to organizational goals. Each blank on a budget form forces a question into a manager's mind. With the old technology, the sheer time required to fill in the blanks prevented managers from trying out several alternative combinations of numbers and looking down the road to see the implications of each.

New spreadsheet technology not only speeds the budgeting process by allowing managers to "plug in" numbers faster; it also improves the quality of those budgets by letting managers try out a variety of "what if" scenarios and compare the outcomes. If a business is trying to project revenues, say, it can run through several iterations based on possible changes in the market in a very short period of time.

A first run-through might assume a regulatory change that bolsters the sales of one product. In another, the absence of the new law might cause sales to remain flat. By using computer models to test various assumptions, managers can think more carefully about plans and expenditures associated with them and then follow these ideas through to their logical conclusions. In this way, the technology drives management to better anticipate and prepare for contingencies. Also, since individual unit budgets can be almost immediately consolidated into overall corporate financial plans, the process helps companies to coordinate diverse activities.

The new technology also lets managers continuously update budgets based on actual performance. Organizations are no longer bound to immediately out-of-date documents. They can quickly change plans in midstream based on performance data. For instance, a telecommunications network can quickly notify manufacturing to step up production as actual sales exceed the forecast. Similarly, the effect of cost overruns on end-of-month profits can be projected as soon as they occur.

In short, information technology permits turning the budget into a meaningful set of instructions that can facilitate optimization of the company's performance under changing conditions. The controller of a large U.S. corporation claims that quickly consolidated on-line spreadsheets for each department and business unit have improved tenfold his company's ability to coordinate action under various alternatives. Moreover, less staff is needed to meet budget preparation deadlines.

Adaptation to Change

More powerful and flexible data architectures help companies adapt to regulatory or other environmental changes. When the 1986 tax law shifted the game rules for insurance companies, one company quickly capitalized on the change. Within weeks of the law's passage, the company launched a campaign to educate its agents and customers about the statute's ramifications and the desirability of repaying loans against insurance policies. While companies whose customer files were policy-oriented scrambled to deliver a coherent message to their clients, this company's computer system produced thousands of individually tailored reports that explained in a few pages how the new rules would affect its policyholders.

The point of the program was to persuade customers to pay back loans against their whole-life policies, since loan interest was no longer tax-deductible and the cash-value buildup on a policy receives favorable tax treatment. (Customers, of course, were in the habit of borrowing against the cash value of their policies at a low rate, deducting the interest on those loans, and pouring the money into high-yield Treasury bills. The net effect was a huge drain on company coffers.) This innovative company succeeded in convincing customers to repay tens of millions of dollars on their loans and at the same time generated massive new sales of single-premium life insurance, which is both liquid and nontaxable under the new law. The ability to respond to environmental change paid a handsome dividend. The flexibility built into the system, of course, was almost impossible to justify at the time the investment was made. Afterward the firm wondered how they could have lived without it.

Solutions for Production

The increased power and versatility of new control systems help managers identify trouble spots in their administrative, field, or factory operations.

One of the widest uses of IT is in production facilities, where monitoring systems track errors per hour, flag equipment downtime, measure machine speeds, and assess worker productivity—allowing managers to remedy production problems before they become disasters. Conventional systems force managers to rely on someone's spotting the variation in a machine's production, or to wait until a piece of equipment breaks completely. Modern systems, however, can detect even the slightest deviation in human or machine performance. Early detection allows early correction, thereby improving the economics of manufacturing.

Examples of this application abound. One cigarette manufacturer has installed an automated system that regularly pulls cigarettes off the line and puts them through 20 tests, noting the smallest inconsistency in quality. Paper companies use sophisticated monitoring devices to detect variations in paper thickness or color that are invisible to the human eye. The precision with which these machines detect slight flaws allows workers to quickly adjust equipment—or their own tasks—as needed. As a refinement of earlier versions of this system, the machine operators and the system designers worked together to develop a set of dynamic graphs on display terminals showing paper thickness versus machine settings. This permits even better control of the paper-making process.

Facts to Make the Sale

Information technology can help management align control and sales-incentive measures with the realities of the market. Failure to use that ability can have embarrassing results. As noted earlier, a prominent retail bank sent salespeople to call on upscale clients with the intention of selling them new financial products. Unfortunately, the bank lacked data on each customer's total holdings. When through ignorance of these holdings, the salespeople pushed products that were wildly inappropriate for the clients, their image as financial counselors was quickly undermined. The bank should have made the investment in its control systems first. The outmoded systems had thwarted efforts to better serve customer needs, and ultimately the bank had to cancel its well-conceived but impossible-to-execute campaign.

Some companies have used IT to spread their sales tentacles ever closer to the customer without relinquishing coordination and control at the top. Banks and travel agencies, for instance, use computer systems to execute transactions at remote sites and instantly post them to centralized files. Automatic teller machines and travel agent terminals have allowed these innovative companies to shift the point of purchase nearer to customers while retaining timely records that top management can easily access.

Opportunities to reshape customer relations take many forms. Consider the case of a trust officer who wants to court the beneficiaries of a trust so that when the trust initiator dies, the money will stay at the bank. In a large bank that handles 10,000 trusts, information about the beneficiaries, many of whom are children, is likely to be buried in computer files or in paper archives. With the right information and an automated "tickler" system, the trust officer can send credit applications to these young beneficiaries as they come of age, thereby founding early relationships with them.

Tracking Inventory and Sales

New inventory tracking systems let companies continuously trace an order, update account balances, monitor inventory, and alert manufacturing and suppliers to upcoming requirements. Companies have applied such systems to control in a variety of ways. An electric sign company installed a sophisticated production control system that pipes orders directly to manufacturing. Under the old arrangement, orders took a week longer to trickle down to the factory floor. The production manager never knew what was in the pipeline, so she could not prepare the materials and staff ahead of time. Production bottlenecks and huge inventories were a way of life. The new system drives down inventory costs by eliminating the need to overstock expensive materials, and it ensures that capacity is better used throughout the 22-step manufacturing process.

Some systems amplify the benefits of low inventory without shortages by linking the order-entry function to suppliers. An automobile manufacturer has electronic ties to its suppliers, which now receive up-to-the-minute information from the company's order-entry system. The supplier can then ensure that necessary materials arrive on time. The system has proved so successful that the manufacturer has reduced its investment in inventory and warehouses—and the savings more than offset the system's cost.

An inventory monitoring system can also help managers get the product to the market where it is selling best. To be most useful, the procedure must be able to capture information and manipulate it quickly. One variety-store chain bought a scanner-based inventory system for its outlets. The old system had used a punch card at the end of each stack of 12 products to signal the need to reorder, but while items were trickling out of stores, corporate management had no idea what was selling in which areas, or how quickly.

Today a wand at the checkout counter reads the bar code off each item sold, and headquarters polls every store across the country every night for inventory data. In this way, management can assess customer trends on a daily basis. An item that turns quickly in 32 upscale locations might stall in inner-city stores, and vice versa. The new system allows managers to tailor product mix to clientele and helps identify emerging market niches that demand new product designs.

Automated order entry and inventory tracking can help companies vary their sales and pricing strategies between regions or customer types and keep their sales force informed of price changes. One national food company with its own truck fleet faced a tough problem: each sales region required its own pricing strategy, and each store its own product mix. What's more, the company wanted to base its strategy for each store on a combination of the items sold and the number of stale items left over from the previous day. Clearly drivers could not sift through customer records every night or new prices from headquarters every morning and still be expected to make their rounds.

The company installed microcomputers in more than 10,000 delivery trucks. Each morning, each driver's PC receives from a headquarters mainframe computer the subregion's prices and recommended stock mix. Every night, the company receives data in electronic form from each driver on what items were delivered and what stale items were removed from the shelves to help it determine the next day's recommendations.

Effective Incentive Systems

Technology can help managers create more effective incentive systems—from corporate profit-sharing plans that eliminate internal rivalries to schemes that automatically pay factory workers bonuses for meeting deadlines. A simple form of automated incentive system in one company continuously tallies sales commissions and allows salespeople to access their records. Salespersons' reviews of how far they are from meeting their quota may motivate them to push harder.

Additionally, incentive-based measurement systems can identify and track the contribution of a working unit that may otherwise go unrecognized. The automotive industry has found this capability attractive. The first dealer a customer visits usually invests a lot of time explaining the various models and demonstrating their features. Nonetheless, the customer may buy the car from a different dealer, who has done far less work but offers a slightly lower price. Knowing this pattern, the first dealer may do a hasty job of educating the customer and try to close the deal quickly. Although automakers may not like this situation, the industry's commission structure, which measures only sales, supports it. One manufacturer is now considering a customer tracking system that would modestly reward a salesperson who makes an initial presentation even though another dealer makes the sale.

Some organizations use innovative systems to influence customers to buy more. With sophisticated on-line analysis, a company can base a customer's discounts on total volume rather than on each other. A contact lens company offers a consignment inventory to opticians who can turn it over 13 times a year. Since opticians can fill 65 percent of their orders from that inventory and get paid on the spot instead of a week later, they are spurred to sell heavily from that manufacturer's line as opposed to some other firm's. Moreover, fast information tells the company and the opticians whether the stores are on schedule to meet their turnover quotas. This system dramatically boosted the lens company's market share over a period of several years.

Different Cost Structures and Asset Investment Levels

Over a period of time, genuinely different cost structures and asset levels may appear. No firm is more illustrative of this than Bergen Brunswig, a $4 billion sales drug wholesaler. In 1970 there were 1,000 firms in the drug wholesale industry, with no firm holding more tha 1.5 percent of the market. Bergen Brunswig's operations costs-to-sales ratio was 16 percent, typical of the industry. In 1989, in a vastly consolidated industry of 200 firms, the top five firms (of which Bergen Brunswig was one) in aggregate held 70 percent of the market. Bergen Brunswig's operations costs-to-sales ratio had shrunk to 2 percent. There was no room left for a 16 percent performance.

Three aspects of this story are important. The first is that these changes evolved over 20 years. The possibilities enabled by information technology can take a long time to play out, both because of the increasing capabilities of the technology and because of the difficulties of change management. When speaking of the competitive uses of technology, we are not talking about a quick checker game but about a chess game that can go on for years. Secondly, in Bergen Brunswig's opinion (1988 company history), the primary driver was information technology, as they slashed operating costs, quintupled the sales revenue handled per marketing representative, and completely transformed the operating structure of the warehouse. Thirdly, on-line ordering to suppliers had shrunk the inventory-to-sales ratio. This type of infrastructure transformation, while not as glamorous as some of the other examples, is absolutely fundamental to survival and competitiveness.

"Flattening" the Organization

The new technologies are allowing very different forms of organizations to emerge. As noted earlier, by facilitating information manipulation, the technology has enabled one or more layers of hierarchy to be eliminated in a number of settings, reducing distance from top to bottom of the organization.

Video conferencing, video cassettes, voice mail, and so on, allow the top of the organization to appear psychologically closer to the middle and the bottom. The CEO and the divisional president now *seem* to be closer and much more real to the managers and staff in the middle of the organization. Some of the techniques used for communicating in the political world have come to the corporate environment. The *form* of communication is changing.

Finally, in this area we come to the networked organization. Voice and electronic mail have radically altered the patterns of communication inside organizations as individuals are able to identify and interact with pockets of expertise they would have been totally unaware of a decade ago. Several years ago one of the authors watched with fascination as a senior sales representative, reacting to a sudden market opportunity, used his firm's electronic mail system to assemble a 200-page proposal in 48 hours with the help of seven sources around the globe whom he had never met within the firm. (The proposal was accepted.) The reach of the network to new sources of expertise and the shrinkage of time make this capability a genuine competitive advantage—albeit one that is extremely hard to justify objectively.

Controlled Complexity—An Example

The ability of some companies to use the technology to execute very complex micromarketing campaigns can put unresponsive organizations at an extraordinary competitive disadvantage. A 1989 interview with the former chairman of People's Express Airlines (chairman until its demise) illustrates this point. He noted that his airline had used a very limited amount of information technology, particularly in its fare structuring. They had only a single weekly fare for any seat on each route; time of day, day of week, and actual loading factors were all irrelevant. He noted that, in his judgment, the key date of their death was January 19, 1985. That was the day when American Airlines introduced their "internal yield management system," which allows them, if desired, to set a different fare for each seat on every flight on a particular route. With that capability, he noted that on every route American flew head-to-head with People Express, depending on anticipated flight loading between 1 and 100, deep/deep/deep discount seats were assigned, with the deep/deep/deep discount seats' fare being $5 below the prevailing People Express fare. American then launched a national advertising campaign.

> Call your travel agent and find out who the *real* low-cost airline is. It is not People Express. It is American Airlines.

Within 20 minutes of the time People Express announced a fare change for a route, American had adjusted its deep/deep/deep discount fare to

$5 below the new People Express fare and electronically communicated it to travel agents all over the United States and the world.

Competing against that level of managed complexity is extraordinarily difficult.

SUMMARY

Because changes in organization control systems affect all areas of the corporation, changes in them can be extraordinarily disruptive, with the technical issues and their associated costs being the lesser part of the challenge. For this reason, managers should think long and hard about the changes and their many implications before going forward.

As noted earlier, the technology itself is organizationally neutral. It does not favor centralization over decentralization or one control philosophy over another. It simply offers top managers choices they have not had before. As a by-product, local managers in the elevator company lost some autonomy, and their noses were out of joint for awhile. On the other hand, supermarket automated control systems gave store managers more information, which helped them make better decisions at the store level.

Such choices must be made consciously, giving full attention to the practical details of implementation. For example, reporting relationships may be impaired. Taking away or adding decision-making power may demand that a different type of manager be placed in some posts. The blurring of operational and managerial control may also require restructuring and redefinition of managers' roles.

There is danger, too, in failing to consider all the strategic advantages to be gained from the creative new controls and organization structures. One competitor in the elevator industry copied the other's move to centralize service records. The copycat company, however, went a step further: it identified all of its elevators that chronically failed because of age rather than some defect and then approached the owners of those elevators with proposals to rebuild the units. The innovator has defined a new, very profitable market, at least temporarily.

Expensive data storage, sluggish retrieval, and complex systems that overwhelm their would-be users are all relics of the past. The technology now exists to transform the internal workings of the organization. Consequently, it is appropriate to step back and ponder whether decentralized units are really aligned to company goals, and whether incentive systems are helping or hurting this alignment. Can technology offer new solutions to these issues in your setting?

Case 5–1

FAIRFIELD INN (A)

Mike Ruffer, the vice president and general manager of Fairfield Inn, Marriott's new entry into the economy/limited-service motel industry, summarized the dilemma facing Fairfield Inn's top executives in 1989:

How does a new chain with limited ad dollars take on competitors like Days Inn, Hampton Inn and Red Roof Inn—each with more than 200 units already operating? When we started Fairfield Inn, we knew that it was going to be a distribution game, but now in the face of rapid room supply increases and greater competition, the established players are making it a marketing and ad spending game as well.

Ruffer paused and looked out of his window at Marriott's corporate headquarters located about a half mile away in a Bethesda, Maryland, office park. He continued:

The dynamics of the business have changed considerably in the past 2½ years. Our original recommendation called for a portion of our unit growth to come from franchising. Yet, when Bill Marriott nixed the idea because of his desire to have full control over the operations, we were still confident that we could successfully establish a meaningful presence and achieve good unit distribution.

Since then, however, the economy category has experienced annual, double-digit growth in room supply—most of it occurring in the chains that are predominantly franchise-focused. Good sites, which have typically been scarce and costly, are becoming more so. And due to the rapid growth of other chains, we not only run the risk of being preempted from entering markets, but the growth of these other competitors greatly increases the size of their marketing war chest in the battle for the customer.

Our preference in Marriott has historically been to manage our own operations rather than employ a franchising strategy. Yet, if we aren't able to increase our rollout rate, the true unit potential of this new business may never be fully realized.

Company Background

Fairfield Inn, with 25 properties open in March 1989, was the newest concept in Marriott's lodging and food services empire. In 1988, the Marriott Corporation had sales of over $7.3 billion, an operating income of $398 million and a net income of $232 million. (In the past year, Marriott stock had traded in a range of $26 to $35, and there were 108.7 million shares outstanding.)

Marriott Corporation traced its roots back to the peak of the Great Depression. On May 20, 1927, Charles Lindberg took off in the *Spirit of St. Louis* on his historic trans-Atlantic flight, Babe Ruth was in the midst of his 60-home-run year, and J. Willard Marriott and his wife, Alice, opened a nine-stool root beer stand named The Hot Shoppe in Washington, D.C.

By 1989, the Marriott Corporation had more than 230,000 employees, was serving more than 5 million meals daily, and was developing over $1 billion of real estate every year as one of the 10 largest real estate

Kenneth Ray prepared this case under the supervision of Professor James L. Heskett as the basis for class discussion rather than to illustrate either effective or ineffective handling of an administrative situation.

developers in the United States. The corporation was divided into three major divisions: Contract Services, Restaurants, and Lodging.

Contract Services

Marriott's Contract Services provided 44 percent of the company sales and 32 percent of its operating income in 1988. The best known of these services was probably Marriott's In-Flite Services, the company's airline catering operations. Marriott pioneered this business in 1939 and by 1989 provided food and other services to more than 140 airlines at 92 flight kitchens located in 70 airports throughout the world. Marriott's Contract Services also included Education Services, which provided food services to 585 colleges and high schools. Health Care Services handled food services at over 400 hospitals and retirement centers.

Restaurants

J. Willard and Alice Marriott's single Hot Shoppe had been expanded to a restaurant operation encompassing more than 1,000 owned and franchised popularly priced restaurants that included Bob's Big Boy, Roy Rogers, Hot Shoppes, and Travel Plazas by Marriott. In 1988, this division delivered 13 percent of Marriott's sales and 16 percent of its operating income.

Lodging

Marriott's Lodging Group encompassed 451 hotels with more than 118,000 rooms. Marriott was America's leading operator (as opposed to franchisor) of hotel rooms. Lodging operations represented 43 percent of sales and 52 percent of operating income in 1988. The lodging group, including Fairfield Inn, was subdivided into five distinct segments.

Marriott Hotels and Resorts were full-service hotels in the luxury/quality segment. In 1988, the system comprised 192 hotels in 38 states and 13 countries and totaled more than 83,000 rooms. The cost of a room ranged between $75 and $195 a night.

The first Marriott Suites hotel opened in early 1987 in Atlanta. This full-service chain provided guests with their choice of one- and two-bedroom suites, a restaurant, a lounge, and several meeting rooms. Three more Marriott Suite hotels opened in 1988, and the company planned to have a total of 40 open by 1993. Room rates typically ranged from $85 to $125.

Residence Inn by Marriott was America's leading moderate-price, extended-stay suite concept and was acquired by Marriott in July 1987. The typical Residence Inn guest stayed for five or more consecutive nights. Guests were usually corporate employees who were in the process of being relocated to a new city, on some sort of temporary project assignment, or working in some kind of consulting capacity. At the end of 1988, there were 130 Residence Inns in 37 states with nearly 15,000 suites. Room rates ranged between $65 and $90.

Courtyard by Marriott was a lodging concept that was only six years old and focused on the *moderate-price segment* of the hotel industry. A property normally had 150 rooms, a restaurant, a lounge, and several meeting rooms. In 1988, Courtyard had 111 properties with 16,000 rooms in 27 states. Rates ranged from $50 to $88 each night.

The Fairfield Inn Decision

The decision to venture into the economy/limited-service (ELS) segment (below $45 a night) was not an easy one and raised several questions for Marriott's senior management. They included the following:

1. Could Marriott compete as a late entry in a market segment already crowded with Red Roof Inns, Holiday Corporation's Hampton Inn, Days Inn, La Quinta, Comfort Inns, and 45 other regional or state chains?

2. Would Marriott be jeopardizing its Courtyard clientele or cannibalizing some of its existing business by selling guests down to an economy-priced product?
3. Could Marriott design a product and property that was attractive enough to build a thriving business, yet cost-effective enough to meet Marriott's corporate net present value goals and its 12 percent target internal rate of return for new development projects?

Mark Pacala, Fairfield's vice president of operations, was one of the strategists with Marriott's Corporate Planning Department who first looked at the ELS segment in 1985 as a possible growth opportunity for Marriott. According to him:

> Going ahead with Fairfield Inn was a very tough decision. The market was growing rapidly and established competitors had already built strong brand names with a consistent product. We knew we'd be walking into the middle of a share-grab game.
>
> The no-go position was that we didn't know anything about this market segment, Marriott was too quality-oriented, we might tend to overinvest (hence, couldn't meet IRR goals because of high costs), and we would be entering too late into this market.
>
> The go position was that it's the second biggest segment in the lodging industry and the fastest growing. It would allow us to diversify. There was no one dominant national player, so we could take a little bit of share from everybody. Lastly, if things didn't work out, we projected that we could recover our costs by selling out to one of the established chains.

Despite its initial reservations, Marriott's Corporate Finance Committee approved the Fairfield Inn planning group's original request for $10.0 million to develop two five-property ELS test markets. In December 1985 approval was given, and in October 1987 the first Fairfield Inn opened in Atlanta.

The Economy, Limited-Service (ELS) Hotel Business

The economy segment of the U.S. lodging industry accounted for as much as 28 percent of all available rooms in 1988. Economy properties' room rents normally fell in the $25 to $45 per-night range. Economy hotels typically did not have restaurants, luxurious lobbies, or extensive meeting facilities. One authority estimated that for these reasons, economy hotels could break even with occupancy rates between 52 and 55 percent, about 10 to 12 occupancy points below the level at which full service properties tended to break even.

The top 50 ELS lodging chains had a combined total of 5,042 properties and 498,800 rooms at the end of 1987, a year in which occupancy rates for the entire ELS segment firmed up. Occupancies are shown in Exhibit 1.

The ELS segment was the fastest growing part of the U.S. lodging industry. In 1987, the segment expanded with 606 properties and 67,800 rooms. This translated to growth rates of 13.7 percent and 15.6 percent, respectively, in number of properties and number of rooms. In 1988, market experts anticipated that just over 1,000 properties with 102,200 rooms would be added to the ELS

EXHIBIT 1   Occupancy Rates, Lodging Industry and Economy/Limited-Service Segment, 1982–1987

Year	Entire Lodging Industry	Economy/Limited-Service Segment
1982	64.6%	65.6%
1983	65.2	65.3
1984	65.9	65.2
1985	64.4	64.0
1986	64.7	62.7
1987	65.6	63.5

segment. Projected growth rates for several of the leading chains in the segment are included in Exhibit 2.

The expansion of the segment paralleled corporate America's increased emphasis on controlling travel and entertainment (T&E) expenses. American Express's biennial Survey of Business Travel Management noted that "the number of chief executive officers and senior financial managers who rate rising T&E costs as a 'top concern' has increased from 45 percent to 55 percent in the past two years."

In 1990, industry experts estimated that American companies would spend at least $115 billion on T&E expenses, up from the $95 billion spent in 1988. While air travel costs were the largest single expenditure, responsible for 40 percent of every T&E dollar, lodging was next, accounting for 23 percent of every T&E dollar.

Established Competition

Days Inn of America, based in Atlanta, with 84,800 rooms and 590 properties throughout America, was the largest ELS chain in 1987. It owned 12 percent of its hotels and franchised the rest. In 1988, Days Inn opened 163 new properties and added 22,000 rooms. Occupancy rates for the chain were between 63 percent to 68 percent. Although Days Inn room rates averaged between $35 and $40 per night, published room rates varied from $18 to $109 a night depending on the location of the property. Days Inn accounted for 17 percent of all rooms in the ELS segment in 1987.

Motel 6's 48,800 rooms and 431 properties ranked it as the second largest economy chain in the United States in 1988. All of the properties were owned and operated by Motel 6. Occupancies ranged from 70 percent to 75 percent, and its published room rates ranged from $17.95 to $28.95. In 1987, Motel 6 initiated a major radio advertising campaign that had spokesperson Tom Bodette telling travelers that "We'll leave a light on for you." Bodette's folksy voice and inviting manner increased the awareness levels of Motel 6 within its target market.

EXHIBIT 2 Projected Economy Lodging Capacities

	Number of Rooms 1986[a]	Number of Rooms 1987	Number of Rooms 1988	Number of Rooms 1989[b]	Number of Rooms 1995[c]	Annual Growth Rate[d]
Days Inn	49,500	66,400	84,800	69,000	137,000	12%
Hampton	11,600	13,400	19,100	23,000	85,000	25
La Quinta	24,100	23,500	25,200	25,700	85,000	15
Comfort Inn	18,200	23,800	33,100	44,500	64,000	15
Red Roof	16,500	17,600	19,500	21,500	50,000	13
Fairfield	—	NA	265	2,400	49,500	

[a]As of January 1, based on annual information prepared by Laventhal and Horwath and published in *Hotel and Motel Management* magazine.

[b]The number of rooms for Days Inn was adjusted downward to reflect the amount of their room inventory that is effectively being sold at less than $45 per night, comparable to economy lodging.

[c]Estimates made in 1986.

[d]For three years prior to January 1, 1986.

Comfort Inn, headquartered in Silver Spring, Maryland, was the third largest ELS chain in the United States, with 375 properties and 33,700 rooms. Comfort Inns were 100 percent franchised. Its units' occupancies varied between 65 percent and 70 percent, and published room rates were from $30 to $50 per night.

Red Roof Inn was founded in Ohio in 1964 and opened its 200th property in Orlando in 1989. All Red Roof Inns were owned by the company. New Red Roof Inns had been opened at the rate of about 15 a year for the past three years. Its occupancies ranged from 77 percent to 82 percent, and room rates averaged between $35 and $40 a night.

Holiday Corporation's Hampton Inn had the most ambitious growth plans of all ELS chains. By 1988, Hampton Inn had 152 properties and more than 19,000 rooms. Holiday Corp. retained direct ownership of 12 percent of the properties and franchised 88 percent of the chain. Room rates ranged from $29 to $68 a night.

In a 1986 meeting of the Holiday Corp.'s limited-service hotel division, Ray Schultz, Hampton Inn's president, told managers, owners, and operators in attendance that, "We're not the biggest yet, but we will be. Don't get greedy. Stay away from raising rates. Operate lean and efficiently. And hire, train, and motivate good people."[1]

Michael Rose, chairman and CEO of Hampton's parent company, emphasized that, "In a survey of Hampton customers, 98 percent said they would use a Hampton Inn again. Two-thirds said they would actually go out of their way to stay at a Hampton Inn hotel. . . . Design has been an important factor, but in the long term, outstanding customer service is the key to success."[2] According to Hampton's President Schultz:

We basically are competing in the upper and middle ranges of the limited-service segment. We see our main competitor (as of 1986) as being the La Quintas, the Comforts, the Days Inns. . . . We're going into a "burst" mode of advertising, where periodically we'll attempt to make travelers aware of our product. We're aiming for national awareness. . . . We're finding that new Inns are running in the high 50s or low 60s "percentagewise" (in occupancy). After about six months, they're in the middle 60s. After a year, occupancy rates are typically in the 70 percent range. . . . We made aggressive plans, and we're fulfilling them, so I'm not so surprised that we're growing so fast. The competitors around us are the ones who are surprised.[3]

Market Analysis and Fairfield's Positioning

The size of the entire ELS segment was estimated at 285 million room nights annually in 1985. The market was broadly divided into business travelers, who accounted for 178 million room nights, and pleasure travelers, who purchased 107 million room nights. Overall demand growth in the ELS segment was expected to range from 4 to 6 percent each year throughout the next decade. Fairfield Inn was designed for the transient market, business and pleasure travelers who were seeking clean, comfortable, and convenient lodging in the $30 to $40 price range. Its anticipated guest mix was 65 percent business transients and 35 percent pleasure transients.

Business travelers in the economy segment usually traveled by auto and followed

---

[1] Bill Gillette, "Hampton Plans to Rule Limited-Service Market," *Hotel & Motel Management,* June 30, 1986, p. 2.

[2] Ibid.

[3] Bill Gillette, "Schultz Leading Chain's Growth," *Hotel & Motel Management,* June 30, 1986, p. 38.

regional drive patterns in the course of their business and sales calls. In deciding where to stay for the night, the most important attributes for these travelers were cleanliness; overall value for the money spent; secure feeling; friendly, efficient employees; and overall service. Traveler comments obtained from focus group interviews conducted for Fairfield Inn's management appear in Exhibit 3.

According to Marriott's in-house research, business travelers could be subdivided into two basic traveler segments, "functional travelers" and "stylish travelers." Fairfield Inn's strategy was to make the functional business traveler the primary customer group; in 1985, this segment was estimated to comprise 66 percent of business travelers purchasing 72 percent of room nights occupied by business travelers.

Functional and stylish travelers possessed different attitudes toward lodging and had different demographic and travel profiles. The functional business traveler wanted the basic amenities (clean room, good price/value, and consistency) but didn't need lots of extras. Functional travelers preferred motels like Fairfield Inn, Red Roof, and Knights Inn. Stylish travelers wanted the basics plus some food and beverage service, business services and meeting rooms, and recreational facilities. Stylish travelers tended to prefer motels like Hampton Inn, Signature Inn, and La Quinta Motor Inn.

Fairfield Inn targeted the functional traveler group because this group was composed of the most frequent travelers, was the largest economy consumer group, and generated the most potential new room nights. Market research indicated that the vast majority of travelers within this price segment were new Marriott customers and not established Courtyard clientele. Also, the weekend pleasure customers' lodging needs were quite similar to those of the functional business traveler, so Fairfield's product and price allowed Marriott's new brand to attract the weekend pleasure traveler.

Market analyses conducted by Fairfield Inn's management showed four key customer target groups among frequent automobile travelers who were current users of other economy-price hotels:

1. Traveling salespeople or regional managers were travelers with an assigned territory to cover. They had fairly strict per diem allowances for travel and lodging. They desired a good clean room that was also conducive to working at night.
2. Government and military employees had a rigid per diem budget that they were allowed to spend on lodging. Economy hotels met their needs quite well.
3. Self-employed businesspeople tried to minimize expenses by staying in reasonably priced lodging. Since all bills were paid out of their own pockets, members of this group were rate-sensitive and didn't want to be charged for services not used.
4. Extended stayers were defined as guests staying more than a week. Typically, these people were relocating or part of a project team.

Additionally, Fairfield Inn's management wanted to set a price high enough to discourage truckers and construction crews as guests. They wanted to exude the image of being a businessperson's hotel during the week.

Guest tracking surveys conducted in 1988 confirmed that Marriott's first 15 ELS properties were reaching their target customers. Fairfield Inn's weekday guest was an over-the-road (as opposed to air traveling) salesperson who was about 40 years old, made 33 business trips a year, and had a personal income of $52,600.

Focus groups conducted with ELS hotel customers indicated that pleasure travelers

---

EXHIBIT 3 Customer Comments Regarding Fairfield Inn

About the importance of price . . .

"The company sets the limit for us. They say 'Anything over $45 and you pay the difference.' "

"I often work on a per diem basis. You can go to a really nice hotel and eat at McDonald's or you can stay at a cheap place and eat steak."

"I don't have any limit, but I don't spend an extra $30 for something I don't think I need. I might find something better to spend it for."

"I'm on straight commission. I'm an independent contractor, so I set my own limit and I look for a fair price."

Selecting a place to stay . . .

"I've been on the highways for 40 years, and it gets to where you can pretty well drive by them and tell which ones are good."

"I want to drive up to the room. I don't like all these places they're making now where you've got to walk through the lobby, drag all your junk with you and drag it all back out with you."

"I want the convenience of being able to carry my files in and being able to do my paperwork in the evening."

"Some places go out of their way to make you feel at home and you want to go after a place like that. That means a lot."

About the competition . . .

"I prefer Hampton over Red Roof. The rooms were much nicer—they were much prettier. I just like the way the rooms were done. They have more luxury than Red Roof. I don't think Hampton is considered a budget hotel."

"Knights Inn transcends tackiness—purple bed sheets. I won't go back."

"One thing I like about Knights Inn is you can pack right at your door."

"It's like a White Castle that jumps right out at you . . . that red roof. They have a good sign that catches your eye."

"Red Roofs are at good locations. They work the exits very well."

---

wanted a well-run, secure, inexpensive place to spend the night while on the road to some other destination or to use as a "base camp" for visiting friends or family within the local area.

The ELS pleasure traveler represented a broad segment of the U.S. population. Marriott researchers estimated that 25 percent of U.S. families stayed in economy lodging at least one night each year for pleasure travel. Broadly speaking, these customers lived within a 300-mile radius of the hotel and drove there with their family. Marriott's research showed that many travelers who stayed in higher-priced lodging while on business also preferred to stay in ELS lodging when traveling for pleasure. The typical weekend guest at Fairfield Inn was 40 years of age, but had a lower personal income than weekday guests.

EXHIBIT 3   (Continued)

Choosing a place to stay . . .

"It's all a matter of economics. When you're traveling to a location and not planning on spending the whole day at a motel, you drive till you sleep, sleep, then you get up and go again."

"My wife gives the final say on where we'll stay."

"I really like the little book with the little map that says 'here it is,' you go down this street and turn and there it is!"

"I look at billboards. As you're driving into town you're trying to spot something that might ring a bell in your mind—somewhere you've stayed before or something you've heard."

"If the outside of the hotel is shabby-looking, I always think the inside is going to be like that. I'm not talking real fancy. It can be just a neat appearance on the outside and all the lights are working. Normally, the inside will be neat also."

Some expectations . . .

"Whether it's $29.95 or $49.94 or $95.99 a night, you want your motel to be as comfortable as home, if possible. That's what you're looking for. You don't want to get hassled when you complain about a drippy faucet. You want a place that's managed."

"Courteous people at the desk. If they have to pay those people a little more money, they're going to be nice to me—especially when there's a problem. That's one of my biggies."

"It doesn't matter if they're a clerk or a manager, they ought to be polite."

About the rooms . . .

"As long as it's clean and it's tidy and it's sanitary, I have no problem."

"If I'm staying just a short while, all I really want is a good bed to sleep in and a clean bathroom to take care of business the next morning, and I don't need lots of space. Even with children you don't need lots of space."

"Once you close your eyes, all rooms are the same size anyway."

The Fairfield Inn Concept

After completing the initial feasibility studies, the real challenge for Fairfield Inn's operating managers was in designing, producing, implementing, and operating a Fairfield Inn concept. Mike Ruffer clearly delineated the expectations for Fairfield Inn:

> In any lodging segment that we or Marriott compete in our objective going in is not to be the biggest; we do, however, want to be best of the class. Our long-term success is more dependent upon how well we serve our guests time and again. Consistently. Superior hospitality and execution day-to-day will let us "win" over time.

The mission statement that was developed by Fairfield Inn's management team reflected a desire to be the best:

At Fairfield Inn, our team's mission is to . . .

- Impress our guests.
- Have committed employees pursuing excellence.
- Recognize and reward excellent performance.

Mel Warriner, vice president of human resources commented, "You'll notice we don't use the word satisfy. It's too mediocre. We are hanging our strategic hat on service. We want the guest to leave and say, 'Wow, this was different.' "

Fairfield Inn's rooms rented for $36 per night, and each property had about 130 rooms. Fairfield Inn management anticipated that established properties would have an annual occupancy rate of 78 percent.

Fairfield Inn's amenities package was designed using surveys that asked experienced ELS customers what they wanted. According to Bob Ziegler, Fairfield's director of marketing communications: "We sampled more than 600 people. We screened them on several criteria, whether they took 6 or more business trips a year, expected to pay between $20 and $45 a night when they were paying for their own lodging, and stayed in competitive hotels during the past year."

Each Fairfield Inn offered guests king-size beds, free cable television, remote-control television, thick towels, free local phone calls, large comfortable chair, large work desk (45 × 28 inches), alarm clock, free coffee and tea in the lobby, swimming pool, inside or outside room entry, smoking or nonsmoking rooms, long-cord telephones, separate full-length mirror, a meeting room just off the lobby, and vending machines with a variety of snacks, juices, and soft drinks.

Fairfield Inn's top management realized early on that if its concept was going to succeed in an already-crowded ELS segment, it would have to successfully combine an efficient, attractive property with a highly motivated staff. As Mel Warriner put it, "Too often employees are just marking time. At Fairfield, we are committing ourselves to reducing turnover in housekeeping and staff levels dramatically below the industry's 150 to 200 percent per-year average. We hire people who like to make people smile. We have designed what we feel is an innovative pay-for-performance system that encourages the pursuit of excellence." Management called this the Scorecard System.

The Scorecard System

According to Robert J. McCarthy, Fairfield's vice president of marketing, "Scorecard is the single most unique thing we are doing. It's not a typical hotel amenity, but it may be our most powerful amenity."

Each Fairfield Inn check-out counter was equipped with two Scorecard computer monitors. When a guest checked out, it was the guest service representative's (or GSR, the equivalent of a front-desk clerk at Fairfield) responsibility to cheerfully ask the customer to rate the quality of his or her stay and the services he or she received by entering either excellent, average, or poor on the Scoreboard monitor's keypad.

The complete Scorecard system involved six questions (listed in Exhibit 4), but customers only answered four questions during each checkout. The question about the cleanliness of the room was answered by every guest, while the software program rotated the remaining five questions in the other three Scorecard slots. These other questions queried the guest about the friendliness and efficiency of the clerk at arrival and checkout, an overall rating of this Fairfield Inn, value for the price paid, and an overall rating of cleanliness and staff hospitality.

To facilitate use of the Scorecard, each GSR and guest room attendant (GRA or housekeeper) was assigned a special employee code number. Scorecard's software system automatically matched each guest's rating for every question to the appropriate service personnel. In this way, the ratings produced a performance "scorecard" for the property and every employee on the property that regularly came in contact with guests, as shown in Exhibit 4.

EXHIBIT 4 Guest Scorecard Period Report

Atlanta Report

Period 13: Quarter 4

Fiscal Week 12-31-89 to 01-07-90
Page 1

Question	This Period				Previous Period Average	Quarter to Date Average
	# of Resp.	# of Excl.	# of Ave.	# of Poor	Average		

Question	# of Resp.	# of Excl.	# of Ave.	# of Poor	Average	Previous Period Average	Quarter to Date Average
Friendliness and efficiency of clerk at check-in	299	287	12	0	98.0	95.5	96.6
Friendliness and efficiency of clerk at check-out	308	300	7	1	98.5	96.8	97.6
Cleanliness of room	510	482	27	1	97.2	95.7	96.9
Overall rating of this Fairfield Inn	319	290	29	0	95.5	92.9	94.2
Value for the price paid	301	256	42	3	92.0	89.2	91.3
Overall Inn cleanliness and staff hospitality	286	272	14	0	97.6	95.9	96.8
Capture rate (responses/check-outs)					42.4%	26.7%	36.2%

Current period capture rate calculation

1128 check-outs with responses

2660 total check-outs

195

The Scorecard ratings played a major role in the incentive compensation levels of each employee at the Inn. They were published monthly and posted in the break room at each Fairfield Inn. A GSR or GRA was able to earn a bonus of up to 10 percent of salary every quarter with 50 percent of the bonus based on individual performance and 50 percent based on the entire staff's performance at each property. Fairfield Inn's base wages for each position ranked in the top quarter among salaries offered by local hotels and motels.

Joanne Eckhardt, a GSR in Detroit, commented:

> Scorecard gives corporate an immediate rating on a guest stay since we're all logged in. It gives credit where credit is due. You're not getting the same amount of pay as everyone else. It's very fair. With Holiday Inn (her previous employer) there was no incentive and no option to progress within the system. It was like you were expendable. Here at Fairfield Inn, I've seen them promote front-desk clerks into management, or if you're happy doing what you're doing, they recognize and reward you.

Linda Wilson, another GSR, said:

> I love to see it when guests checking out push excellent. At Signature Inn, the only people who ever got a bonus check were the front-desk crew and the manager. Housekeeping, maintenance, and laundry got absolutely nothing. They tried to keep bonuses really hush-hush. Back then, I was assistant supervisor of housecleaning and it really made me mad that the front desk got a bonus and we didn't. They said that front desk sells the hotel, but what do you think happens if the guest walks into a room that's dirty. At Fairfield, we're a team.

According to Deneige Teague, a guest linen attendant (laundry room):

> The money is nice. No other hotel company offers it. My bonus is based on the Inn's over-

all rating. Here, we are very proud of what we do. It's our property. When someone walks in that room, we all have the same idea—to make sure they get a great room and come back again.

Scorecard ratings seemed to serve as a focal point for some good-natured competition among each Inn's staff and across the various Fairfield locations. Joyce Smith, a GRA, said, "Every time the ratings get posted we all rush up to see how well we did. Everybody takes care of their own section of rooms and wants to have the cleanest rooms in the hotel." Rob Munro, a guest room supervisor, added:

> Scorecard is an incentive. We try and encourage the GRAs to take great pride in their work. Each day I will review two rooms (out of the 14 assigned daily to each GRA) with the person. I try to be really positive because we want to keep the person from getting discouraged. They are going to make a lot of mistakes initially—water-spotted chrome, a stopper not in the tub, or dust on the chair legs. Fairfield is very particular. We don't have a lot of extras, so we want everything to be absolutely clean. Some of our high standards come from our hiring. We get people with good attitudes and good personalities. But it's up to the supervisors and managers to provide the right working environment.

Personnel Selection

The Scorecard system and Fairfield's focus on hospitality was based upon hiring good people from the start and developing a strong relationship among the entire staff during the pre-opening stages of a property.

Fairfield Inn managers made their employee selections after evaluating the potential candidates in a series of personal interviews (as many as three rounds) and on the basis of a personality skills profile test designed by Selection Research Institute.

"Generally, we like to hire people who enjoy pleasing other people. For GRAs, we try to identify people who like to clean and enjoy housework. Similarly, for our maintenance jobs we focus on finding people who enjoy fixing things. Part of the six-to-eight-week training program for Fairfield managers is a three-day seminar on how to interview job candidates and how to evaluate the personality skills test," commented Mark Pacala.

Sue Graves, Fairfield's Detroit area manager, who supervised six area properties, remembered opening up the airport property a year earlier: "When we opened that Detroit property we were running about two weeks behind (in construction and finishing), so that allowed me and the assistant managers to interview more people," she said. "We interviewed over 500 people to fill 19 positions at the first property, and in the last 90 days we haven't had any turnover."

Another way that Fairfield management had generated a tremendous amount of enthusiasm among the hourly employees at each hotel was through a team-building exercise in the pre-opening meeting where management and hourly employees had a round-table discussion of mutual expectations.

The team-building discussion began with employees and management generating a list of what they would want if they each were a guest at this Fairfield Inn. The next segment of the team-building exercise encouraged hourly employees to generate a list of expectations for each other. At the Warren property, a suburb of Detroit, the employee promises to each other were: dependability, teamwork, positivity, consideration, honesty, reliability, loyalty, integrity, encourage others, pats on the back, caring, understanding, jokes, a sense of humor, camaraderie, friendship, communication, lightheartedness, and to not sweat the small stuff.

Next, the hourly employees generated a list of their expectations from management.

At Canton, these expectations included: sensitivity, respect, a second chance, empathy, fairness, friendship, protection, creativity, teach us, keep us informed, keep us a part of decisions, stand by us, listen to our ideas, money, sense of humor, understanding, support, and patience.

At each Fairfield Inn, the posters that had been generated in the team-building exercise were prominently displayed in the employee break room located next to the property manager's office.

Organization

Each Fairfield Inn had a staff of about 21 employees to run the property. The staff was composed of a manger, assistant manager, and 19 hourly employees: four GSRs, 11 GRAs, one guest room supervisor, one maintenance chief, one custodial facility attendant, and one guest linen attendant.

The regional support group for each cluster of 10 to 12 Fairfield Inns was composed of a field marketing manager and an area manager. The area manager was directly responsible to headquarters for the performance of each Inn in his or her region.

Fairfield's decentralized organization was combined with a highly centralized operations system. Each Fairfield Inn was directly linked to a central computer at the Bethesda headquarters through an in-house system known as "The Coordinator." The resulting "flat" organization structure allowed each property manager to focus on "impressing the guest."

"The administrative load is really minimal. It's like night-and-day when compared to the inventory and labor reports I had to complete in another Marriott group. Not having tons of paperwork allows you to be out with your guests. Every morning, I try to be out at the front desk or lobby between 7:30 A.M. and 9:00 A.M. so I can personally greet and get to know our guests," commented Norm Bartlemay, the manager at Detroit's Canton property.

Guest and Employee Incentives

Another program developed by Fairfield Inn in 1988 was the creation of a discretionary promotions fund. The fund gave property managers the opportunity to provide special events and promotions for both their employees and guests. Each manager was allocated $175 every month to spend on employee incentives and $125 to use on guest incentives.

At the Detroit airport property, a "hospitality committee" composed of the maintenance chief, one guest room attendant, and an assistant manager determined how to allocate the money for guest incentives. In recent months, regular guests had been surprised with gift certificates to Bob Evans restaurants, green carnations on St. Patrick's Day, and Easter baskets full of jelly beans in their rooms.

For the employees, incentives usually took the form of cash bonuses and gift certificates. For example, in March 1989 at the Warren property, the winner of the month's "White Glove Award," the person scoring highest on daily room inspections, had his/her choice of $25 cash, a $25 dinner certificate for a local restaurant, or an equivalent amount of movie passes. Additionally, the winner's name was prominently displayed in the break room for the next month.

At the Madison Heights property, manager Joan Susinskas handed out Easter baskets hand-stuffed with goodies to each of the team members when the employees came into her office to pick up their weekly paychecks. At the Warren property, people were talking about the employee Easter Egg hunt scheduled for the next day. Associate manager Mary Von Koughnett had already generated a great deal of excitement by announcing that plastic eggs stuffed with various amounts of cash would be scattered throughout the property. After the "hunt," a coffee-and-donuts breakfast was scheduled for all employees. According to Koughnett, "With a staff of 15, it's real important to know how to deal with each one individually as well as in a group. You've got to make your employees feel like they are kings and queens. If someone calls in sick, we want to call back later in the day to see if anyone can bring over anything. We've become a really close group that cares about each other. At this property, our turnover has been almost nil. Last week, I had to hire the first new person since we opened last August (eight months previously).

Fairfield Inn also had developed a unique paid leave program for its employees. The program was designed to reduce the industry's traditionally high absenteeism and high turnover rates among GRAs and GSRs.

Each employee was initially given a week of vacation per year. For every month with perfect attendance (not missing any scheduled work days or not failing to arrange for a substitute), the employee would "earn" a half day of paid leave. Perfect attendance for a quarter would earn the employee one full day of paid leave in addition to the three half days already earned for perfect attendance during each month of the quarter. Thus, an employee who had perfect attendance for a year would earn 10 extra days of paid leave (4 quarters × 2.5 earned days), for a total of three weeks of vacation and paid leave.

Although the paid leave program had been in effect for less than a year in 1989, it appeared that Fairfield Inn had been successful in reducing its turnover versus the industry average. Mel Warriner reported, "Rough numbers from last quarter indicated that the annualized turnover of our hourly employees was about 91 percent, or approximately half the industry rate. Additionally, 85 to 90 percent of the eligible employees had earned some bonus leave during the last quarter. The turnover among our managers was 4 percent compared to the 15 percent management turnover rate that is normal in Marriott's full-service chains."

Another incentive designed to help Fairfield managers compensate for the inevitable GRA staffing problems was the Bonus Pay Program. Normally, GRAs were expected to clean 14 rooms during a seven-hour shift. However, GRAs were given the opportunity to clean additional rooms when unexpectedly high occupancies or a GRA's absence required that more rooms be cleaned per GRA. If the GRAs were able to complete cleaning the additional rooms during their shift, they would be compensated in cash at the end of the shift. The bonus was equal to one-half the employee's hourly rate for each room cleaned. Instead of the cash bonus, the employee could also choose to remain on the time clock for 30 minutes longer for each additional room assigned.

Economics

Occupancy rates, room rates, operating expenses, and investment costs were the major variables determining whether or not a Fairfield Inn property would be successful.

Fairfield Inn's development costs for a particular site were typically between $4.5 and $5.0 million. This included land (2.1 acres versus the 4 acres needed for a Courtyard), building and systems, FF&E (furniture, fixtures, and equipment), opening inventory, fees, and construction interest. Marriott usually funded 100 percent of the investment internally, then sold the entire property to outside investors (e.g., through a real estate syndication), and retained a management contract for operating the property. (Pro-forma operating statements for a typical Inn are shown in Exhibits 5 and 6.)

Options for Future Growth

In 1989, Mike Ruffer and the rest of the Fairfield Inn management team were faced with three basic questions regarding the

---

EXHIBIT 5 Fairfield Inn Investment Assumptions (105-room inn)

	Fairfield Low	Fairfield High	Per Room Low	Per Room High
Land	$ 528,000	$1,410,000	$ 5,029	$13,429
Building and Systems	2,425,000	3,190,000	23,095	30,381
FF&E[a]	480,000	480,000	4,571	4,571
Fees	140,000	160,000	1,333	1,524
Construction Interest	140,000	270,000	1,333	2,571
Total	$3,713,000	$5,510,000	$35,361	$52,476
Pre-opening Expenses	135,000	135,000		
Working Capital	15,000	15,000		
Capitalized Development	56,000	56,000		
Total	$3,919,000	$5,716,000		

[a]Fixtures, furniture, and equipment.

EXHIBIT 6   Fairfield Inn Economics (105-room inn)

(Percentages of total revenues—year 4 of stabilized operations)	
Revenues	
Rooms	96.0%
Telephone	3.0
Other	1.0
Total	100.0%
Department profits[a]	
Rooms	74.6
Telephone and other	32.1
Total (average of the two)	72.9%
Deductions	
General and administration	7.3
Heat, light, and power	4.8
Repair and maintenance	3.6
Group insurance	1.6
Reservations	1.4
National marketing	2.5
Local marketing	3.3
Other	4.0
Total	28.5%
House profit	44.4%

Owned		*Syndicated*		*Franchised*	
House profit	44.4%	Management fee	4.0%	Royalties	4.0%
Depreciation	(10.8)	Chain services fee[b]	1.5	Franchising overhead	(1.2)
Property taxes	(4.4)	Incentive fee	4.5		
Corporate and division overhead	(4.0)	Corporate and division overhead	(4.0)		
Interest	(20.0)				
Total	5.2%		6.0%		2.8%

[a]After direct costs of labor, material, and commissions.
[b]The chain services fee is a "cost pass through" to cover costs of area managers and central accounting functions.

---

growth of Marriott's newest hotel chain: (1) Do we follow the traditional Marriott strategy of operating but not owning facilities? (2) If we don't, should we use a "standard" franchising approach (like Hampton Inn), or do we use a "McDonald's approach" to franchising? (3) Is there some appropriate mix of these alternatives?

The decision to grow internally versus expanding through franchising would have a large effect on the ultimate size of the Fairfield Inn chain. In 1986, an internal Marriott group completed an intensive study of site opportunities for an ELS chain. The report concluded that Fairfield Inn could grow to 350 units in a company-managed scenario or to 500 units in a franchising scenario.

Franchising would give Fairfield Inn access to many good undeveloped locations that were owned by developers and individuals unwilling to sell, but who wanted to use their land as an equity stake in a commercial project. Fairfield Inn's projected roll-out schedules under each scenario are shown in Exhibit 7.

Franchising Options

The Fairfield Inn concept seemed to be an ideal candidate for franchising. The product was relatively simple, a hotel without food and beverage operations where furniture, fixtures, and equipment could be controlled through a tightly worded franchise agreement. Additionally, Marriott's history showed that the company was able to successfully manage "formula systems." Lastly, by linking the franchisee with ancillary support services (property management system, reservations network, group health insurance, etc.), Fairfield corporate would be able to maintain leverage with future franchisees and provide operations expertise.

Fairfield's ancillary services would create additional value for franchisees by providing them with benefits unavailable to an independent operator. Fairfield's management would in all likelihood price these services at a break-even level for Marriott. By pricing at its cost, Marriott could not be accused of "tying arrangements."[4] In fast-food restaurants, McDonald's had successfully used a similar strategy to increase the real and perceived value of the McDonald's system for its franchisees.

However, under a franchise system, Fairfield Inn would lose control over prices. Federal laws dictated that franchisees had to be able to set their own prices.[5] One challenge for management under franchising would be to influence pricing among franchisees so that their room rates were consistent with Fairfield's desired position in the ELS segment.

Franchising would also impact the revenues that Fairfield Inn would deliver to Marriott. Fairfield Inn's competitors offered a variety of franchise packages. This suggested that Mike Ruffer and his management team would have a tremendous amount of flexibility in structuring any franchise agreement if they elected to franchise. Under franchising, Fairfield Inn's management group estimated the net present value generated by each property was approximately $400,000 for Marriott in 1988 dollars while also delivering an 18.0 percent cash-on-cash return to the franchisee. (This compared with an estimated net present value for a Marriott-owned property of $450,000 in 1988 dollars.) Under franchising, Marriott's initial investment would be reduced significantly.

Two potential franchising approaches were known in-house as the "Standard" and the "McDonald's" franchising plans.

---

[4] A tying arrangement is one in which the seller, with market power, conditions the sale of one product (the franchise) on the purchase from the seller (or a third party in which the seller has an interest) of a separate product, at a higher price than the buyer would have paid had both tying and tied products been purchased from other sources. Tying arrangements are violations of the antitrust laws and are not subject to economic justification.

[5] As of 1989, establishment by a franchisor of the prices which franchisees charge for any product was a violation of Section 1 of the Sherman Act, regardless of whether the purpose of the arrangement was to raise, lower, or stabilize retail prices. A franchisor could suggest retail prices so long as it did not attempt to coerce franchisees to comply with its "suggestions."

EXHIBIT 7 Fairfield Inn Roll-Out Scenarios (as projected in 1986)

	1986	1987	1988	1989	1990	1991	1992	1993	1994	1995	1996
				Fully Owned							
Units opened during year	1	16	42	50	50	40	40	40	40	31	0
Cumulative	1	17	59	109	159	199	239	279	319	350	350
				Fully Franchised							
Units opened during year	0	0	10	50	100	125	150	65	0	0	0
Cumulative	0	0	10	60	160	285	435	500	500	500	500

The Standard Plan

The primary target under a "standard plan" would be management companies with in-house development and construction management abilities as well as lodging operations experience. Existing franchisees of other Marriott lodging concepts would provide a core of qualified franchisees who could finance, develop, construct, and staff their properties. The franchise terms would be a 20-year agreement with no renewal. Marriott would receive a 4 percent royalty on gross revenues and a $45,000 application fee.

Under the Standard plan, the overall number of projects developed would be increased because of sites brought in by franchisees. Only franchisees that were meeting operational performance criteria would be encouraged to build additional properties. The franchisee would manage construction, and Marriott would approve a general contractor. Marriott would control construction quality with a thorough design guide and with inspection visits to the construction site during key phases of development. The granting of the actual franchise would be contingent on the construction being completed satisfactorily.

A franchisee would need to arrange his or her own financing.

The "McDonald's" Plan

Under this plan, the primary target would be experienced hotel operators wanting to acquire their own property. These franchisees would have a demonstrated ability to meet Marriott operating standards. They would be required to personally participate in the business, thus most likely limiting them to one inn each. The franchise agreement would be for 20 years with no renewal. Marriott would receive a 4 percent royalty of gross revenues plus lease payments for the land and building. A $45,000 fee would be payable with application for a franchise.

Marriott would handle virtually all development. This would include analyzing market potential, conducting feasibility studies, and site selection and the approval process. Additionally, Marriott would construct each inn.

Marriott would retain title to the land and building while the property would be leased to the franchisee. Franchisees would finance the remainder of the investment on their own.

Syndication

Fairfield Inn's third option for future growth was to follow a frequently used Marriott strategy of syndicating the properties.

As Bill Marriott, Jr., explained in his 1988 letter to shareholders, "We extend our competitive advantage by using innovative financing techniques to minimize internal capital needs and access the lowest cost of capital available. We have 'decapitalized' our lodging business by selling hotels while retaining operating control under long-term agreements. We earn development fees by designing and constructing hotels for sales to investors and management fees for operating the hotels successfully."

A simplified syndication process followed these steps:

1. Marriott buys the land and develops the sites.
2. Marriott builds a Fairfield Inn on each piece of land.
3. When properties are open, they are sold via a public or private syndication, in groups.
4. After the sale, a syndicate of investors has ownership of all properties in the block while Marriott staffs the hotel with its own employees for a management fee of 4 to 5 percent of revenues and an incentive fee based on operating results.

Each syndication by Marriott was different, but it was becoming typical for Marriott to offer a guaranteed return for the first three years to the investors. If Fairfield was going to syndicate, investors would expect about a 9 percent cash-on-cash return after-tax, according to Richard Palmer, Fairfield Inn's vice president of finance. In the case of a cash-flow shortfall for the properties, Marriott's syndication agreement usually guaranteed covering the debt-service payments for the first three years in addition to the guaranteed return to investors.

In a syndication, Marriott would earn development fees ranging from 2 to 5 percent based on a $5 million investment for each property. However, the transaction costs of a syndication, which included investment banker fees, printing and distribution costs, and closing costs, were estimated by Palmer to be in the neighborhood of 5 percent of the value of the properties to be syndicated. The syndication option had virtually the same corporate overhead costs as the owned option. Franchising would require less overhead per property.

Under a syndication scenario, Fairfield Inn's internal growth would provide a working environment with numerous opportunities for employees at every level to move up. However, it would also stretch the organization to find, hire, and train enough people to staff each property. Lastly, under a rapid expansion strategy, whether syndicated or franchised, Fairfield Inn would be challenged to ensure that standards of excellence for customer service were consistent across the chain at each new property.

Mark Pacala commented:

> It seems that the most important issue facing Fairfield Inn is how committed the employees will be to guest service under each growth option. Right now, we've created a very special environment for employees. We're new, it's exciting, and we've only got 25 properties. There seem to be three components that are of critical importance to our future. First, can we require that franchisees use Scorecard? Second, can we insist that they compensate their people based on Scorecard performance? Third, can we get them to recruit based on the Fairfield Inn selection techniques that we use? The culture of Fairfield Inn will ultimately determine how successful we are in the ELS segment.

Case 5–2

OTISLINE (A)

When elevators are running really well, people do not notice them. . . . Our objective is to go unnoticed.

Bob Smith
Executive Vice President
Chief Operating Officer
Otis Elevator

In late November 1985, John Miller, director of information systems for Otis Elevator North American Operations, contemplated the future of OTISLINE,* a computer application developed to improve Otis Elevator's responsiveness to its service customers. The nationwide implementation of OTISLINE was under way, and the company was considering several other applications that could use the system's infrastructure.

Company Overview

Otis Elevator, a subsidiary of United Technologies Corporation, was the world leader in elevator sales and service (i.e., maintenance). Its 1984 revenue of $2 billion represented 13 percent of United Technologies' total revenue.[1] Otis Elevator was organized into four geographic divisions: North American Operations, Latin American Operations, Pacific Area Operations, and European Transcontinental Operations.

Otis Elevator, named for the company's founder, Elisha Graves Otis, described its business as the design, manufacture, installation, and service of elevators and related products, including escalators and moving sidewalks. By the end of the nineteenth century, Otis's name was known worldwide and had become synonymous with one of the most useful and dramatic inventions of the century, the passenger elevator.[2] Exhibit 1, an excerpt from the company history, *Going Up,* describes the events leading up to the installation of the first passenger elevator.

The Otis name connoted technological leadership, reliability, and quality. Since Otis Elevator was perceived to be the best, customers were willing to pay a premium for its products. The company marketed three elevator lines: Otis Hydraulics for low-rise buildings (up to 6 stories), Otis Geared for

---

[1] *1984 Annual Report,* United Technologies Corporation.

[2] Jean Gavois, *Going Up* (Hartford, Conn.: 1983), p. 74.

Research Assistant Donna Stoddard prepared this case under the supervision of Professor Warren McFarlan as the basis for class discussion rather than to illustrate either effective or ineffective handling of an administrative situation. The names of Otis Elevator employees have been disguised.

*"OtisLine" is a registered servicemark of Otis Elevator Company.

EXHIBIT 1 The First Elevators

31128

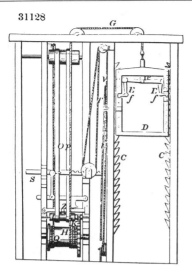

The story of Elisha Graves Otis is a textbook tale of inventiveness, opportunity and enterprise. Along with other folk heroes of Victorian America, Otis took his place in books of precept and example. Imagine the scene: a small factory in Yonkers, making cheap iron bedsteads. The young Elisha Otis, master mechanic and inventor of a system for raising and lowering beds, contemplates the arid prospect of his future. Then in comes Mr. Newhouse from Hudson Street, New York, to ask if Mr. Otis could adapt his safety elevator to the problem of shifting merchandise. Could he, in fact, build him two elevators for hauling goods rather than lifting bedsteads. Two years later there were 27 Otis elevators in service in New York, and the foundations had been laid for enduring fame and fortune. Otis demonstrated his safety elevator in characteristically dramatic fashion at the New York Crystal Palace exhibition in 1853. He had himself hoisted up on the elevator platform, in full view of alarmed spectators and delighted journalists, and promptly cut the suspension cord. Nothing happened; the rack and pinion safety lock ensured that he was *All safe, Gentlemen!* The first passenger elevator was installed in E. V. Haughwout and Co.'s store on Broadway in 1857; it was the talk, and envy, of the town, attracting thousands of visitors.
Otis Collection.

BROADWAY: THE STORE OF MESSRS. E. V. HAUGHWOUT AND CO.

mid-rise buildings (up to 24 stories), and Otis Gearless for high-rise buildings. Otis had been most successful in selling elevators for projects that were large, that required customized elevators (atrium elevators, for example), or that required state-of-the-art elevator technology. Otis Elevator's large, highly regarded service organization often led customers to prefer an Otis elevator over another manufacturer's product.

In the late 1970s, microprocessor technology transformed the design of elevators, replacing the outdated mechanical elevator control systems. Otis Elevator's Elevonic 401, with three microcomputer-based control units, was one of the most advanced elevator systems at this time.[3] Exhibit 2 gives a description of the Elevonic 401. Microcomputer technology enabled Otis Elevator North American Operations (NAO) to increase its market share significantly between 1980 and 1984. Management believed that microcomputer technology would also help shape the future of the service business.

Elevator Industry Overview

By 1985, new equipment sales and service of elevators in North America represented approximately $1 billion and $2 billion markets, respectively. The industry was very competitive, with Otis, Westinghouse, Dover, Montgomery, Schindler, U.S. Elevator, and Fujitec the major manufacturers. Otis, however, was the leader in both sales and service. Because elevator sales were directly correlated to the building cycle, they were cyclical, but the elevator service market was very stable. Elevator manufacturers often accepted a low margin on the sale of an elevator in order to obtain the service contract since service accounted for a significantly higher portion of profits.

---

[3]*Elevonic* is a registered trademark of Otis Elevator.

The service market attracted many participants because of its steady demand and high profitability. Consequently, thousands of elevator service companies existed, including both elevator manufacturers and many small companies devoted exclusively to elevator service. These companies could service elevators from almost any manufacturer since all elevators made prior to the introduction of microprocessor-based elevator control systems used similar electromechanical technology.

For a small building project, the elevator manufacturer was selected by the contractor, architect, or building owner. Larger projects often involved all three parties in the decision-making process. They selected a manufacturer on the basis of ability to satisfy the elevator performance specifications and architectural requirements, price, and reputation.

An elevator service company was selected on the basis of responsiveness, quality, and price. An elevator manufacturer was typically awarded 60 percent to 80 percent of the service contracts for its newly installed elevators. As a building aged and competition for tenants increased, the cost of service often became the major consideration, and the lowest bidder received the service contract. Since servicing elevators with microprocessor-based control systems often required the use of proprietary maintenance devices, the manufacturer was more likely to keep these service contracts. Many elevator manufacturers offered discounts for long-term service contracts in an effort to attract and maintain service customers.

North American Operations Overview

North American Operations, with 8,000 employees at the end of 1985, was the second-largest division of Otis Elevator. The scope of its business necessitated a large, geographically dispersed field organization. Exhibit 3 shows the NAO organization chart.

EXHIBIT 2   Description of Elevonic 401

System Hardware

The advent of microprocessor technology has enabled Otis to reassign elevator control strategies from hardware to microcomputer software.

Elevonic 401 control hardware is an integrated network of three microcomputer-based control units; a

Group Controller (in the machine room) to make dispatching decisions and call assignments; a

Car Controller (one per car in the machine room) to govern the operation and motion of the car; and a

Cab Controller (mounted behind the car operating panel) to interface with control hardware on the car, communicate cab data (e.g. passenger load, car calls) with the car controller, and control car-operating panel speech synthesis, visual display functions and coded secure entry.

Transducers, the sensors of the system, together with the car controller, form the closed loop structure that provides feedback that enables corrections to be made within milliseconds.

The group and car controllers employ the latest microprocessor technology. They differ in the number of cards in their card files and in the resident software. Although control hardware is standard for all Otis high-rise duties, and designed to suit practically all building specifications, custom software is added to personalize the controllers for each building's specific requirements.

The cab controller serves as a bi-directional information link between the cab mounted devices (car call buttons, load weighing transduc-

ers, speech synthesizer, secure entry modules) and the car controller. Multiplexing (transmitting hundreds of signals back and forth over a single pair of wires) between controllers significantly reduces the number of wires required for communication between controllers and peripheral devices. For example, while previous systems required an average of three traveling cables, the new Elevonic 401 system utilizes just one.

System hardware determines the quantity and quality of input received by the control system, permitting control decisions and corrective actions to be made and implemented within milliseconds. Digital measurement yields such benefits as the precise control knowledge of car velocity, acceleration, and position.

Transducer feedback, obtained as digital numbers, is compared by the controller with the prescribed specifications. The difference, or error, is driven toward zero to enforce the specified flight pattern programmed in the computer.

The hardware components of the new Elevonic 401 system permit placing total operating authority under software control. Minimum physical or mechanical adjustments are required to maintain control. Changes in strategy and performance requirements are implemented in the software. The result is more precise, more efficient control, with the capacity to control a greater number of functions with much greater flexibility—making instantaneous decisions based on real time conditions.

Branch offices and smaller field offices reported to district offices, which bore profit and loss responsibility. (Hereafter, district, branch, and smaller field offices will be referred to as "field" offices.) Field offices handled both sales and service and ranged in size from one or two people in outlying areas to as many as 100 people in large metropolitan areas. NAO's customer base was equally diverse; Otis installed elevators in buildings ranging from 2 stories to the 110-story World Trade Center in New York City.

EXHIBIT 3 NAO Organization Chart

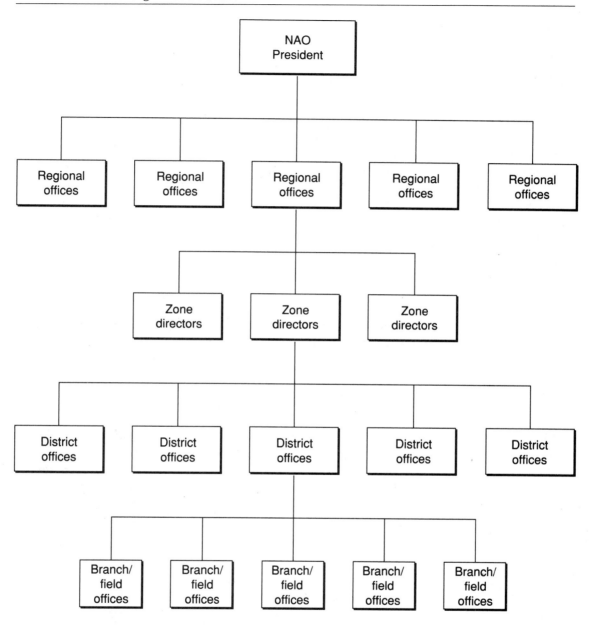

Regional offices are geographically dispersed throughout North America.

Zone directors have three to five district managers reporting to them.

District managers have two to six branch/field offices reporting to them.

NAO Information Services

NAO installed its first computer, an IBM 1401, in 1965 to automate maintenance billing. From 1965 until 1978, the computer was used for production control and accounting. From 1978 to 1981, on-line capabilities expanded its uses to include data entry and inquiry for inventory control and accounting.

In 1981, Otis implemented a company-wide cost-reduction drive to improve NAO's profitability. Bob Smith, then president of NAO, asked John Miller to suspend all efforts in new systems development until a clear course of applications could be charted. Smith was concerned that the company was spending its applications development resources to automate old manual procedures rather than to establish new, helpful systems. Sixty percent of the programmers were laid off, no hardware upgrades were allowed, and no new applications were implemented. The work load was cut back as much as possible since the system in place (an IBM 370/158) was often running at 100 percent.

The year 1982 was one of transition for NAO's information services area. With the cost-reduction program completed, management began to assess the ability of information services to improve the quality of its maintenance service.

In late 1981, NAO had begun to investigate the feasibility of using information technology to establish a centralized customer service department (on either a regional or a divisionwide basis) to accept customer requests for elevator maintenance during nonworking hours, that is, non-prime-time callbacks. (A callback is a customer request for elevator maintenance.) Otis and other elevator service companies were then using commercial answering services for non-prime-time callbacks. Otis supplied the answering service with a duty roster from which it selected a service mechanic to dispatch to the customer. In small cities, the same answering service was commonly used by several elevator service companies. During prime time (regular working hours), the customer called the local NAO field office, where an Otis employee accepted the call and dispatched the appropriate service mechanic.

Customers assess the quality of an elevator company's service offerings mainly by its responsiveness to callbacks. The callback response time is the time it takes a service mechanic to arrive on site after the customer reaches Otis Elevator (or its answering service). Although Otis received assurances from the local answering services that it would be promptly notified of a customer callback, the quality of the answering services varied greatly. In a videotape that described the need for the centralized customer service department, Bob Smith stated, "A commercial answering service does not have the same interest that we have to get service to the customer as fast as possible."

By August 1982, a centralized customer service system had been successfully piloted in a major eastern market, and Otis management decided to create a North American customer service center to dispatch service mechanics, in response to callbacks, 24 hours a day. A project team composed of individuals from many functional areas, including information services, was selected to implement this concept, which was called OTISLINE.

An IBM 3083 was installed in early 1983 to replace the IBM 370/158, and by 1985 extensive peripheral equipment, including state-of-the-art direct-access storage devices, tape drives, and telecommunications equipment, had been installed. These additional resources were acquired to support the OTISLINE customer service center. The 1985 NAO information services budget was more than twice as large as the 1982 budget.

Most of the 2,300 service mechanics employed by NAO in 1985 had assigned routes and were responsible both for callbacks and for preventive maintenance for specific elevator customers. NAO calculated that reducing callbacks for each installed elevator by one a year would save Otis $5 million annually. Out-of-service elevators not only irritated customers and handicapped their businesses but also affected their opinion of the quality of an Otis elevator.

OTISLINE Overview

Brad Robertson, director of service operations, was the leader of the OTISLINE development team and was responsible for the implementation and management of the OTISLINE customer service center. During the development of OTISLINE, Robertson reported to the vice president of finance; after an August 1985 reorganization, he reported to the vice president of marketing.

In describing OTISLINE, Robertson stated:

> OTISLINE improved the visibility of our service business and helped management and local office personnel to provide quality service to our customers more effectively. Our responsiveness to customer callback requests has been greatly enhanced. OTISLINE's reporting functions provided district, regional, and NAO headquarters management with a significant amount of information on the quality of service rendered to our customers. Prior to OTISLINE, management became aware of many service problems only if there was a customer complaint. OTISLINE has allowed us to produce "excess" callback reports for various levels of management. For example, elevators receiving three or more callbacks in a month are reported to the district manager; those receiving eight or more in 90 days are reported to the regional vice president. Critical situations are reported to the president.
>
> The excess callback reports highlight problem installations and have enhanced our abil-

ity to quickly diagnose problems that may be due to a specific component malfunction. With this information, local office management (or engineering management if the problem is with a component malfunction) can focus resources on key problem areas.

The success of OTISLINE is attributable to top management support of the project, which fostered cooperation among functional areas and provided the resources and motivation required to "make it happen."

OTISLINE not only improved the quality of NAO's customer service; it also changed the way NAO does business. The OTISLINE system affected almost all of NAO's business functions, including information services, customer service, service mechanic dispatching and control, and service marketing and engineering. In addition, its infrastructure has been used to support applications that enhance the productivity of elevator sales representatives and service mechanics. In the future, OTISLINE may interface directly with installed elevators by means of remote diagnostic technology.

Following is a description of OTISLINE's impact on specific business activities.

Information Services

The OTISLINE application is a part of NAO's Service Management System (SMS), an integrated database management system (Exhibit 4). Prior to OTISLINE, the SMS database contained the customer master file (customer name, building location, contract information) and other information that was used to monitor and control the service business, such as route information and service price estimating data. With OTISLINE, the SMS was expanded to include *all* maintenance activity for elevators under a service contract. Some applications, such as service price estimating, were improved, and new applications such as billing will be added. The SMS database is accessed and updated by an

EXHIBIT 4   NAO Service Management System

OTISLINE dispatcher through a display attached to the IBM 3083 host computer. Designed in the late 1970s, the SMS database significantly shortened the time required to develop OTISLINE. According to Tim Clark, manager of systems development, the development of the OTISLINE application would have taken four to five years if the SMS database had not already been in place.

The OTISLINE application was designed to enable the OTISLINE dispatcher to respond to a customer in less than a second by giving the dispatcher a local display and by engineering short database paths to the necessary information. Subsecond response time was an important design element because experience had shown that when more than 2 percent of transactions had longer than a five-second response time, the time taken to handle customer service requests was unacceptable.

Because of the strategic nature of the OTISLINE application, a large portion of the information services budget was earmarked for its support. The data center operations budget was also increased significantly to support OTISLINE's stringent response-time and performance requirements. New methodologies of systems development are being introduced as a direct result of OTISLINE. By the end of 1985, 37 local terminals had been installed at the OTISLINE Service Center; future plans called for the installation of 150 personal computers in the field offices with OTISLINE inquiry capability.

Customer Service

The OTISLINE Service Center was staffed by highly skilled dispatchers. About half of them had college degrees, and many spoke two languages. New hires received from four to six weeks of in-house training, covering

- The OTISLINE software (the dispatching system).
- The IBM display.
- Operation of the phone system.
- Appropriate telephone salutations and courtesies.
- Listening and customer satisfaction skills.
- Overview of Otis Elevator organization structure.
- Elevator terminology and possible system problems.

The objective of the training was to ensure the dispatcher's ability to handle customer calls in an efficient and effective manner. The company held periodic seminars to update the dispatchers on system changes, to review sample dialogues for situations that were likely to be encountered (for example, an irritated customer or a trapped-in-an-elevator scenario), and to discuss the criteria used to assess dispatcher performance.

OTISLINE dispatchers were trained to be courteous, sensitive, and efficient and to speak clearly. They were taught to update the database with information obtained during a call, thus allowing quicker identification of both the building and the elevator during subsequent calls from the same customer. Periodically, a supervisor or manager listened in as a dispatcher handled a call and then completed a dispatcher evaluation form and reviewed it with the dispatcher.

Customers accessed OTISLINE by calling a toll-free number connecting them to the North American customer service center. Incoming calls were distributed either to the next available dispatcher or to a specific dispatcher (calls from a French-speaking province in Canada, for example, would be routed to a French-speaking dispatcher). Calls coming in on designated lines were moved automatically to the head of the queue.

The telephone system produced a variety of statistics. Reports showed the amount of time each dispatcher was available to accept calls during the shift, thus enabling Otis to measure dispatcher performance against department standards and averages. The system also produced statistics on how long customers had to wait for an available dispatcher. This information helped management determine when to employ additional staff in order to maintain a high level of responsiveness.

The OTISLINE application display screens were designed to lead the dispatcher and the customer quickly through a series of questions to identify the building and elevator needing service. When a customer call was received, the OTISLINE dispatcher filled in the display screen. OTISLINE could recognize a building and elevator in four different ways: (1) the building identification number; (2) the telephone number; (3) the building name, city, and state; or (4) the building address, city, and state. A "no hit" situation was encountered if the building and elevator needing service could not be identified using one of these criteria. The dispatcher then was expected to assure the customer that a service mechanic would be dispatched, end the call, and use alternate procedures to find the information on the building and elevator. If a "hit," or identification, was made, the dispatcher verified the building address and elevator identification number, ended the call, and logged the service request. Another dispatcher then paged the appropriate mechanic.

The OTISLINE Service Center was organized to promote dispatcher efficiency. During a shift, each dispatcher was usually assigned one function: to accept calls, to page service mechanics, or to handle new equipment sales (described later). Thus one callback request often involved four OTISLINE dispatchers: one to log the service request, one to page the service mechanic, one to receive the call from the service mechanic, and one to log the situation resolution data from the service mechanic's "closing" call.

By the end of 1985, 11 of the 47 NAO districts were using OTISLINE for 24-hour dispatch of service mechanics. The service center received 4,300 calls on an average weekday. However, the center would be expected to handle 10,000 incoming calls per day as soon as the system was implemented for all of the districts. Customer calls accounted for one-third of the total calls, 75 percent of which were service requests. The majority of the calls were from service mechanics who had been paged or had just closed a callback.

Dispatching and Control of Service Mechanics

Prior to OTISLINE, each field office handled the dispatching of service mechanics during normal working hours and used answering services after hours and on weekends and holidays. Service mechanics were required to complete a written report for each callback. These reports provided the data for a callback and repair history log that the field office's service desk representative maintained. This log was used by the local office to support daily operations and by the engineering department to flag problems and establish preventive maintenance procedures. Since these logs were maintained manually, the preparation of summary reports was very time-consuming. Thus callback data were reported to district, region, or NAO headquarters only upon request.

With OTISLINE, instead of filing a written report for each callback, the service mechanics called OTISLINE, described the situation when they arrived at the building, and reported the steps taken to repair the elevator. The service mechanics carried a pocket notebook in which they recorded information on each service call. The notebook also listed the questions they would need to answer for the OTISLINE dispatcher when completing the callback report.

One measure of performance in field offices was the number of callbacks received. Prior to OTISLINE, the accuracy and consistency of callback reports varied from office to office. Identifying chronically malfunctioning components and other recurring problems was difficult because detailed information was not yet stored in a central database.

With OTISLINE, the quality and timeliness of information available to district, region, and NAO management increased significantly. All customers (including large installations with on-site service mechanics) now called OTISLINE to request service. The OTISLINE dispatcher then paged the service mechanic to request service on a particular elevator. All data about service calls were stored in a central computer (see Exhibit 5), so the local offices no longer needed to keep manual elevator maintenance history logs.

Initially, some field office managers were skeptical of the OTISLINE concept. They felt that the system would decrease their

---

EXHIBIT 5 Callback Data Stored Online

Elevator identification

Date/time service requested

Requestor of service

Time service mechanic notified

Time service mechanic arrived on site

Condition of elevator on arrival

Time elevator back in service

Repair action taken

Service mechanic responding to request

Maintenance supervisor

Cause of malfunction or problem

Reprinted with permission of Otis Elevator.

control over the dispatching of service mechanics for callbacks and that therefore they would not know the location of their service mechanics throughout the day. OTISLINE is being improved to address these concerns. Personal computers with OTISLINE inquiry capability will be installed in field offices to enable local management to track callback activity in their territories.

Bob Smith noted that although centralizing service mechanic dispatching seemed contrary to NAO's decentralized organization, the quality and reliability of Otis products provided Otis's edge over its competitors. With OTISLINE, service and engineering managers had the information they needed to continue to boost the quality and reliability of Otis products.

Marketing—New Equipment Sales

The company also used OTISLINE to support elevator sales. New equipment sales representatives could access the New Equipment Sales (NES) application by calling OTISLINE. NES was an integrated database management system designed to automate the production of status reports on elevator sales prospects. It had three primary components: negotiation, estimation, and disposition.

Negotiation allowed the new equipment sales representatives to organize data about new equipment projects and to communicate the status of those projects to the appropriate managers.

Estimation provided cost estimates and configurations for certain new products that could be used by the new equipment sales representative and local office to determine the elevator sales price.

Disposition provided the mechanism to record the outcome of a negotiation as a customer decision to purchase an elevator from Otis, as a competitive loss, or as an abandoned effort.

NES made data about competitive losses and performance of new equipment sales representatives easily accessible to management. In the future, when a negotiation becomes a sale, the NES information will be used to establish a record in SMS.

Marketing—Service

A brochure published in 1984 to describe OTISLINE to the NAO service mechanics listed six components of Otis Elevator's philosophy of service: responsiveness, reliability, innovation, communication, teamwork, and customer satisfaction. OTISLINE addressed all of these elements.

Responsiveness. OTISLINE dramatically improved NAO's responsiveness to customer maintenance requests. The system kept track of the status of the response to customers' calls. If the service mechanic assigned to a route was unable to take a call, either an alternate service mechanic or the service supervisor was paged. Response time was especially critical for certain customers such as hospitals and buildings with only one elevator. Backed by OTISLINE, the company began to offer a guaranteed response time to these customers. The system also produced reports of response-time statistics that could be reviewed with customers.

Reliability. OTISLINE dispatchers updated the SMS to maintain data on actions that had been necessary to repair out-of-service elevators. This data could be used by management to allocate resources to locations with recurring problems and by engineering to spot trends that indicated elevator design problems.

Innovation. As the leader in the industry, Otis was expected to deliver more than its competitors. NAO was the first to offer a professionally staffed customer service center.

Communication. OTISLINE improved communication between Otis customers and the service and sales departments. It also provided a more effective way for service and sales departments to submit reports to management.

Teamwork. The OTISLINE dispatcher was one of many members of the team concerned with providing a high level of service to Otis customers.

Customer Satisfaction. Customer satisfaction, as measured by a reduction in both the volume of complaints and service calls, improved as a result of the implementation of OTISLINE. The United Technologies 1985 *Annual Report* noted that Otis strengthened its number one share of the service market in North America. OTISLINE contributed to NAO's ability to improve service quality and to compete successfully with lower-priced independent service companies.

Future Applications

Bob Smith felt sure that information technology could be used in many ways to further enhance Otis Elevator's marketing of service.

Remote Elevator Monitoring (REM). Otis Elevator had been testing REM, an application by which a microprocessor-based elevator could monitor its control system and log performance statistics directly onto a distant computer. In the pilot installations, elevators communicated problems to a personal computer at NAO headquarters. The personal computer then analyzed the problems and produced trouble reports used to dispatch service mechanics before the elevator went out of service.

Further development of REM would enable an elevator to communicate with a central computer that would determine the cause of the problems, transmit a message to the OTISLINE system, and dispatch a service mechanic.

The great advantage of REM is its ability to identify problems before an elevator is out of service. The service mechanics could adjust running elevators to keep them operating at maximum performance levels, and NAO could handle specific problems before customers were even aware of them.

In-Car Phones. The most sensitive kind of callback occurred when passengers were trapped in an elevator. Many Otis elevators were equipped with a telephone with which the passenger could automatically reach the OTISLINE dispatcher to notify the service department of the situation. The OTISLINE phone system recognized calls coming in on these lines and moved such calls to the head of the queue. The OTISLINE dispatcher was then alerted via a message on the telephone display or an audible beep that an emergency call had been received. The dispatcher could then work with the passenger to identify the location of the elevator and dispatch a service mechanic immediately.

Replacement of Service Mechanic Pagers with Hand-Held Terminals. Field service mechanics were contacted using pagers. Eventually these pagers could be replaced with hand-held terminals through which the OTISLINE dispatcher could send a message directly to the service mechanic, thus eliminating the need for service mechanics to call in for messages. The service mechanic could also use the hand-held terminal to complete callback reports and to order parts for out-of-service elevators.

New Equipment Ordering. NES could be expanded to include files for new equipment orders. When the new equipment sales representative called in to report that a project had resulted in a sale, he or she could also place the order for the elevator. This information could be transmitted directly to the plant, thereby shortening the lead time for manufacturing the elevator. Moreover, by reducing the amount of time taken to notify the plant of an order, NES could improve management of the plant's raw material inventory.

Contract Management.   After Otis made a sale, its ability to monitor and abide by the customer's installation schedule was extremely important. Slippages in the installation schedule could be caused by building contractor delays, by technical problems encountered by the Otis superintendent at the construction site, or by elevator manufacturing delays. Both Otis and building management had to be aware of these problems. A personal computer could be installed at the construction site so the construction superintendent could document slippages in the schedule. This information could be communicated to the factory and to others involved in the installation and could be used to keep both Otis management and the building owner aware of the reasons for changes in the installation schedule.

Telemarketing of Service.   The SMS database contains information on all installed Otis elevators in North America. The OTISLINE facility could be used to contact those customers whose service contract was not with Otis. The OTISLINE dispatcher could find out when the current elevator maintenance contracts would expire and could produce a prospect list to be distributed monthly to the service sales representatives.

In a 1985 NAO management newsletter, Bob Smith stated:

> The real significance of OTISLINE is its ability to collapse both distance and time, resulting in faster responses to customer problems, better maintenance procedures, and, ultimately more reliable elevators. . . . This can translate into real competitive advantage. We're confident that it will, and we are investing accordingly.

Chapter 6

Information-Enabled Alliances

Information technology empowers companies to compete, interestingly enough, by allowing them new ways to cooperate. One way is through the information partnership facilitated by the sharing of data between organizations.

THE ALLEGIS EXAMPLE

This competition through cooperation can be illustrated by a notable failure. Allegis Corporation was the brainchild of United Airlines, which acquired Hertz Rent A Car and Westin Hotels in hopes of creating an integrated travel company with real synergies in the eyes of the end customer. The venture was quickly torpedoed by skepticism on Wall Street, where great fear was expressed that the firm was getting involved in businesses whose operations they did not fully understand. Nobody speaks of the Allegis Corporation today without using the word *fiasco*, as the company was forced to divest itself of its pieces at great loss. Yet in retrospect it is hard to imagine a more prescient effort to form a market coalition that exploits the power of information technology.

The Allegis idea seemed to offer something for everyone. From the United Airlines customers' point of view, by renting a Hertz car and staying a Westin hotel, they could earn "frequent flyer" miles on United. The participant divisions could benefit by sharing databases supported by powerful means to transmit, log, and retrieve information. Furthermore, the company could present itself to the customer as a single source of travel services, incentives, and support. Eventually, one could imagine Allegis customizing travel programs for a large number of regular customers.

Implications.   Allegis's hard lesson—and everybody else's excellent one—was that the partnerships engendered by information systems *need not be based on ownership.* Managers of companies in reciprocal industries can plan and coordinate common approaches to customers through relational databases without taking each other over. In retrospect, Wall Street quite rightly reckoned that although United's top managers could develop synergies in servicing customers, they were not likely to enjoy any operational advantages. Indeed the real and legitimate fear was that airline executives would not know how to manage these myriad businesses with specialized operating problems. The insurance industry, with many participants recovering from forays into the "financial supermarket," is learning this same lesson.

The real opportunity, it turns out, is in joining forces *without* merging, the way American Airlines has allied with Citibank. In this arrangement, air mileage credit in the airline's frequent flyer program is awarded to credit card users—one mile for every dollar spent on the card. American has thus increased the loyalty of its customers, and the credit card company has gained access to a new, highly credit-worthy customer base for cross-marketing. This partnership has been expanded to include MCI, a major long distance telephone company, which offers multiple airline frequent flyer miles for each dollar of long-distance billing. Citibank, the largest issuer of Visa and Master-Cards, recently initiated a partnership to steer its 14.6 million Visa card holders to MCI, a response to AT&T's entry into credit cards (the Universal card). American Airlines soon thereafter entered a partnership with Hilton Hotels and Budget Rent-A-Car to build a joint travel service with an investment/contribution from each partner. They have recently added Marriott Hotels and are discussing arrangements with others in the industry. Their next planned move is to provide convention services for cities.

BENEFITS OF INFORMATION PARTNERING

Through an information partnership, diverse companies can offer novel incentives and services or participate in joint marketing programs. They can take advantage of new channels of distribution and introduce operational efficiencies and revenue enhancements. Partnerships enhance opportunities for scale and cross-selling. They can make small companies look, feel, and act big as they reach for customers once beyond their grasp. They can also make big companies look small and close as they target and service custom markets. Information-enabled partnerships, in short, provide a new basis for differentiation. Many more of them will be appearing in the coming decade.

These new forms of market cooperation pass large volumes of electronic data precisely, instantaneously, and relatively cheaply. New computer speeds and cheaper mass storage devices mean that information can be archived, cross-correlated, and retrieved much faster and less expensively than before—and in ways that are customized for recipients. Additionally, the widespread emergence of fiber-optic networks has greatly improved cost-effective delivery of information to remote locations.

Additionally, managers whenever possible are anxious to lessen their financial and technical exposure. Partnerships allow them to share investments in hardware and software as well as the considerable expense of learning how to use both. The cost of developing certain configurations of software is particularly great, posing huge problems for small and mid-size companies that compete against large companies. Software investments may be denominated in hundreds of millions of dollars, which creates impenetrable entry barriers for smaller competitors—unless a number of them consolidate their purchasing power. (The authors have encountered more than one hundred system development projects in the past two years that cost over one hundred million dollars.)

Likewise, as discussed in detail elsewhere, the management cost of organizational learning in this rapidly changing technical environment is mushrooming. While there is no shortcut to learning, information partnerships provide a way to reduce risks in leading-edge technology investments by sharing expenses and exposure. End-customers should provide additional pressure to support this trend. Desktop clutter has led to a demand for simplification. Users want simple, user-friendly interfaces that will enable them to reach out to a variety of services both within and without the firm through a single device and with a minimum of confusing detail. This implies that users want companies to cooperate, at least, on data interface standards where possible and, in fact, they have brought pressure to bear in this regard. Users also continue to demand higher service levels, including faster response time, broader access to data files, and increasingly customized service. Partnerships provide scale and clout for helping companies to satisfy customers in this regard.

KINDS OF INFORMATION-ENABLED ALLIANCES

In response to these opportunities and pressures, four kinds of information partnerships have emerged: joint marketing partnerships, intra-industry partnerships, customer–supplier partnerships, and IT vendor–driven partnerships.

Joint Marketing Partnerships

Information technology offers companies an important new option: coordinate with rivals where there is an advantage in doing so, and specialize where it continues to make sense.

The effort by IBM and Sears to market Prodigy is an example of such an effort. At a cost of more than $500 million, these companies have assembled a package of more than 400 electronic data services—home banking, stock market quotations, restaurant reservations, and so on—to be delivered across a standard telephone network to millions of American homes. Individually, these services would be used so infrequently—and cost so much to get hooked into—that few customers would be likely to find any one of them practical. IBM and Sears have perceived that these services have considerable appeal when bundled together. By selling advertising space around the edge of the screen, the partners are able to deliver the product to a home for only $130 per year irrespective of usage.

In another setting, travel companies are making use of electronic linkages to establish combined marketing programs—common customer databases, joint purchasing incentives, and so on—so that airlines, hotels, car rental companies, and bank credit cards are all being combined into a single electronic marketing effort. Spearheading this are such information networks as American Airlines' SABRE, which reaches into thousands of travel agencies and firms. Today all major U.S. airlines are involved in one partnering agreement or another.

In the airline industry, the scale needed to develop and manage a reservation system for travel agencies and individual client firms is beyond the reach of the medium-sized airlines, most of which have become clients of (and hostages to) the reservation information systems of the bigger carriers. In Europe, two major coalitions have been created, the Amadeus Coalition and the Galileo Coalition; software for Amadeus is built around System One, the computer reservation system of Continental Airlines, and Galileo is built around United's software. Of course, there are only a limited number of airlines, and the credit card industry is extremely fragmented. Banks that held back in establishing partnerships with airlines found themselves frozen out once the early movers had made their deals. The painful fact is that the dynamic competitive environment punishes procrastination as much as it does strategic blunders. The first movers may have the capacity to build lasting barriers to entry that punish late entrants. More recently, marketing alliances have been formed among banks, grocery chains, and food companies.

In marketing partnerships, participant companies gain access both to new customers and territories and to economies of scale through cost-sharing. Sharing allows the provider of the data channel to sell excess capacity in the channel, to ensure that the company's image and market position will not be compromised, and to reach customers once thought too expensive to reach. From the customer's perspective, life is simplified when several needed products arrive through a single channel.

The path to these joint marketing programs may be forged with either offensive or defensive objectives in mind. A market leader—as for example, American Airlines—may seize the initiative and establish an imperative for participation, all the while controlling the partnership structure. On the other hand, Johnson & Johnson's development of the COACT system was primarily in response to its concerns that previous initiatives by American Hospital Supply were hurting its sales—clearly a defensive action. Another example of defensive maneuvering is that of Texas Air. A significant motivation for its acquisition of Eastern Airlines was to obtain their reservation system channel as a weapon to partially negate the impact of United and American in the travel agencies, which was seen as unfavorably impacting Texas Air's market share and ability to grow.

Intra-Industry Partnerships

The most important and potentially difficult to manage information partnerships evolve not among companies offering complementary services, but among small or mid-sized competitors who see an opportunity or need to pool resources in order to stay in the game competitively. The ATM banking networks constitute an industry that provides nationwide access to previously *regional* products.

A particularly interesting case is the alliance of 18 mid-sized paper companies that has developed a global electronic information system to link them with hundreds of key customers and international sales offices. Costing $50 million to develop, it was targeted at providing a speed and quality of response that would have been technically and financially unattainable by any of the individual participants acting in their own behalf. With combined sales of nearly $4 billion, these companies made this investment because they could see that to compete effectively in their service-oriented business they must provide on-line, global data interchange with key customers on order-entry inventory-status product specifications. The alternative was to be driven from key markets by large competitors providing these services. Thus the partnership was driven by the fear of losing. They wanted to provide customers a virtually instantaneous means of placing status inquiries and orders, in contrast with the previous industry norm of 12-day processing cycles. They were all genuinely uneasy about joining the proprietary information networks of their big, global competitors, because they were aware of the harsh penalties and aggressive charging practices in some other industries.

In reaction to the high charges exacted by the airlines' systems, a group of hotels has been actively examining ways to establish their own hotel reservation system. They believe that as a group they might bring enough "critical mass" to the market that they will be able to sharply reduce charges per reservation. This in turn has attracted the interest of a major airline.

Another coalition among competitors is the Insurance Value-Added Network Services (IVANS), which links hundreds of insurance companies' home offices and thousands of independent agents. IVANS permits independent agents across the United States access to distant property and casualty insurance companies for policy issuance, price quotation, and other policy management services. It was initiated and created by the industry trade association ACORD.

These insurance companies were all concerned that several larger companies had invested in electronic channels of their own, giving them the potential to monopolize the business of the independent agents. The IVANS interface presents independent agents with a roster of smaller insurance companies and a level playing field—which benefits the agent, of course, who is concerned about maintaining the competitive environment ensured by multiple providers.

Understandably enough, ACORD's position as a trade organization allows it to be perceived as the fairest, and hence most effective, broker of a collaborative system among businesses. In a similar vein, MEMA/Transnet, which connects hundreds of manufacturers and thousands of retailers in the auto parts industry, resulted from actions by the Motor and Equipment Manufacturers Association (MEMA).

Sometimes, however, suppliers and customers are so fragmented that neither side has the vision or resources to put together any kind of system. In these settings a third party may be positioned to perform this function. The American Gem Market System is an example of this. Put together by a third party independently financed for this purpose, American Gem Market System linked dozens of gem suppliers with hundreds of jewelry stores, in effect replacing what had been a complex interpersonal network. Gems were now traded between partners who had no personal knowledge of each other but who trusted the integrity and reliability of the network provider. Unfortunately, the network provider was unable to attract enough customers and it ultimately failed.

Some intra-industry partnerships are so important to a country or other political body that they are initiated and led by government. An example is the TradeNet system of Singapore, which links the management and operations activities of the world's largest port. The Singapore government has spent an amount approaching $50 million to develop this system for linking trade agents—freight forwarders, shipping companies, banks, and insurance companies—with relevant government agencies—customs officials, immigration officials, and others. Clearing the port used to take a vessel two to four days; now it takes as little as ten minutes. It is hoped that this dramatic reduction in the time ships remain in port will help ensure that Singapore remains a port of choice in Southeast Asia, where the competition among ports is growing.

Customer–Supplier Partnerships

Some information partnerships are built on data networks set up by suppliers to service customers. A good illustration of this noted earlier is the interorganizational system of Baxter Healthcare (formerly American Hospital Supply), a medical equipment and healthcare supplier. Today Baxter Healthcare offers its customers a wide variety of medical supplies manufactured by Baxter and its competitors as well as many other products, including office supplies.

The system has created a platform, a single interface, for buyers to reach their many suppliers and for the participating suppliers to reach new customers at dramatically lower costs. From the viewpoint of Baxter, this system is evolving into a major new revenue stream through its offering of a package of multivendor services. Since its introduction, the system has been one of dynamic reconfiguration and redevelopment—and to some extent, so have the participating companies. Equally important by developing this platform, it allowed Baxter to forestall another company developing their own proprietary platform that could put Baxter at significant disadvantage.

Another example involves a retail grocery chain that has renegotiated its relationship with a supplier of disposable diapers, one of its very profitable, high-turnover items. Under the new partnership agreement, when a shipment of diapers leaves the retailer's warehouse, notice is sent to the manufacturer. No order is transmitted, no delivery schedule is requested. The manufacturer is bound by a performance contract to keep the warehouse sufficiently stocked, and this system provides it the information it needs to ensure this. This partnership is intended to reduce inventories in the retailer's warehouse and to facilitate full-scale coordination and mutual cost reduction, and it appears to be effective. Paperwork has been significantly reduced on both sides (orders, quotes, complicated billing, and so on), production schedules are now more responsive, and each company has trimmed its operations staff.

IT Vendor–Driven Partnerships

On the one hand, these partnerships allow a technology vendor to bring its technology to a new market and, on the other hand, they provide a platform for industry participants to offer novel, technologically sophisticated customer services. General Electric Information Services and Automatic Data Processing are examples of firms that have successfully provided such data interchange platforms. These information companies can become the strategic linchpin for an organization that wishes to pioneer such services.

A good example of this is ESAB, a large European welding-supplies and equipment company that tripled in size between 1973 and 1987 —a period when sales fell off by half in the industry as a whole. A key to the company's growth was an alliance with a large independent network vendor. It used that third party's information services to facilitate acquiring and rationalizing failing companies throughout Europe: closing their plants and moving production of what had been local brands to a central plant in Sweden, while providing the customers an on-line order-entry service. ESAB did not have the IT development resources in-house to build such a Europe-wide telecommunications system.

From the customers' point of view, the old companies' local offices still provided goods and services. In fact, the information system governed the company's production schedule, manufacturing, and shipping so that customers received products, usually overnight, without realizing they were no longer dealing with a local manufacturer. This strategy enabled costs to be slashed dramatically. ESAB has, in effect, replaced inventory and plants with information, using a technology that would have been extremely costly to develop from scratch.

In another type of partnership an information vendor forms a research alliance with a major customer. A common form of this is the joint establishment of a "beta site"—where a manufacturer tests a new technology with selected clients in order to both debug it and learn the extent of its uses. Such coalitions provide advantages to both parties. The vendors gain valuable insight into the practical field problems associated with their technology. Their ability to resolve their customers' problems, especially those of prestige accounts, gives vendors' sales forces highly visible references for further promotion. The customer learns and participates in a new technology that may otherwise be beyond its skill and financial resources and gets a head start in introducing it to appropriate markets.

LAYING THE FOUNDATION FOR A SUCCESSFUL PARTNERSHIP

At its core, partnership is strategy. As a manager starts forward, questions must continually be asked: What lines of business should I provide exclusively, and where should I move to leverage my activities through partnering? What are the appropriate adjunct services that I can use to drive my products to new markets? Where can I profitably offer joint purchasing incentives without confusing or eroding my existing customer base?

Like most activities in the practical world, partnerships are not a sure bet. They can fail because of overly optimistic assessments of the benefits accruing to the several parties or because of inadequate attention to the difficult challenges of administering the relationship. While no single formula will ensure successful partnerships, our research has identified some characteristics of successful partnerships.

Shared Vision at the Top. It may seem a cliché by now, but there are really no substitutes for champions in senior management. If a partnership is to overcome the inevitable divergence of interest among companies, top executives must share both viscerally and intellectually an understanding of the specific benefits of collaboration—cost reductions, new customers, cross-selling. Because of its potential impact, partnering is a strategic matter that needs the stubborn vision of the corporate strategists. For example, the airlines and credit card accord emerged only because their CEOs hammered out details in face-to-face discussions. Neither side was looking for a quick killing; both sought a long-term, mutually profitable relationship.

Reciprocal Skills in Information Technology. Competence in such areas as telecommunications, database design, and programming must be reasonably sophisticated in all partners, and very sophisticated in the partner that is leading the development of the information platform. Minimally, all participant companies must be able to manage telecommunications networks, have high standards of internal quality control (at least with respect to data handling), and be accustomed to working with very large databases. Many companies that have tried to initiate electronic data-interchange agreements have been shocked to find that their potential partners were unable to assimilate even modest data technologies and applications.

Concrete Plans for an Early Success. Partnerships grow from strength to strength. It is important to plan the introduction of the system so that people across participating companies can experience at least limited positive results at the start. Early successes, perhaps at pilot installations in key regions, create a sense of accomplishment and commitment.

Usually, partners must expend considerable effort in testing their hardware and software to ensure that their general direction is technically feasible. Most specifically, they should not settle for the lowest common technical denominator between the organizations. Rather, the more competent side must assist in helping to upgrade the technical or business environment of its partner.

Persistence in the Development of Usable Information. Mere ownership of a database—say, of a company's current customers—is no guarantee that information is organized in a form that can pass beyond corporate boundaries to partners. In fact, often the most expensive and time-consuming prelude to partnership is organization of data so that it can be usefully and cost-effectively transmitted.

The information must be packaged in ways that make it immediately useful to others without compromising the confidentiality of the company's secrets. In reality, information must be packaged for all partners *by* all partners. This requires the joint design of data definitions, formats, relationships, and search patterns.

Coordination on Business Procedures. Partnering involves a great deal more than the mere sharing of data. For companies to share data effectively involves a considerable degree of procedural integration across the company lines. A joint team is needed for developing the initial system, and an ongoing task force is needed for guiding its evolution. The partners must involve themselves in such mundane tasks as defining common procedures and common standards of systems development and maintenance. They must develop common codes for products, customers, and data communications as well as articulated procedures for surfacing conflicts, addressing perceived injustices, and rethinking the terms of the partnership when it becomes necessary.

For example, one partnership we have tracked was recently on the verge of collapse because the partner receiving data had not brought its business systems into line with the other partner's systems. For the partnership system to operate, the receiving firm had to first print out all incoming documents and then manually recode and rekey the information to make it compatible with its database architecture.

Appropriate Business Architecture. Partnering companies must establish structures and guidelines that ensure fairness and profit on both sides. This involves agreeing on rules that will help to assure equal treatment under the system. It also includes addressing possible asymmetries in the partners' underlying interests. That is, the deal should be structured so that partners are not required to contribute more than they can afford and so that they will profit from the system roughly in proportion to what they have contributed.

The sources of potential problems in this area are multitudinous. For example, in the airline industry, the issue of "screen bias"—the listing of competing airlines' flights below those of the lead partner—has been as explosive as exorbitant charging. Additionally, some airlines have contended that American and United have examined their competing partners' booking data to gain insight into competitive market positioning while denying their "partners" access to this data. American and United have denied the charge.

In another setting a small, start-up book distribution company approached a major retailer with the idea of using the retailer's sales data to identify customers' potential interests in books. This would allow the book distributor to promote books about gardening to recent purchasers of gardening tools, for example. As the discussions evolved, however, examination of the retailer's sales data revealed that the two companies would have had to integrate 11 different databases in order to accomplish the joint venture, a task too expensive and risky for the undercapitalized book distributor.

SUMMARY

In the past, the focus of IT thinking and research was on applications for the individual company's management of its information. This led to intense discussion of the chief information officer's role in deployment of IT resources inside the company and the structure and nature of appropriate planning and control systems. More recently, extensive work has been done to develop better understanding of the technical and administrative issues involved in preparing and managing ongoing electronic interorganizational system (IOS) links between a company and its customers and suppliers.

Today, however, the opportunities are broader, and senior managers are discussing the establishment of strategic information partnerships with other companies and in fact implementing them within their industry and without. In tomorrow's business environment, many more companies will find it necessary to analyze and develop these collaborative IT relationships.

Questions for the General Manager

In conclusion, we offer four questions for the general manager:

1.   Is your company vulnerable to new information partnering, and are there ways to forge alliances of your own to preempt them? In reality, alliances produce many more losers than winners, since in many settings early movers freeze others out of the game or build economies of scale that are hard to replicate. Timing is crucial. If you start too early, you and your partners may get into technical trouble or face a market that does not know it wants your product. (The field is filled with examples of this.) If you start too late, the window of opportunity will close, and real exposure will exist for competitors to damage you.

2. Does your business strategy realistically assess the implications of the transfer of power and authority to partners in any prospective electronic partnering arrangements? False steps can be extraordinarily expensive and time-consuming to correct.

3. Are your potential partners financially viable, and do they represent the right collection of players for potential synergy? In selecting these partners, have you analyzed the set of future options that you may be foreclosing? Today's short-term opportunity is often tomorrow's strategic liability.

4. Is the technical infrastructure you have in place the right one to effect and manage the kinds of strategic alliances you are considering? Are you overreaching your skills or contemplating an approach that does not use your most accessible technical capabilities?

Case 6–1

SINGAPORE TRADENET: A TALE OF ONE CITY

As the sun rose over the island of Borneo, the container ship *Kobayashi Maru* rounded the southern tip of Singapore Island from the South China Sea, bound for the Port of Singapore near the heart of the city. The captain knew the crew would be disappointed by their short stay in port that would prevent many from taking shore leave in town. In spite of the extensive off-loading and on-loading planned at the container terminal, the *Kobayashi Maru* would be putting to sea by nightfall. Singapore's state-of-the-art shipping facilities could turn an average-sized container ship around in under 10 hours, as opposed to 20 hours or more for most ports. A major factor in this was the new TradeNet system. Early this morning the captain had sent his ship's cargo manifests in electronic form to the freight forwarders in Singapore. Within two hours, using TradeNet, the freight forwarders had already obtained import permits, cleared customs, and paid duties for all cargo going ashore, and had received export permits for the ship's outbound cargo. Together with the other systems in the Singapore port, the days of the long layover in Singapore City were over. Shipping there was now strictly business.

Trade in Singapore

Singapore is a city state of 2.6 million people occupying a 625-square-kilometer island at the southern tip of the Malaysian Peninsula. The country is prosperous, having sustained remarkable economic growth during the past 20 years. GNP in 1989 was US$23.84 billion, and per capita GNP was US$9,000. With a literacy rate of over 87 percent and a life expectancy of 74 years, Singapore is on the verge of moving into the club of developed nations. The government has adopted a public position that the country will be recognized as a developed nation by the year 2000.

Singapore's location, between the Pacific and Indian oceans, has made it a key strategic port for any interested in trade in and around Asia (see Exhibit 1). Its position at the tip of the Malaysian peninsula, at the bend in the long sea trade route between the Indian Ocean and South China Sea, has been the crucial factor in Singapore's development since its founding in 1819, and is a major source of the country's remarkable economic growth since becoming an independent republic in 1966.

As of 1989 Singapore had the largest port in the world in gross tonnage, and in bunkering activity (transshipment of oil and oil products). It was the second-largest port in container handling, behind only Hong Kong. Singapore was significantly ahead of Rotterdam, the third-largest port. Singapore had also built the region's busiest airport, and in 1989 began expanding the airport with new passenger and cargo facilities to be ready in 1991. Trade had grown to be a highly signif-

This case was prepared by Marvin Bower Fellow John King and Professor Benn Konsynski to be used as a basis for class discussion rather than to illustrate either effective or ineffective handling of an administrative situation.

EXHIBIT 1   South East Asia

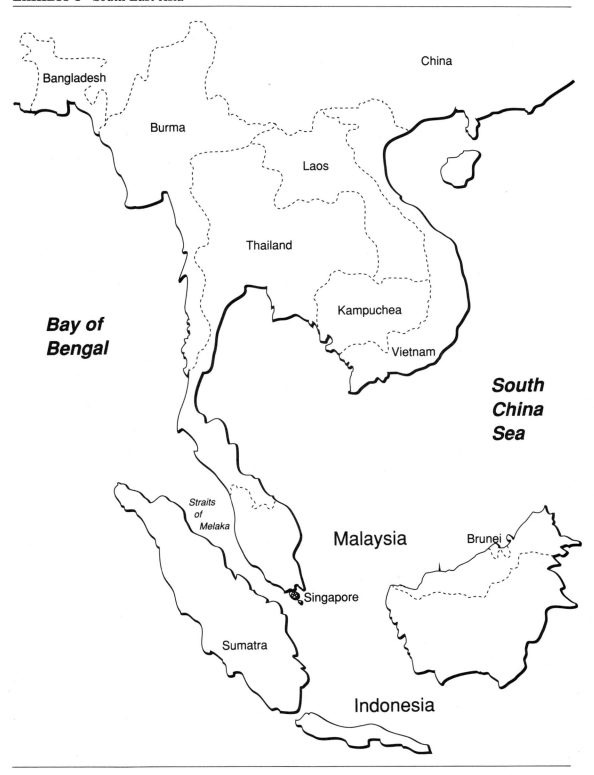

icant component of Singapore's economy. In 1990, external trade alone equaled 3.5 times the country's GDP. Though Singapore was a city state the size of Philadelphia in land and population, in 1989 it was among the top 20 trading nations of the world.

Trade Documentation

Modern trade revolves around transactions involving information on facts, parties at interest, and exchanges. *Facts* include the cargoes that are being shipped, the values of the cargoes, the vessels that carry them, their points of origin and destination, and the dates of departure and arrival. *Parties at interest* include the owners of the cargoes who are shipping them, and the recipients who will receive them, as well as all the intermediaries of agents, freight forwarders, shipping companies, banks, insurance companies, port authorities, and government customs and control agencies. *Exchange transactions* are the actual interchange of goods and information at the intersections of facts and parties at interest, and include transfer of cargo custody, payments of various fees and duties, and payments among the parties buying and selling the cargoes.

Trade documentation links these crucial information components together through manifests, bills of lading, letters of credit, customs declarations, and all manner of receipts and reports. Trade documentation in a busy port like Singapore is a complex and expensive activity. Yeo Seng Teck, chief executive officer of the Trade Development Board (TDB), a statutory board[1] responsible for managing all incoming and outgoing trade activities, explained the situation his agency faced in 1987:

> Our agency (TDB) was loaded with paperwork. In 1987 we were handling about 10,000 declarations each day, and the number was rising. And TDB was only part of the system. The trade process involves agencies such as the port authorities, customs, and so on, each with its own rules. At least four documents had to be completed for each incoming or outgoing shipment. In complicated cases as many as 20 forms might be required. Shipping agents and freight forwarders prepared these reports and physically carried them to service centers where they would be handled manually by government officials and clerks. Two-day turnaround was common. The cost of these transactions was high for all concerned. Swedish and U.S. studies of the costs of trade documentation in those countries estimated the cost at 4–7 percent of the values of goods shipped. And such transactions are error-prone. A British study estimated that half of all letter of credit applications were turned down on first application due to errors in completion. This seemed like a lot of work with little payoff. It also provided an opportunity for us. Singapore is a small country. We have no natural resources. Our population has stabilized. We know we cannot compete by just bringing in new labor. If we are to be successful, we must improve our competitiveness in every way, and especially in external trade, which is our largest business sector. This means cutting costs. That 4–7 percent was the best place to start.

---

[1]Statutory boards are an important feature of Singapore's economic structure, responsible for operating vital utilities (e.g., telephone and subway system), major installations (e.g., the airport and the port), major construction enterprises (e.g., the Urban Redevelopment Authority), and analytical functions (e.g., the Economic Development Board). Each entity with the term "board" or "authority" in its title mentioned in this case is a statutory board. These boards are created by the government through enabling legislation, but they are *not* government departments. They are typically tied through their enabling legislation to particular ministries of government, but they are not-for-profit corporations whose directorships consist of a mix of leaders from government, the private sector, and labor organizations. They generally must operate without government subsidy, and can retain surplus earnings to expand their programs.

The TradeNet System

TradeNet is a system supporting Electronic Data Interchange (EDI), providing for computer-to-computer exchange of intercompany business documents in a format conforming to an established public standard. The TradeNet system connects members of the Singapore trading community with links provided for eventual interaction with EDI systems on an international level (see Exhibit 2). The TradeNet system (see Exhibit 3) utilizes software running on a large IBM mainframe computer owned and operated by Singapore Network Services Pte. Ltd. This system is linked via telephone dial-up or leased lines to all the members of the trading community, each of whom uses terminals or its own computer systems to interact with the system.

A user, such as a freight forwarder, will utilize the Application Interface (see Exhibit 4) on its local computer system to complete the required TradeNet application forms. The local system translates the data from the form into EDIFACT (an international electronic document standard). A communications program then transmits the EDIFACT document to the TradeNet mainframe. At the mainframe, the Information Exchange Interface receives the information, determines the nature of the transaction that the document represents, who it is from, and what is being requested. A typical request might be for an approval from TDB and Customs and Excise to release an incoming shipment for delivery to a destination within Singapore, or to release a shipment that is being exported from Singapore. Relevant data are forwarded to appropriate destinations, such as the TDB, Customs, and any other agency with jurisdiction over particular trade-associated requests. The Applications Manager module and the Session Manager module keep track of the transaction, store data for future use, and forward system use information to the User and System Monitor module, which will eventually bill the user's organization for use of TradeNet.

The Trade Development Board, TDB, and the Customs and Excise agency are the principal governmental agencies with whom traders interact via TradeNet, but the system can also provide data on a shipment status to other interested parties such as the port or airport authorities. TradeNet also has the ability to support certain financial transactions. A freight forwarder, for example, might send a message to its bank ordering a payment to be made to another freight forwarder for services rendered on a given shipment. TradeNet also supports direct GIRO interbank funds transfer.

Planning TradeNet

TradeNet resulted from discussions on environmental factors and government policies and programs in the 1980s. As part of its program of general economic development during the 1970s, a number of opportunities for Singapore's economic growth were explored. These explorations suggested that the broad field of information technology (IT) provided special opportunities for the country. Accordingly, a blue-ribbon Committee on National Computerization was established by the government to develop specific recommendations on ways Singapore could pursue a future in the growing information technology field. In 1980 the CNC issued a report stating that Singapore could become one of the world's leaders in the creation and use of information technologies. To do so, however, the country would have to mobilize its efforts and create a coherent plan of development. In particular, it was necessary to build Singapore's IT human infrastructure. Only 850 IT professionals were available in the country in 1980. The CNC estimated that 10,000 would be needed by 1990 to accomplish its goals. Computer education at all levels of school became a priority. Also, the country needed to gain practical experi-

EXHIBIT 2   The TradeNet Community

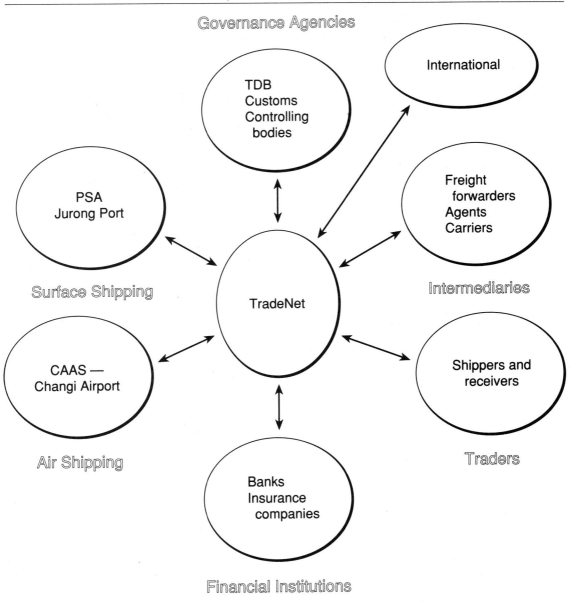

Governance Agencies

TDB
Customs
Controlling
bodies

International

PSA
Jurong Port

Freight
forwarders
Agents
Carriers

Surface Shipping

TradeNet

Intermediaries

CAAS —
Changi Airport

Shippers and
receivers

Air Shipping

Traders

Banks
Insurance
companies

Financial Institutions

ence with the technology. A special statutory board, the National Computer Board (NCB), was created under the Ministry of Finance and charged with creating development programs that would build Singapore into an IT Society. NCB's first major effort, the Government Computerization Project, focused on bringing computerization to government agencies, and greatly expanded the skill base. The education programs worked well,

EXHIBIT 3 TradeNet Structure

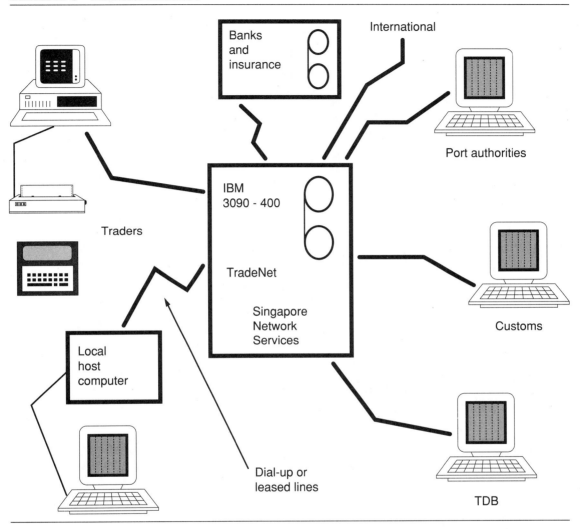

and by 1986 there were nearly 4,000 IT professionals available in the country. These initiatives provided the base for more ambitious undertakings.

In 1985 a recession hit Singapore, causing concern about the country's economic future, and in particular, the immediate goals of national economic development. A high-level committee convened to consider options, and named improvement in external trade as a major goal. This report resulted in concentration on the application of IT to both the port and the airport, and was an important mobilizing factor leading to TradeNet. Also in 1986, Singapore's main shipping competitor, Hong Kong, revealed that it was working toward creation of a trade-oriented EDI system to be called Hotline (later renamed TradeLink).

Trade is clearly a multilateral phenomenon, involving many groups with differing

EXHIBIT 4 TradeNet Schematic

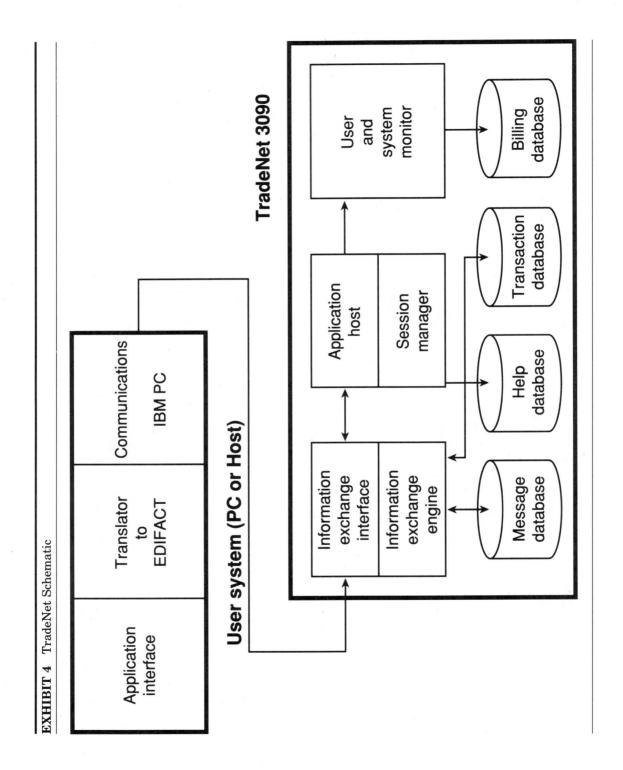

interests. No single organization could create a workable computer system for trade. Whatever was done, it would have to be built on agreements among a large number of interest groups. Philip Yeo, chairman of the Economic Development Board (EDB) and National Computer Board (NCB), and a graduate of a well-known U.S. East Coast MBA program, met with Yeo Seng Teck, chairman of the Trade Development Board (TDB), to discuss ways to proceed. As Yeo Seng Teck recalls,

> Philip and I knew each other well. The small size of our country makes it possible for key people to get to know one another. In fact, people often hold a number of key positions in different agencies through their careers. Philip was chairman of EDB, and I had been CEO of EDB before I moved over to TDB. We both understood the problems. We also knew nothing would happen unless we agreed to push it. So the two Yeos got together and agreed to make it happen.

They brought together a disparate group of influential interests and obtained agreement on "streamlining trade." This meant building technological support, but perhaps more important, it meant changing procedures. The procedures and protocols of many different agencies and organizations had to be streamlined into a set of coherent and simplified procedures that could be automated. This challenge was often more political than technical. TDB was given the task of mobilizing the trade community and became the coordinating entity among the government agencies and statutory boards involved with trade, such as Customs and Excise, the Port of Singapore Authority, and Civil Aviation Authority of Singapore. Yeo Seng Teck called a meeting of the relevant interest groups that would have to come together in agreement if TradeNet were to succeed (see Exhibit 5). Participants included a large, heterogeneous mix of government agencies, companies, hierarchical organizations and voluntary associations. Through several meetings and much discussion all the participants came to agree that significant savings would accrue from reducing the burdens of trade documentation handling. The position was brought forward that streamlining trade would make the entire trading community of Singapore more competitive internationally. Eventually, an "agreement to agree" was reached, and the process of streamlining began.

The most important first step in the process was to develop a detailed understanding of exactly what trade procedures were al-

---

EXHIBIT 5   Interested Parties in the Process

TDB-MTI-EDB-NCB
Port of Singapore Authority
Jurong Town Corporation
Civil Aviation Authority of
  Singapore (Changi Airport)
Customs and Excise
Singapore Telecoms
Other controlling agencies
Singapore National Shipping
  Association

Singapore Freight Forwarders
  Association
Singapore Air Cargo Agents
  Association
Board of Airline Representatives
Federation of Chambers of
  Commerce and Industry

ready being followed. Exhibit 6 depicts the current process review organization. The TradeNet Steering Committee was created to oversee the process, and NCB was appointed to serve as staff to the enterprise. The committee of the whole was subdivided into three working subcommittees, one each for the maritime community (sea shipping), the air community (air shipping), and the government agencies and statutory boards. Individual NCB staffers were appointed to support each subcommittee. The subcommittees met regularly over several months, investigating trade procedures and developing a profile of essential trade documentation activities that must be incorporated in any new set of procedures. Each subcommittee produced a report, and these reports were integrated by NCB staffers and members of

the whole committee into an "Integrated Procedures Report" that served as the focal point of procedural reform discussions.

Automating the existing procedures would produce nothing more than an automated mess. It would be necessary to reduce the 20 + forms involved in trade to a very few, or ideally, one. There was much negotiation, during which organizations with long-standing procedures based on particular forms had to compromise. The result was a single form—actually, a large, formatted computer screen—to serve nearly all trade documentation needs in Singapore. This form would be the substantive core of the new computerized system. Once this agreement was made, the committee prepared a proposal for the creation of TradeNet. At about the same time, TDB began experimenting

EXHIBIT 6   TradeNet Committee Structure

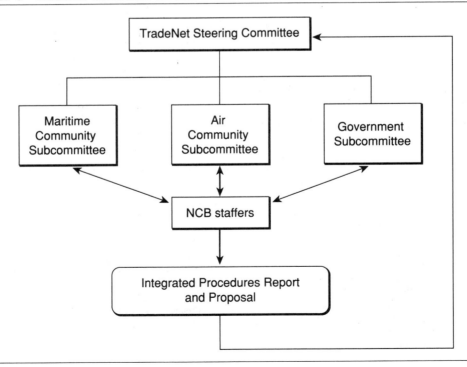

with a prototype on-line system called Trade-Dial-Up, which allowed traders to dial into the TDB computer system and complete trade forms from their local PCs or systems in terminal emulation mode. Completion of the single form made Trade-Dial-Up effective, and the system was used successfully to prove the concept that trade documentation could be completed on-line.

The TradeNet project was reviewed at the highest levels of government, and received the go-ahead. In December of 1986, B. G. Lee, son of the Prime Minister and head of the Ministry of Trade and Industry, publicly announced the TradeNet project. In his announcement he said the new system would be operational within two years. This gave the development team little time, but by its decision the government gave the team full authority and resources to proceed.

Building TradeNet

By February, 1987 the TradeNet team had refined the reports produced in the analysis phase into a set of broad specifications for an EDI system for trade documentation. They issued to a long list of possible vendors and developed a prequalification solicitation, essentially a Request for Information (RFI) that would provide background on which companies could undertake such a project. They also commissioned Price Waterhouse to do a separate study of TradeNet's likely market. The report suggested a potential customer base of about 2,200 firms engaged in trade-related activities in Singapore, plus the various government agencies and statutory boards that would be users of the system. Price Waterhouse was also asked to conduct a study of the basic information processing requirements of firms within the trading community. The objective of this study was to evaluate the potential applications of computers to these firms. It was felt that this information would help firms de-velop applications to make them more productive. But the real objective was to enhance TradeNet's effects. TradeNet would be most useful if it tied directly into the automated systems of the trading firms, and the Price Waterhouse study provided examples of the applications that were needed to enhance TradeNet's value throughout the trading community.

The RFI produced 23 responses, mostly from U.S. and Japanese firms. Most were judged too small or inexperienced to take on the project and were eliminated. To assess the remaining vendors, members of the TradeNet team made visits to EDI installations in the United States and Europe to see the various systems in action. By the summer of 1987, three finalists were chosen: IBM Corporation, McDonnell Douglas Information Systems Company, and General Electric Information Services (GEIS). Each received a formal request for proposal (RFP) in June of 1987. Proposals were received in September. The proposals were reviewed with special emphasis on each company's "staying power" in completing a project of TradeNet's complexity. In December of 1987, a year after TradeNet was announced, IBM was notified that it was the winning bidder.

The specialists in IBM's Singapore office knew that TradeNet was not a trivial system. It would link together a number of existing and new procedural and computerized systems. The project was more of a systems integration effort than a system building effort. To head up the TradeNet technical effort, IBM sent Joe Huber to Singapore. Huber had extensive experience in large-scale systems integration through IBM's Federal Systems Division, which builds special systems for the U.S. government. Huber's first decision was to put the contract negotiations on hold while IBM conducted a "detailed design study" of the proposed system. Basically, he wanted to know what IBM was really getting into. The TradeNet team agreed to IBM's study, even though it would take time, because the study would provide useful information for the actual construction of the system.

Since the TradeNet project was proceeding toward a formal contract with significant commitments, it was time to create an official organization to house the enterprise. The decision was made by the four key statutory boards involved in the project—TDB, the Port of Singapore Authority (PSA), which runs the port facilities, the Civil Aviation Authority of Singapore (CAAS), which runs Changi International Airport, and Singapore Telecoms, which runs the telephone system—to create a for-profit company to own and operate the system. On March 18, 1988, Singapore Network Services Pte. Ltd. was created. TDB owned 55 percent of the SNS shares, and PSA, CAAS, and Telecoms each owned 15 percent. Pearleen Chan, who had been deputy general manager and head of the Government Computerization Project at NCB, was named CEO of SNS. The core staff consisted of only four people, all of them from the original TradeNet committee. Of the original TradeNet team, only Ko Kheng Hwa did not move. He remained at NCB as head of industry computerization.

The detailed design review took three months, and was submitted in April of 1988. The results showed that the system could indeed be built as proposed, and minor modifications were made in the proposed contract to accommodate issues discovered during the review. The final contract between SNS and IBM was signed on May 25, 1988. IBM was the system integration contractor with responsibility for all aspects of the system, except the software that would run at the user site (the application interface, EDIFACT translator, and communications mod-

ule). IBM's partner in the project was a Singapore-based software company, CSA (Computer Systems Advisers, Pte. Ltd.), which would serve as subcontractor.

The general structure of TradeNet as it came to be built is shown in Exhibits 3 and 4. The actual construction of the system depended on adaptation of existing code and writing of new programs. The core of the system, which is shown in Exhibit 4 as the Information Exchange Engine, was a large, proprietary EDI system built for internal IBM use. Nicknamed the "Tampa Engine" for the IBM Information Networks division in Tampa, Florida, where it was created, it consisted of approximately 1.25 million lines of assembly code and had taken many person-years to build.[*] The Tampa Engine required only minor modifications to serve TradeNet purposes: a total of about 3,000 lines of code were altered in the process.

It was expected that the transfer of the Tampa Engine to the TradeNet application would be a modest undertaking. The basic system was in place and proven, and the system engineers (SE's) from Tampa would provide whatever help was needed to transport the system to its new use. However, IBM's Tampa operation was not positioned to provide the requisite support, and IBM Singapore had to handle the installation on its own. The Singapore office added two SE's to its original complement, and dispatched them to Tampa and later to London to study the Tampa Engine in detail and learn how it worked. This proved to be an essential factor in bringing the engine on-line for TradeNet.

In the mean time, IBM and CSA began work on the other components of the TradeNet sys-

---

[*]The "Tampa Engine" refers to the global IBM Information Network service.

tem. CSA had responsibility, under IBM's direction, for writing the Information Exchange Interface, the Application Host, the Session Manager, and the modules associated with system monitoring and user billing. All told, these modules constituted about 250,000 lines of CO-BOL code. CSA's professional staff had little difficulty developing this code, as they made use of the well-developed procedural and design documents produced by the TradeNet team and by IBM in the detailed design review. Also, they were writing for the "target" of the Tampa Engine, and knew the parameters they had to meet. Although they had only six months to develop and test the modules, they were able to make good progress.

During this period, two procedural steps were taken that helped keep the program on track. The first was precipitated by an inevitable problem in complex system integration projects: the emergence of engineering change requests. Any new system poses a dilemma for designers. As the system is built, everyone learns more about what is desirable and undesirable, possible and impossible. Thus, there is a strong temptation to change the design to conform to this new understanding. Huber recognized this problem from his long experience in system integration work, and knew that the most serious consequence in implementing engineering changes was delay. With B. G. Lee's deadline of January 1989 looming, there was no slack in the schedule. To handle this problem, Huber instituted an "Engineering Change Procedure" (ECP) to deal with all changes proposed by SNS. The procedure was straightforward, albeit demanding. Any proposed change was given a thorough assessment in terms of what it would actually require in time and money. The assessment, and the rationale behind it, was documented in an ECP report. This became the basis of negotiation between IBM and SNS.

The first encounter over a proposed change was stressful for the IBM/SNS relationship. As Joe Huber put it,

> The results of the first ECP were startling, especially the projected cost and delay it would cause. Our relations with the customer were probably more tense at this time than any other time in the project. But our numbers were right, and we stood by them. Eventually it became clear to everyone that changes cause cost and delay. Some delays can be accommodated; some cannot. Once everyone accepted the ECP as standard and took the results seriously, it was possible to make quick evaluations of proposed changes and decide whether to implement them or not. Some of the proposed changes were implemented, but many were not.

The ECP was a major breakthrough in the SNS/IBM relationship, because it established a sense of shared purpose in the TradeNet enterprise. Both SNS and IBM were now focused on getting the system up on time; useful changes could wait for later.

The other procedural change was a decision of the top management of the enterprise to engage the SNS systems professionals early in the "customization" phase of the design and development process. This had two effects. Most important, it gave the SNS systems people early access to the major components of the system, and allowed them time to learn in detail how the system was to work. This knowledge was instrumental in developing the customized features of the system for various user communities. Also important, however, the early involvement of the SNS systems people cemented the social bonds between IBM and SNS at the crucial level of technical reality. Thus, SNS systems people became effective boundary spanners between IBM and SNS leadership over important questions about design and implementation that might, under different circumstances, have been a source of serious disputes. This was especially crucial given the deadline. Chan Kah Khuen, a member of the early study team and later head of SNS's technical group, expressed it this way:

> There was real management commitment to this project, and clear agreement on project objectives, so decisions got made fast. This helped build *esprit de corps,* a spirit of teamwork. The teams were also very skilled, with real expertise coming from IBM, CSA and SNS. At times there were 100–200 people working together very closely, and everyone got on well. There were occasionally disagreements over the "gray areas," but these got resolved quickly because management paid attention to the effort and we were a real team.

In the meantime, SNS had let contracts to four local firms to develop the user interface software essential for the trading community that would use TradeNet. The initial implementations were kept relatively simple by standardizing on MS-DOS machines (e.g., the IBM PC) as the target user computer. This was sensible because the availability of low-priced, powerful MS-DOS systems made them the most common system among Singapore's business community. Also, to help keep implementation simple, SNS mandated use of the IBM PC-IE communications software that would link the user host to the TradeNet mainframe over leased or dial-up lines. In spite of the relative simplicity of the task, there were delays and problems in getting the user software ready for January. Considerable energy had to be spent by SNS staff in making the software work correctly. In the end, however, useable packages were created.

Delay-producing changes proposed for TradeNet were usually deferred through use of the ECP, but some essential changes were adopted and implemented. Some delays

were unavoidable. To go live with TradeNet in January of 1989, SNS and IBM decided to concentrate on the basic information exchange and transaction processing components of the system. They delayed implementation of some database capabilities as well as the user billing modules until after the system went live. This allowed the team to concentrate on finishing, testing, and debugging the crucial components of the Information Exchange Interface, the Application Host, the Session Manager, and the Information Exchange Engine.

The progress on TradeNet was also rapid because so much of the essential infrastructure was already in place. Pearleen Chan commented,

> TradeNet is the largest single project undertaken to date in the national effort to build IT capability, but it would have been impossible without the Government Computerization Project that preceded it. Also, without the sophisticated computer systems installed in the various boards and agencies, TradeNet would have had nothing to hook up to. It wouldn't have mattered if we could deliver documents quickly to TDB or Customs, for example, if they simply went into big stacks to be processed manually. The fact that documents flow through TradeNet into the automated systems at TDB and Customs is essential to the main objective of speeding up trade document transactions.

The first transaction on TradeNet was a shipping application sent over a dial-up line by Merchants Air Cargo, an air cargo company owned by Mr. Joseph Low, who had served as the representative of the Singapore Air Cargo Agents Association on the TradeNet committee. The application was submitted on January 1, 1989. Ten minutes later, approval of the shipment was returned to the Merchants Air Cargo offices. TradeNet was operational.

In the next six months, the remaining modules were completed, tested and installed. By June of 1989, all of the original design components of TradeNet were in place, and planning had begun on significant enhancements. The direct capital cost of TradeNet's development, meaning the contract cost to IBM and the other contractors, was more than S$20 million. This does not include the investment made by the various ministries and statutory boards in conceiving the project, developing the requirements and specifications, managing the contracting, or establishing SNS.

Results

The original expectations for TradeNet were ambitious. SNS hoped to capture about 25 percent of the total trade document transactions in the first year of operation, with a subscriber base of about 500. In retrospect, these ambitious expectations looked conservative. By December of 1989, TradeNet had 850 out of about 2,200 possible subscribers, and about 45 percent of all trade documentation for sea and air shipments was being handled by the network. The success was so striking that TDB moved forward, from early 1993 to early 1991, the date by which use of TradeNet for all trade transactions would be made mandatory. Most of the larger firms had joined the system by the end of 1989. The balance of the 2,200 potential subscribers were medium and small firms. In anticipation of eventually making use of TradeNet mandatory, SNS began exploring means for facilitating the movement of the medium and smaller sized firms onto the system. As SNS had grown significantly, Pearleen Chan, who had still been working on projects at NCB, moved over to SNS full time in October of 1989. By March of 1990 SNS had grown to a full-time staff of five managers, 40 programmers and sales people, and 10 support staff, and was expanding. It had outgrown its offices and was looking forward to moving into larger quarters in a new build-

ing under construction nearby. Soon, SNS was meeting its operational costs through revenues from TradeNet subscriptions and user fees.

Joining TradeNet cost a company S$750 for a one-time connect charge, with monthly costs of S$30 for a dial-up port and transaction costs of S$0.50 per 1 kilobyte of transmitted information (the average declaration requires 0.7 kilobytes). In addition, the company must have hardware necessary for local processing of the application and transmission of the coded EDIFACT data. The minimum required PC configuration costs about S$4,000, and the software cost between S$1,000 and S$4,000. This poses no problem for large companies, most of whom have significant in-house computer capability. Smaller companies are generally willing to buy the hardware since Singapore offers enticing tax write-offs for computer hardware purchase by small enterprises. Nevertheless, SNS and TDB recognize that not all small companies will wish to spend the capital necessary to join TradeNet right away. Therefore, plans were developed to provide for use of the system via three mechanisms. Small companies may, if they do not wish to make the necessary investments, use the facilities of service centers. If this does not prove to be appealing, they may come to the TDB offices, where data will be captured by TDB. Finally, TDB is considering opening convenient offices where public terminals and assistance can be obtained for modest fee. It is anticipated that these avenues of use will constitute no more than 5 percent of total TradeNet volume.

The costs of a company's overall changes in procedures and protocols required for moving to TradeNet are less clear than the direct costs. For some companies, the conversion is trivial because their own systems are already in place and ready to accommodate the new ways of doing business. For companies not yet used to doing business with computers, the future is less clear. However, many small companies with no prior computing experience have purchased computers and begun to use them, due strictly to the availability of TradeNet.

TradeNet's performance effects are beginning to be noticed. Turnaround time for processing of typical trade documents has been reduced from a minimum of one day and as many as four days to 10 to 15 minutes. Most transactions are actually completed in 10 minutes. This has had a remarkable effect on the subscribers to the system. An example of this can be seen from the experience of MSAS Cargo International, a worldwide multimodal freight forwarder with a major office in Singapore. As Georgiana Yuen, regional systems manager at MSAS, Pte. Ltd. Singapore, expressed it:

> The productivity improvements from TradeNet have been significant. The turnaround is much faster, and we can speed up the movements of shipments to our customers. There are also major logistics improvements. For example, we used to have to send clerks as couriers with documents to various offices here, at Changi International Airport, or downtown. Now there is no need to. The clerks do not have to wait in line and are always here in the office. This saves a lot of time and means better deployment of our staff. Also, we've been able to make better use of our trucks. Fast turnaround makes it possible for us to organize shipments onto outgoing trucks. Mainly, we benefit from improved service to our customers, more effective control of trucks and equipment, and of manpower resources. As a result, we experience higher productivity in our operations. TradeNet has become a key part of our operations.

Great Expectations

While formal analysis of the cost impacts of TradeNet for subscribers have yet to be performed, several freight forwarders report savings of 25–35 percent in handling trade documentation. Expectations of benefits by TradeNet subscribers are significant. They are indicated by the experiences of Merchants Air Cargo, Pte. Ltd., a freight forwarder based at Changi International Airport. MAC has been an innovator in the use of computers for its operations for several years. By 1984 it had computerized most of its back office functions (accounting, statistics, etc.) using a NEC ASTRA minicomputer. Its software was custom-built by an outside contractor, but over time it took all system support activities in-house. In 1985 it embarked on computerizing significant aspects of its operations, but since most transactions involving shipments were tied to outside entities that were not computerized, the full potential of computerized operations was difficult to realize. MAC was a participant in TDB's Trade Dial-Up experiments in 1986–87, which confirmed the potential of computerization of trade documentation functions. And MAC served as one of the exemplary sites for development of the requirements described in the Air Community Subcommittee report. MAC continued to develop its in-house computer capabilities during the period when TradeNet was being constructed. It expanded its minicomputer system, and installed new terminals that gave it a terminal-to-employee ratio of 1:2. When TradeNet went on-line, MAC sent the first transaction over the system.

Mr. Joseph Low, president of MAC, characterizes the potential of TradeNet for his company and for his industry:

> TradeNet really makes our business work more efficiently. It is a 24-hour per-day system, which is a big improvement over having to work through offices that are only open eight hours a day. We can integrate our operations now. For example, we can get information on an incoming shipment prior to the arrival of the aircraft it is on, submit the documents, get the shipment cleared, and meet

the plane with all the finished documents in hand. We can get shipments to customers very quickly this way. Also, we can clear whole collections of shipments in a single transaction, which speeds things up. And we can consolidate shipments on our trucks, which saves time and money. We also save money by not having to send people out to stand in line in queues, waiting to have documents cleared. Since we are computerized in our own operations, we also save money and time by automatically completing most of the TradeNet documentation using information already entered in our own system. Between 60 and 70 percent of the information required for each TradeNet submission is automatically transferred from our own system each time we prepare documentation forms. When the additional capabilities for banking and insurance interactions are installed, the benefits will be greater. Even now, we are completely dependent on our systems. A couple of months ago we had a major power failure here, and the systems were all down. Everyone sat around, unable to work. But I don't mind that. The payoffs are worth it.

The expectation of benefits for the subscribers is matched by the benefits to the various government agencies and statutory boards that use the system. For example, Customs and Excise has found TradeNet to be a major adjunct to its operations. As Customs and Excise Director General Lee Yew Kim expressed it,

TradeNet is part of our larger scheme to improve performance through use of computers. Our earlier computerization efforts made our important procedural reforms work to our advantage. We were able to turn Customs and Excise into an agency that helps speed up trade, not slow it down. For example, we went from a procedure of post-approval of applications to pre-approval. Duties are now prepaid and post-approval checks on an audit basis are then made. Violators are subject to penalties, such as fines and their subsequent shipments are inspected. This makes them uncompetitive, so the responsible companies

never even try to avoid customs checks. This procedure change improved throughput dramatically, but most important, it made it possible for our computers to interface directly with TradeNet. We are also using TradeNet as the vehicle for payment of customs duties, which means we get paid much faster. Only a fraction of the traders are paying via TradeNet now, but this will grow rapidly.

Benefits to the TDB, the "clearinghouse" for trade documentation in Singapore, have been substantial in both direct and indirect ways. TDB CEO Yeo Seng Teck summarized the short-run and long-run benefits this way:

We haven't done a detailed study of the benefits yet, but the system is clearly a success. We have about 50 percent of the transactions going through the system now, and we expect to have 90 percent by the end of 1990. We'll cut over to use of TradeNet for almost all transactions around that time. The local benefits of TradeNet are very nice, but the big payoffs for us are international. TDB is not a trade *control* agency; it is a trade *facilitator*. We are trade promoters. TradeNet facilitates trade. It makes it easier to do business in Singapore. That draws foreign investment to our economy, and makes us competitive internationally. We are very happy to say that Hong Kong is now looking to us for inspiration.

TradeNet, in conjunction with information systems innovations in the port and airport, permits faster total turnaround for ships and aircraft. For example, the Port of Singapore Authority has installed sophisticated computer-based systems that facilitate registration of incoming vessels, deployment of vessels to port facilities (e.g., container cranes), optimization of off-loading and on-loading sequences, and discharging of vessels that are ready to leave. Similarly, systems have been installed to facilitate movement of cargoes within the free-trade zone, into and out of the free-trade zone, into and out of Customs warehouses, and between the port and the airport. The total package of aids to trade is making Singapore into one of the world's most efficient trading centers.

Beyond TradeNet

TradeNet launches Singapore's full entry into the development and deployment of EDI services. SNS was created not only as the owner and custodian of TradeNet, but as a company that would develop and deploy value-added networks throughout the Singapore economy. Already, TradeNet offers interbank GIRO service for electronic payments. This facility is being used by Customs and Excise, and will be expanded substantially for all users. In addition, TradeNet will offer interorganizational interchange of many kinds of business documents among subscribers, including invoice, purchase orders, delivery orders, debit and credit notes, and so on. These are intended to facilitate such business practices as just-in-time inventory control and direct store delivery. TradeNet also will be linked to the international trade community.

Beyond the trade sector, SNS is working on EDI networks for the health-care, legal, retailing, and manufacturing sectors. A health-care network called MediNet is being planned to link hospitals, laboratories, pharmacies, drug distributors, private clinics, and medical supply companies. Among the information to be exchanged in this system are hospital payments via the third-party payments system; public health data that must be reported to government authorities; purchase orders, invoices, and delivery orders for drugs and medical supplies; and patient medical records. The system will also provide access to international medical data bases. Preliminary designs are also under way for a supplier-manufacturer network that will permit international multinationals in the electronics industry to order and pay for components from local suppliers. In time, exchange of computer-aided design (CAD) files will be provided via this system, and the system will contain the ability to translate such files from one protocol to another (e.g., between AutoCAD and other formats). Similar network utilities are being designed to link major chain stores with suppliers, incorporating data collected from point-of-sale terminals. As Pearleen Chan notes,

> Our vision is to extend the use of EDI through every sector of Singapore economy, to create a more conducive environment for doing business, and to give our companies a truly competitive edge. I believe we will see tremendous growth in the EDI industry over the next decade. We at SNS will do our best to be among the leaders in this business.

Case 6–2

SINGAPORE LEADERSHIP: A TALE OF ONE CITY

Lee Kuan Yew, the prime minister of the Republic of Singapore, is usually credited with the "Singapore Miracle." Cambridge-educated and widely regarded as a brilliant strategist, Lee has been the central figure in Singapore politics since before the founding of the Republic in 1959. Admirers say he embodies all that is good about Asia. Singapore's rapid economic progress (see Exhibit 1) is accompanied by litter-free streets, a low crime rate, and a high level of public amenities and services. Lee's critics, however, point at Singapore's strict laws governing everyday behavior (e.g., rigorously enforced rules against spitting and other minor infractions) and suppression of criticism of the government as a high cost the citizens of Singapore pay for their progress.

Lee has used his People's Action Party (PAP) to create a functioning multi-racial, multi-lingual, multi-religious society. The Republic is a parliamentary democracy, with an elected parliament that elects a president every four years. The president appoints the prime minister and cabinet. Ethnic Chinese make up a significant percent of the population, followed by Malays, Indians, and "Europeans." To help balance the different interests in the society, representation by non-Chinese in Parliament is based on group representation constituencies (GRCs). Opposition parties are allowed to hold up to three of the 81 seats in Parliament as non-constituency members of parliament (MPs), if fewer than three opposition MPs are returned in the elections. Over the years, PAP has remained strong, currently holding 80 of the 81 seats.

The central question in Singapore politics has for some years concerned Lee's succes-sor. Recent events have set the stage for the immediate succession when Lee retires to the position of a regular cabinet member at the end of 1990. Goh Chok Tong, currently 1st deputy prime minister and 1st minister of defense, has been named to become prime minister at that time. Lately Goh has become quite visible, for example making policy statements in the sensitive area of relations between Singapore and neighboring Malaysia. Recently, Goh was asked if his assumption of the prime minister's job signaled a long-term direction for the country, or whether he was taking the job as an "interim measure" in anticipation of another prime minister down the line. Goh's said a "substantial" victory in the September 1993 election would make him secure in his position, but he also said he would not remain in the office for "long."

The most widely rumored successor to Goh is the oldest son of Lee Kuan Yew, Lee Hsien Loong, known popularly as B. G. (Brigadier General) Lee for his status in Singapore's armed forces. Educated at Cambridge, Harvard, and the U.S. Army General Staff College, he has held important government positions, including 2nd minister of defense and minister of trade and industry. He also has been involved in many key policy debates re-

This case was prepared by Marvin Bower Fellow John King and Professor Benn Konsynski to be used as a basis for class discussion rather than to illustrate either effective or ineffective handling of an administrative situation.

EXHIBIT 1 Comparative Statistics for Singapore, 1965 and 1988

Item	1965	1988
Population at mid-year	1.89 million	2.65 million
GDP (1985 market prices)	6.62 billion	47.9 billion
Indigenous GDP per capita	1,692	15,999
External trade (imported and export)	6.8 billion	167.28 billion
Students enrolled in school	15,000	77,000
Labor force	723,000	1,282,000
Sea cargo handled (tons)	15.1 million	142 million
Air cargo handled (tons)	21,100	512,500
Official foreign reserves	14.2 million	33.28 billion
Balance of payment (current acct.)	-150,000	3.34 billion

Source: Singapore Economic Development Board, 1990.

garding the future of Singapore. Political commentators have compared him with his illustrious father. Regarding competitiveness of nations, B. G. Lee said:

> What's important is not just the cost of labor. The key is total productivity. There's the labor cost, infrastructure, inventiveness of the leading edge of technology and the quality of the production process. Not just individual workers but the way whole plants are organized and structured and efficiency is squeezed out of fallible human digits.
>
> In Singapore we have an appreciation for how fragile we are. Why are we here? There is nothing special about this island. It is just one of 18,000 islands in the region. But here you can do business. You have banks, telephones, airports that work, factories that are up and running in six to nine months. What makes it special? The only thing which makes it special is that the place is revved to 99 percent of what it is capable of. And unless you can always run at that efficiency, you'll just sink. There's no reason to be here. Do we have hydroelectric power? Timber, tin, gold, gas? We have none. But if we want to continue to be here, we have to be special.[1]

Being "special" in the Singaporean sense has translated into active government programs fostering economic links with other countries, the encouragement of overseas investment, the establishment of an assertive diplomacy, and the development of "interna-

---

[1]Brian Kelly and Mark London, *The Four Little Dragons* (New York: Simon and Schuster, 1989), pp. 385, 387.

tional networking." The fiscal system of Singapore has been characterized as 75 percent private and 25 percent government, with high levels of public investment in infrastructure and the maintenance of sound monetary policy. In recent years the country has built state-of-the-art transportation infrastructure, including world-class container ports, airport facilities, highways, and a subway system. It also has an advanced telephone and data communications network. Much effort is focused on building the capabilities of the country's small and medium-sized enterprises through tax credits and other incentives to encourage investment in computing technology and the hiring of consultants to improve know-how at the firm level.

Case 6-3

HONG KONG TRADELINK:
NEWS FROM THE SECOND CITY

This brief background on Hong Kong, the Tradelink project, and the Hotline project that preceded Tradelink, is drawn from various public record sources. The excepts from newspaper articles that follow cover the period between November 1988 and May 1990. For the most part, the articles are excerpted from the *South China Morning Post.*

Background on Hong Kong

Hong Kong was established by the United Kingdom in the early 19th century as a trading colony, part of the British Empire. The colony was built upon Hong Kong Island, which was ceded to the U.K. in perpetuity by the Chinese government. As the colony grew, it expanded beyond the island, and eventually came to occupy a significant part of the mainland (the New Territories) leased by the Chinese government to the U.K. for the period 1898–1997. After extensive negotiations between the U.K. and the People's Republic of China during the mid- to late 1980s, a joint agreement was reached whereby Hong Kong would become part of the PRC in 1997. However, the memorandum of understanding stipulates that Hong Kong will retain its special political and economic character for 50 years past the 1997 hand-over.

Hong Kong is administered by a governor appointed by the Queen of England, though as a practical matter the governor reports to U.K. Foreign Office. The governor is assisted by two councils, a Legislative Council that enacts local legislation and sets budgetary authority; and an advisory Executive Council. Administration of the Hong Kong Government (HKG) is managed by the chief secretary (formerly called the colonial secretary), to whom most of the secretaries running major HKG agencies report. The attorney general and the finance secretary also report to the chief secretary, though they have more of a peer status with the chief secretary than do the other secretaries. The attorney general is responsible for all Crown prosecutions, while the finance secretary is responsible for the treasury, trade and industry, government data processing, and other key administrative functions. Numerous advisory committees involving government officials and citizens help with particular policy issues.

Background on Trade-Related Electronic Data Interchange in Hong Kong

In 1983 the Hong Kong Trade Facilitation Council (TFC), a nonprofit organization of traders, facility authorities (e.g., the port authority), and trade-related agencies of the Hong Kong government, began looking into the possibility of improving trade activities in Hong Kong through use of Electronic Data Interchange (EDI). A study was organized within the TFC to outline a possible

Marvin Bower Fellow John King and Professor Benn Konsynski prepared this material as the basis for class discussion rather than to illustrate either effective or ineffective handling of an administrative situation.

EDI project, and in 1984 the TFC made public plans for the construction of a system called *Hotline*. Hotline was proposed as a centralized data base system of consignment data on all goods exchanged through external trade mechanisms.

The HKG, which had been instrumental in creation of the TFC and was its initial underwriter, was approached to fund the Hotline project. The HKG had problems with the proposal on substantive and procedural grounds. None of the HKG officials who would have to approve the Hotline project and provide funding understood what was being proposed in detail, so it was not easy to sell the concept. No other trade-related EDI was operating in the world, and only limited discussion and planning had taken place in those places contemplating it. Also, TFC had been started with initial support by the HKG, but it was the intent from the beginning to have TFC a self-supporting entity very soon after creation. HKG support of Hotline would have significantly increased the government's obligations to TFC, and to the thinking of HKG officials, there were not sound grounds for making the investment in the first place.

The HKG response to the Hotline project was that the private sector stood to benefit most from Hotline, and therefore it should undertake the project if it felt the benefits worthwhile. While rational from a market perspective, this suggestion met severe institutional resistance among the members of the trading company. A survey of interested companies revealed the widespread sentiment that the information contained in such a system would be proprietary and competitively sensitive. The HKG, in the minds of the various companies, was the only entity that could undertake the project and guarantee fair and equal treatment of all users. Thus, the key blocs within the TFC—the HKG and the private companies

involved in trade—were at a deadlock on Hotline.

From 1984–1987 the EDI issue was dormant. None of the TFC parties could devise a means of breaking out of the deadlock, and for a while, interest in the issue waned. However, in 1987 several key events occurred that restarted discussions. One was the establishment of the United Nations EDIFACT standard for EDI. This greatly increased the probability that a single EDI format would be adopted for trading use. Another, more local stimulus was the announcement by the Singapore government of a crash program to develop a trade-related EDI system called TradeNet. TradeNet was to use the EDIFACT standard, and it was targeted to be working within two years. This announcement was significant because Singapore, as Hong Kong's nearest and largest trading competitor, was clearly viewing EDI as a major source of competitive advantage in trade. Also at about this time other, less ambitious trade-related EDI projects were being announced in Norway, the U.K., and other countries. It seemed to some members of the TFC that EDI had moved from "desirable" status to "necessary" status in Hong Kong's trade future. And there was official support for moving forward provided by the Hong Kong Government's Advisory Board on Science and Technology, which recommended that the government help make some kind of EDI project happen.

In late 1987 several companies that were members of the TFC decided to pull out of TFC and form their own EDI consortium for the purpose of commissioning and funding a major study of the viability of a trade-related EDI system for Hong Kong. They formed a special company called Tradelink, and commissioned a major consultancy study with the firm Coopers and Lybrand. The HKG, desiring to keep a hand in the ongoing discussion, contributed 10 percent to the cost of the consultancy.

Excerpts from Articles on Trade-Related EDI from Hong Kong Newspapers

Eight Hong Kong Companies Have Started Work on Tradelink Computer Network

Eight Hong Kong companies have begun work on an international computer network linking Hong Kong's freight carriers, banks and trading companies. These are China Resources, Hong Kong Air and Cargo Terminals, Hong Kong International Terminals, Maersk Line (HK), Modern Terminals, Swire Pacific, Standard Chartered Bank and the Hong Kong and Shanghai Bank. The government is not a shareholder of the new company, TRADELINK Electronic Document Services. The formation of TRADELINK is in response to the increasing use of electronic data interchange (EDI) systems to reduce paperwork. TRADELINK is expected to begin operation in 1990, almost a year after Singapore is scheduled to launch its EDI, Tradenet.

Shipping Times 11/1/88, p. 1.

Tradelink Computerised Paperwork System Given Go Ahead

A final report from Coopers and Lybrand on the practicalities of setting up a computerised network to handle trade paperwork in the territory will recommend that the project goes ahead despite concerns over its economic viability. The TRADELINK consortium proposing the project is expected to decide whether to provide a paperless trading service in Hong Kong before October 4, when the group will participate in a conference on electronic document interchange (EDI).

South China Morning Post (Business News) 8/27/89, p. 3.

Tradelink Denies Dropping Plans for Electronic Data Interchange Service

TRADELINK, the consortium of 11 companies set up to establish a comprehensive EDI service in Hong Kong, has said no decision on the project has been made. An EDI feasibility study by Coopers and Lybrand is believed to have run over its HK$6 million government provided funding and is already two months overdue. TRADELINK did not say whether Coopers' draft report had recommended the project be abandoned. TRADELINK project manager Juletta Broomfield said a statement would probably be made in October.

South China Morning Post (Business News) 8/22/89, p. 11.

Cable and Wireless to Launch EDI System

Cable and Wireless has decided not to wait for the findings of a feasibility study commissioned by the TRADELINK consortium about an electronic data interchange (EDI) system in Hong Kong. The company will launch its own EDI system in Hong Kong on June 5, about a month before the results of the Coopers and Lybrand study are handed to TRADELINK. According to Cable and Wireless, the move is nothing unusual. Plans for the system, to be called Intertrade, have been underway since early last year, well before TRADELINK was formed.

South China Morning Post (Business News) 9/9/89, p. 11.

Tradelink Announcement on EDI Expected Next Month

TRADELINK Electronic Document Services is next month expected to make a preliminary announcement on its role in setting up a territory-wide electronic data interchange (EDI). The group—composed of 11 Hong Kong organisations—is investigating the feasibility of EDI in Hong Kong. Anthony Charter, managing director of Hong Kong Air Cargo Terminals and newly appointed chairman of TRADELINK, said: "EDI has already proved its worth in the highly competitive air transport industry and I am not in any doubt that it will become an essential way of doing business for much of Hong Kong's trading community in the future. The only question that has to be resolved is to what extent Hong Kong would benefit from a coordinated approach."

South China Morning Post (Business News) 9/4/89, p. 3.

Agenda: Electronic Data Conference

With so many people (still) waiting to hear the recommendations of the Coopers and Lybrand report commissioned by TRADELINK on the feasibility of electronic data interchange in Hong Kong, the two-day EDI Asia '89 conference which starts at the Exhibition Centre today should generate a lot of interest. . . . TRADELINK's new chairman, Anthony Charter, will reveal all tomorrow when he delivers a talk on the Coopers and Lybrand consultancy study and the future role of TRADELINK in the application of EDI in Hong Kong. For most observers, the question of whether or not EDI is the wave of the future for Hong Kong has already been answered. It will be. The questions that remain are when substantial services will be adopted by Hong Kong, who will provide the services (and the hardware involved), and what kind of system will be implemented. The principal sponsor of the conference program is everyone's favourite computer monolith, Big Blue. Then, sponsoring everything from speeches to lunches to cocktail receptions, is Hewlett Packard, American Telephone and Telegraph, Digital Equipment, ICL, Hong Kong Telephone, Cable and Wireless, Intertrade, NYNEX, McDonnell Douglas Information Systems, International Network Services, Singapore, Computer Systems and even relational database specialist Oracle. Not to be seen left out of the event, the Government is also involved in the sponsorship program through both the Hong Kong Productivity Council and the Hong Kong Trade Facilitation Council.

South China Morning Post (Business News) 10/3/89, p. 12.

Tradelink Electronic Scheme to Process Trade Documents Under Study

By James Riley

The Government is considering a proposal that would allow a private company to provide an exclusive franchise service to process government-related trade documents electronically, according to Secretary for the Treasury Hamish McCleod. The proposal was submitted last week by TRADELINK . . . TRADELINK's initiative to form a public and private sector "partnership" to process government trade documents was also under consideration, he said. "We do not rule out, at this stage, any possible options in developing trade related EDI in Hong Kong," Mr McCleod said. TRADELINK chairman Anthony Charter said the report had found that the potential market for EDI services could be as high as $10 billion by the turn of the century, but that due to constraints unique to Hong Kong, the realisable market had been estimated between $1 billion and $1.5 billion. He said the market size was restricted by the resistance of smaller companies to computerisation; a lack of standards for the development of Chinese language EDI; a low awareness of the real cost of handling paper documents; and the legal constraints that electronic documents presented. The granting of an exclusive franchise would help overcome these constraints, and speed the overall adoption of paperless trading in Hong Kong, he added. The franchise should be granted in return for an obligation to explore low cost access to EDI for Hong Kong's numerous small traders and to help develop and establish Chinese-language EDI standards. . . . Mr Charter said the setting up of an EDI service could require an investment of up to $500 million over the next 10 years. Mr Charter said that while the EDI gateway to the government should be franchised, the open market should dictate the development of electronic document gateways between domestic trading partners, and between Hong Kong and overseas trading partners.

South China Morning Post (Business News) 10/5/89, p. 1.

Data Interchange Seminars Offered

The latest in a series of seminars organised by TRADELINK to prepare Hong Kong business for the advent of EDI. . . . "Although EDI is correctly described as a business function rather than a technological one, its implementation demands specialist software and telecommunications links," seminar leader John Sanders said. "Therefore the businessman needs to have a broad understanding of the technical issues involved, so that he knows the right questions to ask suppliers, and can be sure of acquiring the right software and communications services," he added.

Mr Sanders said that because TRADELINK was independent of any vendor, the seminar would not make specific recommendations for any particular EDI product or service. . . .

South China Morning Post (Business News) 10/16/89, p. 4.

World Not Ready for EDI Implementation

By Keith Cameron

It seems that we are subjected to "experts" talking on Electronic Data Interchange (EDI) on a daily basis. The questions which loom up in my mind are: Are the "experts" talking to the right audience? And, even if they are, does the audience understand what they are talking about? It hardly needed a multi-million dollar consultancy study to tell us that there was a myriad of small companies here that would need training in the fundamentals of information technology before any standardised electronic document exchange could be introduced. Taxpayers' funds paid for part of the TRADELINK study, for which we are now told that the consultants were given the wrong terms of reference. The TRADELINK organisation is claiming that all is not lost because of that and has turned to Government for a commitment of exclusivity for electronic document handling. This, it said, would enable EDI to be introduced on a commercial basis, provided it was linked to a Government-backed no-loss guarantee for the trading organisation. Commercial Utopia supreme, it would appear. While I have no argument with preparing for the day when all documents will be transferred electronically, I believe that the hype about EDI today is misplaced and premature. There is much to be done worldwide before a total EDI environment can exist, and most of the responsibility lies at the user end, not with the technologists, although some important technological implementations must occur. International standards for documentation must be agreed and implemented by all parties for EDI to be successful. Anyone who has been remotely connected with the freight and shipping industry will be aware that this is no mean task. It not only involves a collaboration between private industry, but it also demands conformity by relevant government bodies all over 'he world. . . . I do not mean to discourage the activity which surrounds EDI in Hong Kong today, but I do think that it could be a little more pragmatic and less theoretical.

South China Morning Post (Business News) 10/31/89, p. 13.

Firms Urged to Seize Lead in EDI Growth

BANKS in Hong Kong and other major banking and finance centres could lose their traditional data interchange business unless they take the lead in developing a standard global electronic data interchange (EDI) network, according to a banking and finance computer consultant. . . . While stressing that "what Hong Kong and Singapore are doing is a step in the right direction", Mr Griggs said that, like other major trading centres, "they are responding to market pressures in the fight to remain competitive". Many of the systems now in use worldwide, he said, were solving documentation and information problems and leading to systems that would easily extend to taking over much of the traditional banking aspects of trade finance. "Unfortunately, banks generally are not part of the movement and are in danger of being left out," Mr Griggs said.

South China Morning Post (Business News) 11/2/89, p. 14.

Group Steps Up Campaign on Data Exchange

By James Riley

The TRADELINK consortium has intensified its lobbying of the government for an exclusive franchise to computerise the processing of all government trade related documents. The proposal has drawn heavy criticism from some sectors of the high technology industry which claim that electronic document processing would be better serviced in a free-market environment. . . . The controversial proposal would include a safety net of government subsidies to ensure its profitability during its introduction. TRADELINK chairman Anthony Charter said the project would require a total investment of "considerably more" than $500 million over 10 years. Mr Charter said an exclusive franchise should be granted for EDI processing of government documents to ensure that a system of standards was established, and that the territory's vast number of small trading companies were encouraged to adopt the system. He warned that unless the government said it intended to adopt EDI before the end of the year, it was likely that the TRADELINK members would withdraw the proposal and dissolve the company. The group said it had spent $14 million investigating EDI in Hong Kong. . . . Mr Charter said unless Hong Kong traders adopted EDI practices they could become less competitive in international markets. "I believe (EDI) should be ranked at least equal in priority to major physical infrastructure projects like the new airport," Mr Charter said. "In this situation where you have a slow take (of EDI) in the early years, there is an implied subsidy that would be required from government," he said. "They subsidise roads and they subsidise airports—this is part of the infrastructure and if necessary they should subsidise it in the early years until it can stand on its own feet." The Hong Kong Information Technology Federation (HKITF), a 120-member high technology industry group, has responded coolly to the TRADELINK proposal.

South China Morning Post (Business News) 11/16/89, p. 4.

Council to Promote Joint Research Urged

By James Riley

LEGISLATIVE Councillor Professor Poon Chung-Kwong last week urged the Government to establish an autonomous council to coordinate joint research efforts between the public and private sectors. Professor Poon, who is also the chairman of the Government's Committee on Science and Technology and the head of Hong Kong University's science faculty, said Hong Kong lacked a centralised body to formulate and implement long-term technology projects. . . . The recent proposal by the TRADELINK consortium that it be granted a franchise to establish an electronic data interchange gateway to Government was a good example of where an established and powerful committee could be of use in making technology decisions, he said.

South China Morning Post (Business News) 11/21/89, p. 13.

Tradelink Makes Its Case for EDI to IT Federation

By James Riley

In an attempt to bolster support for its electronic data interchange (EDI) initiative, TRADELINK last week met with Hong Kong Information Technology Federation (HKITF) representatives in the hope of winning support from the powerful trade group. . . . There were some committee members that felt that if a franchise were granted, it be for an EDI gateway alone, and should not include any pre-processing. . . .

South China Morning Post (Business News) 11/28/89, p. 12.

Government to Decide on Trade Uses of EDI

By James Riley

The trading community in Hong Kong should know by the end of the month whether or not the Government is serious about plans to introduce electronic data interchange (EDI) to Hong Kong. Whatever the Government decides about its EDI plans, any announcement on the subject is likely to raise plenty of eyebrows among the local trading community. . . . The Government has given TRADELINK a commitment that it will indicate by the end of the month whether the group should proceed with further investigation and pilot projects—or that it deems the idea unfeasible. The Government's thinking on the proposal is not known, so it is impossible to guess whether or not the investment in TRADELINK by its shareholders will eventually pay its own way. But even if TRADELINK should disband, the company has already been an outstanding success as the principal impetus behind all the current talk about the EDI concept.

South China Morning Post (Business News) 3/4/90, p. 12.

Seminar on Paperless Trade

By Ian Lewis

The Hong Kong Shippers' Council is organising a one-day seminar to increase awareness of existing paperless communication systems while businesses wait for the TRADELINK Electronic Data Interchange (EDI) network to start up. The seminar is organised in conjunction with Intertrade, an EDI service run by Cable and Wireless (HK), and will be presented by Cantonese at the Hong Kong Convention and Exhibition Centre on April 12. . . .

South China Morning Post (Business News) 3/13/90, p. 4.

HK "Will Lose Out Without More IT"

By James Riley

The Hong Kong business community must become more aware of the opportunities that information technology (IT) offers and the problems that must be overcome in implementing that technology if the territory is to remain competitive in the region Legislative Councillor Mr Stephen Cheong Kam-Cheun said yesterday. Officially announcing the local industry's biggest-ever technology event, Information Technology Week (IT Week)—which is scheduled for September—Mr Cheong said Hong Kong had fallen behind some Asian competitors in the adoption of technology. There were key technology issues facing Hong Kong that had to be addressed as soon as possible if the territory were to maintain its position in Asia as a financial and industrial centre. . . . "Hong kong has had the misfortune of falling behind other territories like Taiwan, Korea and Singapore," Mr Cheong said. "It is now our duty and our hope that we will catch up—and given the Hong Kong people's tremendous appetite for learning and tremendous energy I am sure that we can get on with it," he said. . . .

South China Morning Post (Business News) 3/20/90, p. 12.

Government in EDI Venture with TRADELINK

By James Riley

The Government plans to set up a joint-venture project with TRADELINK Electronic Document Services to develop a system of "paperless trading", the acting Secretary for Trade and Industry, Mr Joseph Wong Wing-Ping announced yesterday. Funding for the $9 million venture will be shared equally by the government and TRADELINK. The project will develop a business plan and technical specifications for a long awaited community-wide system of electronic data interchange (EDI) for Hong Kong. Called SPEDI—Shared Project for EDI—the study will be completed by the end of the year.

South China Morning Post (Business News) 3/21/90, p. 3.

EDI Joint Venture "Half-Hearted Step"

By James Riley

Local industry groups have responded coolly to the Government's announcement last week that it had entered a $9 million joint venture, Shared Project for EDI (SPEDI), with TRADELINK to develop a business plan for the introduction of electronic data interchange (EDI) in Hong Kong. Spokesmen for the Hong Kong Telecommunication Users Group and the Hong Kong Information Technology Federation's EDI committee said the joint venture was a half-hearted step forward, and complained that the Government was still dragging its feet in making a solid commitment to adopting paperless trading practices. The spokesmen questioned the likely benefits that would be derived from the study, given its limited $9 million budget, and expressed concern that it would simply retrace the steps of the consultancy study carried out by Coopers and Lybrand on behalf of TRADELINK last year. "I am extremely disappointed," said HKITF EDI committee chairman Mr Roy Grubb. "We believe that the Government should be taking the bull by the horns and doing (EDI) for themselves—at the very least for their own paperwork." . . .

South China Morning Post (Business News) 3/27/90, p. 12.

Talks on Chinese EDI

Talks between Hong Kong and mainland electronic data interchange (EDI) experts to develop Chinese-language messaging standards have been scheduled for later this year following an exploratory meeting of representatives in Beijing recently. The discussions will aim to establish common character sets and internal codes for Chinese language data processing, Chinese versions of UN-EDIFACT (the international message standard for EDI), and trading terms and definitions. With the involvement of Taiwan, also represented at the Beijing meeting, it should be possible to develop Chinese language applications of EDI that can be used throughout China, Hong Kong and Taiwan, and internationally.

South China Morning Post (Business News) 5/22/90, p. 12.

Chapter 7

IT Architectural Alternatives

THE EVOLVING IT ENVIRONMENT

Instability and evolution in the organization structure for delivering IT support have been enduring features of the information technology (IT) environment. In the past decade changes in technology and corporate strategy have repeatedly challenged existing organizational structures for delivering IT support and have led to major reorganizations. Several key reasons lie behind this.

Technological Change

First, both for efficiency and effectiveness reasons, IT in the 1990s incorporates the technologies of office support, image processing, data and voice communications, and data processing. Ideally, all of these technologies are managed in a coordinated, integrated manner. Developing this coordination has not always been easy. In many organizations in the 1960s and 1970s each of these technologies had a different set of implementation issues and was marketed to the company separately. Quite independent internal organizational structures within the firm developed for managing each technology. Very few of these organizations had the necessary staff or the required mix of skills for the new technology or for facilitating its integration with other technologies. The varied managerial histories and decision processes associated with each of these technologies has made their integration exceptionally difficult, and this difficulty continues today. In most firms, the organization of information technology has evolved by experience to its present structure.

Second, ensuring the success of information technologies new to the organization often requires approaches that are quite different from those used with mainframes/minicomputer technologies with which the organization has had more experience. New organization structures have emerged to facilitate handling this problem. The trend is to shift more IT responsibility to the using group.

Third, where the firm's data and computer hardware resources should be located organizationally often requires rethinking. The dramatic hardware performance improvements (in all three technologies) in the past two decades allows very different organizational solutions today than were possible in the early 1970s. These improvements have been facilitated by the technology shifts from the vacuum tube to the very large-scale integrated circuits in computers and from copper wire to optical fiber in telecommunications. In each case vastly improved cost-performance ratios resulted. Equally significant, integrated circuits have permitted development of stand-alone personal computer systems and of office support systems that can be tailored to provide highly specific service for any desired location.

Technological change, then, has brought a dramatic shift in the type of information services being delivered to users and in what constitutes the best organizational structure for delivering them. This new structure involves not only the coordination of data processing, teleprocessing, and office support, but also affords opportunities to change the physical and organizational placements of the firm's technical and staff IT resources. Technical resources include such items as computers, word processors, image processors, private telephone exchanges, and intelligent terminals. Staff resources consist of all the individuals responsible for operating these technologies, developing new applications, or maintaining them.

Productivity improvements will continue as still smaller, more reliable circuits are developed. Table 7–1 shows the cost and performance trends per individual unit and circuit based upon known chip technology. The combination of these reductions in cost, increases in capacity, and the past decade's explosive developments in software have brought linked desktop computers to most office workers' desks.

Environmental Factors

In addition to technology changes, several nontechnological factors have prompted reexamination of effective organization of IT services inside the firm.

Human Resources.   The United States has a significant shortage of competent, skilled people who can translate technology into ongoing systems and processes within organizations. These shortages, severe in 1991, are likely to continue in the coming decade as our appetite for complex systems continues to grow. The slow growth problems that

TABLE 7–1   Cost and Performance of Electronics, 1958–the 1990s

Technology	1958 Vacuum Tube	1966 Transistor	1972 IC[a]	1980 LSI[b]	1992 CMOS[c]
Dollars per unit	$ 8.00	$ 0.25	$0.02	$0.001	$ 0
Bits stored per unit	1/32	1	1K	64K	16M
Dollars/logic unit	$160.0	$12.0	$ .200	.008	.0006
Access time	16×10^{-3}	4×10^{-6}	40×10^{-9}	2×10^{-10}	50×10^{-12}

[a]Integrated circuit.
[b]Large-scale integrated circuit.
[c]Complemental metal oxide semiconductor.

Source: Georges Anderla and Anthony Dunning, *Computer Strategies 1990–9, Technologies-Costs-Markets,* John Wiley & Sons, p. 18.

have beset the hardware manufacturers have not hit the software and system developers. Partially offsetting this has been the development of user-friendly technologies that allow faster applications to be developed by less-skilled individuals.

Telecommunications Environment.   The highly reliable, inexpensive digital telecommunications systems that have been developed in the United States and the "explosion" of optical fiber provide the potential for dramatically different services in the next decade. The economics and reliability of telecommunications in the rest of the world, however, differ from those in the United States and Canada, and this presents unique environments for the immediate future.

In Western Europe, excessive tariffs (often dramatically higher than in the United States and Canada) and inordinate installation delays have significantly slowed the growth of certain services. During the 1990s, however, better coordination of government-owned systems, increased privatization, and more cost-effective, time-responsive environments are likely to emerge.

In Latin America and other less developed areas, systems and infrastructure reliability problems are combined with the problems encountered in Europe. For example, because of an unacceptable level of communication breakdowns (some more than 24 hours in duration), several South American companies were forced to shut down a sophisticated on-line system supporting multiple branches and to seek solutions that addressed realistically the unreliability of the infrastructure. In another situation, a company was able to achieve acceptable reliability only by gaining permission to construct and maintain its own network of microwave towers. For multinationals this state of affairs poses important problems in developing international networks and common standards and has forced them to be flexible. Recent expansion of satellite links is ameliorating the problem, and paving the way for the inevitable fiber-linked global village. Managing the timing is the key challenge.

Supply–Demand Imbalances.   Legitimate user demand for IT support continues to vastly exceed the supply available from an IT organization. Business-justified applications waiting to be implemented and exceeding available IT staff resources by three or more years—the norm rather than the exception—lead to a perception of unsatisfactory support and to dissatisfaction with the central IT organization. This dissatisfaction is intensified when users want types of support that the company cannot afford at the time.

Widespread user frustration provides additional momentum for end-user computing, personal computers, and so on, as alternative ways to meet legitimate needs or to circumvent oppressive financial controls. Personal computer technologies have increasingly permitted users to bypass central IT control, which is helping to relieve some of these frustrations. In addition, users' confidence in their ability to develop and operate a computer system because of their experience on personal computers has grown, and the growth is likely to continue.

Systems Design Philosophy.   A fundamental shift has occurred in computer-based systems design philosophy. The prevailing practice in the 1960s and early 1970s involved writing computer programs that intermixed data processing instructions and data elements within the program structure. Today, however, the management of data elements and their architecture are clearly separated from the computer program instructions. Additionally, large amounts of external software are being acquired to be inserted into these systems. Implementing these shifts while coping with legitimate changes in business processing needs is placing enormous pressures on IT organizations. They must balance investing human resources in new systems developments against redesigning old systems to increase their relevance, while ensuring reliable operation of the old systems until the updated ones can be installed. Computer-assisted software engineering is maturing as IBM offers the potential of automated programming in its new depository architecture.

Combined with changing computer hardware economics, these factors have made organization structures designed in the early 1970s seem seriously flawed, and major reappraisals are in order for many firms. Succeeding sections of this chapter deal with the need for and challenges in merging the disparate technologies, various approaches for assimilating IT, and the issues involved in selecting an appropriate centralization/decentralization balance of data and hardware.

MERGING THE "ISLANDS" OF INFORMATION TECHNOLOGY

Problems in the speedy integration of data processing, telecommunications, and office support largely result from these technologies' very different management practices (as shown in Table 7–2). The following paragraphs analyze these differences.

1920. In 1920, an operational style of information services, elements of which persist to this day, was in place in most corporations. The manager and his or her secretary were supported by three forms of information services, each using a different technology. For word processing, the typewriter was the main machine for generating legible words for distribution; a file cabinet served as the main storage device for output, and the various organization units were linked by secretaries moving paper from one unit to another. Data processing, if automated at all, was dependent upon card-sorting machines to develop sums and balances, using as input punched cards that served as memory for this system. The telecommunications system consisted of wires and messages that were manipulated by operator control of electromechanical switches to connect parties. The telecommunications system had no storage capacity.

Also in 1920 (as shown in Table 7–3), the designers of the three "islands" (office support, data processing, and telecommunications) had significantly different roles. For office support, the office manager directed the design, heavily influenced by the whim of his or her manager. Although office system studies were emerging, word processing was the primary means of facilitating secretarial work. The primary means of obtaining new equipment was through purchasing agents and it involved selecting typewriters, dictaphones, and file cabinets from a wide variety of medium-sized companies. Standardization was not critical. Data processing was the domain of the controller-accountant, and its design activity was carried out by either the chief accountant or a card systems manager, whose job it was to design the protocols for processing information. Both data processing and teleprocessing were sufficiently complex and expensive that they required that managers develop an explicit plan of action.

A key difference between data processing and telephones, starting in the 1920s, was that the service of data processing was normally purchased and maintained as a system from one supplier. Thus, from the beginning, a systems relationship existed between buyer and seller. Teleprocessing, however, evolved as a purchased service. As AT&T made available a network of less-expensive inner-city telephones, companies responded by ordering the phones, and the utility developed a monopoly of telephone service. All three islands, therefore, were

TABLE 7–2 Information Technology Equipment, 1920–1990s

	Islands of Technology								
	1920			*1965*			*1990*		
Functions of the Technology	*Word Processing*	*Data Processing*	*Communication*	*Word Processing*	*Data Processing*	*Communication*	*Word Processing*	*Data Processing*	*Communication*
Human-to-machine translation	Shorthand Dictaphone	Form Keypunch	Telephone	Shorthand Dictaphone	Form Keypunch	Telephone	Dictaphone Terminal Audio input	Terminal	Telephone Terminal
Manipulation of data	Typewriter	Card sort	Switch	Typewriter	Computer	Computer	Computer	Computer	Computer
Memory	File cabinet	Cards	None	File cabinet	Computer	None	Computer	Computer	Computer
Linkage	Secretary	Operator	Operator	Secretary	Computer	Computer	Computer	Computer	Computer

TABLE 7–3 Information Technology Human Roles, 1920–1990s

	Islands of Technology								
	1920			*1965*			*1986*		
Roles	*Word Processing*	*Data Processing*	*Communication*	*Word Processing*	*Data Processing*	*Communication*	*Word Processing*	*Data Processing*	*Communication*
Designer	Office manager	Card designer	AT&T	Office system analyst	System analyst	AT&T	System analyst	System analyst	System analyst
Operator	Secretary	Machine operator	AT&T	Secretary	Operator	AT&T	Manager Secretary Editor	Manager Secretary Operator	Manager Secretary Multiple suppliers
Maintainer	Many companies	Single supplier	AT&T	Many companies	Single supplier	AT&T	Many companies or single supplier	Multiple suppliers	Multiple suppliers Other
User	Manager	Accountant	Manager	Manager	Manager Accountant	Everybody	Everybody	Everybody	Everybody

served in a different manner in 1920: one by many companies, one by a single systems supplier, and one by a public utility.

1965.   In 1965 the servicing and management of all three islands were still institutionalized in the 1920s pattern. Office support had a design content, but it was still very much influenced by the individual manager and centered around the secretary. Services, such as typewriters and reproducing systems, were purchased as independent units from a range of competitors offering similar technology. There was little long-term planning, and designs and systems evolved in response to available new technical units. Data processing, however, had become an increasingly complex management process, requiring serious evaluation of major capital investments in computers and software and multiyear project management of the design and development of systems support. In addition, all users needed extensive training sessions so that they could take full advantage of the productivity offered by the new system. At times even the corporate organization was changed to accommodate the problems and the new potential created by computer technology. AT&T completely dominated the provision of communications service in 1965; from a user's perspective, management of communications was a passive purchase problem. In some organizations, managing communications implied placing three-minute egg timers beside telephones as an aid in reducing the length of calls.

Today.   Today the management concerns for office support and telecommunications are integrated with those of data processing for three important reasons. First, all three areas now require large capital investments, involve large protracted projects with complex implementations, and may need extensive user training. Further, significant portions of all three services are increasingly being purchased from single suppliers. The corporate managers of these activities, however, are still learning how to handle these very different situations. A special challenge for office support has been the move from multiple vendors with small, individual dollar purchases to a single vendor that provides integrated support. The size of the purchase decisions and the complexity of the applications are several orders of magnitude larger and more complex than those of the 1970s, as networks of thousands of intelligent terminals are being created. For telecommunications the problem is that of breaking the habit of relying on a service purchased from a public utility and, instead, considering multiple sources in making large-capital-investment decisions that may include creating significant in-house networks. Both cases involve a sharp departure from past practices and require a type of management skill that was added to the data processing function in the 1970s.

The second reason for the integration of management concerns is that, to an increasing extent, key sectors of all three islands are physically linked in a network. For example, in a typical mid-sized manufacturing company the same WATS line may be used over a 24-hour period to support on-line data communications, normal voice communication, and an electronic mail message-switching system. A problem of one island, therefore, can no longer be addressed independently of the needs of the other two.

Third, complicating the situation today, dominant suppliers for each island market their products as the natural technological base for coordinated automation of the other islands. Some examples:

- IBM has attempted to extend its data processing base into office support and communications products.
- AT&T is attempting to extend its communications base into products targeted at data processing and office support; it has augmented its line of computers with its acquisition of NCR.
- Xerox is attempting to expand its office support effort into communications and data processing.

Failure to address these management issues appropriately places an organization at great risk. In the past decade most U.S. organizations have consolidated at least policy control and, in the majority of cases, management of the islands in a single IT unit at either corporate or divisional level. The main reasons for this include:

1. Decisions in each island now involve large amounts of money and complex technical/cost evaluations. Similar staff backgrounds are needed in each case to do the appropriate analysis.
2. Great similarity exists in the type of project management skills and staff needed to implement applications of these three technologies.
3. Most applications now require integrated technological networks to handle computing, telecommunications, and office support.

MANAGING THE ASSIMILATION OF EMERGING INFORMATION TECHNOLOGY

Chapters 3, 4 and 5 focused on how developments in information technology have facilitated many new strategic applications. Indeed, as noted, many companies depend heavily on this technology to operationalize and implement their competitive business strategy. For them, relevant new technology (for example, expert systems) must be identified and exploited as quickly as possible. Sustaining a high rate of product innovation, assimilating new vendors, and carefully evaluating new technology options each pose significant organizational challenges as these firms balance the need to run day-to-day operations smoothly while appropriately investigating and assimilating new technologies.

Two key steps must be taken to address this problem. First, corporate management needs to take a *contingency* approach to administrative systems for managing technology assimilation. Each technology requires different management approaches at various points of its life cycle. Introducing technologies to a firm requires an organizational learning perspective as opposed to considering only cost and efficiency. (These concepts are well grounded in organizational theory research. For example, the work of Chris Argyris and Donald Schon[1] describing how organizations successfully exploit new technologies has been particularly helpful.)

The second step is careful consideration of the establishment of a new unit in the IT structure called *emerging technologies (ET)*. This unit, which has been installed successfully in a number of settings, manages the identification and introduction of new technology with high payoff potential.

The Four Phases of IT Assimilation

The notion of information technology being assimilated in stages has been discussed since the mid-1970s. The pivotal work was introduced by Cyrus Gibson and Richard Nolan.[2] Focusing on large-scale computer technology and the development of centralized data processing departments during the late 1960s and early 1970s, they described four stages of assimilating data processing (essentially batch-oriented) technology.

As pointed out in Chapter 2, we have refined this idea when we speak of a company's "portfolio" of information technologies. Each technology application in an individual firm progresses through a set of phases that relate to Nolan and Gibson's original stages and that is also consistent with the organizational change concepts developed by Edgar Schein.[3] These phases are characterized in Figure 7–1 as investment/project initiation, technology learning and adaptation, rationalization/management control, and maturity/widespread technology transfer.

Phase 1. The first phase is initiated by a decision to invest in a new (to the organization) information-processing technology. It involves

---

[1]C. Argyris and D. A. Schon, *Organizational Learning: A Theory of Action Perspective* (Reading, Mass.: Addison-Wesley Publishing, 1978).

[2]R. L. Nolan and C. F. Gibson, "Managing the Four Stages of EDP Growth," *Harvard Business Review,* January–February 1974, pp. 76–88.

[3]Edgar Schein, "Management Development as a Process of Influence," *Industrial Management Review* 2 (1961), pp. 59–77.

FIGURE 7-1   Phases of IT Assimilation

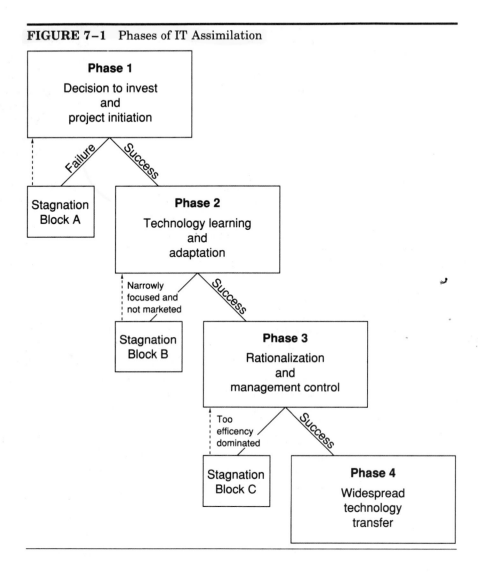

one or more complementary project development efforts and initial individual training. These projects are characterized by a lack of precision in both their costs and ultimate stream of benefits and, where possible, are confined to test markets and/or plants. The resulting systems, in retrospect, often seem quite clumsy. Each step of the project life cycle is characterized by much uncertainty, and considerable learning takes place. The second phase follows unless there is a disaster in Phase 1 —such as vendor failure, discovery that the technology is inappropriate to the firm, or poor user involvement—that results in "Stagnation Block A."

Stagnation Block A typically generates a two-year lag before new investments in this technology are attempted again, usually accompanied by a complete change of personnel. The decision to disinvest is normally a result of there being increased work and little benefit from the system. Sources of these problems may be vendor failure, lack of genuine management attention to the effort, incompetent project management, poor fit of technology to organizations, or merely bad choice. Rarely are the causes recognized immediately. The complexity and time requirements of implementing new information technology normally hide perception of the developing failure for 18 to 36 months. The project typically is not a clear technological disaster, but rather, an ambiguous situation that is perceived as adding more work to the organization with little perceived benefit. Rejection of the system follows. All aborted projects of this type that were studied had significant cost overruns. Each failure created anxieties and prevented development of coordinated momentum. Typically, organizations frozen in this state end up purchasing more services of a familiar technology. They become relatively adept at adapting this familiar technology to their use but become vulnerable to obsolescence.

At the CEO's urging, an insurance company launched a major desktop Executive Information System (EIS) project to put a device on every senior executive's desk. Eight months into the process, the CEO had to retire suddenly for health reasons. Without its key sponsor, the project died over the next six months. Only today, three years later, is the problem far enough in the past that the company is willing to start over, and it is significantly behind the state of the art.

Phase 2.   The second phase involves learning how to adapt the new technology to particular tasks beyond those identified in the initial proposal. As learning occurs, the actual benefits coming from the projects in this phase are often quite different from those anticipated. Again, retrospectively, the resulting systems look clumsy. Although the project life cycles in this phase are not characterized by great technical problems, they tend to be hard to plan. A study of 37 office support sites showed that in none of them was the first utilization of technology implemented as originally planned.[4] In each case, significant learning took place during implementation. Indeed, many of the competitive successes discussed in Chapters 3, 4 and 5 evolved over a decade or more as the systems were successively refined through new technologies and experience. If the second phase is managed in an adaptive manner that permits managers to capture, develop, and refine new understanding of

---

[4]Kathleen Curley, *Word Processing—First Step to the Office of the Future* (New York: Praeger Publishers, 1983).

how this technology could be more helpful, the organization moves to Phase 3. Failure to learn from the first applications and to effectively disseminate this learning leads to "Stagnation Block B."

A typical Stagnation Block B situation occurred in a large manufacturing company and involved automation of clerical word processing activities that were under the control of a very cost-conscious accounting function. Highly conservative in its approach to data processing technology, the firm had developed automated accounting systems centrally controlled in a relatively outmoded computer operating system, and it had no plans to enter into database systems. Focusing on only word processing for its mass mailing activities in order to save costs, it forfeited additional benefits. After three years of use, mass mailing was the only activity on its word processing system. Only with new management did the company solicit a proposal that led to the understanding of how this architecture could be the base for an executive information system and many other applications. The organization, however, had been frozen in underutilization for an unconscionably long period.

Phase 3.   This phase typically involves a significant change in the organization's approach to the technology, continued evolution of the uses of technology to ones not originally considered, and most important, development of precise controls for guiding the design and implementation of systems that use these technologies (to ensure that later applications can be implemented more cost-efficiently than the earlier ones). In this phase the various aspects of the project life cycle are analyzed, with the roles of IT staff and user becoming clearer and the results more predictable.

If, in Phase 3, control for efficiency does not excessively dominate and room is left for broader objectives of effectiveness, then the organization moves into Phase 4, which involves broad-based communication and implementation of the technology to other groups in the organization. "Stagnation Block C" is reached if excessive controls are developed that are so onerous as to inhibit legitimate, profitable expansion in the use of technology. An example of Stagnation Block C with respect to data processing is the case of a manufacturing company that built a large-scale, centralized distribution center and redesigned all its systems to support this structure. To justify the expense of this new center, it focused on gaining all possible cost economies of a very standardized, highly efficient distribution center. In its single-minded effort to gain this efficiency, the organization became so focused on standard procedures and cost squeezing that it lost its ability and enthusiasm for innovation and change utilizing this technology. This served to discourage users who had useful new ideas. Further, the rigorous protocols of the standard programs in the branches irritated users and helped set the stage for surreptitious branch-office support experimentation (Phase 1 in a different technology). Too rigorous an emphasis on control prevented logical growth.

Phase 4.   This final phase can be characterized as a program of technological diffusion. Here firms take the experience they have gained in one operating division and expand its use throughout the corporation.

Quite naturally, as time passes, new technologies will emerge that offer the firm the opportunity either to move into new applications areas or to restructure old ones. A firm is thus confronted over time with a series of waves of new technologies and at any one time is adapting to managing and assimilating several technologies, each in a different phase (see Figure 7–1). For example, a financial organization studied in 1990 was in Phase 4 in terms of its ability to conceptualize and utilize enhancements to its demand-deposit accounting (check processing) systems over a multiyear period. At the same time, it was in Phase 3 in terms of organizing protocols to roll out a new type of branch platform work station that had been successfully piloted in its branches and was now ready for systemwide use. It had recently made an investment in image processing in two departments, and although the firm was highly optimistic about the long-term results, it was clearly in Phase 1 with respect to this technology. Finally, it had just been decided that executive information systems was an important technology, and the firm was at the beginning of Phase 1 in terms of planning what to acquire and how to place it on the desks of key senior managers.

For organizational structure planning, the four phases can be grouped into two broader categories. Phases 1 and 2 comprise a category called *innovation phases,* and Phases 3 and 4 can be grouped as *control phases*. The differences between them can be described as forecasting, assessing, learning, creating, and testing (innovation) versus general usage, acceptance, and support (control).

Work in this area suggests that different parts of the organization will (or should) be responsible for these two functions. Keeping innovation-phase activities separate from control-phase activities helps ensure that the efficiency goals of one do not blunt the effectiveness goals of the other. This idea initially emerged from the organizational behavior literature. For example, James March and Herbert Simon, in their classic book on organizations,[5] referred to the innovation versus control phases as *unprogrammed* versus *programmed* activity. To enable and encourage unprogrammed or innovative activity, they recommended that organizations make special and separate provisions for it. This would frequently involve creating special units for the innovative purpose.

---

[5]J. S. March and H. A. Simon, *Organizations* (New York: John Wiley & Sons, 1958).

Managing the Emerging Technology (ET) Group

Increasingly, a new, explicitly separate organization unit to address innovation-phase technology exploitation and management appears to be a promising approach. Called the *emerging technology (ET) group,* it often resides initially in the IT organization on a level equal with applications development and operations departments. A historical analysis of 12 firms found that the key difference between leading and lagging financial institutions, airlines, and manufacturers was the early formation of an ET group. In some large, strategic IT organizations, the ET unit has been placed outside the IT department to help ensure that it is not swamped by the IT control philosophy.

Three issues must be dealt with by general management in structuring the ET group: organization, management control, and leadership (Table 7–4). The following paragraphs address these three issues in relation to the innovation and control phases. Because the innovation phase is more troublesome for most organizations, it is discussed in more detail.

Innovation Phase.   The atmosphere within the ET group should be exploratory and experimental. Examples of current technologies that such a group might be exploring are interorganization image processing and small-scale expert systems. The organizational structures and management controls are loose and informal. Cost accounting and reporting are flexible (though accuracy is essential), and little or no requirement exists for pro forma project cost-benefit analysis. The leadership style resembles what Hersey et al. refer to as "participating"; that is, the distinctions between leaders and subordinates are somewhat clouded, and the lines of communication are shortened. The level of attention to relationships is high compared to that of task orientation. As noted earlier, this informality is key to innovation and organizational learning.

TABLE 7–4   Characteristics of Effective Management of Emerging Technology (ET) Groups by Phase

	Characteristic	
Management Issue	*Innovation-Phase Effectiveness*	*Control-Phase Efficiency*
Organization	Organic (ET)	Mechanistic (traditional IT)
Management control	Loose, informal	Tight
Leadership	Participating	Directive (telling, delegating)

A study of the tobacco industry[6] referred to such informality as *organizational slack* and stated that "the creation or utilization of slack normally requires the temporary relaxation of performance standards." In the effective companies standards of efficiency were greatly reduced during the early testing phases of a new IT innovation. Organizations strategically dependent on IT should view innovation-phase activities as an integral part of their ongoing response to pressures to adapt to changing environments and should fund them appropriately.

Illustrative of the pressure and responses that lead to establishment of a separate department is the dramatic growth of "information centers" in response to end-user computing. These facilities are generally staffed with nontraditional data processing professionals and have very different accounting, justification, and cost-benefit systems. Firms that are strategically dependent on IT cannot afford to establish such centers reactively. They must proactively forecast, assess, and test appropriate technology to introduce it at an early stage. These activities are unlikely to occur without specific responsibility being assigned to a person or an organizational unit. The role of this unit may be seen as being similar to that of a corporate R&D department.

Two key features contained in a position analysis for ET are noteworthy because of their deviation from the general corporate R&D model. The first is that the manager of ET and the department staff serve primarily as facilitators as opposed to gurus. This implies the use of professionals outside the ET organization to forecast, track, and assess specific technology evolution. For example, a person in the database administrator's organization might be partially funded by ET to forecast, track, and test new database management system products. The second feature is that ET is responsible for what we call *intraorganizational technology transfer*. This refers to the role of designing and managing the Phase-2 introduction and diffusion of the targeted technology in the company. This is the key role of an ET group when contributing to the broad-based learning in a company. ET must first facilitate the development of user-oriented, creative pilot applications of the new technology. They then participate in discussions about how the new applications can best be developed and implemented, the education and training needs of users and IT professionals for using the new technology, and the changes in strategy or structure that may result from implementing the new technology and associated applications.

After the personnel directly involved with the new technology (the ET group) develop the ability to support it, general management then decides whether to provide additional resources to continue the diffu-

---

[6]R. Miles, *Coffin Nails and Corporate Strategies* (Englewood Cliffs, N. J.: Prentice-Hall, 1982).

sion of the technology throughout the organization (Phase 2). With requisite support of senior management, the ET group begins to teach others throughout the organization how to utilize it and encourages experimentation. A chief concern of the ET manager at this point becomes how to market it effectively to the rest of the organization. (In some organizations the job of selling the new technology is easy because the organizational culture encourages innovation and experimentation.) In the words of March and Simon, innovation in such companies is "institutionalized."[7]

Again the cultural differences between laboratory and operations are important. Part of the task of successfully selling this technology to other parts of the organization is finding a way to translate the unique language associated with the technology to a language compatible with the larger organizational culture. It was noted in a study of the electronics industry that these cultural differences exist more in the minds of the organizational participants than in any objective reality. The "artifacts" identified in the study resulted from the natural tendency of people "when faced with problems in human organizations of an intractable nature, to find relief in attributing the difficulties to the wrong-headedness, stupidity, or delinquency of the others with whom they had to deal."[8]

The issue is not whether the cultural differences exist only in the minds of the participants but, rather, given that they do exist somewhere, what can be done about them. The study identified two useful solutions employed by the sample companies. One solution was assigning members of the design department to supervise production activity and production personnel to supervise the design activity. For IT this means assigning responsibility for user implementation work to ET staff, as well as putting the user in charge of ET group projects. To be effective, this solution must be implemented with consideration for the wide gaps in technical expertise between subordinates and their managers. (Usually the subordinates know more about the technology or business process than the manager does.) However, this has proven to be a viable approach when the key individuals are chosen carefully.

A second solution was effective in other settings. It is the creation of special intermediaries to serve as liaison between the design department and production shops in the organizations. IT steering committees and user department analysts are examples of these intermediaries which have worked effectively in the IT environment. This strategy unfortunately increases the bureaucracy of the organization structure,

---

[7]March and Simon, *Organizations* (see footnote 4).

[8]Burns and Stalker, *Management of Innovation* (London: Tavistock Publishing, 1979), p. 53.

but for many organizations has proven to be a very effective solution to improved communication.

ET managers must analyze existing or potential resistance by organization members to the change brought about by the new technology. Resistance to change often stems from the reluctance of organization members to disturb delicately balanced power and status structures. ET managers need to adopt a "selling" leadership style, which is characterized by high task orientation and high levels of interpersonal interaction. Major organizational changes threaten long-established power positions and open up opportunities for new ones to develop. The advocate of a new technology who is insensitive to the political ramifications of the new system will face unpleasant, unanticipated consequences.

Once the range of potential uses of the new technology has been generated and appropriate users are acquainted with the new technology, management must make a decision about putting the technology permanently into place. At this juncture the assimilation project moves from the innovative phases to the control phases.

Control Phase.　The focus of the control phase is to develop and install controls for the new technology. Whereas the main concern during the innovation phase was the *effectiveness* of the technology, control-phase management is concerned with *efficiency*. In installing the necessary controls over the technology, management's task is to define the goals and criteria for technology utilization. The most effective leadership style here is one of "informing," with lower interpersonal involvement relative to task orientation. During this phase the organizational users (non-IT staff) are better able to judge the appropriateness and feasibility of the new technology to their tasks than they were during the innovation phase. The traditional IT organization and associated administrative systems are generally appropriate for this task.

For technologies in the later aspects of the control phase, IT managers typically exhibit a "delegating" leadership style. Interpersonal involvement and task orientation are low. With operation procedures now well understood and awareness high, the effective managers let subordinates "run the show."

PATTERNS OF HARDWARE/DATA DISTRIBUTION

As technology capabilities evolve (apart from issues in handling emerging technology), another key organizational issue concerns the physical location of the data and hardware elements. (Issues associated with the location of the development staff are dealt with in the next chapter.) At one extreme is the organization that has a large centralized hub connected by telecommunications links to remote input/output devices. At the other extreme is the organization with a small or nonexistent hub, most or all of its data and hardware being distributed to users. Between these two extremes lies a rich variety of intermediate alternatives.

The early solutions to this organizational problem were heavily influenced by technology. The high cost of hardware and the significant economies of scale associated with it in the early 1960s made consolidation of processing power into large data centers very cost effective. In contrast, the cost characteristics of the technology of the 1990s permit but do not demand cost-effective organizational alternatives. (In the 1990s technological efficiency of hardware per se is not a prime reason for having a large central data center.)

Pressures toward a Large Central Hub of a Distributed Network

In order to retain market share as the difference in efficiency between large and small computers has eroded, the vendors of large computers are suggesting that many members of an organization have a critical need to access the same large data files. Hence one ideal structure of an information service is a large central processing unit with massive data files connected by a telecommunications network to a wide array of intelligent devices (often at great distance). The alternative is a network of powerful intelligent terminals containing most of the organization's data files linked to each other. This dichotomy poses a set of complex architectural decisions.

Resolution of the IT organizational-structure problem depends on the key factors of management control, technology, data, professional services, and organizational fit. The impact of each of these factors is discussed here, with Table 7–5 presenting a summary.

Management Control.   The ability to attract, develop, maintain, and manage staffs and controls in order to assure high-quality, cost-effective operation of existing systems is a key reason for a strong central processing unit (CPU). The argument is that a more professional, less-expensive, higher-quality operation (from the user's perspective) can be put together in a single large unit than through the operation of a series of smaller units. A dominant trend of the early 1990s is the notion of data-center consolidation for reducing costs by eliminating duplicate software charges, technical support staff, operations, and so on. It was the primary force behind one large decentralized company's decision not to eliminate its corporate data center and move to regional centers. In the final analysis, the firm's management was unconvinced that eight small data centers could be run as efficiently in aggregate and that even if they could, the cost and trauma of making the transition would be justifiable. The company felt that

TABLE 7–5 Pressures on Balancing the Hardware/Data Distribution

Pressure	Toward Increasing the Hub	Toward Increasing Distribution
Management control	More professional operation. Flexible backup. Efficient use of personnel.	User control. User responsiveness. Simpler control. Improvement in local reliability.
Technology	Access to large-scale capacity. Efficient use of capacity.	Efficiency of small scale. Reduction of telecommunications costs.
Data	Multiple access to common data. Assurance of data standards. Security control.	Easier access. Fit with field needs. Data relevant to only one branch.
Professional services	Availablity of specialized staff. Reduced turnover disruption. Richer professional career paths.	Stability of work force. User career paths.
Organizational fit	Corporate style: centralized. Corporate style: functional. IT centralized from the beginning.	Corporate style: decentralized. Business need: transnationals.

through its critical mass, the corporate data center permitted retention of skills for corporatewide use that could not be attracted or retained in a series of smaller data centers. They decided to keep the operation and maintenance of all three technologies central, and to emphasize user input to projects in the design and construction phases through development departments in the several divisions.

In 1990 a large aerospace company consolidated eleven data centers to two. This produced savings of nearly $50 million by eliminating 350 jobs and duplicate software rentals, and management believed it also provided a higher degree of control.

Further, provision of better backup occurs through the ability to have multiple CPUs in a single site. When hardware failure occurs in one CPU, the network can be switched from one machine to another by simply pushing a button. Obviously this does not address the concern that a major environmental disaster could strike the center.

Technology. Another justification for a large hub is its ability to provide very large-scale processing capacity for users who need it but whose need is insufficient to justify their own independent processing system. In a day of rapid explosion in inexpensive, powerful computing, it is easy for users to do significant amounts of their computing on desktop computers or stand-alone minicomputers. At the same time, however, some users have huge "number crunching" problems—such as large linear programming models, petroleum geological reservoir mapping programs, and weather forecasting models—that require the largest available computing capacity. The larger the computer capacity available, the more value-added detail they can profitably build into the infrastructure of their computer programs.

Many firms see consolidation as an opportunity to better manage aggregate computing capacity in the company, thus reducing total hardware expenditures. When many machines are present in an organization and each is loaded to 70 percent, the perception may be that the "waste" of a vast number of CPU cycles could be eliminated if the processing was consolidated. Although such thinking was an important issue in the technology economics of the 1960s, its significance as a decision element has largely disappeared. The ability to eliminate duplicate software rentals and reduce operating staff remain important reasons for consolidation.

Data. Another pressure for the large central hub is the ability to provide instantaneous, controlled, multiple-user access to common corporate data files on a need-to-know basis. An absolutely essential need since the early days for organizations such as airlines and railroads, this access has become economically desirable in many other settings. Management of data at the hub is also very effective for controlling access and thus security. The issue has become extraordinarily complex, however. Where there is high local need for file access and only occasional need outside the area, locally sited files linked by telecommunications has proven to be a highly satisfactory and less expensive alternative. The geographic dispersal of data files is a very important and complex issue to study.

Professional Services. In itself, the sizable staff required for a large IT data center enhances the organization's ability to attract and retain a specialized technical staff. The ability to work on complex problems and share expertise with other professionals provides a desirable air of excitement, which helps to attract competent IT specialists to the firms and to keep them involved and excited about their work. Availability of these skills in the organization permits individual units to undertake complex tasks as needed without incurring undue risks. Furthermore, when staff and/or skills are limited, consolidation in a single unit permits better deployment of them. Additionally, having the large staff resources at a hub permits more comfortable adaptation to inevitable turnover problems. Resignation of one person in a distributed three-person group is normally more disruptive than five resignations in a group of 100.

For the ambitious individual who wants to remain in the IT field, the large unit provides more opportunity for stimulation and personal development. Perceived opportunity for technical and professional growth has proven to be a key element in reducing turnover. The opportunity for professional growth is a critical weapon in battling the so-called burnout problem.

Organizational Fit. In a centralized organization, the above-mentioned factors take on particular weight, since they lead to congruency between IT structure and overall corporate structure and help to eliminate friction. This point is particularly important for organizations where IT hardware was introduced in a centralized fashion and the company adapted its management practices to IT's location in this way. Reversal of such a structure can be tumultuous.

Pressures toward a Distributed Network

Other pressures push toward the placement of significant processing capacity and data in the hands of the users and only limited or non-existent processing power at the hub of the network.

Management Control. Most important among these pressures is that the distributed network structure better satisfies the user's expectation of control. The ability to handle most transactions locally is consistent with users' desires to maintain a firm grip on their operation. The concept of locally managed data files suggests that the user will be the first person to hear about deviations from planned performance of the unit and hence have an opportunity to analyze and communicate on a planned basis his or her understanding of what has transpired. Further, there now exist a greater number of user-managers with long experience in IT activities who have an understanding of systems and their management needs. These individuals are justifiably confident in their ability to manage IT hardware and data.

The user is offered better guarantees of stability in response time by being removed from the fluctuations in demand on the corporate network. The ability to implement a guaranteed response time on certain applications has been found to be very important to the user.

A distributed network also permits the user to predict in advance more accurately what the costs of computer use are likely to be. Not infrequently the distributed network appears to offer the possibility of lower costs (a careful cost analysis, however, sometimes reverses this conclusion).

Distribution of processing power to the user offers the potential to reduce corporate vulnerability to a massive failure in the corporate data center. A network of local work stations can keep key aspects of an operation going during a service interruption at the main location. A large forest products company decentralized to local fabricators all raw-material and product decisions through installation of a network of work stations with substantial local file storage capacity and processing capability. This reduced the volatility of on-line demand at the corporate computer center and increased the productivity of both corporate and distributed users. Reuters news service scatters key pieces of its database around the globe, and each module has multiple communications paths into it. If a large-scale disaster should occur in any location, the network will not collapse but will only slightly degrade. This system will work for information services, but it would be unviable for an airline reservation system, for example, where an informed opinion (as to whether a seat on a particular flight is or is not sold) must exist in a single setting.

From the user's perspective the distributed network offers a simpler environment, in terms of feeding work into the system and constructing the operating system. The red tape and delay of routing work to a data entry department are eliminated, and the necessary processing procedures can be built right into the ongoing operation of the user department. (Surprisingly, in some cases regaining this control has been viewed with trepidation by the user, although after the fact it is a "non-issue.") Similarly, the new desktop software has dramatically simplified the task of user/technology communication. (In the jargon of the trade, they are "user friendly.") Today's graphic/user interfaces, executive information systems, and electronic mail systems have revolutionized the use of the technology and have propelled such firms as Apple, Microsoft, and COMSHARE to the forefront.

Technology. In the early days the efficiency of large central processing units was superior to that of smaller units. Today, however, several important changes have occurred:

1. The economics of CPUs and memories in relation to their size have altered. The rule that the power of computers rises as the square of the price (commonly called *Grosch's law*) no longer applies.
2. The economics of Grosch's law never did apply to peripheral units and other elements of the network. The CPU and internal memory costs are a much smaller percentage of the total hardware expenditures today than they were in 1970, with network and peripheral unit costs being the dominant hardware items.
3. The percentage of hardware costs as a part of the total IT budget has dropped dramatically over the past decade as personnel, telecommunications, and other operating and development costs have risen. (In several industries teleprocessing investment and ex-

penses constitute more than half of the computer configuration expenditures.) Efficiency of hardware utilization is consequently not the burning issue it was a decade ago, except for a limited number of super computer applications. Considering these factors, as well as the much slower reduction in telecommunications costs (11 percent per year) and the explosion of user needs for on-line access to data files that can be generated and stored locally, the economic case for a large hub has been totally reversed in many cases.

4. As more systems are purchased rather than made, users are becoming better informed in the procedures of selecting and managing a local system.

Data.   Universal access by users to all data files is not a uniformly desired goal. Due to telecommunications costs and most users' infrequent need to access data files at other sites, it is often uneconomical or undesirable to provide central access to all data. Further, building in the inability to interrelate data from different segments of the firm may in fact be part of corporate strategy.

As a case in point, consider a large decentralized financial services company with a central corporate computing center that serves its four divisions. (All development staff reside in the division.) Almost no common application or data file exists between even two of the divisions in the company except for personnel. Even if its survival depended on it, the company could not identify in less than 24 hours its total relationship with any individual customer. In senior management's judgment, this lack of data relationships between divisions appropriately reinforces the company's highly decentralized structure; indeed there could be significant negative implications in terms of units poaching on each other's customers. No pressure exists anywhere in the organization for change. The corporate computing center, an organizational anomaly, was conceived as a cost-efficient way of permitting each division to develop its network of individual systems. In place for several years, no need has yet emerged for managers to develop common systems or to share data.

Technicians can readily suggest interesting approaches for providing information that has no practical use. Indeed those ostensibly sound suggestions if implemented would destabilize soundly conceived organizational structures.

Professional Services.   Moving technical support functions away from an urban area offers the opportunity to reduce employee turnover, the bane of metropolitan-area IT departments. Recruiting and training can be more difficult in such settings, but once the employees are there, and if they are sensitively managed, the relative scarcity of "headhunters" and nearby attractive employers reduces turnover pressures.

When the IT staff is closely linked to the user organization, it becomes easier to plan employee promotions that may move technical personnel from the IT organization into user departments. This is critical for the department with low employee turnover, as the former change agents begin to develop "middle-age spread" and burnout symptoms. Two-way staff transfers between user departments and IT are a growing trend for expanding the experience base and facilitating closer user–IT relations. This is discussed further in the next chapter.

Organizational Fit.   In many settings the controls implicit in the distributed approach better fit the corporation's organization structure and general leadership style. This is particularly true for highly decentralized structures (or organizations that wish to evolve in that direction) and for organizations that are geographically very diverse.

Finally, widely distributed facilities fit the needs of many multinational organizations. Although airline reservation data, shipping container operations, and certain kinds of banking transactions must flow through a central location, the overwhelming amount of work in many settings is more effectively managed in the local country, with communication to corporate headquarters either by fax, mail or delivery service, telecommunications link, or some other means, depending on the organization's management style, size of unit, and so on.

Assessing the appropriateness of a particular hardware–data configuration for an organization is very challenging. In all but the most decentralized of organizations, there is a strong need for central control over standards and operating procedures. The changes in technology, however, both permit and make desirable in many settings the distribution of significant amounts of the hardware operations and data handling. What in a previous technology was an either/or situation, today is a wide portfolio of difficult options, as we move to ever more networked organizations.

SUMMARY

The trend to merge technologies and the ability to distribute data and hardware must be carefully managed in combination, because they are interdependent. Since firms vary in their use of IT, history, culture, and business strategy, they may appropriately develop radically different structures. When new needs arise for central integrated files in industries in which IT is *strategic* (such as banking and insurance), there is a strong tendency to accelerate the merging of all services into single-site support systems, often at the cost of great organization disruption. (Industries in which IT is *supportive* can move more slowly.)

On the other hand, even some banks have maintained distributed stand-alone systems providing similar support. Key reasons for these structures lie in the bank's internal culture, geography, and other factors relating to its business practices.

Periodic reexamination of the organization's deployment of hardware and software resources for the IT function should have high priority. Changing technology economics, merging of formerly disparate technologies whose managerial traditions differ, and the problems of managing technology innovation have made obsolete many organizational structures that were appropriate as late as the mid-1980s. To ensure that these issues are being properly addressed, six steps must be taken:

1. Establish, as part of the objectives of a permanent corporate policy group, the development of a program to periodically review IT architecture. Foremost, this involves balancing the desires for a strong hub against the advantage of a strongly distributed approach and ensuring that different technologies are being guided appropriately. A structure that is appropriate for the technology and competitive environment of 1993 may not be appropriate in 1997.

2. Ensure that uniformity in management practice is not pushed too far and that appropriate diversity is accommodated. It may be appropriate for the different parts of the organization to evolve different patterns of support for hardware and data. (Just because four units are supported out of a central hardware facility does not automatically imply that it is appropriate for the fifth). Differing phases of development of specific technologies and geographical distance from potential central service support, for example, are valid reasons for different approaches.

3. Show particular sensitivity to the needs of international activities. What works in the United States may not work at all in Thailand. Neither companies that operate primarily in a single country nor transnationals that operate in many countries can assume that enforcing the same approaches in all countries is appropriate. Each country has different cost and quality structures of telecommunications, different levels of IT achievement, different reservoirs of technical skills, different cultures, and so on. These differences are likely to endure for some time. A common hardware/data architecture standard will have to be flexible.

4. Address these issues in a broad strategic fashion. The arguments and reasoning leading to a set of solutions are more complex than simply the current economics of hardware or deciding which persons should have access to particular data files. Corporate organization structure, corporate strategy and direction, availability of human resources, and current operating administrative processes are other critical inputs. In both practice and writing, the technicians and information theorists have tended to oversimplify a very complex set of problems and options.

5. Ensure adequate innovation-phase investment; that is, investments in experimental studies, pilot studies of new technologies, and development of prototypes. Attention must be paid to ensure that proven expertise is being distributed appropriately within the firm, even to places where the technology's availability or potential may not be obvious. Establishing an ET group is a highly effective approach, particularly for firms that have high strategic dependence on information technology. Firms that have strong commitments to R&D in non-IT areas have found it easier to deal with these issues than firms that lack a strong research tradition.

6. Ensure an appropriate balance between long-term and short-term needs. A distributed structure optimally designed for the current technology and economics may fit rather poorly five years from now. It may make sense to postpone feature development or to design an approach that is clumsy in today's technology but which will be quite efficient in the anticipated technologies five years in the future.

Case 7–1

PROFILING AT NATIONAL MUTUAL (A)

In 1989, National Mutual Life Association of Australia seemed poised to become the number one life insurance office in the country; by some measures, such as single-premium business sold, it had already won the battle. With its success in life insurance assured, National Mutual set its sights on a broader horizon—the total financial services market. During the 1980s, the company had rapidly expanded its investment product line, moved into new areas of business, increased its overseas operations, and greatly enlarged its sole agency force. In the 1990s, management intended to establish an international reputation as a first-class financial services institution.

However, these initiatives had already exacted a price by exacerbating direct-sales force organizations' perennial problems:

- The training of agents: keeping the agents up-to-date on the new product offerings and strategies.
- The high cost of distribution.
- Agent productivity and retention.
- Maintaining a strategic marketing advantage.
- Ensuring that the customer receives high-quality service.

National Mutual had recently performed a feasibility study on using Client Profiling—a financial-planning expert system produced by Applied Expert Systems of Cambridge, Massachusetts. Management was convinced that the system could act as a conduit for financial planning expertise and product positioning from the head office to the field. The possible impacts of the technology were far-reaching, even dizzying—creating a crucial competitive edge in customer service and transforming the traditional methods of selling. The responsibility for successfully implementing the system was given to Neville Mears and the Profiling team.

The Australian Life Insurance Industry

In 1989, the population of Australia was approximately 17 million people, with over 10 million of those residents living in its five major cities (Melbourne, Sydney, Brisbane, Adelaide, and Perth). National Mutual (NM) was headquartered in Melbourne. National Mutual Life Association was the second-largest life insurance company in Australia, close behind the reigning AMP Society. In fact, since 1987, National Mutual had written more insurance than AMP, and in 1989 National Mutual became the first Australian-based life insurance office to have worldwide sales of over $3 billion, placing it just within the top 50 life insurers in the world. With an asset base of about $23 billion, the company had a 20 percent share of the Australian market. Together, National Mutual and AMP shared about half the total Australian market, dominating the other 57 registered life insurance offices in

Research Associate Audris Wong prepared this case under the supervision of Professor John Sviokla as the basis for class discussion rather than to illustrate either effective or ineffective handling of an administrative situation.

Australia. Exhibit 1 lists the top 10 life insurers in Australia in 1988 and 1989.

Throughout the 1980s, the life insurance industry had become increasingly competitive. Deregulation in 1984 allowed trading banks to enter the insurance business and vice versa. Larger banks rapidly picked up 8 percent of the insurance market, drawing on a ready-made distribution channel of vast branch systems and existing client bases. Also, a number of foreign firms—primarily American and British—opened offices in Australia.

In the mid-'80s, National Mutual obtained a retail banking license and established a number of new subsidiaries to market a variety of investment products. As a full-service insurance and investment firm, the company established its presence in Hong Kong and the United States to complement its operations in New Zealand and Great Britain. See Exhibit 2 for a listing of National Mutual's subsidiaries and associates. The AMP Society also owned a 50 percent interest in a bank and had bought other investment firms as well. This transformation in the Australian market mirrored changes in the life insurance business in other major markets such as the United States and England. The nature of insurance was changing as the number and types of investment products available to the general public grew. Traditional life insurance was beginning to be regarded as part of a larger financial portfolio and, in that sense, had to compete against a variety of investment products.

With so many investment alternatives becoming available to the general public, the financial-planning business flourished. In 1987, the International Association of Financial Planners (IAFP) organized an Australian chapter. IAFP/Australia lobbied for direct regulation of the financial-planning industry and maintained a registry of financial planners who met certain educational and planning practice criteria. The AMP Society tied its financial-planning services to its direct or captive agency force by using a "shopfront" approach: certain agencies were designated as financial services shops which would provide comprehensive financial planning. National Mutual had bought a controlling interest in Godfrey Weston, an investment advisory firm, which had approximately 150 professionals in the planning business. Godfrey Weston served as a new distribution channel for National Mutual products although its advice was independent. Godfrey Weston was free to recommend and sell other companies' products as well.

National Mutual Life Association of Australia

In 1989, the National Mutual Group was arranged into five divisions under Chairman of the Board Baillieu Myer and CEO Eric Mayer: Overseas Operations, International Investment House, Group Finance & Actuary, Australia Operations, and Strategy & Group Services. See Exhibit 3 for an organizational chart. Gil Hoskins was in charge of Australia Operations, and under him Pat Manning was the general manager for Agency, the primary distribution system for National Mutual products and services. One division of Agency was Agency Management and Development, which was headed by John Oates. Neville Mears reported to Oates as the project manager for Client Profiling.

The agency force was organized into branches, with one Branch Manager Agency (BMA) per Australian state (New South Wales, Victoria, Queensland, Western Australia, South Australia, and Tasmania.) Each branch might have anywhere from one to five Regional Managers Agency (RMA). Each RMA was responsible for from six to twelve Divisional Sales Offices (DSO). The

EXHIBIT 1 Top 10 Australian Life Insurance Offices

Company	Market Share Percentage		New Annual Premiums (millions) Ordinary, Superannuation, and Annuity			Single Premium Business (millions)	
	Rank	Dec 1988	Rank	1989	1988	Rank	March 1989
AMP Society	1	32.44	1	$734.837	$559.477	2	$1,255.8
NatMut Life	2	23.57	2	546.868	351.483	1	1,884.8
Colonial Mutual	3	5.82	3	155.453	85.995	7	427.6
Prudential	4	5.53	4	124.332	73.662	11	228.6
Merc Mutual	5	5.18	5	88.434	82.681	3	651.1
MLC	6	3.58	7	85.266	64.901	4	580.2
Capita	7	3.04	6	86.506	50.185	6	490.6
Legal & General	8	2.41	8	55.109	43.627	8	359.4
Westpac	9	1.96	9	50.156	20.741	12	165.4
Zurich	10	1.88	*	*	*	13	135.4
Industry Total		85.41		$ 2.29 billion	$ 1.64 billion		$ 8.46 billion

EXHIBIT 2   National Mutual Domestic and Foreign Subsidiaries and Associates (at 9/89)

National Mutual, Australia

ACC Holdings Ltd.
Australian Casualty Company Ltd.
Bongiorno Financial Services Ltd.
Godfrey Weston, Ltd.
National Mutual Assets Management Ltd.
National Mutual Funds Management Ltd.
National Mutual Life Nominees, Ltd.
National Mutual Portfolio Management Ltd.
National Mutual Property Services (Aust) Pty., Ltd.
National Mutual Security Ltd.
National Mutual Trustees Limited
Nexis Proprietary Ltd.
NM Rural Enterprises Pty Ltd.
NM Superannuation Pty, Ltd.
NM Travel Pty Ltd.
Palmer Gould Evans Pty Ltd.
PGE (Australasia) Pty Ltd.
Silverton Limited

Associated Companies

Capel Court Corporation Ltd.
Capel Court Powell Ltd.
Helm Corporation Limited
National Commercial Union, Ltd.
National Mutual Royal Bank Ltd.
National Mutual Royal Savings Bank Ltd.
Swann Insurance (Aust) Pty Limited
Town & Country Building Society

National Mutual, Overseas

Financial Administration Systems Limited
Integrity Life Insurance Company (United States)
National Mutual Assets Management New Zealand Ltd.
National Mutual Bank New Zealand Limited
National Mutual Finance Limited
National Mutual Fund Management Co. Ltd, Hong Kong
National Mutual Fund Management New Zealand Ltd.
National Mutual Insurance Company (Bermuda) Ltd.
National Mutual Insurance Company Ltd.
National Mutual Investment Management Limited
National Mutual Investment Services Ltd.
National Mutual Permanent Building Society
National Mutual Insurance Co. Ltd. (Hong Kong)
NM Financial Management Limited (United Kingdom)
NM Life Assurance Ltd.
NM Unit Trust Managers Ltd.

EXHIBIT 3 Partial Organizational Structure (at 4/1/89)

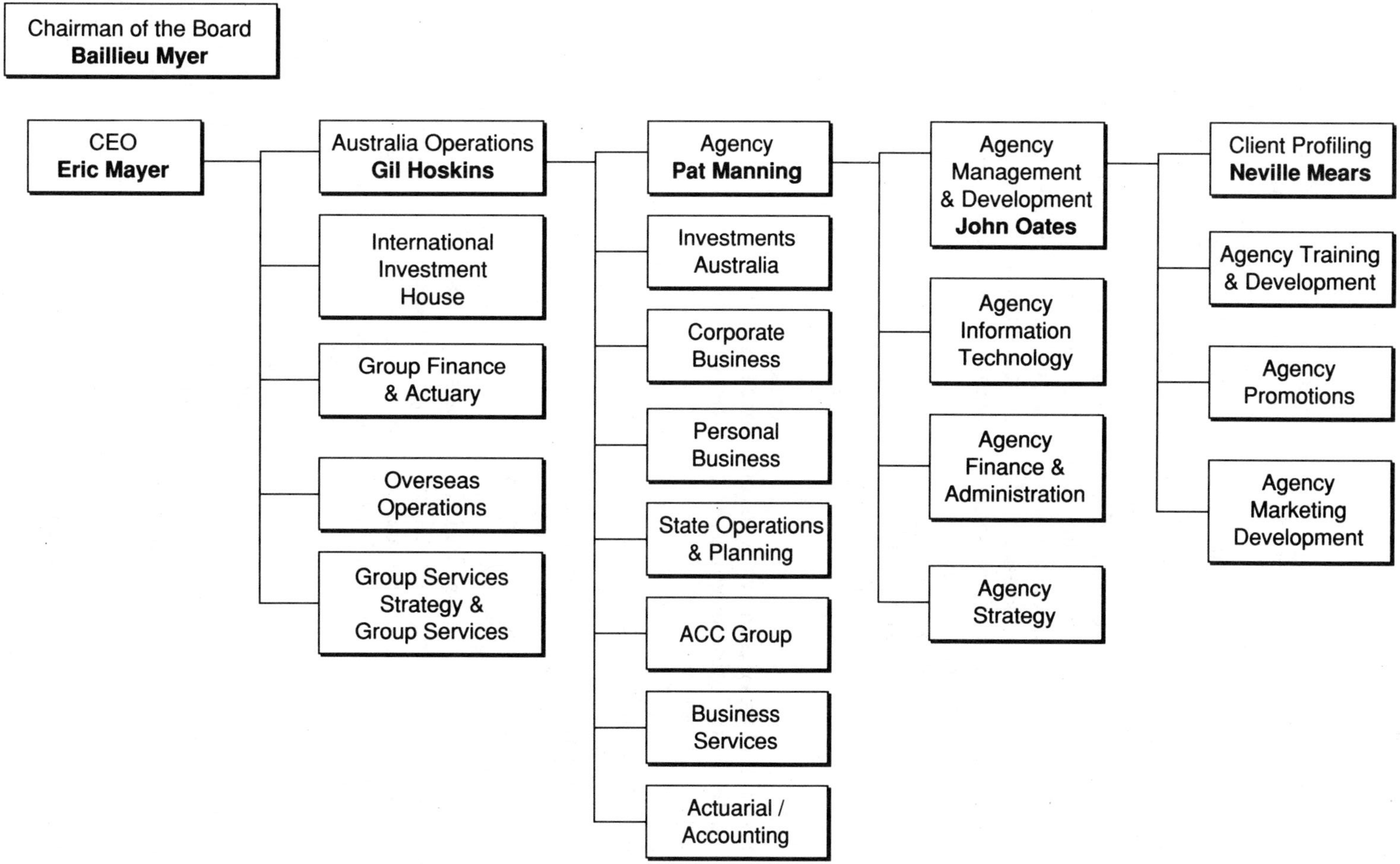

Chairman of the Board
Baillieu Myer

CEO
Eric Mayer

Australia Operations
Gil Hoskins

International Investment House

Group Finance & Actuary

Overseas Operations

Group Services Strategy & Group Services

Agency
Pat Manning

Investments Australia

Corporate Business

Personal Business

State Operations & Planning

ACC Group

Business Services

Actuarial / Accounting

Agency Management & Development
John Oates

Agency Information Technology

Agency Finance & Administration

Agency Strategy

Client Profiling
Neville Mears

Agency Training & Development

Agency Promotions

Agency Marketing Development

This chart shows the reporting structure and is not illustrative of seniority.

DSO was a unit of 10 to 40 agents, operated by a Divisional Manager Agency (DMA). See Exhibit 4 for a graphic representation of the field sales force organization. This hierarchy was organized into a highly decentralized agency structure. DMAs showed a great deal of independence, and in turn, agents could be highly independent from their DSOs. While the agency force was largely captive, several agencies had incorporated themselves under a different name and, while associated with National Mutual, presented themselves as independent businesses. For example, an agency that specialized in financial planning or industrial insurance might incorporate to signify a greater professionalism and specialization.

The Agency Force

National Mutual had three primary types of arrangements for distributing products: sole agents, associate agents, and special investment advisers. In early 1990, the company had a soliciting force of 3,500 sole agents—a direct sales or "captive" agency force in which National Mutual supported agents who sold only National Mutual products. This distribution system was considerably more expensive than selling through independent agents.[1] National Mutual had the additional costs of maintaining agencies and training agents as well as the usual costs of maintaining a line of insurance and investment products. The company had an agent turnover rate of 95 percent over five years—a typical retention rate for a large, diversified insurance company.

In the second tier of the sales force were approximately 1,200 associate agents. Associate agents were usually professionals, of-

ten accountants. These agents could sell NM products through a NM agent, often by making commission-splitting arrangements on an individual basis between the agent and associate agent. Lastly, some 50 special investment advisers were separately registered to sell only NM single-premium products (not annual-premium products) such as Approved Deposit Funds and Insurance Bonds. Typically, these people worked in the investment advisory business and did not wish to be restricted by a sole agency agreement, i.e., marketing only National Mutual products.

National Mutual planned to expand both its sole and its associate agency force. The company hoped to recruit and train more sophisticated agents in the face of a more sophisticated and financially aware clientele. These goals were eternally challenging given the high agent turnover that most insurance companies experience in fielding an agency force. Increasing product innovation escalated the problem.

In 1980, National Mutual, like the rest of the life insurance industry, had two basic products: permanent insurance (e.g., "whole of life") and term insurance. In the 1980s, the company moved first to "unbundle" contracts into their insurance and investment components. It then moved to add single-premium "insurance bonds," which paid a guaranteed investment return over a fixed time horizon. The innovations flourished and by 1989, National Mutual backed more than three dozen base products with many more options and features in terms of payment schedules, riders, and investment options. To better inform agents and influence their selling patterns, National Mutual had pursued the traditional solutions of improving and increasing training. The growing size of the agency force, however, was stretching the resources of Agency Administration and Development.

---

[1]Studies in the United States had shown that a direct salesforce is approximately 7 percent more expensive than "independent" agents.

EXHIBIT 4 Organization of Field Force

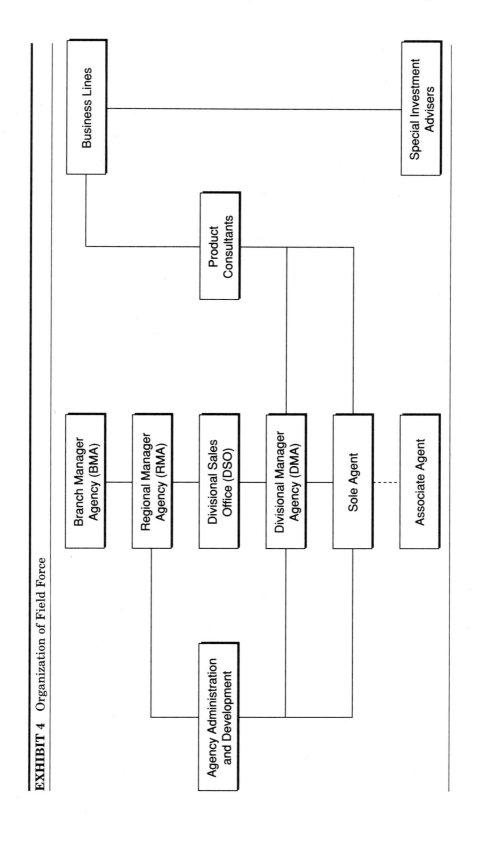

With so many products to support, the business units introduced the "product consultant," whose job was to get agents to adopt new products. National Mutual had an estimated 200 product consultants in Australia. As the local manager, the DMA received bonuses and incentives based primarily on the commission volume brought in by the agents. Therefore, local management had little incentive to "push" a new product unless there was significant compensation associated with it. In addition, local management had other significant responsibilities, including agent training, recruiting, and office management. Getting agents to use new or different products became the role of the product consultant, whose compensation was linked to the volume of their products sold by the local office. In effect the consultants were "selling" the agent on the idea of trying a new product. Moreover, the competition for the agent's time was significant, as many different product consultants might visit an agent over the week or month.

Field Salesforce Technology and Training

National Mutual had a large Agency Information Technology department, offering a number of innovations throughout the 1980s to aid field sales personnel. By 1989, most agencies were equipped with a tool kit of computer support known as MENTOR, which operated on IBM-compatible equipment, including the agents' Toshiba 1200 laptop computers. In the field, sole agents usually had available to them a product illustration system call COBBER, a prospecting and client database called ICIS, and a link to the head office mainframe to obtain information on past and pending policies, as well as MultiMate and Lotus 1-2-3. Not all DSOs actively supported these systems, and an agent was usually free to operate without

these information tools if he or she so chose. Agents were trained on these systems by the DMA or, at the beginning of their training, participated in one-day workshops run by Agency Development and Training.

After recruitment by the DMA, a sole agent's sales training began with Pre-Appointment Training (PAT). The DMA taught a PAT basic selling course and might accompany a trainee on some sales calls. The PAT program gave recruits a chance to experience the job firsthand before the agent was put on contract. Once hired, he or she attended a two- to three-week training program that taught selling techniques, client management, and the use of some computer support tools. Exhibit 5 shows a sample breakdown of the selling process and necessary agent skills as they might be taught to new agents: (1) Product Knowledge; (2) Prospecting; (3) The Approach; (4) Establishing Needs; (5) The Presentation; (6) Closing the Sale; and (7) Follow Through. The agent's DMA might continue training at the DSO, but otherwise the agent's basic training was over. Many agents took advantage of the courses offered by the Australian Lifewriters Association, such as financial planning, investments, and corporate superannuation, and were encouraged to do so through credits in sales competitions. National Mutual had the highest representation of any company in such courses and over the past few years management had reaffirmed its commitment to additional training many times. Agents often specialized their markets according to personal ability or as trained by the DMA who might have experience in particular fields.

The independence of the agent force made National Mutual's attempts to initiate cultural change difficult. Management was greatly concerned with the prevalence of "policy floggers," agents who sold only one or a handful of products, usually those products that were easiest to learn and paid the high-

EXHIBIT 5 A Sample Breakdown of the Traditional Selling Process*

1. Product Knowledge
One of the key components of being a top agent, product knowledge is understanding and being able to communicate what National Mutual products can do for the customer. With NM's rapidly expanding product line, keeping up-to-date is extremely difficult.

2. Prospecting
Finding potential clients to contact. An agent can spend up to 20 hours a week prospecting and making cold calls.

3. The Approach
The initial interview. These first impressions will establish the agent-customer relationship. All NM agents (and most employees) are given personality tests to help them create a winning approach.

4. Establishing Needs
The agent must convincingly uncover the customers' insurance needs, as well as their ability to buy NM products. This is where the CIMER process might take place. Needs must be exposed before a discussion of products can take place.

5. The Presentation
How National Mutual products can meet the customer's needs makes up the presentation. Agents describe what products and in what amounts are suitable for the customer, plus reaffirm NM's advantages over its competitors.

6. Closing the Sale
Closing the sale hinges on convincing the customer of the urgency of fulfilling his or her exposed needs. Coaxing the customer to buy depends on how well all the previous steps of selling have been mastered.

7. Follow Through
Once the sale is closed, agents should maintain and cultivate the relationship they have built with their clients. This includes excellent customer service, asking for referrals, and checking up on the clients periodically to see if their needs have changed.

*Note: Within the traditional selling process most agents will endeavor to complete steps 3 through 6 in a one-interview situation. (Therefore, adoption of the Profiling concept, which necessitates two interviews, is in effect a cultural change.)

est commissions. A number of studies conducted by the Life Insurance Marketing Research Association (LIMRA) in the United States had shown that client retention increased dramatically when a client purchased more than one product from a company. Consequently, management felt that the "one-off" sales approach led to weaker relationships between NM and the client, as well as providing an insufficient representation of the full line of products and services that the company could bring to bear.

Management at National Mutual was also aware of the growing, global tide of consumer concern. Consumerism had resulted in significant legislative initiatives; in the United States, the distribution of life insurance and investment products had been considerably regulated. In 1989 the United Kingdom passed a law that required any person selling financial products to first produce a financial plan and to keep records of that plan for seven years, so that planners could prove they had "sufficient client knowledge" and that the individual planner had provided "best advice" to the purchasing consumer. A financial-planning expert system like Client Profiling in the hands of every agent might potentially serve as a means toward ensuring "best advice" and an independent view of the client's situation. Given the fact that legal innovations had a history of moving across from the United Kingdom and United States to Australia, the issue was salient in management's mind.

Client Profiling—The System

Client Profiling was developed by Applied Expert Systems (APEX) of Cambridge, Massachusetts. It was designed to perform comprehensive financial planning in the areas of cash management, risk management, income protection, general insurance, education funding, wills, credit management, investment planning, and retirement planning. Profiling also provided a net-worth restructuring statement to guide clients to a more healthy financial balance sheet through a strategy of asset diversification. Its primary market was couples, families, and individuals with joint incomes above approximately $30,000 and below $150,000.

The profiling process had three parts: an extensive questionnaire, a professional-looking "Personal Financial Profile" (Client's Report),

and an Agent's Report. Exhibit 6 shows an overview of this process. The questionnaire required the client to gather extensive financial and personal data, including future goals such as buying a new home or financing a wedding. The profile then made generic recommendations such as "Purchase an income protection policy for Albert with a weekly benefit of $790 for sickness or accident to age 65." The profile used computed text to prepare a plan that seemed to be written to the client's personal situation, as opposed to "boilerplate" text with numbers inserted. The Agent's Report matched specific National Mutual products to these recommendations. The above recommendation would reference "PRODUCT NAME: Professional Income Protection," followed by a list of "Selling Points." See Exhibits 7 and 8 for sample pages of the Client's Report and Agent's Report.

In short, with the financial data given in the questionnaire, the expert financial planning logic of the system (over 2,000 rules) presented a comprehensive financial picture and exposed the client's insurance and investment needs. The client received a professional-looking document that detailed his or her financial situation and pinpointed areas for improvement plus a strategy for meeting future goals. The agent worked from this document and the Agent's Report which explained which National Mutual products were a suitable match to the client's needs.

IBM introduced National Mutual to APEX in mid-1986. Eric Mayer and Gil Hoskins immediately saw tremendous potential to acquire expert-systems expertise and hoped it would increase the productivity of their sole agents and gain a competitive edge. Unlike its arrangement with Godfrey Weston, National Mutual's potential purchase of Client Profiling offered the opportunity to extend financial planning services to all of National Mutual's agents and clients. Client Profiling would offer sound financial-

EXHIBIT 6   Profiling Overview

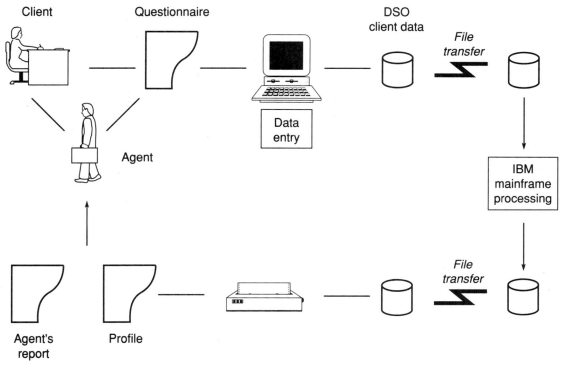

Client   Questionnaire   DSO
                                                      client data   *File transfer*

                                        Data entry

                                                      Agent

                                                                           IBM mainframe processing

                                                                           File transfer

Agent's report   Profile

planning advice and still be tied to its sole agency force.

Test Results and Expected Returns

In January 1988, APEX and National Mutual agreed to initiate a commercial and technical feasibility study. Together they conducted a targeted test with six agents. The results indicated that the close ratio of sales to interviews moved from one sale in three interviews to four sales out of five interviews. The average premium sale increased to A$2900, compared to the Australian average premium sale of A$1400.[2] Four to five referrals could be expected from each satisfied client. Agent retention was expected to dramatically improve as Client Profiling expanded the agents' role, helped them move into a high-income market, and in general, made "better" agents.

With Client Profiling, agents were expected to sell to genuine client needs. Previous National Mutual studies had shown that a full "needs analysis" often resulted in bigger sales and a greater variety of products suggested to the client. Furthermore, through cross-selling, where the client buys more than one product from National Mutual, agents would build stronger and multiple relationships with their clients. Moreover, the company hoped that clients would see National Mutual as not just a life insurance company, but also as their in-

---

[2]US$1 = A$1.2.

EXHIBIT 7   Client's Report: Sample Pages (page 1 of 4)

SUMMARY OF OUR RECOMMENDATIONS

Cash Management

1. Monitor your spending so that you will be able to continue your saving to meet your goals.
2. Set up a cash reserve of $2,527 in a Statement Savings Account. Ensure that you have a line of credit for at least $5,055.

Special Cash Need

3. Set aside $7,660 of your assets to buy a new car.

Special Cash Need

4. Allocate $511 of annual increasing savings to fund your daughter's wedding.

Risk Management

5. Purchase at least $461,785 of life insurance on Albert's life in addition to his existing coverage to provide funds for high priority needs.
6. Also purchase at least $96,900 of life insurance on Catherine's life to provide funds for high-priority needs.

Income Protection

7. Purchase an Income Protection policy for Albert with a weekly benefit of $790 for sickness or accident to age 65.

General Insurance

8. Review the cover for your primary residence. Ensure that the cover for all your home contents, personal property, and personal liability is adequate. Make sure you have an inflation rider on this policy.
9. Review your car insurance to determine if your cover is adequate. Elect the highest excess with which you feel comfortable.

Education Funding

10. Set aside $5,113 of your assets and allocate $1,896 of your annual savings to partially fund the education of your children.

Wills

11. Have a will prepared for Catherine. Review Albert's will immediately.
12. Consider the execution of "Enduring Power of Attorney" documents.

Credit Management

13. Review your loan situation.

EXHIBIT 7 Client's Report: Sample Pages (continued) (page 2 of 4)

Risk Management

The following represents an analysis of capital and future income needs in the event of the premature death of either of you. Properties and other non-repositionable assets are not considered realisable, because they cannot be expected to be easily cashed in the event of death. Therefore they are not included in the Capital Needs Summary table. Non-taxable income, other taxable income, and investment and interest income are not taken into account in the Future Income Needs table as the level of income could alter in the event of death. In consultation with your Agent or Financial Adviser you may wish to review the recommendations.

Because you did not specify the amount of survivor income, we estimate that your family would need 75 percent of Albert's current earnings, or $3,438 a month indexed for inflation, during the period when your children are dependent on the survivor for support.

Since you did not specify the amount of survivor income after your children are independent, we have estimated that the survivor will require 67 percent of Albert's current earnings, or $3,071 a month indexed for inflation.

For the purposes of this Profile, it is assumed that Social Security benefits will not be available.

Recommendation #5: Purchase at least $461,785 of life insurance on Albert's life in addition to his existing coverage to provide funds for high-priority needs.

Explanation: The following tables are an analysis of Catherine's capital and future income needs situation in the event of Albert's premature death.

Capital Needs Summary for Catherine if Albert Dies Today

	$	$
Realisable Assets	15,300	
Superannuation Lump Sum Proceeds	374,500	
Insurance Proceeds	40,000	
Social Security	0	
Total Capital Assets Available		429,800
Less: Funeral Expenses	5,000	
Administrative Expenses	21,490	
Education Fund	27,345	
Other Lump Sum Needs*	2,000	
Mortgages	74,000	
Debts	1,700	
Cash Reserve	1,390	
Total Immediate Cash Needs		132,925

*Other Lump Sum Needs is for donation to RSPCA.

A. Capital Available after Cash Needs: $296,875

EXHIBIT 7   Client's Report: Sample Pages (continued) (page 3 of 4)

Analysis of Future Income Needs in Today's Dollars

	Catherine with Children (8 years)	Catherine Alone (20 years)	Catherine During Retirement
	$	$	$
Monthly Need	3,438	3,071	3,071
Sources of Income:			
Catherine's Income	0	0	0
Survivor Benefits:			
Social Security	0	0	0
Total Income	0	0	0
Net Need	3,438	3,071	3,071
Capital Needed for Income*	282,406	340,720	135,534

B. Total Capital Needed for Income:	$758,660

Total Capital Required (B − A): $461,785

- *Assumptions:* This capital is invested at 11% with the monthly need inflated at 6% being drawn against the capital.

The above capital needs analysis indicates:

- If Albert died today there would be adequate assets to cover immediate needs.
- There would be sufficient resources to provide Catherine with income during the time that your children will rely on her for support.
- There would be insufficient resources to provide Catherine with ongoing income after your children become independent.

Meeting immediate cash needs after death is a high priority. Providing income during the period when your children are dependent on Catherine for support is another high priority. You have adequate capital to meet your two most pressing needs.

However, to also cover Catherine's estimated ongoing income needs after your children are no longer dependent, the total capital required becomes $461,785. The most cost-effective way (and often the only way) to generate this capital is through insurance.

Since the majority of Albert's life insurance is employer-provided, he should review his capital needs again in the event of a change in his financial, personal, or especially his work situation.

EXHIBIT 7   Client's Report: Sample Pages (continued) (page 4 of 4)

Guide to Implementing Our Recommendations

Net Worth Restructuring Statement

This chart shows how our recommendations affect the balance sheet of your financial position. You should read it from left to right. The *Decreases* column shows funds taken out of assets and reductions of debts; the *Increases* column shows funds added to assets and increments of liabilities. These shifts in the composition of your net worth result in the *Recommended Position,* with *Position Today* as the starting point.

Repositionable Assets	*Position Today*	−	*Decreases*	+	*Increases*	=	*Recommended Position*
	$		$		$		$
Statement Savings Account(s)	3,300		773		0		2,527
Savings Investment Account(s)	5,000		4,304		0		696
Cheque Without Interest Account(s)	500		500		0		0
Guaranteed Insurance Bond(s)	0		0		5,577		5,577
Total	**8,800**						**8,800**
Invested Assets							
Other Invested Asset(s)	6,500		0		0		6,500
Total	**6,500**						**6,500**
Non-Repositionable Assets							
Life Insurance Cash Value	3,000		0		0		3,000
Motor Vehicles	10,500		0		0		10,500
Primary Residence	135,000		0		0		135,000
Land	15,000		0		0		15,000
Albert's Super Fund(s)	123,000		0		0		123,000
Other Non-Repositionable Asset(s)	15,000		0		0		15,000
Total	**301,500**						**301,500**
Total Assets	**316,800**						**316,800**
Liabilities							
Home Loan	74,000		0		0		74,000
Credit Card Debt	1,700		0		0		1,700
Total	**75,700**						**75,700**
Net Worth	**241,100**						**241,100**

EXHIBIT 8   Agent's Report: Sample Pages (page 1 of 3)

Initiating Agent Name:	John Sample
Agent Name:	Branch Direct
Agent Division:	Branch Direct
Plan Date:	12/11/1990

AGENT'S REPORT
for
Albert and Catherine Friendly

The clients have indicated that their principal financial objectives are:
- To buy a new car
- To fund their daughter's wedding
- To fund their children's education

Action Plan

Call Albert and Catherine to set up an appointment to present this plan.
Let them know that someone else prepared this plan. You may disagree with some recommendations or have other ideas.

Client Summary

Albert Friendly   Catherine Friendly
Age: 44   Age: 37
Computer Programmer   Home Duties
Employee

Home:	24/2001 Space Odyssey Drive
	Apollo Bay
	VIC 3233
Telephone:	052 381 2274 (Home)
	052 26784 (Work)
Dependents:	David, 10 year-old son, Kelly, 16 year-old daughter
Income:	$ 56,780
Assets:	$316,800
Liabilities:	$ 75,700
Net Worth:	$241,100
Annual Savings Capability:	$ 4,490
Effective Tax Rate:	31%
Client Marginal Tax Rate:	47%

EXHIBIT 8   Agent's Report: Sample Pages Continued (page 2 of 3)

Sources and Uses of Funds

Summary of Funding Sources

	Funds Available ($)
Repositionable Assets	15,300
Annual Savings Capability	4,490

Allocation of Funds by Need

Funding Needs		*Funds Allocated*	*Additional Funds Required*
Amount	*Purpose*		
$		$	$
	Establish a Cash Reserve		
2,527	Sources: Assets	2,527	
	Education Costs		
27,345	Sources: Assets	5,113	11,681 or
	Annual Savings	1,896	1,226
	To buy a new car		
7,660	Sources: Assets	7,660	
	To fund their daughter's wedding		
2,751	Sources: Annual Savings	511	
	Personal Insurance		
2,083	Sources: Annual Savings	2,083	

vestment adviser. National Mutual foresaw better business retention and a more stable, better-paid, more productive agency force. In principle, Client Profiling had the potential to make all National Mutual agents an extension of the full-service financial services institution it aimed to be.

A decision was reached in July 1988 to proceed with the development of Client Profiling for the Australian environment. The initial contract with APEX required the payment of some A$2.5 million for the development work. It also called for the annual payment of "per profile" success fees over five years. These fees were based on a sliding scale to encourage early delivery of the system and incorporated absolute minimums and maximums.

Within the A$3 million contract there were four important negotiation points requested by Mayer and Hoskins:

1. Self-sufficiency. National Mutual wanted to be able to maintain and upgrade the system in the future with the expert-system development platform.
2. Exclusivity. Exclusive rights to the system throughout Australia.
3. IBM operation. Conversion of the computer system from DEC equipment to IBM equipment.
4. The availability of the Australian system by April 1989. APEX had originally planned for a launch of Profiling within National Mutual in 1990. Mayer and

---

EXHIBIT 8   Agent's Report: Sample Pages (continued) (page 3 of 3)

Recommendation #5: Buy Life Insurance for Albert

Recommended Premium: $1,016 annually $91 monthly

Recommended Sum Insured: $461,785

Product Name: Annual Renewable Term

Contact: Contact your local product consultant or Alan O'Donnell, Technical Officer
    Ph: 03 2873694

Selling Points:

- Consumer Price Index (C.P.I.) linked.
- Range of supplementary benefits available.
- Renewable each year up to age 70.
- Option to convert to permanent insurance.
- Cover provides for dependents or covers a debt in the event of death.
- Non-smoker rates available.
- Discounted premium for sums insured over $200,000.

Recommendation #6: Buy Life Insurance for Catherine

Recommended Premium: $348 annually $32 monthly
Recommended Sum Insured: $96,900

Product Name: Annual Renewable Term

Contact: Contact your local product consultant or Alan O'Donnell, Technical Officer
    Ph: 03 2873694

Selling Points:

- Consumer Price Index (C.P.I.) linked.
- Range of supplementary benefits available.
- Renewable each year up to age 70.
- Option to convert to permanent insurance.

Hoskins insisted that a workable Australian version of Client Profiling be available sooner—in early 1989. Despite its reservations that the re-engineering process had never been turned around in such a short time, APEX managed to complete a workable Australian version by March 1989.

The Implementation Approach

Early on, management decided to create a centralized group that would be solely responsible for successfully implementing Client Profiling, i.e., bringing the product to completion for use by the National Mutual agents, conducting training, and tracking the use of the system. Neville Mears was pulled off other projects in Agency Development to work full-time as the project manager for the newly created Profiling department.

Mears put together a team of three knowledge engineers, two systems engineers, three Profiling experts, and one administrative assistant. Mears himself was a 25-year veteran of National Mutual and had won the Managers Award in 1986 for developing a customer service event-tracking system that was used throughout National Mutual's internal network. See Exhibit 9 for an organization chart of the initial profiling group.

The knowledge engineers worked on building the product knowledge base and refining the system's recommendations. The Profiling experts were in charge of training and of monitoring the progress of implementation, and also acted as clearinghouses of information and provided a helpline for agents. These people had a variety of National Mutual experiences as agents and as part of Agency Development and Training. The systems manager was responsible for overseeing the flow of data. A long-associated independent contractor designed Profiling's input screens; he had also developed the data entry screens for COBBER and ICIS.

The original implementation strategy as planned in January 1989, was scheduled as follows:

Pilot. To commence April 4, 1989. Thirty-five sole agents across Australia, selected to be representative of potential Client Profiling users, participated in the pilot over a three-month period. The agents varied in terms of age, experience, and performance.

Limited Deployment. To commence July 3, 1989. Divisional Managers Agency were to commit to involving one agent in each DSO that had mainframe computer access—a total of about 150 agents. Three main goals of the limited deployment phase were: first, to develop some degree of Profiling expertise within each DSO; second, to engender a degree of demand from those agents not involved in limited deployment; and third, to allow time to refine the system and to develop training support materials based on feedback from the pilot. To develop interest, DMAs were supposed to profile each agent within their DSOs.

Full-Scale National Rollout. To commence October 2, 1989, with an Agency Managers meeting to generate enthusiasm and commitment from each DMA. The strategy of the national rollout was to make the tool available to

---

EXHIBIT 9   Client Profiling Team

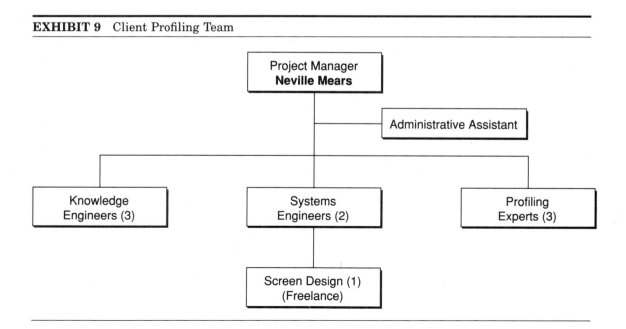

all agents and let their interests dictate whether or not to adopt Profiling.

Expected Challenges in the Implementation Process

Historically, National Mutual's agents were trained to discover and sell to the client's greatest exposed need and close the sale in one interview. This process used only five numbers and was called CIMER, which stood for Clean-up (amount needed to cover outstanding debts and funeral expenses), Income, Mortgage, Education (amount needed to provide for dependents' education), and Retirement. However, during the mid-'80s, Agency Development introduced the "consultative" selling process, which encouraged a "two-call" sale.

The Client Profiling process involved two or three interviews. The first introduced the financial planning process and gathered preliminary data. Once the questionnaire was completed—which could take one to two interviews—the agent input the data at the DSO and sent it to the home office in Melbourne to be processed into a report. At the next interview—scheduled for about a week later—the agent would present the report, review its major recommendations, and hope to close a sale. Client Profiling would require agents to gather even more data from their clients and hold more interviews than with consultative selling. In short, with Profiling, the agent's relationship to the client was to become even more interactive and consultative.

The complexity of the data collection and the professionalism of the multiple-interview sales process was targeted to create an air of quality and sophistication that competitors would find hard to copy. Many at National Mutual felt that the future of life insurance would inevitably involve financial planning. From the beginning, NM management saw Client Profiling as a tool that could be used to help to effect a cultural change in the way in which agents sell business. In their view, the organizational change necessary to make implementation successful would take three to five years to introduce, and Profiling might ultimately reach 80 percent of all agents.

Case 7-2

PROFILING AT NATIONAL MUTUAL (B)

The Pilot began as scheduled on April 4, 1989. Neville Mears invited 29 agents and their DMAs to Melbourne for the launch. The launch stressed that the pilot agents were an elite group whose performance would set the tone for the whole Client Profiling effort. Unintentionally, the end of the pilot coincided with the end of the tax year, June 30 — the busiest time of the year for a high proportion of pilot agents who were heavily involved in personal and corporate superannuation (e.g., pension business).

Pilot Results

The pilot results and pilot agent backgrounds are summarized in Exhibit 1. The pilot results suggested these potential benefits:

- Prospecting. Agents who showed a sample report to prospects generally found it much easier to make appointments.
- Referred Leads. When asked, a client usually will give an average of four referred leads per profile.
- Number of Profiles to Sales Success Rate. The pilot produced an average of 0.33 profiles per agent work week across all agents, including those pilot agents who did none. For a division of 20 agents, that would mean 6.6 profiles per week. A sale could be expected to be made in 80 percent of all cases.
- Average Sale. The pilot produced an average sale of A$3,053 per profile, calculated by taking the total business attributed to Profiling and dividing by the total number of profiles (183). The current average sale, before Profiling, was around A$1700. If an agent did just one profile per week over 40

weeks, over A$120,000 in annualized premiums per annum was expected to be realized.
- Other expected agent benefits included: (1) saving time when dealing with the client who cannot afford to take any business, i.e., the questionnaire and profile reveal a more accurate financial picture; (2) significantly enhanced credibility with the prospects, therefore a stronger agent/client relationship; (3) an easier and quicker opportunity to move up-market.

The pilot also revealed the need for certain changes:

- The time taken to collect client data proved to be a major barrier to agent adoption. Questionnaires and guidelines needed to be simplified. The Client Profiling team developed a new questionnaire that required only 10 mandatory questions necessary to produce a profile and urged agents to make approximations and educated guesses. The less detailed the data, the less detailed the plan.
- There were some inadequacies or errors in the specifications of the expert logic. While these could eventually be fixed, these problems and the agents' perception of faulty expert logic seriously undermined the program's credibility. Mears decided to add a quality assurance expert to the Client Profiling team.

Research Associate Audris S. Wong prepared this case under the supervision of Professor John Sviokla as the basis for class discussion rather than to illustrate either effective or ineffective handling of an administrative situation.

EXHIBIT 1 Pilot Agent Selection

STATE/ Division	DSO[a] CLASS M/R/C	QREM[b] – ($000s)				SERVICE (Years)				AGE (Years)			Names	Total Profiles During Pilot
		<20	35	50	>99	<1	2	5	>9	<25	26–45	>45		
VICTORIA														
St. Kilda Road	M				X				X			X	Ken Boyd	0
City Central	M				X				X			X	Geoff Lancaster	28
City Central	M				X				X			X	Frank Maloney	1
Doncaster	M				X			X				X	G. Graham-Smith	0
Doncaster	M				X		X					X	Barry Sanders	4
Waverley	M				X				X		X		Bill Haywood	3
Waverley	M				X		X				X		Tim Donohue	1
Brighton	M		X				X				X		Blair Freeman	10
Boronia	M			X					X		X		David Hansen	4
Essendon	M			X				X			X		Tony Rulli	8
Essendon	M		X				X			X			Clyde Keam	1
Ballarat	R	X				X				X			Chris Duke	8
Ballarat	R				X				X		X		Ian Forbes	3
North East	R			X					X		X		Gerald Beckton	2
North East	R		X						X			X	Geoff Bock	2
Bendigo	C				X				X			X	Les Roberts	1
Bendigo	C		X				X				X		Garry Jones	5
SOUTH AUSTRALIA														
North Adelaide	M				X				X		X		Jeffery Bradley	6
Southern	M		X				X				X		Peter Butters	2
North Adelaide	M		X				X				X		Daryl Ross	5
TASMANIA														
Launceston	R		X					X				X	Bert Montauban	1
Launceston	R		X					X			X		Michael Menzie	2
NEW SOUTH WALES														
North Sydney	M		X				X				X		Bill Saroukas	1
Manly	M		X					X				X	Brian Carmody	9
Manly	M			X			X			X			Robert Hutton	6
Parramatta	M			X			X					X	Vic Hankins	2
Bondi	M			X				X			X		Melinda Kullberg	12
Bondi	M		X				X			X			David Burman	3
WEST AUSTRALIA														
Metro	M			X				X			X		Peter Tucker	5
Metro	M			X			X				X		Rod Shaw	15
QUEENSLAND														
Milton	M		X				X				X		Murray Hilton	11
Garden City	M		X						X			X	David Laycock	11
Toowoomba	C			X					X			X	Warren Savill	5
Garden City	M			X				X			X		John Casey	2

M = metropolitan	25 M	1 < $20,000				1 < 1				4 < 25				
R = regional	6 R	12 $35,000				12 2				18 26 – 45				
C = country	3 C	10 $50,000				9 5				12 > 45				
		11 > $99,000				12 > 9								

[a] DSO = District Sales Office

[b] QREM = Qualifying Remuneration is an individual performance measure based on amount and type of product sold by an agent.

- The client report seemed too long and too complex. In a memo to DMAs, Mears warned that while the product was complex, the process was not. Yet the effort implied by the product's complexity discouraged agents from committing to its use.

In general, the pilot reaffirmed to National Mutual management the enormous cultural change that adoption would require from agents. Agents were unwilling to change their selling strategies, and surveys showed that a third of the DMAs had a neutral or negative attitude to the pilot. A significant number said that they could give little time to basic Profiling training.

Overall, Mears felt that implementation was going slower than he had expected. The number of profiles seemed low, as did enthusiasm from DMAs and branch general managers. Pat Manning, head of Agency, had pledged that Client Profiling had at least three years to prove itself:

> We won't know for four more years if Profiling is a success or not. I won't entertain a review of the Profiling decision for at least three years. We are going to do Profiling because it is central to our strategy. Cultural change takes years and we are going to have a go at it.

Manning felt that the DMAs could not be relied upon to motivate agents and that consultants should be used to train and inform agents, generate demand for Client Profiling, and be paid on the same basis as product consultants, i.e., based on the number of profiles produced in the consultant's region. Profiling, Manning believed, had to be sold to the agent.

John Oates, head of Agency Development, took a similar view. Client Profiling should have been introduced as a new product, with the consultants funded by part of the charging fees. He foresaw that a significant innovation such as Profiling would take years to be accepted and then would suddenly bloom. National Mutual was a company that continually underwent change to stay active and flexible. Its greatest worry with Client Profiling was that the system's potential competitive advantage would be lost if implementation was delayed.

Case 7–3

CAPITAL HOLDING CORPORATION

We have made some dramatic changes in the past 18 months. One way to describe it is to say we have become focused. We believe our success will come by differentiating ourselves through customer service and integrated asset/liability management. The entire corporation is working toward implementing this umbrella strategy. We think we can improve our cost control as well. There are opportunities for us to streamline our processes and to share expertise across our affiliates. Time-based management holds great potential for us. We are empowering our employees to put decisions and tools as close as possible to the firing line.

Irv Bailey, *Chairman, President and Chief Executive Officer*
Capital Holding Corporation

Irv Bailey, chief investment officer at Capital Holding Corporation (CHC) since 1981, took the reins of the corporation in the fall of 1987. Tom Simons, the charismatic leader who preceded him, remained as chairman until his untimely death in mid-1988. Bailey's strategic vision was to build competitive advantage by driving down costs and becoming market driven. He also saw a major untapped opportunity for synergy between business units.

By June 1989, the corporation had reorganized around four major business lines, developed a statement of values and guiding principles, and established strategic plans for each of the business units. Some questions remained unanswered despite the considerable progress Bailey and his team had made. Executives were undecided about the potential for cost savings through consolidation across the retail businesses. Further, they had not been able to reach a consensus about how the holding company itself could best contribute to value added. A consultant study was under way to analyze the costs and benefits of combining CHC's data centers into a single information systems util-

ity. In March, the chief information officer of Agency Group (CIO-AG), who also informally coordinated systems activities for AIG and the corporate headquarters group, had left the company, and management had decided to postpone replacing him until these issues were resolved.

Company Overview

At the end of 1988, CHC, headquartered in Louisville, Kentucky, was one of the 10 largest stockholder-owned insurance companies in the United States. CHC ranked number 371 in terms of market value in *Business Week*'s 1989 top 1,000 list. It was the 20th-largest insurance company in the nation, with more than $2 billion in revenues. CHC had almost 8,000 employees at the end of 1988. (See *Appendix A* for an overview of the

Professors Jane Linder, Donna Stoddard, and Benn Konsynski prepared this case as the basis for class discussion rather than to illustrate either effective or ineffective handling of an administrative situation.

Copyright © 1987 by the President and Fellows of Harvard College. Harvard Business School case 9-187-169.

insurance industry and a glossary of insurance terms.)

The original kernel of CHC was Commonwealth Life Insurance Company of Kentucky, founded in 1904. CHC was formed by Commonwealth in 1969 to facilitate growth through the acquisition of other life insurance companies, and its record had been quite impressive. From 1968 to 1988, CHC acquired 14 insurance companies and a bank, driving its assets from $360 million to almost $13 billion. In the same period, profits went from $9 million to $190 million. (*Appendix B* shows financial statistics.)

Prior to the early 1980s, most of CHC's insurance companies distributed "debit insurance" through home service. Small policies were sold mostly to blue collar or rural workers by agents who went door to door to collect monthly premium payments. In 1988, the company no longer sold only debit policies, but continued to focus on the middle-income market. CHC targeted customers whose household income ranged from $15,000 to $50,000. The firm's research showed that this market represented 44 percent of all U.S. households and tended to be less competitive than the upscale segment.

From 1978 through early 1989, CHC diversified both its product lines and its distribution channels. Three major initiatives were implemented through an aggressive acquisition strategy. First, CHC moved into direct-response marketing by acquiring National Liberty Corporation (NLC) in 1981 and Worldwide Insurance Group at the end of 1986. Second, CHC reached into other financial service sectors when it acquired First Deposit Corporation, a "nonbank" bank holding company, in 1984. Third, CHC continued to expand its geographic coverage in the southeastern part of the United States through smaller acquisitions that complemented its agent system. Additionally, CHC developed a series of innovative investment products that carried flexible interest rates. Capital Initiatives Corporation was formed to market these products through bank trust officers and stock brokers.

Simons's vision was that CHC's business units would operate autonomously, but with communication bridges among them to promote synergy. (Exhibit 1 shows the 1986 organizational structure.) The reality was quite different. Products were not shared across the business units, and cooperative efforts, with a few exceptions such as integrated investment strategies, were negligible. In September 1987, Irv Bailey was named president and chief operating officer, and the corporation was reorganized to improve its internal workings. The corporation's businesses were formed into four distinct units: Agency Group, Direct Response Group (DRG), Accumulation and Investment Group (AIG), and First Deposit Corporation (FDC). (Exhibit 2 shows the 1989 organizational structure.)

Agency Group

The Agency Group sold basic life and health insurance through two affiliates: Commonwealth Insurance, headquartered in Louisville, and Peoples Security, whose home office was in Durham, North Carolina. The Agency Group companies were focused squarely on the middle-income market in the southeast region of the United States. Their objective was to improve operating earnings in a mature market by providing high-quality products and services for low cost. This was done by segmenting markets to match the right agent with the right products to the right customer. The result was higher agent income, less agent turnover, a declining lapse rate, and greater profitability. Agency Group marketed primary insurance coverage through home service agents. (Exhibit 3 shows a portfolio of Agency Group products.) Each agent was employed directly

EXHIBIT 1 Capital Holding Corporation: 1986 Corporate Organization Structure

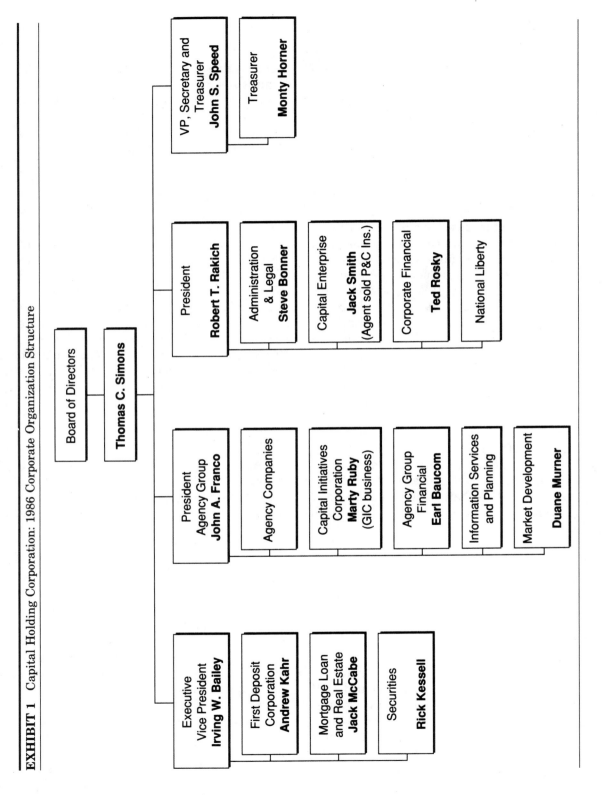

Board of Directors

Thomas C. Simons

Executive Vice President
Irving W. Bailey

- First Deposit Corporation
  Andrew Kahr
- Mortgage Loan and Real Estate
  Jack McCabe
- Securities
  Rick Kessell

President Agency Group
John A. Franco

- Agency Companies
- Capital Initiatives Corporation
  Marty Ruby
  (GIC business)
- Agency Group Financial
  Earl Baucom
- Information Services and Planning
- Market Development
  Duane Murner

President
Robert T. Rakich

- Administration & Legal
  Steve Bonner
- Capital Enterprise
  Jack Smith
  (Agent sold P&C Ins.)
- Corporate Financial
  Ted Rosky
- National Liberty

VP, Secretary and Treasurer
John S. Speed

- Treasurer
  Monty Horner

EXHIBIT 2 Capital Holding Corporation: 1989 Organization Chart

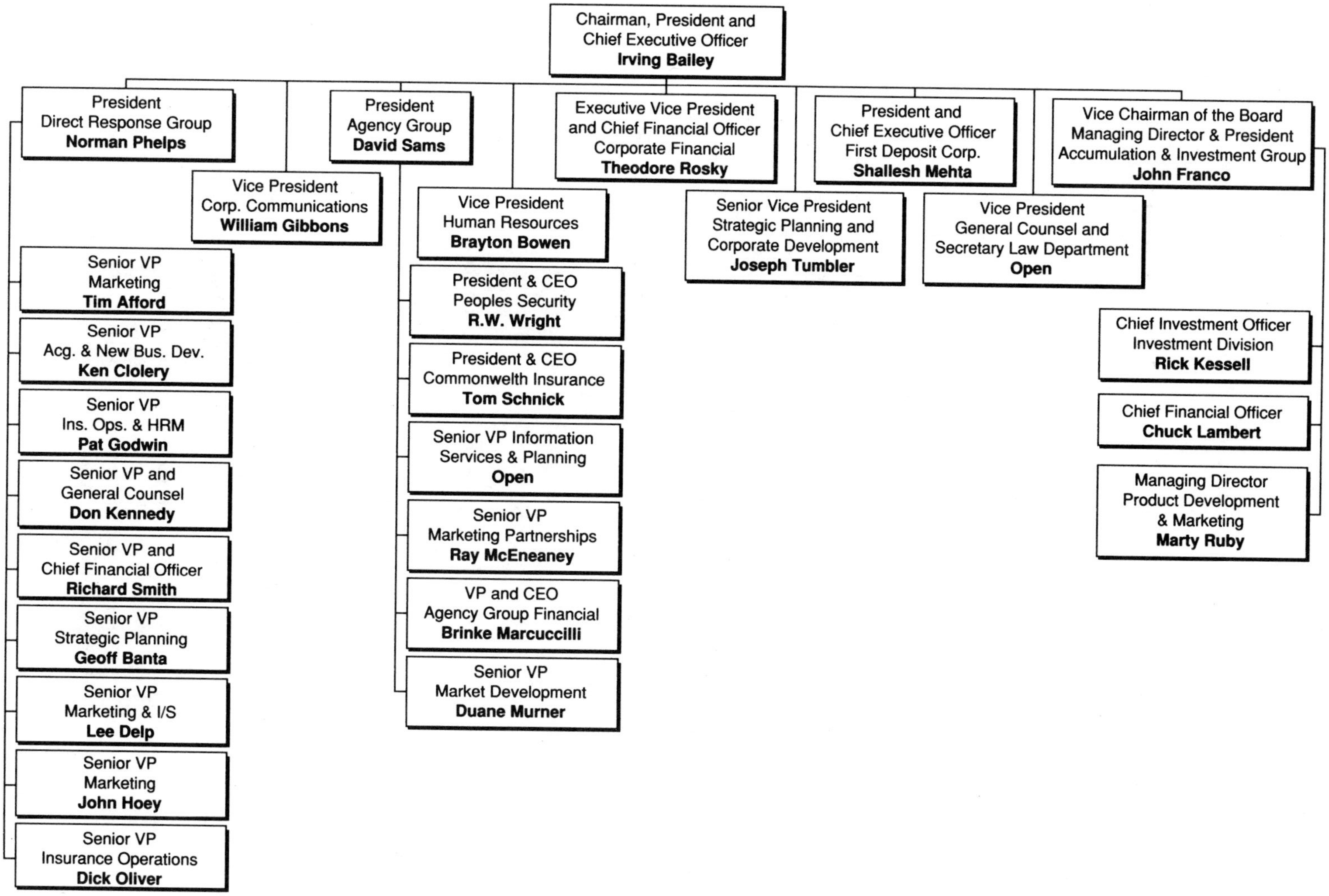

Chairman, President and Chief Executive Officer
Irving Bailey

- Executive Vice President and Chief Financial Officer Corporate Financial
Theodore Rosky
  - Senior Vice President Strategic Planning and Corporate Development
  Joseph Tumbler

- President and Chief Executive Officer First Deposit Corp.
Shallesh Mehta
  - Vice President General Counsel and Secretary Law Department
  Open

- Vice Chairman of the Board Managing Director & President Accumulation & Investment Group
John Franco
  - Chief Investment Officer Investment Division
  Rick Kessell
  - Chief Financial Officer
  Chuck Lambert
  - Managing Director Product Development & Marketing
  Marty Ruby

- President Agency Group
David Sams
  - Vice President Human Resources
  Brayton Bowen
  - President & CEO Peoples Security
  R.W. Wright
  - President & CEO Commonwelth Insurance
  Tom Schnick
  - Senior VP Information Services & Planning
  Open
  - Senior VP Marketing Partnerships
  Ray McEneaney
  - VP and CEO Agency Group Financial
  Brinke Marcuccilli
  - Senior VP Market Development
  Duane Murner

- President Direct Response Group
Norman Phelps
  - Vice President Corp. Communications
  William Gibbons
  - Senior VP Marketing
  Tim Afford
  - Senior VP Acg. & New Bus. Dev.
  Ken Clolery
  - Senior VP Ins. Ops. & HRM
  Pat Godwin
  - Senior VP and General Counsel
  Don Kennedy
  - Senior VP and Chief Financial Officer
  Richard Smith
  - Senior VP Strategic Planning
  Geoff Banta
  - Senior VP Marketing & I/S
  Lee Delp
  - Senior VP Marketing
  John Hoey
  - Senior VP Insurance Operations
  Dick Oliver

311

EXHIBIT 3 Capital Holding Corporation: Agency Group Product Portfolio

---

Year Announced	
•	Whole life [1,2][a]
•	20 Pay Life [1,2]
•	Debit fire [1]
•	Cancer [1,2,3]
1965	Automobile [3]
	Homeowner's [3]
1979	Capitalizer, an adjustable-premium whole-life policy [no longer sold]
1981	UniversaLife [2,3]
	UniversAnnuity, an annuity designed for IRAs [2,3]
	Econolife 20, an increasing-premium whole-life policy [no longer sold]
1982	Umbrella Liability [3]
	Life Annuities [2,3]
	Flexible Premium Annuities [2,3]
1983	Guaranteed Acceptance Plan [1,2]
1984	UniversaLife, introduced two new versions
	CAP/CARE, a cost-containment health insurance product [no longer sold]
1985	Group annuities [no longer sold]
1986	Classic Plus, an interest-sensitive whole-life product [1,2,3]
	Protector Plus, a term product [1,2,3]
	Protector Decreasing Term [1,2,3]
	UniversaLife Plus[b] [2,3]
1987	Increasing Death Benefit, a whole life product [1,2]
	Accident[b] [1,2,3]
1988	Living Payout Benefit, a product to compensate the terminally ill [2,3]
	Home Income Security Plan, a reverse mortgage

[a]Whole life, 20 pay life, debit fire, and cancer insurance have been available for decades.

[b]Term insurance and accident insurance have always been a part of the CHC product portfolio. New products were introduced in 1986 and 1987 respectively.

(With the COMPASS program, this product is targeted to be sold by [1] a service representative, [2] an account representative, or [3] a sales representative.)

---

in one of CHC's 120 agencies and was typically assigned to a geographical area with 6,000 to 12,000 residents. An agent was expected to maintain an active client list of 500 to 600 customers and to close two sales per week.

David Sams, a 23-year veteran of CHC, had been heavily involved for four years in the development and implementation of a strategic plan for the group, first as CEO of Commonwealth Life Insurance Company, then as president of Agency Group. Sams articulated four major strategies for the coming years:

- Field management and market segmentation through the COMPASS program.
- Streamlining operations to achieve an optimal balance between high quality and low cost.
- Marketing partnerships with other insurance firms.
- Active management of each of the elements of profitability—pricing, production, persistency, claims, and spending.

COMPASS was Agency Group's market segmentation strategy. Agency Group divided its target market into three categories of customers, based primarily on household income. The COMPASS program tailored agent assignment, training, the sales process, the product portfolio, and agent compensation to the three market segments in order to provide the right products and level of service for each customer group. (See Exhibit 4.)

The first segment included customers with income between $0 and $15,000. These customers were assigned to *service representatives* who focused primarily on maintaining the in-force book of business rather than making new sales. A service representative's product portfolio included the simplest products such as juvenile plans and final expense coverage, and compensation was linked primarily to keeping policies in force.

The second and largest category of customers, with household incomes between $15,000

and $25,000, was served by *account representatives*. This group of agents was charged with maintaining the current block of business and showing reasonable amounts of in-force premium growth. They sold traditional term and whole life products, interest-sensitive products with face value under $50,000, and some medical expense coverage. Account representatives earned commissions on new sales in addition to compensation for keeping polices in force.

Sales representatives were assigned to the third category, households with incomes in the $25,000 to $50,000 range. This segment did not rely on personal collection of premiums; therefore agents concentrated on new business activity largely with interest-sensitive and accumulation products. This third group of agents used property and casualty products, principally homeowner's insurance, as a means of generating leads and making initial contact with prospects. The majority of a sales representative's pay was in the form of commissions.

After spending almost four years implementing the COMPASS program throughout the field sales force, executives were pleased with the financial results. Sams said, "We have reduced the number of field agents by over 20 percent, to 2,400. Our agents are better off now because more customers and more policies are spread over fewer agents. We are looking for better productivity, and they're delivering." The policy lapse rate, a key determinant of the group's profitability had improved from almost 25 percent in 1983 to 17.6 percent in 1988. Annual agent turnover was down to about 30 percent, and operating earnings had increased as well. (See Exhibit 5).

Location Selling

In the mid 1980s, CHC had experimented with selling insurance through bank branches in a joint venture with Bank of America. CHC had sold auto, homeowner's,

EXHIBIT 4   Capital Holding Corporation: COMPASS—Customer Segments

Type of Agent	*Service Representative*	*Account Representative*	*Sales Representative*
Customer Segment Household Income	$15,000 or less	$15,000–$25,000	$25,000–$50,000
Type of Products Sold	Maintain and service in-force block of insurance	Traditional interest-sensitive products	Property and casualty, interest-sensitive products, and accumulation products
Projected Agent Income	$21,000	$25,000	$35,000

EXHIBIT 5   Capital Holding Corporation: Agency Group Performance Indicators (individual life and health)

	1988	1983	Compound growth rate
Policy termination rate	17.6%	24.9%	
Revenues			
Amount (millions)	$489.7	$422.6	3.0%
Per agent (thousands)	$200.7	$130.2	9.0%
Pretax operating earnings			
Amount (millions)	$130.6	$105.3	4.4%
Per employee (thousands)	$ 27.9	$ 17.4	9.9%

and life insurance in Bakersfield and Santa Barbara, California. Because of poor results, this program was abandoned in 1986.

A similar venture with Kroger supermarkets proved somewhat more effective. In 1986, CHC began to establish financial centers in supermarkets. By the end of 1988, 25 centers were operating in five states. Initially conceived as full-service insurance offices, the Kroger centers had been repositioned as "prospecting" locations. Agents, especially new employees, worked at the centers to generate leads. They pursued the sales with traditional visits to the client's home.

Information Technology at Agency Group

Beginning in the late 1970s, CHC initiated project ECLIPSE—a massive back-office automation project designed to eliminate the multiple, outmoded administrative systems in the Agency Group. In the words of one executive, "Project ECLIPSE was a disaster." In its efforts to implement ECLIPSE rapidly among all the Agency Group companies, CHC had failed to assess the affiliates' unique accounting systems thoroughly. They encountered significant problems converting thousands of different policy variations to a single system.

After the problems were resolved, a new chief information officer was hired in 1985 to make the system function in a more strategic way. The system became a platform for further progress. Although the CIO-AG reported to the president of Agency Group, he also wore a corporate hat. Simons, chief executive at the time, looked to him to create information systems (I/S) synergies across CHC's business units.

By the end of 1986, the master files of all of the Agency Group marketing affiliates could interface with the compensation and field accounting elements of the ECLIPSE system. The payoff was that the new interest-sensitive products that had been developed under the ECLIPSE architecture were available to all of the units. ECLIPSE set standards for back-office processing, agent compensation and performance measurement, premium collection, and client tracking.

As of the end of May 1989, Agency Group was two weeks away from the final ECLIPSE milestone. Commonwealth Life Insurance's existing business would be fully converted. Sams stated, "We are aiming for one way of doing business—one set of processes and procedures. The standards that we've implemented through ECLIPSE help us achieve this goal. At some point, however, we will have to consider converting the system to database technology." According to Brinke Marcuccilli, Agency Group chief financial officer, the total cost of ECLIPSE development and implementation was undocumented. From the project's inception through 1984, $67.0 million was capitalized, but expenditures since that time had been expensed as they were incurred.

While the ECLIPSE project was under way, several other technology projects formed the foundation for COMPASS implementation. (See Exhibit 6.) A client management system was developed to help the agent keep track of existing clients and their needs. Agents were encouraged to develop relationships with clients that would enable them to conduct an annual review of household insurance needs. Agents completed a standard personal financial review form, which was entered in the computer at headquarters. The system produced a needs analysis and set of recommended coverage levels and products that the agent could review with the customer. Duane Murner, senior vice president of market development for Agency Group, believed that CHC's client management system gave them a competitive advantage because no other insurance company had a comparable system in place.

A second IT application that was developed to support COMPASS was "Customer Triggers." This application scanned a database of CHC customers and highlighted those who were in an agent's territory, but who were not current clients of the agent. (These customers may have been sold insurance by a previous agent assigned to the territory, for example.) This listing provided the agent with customer information such as age, term insurance in force that could be converted to universal or whole life, and a listing of other Agency Group relationships.

A third application developed with COMPASS was the "Leads Management System." Agents were provided with cards on which they recorded information about prospective customers. When they met a potential client, they filled in the individual's name and a trigger date that was not longer than one month in the future. These cards were turned in at the agency, and the information was entered into the central computer. Periodically, agents received reports that reminded them to contact these customers.

In early 1989, the CIO-AG left the company. Sams decided to implement a temporary reporting structure until the corporation's strategic planning efforts were completed. Sams commented, "He was an able and intense guy. I want to let the dust

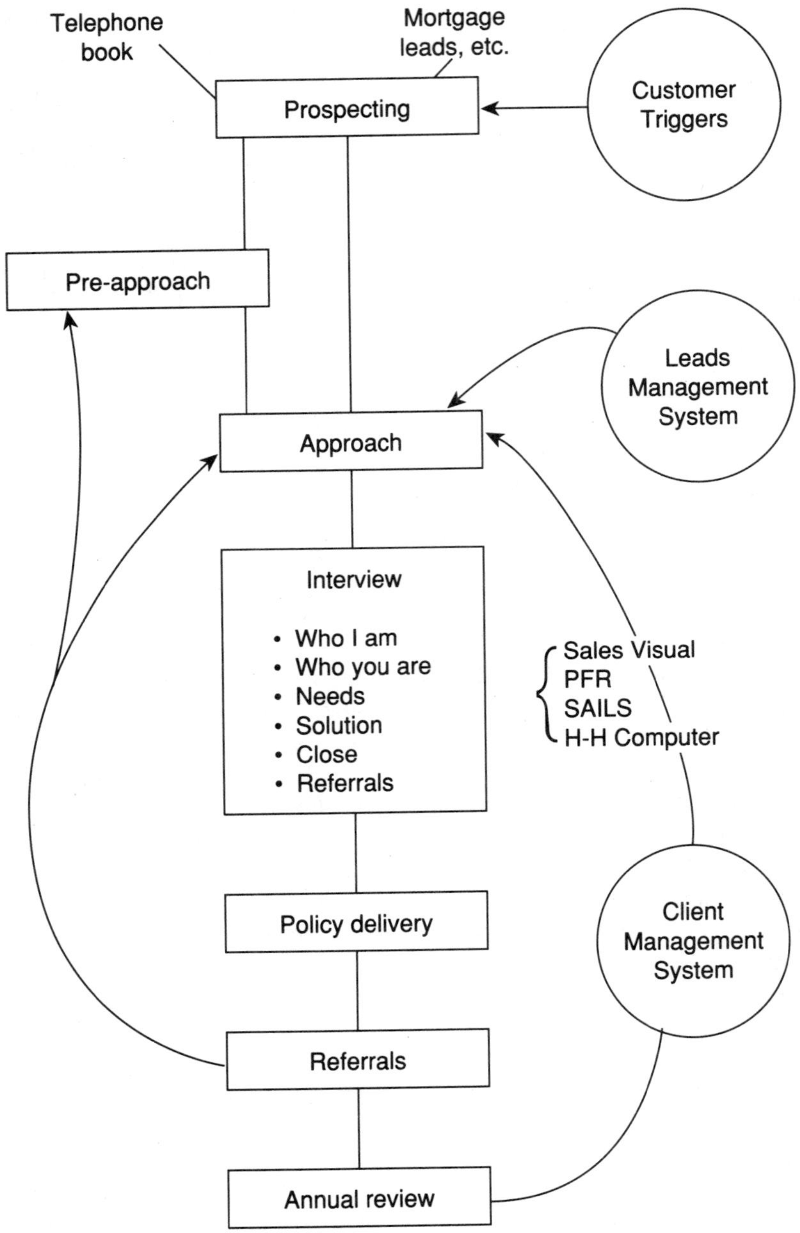

EXHIBIT 6   Capital Holding Corporation: CHC Agent Sales Process

settle a little before deciding on the appropriate structure for I/S, and we'll fill the job based on the structure we want." Dean Quillet, formerly the vice president for systems development, assumed responsibility for most of the group, reporting to Sams. The staff, which supported the Accumulation and Investment Group, was transferred from Quillet's organization to AIG. The individual in charge of project LISTEN reported directly to Sams.

Project LISTEN was Agency Group's next horizon. What COMPASS was to the front office, LISTEN was to the back. The project included an array of studies of the product development, new business and underwriting, and policyholder services areas. The purpose was to gain a clear understanding of how the Agency Group operated and how service and operating efficiencies could be improved. Begun in 1986, LISTEN's study phase was scheduled to be completed in mid-1989. Several executives had high hopes for its contribution to expense savings. Ted Rosky, chief financial officer, stated, "LISTEN will enable us to reconfigure the back office to smooth the work flows. Through technology, we will be able to move some of the functions out to the field office, as close to the customer as he or she wants it to be. The ultimate may well be to have agents use laptop computers to gather data and underwrite policies overnight on a distributed basis. This effort is far from complete." The total expenditure on LISTEN during 1988 and 1989 was expected to be about $3.1 million, two-thirds of which was for consulting services.

Capital Holding had purchased a packaged executive information system (EIS) in 1988 with an eye toward putting information at management's fingertips. Quillet said that AIG was further along in its use of the system than Agency Group was. "The trick is to define the information that needs to be available, then to get it there. With project LISTEN, we are redefining the way we want to operate and the information we want to look at, so that has slowed up our use of the system." Quillet expected that Agency Group's and AIG's use of the EIS system would be totally different because of different management information needs.

Direct Response Group

Direct Response Group consisted of two firms: National Liberty sold life and health insurance, and Worldwide Insurance was a property/casualty underwriter. Both marketed their products through direct response channels—television, telephone, and direct mail. NLC was best known for its ads featuring celebrity endorsers such as Lorne Green, Michael Landon, Art Linkletter, Ed Asner, and Tennessee Ernie Ford. In addition to television commercials, newspaper inserts and direct-mail advertising were used to make contact with prospects. For example, in response to a TV advertisement targeting veterans and featuring Roger Staubach, a prospect might call in to request more information on a life insurance product. A kit describing the product would be mailed to the potential customer. These mailings might be followed up with a phone call from a telemarketing sales representative who would attempt to close the sale.

Both Direct Response Group and Agency Group retailed insurance to middle-market customers, but the two business units differed in several important ways. Agency Group sold basic coverage while DRG focused on supplemental insurance. Key products for DRG included hospital indemnity that paid the subscriber during a hospital stay, home health care to cover convalescence costs, and Medicare supplement that covered medical bills and deductibles that fell outside of the federal reimbursement program. DRG's products tended to be simpler than Agency Group's because most were sold without benefit of personal contact or explanation. DRG marketed nationwide, while Agency Group was a regional player. Finally, the mix of fixed and variable costs was different for the two units. Much of Agency Group's policy-acquisition expenses were variable: agents were compensated primarily by commission for generating new business. DRG's expenses, in contrast, were heavily front-end loaded. Norm Phelps, president of DRG, estimated that between 85 percent and 150 percent of a product's first-year premium was spent in marketing costs before a single policy was sold. CHC did not have good data as to the extent of overlap between Agency Group's customer profile and that of DRG.

When CHC began direct-response distribution, the group's financial performance was excellent. In 1986, National Liberty was touted as having one of the fastest-growing distribution channels in the insurance industry. By 1989, however, the picture looked different. Phelps explained, "In the past two years, we have discovered that direct response insurance is a slow-growth business. We had annuity products mixed in with our life and health insurance results, and what was happening to the core business was not easily discernable. We were growing and exceeding profit goals. No one looked underneath the covers. When we took the annuities out, we found that the basic insurance business hadn't been growing for years, and our persistency was terrible. The days of mass marketing are over. We have to move toward customer segmentation and relationship marketing to improve our value to the customer, to increase response rates, and to turn persistency around."

To support this strategic direction, Phelps began a broad program of change at National Liberty and Worldwide. They began to rely more heavily on personal telephone contact and on products tailored to specific market segments. A force of 40 "tele-agents" was created out of the telemarketing staff of 500. These individuals were assigned to specific clients and encouraged to form a personal relationship. The agents exchanged pictures with their customers and, in some cases, visited their homes.

Products were also more carefully tailored to market niches. The newly developed Medicare supplement was an example. It was designed through careful consumer research and advertised with an upbeat, positive message about product features and caring service. *Consumer Reports* labeled it a "best buy," in the May 1989 magazine. This product's persistency compared very favorably with some of DRG's past mass marketing efforts. In extreme cases, more than 50 percent of the policies sold in the past had lapsed within the first three months. Phelps explained, "We never had to be this sophisticated before. If we are really serious about treating the customers *one by one,* we will have to have a series of modular product components on the shelf. Every time we talk to someone on the phone, we could combine these components to meet their exact need. If we're good at listening, the product will always be changing. The technology hurdles are significant, though."

Financial results at DRG had not yet begun to reflect the new strategic focus. Phelps remarked, "The excitement of a new vision has subsided, and we are faced with the hard job of implementation. If we can't pull it off, it will be because we have run out of time. The board's patience will not last forever. We cannot continue to operate in the time frames that used to be comfortable—we simply have to be willing to execute. The organization doesn't think as frenetically as I'd like it to think."

Information Technology at DRG

DRG's strategic shift had a major impact on the information systems support the organization required. Pete Cola, vice president of information systems remarked, "When Norm came in 1987, we had consultants work with us on strategy. Our internal view at the time was that our strength was in marketing. The consultants said that our real advantages lay in telemarketing and information systems. That insight caused us to change the way we do business, and information systems got a big piece of the action."

In January 1989, National Liberty implemented the client prospect database. Initially, it contained only TV inquiry leads, about 1.5 million names. By August, the I/S team planned to build automatic linkages between the database and the company's administrative and claims processing systems and load all in-force policy records on the files. By the end of the summer, the complete database would carry information about 2.5 million policies with 1.7 million households. The database would become the foundation for an on-line sales and service support system. Telephone-based service representatives and sales agents would have access to all information about a customer household when they were in phone contact.

Cola planned to include Worldwide's book of business in the database as well. By early 1990, Worldwide's policy and customer data would be loaded onto the DRG database so that any product could be sold or serviced from either location. The two completely different sets of administrative systems would be integrated to give sales and service personnel the image of dealing with one I/S infrastructure. (Exhibit 7 contrasts CHC's data centers.)

NLC had made a major commitment to CASE technology to manage the growing I/S workload. Cola beamed, "The I/S organization at National Liberty Corporation successfully transformed itself from a process-oriented COBOL, Assembler VSAM shop, to an organization focused on architecture, information, CASE, and relational database. This was accomplished in one year, with no increase in staff and with no application systems failures. We delivered a major application system that was comprised of 32 DB2 tables, 45 online CICS screens,

EXHIBIT 7   Capital Holding Corporation: 1989 I/S Installation Overview

	Louisville Facility (Agency)	*Valley Forge Facility (NLC)*	*St. Louis Facility (Worldwide)*
Budget, 1989	$31.3M[a]	$16M	$6M
Staff	332[a]	225	84
Mainframe	IBM 3084 IBM 3081	IBM 3090	IBM 3081
Disk capacity (Gigabytes)	189.2	162.5	45.0
Primary operating system	MVS/XA	MVS/XA	MVS/XA
Number of installed terminals	900	1200	700
Online transactions/day	410K	265K	380K
Batch jobs/day	3,600	3,050	1,250

[a]Includes AIG budget of $4.2 million and staff of about 30 at Louisville.

450,000 lines of code, and a transaction rate of 10,000 per day. This was accomplished while establishing our new development platform that required us to restructure our organization, establish a new planning and development methodology, adopt the principles and tools for data modeling, establish a CASE environment, and implement a relational database management system." Spending for strategic systems projects was approximately $1.5 million. Cola stated it would probably remain at this level throughout the five-year implementation of the plan.

Cola's group was also developing a project management and scheduling system to manage marketing programs more effectively. Many of the individual elements in marketing production, which reported to Cola, had already been automated. Copy was created with word processing, and artwork and graphics were added with desktop publishing software on Macintosh computers. National Liberty was also in the process of implementing a system to support purchasing.

A major challenge was to reorganize the workflow in the product development and production process. In the past, according to Phelps, marketers had "always gotten whatever they wanted. They drove everything. Today, artists, copywriters, and purchasing and production people have to be equal members of the team." Cola's aim was to break his marketing operations organization into cross-functional teams what would be physically located together in order to squeeze time and redundancy out of the process. He stated, "Technology is the enabling platform for this reorganization."

Phelps stated that the CIO-AG's departure had not affected DRG because DRG's computing resources were separate from CHC's corporate information systems group. "We don't need a CIO at the holding company level. Right now it's difficult to inter-

ject a drive for CHC common systems in an organization that is already dealing with too much change. The danger is that we could get further apart by operating separately, but there's not a lot of support for giving up a piece of your destiny to someone else. Ultimately, we will need some common standards throughout CHC. The question is timing and priority."

Accumulation and Investment Group

The Accumulation and Investment Group (AIG) was formed in September 1987 when CHC restructured its operations. It was Bailey's recommendation that the corporation should manage its accumulation business in an integrated way in order to improve the strategic potential in this business line. AIG was formed by combining the investment division which had been run by Bailey, with National Liberty's single-premium deferred annuity business and Agency Group's wholesale business lines centered on guaranteed interest contracts (GICs). GICs were similar to certificates of deposit in the retail market, but were wholesaled through pension consultants and bank trust managers. AIG's most successful products were indexed GICs, which were unique in the industry because their interest rates floated with a market index. AIG's annuities were sold to individual conservative investors through stock brokers, banks, and savings and loans.

Bailey stated, "Organizational barriers were impeding effective management of the investment business. The key players were working to different agendas because they were attached to different business units. We pulled the pieces of AIG together to give it focus and attention. As the accumulation business becomes increasingly dominant in our asset base, we must reduce its risk through new products, new investment techniques, and product balance. We must improve the sophistication of our asset/liability techniques, and we must also find ways to maintain superior investment results, which become increasingly difficult with size."

Integration was the key word at AIG. The informal collaboration among investment officers, financial people, and marketers that had started through the Asset/Liability Management Committee was institutionalized when AIG was formed. Franco explained, "Most financial service firms design and sell an investment product without thinking much about the asset management side of the equation. Our marketers, financial, and investment professionals work together to design the product and its related investment strategy up front. We do our homework in an integrative way. Plus we are a very low-cost shop. Others may spend as much as 0.5 percent of assets per year on operating costs. Our costs are 0.3 percent, so we don't have to take as much investment risk as others do in order to earn a fair return."

In 1989, AIG was by far the fastest growing component of CHC. It accounted for 70 percent of the corporation's invested assets and 23 percent of the profits. Staff had grown from 50 in 1987 to 190 in 1989.[1] John Franco, president of AIG, described Capital Holding's approach to this part of its business as unique in the industry. "We are in the business of using integrated risk management techniques to exploit profitable spread-making opportunities. We make money by: (1) being a niche marketer and enjoying niche market pricing for the risks we assume; (2) being a low-cost producer; and (3) effectively integrating the structure of assets and liabilities." AIG had shown its ability to deliver acceptable returns under both good and bad

economic conditions. (See Exhibit 8.) Franco expected that AIG could control $30 billion in assets and account for 50 percent of the corporation's profits within 10 years.

One of the key elements in implementing Franco's strategy was an empowered work force. Franco stated, "We may have the only sales force in America that is compensated by profitability. We pay people to produce profits." Management systems were in place to track many individuals' contribution to the bottom line of the division on a monthly basis. One manager who had recently transferred from Agency Group to AIG remarked that the cultures of the two organizations were totally different. "Agency Group is big, with lots of layers. AIG, on the other hand, is small and entrepreneurial. There are few procedures—we have to do things in a different way here."

Information Technology at AIG

Franco believed that AIG had not begun to exploit information technology fully. The group had a patchwork quilt of batch and PC systems to support its operations. In April, 18 members of Agency Group's I/S organization were transferred to AIG to form the nucleus of a technology organization for that business. Because AIG's product line was an amalgamation of investment products that had previously been sold by CHC's separate divisions, AIG's I/S resources were similarly distributed. As of June 1989, the majority of the 35-person I/S staff resided in Louisville, but the group also included five people in Valley Forge to support NLC-originated annuities and GICs. AIG's 1989 information technology budget was $4.2 million.

Franco explained that the I/S vision was completed in late May, and the strategy with timelines and costs would be done in approximately two months. He anticipated that the action items that would result would keep the I/S organization busy for five years.

---

[1]Approximately 20 of these were new positions, and the remainder were jobs that were moved to the AIG group from other parts of CHC.

EXHIBIT 8 Capital Holding Corporation: Accumulation and Investment Group

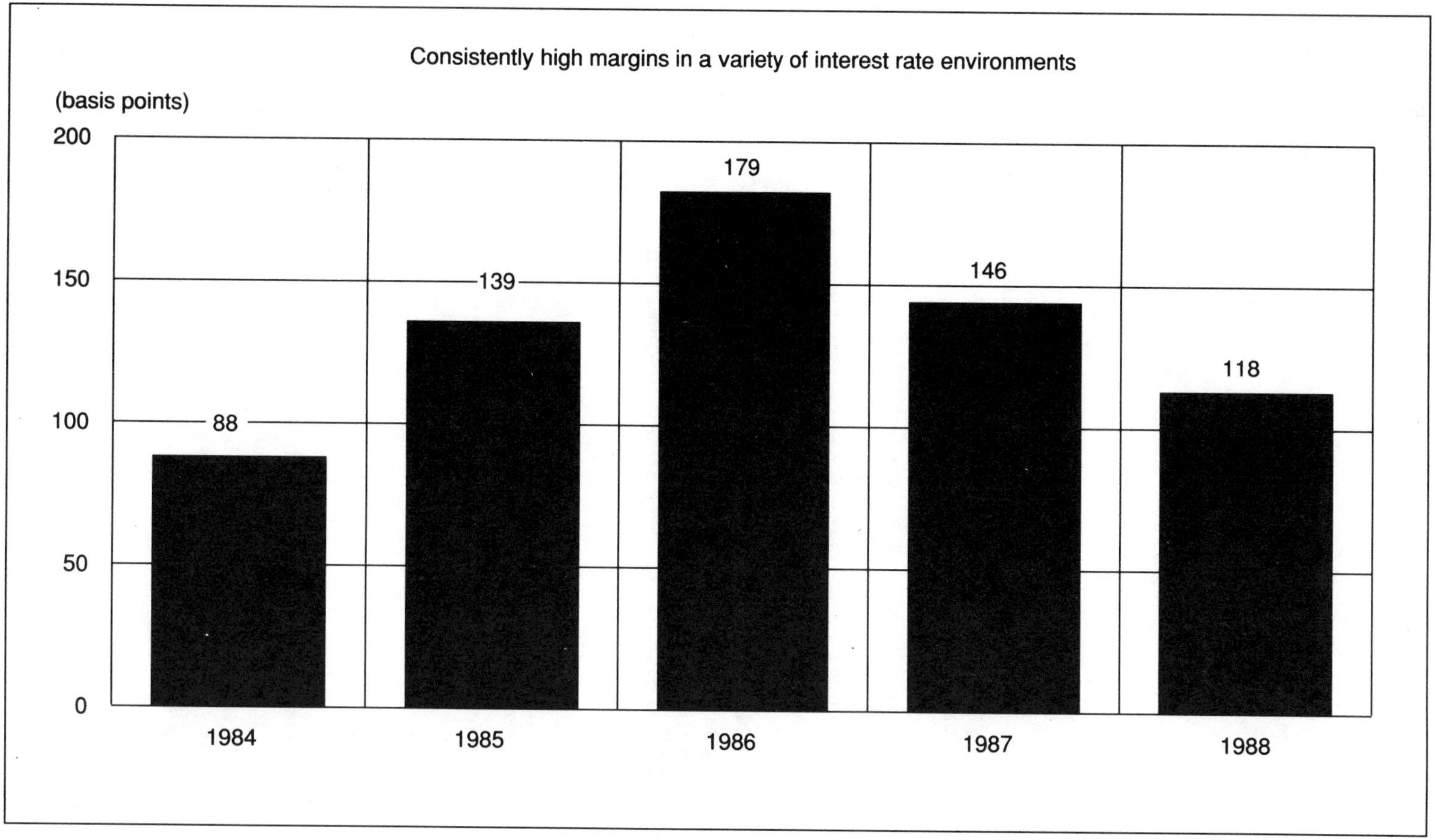

Consistently high margins in a variety of interest rate environments

(basis points)

Year	Value
1984	88
1985	139
1986	179
1987	146
1988	118

Franco noted, "We've got much of what Wall Street has, but it doesn't yet do all that we need. The models are simplistic. We need real-time models with an ability to alter asset or liability portfolio structures in a dynamic way."

First Deposit Corporation

In the early 1980s, CHC began to look for possible acquisitions in the banking industry. Executives saw interesting potential synergies between their insurance business and banking services to middle-market customers. Irv Bailey noted, "A small subsidiary of Parker Pen was brought to our attention. Parker Pen had wanted to get into the financial services business, and had hired a young financial services wizard named Andrew Kahr, who had some of the finest product development credentials around. He is credited with developing the Merrill Lynch Cash Management Account and the Schwab One account. First Deposit Corporation (FDC) with its savings and loan charter, bank charter, insurance charter, and its emphasis on direct-response marketing exceeded our expectation." CHC purchased 80 percent of the stock of FDC from Parker Pen in 1984. CHC viewed FDC as a cash-hungry company with strong potential, in need of solid financial backing.

FDC's primary product was a credit card, sold through the mail. It had unique features that made it attractive to adults who were typically in their 30s, had above-average earnings, and a willingness to incur and manage debt to live a fuller life-style. Carefully controlled direct marketing and strict credit underwriting procedures produced low delinquency rates. At the end of 1985, it had outstanding balances of $150 million, from a standing start at the beginning of the year. By the end of 1988, FDC had increased its balances to $1.6 billion, had begun to market CDs through the mail, and had become highly profitable. FDC used a service bureau for its information technology requirements.

Corporate Staff

In addition to the four-line business units, CHC had four central staff groups with a total of 224 employees at the end of 1988: corporate finance, human resources, corporate communications, and strategic planning. Rosky headed the corporate finance group and was responsible for corporate financial reporting and budgeting. The budgeting process included preparing a three-year profit plan to which executives' incentive compensation was tied. Rosky stated that one of his aims was to make regular financial reporting a "seamless" process. As of the time of the case, the divisions all used the same software packages for budgeting and disbursements, but other financial systems varied across the lines of business. Each business unit had its own chart of accounts. Rosky's group prepared a quarterly corporate financial statement by manually entering division results into a home-grown personal computer system. More frequent, or detailed divisional financial control was a low corporate priority because division presidents were charged with managing their own bottom lines.

Brayton Bowen, vice president of human resources, had been with CHC for under three years. When he joined the firm, he asked a respected consulting firm to assess CHC's human resources function. The review stated, "CHC's predominant image of HR seems focused on Personnel Administration, with a strong emphasis on the administrative, and on minimizing these costs. Not surprisingly, few see any reason why HR should expand, and many reasons why it should not. ... Most senior people can barely credit the notion that, for example, HR could usefully contribute to organization design and structure decisions." In the two years since the report, CHC had developed, if anything, less appetite for strong corporate staff functions. For example, the lack of cross-divisional financial data prevented Bowen from analyzing information such as CHC recruiting expenses. Similarly, the initiative to implement a corporate HRI system to access HR data across the organization was still being met with resistance by the business units, and no consolidated reporting capability had been realized.

Bill Gibbons, vice president of corporate communications, joined CHC in 1988. He and his staff of 17 were responsible for preparing shareholder reports, handling investor relations, and managing media relations, advertising, community relations programs, and the corporate identity initiative. Gibbons explained that, under Bailey's leadership, corporate staff groups such as his had to tighten their belts, adopt a value-added focus, and manage through consensus with the division presidents.

Joe Tumbler, senior vice president of planning and corporate development, had been with CHC 18 months. He was one of the two staff officers on the operations and policy committee (OPC), Bailey's strategic decision-making body. Tumbler was responsible for acquisition activities and the strategic planning process for CHC.

Looking to the Future

"We have an entirely new model of the corporation. We are focused on the customer, on differentiating our products through service, on becoming a low-cost producer, on empowering our employees, and on time-based management," Bailey summarized. Three studies were under way to help CHC understand what the next steps should be.

1. CHC had retained a consulting firm to help it determine the costs and benefits of consolidating the corporation's two major data centers into a single information technology utility. CHC executives expected that the savings from such an endeavor might possibly be significant, but they wanted to understand the other tradeoffs as well. Executives had asked the consultants to recommend a structure and appropriate set of responsibilities for a corporate hardware utility.

Tumbler stated, "We have an opportunity to consolidate the processing utility, but it needs to be harmonious with and responsive to the needs of the business units. It is imperative that the business units approach their customers in a different way, and we can't slow that down with an I/S infrastructure that may have a different set of priorities. The first step may be consolidating the hardware and technical support under common management. And, we can certainly create a central focal point for systems planning—taking a long-term view of how we put technology to best use for CHC. But we have to place systems development as close to the line and as close to our customers as possible."

2. CHC was considering consolidating the retail market research function. Staff from Agency Group in Louisville and DRG in Valley Forge would be combined into an initial unit of six to eight people. Sams described its function as "world-class market research. By combining resources, we will get a high-caliber staff of very creative people who can tell us where we stand in the marketplace. Product development will continue to be decentralized in the business units."

3. Finally, CHC was working toward commissioning a study group that would investigate a new distribution concept combining the strengths of agent and direct-response marketing. Sams stated the purpose was to "take advantage of both distribution systems. The most difficult job for agents is finding prospects. If we can make that job easier and economically viable by using the

direct-response experience, that's great. Our objective is to make the whole more valuable than the sum of the parts." Phelps continued, "This is a threatening idea to some people. We have a lot of history of trying to get synergy, but the cultures of the two groups are dramatically different. We may have to 'wall off' whatever we do in order to get it started." Tumbler added, "The concept we're talking about is different from cross-selling, it's real marketing coherence. We want to tailor services, as well as products, to meet our customers' needs."

Sams and Phelps were meeting to articulate a clear mission for the task force. They anticipated that it would begin its work in July, and expected to see some initial recommendations by the end of the year.

Bailey concluded, "Synergies are still a principal thrust. But we are not thinking about forming a single retail business right now. It's just not being packaged that way. In 1986, there were big walls between the business units. These have been broken down in the past year and a half. We have done a lot to solidify the trust among the top executives." The only piece of the corporate strategic plan that remained unfinished was the role of the holding company. Senior executives were struggling through a process of defining exactly what value-added Capital Holding itself would provide. Bailey anticipated that the need for a CIO to frame and implement corporate I/S strategy would emerge as this vision was articulated.

Appendix A

Capital Holding Corporation: Overview of the Insurance Industry

The insurance industry offers four basic types of coverage: life, health, property-casualty, and annuities. The product lines of many of the major companies include all three types, though some specialize in one area or another. For example, most of Prudential's premium revenue in 1988 was derived from life insurance, and Fireman's Fund specialized in property and casualty insurance.

The majority of an insurance company's income is derived from premiums. The remainder consists primarily of earnings on investments. A factor that significantly affects an insurance company's profitability is the policy lapse rate. Most of the costs of an insurance contract—agent commissions and distribution costs, for example—are incurred during the first few years of the policy, thus companies' profits are tied directly to policyholder persistency.

The insurance industry entered a period of unprecedented change in the early 1980s. This once complacent and conservative industry was faced with high levels of inflation and record-high interest rates. Inflation impacted policy values. Consumers wanted products that would keep pace with market interest rates and thus moved their savings from low-yielding whole life insurance policies to higher-yielding investments such as stocks, bonds, and money market funds. New competitors, from banks and savings and loans to mutual fund companies, threatened the insurance industry's share of consumer savings. Many firms within the industry began to offer interest-sensitive products such as universal life and single-premium annuities to counter the trend. These products promised investment yields that were tied to the current interest rate. Product development, a function that was weak in most of the industry's players, became critical. Expense management also assumed more importance as competition intensified.

With increased pressure on product development and on margins, information technology requirements soared. Insurance, like many other service businesses, had always been information-intensive, the focus of the applications changed. Insurance companies were among the first and most enthusiastic users of data processing in the 1950s and 1960s to handle the routine transactions associated with servicing policies. In the 1980s, information systems moved out of the back office. Effective I/S support was required to develop, administer, and sell many of the new products that were introduced. An industry executive estimated that one of the new, more complex policies required five times the processing power of a traditional term insurance policy. I/S also played a key role in improving the productivity of the agent sales force and made it possible for companies to exploit new channels of distribution.

The Tax Reform Act of 1986 had a positive impact on the accumulation segment of the insurance market. Income earned on insurance contracts and deferred annuities was not taxable until it was distributed. The benefits of these products became more attractive than nontax-deductible IRA contributions.

Glossary of Insurance Terms

Accumulation An insurance-based product whose main focus is saving, not protection.

Annuity An agreement by an insurance company to make periodic payments that continue during the lifetime of the annuitant or for a specified period.

Deferred Annuity An annuity contract that provides for the initiation of payments at some designated future date in contrast to one in which payment begins immediately on purchase.

Single-Premium Policy An insurance policy paid for in a single premium in advance rather than in annual premiums over a period of time.

Term Insurance The type of life insurance that provides protection only for a specified period of time. It does not build up the cash value that is created with whole life insurance.

Universal Life Insurance A flexible-premium life insurance policy under which the policyholder may change the death benefit from time to time (with satisfactory evidence of insurability for increases) and vary the amount or timing of premium payments.

Variable Life Insurance Insurance in which the insurance amount and cash value may fluctuate during the term of the policy. The variable may be some index such as the Consumer Price Index or an index of securities.

Whole Life Insurance Insurance which may be kept in force for a person's whole life and which pays a benefit upon his death, whenever that may be. All whole life policies build up a cash value. Premiums may be payable for a specified number of years (limited payment life) or for life (straight life).

Appendix B Capital Holding Corporation: Consolidated Statements of Operations

Year Ended December 31,	*1988*	*1987*[a]	*1986*[a]
(Dollars in Thousands Except Per Common Share)			
Revenues			
Premiums and other considerations	$ 982,441	$ 969,398	$ 854,438
Investment income, net of expenses	1,018,892	764,651	586,606
Realized investment gain	25,310	14,302	169,341
Other income, net	19,223	36,341	29,968
Total Revenues	2,045,866	1,784,692	1,640,353
Benefits and Expenses			
Benefits and claims	652,425	612,020	516,744
Increase in benefit and contract reserves	566,023	415,418	296,570
Commissions, net	65,146	60,678	59,916
General, administrative and other expenses, net	288,050	258,540	189,813
Amortization:			
Deferred policy and loan acquisition costs	149,314	125,122	165,307
Value of insurance in force purchased	12,088	12,470	15,457
Goodwill	4,869	4,755	4,705
Interest expense	48,772	43,727	40,898
Loss on debenture redemption	-	-	16,195
Total Benefits and Expenses	1,786,687	1,532,730	1,305,605
Income before Federal Income Tax	259,179	251,962	334,748
Federal Income Tax	69,315	73,371	61,734
Net Income before Cumulative Effect of Change in Accounting Principle	189,864	178,591	273,014
Cumulative Effect of Change in Accounting Principle	-	-	(104,069)
Net Income	189,864	178,591	168,945
Provision for Dividends on Preferred Stock	7,323	6,989	7,079
Net Income Applicable to Common Stock	$ 182,541	$ 171,602	$ 161,866
Per Common Share:			
Net Income before Cumulative Effect of Change in Accounting Principle	$ 4.00	$ 3.49	5.24
Cumulative Effect of Change in Accounting Principle	-	-	(2.05)
Net Income	$ 4.00	$ 3.49	$ 3.19

[a]Restated to reflect a change in accounting policy.

Appendix B   (continued)

Business Segment Data

Year Ended December 31,	1988	1987	1986	1985	1984	1983
(Dollars in Thousands)						
Premiums, premium equivalents and other considerations:						
Agency Group[a]						
Life (includes premium equivalents)	$ 271,112	$ 265,803	$254,400	$255,141	$250,914	$255,919
Health	38,069	31,923	29,604	27,679	26,026	27,057
Other product lines	30,018	22,641	21,424	20,226	19,561	22,063
Subtotal	339,199	320,367	305,428	303,046	296,501	305,039
Life premium equivalents	(42,798)	(44,465)	(26,741)	(17,191)	(10,983)	(8,602)
Total Agency Group	296,401	275,902	278,687	285,855	285,518	296,437
Direct Response Group Life	196,057	190,677	170,165	145,147	123,914	95,085
Health	206,616	231,359	244,610	252,681	246,946	229,259
Property and casualty	158,054	163,488	26,786	26,887	22,525	15,657
Other product lines	12,666	14,634	16,878	19,264	20,841	23,246
Total Direct Response Group	573,393	600,158	458,439	443,979	414,226	363,246
Accumulation and Investment Group	97,502	63,846	29,783	22,737	4,120	4,056
Corporate and Other	15,145	29,492	87,529	97,876	100,718	99,212
Consolidated Premiums and Other Considerations	$ 982,441	$ 969,398	$854,438	$850,447	$804,582	$762,951
Increase in Accumulation and Investment Group policyholder deposits:						
Institutional	$1,384,839	$ 884,101	$364,343	$321,470	$155,146	$120,245
Retail	429,252	631,412	428,647	456,113	390,467	390,607
Total Increase in Policyholder Deposits	$1,814,091	$1,515,513	$792,990	$777,583	$545,613	$510,852
Revenues:						
Agency Group[a]						
Life (includes premium equivalents)	$ 446,025	$ 436,187	$421,266	$410,170	$402,023	$393,281
Health	43,634	35,654	33,361	30,895	28,646	29,317
Other product lines	47,205	36,800	35,929	55,456	37,719	39,241
Realized investment gain (loss)	(3,577)	51,222	49,067	(16,499)	12,240	(13,919)
Subtotal	533,287	559,863	539,623	480,022	480,628	447,920
Life premium equivalents	(42,798)	(44,465)	(26,741)	(17,191)	(10,983)	(8,602)
Total Agency Group	490,489	515,398	512,882	462,831	469,645	439,318
Direct Response Group Life	231,364	222,046	198,050	167,350	141,211	108,108
Health	221,511	246,302	259,694	267,351	260,261	241,664
Property and casualty	175,979	174,836	29,685	29,701	25,195	17,323
Other product lines	24,974	23,242	22,930	25,467	27,107	30,059
Realized investment gain	11,797	12,972	25,876	689	3,309	2,976
Total Direct Response Group	665,625	679,398	536,235	490,558	457,083	400,130

[a]In disclosures of Agency Group segment data, life premium equivalents are included, which adjust premiums to amounts as received from policyholders, for comparative purposes and then these equivalents are removed from the segment total.

Appendix B (continued)

Year Ended December 31,	Business Segment Data					
	1988	1987	1986	1985	1984	1983
(Dollars in Thousands)						
Accumulation and Investment Group						
Institutional	234,786	146,327	78,731	51,780	26,556	8,134
Retail	381,620	295,558	225,741	185,352	126,537	78,021
Realized investment gain (loss)	20,753	(49,862)	88,407	30,175	(1,582)	7,611
Total Accumulation and Investment Group	637,159	392,023	392,879	267,307	151,511	93,766
Banking	248,897	130,722	49,902	18,290	2,083	-
Corporate and Other						
Realized investment gain (loss)	(3,663)	(30)	5,991	(9,019)	(20,579)	2,204
Other	7,359	67,181	142,464	131,837	142,110	134,790
Total Corporate and Other	3,696	67,151	148,455	122,818	121,531	136,994
Consolidated Revenues	$2,045,866	$1,784,692	$1,640,353	$1,361,804	1,201,853	$1,070,208
Income (loss) before federal income tax:						
Agency Group						
Life	$ 126,974	$ 120,355	$ 115,161	$ 110,060	$ 106,553	$ 101,523
Health	3,608	5,444	5,185	5,445	3,469	3,751
Other product lines	2,449	1,367	1,284	2,357	1,172	908
Subtotal	133,031	127,166	121,630	117,862	111,194	106,182
Realized investment gain (loss), net of related amortization	(3,347)	51,955	47,922	(17,404)	12,240	(13,919)
Total Agency Group	129,684	179,121	169,552	100,458	123,434	92,263
Direct Response Group						
Life	23,961	21,464	20,828	20,643	21,213	16,528
Health	35,541	36,034	36,376	32,536	25,266	15,559
Property and casualty	7,985	4,535	(2,346)	(3,248)	(7,268)	(1,786)
Other product lines	(661)	(1,284)	(1,375)	(1,375)	(1,064)	257
Subtotal	66,826	60,749	52,440	48,556	38,147	30,558
Realized investment gain	11,797	12,972	25,876	689	3,309	2,976
Total Direct Response Group	78,623	73,721	78,316	49,245	41,456	33,534
Accumulation and Investment Group						
Institutional	27,825	26,043	19,480	8,574	2,617	845
Retail	35,938	29,779	26,377	16,763	7,839	3,677
Subtotal	63,763	55,822	45,857	25,337	10,456	4,522
Realized investment gain (loss), net of related amortization	19,792	(41,604)	61,355	22,616	(1,650)	4,205

[a]In 1984, includes compliance and implementation cost ($5.5 million) and a provision for adverse persistency on a certain product ($7.5 million) related to the enactment of new tax legislation. In 1983, includes a net charge for corporate restructuring ($3.6 million).

Appendix B   (continued)

Business Segment Data

Year Ended December 31,	1988	1987	1986	1985	1984	1983
(Dollars in Thousands)						
Total Accumulation and Investment						
Group	83,555	14,218	107,212	47,953	8,806	8,727
Banking	13,564	7,125	1,080	(2,352)	(1,588)	-
Corporate and Other Realized investment gain						
(loss)	(3,663)	(30)	5,991	(9,019)	(20,579)	2,204
Other[a]	(42,584)	(22,193)	(27,403)	(18,636)	(19,281)	(13,911)
Total Corporate and Other	(46,247)	(22,223)	(21,412)	(27,655)	(39,860)	(11,707)
Consolidated Income before Federal Income Tax	$ 259,179	$ 251,962	$ 334,748	$ 167,649	$ 132,248	$ 122,817
Assets:						
Agency Group						
Life	$ 2,210,605	$ 2,143,474	$2,078,362	$2,023,456	$1,999,188	$1,954,161
Health	83,939	64,974	57,796	50,926	44,964	41,084
Other product lines	389,173	357,732	354,504	355,932	323,649	305,039
Total Agency Group	2,683,717	2,566,180	2,490,662	2,430,314	2,367,801	2,300,284
Direct Response Group						
Life	630,428	577,542	503,947	405,484	330,852	258,544
Health	403,502	398,782	399,955	389,320	364,506	247,785
Property and casualty	256,222	208,534	149,247	29,404	30,123	22,330
Other product lines	177,120	185,283	196,168	213,071	222,346	313,891
Total Direct Response Group	1,467,272	1,370,141	1,249,317	1,037,279	947,827	842,550
Accumulation and Investment Group						
Institutional	3,077,279	1,817,142	904,392	542,850	231,073	102,220
Retail	3,463,007	2,890,243	2,240,745	1,746,927	1,255,408	849,315
Total Accumulation and Investment Group	6,540,286	4,707,385	3,145,137	2,289,777	1,486,481	951,535
Banking	1,648,898	1,065,016	471,929	177,838	74,754	-
Corporate and Other	623,095	647,770	937,969	786,957	703,718	718,579
Consolidated Assets	$12,963,268	$10,356,492	$8,295,014	$6,722,165	$5,580,581	$4,812,948

[a]In 1984, includes compliance and implementation cost ($5.5 million) and a provision for adverse persistency on a certain product ($7.5 million) related to the enactment of new tax legislation. In 1983, includes a net charge to corporate restructuring ($3.6 million).

Chapter 8

IT Organizational Issues

In the preceding chapter we noted that the management structures needed for guiding new technologies into the organization are quite different from those for the older, established technologies. The corporation must encourage *innovation* by information technology (IT) staff and users with the newer technologies while focusing on *control* and *efficiency* in the more mature technologies. In this chapter we will discuss two aspects of IT management that are rapidly changing: first, the range of organizational alternatives that have emerged for effectively assigning responsibility for IT development, and second, the coordination and location of IT policy formulation between users, IT, and general management.

ORGANIZATION ISSUES IN IT DEVELOPMENT

Policies for guiding the deployment of information technology development staff and activity in the future must deal with two sets of tensions. The first, as noted in the previous chapters, is the balance between *innovation* and *control*. The relative emphasis a firm should place on the aggressive innovation phase varies widely from firm to firm, depending on a broad assessment of the potential strategic impact of information technology on the firm, general corporate willingness to take risk, and so on. If IT is perceived to be of great impact in helping the firm reach its strategic objectives, significantly greater investment in innovation is called for than if it is seen to be merely helpful.

The second set is the tension between *IT dominance* and *user dominance* in the retention of development skills and in the active selection of priorities. The user tends toward short-term need fulfillment (at the expense of long-term IT hygiene and orderly development). IT, on the other hand, can become preoccupied with the mastery of technology and an orderly development plan at the risk of slow response to legitimate user needs. Balancing the roles of these two groups is a complex task that must be dealt with in the context of the corporate culture and the potential strategic IT role.

Table 8–1 illustrates some consequences of excessive domination by IT and by users. It shows clearly that very different application portfolios and operating problems emerge in the two settings. This chapter emphasizes the need for experimentation because of the difficulty of anticipating the implications of introducing a new technology. The following four cases illustrate this problem.

Some Examples

Case 1: A Short-Term User-Need Situation, Strategically Important.
The number-one priority in a large machine-tool manufacturer's engineering department was computer-aided design (CAD). Early success

TABLE 8–1   Possible Implications of Excess IT and User Dominance

IT Dominance	*User Dominance*
Too much emphasis on database hygiene.	Too much emphasis on problem focus.
No recent new supplier or new distinct services (too busy with maintenance).	IT says out of control.
All new systems must fit data structure of existing system.	Explosive growth in number of new systems and supporting staff.
All requests for service require system study with benefit identification.	Multiple suppliers delivering services. Frequent change in supplier of specific service.
Standardization dominates; few exceptions.	Lack of standardization and control over data hygiene and system.
IT designs/constructs everything.	Hard evidence of benefits nonexistent.
Benefits of user control over development discussed but never implemented.	Soft evidence of benefits not organized.
Study always shows construction costs less than outside purchase.	Few measurements/objectives for new systems.
Head count of distributed minis and development staff growing surreptitiously.	Technical advice of IT not sought; if received, considered irrelevant.
IT specializing in technical frontiers, not user-oriented markets.	User buying design/construction/maintenance services and even operations from outside.
IT spending 80% on maintenance, 20% on development.	User building networks to own unique needs, not to corporate need.
IT thinks they are in control of all.	Some users are growing rapidly in experience and use, while others feel nothing is relevant because they do not understand.
Users express unhappiness.	No coordinated effort for technology transfer or learning from experience between users.
Portfolio of development opportunities firmly under IT control.	Growth in duplication of technical staffs.
No strong user group exists.	Dramatically rising communications costs because of redundancy.
General management not involved butconcerned.	

had led to a major expansion of the effort. Department personnel modified the digital information design output to enable them to control computer-driven machine tools directly. This work was deliberately kept independent of their bill of materials/cost system, which was in a database format and was maintained by the IT unit.

Short of staff to integrate the new system in their database structure, the user department decided to go ahead despite the major system integration problems that would result. The work was done over the objection of IT management, but the engineering department received full support from senior management because of the project's potential major, immediate impact on shortening the product development life cycle.

The engineers enthusiastically worked on the CAD project to make it work, while the IT unit was decidedly lukewarm. The project slashed development time by half for new designs. The IT database integration issue remains, but realistically, the firm is no worse off in this regard than it was before.

Case 2: User Control to Achieve Automation. A substantial investment in office automation was undertaken by a division of a large consumer products manufacturer with modest up-front cost-benefit justification. Managers and administrative support personnel were encouraged by IT to "use" the systems with only cursory direction and some introductory training on the Wang word processor that was made available to them. After four months, three product managers had developed independent networks to support sales force activities; two had automated portions of their word processing, with substantial savings; two others did little but were encouraging their administrative support staff to "try it out." The users were gaining confidence and pursuing new programs with enthusiasm.

The challenge to the IT management now, after only six months, was to develop and evolve an efficient program with these seven "experienced" users. The IT manager estimated it would take roughly two years to achieve this efficient integration. However, both he and divisional management felt, retrospectively, that it would have been impossible to implement office support with a standard IT-dominated systems study and that the expense of the after-the-fact rationalization was an acceptable price for these benefits. The control over this word processing program contrasted sharply with the strong central control IT was exerting over its mature data processing technologies.

Case 3: Step-by-Step Innovation of a New Technology. A large grocery chain acquired a system of point-of-sales terminals. These terminals were initially purchased by the retail division (with the support of the IT manager) to assist store managers in controlling inventory. They were to be used exclusively within individual stores to accumulate daily sales totals of individual items. These totals would permit individual stores to trigger reorders in case lots at given times.

Once installed, however, these isolated systems were evolved quickly into links to central headquarters at the initiative of corporate management. These links were established to feed data from the stores to new corporate computer programs that provided a measurement of advertising effectiveness and the ability to manage warehouse stock levels chainwide.

Implementation of this nonplanned linkage involved significant extra expense, because the communication protocols in the selected terminals were incompatible with those in the computer at headquarters. Nonetheless, the possibilities and benefits of the resulting system would have been difficult to define in advance, because this eventual use was not considered important when the initial point-of-sale terminals were being installed. Further, in management's opinion, even if the organization had considered it, the ultimate costs of the resulting system would have been seen as prohibitive in relation to benefits (in retrospect, *incorrectly* prohibitive). Success of the first system laid the baseline for the next ones. In an uncertain world, there are limitations to planning.

Case 4: User Innovation as a Source of Productivity.   A large bank introduced an electronic mail system and a word processor system to facilitate its preparation of loan paperwork. The two systems soon evolved to link the bank's loan officers (initially not planned to be clients of either system) to a series of analytical programs—an evolution that developed out of conversations between a loan officer and a consultant. They discovered that the word-processor loan system had bundled with it a powerful analytical tool that could be used by the officers to analyze loan performance. Because of the bank's electronic mail system, this analytical tool could be easily accessed by loan officers (at headquarters and in branches).

After three months of use, the bank faced a series of internal tensions as the costs of both the electronic mail system and the word processing system unexpectedly rose due to this added use. This was compounded by the lack of a formal means to review "experiments" or evaluate unanticipated uses of the systems by participants not initially involved. Eventually a senior management review committee supported the new use of the two systems, and it was permitted to continue. Substantial enhancements were added to the word processing software to make it even more useful to the loan officers.

Implications

These examples are typical of emerging new services that support professionals and managers in doing work. They form the underpinning of our conviction that it is impossible to foresee in advance the full range of consequences of introducing information technology systems. Excessive control and focus on quick results in the early stages can deflect important learning that may result in even more useful applications. Neither IT professionals nor users have outstanding records in anticipating the consequences of new technologies' impacts on organizations. Consequently, a necessary general management role is to help facilitate this assimilation.

This chapter is divided into three sections. The first discusses the pressures on users to gain control, not only over a system's development activities, but when possible, to have the resulting product run on a stand-alone mini or micro system located in their department. The second section identifies the advantages of strong IT development coordination and the potential pitfalls of uncontrolled proliferation of user-developed systems. The third section identifies the core policies that must be implemented by IT management, user management, and general management, respectively, in order to ensure a good result. In our judgment, the general manager's role is particularly critical in creating an environment that facilitates technological change and organizational adaptation.

PRESSURES TOWARD USER DOMINANCE

A number of intense pressures encourage users to exercise stronger control over their systems development resources and acquisition of independent IT resources. These pressures can be clustered into five categories: pent-up user demand, the needs for staffing flexibility, competitive and service growth in the IT market, user desire to control their destiny, and fit with the organization.

Pent-Up User Demand

The backlog of development work facing an IT systems development department is frequently very large in relation to its staff resources; three- to five-year backlogs tend to be the norm. The reasons for these staffing "crunches" are many, and the problems are not easily solved. One reason is that existing systems require sustained maintenance in order to deal with changing regulatory and other business requirements. As more systems have been automated, the maintenance needs have continued to rise, forcing either increases in development staff or the postponement of new work. This problem has been intensified by the shift in systems design philosophy in the early 1970s from one that incorporates data into programs to one that clearly separates database management from processing procedures.

Effecting this one-time conversion has been very expensive in terms of staff resources.

Further, the most challenging, high-status, high-paying jobs tend to be with computer vendors and software houses, which puts great pressure on an organization's IT department. Its most talented staff is tempted to move on to more challenging, perhaps more financially remunerative jobs. Frequently it is easier for the IT systems development unit to get the budget allocations than to find the staff resources to use them. The delays caused by these factors have led to enormous user frustration and a strong desire to take matters into their own hands.

Staff Flexibility and Growth.   The central IT department appears to be unresponsive to users' demands, and user-developed systems and stand-alone minis or micros become attractive to users as a nonconfrontational way of getting work done. Using either their own staffs or outside software houses, users see that they are significantly speeding up the process of obtaining "needed" service.

Staff Professional Growth.   An IT staff decentralized by both their physical and organizational presence in the end-user department helps educate users to the legitimate potential of IT. It also reduces communications problems between IT professionals and end users. Particularly important, it makes it easier to plan employee promotions that rotate IT staff to other (non-IT) jobs within the department, thus enhancing user–IT coordination. This also facilitates the movement of end users to IT positions.

Finally, from the viewpoint of a local department, the protocols of interfacing with the corporate network and of meeting corporate control standards can be very time-consuming and complex. A stand-alone system purchased by a user that is independent of this corporate network may simplify the job of the end user and permit less-skilled staff resources to be utilized. It may require no major changes, particularly if it is a system familiar to one or more employees due to prior experience.

Competitive and Service Growth in the IT Market

Thousands of stand-alone computer systems are available for specific applications. They range from simple accounts-payable systems to complete office automation products. Their existence makes them beguilingly easy solutions to short-term problems. Marketed by hardware and software vendors to end-user managers, the systems' functional features are emphasized, and any technical and software problems are soft-pedaled. For example, most standard word processing systems are marketed without mention of their computer foundation.

A stand-alone local hardware platform may seem particularly attractive to the user, because its on-line response times are faster and more consistent than those of devices that depend on a central unit. The stand-alone unit also provides easy access to on-line systems when needed. With it, the user avoids the problems associated with sharing a many-user system, which can result in a highly variable volume of transactions and lead to variation in response times. Also, the system is seen as operationally simple, needing only an operator to run it when developed. Air conditioning, physical maintenance, and power availability, all of them issues in big IT shops, are less critical in these settings.

Frequently the local solution "appears" to be more cost-effective than work done or purchased by a central IT development group. Not only is there no cumbersome project proposal to be written and defended in front of IT technicians who have their own special agendas, but often a simple up-front price is quoted. Developed under user control, the project is perceived to be both simple and relatively free of red tape.

User Control

The idea of regaining control over a part of their operations, particularly if information technology is a critical part of their units' operations, is very important to users. In many cases this reverses a trend that began 20 years ago in a very different technology. Control in this context has at least three dimensions.

Development.   Users can exercise direct control over systems development priorities. By using either their own staffs or self-selected software houses, which may offer highly specialized skills not present in the firm, users often hope they can get a system functioning in less time than it would take to navigate the priority-setting process in the corporate IT department—and to get staff assigned to the project. A user systems staff is also seen as closer and more responsive to user needs. Development mistakes made by a local group are more easily accepted than those made by a remote group and they are rarely discussed; successes are often topics of conversation.

Maintenance.   Users gain control over systems maintenance priorities. This is because the work will be done either by themselves or by software houses that are dependent upon them for income. The importance of this point is often overlooked initially by the user. Quite often the assumption is that maintenance will be no problem or that it can be performed by a clerk following a manual. A rare occurrence! Needs and desires relentlessly change.

Operations. Users gain control over day-to-day operations. Insulated from the vicissitudes of corporate computer scheduling, users believe they will be able to exert firmer control over the pace of their departments' operations. This is particularly important to small, marginal users of heavily utilized data centers with volatile loads. Today these points are intensified in many users' minds because of previous experiences with service degradation at month-end in large computer systems or with important jobs (to them) not being run because of corporate priorities. Further, as a result of their hands-on experience with home computers, managers are much more confident in their ability to manage a computer operation successfully. Additionally, computer vendors' clever marketing has helped to increase their confidence. In general, however, this experience is of insufficient depth, and the user has more confidence than is warranted.

Fit with the Organization

As the company becomes more decentralized in structure and more geographically diverse, a distributed development function becomes a much better fit and avoids heavy marketing and coordination expenses. Among conglomerates, for example, only a few have tried to centralize development; most leave it with the original units. Heavily decentralized companies such as Capital Holding have closed down their central IT coordinating unit and placed all IT staff in key divisions. Another advantage of distributed development is that if the decision is made to divest the corporation of a unit, the divestiture will be easier to implement if its IT activities are not integrated with the rest of the company.

User Learning

As suggested in the previous chapter, predicting the full ramifications of introducing a new technology is very difficult. On one hand, enthusiastic experimentation by the user can stimulate creativity and produce new approaches to troublesome problems. Systems developed by a central IT unit, on the other hand, must overcome greater user resistance in adoption. This IT challenge simply reflects research in the fields of organization development and control, which has identified organization learning as a principal benefit of organizing in multiple profit centers, rather than by function. As noted earlier, this is increasingly evident in office support and new professional support such as CAD.

Summary

In aggregate, these five pressures represent a powerful argument for a strong user role in systems development and suggest when that role might be the dominant one. The pressures driving users toward purchase, development, *and/or* use of stand-alone, mini-based, and local systems and software can be summarized as *short-term user control*. Stand-alone personal computers and local development have been found to offer users more immediate solutions to the problems under their control and to do so in a climate they perceive as enjoyable. While particular benefits associated with Phase-1 and -2 learning can be achieved by this approach, they may be gained with little regard for information hygiene and less regard for control, as discussed next.

PRESSURES TOWARD IT CONTROL

Countering the arguments of the previous section, pressures exist in many settings to consolidate a firm's IT development resource into a single unit or to at least keep it in two or more large clusters.

Staff Professionalism

As pointed out earlier, a large central IT development staff enhances the organization's ability to recruit and retain (attract and keep challenged) specialized technical personnel. Such a central unit also provides useful support for a small division or unit that does not have its own IT staff and needs occasional access to information technology skills.

Additionally, as the average age of many IT development staffs continues to rise, more and more of the employees are becoming comfortable and set in their ways ("the graying of IT"). The central unit is a useful fulcrum to insert a limited number of high-energy new talent to aid in re-energizing and redirecting older staff. The importance of this is intensified by the fact that salary levels, individual interests, and perceived interpersonal relationships of existing staff often make lateral movement out of the central IT system department undesirable. Many of these people must either be retrained or they will have to be let go. The inability of some firms to manage this is a key reason for the current popularity of outsourcing development to external vendors. It is easier to modernize a centralized unit than one in which the development staff is scattered throughout the firm.

Developing and enforcing better standards of IT management practice is also easier in a large group. Documentation procedures, project management skills, and disciplined maintenance approaches are examples of critical infrastructure items in IT systems development departments. In 1981 a large financial service organization faced with a deteriorating relationship between its central development department and key users was forced to split the development department into a number of smaller units distributed around the company, thereby changing both reporting responsibility and office location. Although the change was initially successful in stimulating new ideas and better relationships with users (many development people came to identify better with users than with technical development issues), by 1987 the quality of IT staff professionalism had dropped so low through neglect that several major project fiascoes occurred that required assistance from an outside service organization. Significant parts of the development function had to be recentralized, and much tighter controls had to be installed over management practices in the remaining distributed development groups. This periodic swing of the centralize/decentralize pendulum has occurred in numerous settings as the benefits of a change over time give way to problems that require redirection.

Central staff expertise is particularly important for supporting user-designed and user-selected computer-based systems. Lacking practical systems design experience and purchased software standards, the user often ignores normal data control procedures, documentation standards, and conventional costing practices. Consequently, purchasing from several suppliers or incrementally from one often results in a clumsy system design that is hard to maintain.

For example, a large financial organization discovered that all of the people who were involved in the design and purchase of software for three of the stand-alone computer systems used to process data on a daily basis had left the company. Further, no formal documentation or operating instructions had been prepared, and all source programs had been lost. All that remained were disk files with object programs on them. The system ran, but why it ran no one knew; and even if the company's survival depended on it, changes would at best have been very difficult and time-consuming to execute.

A recent study of a firm that had invested heavily ($8 million) in personal computers in the past five years showed it had also invested $15 million in systems development for those machines. Locally developed and largely unmanaged, more development money was being spent on the distributed systems than in the central development unit, which had extensive documentation and other controls. The situation was rectified before serious damage occurred.

Feasibility Study Concerns

A user-driven feasibility study may contain major technical mistakes that result in the computer system's being inadequate to handle growing processing requirements or in its having large amounts of excess capacity. Repeatedly, because of inexperienced staff, the feasibility study may underestimate both the complexity of the software needed and the growth in the number of transactions to be handled by the system. (The risk increases if competent technical staff inputs to the feasibility study were limited and if the real business needs were not well understood.)

Additionally, users often focus a feasibility study on a specific service without recognizing that successful first applications tend to generate unanticipated second applications, then third applications, and so forth. Each application appears to require only a modest incremental purchase price and, therefore, does not receive a comprehensive full-cost review. The result may be that in a very short period of time the hardware configuration or software approach selected cannot handle the necessary work. Unless great care was taken in the initial hardware selection and system design process to allow for growth, expansion can result in major business disruptions and very expensive software modifications.

User-driven feasibility studies are more susceptible to recommendations to acquire products from unstable vendors because of some unusually attractive product features. Stability of vendors is an important consideration in this rapidly growing industry sector; significant numbers of software vendors have failed, and a number of hardware manufacturers are in trouble as well. The same trends that hit the pocket calculator and digital watch industries in the late 1970s began to hit this industry sector as it reached a point of maturity in recent years. Stability of the vendors is critical, because many of these systems insinuate themselves into the heart of a department's operations. With software-intensive investments, failure of a hardware vendor can mean both expensive disruption in service provided by the department and intensive, crisis spending efforts to convert the software to another machine unless appropriate standards have been selected. These concerns apply equally to hardware suppliers and to the packages and services provided by software suppliers. A single experience with a product from a failed software vendor provides painful learning.

Some care must be taken on local development, since user groups tend to buy or develop systems tailored to very specific situations, which may lead to long-term maintenance problems. In many environments characterized by local development, there is also poor technology transfer between similar users and thus consequent lack of corporate leverage, an issue of low importance to the local unit.

A large forest products company, organized geographically, combined a system-minded regional manager with an aggressive growth–oriented IT manager who was promoted to responsibility for all administrative support in the region. Within three years their budget for IT was double that of a comparable region. Although their applications were extraordinarily effective, only one was exported to another region. Subsequent review of this unit's work indicated that nearly half of the systems they developed were focused on problems of potentially general interest and consequently could have been exported to other parts of the company.

Corporate Database System

Development of corporate database strategy involves both the collection of data files at a central location for reference by multiple users and the development of networks and procedures that will allow users to access data files easily regardless of their physical location in the firm. A central staff provides a focal point for both conceptualizing and developing the architecture of these systems to serve multiple users across the firm. The need for this corporate database varies widely with the nature of the corporation's activities. A conglomerate usually has much less need for this data across the firm than does a functionally organized, one-product company. Even here, however, electronic mail, videoconferencing, and shared financial performance information have become legitimate needs. If such needs exist, a central department is better able to develop and distribute such systems to users or to coordinate a development process in which key parts of the systems development are farmed out to local development units.

Inevitably the first concern raised when discussing distributed development and hardware in the several business units is that the company will lose the ability to manage and control its data flows—that data of significance to many people beyond those in the originating unit will be locked up in a nonstandardized format in inaccessible locations. Without denying the validity of this concern (there is substantial truth in it in many settings), several mitigating factors demand that such objections be carefully examined in any specific situation.

Timing.   One factor is the issue of timing. In many cases the argument raised against a stand-alone system is the erosion of data as a corporate resource. Allegedly, in order to preserve flexibility for future database design, this stand-alone computer should not be acquired. However, it frequently turns out that this flexibility is not needed as adaptive communication systems can provide control as well as access to distant users. In this context a well-designed stand-alone system may be an equally good (if not better) starting point for these long-term systems as jumping directly from the present set of manual procedures would be. This possibility must be pragmatically assessed.

Abstraction of Data. Another mitigating factor, often overlooked, is the capability for abstracting data, if necessary, from a locally managed system at planned frequent intervals and sending it directly to a central computer. Ordinarily not all information in a stand-alone file is relevant to or needed by other users. Indeed, often only a small percentage is.

On the other hand, locally designed data-handling systems can prove expensive to maintain and to link with each other. The firm must identify in operational terms the data requirements of the central files and provide guidelines for what data can be stored locally and how accessible it should be to others. This problem is exemplified by the branch-office office support systems that generate voluminous records in electronic format. Unless well-designed, these files can be bulky, lock up key data from potential users, and pose potential security problems. For example, a mail-order house recently discovered that each customer representative was using more than 200 disks per day and storing them in boxes by date of order receipt, making aggregate customer information impossible to obtain in a timely manner. A new procedure reduced the number of disks to five.

Organizing and accessing electronic files may require central storage to ensure appropriate security. Managing effective security—a topic of intense interest in a world of "hackers"—is usually easier when all files are in a single location rather than dispersed. Realistically, however, some data is so sensitive that it is best kept off the network, the only way to ensure real security.

Fit with the Corporate Structure and Strategy

Centralized IT development's role is clearest in organizations where there is centrally directed planning and operational control. A large farm-equipment manufacturer with a tradition of central functional control from corporate headquarters successfully implemented a program by which all software for factories and distribution units worldwide was developed by the corporate systems group. As the company grows in size, however, the company's structure is becoming more decentralized. Consequently, the cost of effective central systems development is escalating, and the firm is having to implement a marketing function to educate users on the virtues of central services *and* to decentralize some development functions. It is becoming increasingly common for centralized development groups to have an explicitly defined and staffed internal marketing activity.

Cost Analysis

Because of its practical experience in other systems efforts, a centralized IT development group has the ability to produce a realistic software development estimate (subject to the problems discussed in Chapter 10) that takes into account the interests of the company as a whole. Software development estimates are problematic in user feasibility studies for two key reasons. The first is that most new systems are more software intensive than hardware intensive. Typically software costs are 75 percent to 85 percent of the total cost for a customized system. Few users have had experience in estimating software development costs, and an order-of-magnitude mistake in a feasibility study—particularly if it is an individually developed system and not a "turn-key" (i.e., general purpose) package—is not unknown.

Users also lack understanding of the true costs of an existing service. A major contributor to this is complicated corporate IT charge-out systems, many of which present calculations in terms of utilization of computer resource units that are completely unfathomable to the user. The result is that each month or quarter an unintelligible bill arrives, the amount of which is unpredictable. (In management control environments where the user is held closely responsible for variance from budget, this legitimately causes intense frustration.) A locally developed system, particularly if it is for a stand-alone personal computer, is seen as producing both understandable and predictable costs for the user. Further, since many corporate charge-out systems are designed on a full-cost basis, their charges to the end user seem high and thus offer great inducements to purchase locally. Since much of corporate IT is fixed cost in the short run, many of these savings are false.

Because there are significant fixed-cost elements to a corporate information systems center, particularly in the short run, what appears to the individual user to be an opportunity to reduce costs may be a cost increase for the company—more hardware/software acquired locally and no possible savings at the corporate IT facility. Policies for ensuring that appropriate cost analyses are prepared must be established.

Summary

The pressures toward centralized IT control can be summarized as *long-term information hygiene.* Inexorably over the long run, most (but not all) stand-alone units will become part of a network and need to both receive and share data with other users and systems. In many respects these pressures are not immediately evident when the system is installed but tend to grow in importance with the passage of time.

Policies for managing the trade-offs between the obvious short-term benefits and long-term risks are delicate to administer but necessary.

COORDINATION AND LOCATION OF IT POLICY

Effective management of the tension between IT and users can be managed by establishing clear policies that specify the user domain, the IT domain, and senior management's role. Senior management must play a significant role in ensuring that these policies are developed and that they evolve appropriately over time. Both IT and users must understand the implications of these roles and the possible conflicts.

IT Responsibilities

The following tasks constitute the central core of IT responsibilities — the minimum for managing the long-term information hygiene needs of an organization:

1. Develop procedures to ensure that, for potential IT projects of any size, a comparison is made of internal development versus purchase. If projects are implemented outside the firm or by the user, establish the appropriate professional standards for project control and documentation. These standards must be flexible, since user-developed systems for personal computers pose demands quite different from systems to be run on large mainframe computers. Further, define a process for forcing adherence to the selected standards.
2. Maintain an inventory of installed or planned-to-be-installed information services.
3. Develop and maintain a set of standards that establishes:

   a. Mandatory telecommunication standards.
   b. Standard languages for classes of acquired equipment.
   c. Documentation procedures for different types of systems.
   d. Corporate data dictionary with clear definitions as to which elements must be included. Identification of file maintenance standards and procedures.
   e. Examination procedures for systems developed in local units to ensure that they do not conflict with corporate needs and that any necessary interfaces are constructed.

4. Identify and provide appropriate IT development staff career paths throughout the organization. These include lateral transfers within and between IT units, upward movement within IT, and appropri-

ate outward movement from IT to other functional units. (Although this is more difficult in distributed units, it is still possible.)

5. Establish appropriate internal marketing efforts for IT support. These should exert catch-up pressure and coaching for units that are lagging and slow down units that are pushing too fast into leading edge technologies that they do not understand.

6. Prepare a detailed checklist of questions to be answered in any hardware/software acquisition to ensure that relevant technical and managerial issues are raised. These questions should ask:

   a. Does the proposed system meet corporate communication standards?
   b. For office support systems, has upward growth potential been addressed, and are adequate communication capabilities in place so that local files can be reached from other locations if appropriate?
   c. Are languages being used that are appropriate and that can be maintained over the long term?

7. Identify and maintain relationships with preferred systems suppliers. Before a relationship is established with a vendor, the conditions for entertaining exceptions to the established standards must be agreed upon. For example, size, number of systems in place, and financial structure requirements should be clearly spelled out.

8. Establish education programs for potential users that communicate both the potential and the pitfalls of a new technology and that define the users' roles in ensuring its successful introduction in their departments.

9. Establish an ongoing review of systems for determining which ones have become obsolete and should be redesigned.

These questions apply with particular force to the design of systems that embed themselves in the company's daily operations. Decision support systems do not pose quite the same problems, although the need to obtain data from the rest of the organization is rapidly putting them in the same situation.

These core responsibilities, of course, can be significantly expanded to impose much tighter and more formal controls if the situation warrants it.

User Responsibilities

To assist in the orderly implementation of new IT services and grow in an understanding of their use, cost, and impact on the organization, the following responsibilities should be fulfilled by the user of IT service:

1. Clearly understand the scope of all IT activities supporting the user. Increasingly in the more experienced organizations a user-understandable IT charge-out system has been installed to facilitate this.
2. Realistically appraise the amount of user personnel investment that will be required for each new project, both to develop and to operate the system, in order to ensure a satisfactory service. These costs are often much higher than planned and are frequently ignored.
3. Ensure that comprehensive user input takes place for all IT projects that will support vital aspects of the unit's operations. This might include, for example, nature of service, process of introduction, and level of user training for both staff and managers.
4. Realistically ensure that the IT–user interface is consistent with IT's strategic relevance to the business unit. If it is very important, the interface must be very close. If it is less important, more distance between the parties and more friction can be tolerated.
5. Periodically audit the adequacy of system reliability standards, performance of communications services, and adequacy of security procedures.
6. Participate in the development and maintenance of an IT plan that sets new technology priorities, schedules the transfer of IT among groups, and evaluates a portfolio of projects in light of the company strategy.

These represent the very minimum policies that the users should develop and manage. Depending on the firm's geography, corporate management style, stage of IT development, and mix of technology development phases, expanded levels of user involvement may be appropriate, including full-time assignment of their own staff. As these facets evolve over time, the appropriateness of certain policies will also evolve.

General Management Support and Policy Overview

Distinct from the issues involved in the distribution of IT services is a cluster of broad policy and direction activities that require *senior management perspective*. In the past these activities were built into the structure of a central IT organization. Now, because of the need to link IT to business, IT operations are frequently separated from IT planning. A chemical company reorganized in 1990 to establish a 500-person systems and operations department reporting directly to the head of administrative services, which works on corporate applications. (An additional 400 analysts and programmers are employed in the major divisional staffs.) This department does the implementation and operational IT work of the company on a month-to-month, year-to-year basis. At the same time, a 25- to 30-person IT policy group reports directly to the head of research. This policy group works on overall IT policy and long-range IT strategy formulation for the firm. In a similar vein, a major conglomerate whose development staff and hardware are distributed to key users has a three- to four-person group at headquarters level.

Key responsibilities of a corporate IT policy group should include these:

1. Ensure that an appropriate balance exists between IT and user inputs across the different technologies and that one side is not dominating the other inappropriately. Initiate appropriate personnel and organizational transfers if the situation is out of balance. Establishment of an executive steering committee, for example, is a common response to inadequate user input.

2. Ensure that a comprehensive corporate IT strategy is developed. Particularly in organizations where the resources are widely distributed it is critical that there be a comprehensive overview of technology trends, current corporate use of information technology, and linkage between IT initiatives and overall corporate goals. The resources to be devoted to this effort appropriately varies widely from organization to organization as IT's perceived contribution to corporate strategy, among other things, changes. (This is discussed in more depth in Chapter 13.)

3. Manage the inventory of hardware and software resources and assure that the corporate view extends to the purchasing relationships and contracts. In most settings the corporate group is the appropriate place to identify and manage standard policies for relationships with vendors.

4. Facilitate the development and evolution of appropriate standards for development and operations activities, and ensure that the standards are applied appropriately. In this regard, the corporate policy group plays the combined role of consultant on the one hand and auditor (particularly if there is a weak or nonexistent IT auditing function) on the other hand. This role requires staff that is both technically competent and interpersonally sensitive.

5. Facilitate the transfer of technology from one unit to another. This occurs through recognizing the unit's common systems needs as well as the stimulation of joint projects. Actual transfer requires regular visits to the different operating units, organization of periodic corporate MIS conferences, development of a corporate information systems newsletter, and other means.

6. Actively encourage technical experimentation. A limited program of research is a very appropriate part of the IT function; an important role of the corporate policy group is to ensure that it does not

get swept away in the press of urgent operational issues. Further, the corporate policy group is in a position to encourage patterns of experimentation that smaller units might feel pose undue risk if they are the sole beneficiary.

7. Assume responsibility for developing an appropriate planning and control system to link IT firmly to the company's goals. Planning, system appraisal, charge out, and project management processes should be monitored and (if necessary) encouraged to develop by the policy group. In this context, the group should work closely with the corporate steering committee.

As these responsibilities imply, the corporate IT policy group needs to be staffed with individuals who, in aggregate, have broad technical backgrounds and extensive practical IT administrative experience. Except in very limited numbers, it is not an appropriate department for entry-level staff members.

SUMMARY

Chapters 7 and 8 have focused on the key issues surrounding the organization of information technology for the next decade. A significant revolution has occurred in what is regarded as good managerial practice in this field. Important contributors to this change have been the development of new hardware and software technologies and managerial experience with IT. These technologies not only permit quite different types of services to be delivered, but also offer the potential for quite different ways of delivering these services. Consequently, what constitutes best practice has changed considerably, and the evolution seems likely to continue; many IT organization structures that were effectively put together in the 1970s are being found inappropriate for the 1990s.

The subject of determining the appropriate pattern of distribution of IT resources within the organization is complex and multifaceted. The general manager should develop a program that will encourage appropriate innovation on the one hand while maintaining overall control on the other. The final resolution of these organization and planning issues is inextricably tied to non-IT-oriented aspects of the corporate environment. The leadership style of the person at the top of the organization and that person's view of the future provide one important thrust for redirection. A vision of tight central control presents a different context for these decisions than a vision that emphasizes the autonomy of operating units. Closely associated and linked to this is the corporate organizational structure and culture and the trends occurring within it. Also, the realities of geographical spread of the business units heavily impact on IT organizational and planning possibilities; for example, the corporate headquarters of a large insurance company poses different constraints than the multiple international plants and markets of an automobile manufacturer.

On a less global scale are the present realities of quality and location of existing IT resources (organizationally and physically), which provide the base from which change must be made. Equally important is how responsive and competent current users perceive these resources to be. The unit that is seen (no matter how unfairly or inaccurately) as unresponsive has different organizational challenges than the well-regarded unit. Similarly, the existing and the perceived-appropriate strategic roles of IT on the dimensions of the firm's applications portfolio and operations have important organizational implications. If the firm is in the "support" quadrant, for example, the IT policy unit must realistically be placed lower in the organization structure in order to deal with its perceived lack of burning relevance to corporate strategy.

In dealing with these forces, one is seeking an appropriate balance between innovation and control and between the inputs of the IT specialist and the user. Not only do appropriate answers to these questions vary among companies; different answers and structures are often appropriate for individual units within an organization. In short, there is a series of right questions to ask and there is an identifiable but very complex series of forces that, appropriately analyzed, determine for each organizational unit the direction in which the correct answer lies—for now.

Case 8–1

AIR PRODUCTS AND CHEMICALS, INC.: MIS REORGANIZATION (A)

Air Products' MIS Division had ranked low in both credibility and reputation in 1981. "Things were so bad," said Peter Mather, vice president MIS, "that I personally had to phone the president every time the central computer went down." By 1989, following a decade of change successfully aimed at better serving the needs of the company, the MIS Division's credibility was at an all-time high. "We're now viewed," said Mather, "as partners in change and strategically important to the success of the company."

As one means of effecting this turnaround, Mather had reorganized the Systems Development and Services (SD&S) staff and relocated them physically near or within the company's operating areas. Although SD&S still reported directly to the central MIS Division, Mather believed their presence in these areas would contribute to better working relationships. Then, during a meeting with group vice president of Chemicals, Bob Lovett, in January of 1989, Mather was asked to transfer full responsibility for Chemicals SD&S to the Chemicals Group. Though he had planned to make this move in 12 to 18 months, Mather was concerned that the present timing might not be right.

Company Background

Allentown, Pennsylvania-based Air Products and Chemicals, Inc., had fiscal 1988 sales of $2.4 billion and net income of $214 million. (See Exhibit 1 for Air Products' financial highlights.) Since 1970, company sales had grown at an average rate of 13.5 percent per year, net income at 20 percent per year. Similar growth had occurred in return on equity, dividend distributions, and stock price.

Air Products employed approximately 13,000 people in more than 150 plants worldwide. The company was organized into business segments, a European subsidiary, and central staff organizations for information services, computer-based engineering systems, planning, and other functions. (See Exhibit 2.)

Business Segments

The sale of industrial gases to customers in the steel, metal working, chemical, electronic, petroleum, glass, and rubber industries accounted for more than half of Air Products' revenues. Some of these gases, such as oxygen, nitrogen, and argon, were produced from air by means of low-temperature (cryogenic) separation processes. Others, such as helium and hydrogen, were derived from chemical processes or natural gas.

The Chemicals Group, the second largest segment by sales, manufactured both commodity and specialty chemicals, including ammonia, methanol, alkylamines, urethane intermediates, and various polymers, resins, and catalysts. These chemicals were used in

John W. Preuninger prepared this case under the supervision of Professor Nancy S. Balaguer as the basis for class discussion rather than to illustrate either effective or ineffective handling of an administrative situation.

EXHIBIT 1   Air Products and Chemicals, Inc.: MIS Reorganization

Financial Highlights
(in millions)

	1988	*1987*	*1986*
Sales	$2,431.9	$2,132.2	$1,941.5
Net income	213.7	155.6	4.7
Total assets	2,999.5	2,705.1	2,661.0
Long-term debt	667.9	616.4	698.9

a broad range of applications both within Air Products and by outside customers.

Air Products' Process Systems Area designed, built, and sold air separation plants, heat exchangers for natural gas liquefaction, wastewater treatment systems, and other process systems equipment.

Because the different business segments had very different customer processes, manufacturing technologies, and distribution channels, there was limited need for technology transfer or software or data interchange between them. Consequently, beyond accounting and personnel, each business segment was managed autonomously.

Growth Plans

Air Products' chairman and CEO, Dexter F. Baker, had a plan that called for tripling sales from $2 billion in 1986 to $6 billion by 1996. Seventy percent of this growth was to come from industrial gases, related equipment, and chemical business segments. Within these segments, approximately half of the growth was to come from existing products, half from expansion into new products and applications serving new customer requirements. The remaining 30 percent of growth was to come primarily from environmental/energy markets.

To implement this aggressive growth plan, Air Products focused on product qual-ity and people interactions both within and outside the company. By concentrating on the requirements and expectations of its customers, the company hoped to be able to (1) reduce its costs and (2) react faster to a changing competitive environment.

Though Air Products' low manufacturing and distribution costs provided an important source of competitive advantage, competitors were closing the gap. Consequently, emphasis was placed on reducing production costs and overhead expenses in addition to finding new ways to differentiate company products and services.

Also vital was innovation through the development of new technologies. Research and development costs, which over the years had risen from 2 percent to 3 percent of sales, were expected to grow to 3.5 percent by 1996. In 1988, R&D costs were $72 million.

Management Information Services (MIS)

Information systems were vital to Air Products' day-to-day operations and provided a valuable marketing advantage; senior management viewed Information Services, centralized under the control of Mather, as an important, well-managed organization strategically important to the success and growth of the company. Baker's 20-year in-

EXHIBIT 2   Air Products and Chemicals, Inc.: MIS Reorganization

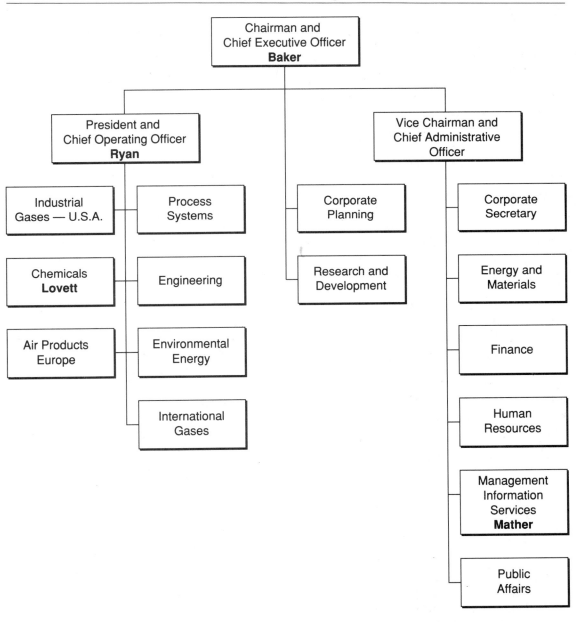

terest in MIS, which extended to how it was to be managed in the future, had made him a strong advocate. Only when he became chairman and CEO did MIS reporting shift from Baker to the vice chairman and chief administrative officer.

Because MIS comprised individuals from diverse fields of expertise including engineering, computer science, and management science, it was relatively easy to combine skills to develop new systems or implement new technologies. According to Mather, "This multi-faceted nature gives us a considerable competitive advantage over other MIS organizations."

Organization of MIS

Each of four directors who reported to Mather (see Exhibit 3) managed a particular function: planning, productivity, and quality; emerging technologies; computing services; and systems development and services. All had been long-term MIS employees at Air Products. Mather also had a manager of MIS in each of the three operating areas and a director of MIS in Europe who reported to him on a functional basis.[1]

Computing Services (CS) was managed by Roger Bast. Air Products' computing complex contained two IBM mainframes and several Tandem, DEC, and Wang minicomputers, to which were connected some 3,000 assorted work stations. Computing Services was responsible for operating the corporate computing and network infrastructure, managing data entry, and handling technical support. This included responsibility for managing (1) the Industrial Gases Division's (IGD) rather complex network, which linked division locations throughout the United States and (2) the MIS customer service activity, which served as the focal point for inquiries and problems regarding all MIS services.

Emerging Technologies (ET), managed by Ray Hoving,[2] was charged with the process of identifying, developing, and tracking new, significant technologies throughout the company. ET had introduced dozens of new technologies to Air Products and, in 1989, was tracking such technologies as personal computer networks, satellite communications, and expert systems. Because many of these technologies could have a critical impact on the MIS infrastructure, coordination with CS was important. Also, as these technologies and their applications could be identified anywhere within Air Products, good communication between ET staff and the operating areas was essential.

Systems Development and Services was managed by Tom Collins. Sieg Mayr, director of Research and Engineering Systems (RES), which was responsible for ensuring that Air Products' R&D and engineering communities maintained a competitive advantage through the effective use of computers and computer-based modeling, reported to Collins. Mayr had a functional reporting relationship to the vice president of Research and Engineering. RES, like ET, transferred new computer-based technologies across operating area boundaries and, thus, maintained a close working relationship with ET staff. The Management Sciences function, which included a strong statistics/mathematics applications staff, developed decision-making and planning applications involving techniques such as regression analysis and linear programming. The Management Sciences manager and SD&S managers (for each of the operating areas and corporate staff) also

---

[1]Air Products defines a functional relationship as a dotted-line reporting relationship to a functional area (e.g., finance, R&D, engineering, MIS).

[2]See "Air Products and Chemicals, Inc. (C): The Emerging Technologies Department," HBS Publishing Division, No. 185-015.

EXHIBIT 3 Air Products and Chemicals, Inc.:: MIS Reorganization

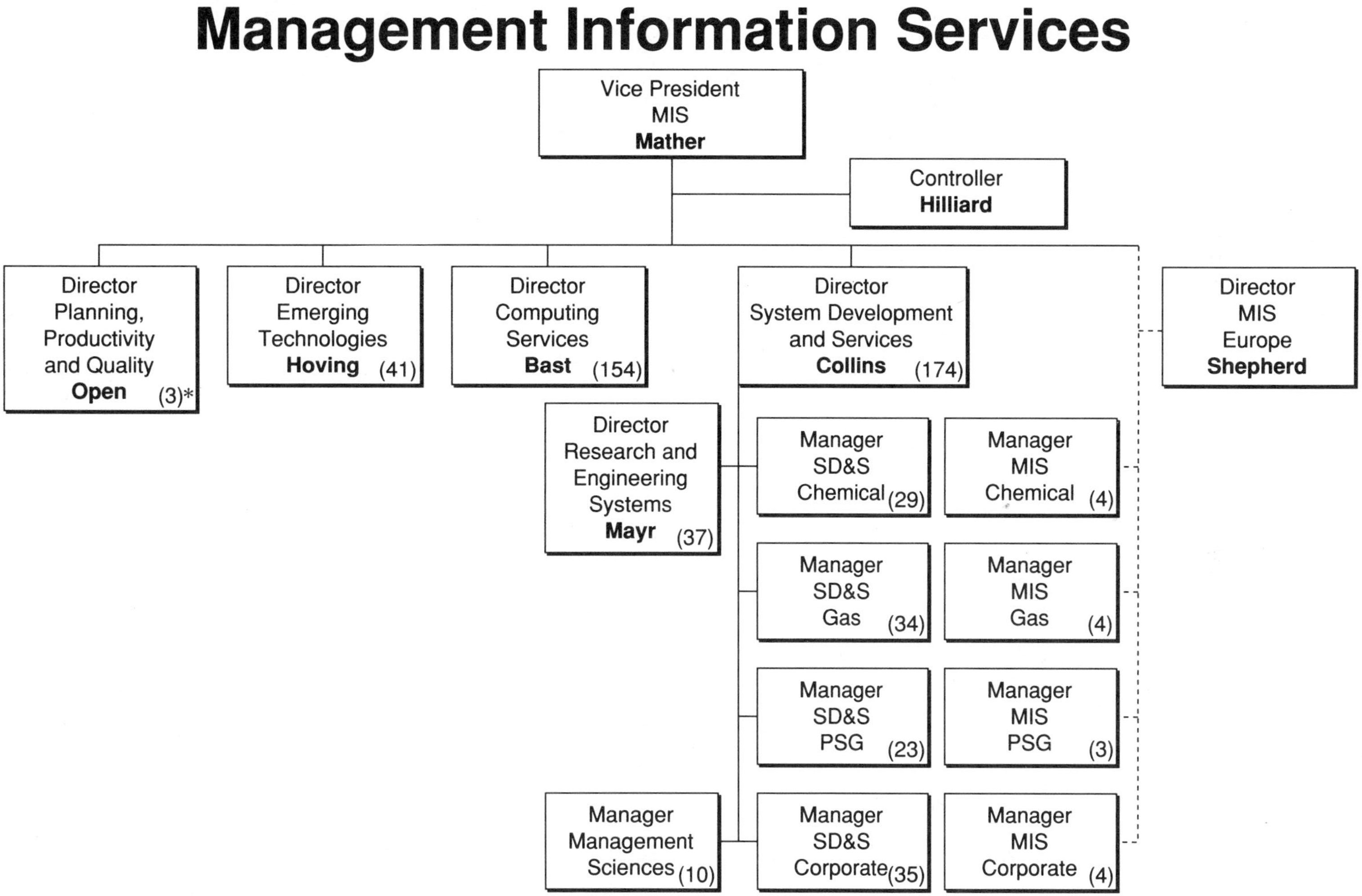

Management Information Services

Vice President MIS **Mather**

Controller **Hilliard**

Director MIS Europe **Shepherd**

Director Planning, Productivity and Quality **Open** (3)*

Director Emerging Technologies **Hoving** (41)

Director Computing Services **Bast** (154)

Director System Development and Services **Collins** (174)

Director Research and Engineering Systems **Mayr** (37)

Manager SD&S Chemical (29)
Manager MIS Chemical (4)

Manager SD&S Gas (34)
Manager MIS Gas (4)

Manager SD&S PSG (23)
Manager MIS PSG (3)

Manager SD&S Corporate (35)
Manager MIS Corporate (4)

Manager Management Sciences (10)

*Numbers in parentheses represent headcount.

355

reported to Collins. These latter departments developed and supported business applications with a staff of systems analysts and programmers.

The Planning, Productivity, and Quality (PP&Q) department handled such tasks as long-range planning, oversight of the MIS total quality process, productivity initiatives, and evaluating new development tools and techniques. It was important for PP&Q to work closely with all MIS organizations, the Corporate Planning and Quality functions, and the operating areas to understand long-term technology directions and requirements and the rate at which the quality process was being assimilated. A director needed to be identified to head this department.

Additionally, Mather had functional relationships with MIS managers located in each of the operating areas and the corporate staff. These managers reported directly to executives within their area of responsibility. For example, the Chemicals Group MIS manager reported to the vice president of Manufacturing, who reported to the Chemicals Group vice president. The Industrial Gases Division MIS manager, on the other hand, reported directly to the IGD vice president.

These MIS managers were responsible for preparing MIS budgets, developing long-range plans, and monitoring the progress of various projects for their operating areas. The SD&S staff who developed business applications, though physically located near or within operating areas, did not report to operating area MIS managers.

Evolution of Systems Development

The evolution of management orientation and systems development alignment at Air Products is shown in Exhibit 4. Prior to 1980, all development work was organized around application type and programmers crossed operating area boundaries. Pro-

grammers with expertise in distribution systems, for example, would work on both gas and chemical distribution applications. All MIS management and staff were housed within the MIS organization, and the style of end-user interface could be characterized as marketing: MIS services were effectively sold to and contracted with operating areas.

A transition that occurred between 1980 and 1986 saw systems development realigned to a market focus by operating area. The intent was to shift the development focus to end-users, or "customers," as they were referred to at Air Products. As the application requirements of the various operating areas tended to be unique, little economy or synergy was to be gained from keeping the development staff organized by system type.

To create a liaison with customers, MIS managers were placed in the operating areas. These managers were assigned no human or financial resources; their responsibility, as noted previously, was to undertake applications planning, prepare area MIS budgets, monitor projects, and represent the operating area within MIS. Though a marketing style interface continued to predominate during this period, the SD&S department was beginning to be seen as a more responsive organization.

In 1986, all systems development staff, except corporate development staff, were physically relocated nearer their respective operating areas. Though the development focus remained on the operating areas, relationships began to exhibit more of a partnership orientation. Involvement with end-users greatly increased. "Project meetings," according to ET Director Hoving,

> were held with end-users where little distinction could be made between MIS and area participants. MIS staff and operating area users would take turns chairing these meetings. I think we really began to see ourselves as part of the same company.

EXHIBIT 4 Air Products and Chemicals, Inc.: MIS Reorganization

	Pre-1980	1980–1986	1987–1992
Design	Focus on Discipline, Business Function	Focus on Discipline, Customer	Focus on Customer
Disciplines	Engineering and Scientific Management Sciences Commercial	SAME + R&D Computing Database KBS, EDI, CAD/CAM Telecommunications Planning Personal Computing	SAME + Telecommunications and Network Management
Exempts (U.S.):	243	Exempts (U.S.): 255	Exempts (U.S.): 235 (FY1987)
Project Orientation	Single discipline Internal competition	Coordinated Multidisciplinary Increased customer involvement	Integrated Multidisciplinary
End User Evolution	Utilize MIS-written programs and systems MIS is intermediary for ad hoc reporting	Development of personal applications on mainframe and PCs Eliminate MIS as intermediary for ad hoc reporting and small systems	Self-sufficient for most small applications and expert systems MIS facilitates application and data integration MIS, in partnership with its customers, develops major database and operational systems
Computing Environment	Mainframe with remote terminals Stand-alone databases	Multiple layers: mainframes, mini, PC Digital PBX, LAN Satellite communications	Integrated layers Distributed field computing Integrated Services: Voice, video, data
	Centralized	Distributed	Integrated
Group MIS Manager	Inside MIS organization	At senior level within Group	At senior level within Group with significant resources
Style	Marketing	Marketing/Responding	Partnership, with customer taking leadership for promoting the use of I.T.

Additionally, MIS began to take a greater functional leadership role. According to Collins, leadership meant more than just servicing user requests; it meant really focusing on the business requirements to meet operating area goals. "There are times," said the SD&S director,

> when a customer will approach us with a request to undertake some development effort. When this happens, the first thing we want to know is: what is the problem and what are the desired results? Oftentimes we can recommend a different course of action and avoid a costly, time-consuming development effort.

RES Director Mayr noted the need for balancing the trade-offs between being a service organization and providing functional leadership. "To optimize the value of MIS," he observed,

> an organization must balance its interactions between providing service and direction. Being a service organization 100 percent of the time means you keep your customer at arm's length and engage in applications development activities requested by the customer. Service organizations only worry about meeting a contract's specifications. They aren't concerned with whether they really create competitive advantage. The risk rests entirely with the customer; there is little added value.
>
> On the other hand, to provide total applications direction 100 percent of the time risks being unresponsive to the customer's business needs. The customer may never accept ownership for the end product and will tend to view MIS as dogmatic. This type of MIS organization is concerned only with working on applications it wants to develop. Little effort is made to truly understand the customer's needs.
>
> At Air Products, we need to both provide service and exercise leadership. This will allow us to maximize our value and become a full-fledged partner.

The Future of MIS at Air Products

Mather wanted to further develop the emerging partnerships between MIS and its customers. He viewed the changes that had occurred in the MIS organization during the 1980s as directed toward this end. Mather, though comfortable with the progress MIS had made, wasn't satisfied. To ensure that MIS continued to play a strategic role in supporting company goals, he outlined the following objectives for MIS's partnership with its Air Products customers: (1) focus information system resources on operating areas' objectives to maximize benefits; (2) increase profitability, quality, and productivity; (3) provide value-added services that differentiate products in the marketplace; (4) assimilate acquisitions; (5) change business practices; and (6) speed new product development. To realize these objectives and continue the evolution of MIS, he planned to transfer to the operating areas by October of 1990 responsibility for all systems development and all associated financial and human resources. While the specifics of this organizational change were not yet fully clear, Mather was comfortable that such a move would address a number of important issues.

First, Mather believed that this change would facilitate greater trust and communication between MIS and the operating areas. Collins, noting that cost center managers often needed to seek consensus from profit center managers prior to making an investment or expenditure, explained that

> it can be difficult to validate the benefits of an MIS investment to an operating area profit center manager. For instance, we undertook a considerable development effort to automate the customer service department in one of our operating areas. Essentially, we were able to improve the productivity of the service representatives so that they could handle about 20 percent more calls per hour. The manager of the customer service depart-

ment was delighted. He could readily see the improvements; we made their lives a lot easier.

To senior managers within the area, however, these benefits were far less visible. While they accepted the value of the project, it was hard for them to see the effect these productivity figures had on the profit and loss statement.

The effectiveness of our relationship thus hinges on a state of trust and credibility. Once we prove we can deliver on projects important to these senior level area managers, we can begin to exercise the functional leadership Mather talks about and propose projects we see as being good investments. Becoming part of the area is probably the best way to facilitate a close working relationship, ensure goal congruence, and develop that trust.

Second, Mather felt that transferring systems development responsibility to the oper-

ating areas would facilitate better investment decisions. Air Products' executives, like executives in many companies, were uncomfortable with the level of growth in their MIS budgets. Costs, as seen in Exhibit 5, had grown by 10 percent per year for the past five years. These costs were charged to the groups on a fully appropriated basis; at the end of the year there was neither over-absorption nor under-absorption. Mather believed that the business areas had to assume ownership of the technology and full responsibility for the benefits and business changes associated with these investments.

MIS Controller Larry Hilliard, explained how the budgeting process worked:

Basically, at the beginning of a budgeting cycle operating area MIS managers and their area customers prepare a list of projects and services they want MIS to undertake. These

---

EXHIBIT 5   Air Products and Chemicals, Inc.: MIS Reorganization

Management Information Services
Expense Trends

	Fiscal Years ($ million)						*FY1989 Increase*	*5-Year CAGR*
	1984	*1985*	*1986*	*1987*	*1988*	*1989*		
Total MIS	$25.8	$28.9	$32.6	$33.2	$37.4	$41.8	4.4	10%
Distributed Services								
Application SW	.1	.2	.3	.4	.5	.5	-	
Search	.7	.9	.9	.7	.8	.8	-	
CAD/CAM	.5	.6	.6	.6	.6	.5	(.1)	
Lab and Process	.5	.4	.7	1.0	1.1	1.5	.4	
PCs	.3	.7	1.2	1.4	1.4	1.9	.5	
Network								
Circuits	.5	.5	.8	1.1	1.2	1.3	.1	
Tandem IGD	-	-	.1	.6	1.4	2.1	.7	
Other NW	2.0	2.2	2.4	2.4	2.4	2.4	-	
NW	2.5	2.7	3.3	4.1	5.0	5.8	.8	
Total Distribution	4.6	5.5	7.0	8.2	9.4	11.0	1.6	19%
Base MIS	21.2	23.4	25.6	25.0	28.0	30.8	2.8	8%

area budgets are then consolidated by us and submitted to corporate for approval. Although our budget has grown considerably over the past five years, we are invariably asked to make cuts. This necessitates our going back to the areas and asking them to make cuts in their projects. It's not an easy task.

Additionally, if you examine the source of growth in the budget (see Exhibits 6 through 9), the fastest-rising item is what we refer to as "pass thru." These are costs for hardware and purchased software systems that are specific to an operating area's systems, like the Tandem network. They are not shared with other areas. The operating areas are clearly driving the growth in these systems.

Comparatively, the growth in MIS corporate overhead hasn't been nearly as great. In fact, MIS employs the same number of professional staff today as it did five years ago. It seems practical to me that the areas should carry pass-thru costs and assets on their own books. There is little value in our doing it for them.

Mather added that there would be considerable benefit in allowing the operating areas to control their own development staff and assets. "Senior operating managers," he explained,

should have the freedom to decide how much they want to spend on MIS, within the restriction of their total operating budget. If they determine the benefits of MIS investments are greater than other investments they can make, that should be their decision. Culling out MIS as a line-item expense that can only grow so much each year ignores the strategic importance of that investment.

The Decision to Proceed and Implementation Issues

A number of senior management changes occurred during 1988 at Air Products. A new president, Frank J. Ryan, was appointed, and three new vice presidents were put in charge of the operating areas. Mather spent time with each to share his vision and plan for the company's MIS resource and to solicit their views for the future.

Bob Lovett, vice president of the Chemicals Group, had just returned from Europe, where Air Products had recently completed a new network that he believed gave them considerable strategic advantage. Consequently, he was very aware of the positive impact MIS could have and was eager to op-

---

EXHIBIT 6   Air Products and Chemicals, Inc.: MIS Reorganization

Management Information Services
Chemicals 1984–1989

Fiscal Year Charge-Out ($ million)

	1984	1985	1986	1987	1988	1989	5-Year CAGR
Production	$ .7	$ .9	$1.1	$1.1	$1.1	$ 1.4	15%
User	1.1	1.2	1.3	1.3	1.3	1.0	0
Support	.8	.9	1.2	1.1	1.3	1.3	10
Pass Thru	.9	1.2	1.6	1.9	1.9	2.6	24
Development	2.1	2.5	2.2	2.2	3.3	5.1	19
	$5.6	$6.7	$7.4	$7.6	$8.9	$11.4	15%

EXHIBIT 7   Air Products and Chemicals, Inc.: MIS Reorganization

Management Information Services
Gas Area 1984–1989

Fiscal Year Charge-Out ($ million)

	1984	1985	1986	1987	1988	1989	5-Year CAGR
Production	$1.3	$1.6	$1.8	$2.1	$ 2.5	$ 2.4	13%
User	.6	.7	.7	.6	.6	.7	3
Support	1.1	1.3	1.5	1.6	1.8	1.8	10
Pass Thru	.7	.9	1.4	1.9	3.1	4.1	42
Development	1.4	1.8	2.1	2.5	2.7	2.8	15
	$5.1	$6.3	$7.5	$8.7	$10.7	$11.8	18%

EXHIBIT 8   Air Products and Chemicals, Inc.: MIS Reorganization

Management Information Services
PSG 1984–1989

Fiscal Year Charge-Out ($ million)

	1984	1985	1986	1987	1988	1989	5-Year CAGR
Production	$ .5	$ .5	$ .7	$ .8	$ .8	$ .8	10%
User	2.1	1.9	2.1	2.0	1.7	1.6	0
Support	1.0	.9	1.0	1.1	1.2	1.0	0
Pass Thru	1.3	1.6	1.8	1.9	2.1	2.2	11
Development	1.9	2.6	2.7	1.8	1.4	2.2	3
	$6.8	$7.5	$8.3	$7.6	$7.2	$7.8	3%

timize it in the Chemicals Group. When Lovett asked that Mather consider transferring to the businesses all MIS resources that directly supported them, Mather announced that he was planning to do this in the longer term and suggested that the Chemicals Group serve as a pilot. Lovett was very receptive.

A chemist by training with an extensive background in research and development, Lovett saw many similarities between R&D and MIS. "When I first got out of the university back in the 1950s," he explained,

most industrial R&D was centralized. In the mid-1960s to mid-1970s, there was a movement toward decentralizing R&D and pushing it into the businesses. This came about because centralized R&D, while functionally excellent, tended not to be responsive to business needs. More recently, there has been a move back to a balanced combination of product line R&D and corporate R&D. The need

EXHIBIT 9   Air Products and Chemicals, Inc.: MIS Reorganization

Management Information Services
Corporate Staff 1984–1989

Fiscal Year Charge-Out ($ million)

	1984	1985	1986	1987	1988	1989	5-Year CAGR
Production	$2.4	$2.6	$2.8	$2.8	$3.3	$3.3	7 %
User	.6	.6	.7	.6	.7	.7	3
Support	1.4	1.4	1.7	1.4	1.6	1.8	5
Pass Thru	.3	.3	.4	.5	.6	.8	22
Development	2.0	1.9	1.8	1.7	1.8	2.4	.4
	$6.7	$6.8	$7.4	$7.0	$8.0	$9.0	6 %

for central functional leadership and a spot where high-quality, high-risk research can be carried out has been recognized, but at the same time the need for responsive, flexible, fast-moving R&D in support of the businesses also has been served.

I feel MIS has reached a stage of development where decentralization makes sense. Hopefully, we can learn from the R&D experience and not go all the way only to recentralize a corporate effort in the years ahead. Moving the part of centralized MIS directly supporting a business to the administrative control of that business is timely. Keeping a strong centralized MIS resource to preserve functional excellence is also desirable.

Mather and Lovett agreed there was no reason to wait until October of 1990; the change could take place immediately. "I know Pete has a lot of issues he wants to work out first," Lovett admitted, "but I'm confident we can address them as we go. To me, this change is probably more significant to the MIS organization than it is to Chemicals." Nevertheless, a number of unresolved issues were bothering Mather.

First, Mather wondered what should be done about the other operating areas? With the vice presidents of Industrial Gases and Process Systems also new to their positions and just getting accustomed to their staffs, perhaps the change might be best undertaken now in all of the operating areas. Should he approach the other vice presidents with the option of transitioning today, or would it be better to test the change in the Chemicals Group first?

Second, Mather was concerned about how to implement the budgeting process with the change. The budget for 1990 was already in preparation under the existing system, in which MIS overhead expenses were charged out as an add-on to other services, such as systems development time. If Mather transferred all systems development, he would have to find a new means of allocating overhead. How should overhead be allocated, he wondered, and was this issue sufficiently important to hold up the transition?

Third, Mather pondered the issue of standards for hardware, software, and communications. Presently, all standards were developed centrally by MIS. With the change, should operating areas develop their own standards or should standard setting remain a central function, and if it did, would this adversely affect the integrity of the plan?

Fourth, Mather wondered how MIS career development should be handled. Currently, it was easy to transfer staff among the different MIS divisions. In fact, most of the MIS directors had served in several departments. Such cross-functional training was believed to be necessary to develop senior MIS executives. In addition, a process for transferring MIS professionals between the operating areas and the central MIS division would have to be considered. Mather wanted MIS professionals to be able to follow career paths both within their MIS operating areas and in the central MIS division. Also, if Mather was to transfer SD&S, which directors or managers should he transfer with the staff?

Finally, Mather wondered, how could he continue to exert some influence over how MIS was treated within the operating areas?

The central nature of the MIS organization facilitated coordination among the various MIS divisions. Would this coordination be adversely impacted? Alternatively, would it make sense to distribute other functions besides SD&S?

Whatever the decision, Mather knew it would have to be approved by the company's Management and Organization Development Committee, which consisted of the chairman, the president, the vice chairman, and the vice president of Human Resources. He wondered how he should position his plan, and upon what conditions or prerequisites he should agree to the change. Finally, because the MIS organization was viewed so positively today, he wondered, "If it ain't broke, why fix it?"

Chapter 9

IT Management Control

The IT management control system is a critical network and set of activities that integrates IT activities with the rest of the firm's operations and ensures that IT is being managed in a cost-efficient, reliable fashion. Whereas the project management system *guides* the life cycle of individual projects (many of which last more than a year) and the firm's planning process takes a multiyear view in assimilating technologies and systems to match the company's evolving needs and strategies, the IT *management control system* focuses primarily on guiding the entirety of the information technology department on a year-to-year basis. The management control system builds on the output of the planning process to develop a portfolio of projects, hardware/software enhancements and additions, facilities plans, and staffing levels for the year. It then monitors their progress, raising red flags for action when appropriate. The broad objectives of an effective IT management control system include these:

1. Facilitate appropriate communication between the user and provider of IT services and provide motivational incentives for them to work together on a day-to-day, month-to-month basis. The management control system must encourage users and IT to act in the best interests of the organization as a whole. It must motivate users to use IT resources appropriately and help them to balance investments in this area against those in other areas.
2. Encourage the effective utilization of the IT department's resources and ensure that users are educated in the potential of existing and evolving technologies. In so doing, it must guide the transfer of technology consistent with strategic needs.
3. Provide the means for efficient management of IT resources and give necessary information for investment decisions. This requires developing the standards for measuring performance and the

means for evaluating performance against the standards to ensure that productivity is being achieved. This should help to facilitate "make" or "buy" decisions and it should ensure that existing services are delivered in a reliable, timely, error-free fashion.

Early IT management control systems tended to be very cost focused, relying heavily, for example, upon return-on-investment (ROI) evaluations of capital investments. These systems proved workable in situations where the technology was installed on a cost-displacement justification basis. However, in firms where the computer was a competitive wedge (such as CAD/CAM or industrial robotics today) or where the technology was pervasively influencing the industry's structure of operations (such as in banking and financial services), cost analysis and displacement alone did not provide appropriate measurements of performance. Development of additional management control techniques has been necessary. For example, several years ago a large metropolitan bank instituted an expensive, complex charge-out system for improving user awareness of costs. Poorly thought out in broad context, the system generated a surge in demand for "cheap" minicomputers and inadequate investment in integrating network services, triggered an overall decline in quality of central IT support in comparison with leading-edge banks, and ultimately created market image and sales difficulties for the bank as a whole. Ultimately the system had to be completely restructured to correct these problems.

Four special inputs now appear to be critical to an appropriate IT management control system structure for an organization:

1. The control system must be adapted to very different software and operations technology in the 1990s than was present in the 1970s. An important part of this adaptation is the development of appropriate sensitivity to the mix of phases of information technologies in the company. The more mature technologies must be managed and controlled in a tighter, more efficient way than those in early phases, which need protective treatment appropriate to a research development activity.
2. Specific factors of the corporate environment determine the appropriate IT management control system. Key issues here are the IT sophistication of users, geographic dispersion of the organization, stability of the management team, the firm's overall size and structure, nature of the relationship between line and staff departments, and so on. These factors influence what is workable.
3. The architecture of the organization's overall management control system and the philosophy underlying it influence IT control systems.
4. The system is affected by the perceived strategic significance of IT, in both the thrust of its applications portfolio and the ever more important dependence on existing automated systems in many settings.

IT EVOLUTION AND MANAGEMENT CONTROL

Software Issues

The management control problem posed by software development has become more complex. An increasing percentage of central data processing software support is for maintenance, while most office support (OS) software is bought. Thus the operational changes necessary for keeping the business running have become intermixed with a stream of small, long-term, service-improving capital investments. Since these two streams are not easily separated in many organizations, controls designed to influence operating expense maintenance are often inappropriately applied to stimulate or choke off systems enhancements that are really capital investments.

A second software issue arises with outside software sourcing. As the percentage of development money devoted to outside software acquisition grows, management control systems designed for an environment where all sourcing was internal are often inappropriate for environments dominated by software make/buy alternatives.

Operations Issues

For IT operations, management control is complex because of the difficulty in measuring and allocating costs in a way that will encourage appropriate behavior. In the short term overall operations costs are relatively fixed and there is considerable volatility in the mix of applications running on a day-to-day basis. The operations cost control problem is further complicated by the cost behavior of IT over time. Technical change has created a world where a replacement computer generally has 4 to 10 times the capacity and costs less. This has created an interesting control issue: Should the cost per unit of IT processing be lower in the early years (to reflect the lower load factor) so that it can be held flat over the life of the unit while permitting full (but not excessive) recovery of costs? Conversely, as utilization grows over the years, should the user's cost per unit of IT processing decline?

An example of coping with this problem is provided by a large insurance company that replaced an IBM 3084 several years ago with an Amdahl V7A, gaining four times the computing capacity at 15 percent less cost. After conversion, the machine was loaded to barely 30 percent capacity. The managers were faced with the choice of either spreading the present costs among their current users or forecasting future costs (assuming future volume activity) and setting a three-year average that would recover costs at the period's end. The first approach would have covered expenses from the start but, through its higher prices, would inhibit the initiation of useful work that was economically justified in the long term. They therefore chose the three-year-average cost as the price basis in order to encourage use and pass on the immediate productivity improvement to their current users. The unabsorbed costs became part of corporate overhead.

The selection of a particular method of cost allocation varies with the firm's experience with technology. In many organizations the current control system gives complete management of office support (OS) to the user and complete management of communications to IT. As we have noted, however, OS and telecommunications are so interrelated that such a separation of management is highly suspect. A critical contemporary problem is to ensure that IT control systems evolve along with changes in the organization's technical environment. For example, a large industrial organization gave free OS technology to stimulate users while simultaneously charging for its traditional database time-sharing decision-support system. Very quickly users started creating their own databases on the OS equipment, which both limited their OS experimentation and underutilized the time-sharing, thereby undercutting the firm's objectives. Our discussion of control structure, while recognizing these issues, does not attempt to resolve them definitively.

Corporate Culture Forces

Growth in User Influence.   A major stimulant to growth in IT usage has been the emergence of a group of users who are familiar with problem solving using information technology. After 20 years it is clear that effective user applications generate ideas for additional applications. This is desirable and healthy, provided a control system exists to encourage appropriate appraisal of the new use's potential costs and benefits (broadly defined) to the organization. The absence of such controls can result in explosive growth (often unprofitable and poorly managed), requiring additional processing capacity every one or two years, or alternatively, in little growth with frustrated users obtaining necessary services surreptitiously (and more expensively). Both situations erode confidence in the IT department and its management control system. Also, for many of the new generation of user demands, articulating their benefits is more difficult than determining their costs. In repeated situations the control system has given the hard cost of an applications implementation undue weight against the soft, but often very strategic, management benefits.

This presents a paradox in the control of information services: while the area is technologically complex, most factors critical to its effective, efficient use are human factors. This poses very familiar management control challenges. A complicating factor is that since both technology and user sophistication are continually changing, the types of applications are also changing. Many individuals are sufficiently set in their ways (reinforced by a control approach) that they find change difficult to implement and thus resist it. As a by-product, these users' perceptions of the change agent (IT department) are often unnecessarily poor. For example, these users attribute all sorts of spurious effects to the introduction of new computer systems, word processors, and so on.

External and Internal Factors.   Forces of change also exist in external items such as new tax laws and in numerous internal strategic items. Internal changes include the addition of new customers and products, moving to new offices, and modifications in the organization. A well-designed management control system recognizes these changes and handles them appropriately.

Geographic and Organizational Structure.   Other important control aspects relate to the organization's geographic dispersion and size. As the number of business sites grows and staff levels increase, substantial changes may be needed in organizational structure, corporate management control, and IT management control. Informal personnel supervision and control that fit the more limited setting can fall apart in the larger, more dispersed setting. Similarly, the nature of relationships between line and staff departments within the company influences expectations about the evolving IT-user relationship and thus the appropriate IT management control.

The organizational structure of the firm plays an important role in the IT management control architecture. A firm with a strong functional organization that maintains the central services function as an unallocated cost center may find it appropriate to keep IT as an unallocated cost center. On the other hand, a firm that is heavily decentralized into profit or investment centers or that has a tradition of charging out for corporate services is propelled down the path of charging for corporate IT activities—and may go as far as setting it up as a profit or investment center. Over time it becomes increasingly difficult to manage with good results an IT organization whose control architecture is sharply different from that of the rest of the firm.

Corporate Planning and Control Process

In concept, the IT planning and management control system should be similar to that of the corporation. Ideally in both cases there is a multiyear plan linked appropriately to the overall business strategy, which in turn is linked to a budget process that allows the responsible managers to negotiate their operating budgets. As such, IT planning/budgeting should be compatible with the overall business planning/budgeting. If business planning primarily consists of an annual budget with periodic follow-up of performance during the year, however, a very difficult environment exists for IT management control. Implementation of any sizable IT change can easily take two or more years—including as much as a year to formulate, select, and refine the appropriate design approach. Thus an IT organization often must maintain at least a three-year view of its activities to ensure that resources are available to meet these demands. In many cases, this extends the IT planning horizon beyond the organization's planning horizon.

To be useful, IT project plans must systematically and precisely identify alternative steps for providing necessary service. For example, to upgrade reservation service in a large hotel chain, the IT department, in concert with key hotel managers, had to project the type of service the hotels would need four years out. This was necessary in order to select the proper terminals and provide an orderly transition to the new system over a 30-month period. A key bottleneck in this massive, one-time, 600-terminal installation was a corporate planning and control approach that extended only one year into the future.

This combination of short corporate time horizons, long IT time horizons, and technical innovation can generate intense corporate management control conflict. These conflicts, which can only be resolved by repeated judgments over time, involve two major clusters of managerial issues.

1. How congruent/similar should the IT management control architecture and process be with that of other parts of the organization? Where differences exist, how can the dissonance best be managed? Should it be allowed to exist long term?
2. How can the tension between sound control and timely innovation best be balanced?

Control typically depends on measuring costs against budgets—actual achievements versus predictions—and returns against investments. Innovation calls for risk taking, gaining trial experience with emerging technologies, relying on faith, and at times moving forward despite a lack of clear objectives. A portfolio excessively balanced in either direction poses grave risks. (As will be discussed in Chapter 10, different companies will appropriately balance their portfolios quite differently.)

Strategic Impact of IT on the Corporation

An important consideration in determining how closely the IT control system should match the business's planning/control process is the strategic importance of IT systems developments for the next three years. If they are very strategic to the firm's achievement of its goals, then close linkage between corporate planning and control and IT planning and control is important, and any differences between the two will cause great difficulty. Additionally, IT investment decisions and key product development innovations must be subject to periodic top-management review.

The control system for these strategic environments must encourage value-based innovations even if only one out of three will pay off. Often in this situation the key challenge is to encourage the generation, evaluation, and management of suggestions for new services from multiple unplanned sources while maintaining adequate control. Several now-defunct brokerage houses and soon-to-be-merged banks were unable to do this.

If IT is not strategic to the business but is more a "factory" or "support" effort, congruency of links to the rest of the business planning and control activities is not as critical. IT can more appropriately develop an independent planning and control process to deal with its need to manage changing user demand and the evolving technology. A "factory" environment, for example, must emphasize efficiency controls, while a "turn-around" should focus upon effective utilization of new technology.

A useful way of looking at management control was developed by Ken Merchant, and we will use it to frame the issues in this chapter. Merchant suggested that controls can be grouped into three categories: results controls, personnel controls, and action controls. The specific mix of these controls that is appropriate to a setting depends on its context.

- *Results* controls are those that focus on the measurement of concrete results; they include such measurements as amount of profit, percentage of variance from the budget, number of items procured/hour versus the budget, and the like.
- *Personnel* controls focus on hiring practices, types of training and testing in place, evaluation procedures, and so on.
- *Action* controls involve the establishment and monitoring of certain protocols and procedures; examples include segregation of duties, establishment of certain task sequences, control of access to certain areas, and so on.

All of these are important in the IT context and will be discussed. Because of the special managerial problems historically associated with results control issues, however, the rest of this chapter pays particular attention to them.

Looking Ahead: Other Aspects of Control

To achieve appropriate results the specific approach to IT management control is tailored to an organization, based on one or more of the dimensions discussed. Further, as circumstances change it will evolve over time. The remainder of the chapter describes additional key factors that influence selection of control architecture (financial), control process (financial and nonfinancial), and the audit function. Briefly defined here, each aspect of control is discussed in depth later in the chapter.

Control Architecture.   *Should the IT function be set up as an unallocated cost center, an allocated cost center, a profit center, or an investment or residual income center? Further, if costs are allocated from the IT function to the users, should the transfer price be market-based, cost-based, cost-plus, split-level, or negotiated?* Each of these alternatives generates quite different behavior and motivation, and each decision is a fundamental decision; once made, it is not lightly changed. Finally, *what nonfinancial measurements should be designed to facilitate effective use of IT?*

Control Process, Financial and Nonfinancial.   *What form of action plan is most appropriate?* Typically this is represented by the annual budget and drives both operations and project development. *What forms of periodic reporting instruments and exception* (against budget targets) *reporting tools are appropriate during the year?* These forms change much more frequently than architectural forms.

Audit Function.   Issues here include ensuring that an IT audit function exists, that it is focused on appropriate problems, and that it is staffed appropriately.

RESULTS CONTROL ARCHITECTURE

Unallocated Cost Center

Establishment of the IT department as an unallocated cost center is a widely used approach that offers many advantages. Its being essentially free to the users stimulates user requests and creates a climate conducive to user experimentation. This is particularly good for technologies in Phase 1 or 2 of their assimilation into the firm. The lack of red tape makes it easier for the IT department to sell its services. All the controversy and acrimony over the IT charge-out process is avoided, since no charge-out system exists. Further, very low expenditures are required for developing and operating IT accounting procedures.

In aggregate, these factors make this a good alternative for situations in which the IT budget is small. Innovation is facilitated in settings where financial resource allocation is not a high-tension activity. A large bank, operating as an unallocated cost center, introduced electronic mail and word processing over a two-year period. It had been decided at the most senior levels that this infrastructure was critical to its long-term operational viability. The lack of an end-user charge-out system was seen as an important facilitator to its introduction.

On the other hand, significant problems can exist when IT is treated as an unallocated cost center. With no financial pressure, the user can quickly perceive IT as a free resource where each user should be sure to get a piece of the action. This can rapidly generate a series of irresponsible user requests for service that may be difficult to turn down. Further, in a situation where staff or financial resources are short, the absence of a charge-out framework increases the possibility of excessive politicization of IT resource-allocation decisions. The unallocated cost center also insulates the IT department from competitive pressures and external measures of performance, permitting the hiding of operational inefficiencies. Further, this approach fits the management control structure of some firms poorly (that is, firms that have a strong tradition of charging out corporate staff services to users). Finally, an unallocated cost center poses particular problems for organizations where IT charges are perceived to be both large and strategic by blurring important revenue/cost trade-offs. In combination, these pressures explain why many firms that start with an unallocated cost center approach evolve forward to another approach, at least for their more mature technologies and users.

One approach widely followed is to keep IT as an unallocated cost center but to inform users through memos what their development and operations charges would be if a charge-out system were in place. Without raising the frictions (described next) associated with charge-out procedures, this shows users that they are not using a free resource of the corporation and gives them an idea of the magnitude of their charges. The approach is often adopted as a transitional measure when a firm is moving IT from an unallocated cost center to some other organizational form. Unfortunately, however, a memo about a charge does not have the same bite as the actual assignment of the charge.

Allocated Cost Center and Charge-Out

From a corporate perspective, establishing the IT department as an allocated cost center has the immediate virtue of helping to stimulate honesty in user requests. This approach fits rather well the later phases of technology assimilation, where the usefulness of the technology has been widely communicated within the firm. While it may open up heated debate about costs, it avoids controversy about whether an internal IT department should be perceived as a profit-making entity. An allocated approach particularly fits environments that have a strong tradition of corporate services charges.

Allocation Problems.   The allocated cost center introduces a series of complexities and frictions, since such a system necessarily has arbitrary elements in it. The following paragraphs suggest some of the practical problems that come from allocating IT department costs to users (whether in a cost center or using some other approach).

The first problem is that the IT charges will be compared to IT charges prepared both by other companies in the same industry and by outside service organizations, raising the possibility of misleading and invidious conclusions. The words *misleading* and *invidious* are related, because the prices prepared by other organizations often have one or more of the following characteristics:

1. The service being priced out is being treated as a by-product rather than as a joint costing problem, and thus the numbers may be *very* misleading.
2. IT is being treated under a management control system different from that of the company making the evaluation (that is, a profit center in one organization and a cost center in the other). Thus the cost comparison is highly misleading, because the charges have been developed under very different bases.
3. An independent IT services firm or an in-house operation selling services to outside customers may deliberately produce an artificially low price as a way of buying short-term market share. Thus their prices may be perceived as fair market when in fact they are nothing of the sort over the long term.

Since the prices produced by other companies are not the result of an efficient market, comparing them to in-house prices may easily produce misleading data for management decisions.

Another issue of concern is innovation. Unless carefully managed, the charge-out system tends to discourage Phase-1 and Phase-2 research projects. These activities must be segregated and managed differently from projects utilizing the more mature technologies. In our view, nothing particularly useful is accomplished by charging 100 percent of all IT costs to the users. Segregating as much as 15 to 25 percent as a separately managed, emerging-technology function and including it in corporate overhead (after careful analysis) is a sound strategy.

On a more technical note, in the majority of companies that are charging out IT costs today, two major concepts underlie the charge-out process:

1. The charge-out system for IT operations costs uses a very complex formula (based on use of computer technology by an application)

that spreads the costs in a supposedly equitable fashion to the ultimate users. Featuring terms such as *XCP*, the concept is that users should bear computer costs in relation to their pro rata use of the underlying resource.

2. The charge-out system ensures that all costs of the activity are passed to consumers of the service. Not infrequently this involves reimbursement by users of all IT operations costs incurred by the firm each month and certainly by year-end.

Rigorous application of these concepts has led to a number of unsatisfactory consequences from the user's perspective. Most important, in many cases the charges are absolutely *unintelligible* and *unpredictable* to the end user, as they are clothed in technical jargon and highly affected by whether it has been a heavy or light month in the IT department. There is no way for the user to predict or control them short of disengaging from the IT activity. This is one reason for the explosion of stand-alone minis and personal computers in the early and mid-1980s.

Not infrequently the charges are highly *unstable*. The same application processing the same amount of data, run at the same time of the week will cost very different amounts from week to week depending on what else happens to be running in the IT department during the week. In addition, if all unallocated costs are charged out to the users at the end of the year, they are often hit with an entirely unwelcome and unanticipated surprise, which generates considerable hostility.

The charges tend to be *artificially high* in relation to incremental costs. As mentioned earlier, this can cause considerable IT–user friction and encourage the user to examine alternatives that may optimize short-term cost behavior at the expense of the long-term strategic interests of the firm.

In addition, in both operations and development this approach makes no attempt to hold IT uniquely responsible for variances in IT efficiency. Rather, all efficiency variances are directly assigned to the ultimate users, which creates additional friction and allegations of IT irresponsibility and mismanagement. Finally, administration of a charge-out system of this type frequently turns out to be very expensive.

These factors in combination have generated a number of charge-out systems that do not satisfactorily meet the needs of many organizations. We believe this is a direct result of the technical and accounting foundations of the system. For most situations, technology and accounting are the wrong disciplines to bring to the problem. The task can be better approached as a problem in applied social psychology: What type of behaviors do you want to trigger in the IT organization and the users? What incentives can be provided to them to help assure that as they move to meet their individual goals, they are moving in a more or less congruent fashion with the overall goals of the corporation?

The design of such a system is a very complex task, requiring trade-offs along many dimensions. As the corporation's needs change, the structures of the charge-out system will also need to change. Critical issues to be dealt with include:

1. Should the system be designed to encourage use of IT services (or components thereof), or should it set high barriers for potential investments?
2. Should the system encourage IT to focus on efficiency or on effectiveness? The answer to this question may well evolve over time.
3. Should the system favor the use of IT department resources or outside resources?
4. What steps must be taken to ensure that the system is congruent with the general control architecture of the organization, or if it is not congruent, to ensure that the deviation is acceptable inside the firm?

Desirable Characteristics. While the answers to these questions will dictate different solutions in different settings, some generalizations that fit most settings and represent the next step in the evolution of a charge-out system are possible. First, for an IT charge-out system to be effective in this environment, it is critical that the users understand it. This means that the system needs to be simple. Again and again, evidence suggests that an IT operations charge-out system that is a gross distortion of the underlying electronics but that the user can understand is vastly preferable to a technically accurate system that no one can comprehend. User understanding that encourages even partial motivation and goal congruence is better than no motivation or goal congruence. In this context, systems that are based on an agreed upon *standard cost* per unit of output are better than those that allocate all costs to whomever happened to use the system. Even better (and a clear trend today) is designing these standards not in IT resource units, but in transactions that users understand (for example, so much per paycheck, so much per order line, so much per inquiry), where the prices of these transactions are established at the beginning of the budget year.

A second desirable characteristic is that the IT operations charge-out system should be *perceived* as fair and reasonable on all sides. In an absolute technical sense it does not have to *be* fair; it is enough that all involved believe that it is a fair and reasonable system. In this vein the IT operations charge-out system should produce replicable results; processing a certain level of transactions at 10 A.M. every Tuesday should cost the same amount week after week. If it does not, an air of skepticism sets in that undermines the system's credibility.

A third desirable characteristic of an IT operations charge-out system is that it should distinguish IT efficiency issues from user utilization of the system. IT operators should be held responsible for its inefficiencies.

Charging month-end or year-end cost efficiency variances to the user usually accomplishes no useful purpose. (It only raises the emotional temperature.) After appropriate analysis of the causes for the variances, they normally should be closed directly to corporate overhead.

IT Maintenance and Development Charges. The issues involved in charging for IT maintenance and systems development are fundamentally different from those of IT operations and must be dealt with separately. In advance of development and maintenance expenditures of any size, a professional contract must be prepared between IT and the users (as though it were a relationship with an outside software company). Elements of a good contract include:

1. The provisions that estimates of job costs are to be prepared by IT and that IT is to be held responsible for all costs in excess of this.
2. Procedures for reestimating and, if necessary, canceling the job if changes in job scope occur.
3. The provision that if a job is bid on a time and materials basis (very frequent in the software industry), a clear understanding must be reached with the user in advance as to what represents such significant change in scope that the contract should be reviewed.

For many systems, such as database systems, the most challenging (sometimes impossible) task is to identify the definable user (or group thereof) with which to write the contract. Further, an answer is needed for this question: If the contract is written with one group of users and others subsequently join, are the new users charged at incremental cost, full cost, or full cost plus (because they have undertaken none of the development risks and are buying into a sure thing)? Neither easy nor general-purpose solutions to these issues are possible.

An Example. One company approached these issues in an effective way in our judgment. It provided computer services to 14 user groups, many of which had very similar needs, spreading *operations expenses* in these ways:

1. Every time a piece of data was inputted or extracted on a computer screen, a standard charge was levied on the user, irrespective of the type of processing system involved. This charge was understandable to the user.
2. Since all costs from the modems out (terminal, line) could be directly associated with a user in a completely understandable fashion, these charges were passed directly to the end user.
3. All report and other paper costs were charged to the user on a standard cost per ton basis, irrespective of the complexity of the system that generated them.

4. All over- or underrecovered variances were analyzed for indications of IT efficiency and then closed directly to a corporate overhead account, bypassing the users.

With respect to *maintenance and development cost,* the following procedures were used:

1. Items budgeted for less than 40 hours were charged directly to the users at a standard rate per hour.
2. Projects budgeted to take more than 40 hours were estimated by the IT organization. If the estimate was acceptable to the user, work would be done. Any variances in relation to the estimate were debited or credited to the IT organization, with the user being billed only the estimated amount.
3. A job-reestimating process was created to handle potential changes in job specification, with the users having the option of accepting the new costs, using the old specifications, or aborting the job.
4. Research and development projects were budgeted separately by the IT organization. IT was accountable to corporate for the costs of these jobs, and the users were not charged for them.

Over a several-year period these procedures did a remarkable job of defusing the tensions in user–IT relationships, enabling them to work together more easily.

Profit Center

A third frequently discussed and used method of management control is the establishment of the IT department as a profit center. Advocates of this approach note that this puts the inside service on the same footing as an outside one and brings the pressures of the marketplace to bear on it. It consequently encourages the IT function to hold costs down through efficiency and to market itself more aggressively inside the company. This structure hastens the emergence of the IT marketing function, which if well managed will improve relationships with users. Further, excess IT capacity tends to be dealt with promptly by IT management, and they are willing to run more risks on the user service side.

Excess capacity also encourages sales of services by the IT department to outside firms, which can turn out to be a mixed blessing. Often priced as incremental sales (rather than on a full-cost basis), not only are these sales unprofitable, but many IT departments—excited by the volatile *hard outside* dollars as opposed to the captive *soft* inside ones— begin to give preferential treatment to outside customers, with a resulting erosion of service to inside users.

Establishing IT as a profit center has other problems. First, significant concern is often raised inside the firm as to whether it is appropriate for an inside *service department* to establish itself as a profit center, particularly when it does not sell any products outside the company. "Profits should come from outside sales, not service department practices" is the dominant complaint. The problem is further complicated when, because of geography, shared data files, and privacy and security reasons, users do not have the legitimate alternative of going outside (unless the entire IT department is out sourced). Therefore, the argument that the profit center is subject to normal market forces is widely perceived by users as spurious.

At least in the short run, setting up the IT activity as a profit center leads to higher user costs, because a profit figure is added to the user costs. Not only can this create user hostility, but in many settings it prevents the user from having legitimate full-cost data from the corporation for external pricing decisions.

In summary, all of these issues must be addressed before an organization adopts a profit center approach. A deceptively intriguing approach on the surface, it has many pitfalls.

Transfer Pricing

When an IT activity is set up as a profit center, establishment of the IT transfer price becomes a critical issue. There are at least four different conceptual approaches, each with specific strengths and weaknesses. (The issues involved are very similar to those of transfer pricing arrangements in general.)

For the purpose of this discussion we will assume that IT operations are being priced in end-user transaction terms (such as so much per paycheck, so much per invoice line, etc.), whereas a fixed-price contract is being written for IT development and maintenance. As described in our earlier discussion on charge-out issues, many other ways exist to approach these items. However, these assumptions are useful for introducing the issues involved.

Cost-Based Price.   Assuming a full-cost method is used, the cost-based price method has the advantage of producing the lowest cost from the user's perspective and is thus likely to generate few user complaints. In this setting, whether IT is a profit center or a cost center is irrelevant, since profits can be earned on internal business only by the internal sales generating positive efficiency variances (obviously sales outside the company can be priced to generate a profit). This approach does not avoid the previously mentioned issue of what constitutes cost and how it should be determined (joint versus by-product, etc.).

A variation of this approach is the **cost-plus** basis. On the positive side, this makes IT generate profits and at the same time provides an understandable number for users to deal with. On the negative side, the users raise both the narrow issue of capriciousness in selection of the "plus" and the broader issue of the general inappropriateness of an internal service department earning profits.

Market-Based Price. A key alternative, the market-based price method is used in some companies, particularly as the availability of outside services has grown. Its implementation, however, poses major problems. The first is the near impossibility in many settings of finding comparable products and services for establishing the market price. Unique databases or process control systems are examples of items for which such data are impossible to find. Even so-called standardized services such as payroll and accounting have so many special ramifications and alternative designs that market prices are very elusive. Also, suppliers of IT services treat some IT products as by-products of other activities and price them accordingly. Still other organizations calculate prices for in-house use; since they make no attempt at rigor, they achieve only "ballpark" figures. Using these figures as market-price surrogates produces spurious results.

Dual Transfer Price.[1] The dual transfer price approach is designed to satisfy the motivational needs of the IT department and the key users simultaneously. As long as a single transfer price is used, it is impossible to come up with a price that will both allow IT to feel that it is earning a fair profit and allow the users to be given prices that will permit them to manage aggregate costs in line with the company's overall interests. The "pain" can be spread around, but in the end it is reallocation of a finite amount of pain as opposed to its elimination. Dual transfer pricing in IT works as follows:

1. The users are charged items at either direct or full cost, depending on the company's overall management control philosophy.
2. The IT department is allocated revenue based on a standard cost of services delivered plus a standard fixed markup (or at a market price if a sound one can be established). Revenue in excess of the planned amount can be derived either from selling more services than planned or from gaining unanticipated cost efficiencies.
3. The difference between the revenue of the IT department and the cost figure charged to the user is posted to an overhead expense account, which is closed to corporate overhead on a monthly basis.

---

[1]Robert G. Eccles, Jr., "Control with Fairness in Transfer Pricing," *Harvard Business Review,* November–December 1983, pp. 149–161.

This method, at least in theory, allows both the IT department and users to be simultaneously motivated to behave in the best overall corporate interest. Users are given appropriate economic trade-offs to consider, while IT is provided incentives to operate efficiently and to sell extra services.

Dual pricing has worked satisfactorily in a number of settings and has dramatically changed the tenor and quality of relationships by permitting the IT group and the users to work together instead of against each other. Its Achilles' heel is that careful attention must be paid to the establishment of the cost target to ensure that the IT group is being asked to stretch enough and is not building excess slack into its budget. Also, its implementation involves some additional accounting work, although not enough to make the idea disabling.

Negotiated Price.   The negotiated-price method is quite difficult to execute in the IT–user arena because the two parties often bring quite different strengths to the negotiating table. For example, systems that interface directly with other systems or that share proprietary data-bases must be run by the central IT department. Hence the negotiating positions of the two parties cannot be considered equal, since the user realistically has no other options.

Summary.   Many potential IT financial control results architectures are possible. None represents a perfect general-purpose solution. The challenge is to pick the one that best fits the company's general management control culture, present user–IT relationships, and current state of IT sophistication. The typical firm has approached these issues in an evolutionary fashion, rather than having selected the right one the first time.

Financial Reporting Process

Budget Objectives.   A key foundation of the IT results control process is the budgeting system. Put together under a very complex set of trade-offs and interlocked with the corporate budgeting process, its first objective is to provide a mechanism for appropriately allocating financial resources. While the planning effort sets the broad framework for the IT activity, the budgeting process ensures fine-tuning in relation to staffing, hardware, and resource levels. A second objective of budgeting is to set a dialogue in motion to ensure that organizational consensus is reached on the specific goals and possible short-term achievements of the IT activity. This is particularly important in organizations where the planning process is not well formed. Finally, the budget establishes a framework around which an early warning system for negative deviations can be built. Without a budget it is difficult to spot deviations in a deteriorating cost situation in time to take appropriate corrective action.

Budget Process. The budget system must involve senior management, IT management, and user groups. Its key outputs include establishing the planned service levels and costs of central operations, the amount of internal development and maintenance support to be implemented, and the amount and form of external services to be acquired. The planned central IT department service levels and their associated costs must flow from review of existing services and the approved application development portfolio as well as user desire for new services. In addition, these planned service levels must take into account long-term systems maintenance needs. The budget must also ensure that there are appropriate controls on purchased IT services for the firm as a whole (software and hardware, such as personal computers). The dialogue between users and the IT department regarding their anticipated needs and usage for the budget year helps generate an understanding of the IT department's goals and constraints that iteratively leads to a better IT plan as well as to clarification of the user's plans.

Example. To ensure that this dialogue occurs, a leading chemical company asks both the users and the IT department to develop two budgets, one for the same amount of dollars and head count as the preceding year and one for 10 percent more dollars and 2 percent more head count. Typically the IT department's proposals involve an expansion of distributed services. To help ensure communication, the main descriptions of key items are stated in user terms—such as the number of personnel records and types of pension planning support—with all the jargon relating to technical support issues being confined to appendixes. Both groups are asked to rank services of critical importance as well as to identify those that are of lower priority or that are likely to be superseded. A senior management group then spends a day reviewing a joint presentation that examines the budget in terms of probable levels of expenditure and develops a tentative ranking of the priority items. This meeting allows senior management to provide overall direction to the final budget negotiations between the two groups. The priorities established in these discussions are then consolidated by the IT manager for final approval. This modified, zero-based budgeting approach is judged to have provided good results in this setting.

Budget Targets. The IT budget must establish benchmark dates for project progress, clarify type and timing of technical changeovers, and identify needed levels and mixes of personnel as well as set spending levels. A further mission is to identify key milestones and completion dates and tie them to the budget. This helps to ensure that periodic review will allow for early detection of variance from the plan. Budgeting the key staff head count and levels is a particularly important management decision. In many situations a major cause of project overruns and delays is lack of talent available to support multiple projects in a timely manner. Shortage of personnel must be dealt with realistically in fitting projects together. (This should be done periodically through the year as well.)

An important benefit of involving users and suppliers in the budget process is the education that results. On the one hand, it helps the IT department to understand the particular needs of each user department and to assess their needs for IT support relative to other departments. On the other hand, the users develop an awareness of what is possible with available technology and better define their potential needs. In one financial institution the budget process is used heavily as a stimulus for innovation. During budget preparation both users and IT staff take many trips to other installations and receive information from their hardware/software suppliers to generate thinking on potential new banking services. Over a several-year period this has significantly improved the relationship between the two groups.

Periodic Reporting.   Effective monitoring of the department's financial performance requires a variety of tools, most of which are common to other settings. These normally include monthly reports that highlight actual performance versus the plan and exception reports as needed. Design and operation of these systems are rather routine. Obvious issues include: (1) Are budget targets readjusted during the year through a forecasting mechanism? (2) If so, is the key performance target actual versus budget or actual versus forecast? (3) Are budgets modified for seasonal factors, or are they prepared on a basis of one-twelfth of the annual expense each month?

The IT financial reporting task is a bit different in that an IT organization requires a matrix cost reporting system as it grows in size. One side of the matrix represents the IT department structure and tracks costs and variances by IT organizational unit. The other side of the matrix tracks costs and variances by programs or projects.

An issue that is beyond the scope of this book is whether budget numbers and actual results should be reported in nominal dollars or in inflation-adjusted dollars. This is an issue of major importance for corporate management control systems today, particularly for multinational firms.

Nonfinancial Reporting Process

At least in an operational sense, the nonfinancial controls are of more importance than the financial ones in assuring management that the day-to-day and month-to-month activities of the IT function remain on target. Critical items here include preparation of regular six-month surveys of user attitudes toward the IT support they are receiving. Such surveys identify problems and provide a benchmark against which progress can be measured over time. Their distribution to the users for completion also clearly communicates that IT is concerned about user perception of service. Problems surfacing in such a survey need to be acted on promptly if the survey is to be an effective control.

Another category of controls are those relating to staff. Reports that monitor personnel turnover trends can provide critical early insight into the problems of this notoriously unstable group. These data allow timely action to be taken on such items as sensitivity of leadership, adequacy of salary levels, and workplace climate. In the same vein, formal training plans and periodic measurement of progress are important management tools for ensuring a professionally relevant group and maintaining morale.

Reports and other procedures that generate absolute measures of operational service levels are very important in IT operations. These include data on such items as trends in network uptime, ability to meet schedules on batch jobs, average transaction response time by type of system, and number of missends and other operational errors *and* a customer complaint log. Critical to the effectiveness of these systems is that they be maintained and adhered to; when quality-control errors are allowed to creep in better performance is shown than is actually present. These issues are discussed further in Chapter 11, with the emphasis that all dimensions of service cannot be optimized simultaneously.

In relation to systems development, reports on development projects in terms of elapsed time and work-months expended (vis-à-vis budget) provide a critical early warning system for assessing overall performance. The type of data needed and appropriately available varies widely by company. The company's maturity in dealing with information technology, the relative strategic role of IT development and operations, and the corporation's general approach to managerial control also influence both the form of these issues and the detail with which they are approached.

IT AUDIT FUNCTION

Located as a part of the office of the general auditor, the IT auditor function provides a vital check and balance on IT activity. The basic elements of its mission are threefold. The first is to ensure that appropriate standards for IT development and operations have been developed and installed consistent with the control architecture. With changes in both technology and the organization's familiarity with it, development of these standards is not a one-time job but requires continuous effort.

The second element is to ensure that these standards are being adhered to by the various operating units. This includes both regular progress reviews and the conduct of surprise audits. Such audits should reduce fraud and loss. Ensuring adherence to these standards should help reduce operations errors and omissions and increase user confidence and satisfaction. Audits also act as a prod toward improving operating efficiency.

The third element is active involvement in the systems' design and maintenance functions to ensure that systems are designed to be easily auditable and that maintenance changes do not create problems. This clearly compromises the supposedly independent mission of the auditor but is a necessary accommodation to the real world. Such involvement helps ensure the smooth running of the final system. Successful execution of all three mission elements helps to reduce the amount of outside assistance needed by the firm.

These seemingly straightforward tasks are very difficult to implement in the real world. The three main causes of this IT auditing difficulty are discussed here.

1. The most important barrier is the difficulty in maintaining necessary auditing staff skills. Operating at the intersection of two disciplines (IT and auditing), good practice demands thorough mastery of both. In fact, because IT auditing is frequently a "dead end" career path, staff members who can be retained are often sufficiently deficient in both disciplines to be ineligible as practitioners in either. Higher salaries and visibly attractive career paths are essential preconditions to reversing this situation.
2. The "art" of IT auditing continually lags behind the challenges posed by new technologies. For example, understanding methodologies for controlling batch systems for computers is not very relevant today for a world dominated by complex operating systems, networks, and on-line technologies. Managing catch-up for such lags poses a key IT auditing challenge for the future.
3. There has been an unevenness of senior management support for IT auditing, due in part to the lack of formally defined requirements from an outside authority. Support for a strong IT auditing function tends to be very episodic, with periods of strong interest following conspicuous internal or external failure. This interest, however, tends to erode rapidly once the calamity is corrected.

The role of the IT auditing function is poorly defined in most organizations at this time. Typically part of the internal auditing organization, and often not reporting to senior management, this is a function that deserves serious consideration at that management level.

SUMMARY

As noted earlier many of the IT management control issues are clearly similar to the general issues of management control that face an organization. Several aspects, however, make them different. The first is posed by the rapid changes in the underlying technology and the long time span required for users to adapt to new technologies. Phase-1 and Phase-2 technologies require a commitment to R&D and user learning that is in direct conflict with the charge-out techniques appropriate for Phase-3 and Phase-4 technologies. It is very easy for an organization to become too uniform in its control system and to try to standardize in order to use systems "efficiently," stamping out appropriate innovation as a by-product. In most organizations today, different divisions (at varying stages of learning, and using varying mixes of technologies) require quite different control approaches. Further, as organizational learning occurs, other control approaches become appropriate. Thus, quite apart from any breakthroughs in the general area of IT control methods, their practice in an organization undergoes continual evolution.

As IT becomes more firmly established in an organization's operation, the penalties of uneven performance of technology may impose very severe consequences for the organization as a whole, and action controls become vital. As a company, department, or system evolves from "turnaround" to "factory" to "support," very different control philosophies become appropriate.

Adding these issues to those discussed at the beginning of the chapter concerning the changing corporate environment and evolving corporate planning and control processes (in a world shifting from "make" to "buy" in software), the full complexity of the IT management control problem is apparent. Different organizations must adopt quite different control approaches, which then must evolve over time to deal with a changing corporate environment, changing strategic role of IT, and changing technologies.

Case 9–1

FRITO-LAY, INC.: FUNDING FOR INFORMATION SYSTEMS

To optimize our overall system, we may need to suboptimize some of the individual components. The trick is to get out in front and take a leadership position, even if you're not sure. There's disaster, which is not taking a position, and there's 'good enough,' which is using technology that does the job.

Charles S. Feld, vice president, Management Services at Frito-Lay, Inc., was speaking in early 1986 about his approach to managing information systems at the Dallas-based snack food company. One of the major changes during Feld's five years as head of Management Services had been the design and implementation of a system for funding certain information systems activities through charges to users. The funding method appeared to Feld to be working well, and the company as a whole was prospering. Some users, however, were questioning the fairness of the system, one describing Feld in jest as "a crook—not only does he get other people to help negotiate his budget, but he's running the only overhead function in the company that shows a positive bottom line."

Feld himself was aware that the funding system might now require some adjustment to keep pace with the evolution of the business and technical environments it had been designed to match. "Whenever anybody tries to lay too much logic on this," he said of his approach to funding, "it falls apart. Nobody ever claimed it was fair—it is primarily a pragmatic approach that made reasonable sense to senior management."

Company Background and Strategy

Frito-Lay, a division of PepsiCo, Inc., produced salty snacks (potato chips, corn chips, tortilla chips, pretzels, etc.), cookies, and other snack foods. The company had 35 manufacturing plants and six regional distribution centers. Frito-Lay products were delivered directly to more than 300,000 retailers by a sales force of some 10,000 route drivers. The company had doubled the number of items in its product line during 1985 and expected similar growth in the future. As snack foods, Frito-Lay products were characterized by perishable raw materials and a limited shelf life. The average selling price of these products was 70 cents. The company had 1985 sales of $2.5 billion and a 1990 revenue goal of $5 billion. (See Exhibit 1.)

Frito-Lay characterized itself as having a lean staff—of the company's 26,000 employees, more than 24,000 were directly involved with making or selling products—and a bias for action. Frito-Lay headquarters employees tended to be relatively young, and were described by Feld as "positive, enthusiastic, and nondefensive."

Frito-Lay's sales had increased rapidly during the 1970s, but by 1982 growth had slowed. The company's routes had finally

This case was prepared as the basis for class discussion rather than to illustrate either effective or ineffective handling of an administrative situation.

EXHIBIT 1   Frito-Lay, Inc.: Funding for Information Systems

PepsiCo Financial Results, 1983–1985
($ in millions)

	1985	1984	1983
Net sales			
Soft drinks	$3,128.5	$2,908.4	$2,940.4
Snack foods[a]	2,847.1	2,709.2	2,430.1
Restaurants	2,081.1	1,833.5	1,529.4
Total	$8,056.7	$7,451.1	$6,899.9
International portion	951.9	963.9	1,128.6
Operating profits			
Soft drinks	263.9	246.4	126.2
Snack foods	401.0	393.9	347.7
Restaurants	194.0	175.2	154.3
Total	$ 858.9	$ 815.5	$ 628.2
International portion	66.7	35.5	(99.1)
Net income	$ 543.7	$ 212.5	$ 284.1

[a]The snack foods business segment included Frito-Lay and PepsiCo Foods International.

Source: PepsiCo, Inc. Annual Report.

covered the entire country, and lower inflation meant fewer price increases. Moreover, other companies, including some very large tobacco, brewing, and consumer products firms, had started to produce snack foods that competed with Frito-Lay's products. In response, Frito-Lay adopted a more complex organizational structure that included a field marketing force, distribution directly from plants to large stores, and a regional focus for products and promotion. The company also gave increased attention to productivity and to new product development. In Feld's view, the keys to Frito-Lay's future success were research and development, which would create new products and new packaging techniques; process engineering, which would lower costs; and information technology which would allow the company to collect, analyze, and use information about its increasingly competitive environment.

Management Services

Until 1970, Frito-Lay had relied entirely on an outside service bureau to perform its data processing chores. In that year, Charlie Feld, then an IBM systems engineer and later a sales representative, was assigned to the Frito-Lay account after the company bought its first in-house computer. Over the next 11 years Feld continued to work with the organization as it brought existing applications in-house and then began to develop new ones. Management Services, as the information systems group was called, reported to the chief financial officer, and one Frito-Lay manager recalled that as late as 1978 the company's applications were "99 percent accounting." Around that time, however, the first on-line applications were installed, and user demand began to grow rapidly. The company purchased its first personal computers in 1982, and the use of time-sharing increased dramatically.

Feld, who during his time at IBM had seen four data processing managers come and go at Frito-Lay, was hired by his former customer in 1981. As he later described the situation, "We were doing important stuff, but we weren't doing it consistently well." Management Services was experiencing 40 percent staff turnover per year and was making heavy use of contract programmers. Many users were dissatisfied with the time it took to get an application developed and with the quality of the resulting software. The general development approach at the time was for users to define systems, which were then designed and built by Management Services staff. Disagreements over whether a given application actually met its specifications were common,

largely because of high employee turnover within Management Services.

In late 1981, Feld hired an outside consulting firm to assess Frito-Lay's use of information systems. The consultants found that the company had developed several significant applications of information systems, and felt that Frito-Lay's overall technology position was strong. The firm, however, found weaknesses in the company's processes and controls for information systems, and criticized underfunding and the lack of organizational stability within Management Services. Most important, the consultants found no clear link between information systems and corporate strategy. "We were staff-driven, not business-driven," Feld said. (See Exhibits 2 and 3).

Feld and others felt that Frito-Lay's approach to funding was responsible for part of the discrepancy. At that time, the company's functional groups (sales, marketing, manufacturing, and distribution) outlined systems projects as part of their annual plans. These systems outlines were submitted to Management Services, which then set development priorities. The user groups had no central contact point with Management Services. The information systems budget was negotiated

---

EXHIBIT 2   Frito-Lay, Inc.: Funding for Information Systems

Management Services Headcount and Budget, 1980–1987
($ in millions)

Year	Headcount	Budget
1980	144	$12
1981	166	16
1982	222	19
1983	252	22
1984	282	26
1985	312	31
1986	325	36
1987	345 (projected)	51 (projected)

EXHIBIT 3   Frito-Lay, Inc.: Management Services Organization Chart (1986)

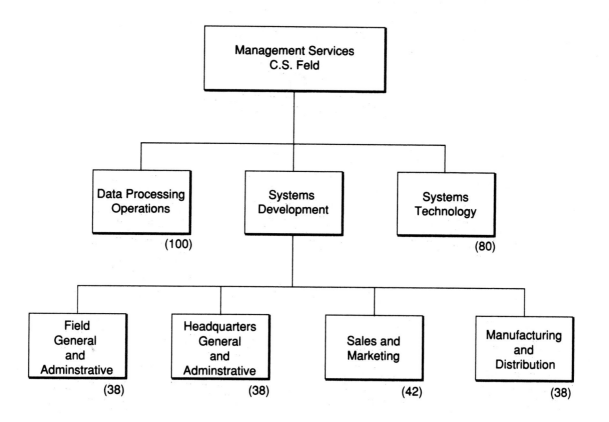

Figures in parentheses indicate the approximate number of personnel in each area.

with top management by Management Services, which then allocated staff to the various functions. Users were not charged for systems development or operation.

Ernest W. Harris, who as director of Distribution Services had designed a vehicle scheduling system that became the company's first on-line application, recalled those earlier days as "a constant struggle to get things onto the data processing queue. It was everyone for themselves to get the available dollars. We never got firm commitments. The relationship tended to be adversarial, with lots of finger-pointing and not much understanding." Harris felt that on-line systems tended to receive relatively low priority. "We had all these batch applications that required maintenance—and who is willing to take a risk and not fix the payroll system?" Harris himself had been able to get what he wanted from Management Services; he described himself as "hard nosed" and said, "I just intimidated my way through that organization. I find that this technique doesn't work so well any more."

Funding for information systems received increased attention after a 1982 corporate edict limiting the growth of general and administrative expenses. The initial cap, 15 percent per year, was quickly reduced to 8 percent. As part of the general and administrative area, Management Services could not continue to increase its spending at the current rate of 35–40 percent per year and at the same time have the area comply with the expense limit. Either the company would have to cut back on information systems development, or it would be necessary to find another way to fund part of the cost.

To address the funding issue, Feld hired Dori Reap, then a member of the corporate planning staff, into a newly created Management Services position, manager of planning and control. As part of this job, Reap was asked to gather data and make recommendations for a new funding system. Reap began by identifying some objectives. First, users should be charged only for things over which they had control; for example, systems development. Second, the funding system should not require a large investment of people or money to develop and administer. Third, it was desirable to move quickly during a "window of opportunity"—personal computers and time-sharing were not yet in heavy use, and it would be some time before the new applications being conceived for sales and manufacturing would require large amounts of money to implement. The immediate impact on user budgets would

therefore be relatively small. Finally, Feld wanted to achieve central control over information systems. At a meeting of Frito-Lay directors, Feld presented his philosophy on this point in a single slide:

Integration is the key to Economics
Control is the key to Integration
Leadership is the key to Control
Vision and Execution are the keys to
 Leadership

Given these objectives and the data she had gathered, Reap developed three funding alternatives. The corporation could do nothing; that is, it could continue to live with the current method. The corporation could charge users at the "micro level," that is, for specific use of hardware, staff time, and so on, meanwhile limiting the growth of the Management Services budget and restricting the functional groups with respect to end-user computing. Or the corporation could aim somewhere in between these options, with some services charged directly to users and others treated as overhead.

System Design and Implementation

The scheme chosen by Management Services, and approved by top management, charged the operating functions (sales, manufacturing, and distribution) directly for system development, and all users for data communications and for end-user hardware (terminals, personal computers, printers, modems, etc.) and software (Lotus 1-2-3, word processing packages, etc.). There were, however, no charges for use of the "central complex"—mainframe hardware and software, operations personnel, etc. In particular, there was no charge for running an applications program. Management Services also took on, as part of its budget, software development for the general and administrative area and all applications maintenance. On this basis, the 1982 budget would have broken down into roughly 20 percent direct user charges and 80 percent overhead.

When the new approach was announced in June 1982, users were told that they would have to include information systems expenses as part of their 1983 budget. As a starting point, users were given a 1983 budget equal to Management Services' budget expenses for 1982 on items that would be charged to users in the future ($3.3 million), plus the additional spending that had already been approved for the second half of that year ($1.5 million). Additions to this initial budget would have to be approved as part of the annual budget review process. Management Services offered to purchase at book value the several hundred personal computers that were already within the company and put them under the same nationwide service agreement that would cover new units purchased centrally. Virtually all of the existing personal computers were transferred to Management Services.

Charging for Equipment and Communications

By the end of 1985, the funding system had gone through its initial shakedown and was operating smoothly. Mary Cass, who with her staff of five was responsible for acquisition, installation, maintenance, and charging for data communications and end-user equipment, described that part of the system. "Our attitude about equipment is, if you want to own it, fine," Cass said, "but if it's not ours, we can't maintain the hardware or software, provide training, or offer network support." There were nearly 1,300 personal computers within Frito-Lay, plus thousands of terminals, printers, plotters, and other peripherals. About twenty units were owned directly by users, the rest by Management Services.

Users who wanted to buy equipment filled out an order form (see Exhibit 4) and got whatever approvals were required by their particular group. The list of standard items was relatively short, but users were free to order any equipment or software they wanted. There was, however, no education, training, user assistance, or other support for items not on Management Services' standard list. Frito-Lay had negotiated volume purchase agreements with a number of suppliers, including IBM, that gave discounts of about 30 percent from retail prices. User prices were set at a level intended to make Cass's group break even each year.

Equipment purchased through Management Services was assembled and tested in Dallas. At that time, special menu-driven software and additional memory were installed on personal computers. The equipment was then delivered directly to the user and set up in its chosen location. Service requests were telephoned to a help desk in Dallas; if the problem appeared to be hardware-related, then an employee of an outside contract maintenance firm would be dispatched to the user's site. Problems not related to hardware were handled directly by the help desk staff.

Data communications was charged at a fixed cost per location, based on the number of units in use and the telephone line charges. (Voice communications was run by a different part of Management Services and was charged for separately.) Cass's group also sent out bills for in-house time-sharing, which had about 150 user accounts. This service cost $4,000 per account per year for unlimited access to the mainframe and a large amount of disk storage. End-user tools, including the statistical package SAS and the report generator FOCUS, were available. There was no charge for using Frito-Lay's electronic mail system, which could be used

EXHIBIT 4   Network Administration Equipment/Software Order Form

General Information

Please fill in all requested information

Contact Name _____

Function _____

Mailing Address (Field) _____

City _____ State _____ Zip _____

Office #/Floor (Hdgs) _____

Phone ( ) _____ Date of Order _____

Order Description

Briefly describe the intent of the order _____

_____

Is host connection desired? YES _____ NO _____ What Systems will you need to access? _____

If a host connection is requested, what is the printer node name you want the device to print to?

_____

Special Instructions

_____

_____

_____

_____

Cross Charge Approval

User agrees to retain hardware for two years. Budget pricing will be determined and announced in July of each year for the following year. Beginning 1/1/86, Field Communications costs are fixed for the year and charged separately from the hardware costs.

For software purchases, user agrees to read and comply with software licensing agreements. Questions should be referred to the Law Department.

_____   _____

_____   _____

_____   _____   _____

Authorized Signatures   Date   Charge Divloc

Total One-Time Charges   _____ (From Pg. 2)
Total Period Charges   _____ (From Pg. 2)

If you have any questions, call (_ _ _) _ _ _ _ _ _ _

Return Completed Forms To: Network Administration
Plano Headquarters-4th floor

For Network Administration Use Only

Project #   _____
Date Order Received   _____
Target Completion Date   _____

order (1)

EXHIBIT 4 (continued)   Equipment List and Pricing

	Qty	One-Time Charge	One-Time Total	Period Charge HDQS	Field	Period Total
Host Terminals						
IBM 3179		50		91	64	
IBM 3278 w/lightpen		60		176	149	
3270-XT w/monitor		160		234	207	
Host Printers						
Medium Speed IBM 3268		195		412	385	
High Speed IBM 3262		300		464	437	
Standalone PC Devices						
PC w/monitor		65		110		
XT w/monitor		65		175		
Compaq		50		76		
PC Printers						
Diablo 630		65		67		
IBM Quietwriter		65		67		
HP Laserjet Plus		90		115		
Epson FX85 (80 Column)		25		26		
Epson FX286 (132 Column)		25		28		
HP Thinkjet		450				
HP 6-pen plotter		50		52		
Software*						
Lotus 1-2-3		325				
OfficeWriter w/speller		290				
GraphWriter		425				
Options Available on 3270-XT*						
PC Graphics		450				
Host Graphics		650				
2nd half-height floppy		333				
2nd half-height hard		700				
AST Card		575				
Other Options						
PC Terminal Furniture		250				
Modem		500				
Power Strip		25				
AB Switch		110				
Other						
Total Charges						

(Record on Page 1)

*If ordering for existing device, please provide the serial number of the system unit in the "Special Instructions" section. In addition, if ordering drives or software, provide the current drive configuration (i.e., full-height hard drive and two half-height floppy drives).

to send messages, documents, and data files, or for the use of other on-line systems.

Asked to assess her group's impact on Frito-Lay's use of information systems, Cass replied, "In a way we stimulate demand, because we make it very easy. Without us the user has to locate a vendor, get three bids, fill out a capital appropriation request, and then worry about service." There had been relatively few complaints about equipment and communications charges, although some users were irritated by the amount of initial paperwork that had to be done, the lack of clear explanation of bills, and the length of time required to fill an order. (On the last point, Dori Reap commented, "We ask for 30 days, but in fact we can do anything in a week.")

Cass foresaw a potential problem as purchased equipment became fully depreciated. Terminals, for example, were on a three-year depreciation schedule with a 3 percent scrap value. "As users see this equipment coming off depreciation," she said, "they may expect to get it for free. We have continually explained that we work on a pooled average cost basis, under which we reduce *everybody's* expense by an appropriate amount as the equipment in the pool becomes fully depreciated. Also, maintenance and communications costs are continually incurred, and we provide lots of service, which is not free." All equipment of the same kind was billed at the same price, regardless of age; the price was adjusted to account for the steady downward trend of equipment costs.

Regarding the equipment policy, Ernest Harris commented, "Charlie Feld has done an extremely good job. He has always let user need drive acquisition—he has tried to coordinate, but never control. Of course, he couldn't have stopped users anyway, and he never could have met the demand for mainframe applications."

Charging for Applications Development

The funding process for applications development was also running smoothly, although with something less than total agreement from users. "I compare it to democracy," Feld said. "It's not perfect, but nobody has come up with anything better."

Under the new process, each functional group had a coordinator who served as the area's key contact with Management Services. The functional coordinator worked with the group during the annual planning process, which began in June, to develop a "wish list" of preliminary designs for desired applications. This list was sent to the group's applications development manager, a member of the Management Services staff who was responsible for liaison with that particular functional group. The applications development manager added to the wish list any projects that Management Services, based on its work with the group, thought the group should have, then prepared a staffing estimate for each project. The project specifications were typically quite vague at this point. "We try to talk with the users," noted Wayne Hyde, the systems development manager for manufacturing, "but a conversation of two hours is really a luxury. We expect ourselves to know enough about the business to know where to go for more information. We may try to sell a preliminary evaluation, two to three months long, for a particularly large or complicated project. Often we can't even get to the preliminary evaluation until the following year, but the eventual result is a better project list and clearer priorities."

After receiving the staffing estimates, users did a benefits assessment and assigned priorities to the projects. The user groups then negotiated with Management Services for staff. There was a fixed pool of developers assigned to each area, and if more were needed, the users and Management Services negotiated jointly for the additional budget required. All development expenses were charged back to users at about $55,000 per person per year. Such charges were essentially fixed once a project had been agreed upon; Charlie Feld noted, "We deliver the project for the estimate, unless the scope changes."

Some negative comments about the new funding system came from managers in the general and administrative area, which was considered "poor" since it had to live within the 8 percent corporate growth guidelines. Mike Miller, the director of accounting, said that it was difficult to get any attention for accounting systems until there was a crisis. Miller noted that in 1985 the clerks in the accounting function had worked almost 90,000 hours of overtime to meet processing and reporting deadlines. Much of this time was spent on tasks that could readily be automated or streamlined. As a result, Miller felt, some staff in his department were becoming frustrated, and morale was dropping. Miller also pointed out that a hand-held computer project now under way in the sales area was consuming a tremendous amount of programming resource. It was more difficult than ever to get approval for upgrading or replacing such "routine" systems as accounts payable or general ledger. Yet precisely these areas were beginning to feel the strain of all the changes under way.

Miller recognized that even the potential automation of the entire accounting group of 600 clerks would not make as large an economic impact on the company as would some of the other development projects that Management Services had under way. Nevertheless, he couldn't help but worry that one of the "routine" systems might become a serious financial or operating control weakness in the future. Feld, who had been listening to Miller's remarks, added, "It's gotten to the point where Management Services is not working on the important things at all— there isn't time. All we work on are the crucial things."

From her new perspective in strategic planning to which she had moved in late 1985, Dori Reap looked back on the funding systems she had helped to create and said, "I think chargeback works great in general, but now it's time to tweak it a bit." Reap's 10-person staff shared a number of personal computers and terminals. By 7:00 a.m., Reap noted, every device was in use and there were lines waiting. "Some of my people are working very long hours and wasting a lot of their $50,000-per-year time. Others are being badly affected by stress. Our accounting system is inadequate, so we have to do lots of work and rework. I only have 10 people on my staff, and I can't afford to let one go so I can afford another computer. What's the solution—do less analysis?"

Another Frito-Lay manager noted that small staff groups without a clearly defined client tended to suffer under the new system. He recalled, for example, that the quality assurance group had wanted a system costing $150,000, about 15 percent of its annual budget. The group could not fit the new system into its annual plan, so it went to the vice president for manufacturing and got his support in asking for more money. The manager continued, "But the more esoteric groups—strategic planning, for instance— have no natural constituency, hence tend not to get much support."

Users generally felt that systems quality had improved markedly under the new funding scheme, as had their relationship with Management Services. From the Management Services perspective, the new system increased central control over development and was an incentive to do good systems planning. There were, however, some complaints. "The system involves a fixed charge for people," one manager noted, "even if there are vacancies. Basically, the user is agreeing to pay for headcount, not for outcomes. Users get no good day-to-day descriptions of the work being done. Systems will say this isn't happening, but trust me—it's exactly what's going on. I'm willing to go on trust over the short term because quality has gotten so much better. But my confidence is based more on the management of the Management Services function than on their control systems. Some people in the company don't have the trust level I do."

Case 9-2

AEROSPACE TECHNOLOGY MANUFACTURING, INC.: INDUSTRY, COMPANY, AND I/S TRANSITIONS

While preparing their 1992 budget, Dave Martin, vice president of Finance, and Bob Enright, director of Information Systems (I/S), were concerned about how to respond to the need to reduce Information Systems (I/S) expenses toward 2–2.5 percent of sales over the next several years. Currently, at 3.5 percent of sales for 1991, they were concerned about how they could effect these changes in a way which would not harm ATMI's competitiveness.

ATMI employed 12,400 people worldwide, including its headquarters in New England. Its products, as a percent of its total 1991 sales to both defense and commercial customers, included domestic aerospace (78 percent), foreign sales (13 percent), and ATMI Support Systems (customer service) (9 percent).

A highly consistent performer throughout the 1970s and early 1980s, ATMI experienced a dramatic loss in 1986. An aggressive restructuring plan helped to restore its profitability in 1987. The situation for the next decade, however, would prove to be difficult. Its existing product lines, in which it has consistently held number one and two market positions, were all in markets which were expected to show little real growth above inflation. Increased profits would only come by either reducing costs or increasing market share against tough competitors. The three dominant factors shaping the markets were:

1. Major long-term reductions in defense spending.

2. Stagnation of the domestic airline market as the result of mergers and consolidations.

3. Excess industry capacity. This is compounded by the shift from mechanical to electrical parts (which do not wear out and, thus, do not require regular service—previously a major source of sales and profits).

Paul Goodman was appointed chief executive officer (Exhibit 1). In taking over the responsibilities of CEO, he was keenly aware that of the six major operating divisions of ATMI's parent corporation, ATMI ranked low in terms of return on sales (ROS), sales growth, and return on shareholders' net worth, a situation unlikely to be rectified without dramatic action.

Company History

ATMI had enjoyed a long, successful history since its founding in 1920. Some of aviation's pioneers were its earliest customers. They trusted its products, and it soon became widely known for building products that withstood the most demanding flight conditions.

Doctoral Candidate CJ Meadows prepared this case under the supervision of Professor F. Warren McFarlan as the basis for class discussion rather than to illustrate either effective or ineffective handling of an administrative situation.

EXHIBIT 1 Aerospace Technologies Manufacturing, Inc. Organization Chart

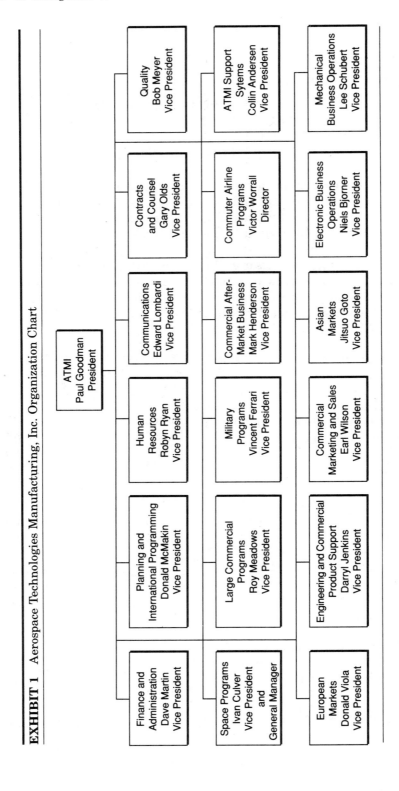

ATMI shared with the nation the greatest adventure of the 20th century by producing the equipment used in the early days of the space program. Over the next 15 years, the company continued its preeminent role in space, providing astronauts with critical equipment. The company also became involved with the project to build America's first manned space station.

ATMI's recent history had been more turbulent, however. After an increase in foreign competition in the automobile and consumer electronics industries and the subsequent collapse of the domestic industry, the U.S. government raised the quality standards on all its aerospace projects. The government insisted that *all* specifications and standards had to be met. However, some of the standards had never been met before, and, indeed, many of the specifications were conflicting. More and more government inspectors went out to ATMI's production facilities. The increased burden of strict compliance put heavy cost pressures on the company.

The *coup de grace* came in 1986 when the processing of all non-conforming material was stopped by the government for a significant period while the company struggled with those items. Halting the flow of military goods in process created factory gridlock, stalling both military and commercial products. Customers experienced delays in their projects as a result of ATMI's delays, and commercial aircraft repair slowed dramatically because replacement parts were unavailable. Customer dissatisfaction grew. Although the company had expected to show sizeable profits that year, ATMI sustained a substantial loss.

In 1988, the company began a major quality movement and hired a consulting firm with significant aerospace experience. To further focus attention on capturing competitive advantage through quality, ATMI began positioning itself to compete for the prestigious Baldrige award (see goals in Exhibit 2), a national quality award given by the U.S. Department of Commerce and presented by the President to American firms excelling in a variety of categories. Emerging as one of the few firms to attain the award against hundreds of competitors would place ATMI in an industry leadership position in the eyes of its current and potential clients. The process itself of improving business practices would yield substantial benefits to the company. Teams were created to begin pursuing the award. Starting in 1987, profits improved but did not meet the parent corporation's standards.

Facing flat sales forecasts and increasing cost pressures, ATMI planned to reduce its workforce by 2,000 people via attrition, voluntary retirements, and layoffs by 1992. All ATMI departments were tasked to reduce their budgets by 30 percent, using as a baseline 1989's budgets, adjusted for inflation.

In addition, inventory reduction was an immediate priority in order to improve cash flow. Inventories had grown as a result of the initiatives to improve customer satisfaction via on-time deliveries. In order to regain the confidence of its customers, the company had increased its spare parts stock to significantly improve its response time for repairs. Long lead times (six to nine months for some products) also necessitated large inventories, but as orders trailed off in late 1990, the company was left with larger inventory than expected. For this reason, cycle times would be a focus in reducing inventory. The real challenge would be to reduce capital investment in inventory without sacrificing customer service. To expedite this process, Paul Goodman, CEO, assigned Donald McMakin, one of ATMI's Vice Presidents, to facilitate improvements in asset management

---

EXHIBIT 2   ATMI Vision, Goals, and Strategy

Vision

Be an internationally recognized producer of high quality aerospace systems and hardware. This will require a process of continuous improvement to meet customer expectations, create employee opportunity, and achieve superior business results.

Goals

Financial performance	Customer satisfaction	Market share	Qualify	Employee satisfaction
Improve by 1993 • ROS of 10% • RNOA of 20%	Meet all commitments we make to our customers, achieving 100% compliance by 1993	Achieve a position of substance—normally as one or two—in all product markets we serve by 1993	Win the Malcom Baldrige Award by 1994	Be the employer of first choice in our market

Measurement

STRATEGY
ATMI is focused on process and cost improvements, to provide predictable financial performance and competitive advantage. Key to success is the development and commitment of our people and suppliers to achieve total quality performance and satisfied customers.

Human resource development training (hrs/employee)

Profitability (ROS)

Total quality performance (Baldrige criteria)

Asset management (RNOA)

ATMI

Long-term growth(%)

Customer satisfaction (commitment compliance)

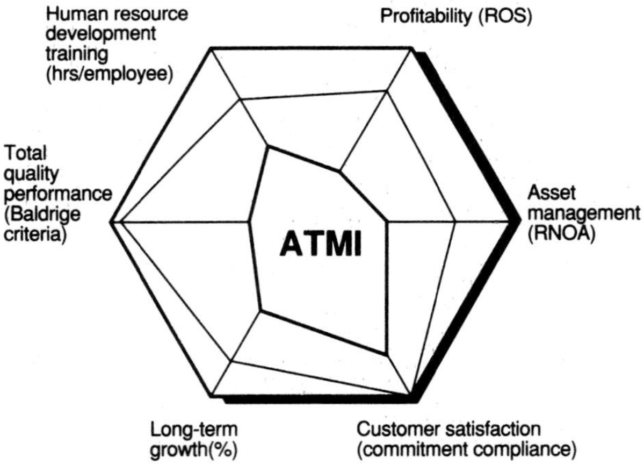

via working capital and, more specifically, inventory reductions. I/S opportunities would be among those investigated, as well as other business opportunities such as reducing lead times and moving some manufacturing to suppliers.

Industry, ATMI, and I/S Stresses

Industry

Like other aerospace firms, ATMI's commercial and military operations had been affected by global industry changes. The 1980s had been a time of aerospace expansion, fueled by growing DOD budgets and airline deregulation. The 1990s, however, were a different story. Terrorist threats, the Gulf War, dramatic increases in jet fuel prices, and overall economic recession had severely influenced the U.S. airline industry. Moreover, the growing success of superpower peace initiatives and related political changes in Eastern Europe combined with overall government deficit spending reductions resulted in dramatic government procurement changes. According to the Aerospace Industries Association, projected sales would decline 3.6 percent in real terms for 1991 over the 1990 figure of $131.3 billion.[1] ATMI expected that it could grow only by increasing market share. In addition to declining sales, foreign competition had increased. The future of the industry might be overseas, or it might remain in the United States. To cope with future changes, ATMI had to move quickly.

ATMI

In 1990, ATMI had to put major cost reductions (30–40 percent) into its pricing for products coming out in 1993 in order to win the necessary contracts and hold market share against the competition's lower prices. Meeting these cost reduction targets would be crucial to meeting its profit goals. Two measures were used by ATMI:

Return on Sales (ROS): Goal = 10 percent by 1993, essentially a 100 percent improvement over 1990

Return on Investment: Goal = 20 percent by 1993, a 70 percent improvement over 1990.

---

[1]1990 Year-End Review and Forecast—An Analysis, Aerospace Industries Association, p.1.

With flat sales projected, reduction of expenses and assets was seen as the only way these targets could be met.

On the revenue side, ATMI's revenue stream faced significant change. In the past, ATMI received revenue from both initial sales and ongoing service on mechanical parts. Since electronic accessories began to replace the traditional electro-mechanical accessories, service revenues, which represented a significant portion of total revenues, were expected to decline. ATMI had to begin realizing improved profitability on original equipment sales.

Assets were a focus because of the high inventory level and inventory carrying costs. Because inventory had to be supported with a large factory parts tracking system, inventory costs worked their way into I/S. To reduce order and inventory costs, the company had to reduce its number of vendors, increase volume per vendor, and create EDI (electronic data interface), MRP (materials requirements planning), JIT (just-in-time), or pull-system links with its vendors.

Another pressure on ATMI was posed by its location. The state in which it operated was noted for high corporate taxes, high wages, high workers' compensation, and high sales tax. Moving its commercial electronics operations to a western city in a "focused facility," ATMI expected to achieve a 40 percent decrease in costs for the facility via lower labor costs, continuous flow manufacturing, and new equipment.

I/S

In the words of Bob Enright, CIO, "Our company is reducing costs. We have to make dramatic cost reductions in all parts of the business. We in Information Systems need to participate." Accordingly, the four most important issues facing I/S were:

- Reducing costs.
- Viewing I/S as a value-added area rather than merely a cost.
- Shifting the I/S approach to support dispersed businesses ("focused facilities").
- Re-engineering—establishing an approach for developing new technology and avoiding the pitfalls of the past, where technology was adapted to the way work was already done and full potential benefits were not realized.

First, even though all I/S costs were charged out to the departments that used its services, Paul Goodman wanted to cut costs "at the source," i.e., remove costs from the I/S department rather than from user departments. The I/S department's $33 million budget would have to be cut to $28 million by 1992. The major I/S costs were broken down as follows:

1. Engineering	= 31%
2. Finance	= 22
3. Manufacturing	= 26
4. Other (e.g., support for space and sea systems, ATMI Support Services, and quality)	= 21
	100 %

Taking costs out of these functions would be very difficult, especially engineering. Since computers had been cheaper than people, over the prior decade, management had given the engineering department more processing capability while holding its headcount constant, a decision made through collaborations between Engineering and I/S. This meant an increase not just in hardware and software costs, but also in maintenance, education, and other costs. In addition to the human vs. machine cost factor, the presence of leading-edge work tools such as electronic design and drafting was seen as critical in helping to attract a high-quality work force. Financial justification of additional investments would be emphasized even more in the future.

The second concern, value-added, can be stated simply as follows: ATMI could not afford to sacrifice projects, software, or equipment that would bring the firm significant net benefit (benefit to the organization minus costs) in the form of greater efficiency or competitive advantage. During cost-cutting times, it is especially important to analyze expenditures carefully to separate expendable ideas and projects from those that more than pay for themselves. To identify these ideas and projects, the head of the systems development function within I/S was placed in charge of a committee which would investigate I/S opportunities for competitive advantage.

Third, I/S would experience a shift, in part, away from supplying I/S services to end users and toward serving independent I/S departments within focused facilities, i.e., "mini-businesses" that would focus on individual product lines (discussed later). Because some focused facilities would have their own separate mainframes and software, ATMI's central I/S department would have to build the standard interface between the facilities and the central computer, act as a coordinator for systems implementation and upgrades, support the network, software, and users, establish standards, and create a training program for employees at the focused facilities (so they could become trainers). These represented new duties and a shift in the I/S service approach.

Finally, re-engineering ATMI's business might prove to be just as important as cost reduction—perhaps more so. Although ATMI had realized benefits from introducing its engineering workstations (including enhanced information and a constant headcount), the company did not realize the full potential benefits from the investment (e.g., by reduced cycle times). I/S and Engineering later initiated a pilot project that would define opportunities for significant cycle time and cost reductions. Other projects might prove necessary to identify re-engineering opportunities.

Current I/S Situation

In January 1990, ATMI's I/S leadership was taken over by Bob Enright, who was elevated from a position as manager of systems development, a position he had held for six years. Reporting to Dave Martin, vice president of Finance, Bob took over the responsibility for ATMI's $33 million Information Systems (I/S) budget and 310 people. By the end of July 1991, the I/S department had been downsized from 310 to 244 (30 from Systems development and the remainder evenly split among the other I/S divisions). His area in 1991 included (Exhibit 3):

Technical Services—data entry, coordination of employee education and education travel, training database, education planning, ad hoc projects (20 people; budget: $1.83 million).

Computer Operations—systems programmers, computer operators and schedulers, etc. (31 people in software support, 41 in operations; budget: $14.33 million).

Exhibit 3 Information Systems Organization Chart

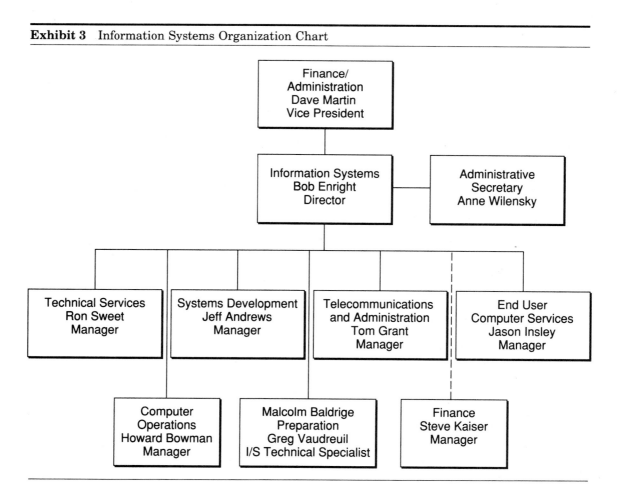

Systems Development—new development and maintenance (106 people; budget: $7.33 million).

Telecommunications and Administration—telecommunications, equipment moves, other I/S administration (28 people in telecommunication, 2 in administration; budget: $8.02 million).

End User Computing Services—software support hotline, information/training center, computer equipment repair (27 people; budget: $1.49 million).

Finance—administrative support for I/S financial operations, e.g., systems for I/S chargeback, I/S purchase and expense tracking, inventory tracking, budget, etc. This section is atypical in that it reports outside I/S (to the assistant controller within the finance/administration area of ATMI) (two people plus some management time; budget: $80,000).

Malcolm Baldrige Preparation—monitoring of the continuous improvement program, identification of opportunities to improve I/S quality for the Baldrige Award (one I/S employee on a small team outside I/S).

Bob Enright and Dave Martin both felt that the headcount had been reduced with little long-term damage to the company. This was evident from both their own personal observations and the lack of any strong negative feedback from other members of management. They were deeply concerned, however, that further downsizing could put ATMI at long-term risk in meeting its goals.

As shown in Exhibit 4, ATMI had an IBM mainframe and a cluster of Digital Equipment (DEC) mainframes which communicated with the IBM. Terminals, engineering workstations (connected in several small local area networks [LANs]), and PCs were connected to the IBM, as well as CADAM (Computer-Aided Design and Manufacturing—two dimensional) and CATIA (3D CAD/CAM) stations, which facilitated the company's 100 percent electronic design and drafting. An AS400 was also connected to the IBM mainframe and was used for manufacturing and shop floor control. The ratio of terminals, PCs, and workstations to salaried workers was almost 1:1.

Changes

To meet the demanding business challenges ahead, three changes (described below) were initiated within the company. These changes were of critical importance at that time and directly influenced the delivery of I/S support.

Corporate I/S Centralization

In early 1990, ATMI's parent corporation had 18 computer centers for its various divisions. Later, the corporation consolidated into 12 systems (see Exhibit 5). ATMI absorbed a sibling company's computer operations in May 1990. Two of ATMI's sibling companies had also consolidated in 1990 into another Data Center, which would be absorbed into ATMI's center in 1994 or 1995, if all went according to plan. The final goal was three sites. The CIOs from the affected divisions would be placed on the Data Center steering committee to ensure close integration with their needs. Centralized functions at these three locations would include payroll, human resources, production scheduling, central accounting, engineering library functions, and standards maintenance. Although ATMI's IBM mainframe, disk storage, and 45 of the 72 people currently in the I/S computer operations department were slated to move to the Data Center (20 miles from ATMI headquarters), other operations staff and the DEC mainframes would remain at headquarters.

Significant cost savings were projected from the data center consolidation via economies of scale. However, the immediate question was how many and how costly the networking problems would be, since the

EXHIBIT 4 Current Systems at ATMI

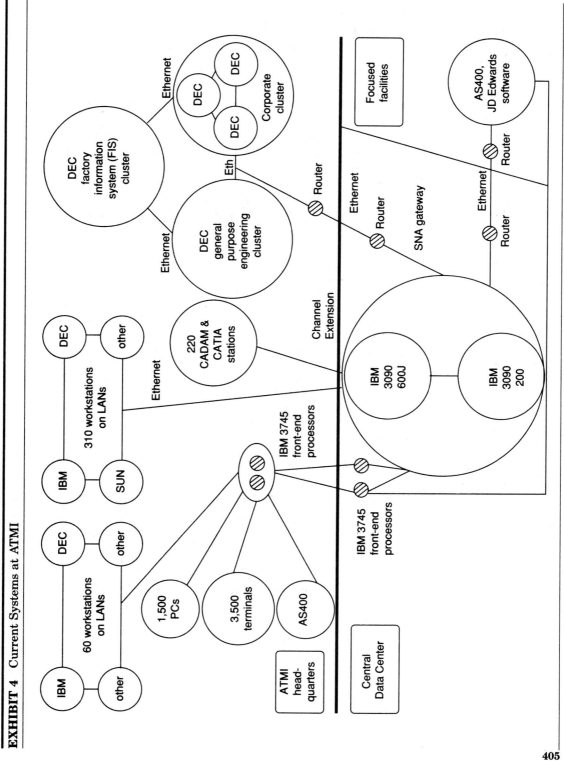

EXHIBIT 5   Data Center Consolidation Schedule

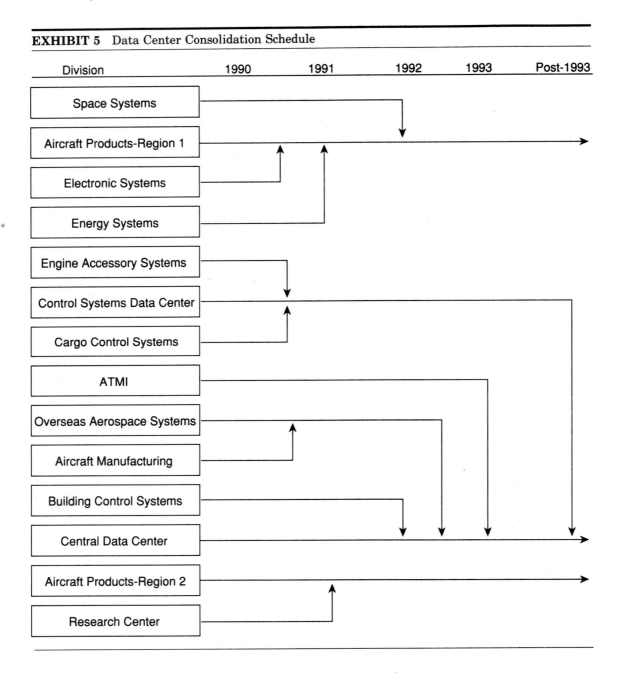

computer operations would become more complex. IBM 3745 front-end processors were to be placed at headquarters and in the Central Data Center (see Exhibit 6), a channel extension would connect the engineering workstations with the Data Center mainframe, and routers connected by Ethernet were to be placed between the DEC mainframes at headquarters and the IBM mainframe at the Data Center. A standard interface between the focused facility mainframes and the Data Center mainframe would be created.

In 1991, ATMI paid $320,000/month for its IBM3090 600J—more than average for such a machine because as ATMI needed more capacity, the company had added onto itsleases several times. If ATMI had a single lease, rather than a base lease and several add-ons, the final lease price would have been less. Although the final mainframe price seemed high, the add-on policy was made with this in mind. Management's intent was to pay a small price when ATMI'S capacity needs were low and pay larger prices for more capacity as needs grew, so that total cost over a long period would be less than if the company had paid for idle capacity early in the life of the computer. One of the benefits of data center consolidation would be the single, newly negotiated lease on a large mainframe at a cheaper per-unit-of-computing price than the current machine.

ATMI's Focused Facilities

ATMI began to migrate into separate commercial and military businesses. Each business would be split into mechanical products and electrical products. Focused facilities (independent mini-businesses) would be created for major product lines or projects, and the I/S function of each facility would be performed by up to five employees. Those that had mainframes would pay up to $1 million per machine for hardware and software. I/S for some of the smaller facilities would be run out of larger facilities or would contain only one or two employees. Only state-of-the-art, mechanical and electronics manufacturing would go to the focused facilities. Although each facility would be expected to be completely independent and to report to a level of management directly under Paul Goodman, a central I/S department would remain at headquarters to act as a focal point for coordinating systems implementation, upgrades, repairs, user training (training trainers only), architectural consistency of application software, and technical support. AS400 and JD Edwards software would be installed at each facility and would hook up to the Data Center to upload financial and operating information.

The underlying philosophy was that separating into focused facilities would push down responsibility and ownership, thus encouraging people to work together to reduce costs, make cultural change, and develop new ideas for competitive advantage. Focused facilities objectives included:

- Cost reduction.
- Reduction in manufacturing cycle time (between shop order release and a finished good).
- Improvement of process yield.
- Improved delivery performance.

A preliminary list of planned facilities included: Commercial Electronic Facility, Commercial Distribution Facility, an Overhaul Facility, Precision Manufacturing Center, and several other facilities being defined. Of these facilities, the Commercial Electronics Facility would open in January 1992 with 60–70 people and would house 250 people by the end of 1994. The Commercial Distribution Facility would open in spring 1992 and house 50–75. In 1993, the Overhaul Facility was scheduled to open (no location yet) with 40–50 people. Another facility was planned at 300–500 people. It was evident from the number of employees to be housed at the new locations that the geogra-

EXHIBIT 6 Preliminary View of Future Systems at ATMI

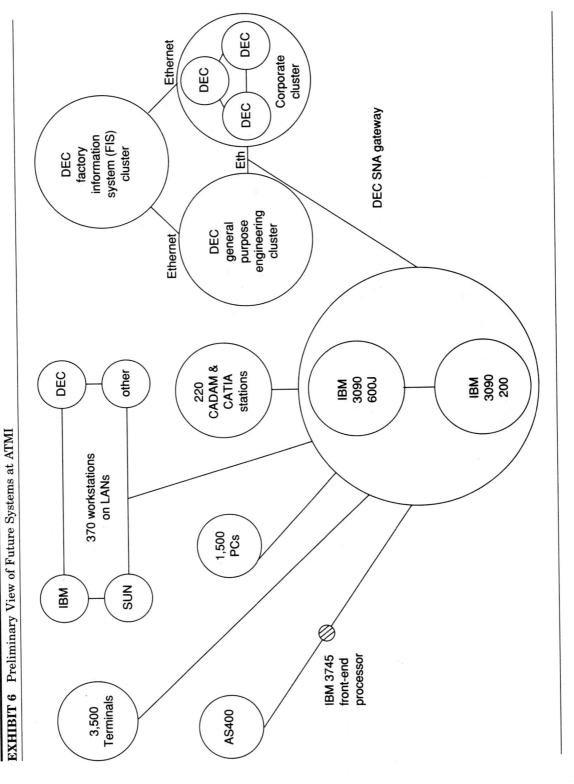

phy, composition, logistics, and communication of ATMI employees would be vastly different in the future.

Downsizing

In thinking about where to make cuts in the I/S budget, Dave Martin was concerned about the following:

1. The ability to size the I/S function at 2–2.5 percent of sales. Many other manufacturers were running at a significantly higher level, and those that ran at equivalent or lower levels often did not include in their I/S budgets all the costs included in ATMI's (e.g., building allocation and I/S employee fringe benefits). Moreover, with the proliferation of the PC and large, widely accessible corporate information systems since the 1970s (when 2–2.5 percent was an industry norm), was this figure really a reasonable figure in 1992 for a firm of ATMI's size?
2. Which I/S areas could be reduced further. About $1.5 million had already been taken out of the systems development staff. But the goal of $28 million for the 1992 budget (discussed below) seemed a long way off.
3. The apparent focus on efficiency vs. effectiveness. In the spirit of cost reduction, a recently proposed project to study ways in which the organization could be restructured with the aid of a consulting firm had been postponed because of the magnitude of the expense. Dave was further concerned by the fact that the basic procedures of the department, including customer service, seemed to be solid—only routine problems had occurred. Would further cuts disrupt this relative smoothness of operation? Of particular concern was that in this austere budget, little concern was being paid to future I/S-stimulated innovations in a company heavily committed to the manufacture and sale of electronic products. ATMI's

innovation and future-oriented outlook would have to be preserved if the company was to survive in the long-run.

In the short-run, however, cuts had to be made. Since 51 percent of the I/S budget consisted of long-term leases, fixed-asset depreciation, lease-mandated equipment maintenance, and other fixed costs which could not be cut within the year, finding costs to cut out of the following year's budget proved to be a particular challenge (Exhibits 7 and 8). Bob Enright believed the budget could be reduced substantially over the next two years, however, as leases ran out and the company refrained from making purchases (thus reducing depreciation). Variable costs (Exhibit 8 – 8 percent of the I/S budget) were examined separately from personnel (Exhibit 8 – 41 percent of the I/S budget) because management aimed at cutting variable and fixed costs before personnel.

The 1989 budget had been $32 million. Adjusted for inflation, the 1992 budget would have been $40 million if kept at the 1989 level. Figuring in Paul Goodman's goal of a 30 percent reduction from that figure brought 1992's budget target to $28 million. More than one year was required to achieve this goal because fixed costs were such a large portion of the budget. The tentative $3 million in net reductions from the 1991 budget of $33 million was proposed as follows (in $000s):

Disk storage lease extension/renegotiation	$ 240
Lease buy outs	500
Software reductions	300
Maintenance reductions	500
Estimated attrition (10 people/6 months)	250
1991 merit-based salary adjustments	500
Inflationary price increases	600
Total	$2,890

EXHIBIT 7 Information Systems Budget History ($000)

	1982 Actuals	1983 Actuals	1984 Actuals	1985 Actuals	1986 Actuals	1987[b] Actuals	1988 Actuals	1989 Actuals	1990 Actuals	1991 Budget
Salaries	$ 3,369.2	$ 4,535.4	$ 5,091.3	$ 5,932.9	$ 6,608.1	$ 7,246.6	$ 8,934.6	$10,122.6	$11,393.7	$10,396.0
Fringe	1,534.6	1,731.2	1,944.0	2,247.5	2,504.5	2,377.7	2,006.5	2,343.3	2,075.3	3,455.3
Equipment	5,120.5	4,883.6	5,854.0	6,598.4	5,520.3	8,315.1	5,228.9	5,558.6	6,272.3	5,697.6
Software	293.5	652.6	977.9	1,021.8	1,628.4	2,444.5	2,387.0	2,216.2	2,727.7	2,520.4
Maintenance						845.1	2,225.1	2,524.8	3,761.7	3,432.4
Supplies	473.3	523.9	582.8	650.7	697.3	931.4	1,066.2	1,263.8	1,174.8	1,017.3
Depreciation	116.7	129.6	180.5	288.3	942.2	3,645.9	4,281.3	4,439.3	4,317.4	4,291.5
Other[a]	1,032.1	526.0	697.5	1,513.5	1,194.4	2,732.7	2,625.7	2,641.7	3,272.5	2,243.9
Total	$11,939.0	$12,982.3	$15,328.0	$18,253.1	$22,095.2	$28,539.0	$28,755.3	$33,110.3	$34,995.4	$33,054.4
[a]Other										
Travel						$ 205.2	$ 125.7	$ 157.2	$ 215.8	$ 156.2
Training						296.0	164.1	144.8	154.3	144.9
Tuition reimbursement						0.0	0.0	0.0	0.0	81.3
Printing/stationery						84.8	7.0	46.4	125.4	98.1
Telephone/postage						911.0	476.7	510.8	1,029.2	818.4
Other rental						35.8	42.2	69.9	83.6	90.7
Professional fees						259.2	608.8	688.1	501.5	49.3
Sundry						3.4	794.2	520.6	682.7	492.2
Plant allocation						937.3	407.0	403.9	480.0	312.8
Total						$ 2,732.7	$ 2,625.7	$ 2,641.7	$ 3,272.5	$ 2,243.9
% of sales	2.2%	2.3%	2.4%	2.7%	3.7%	4.0%	3.4%	3.2%	3.3%	3.3%

1992 estimates: $29 million I/S budget, 3.1% of sales.
[b]Engineering Software Systems and Vax Equipment and Service were added to ISD in 1987.

EXHIBIT 8   1991 I/S Budget ($000)

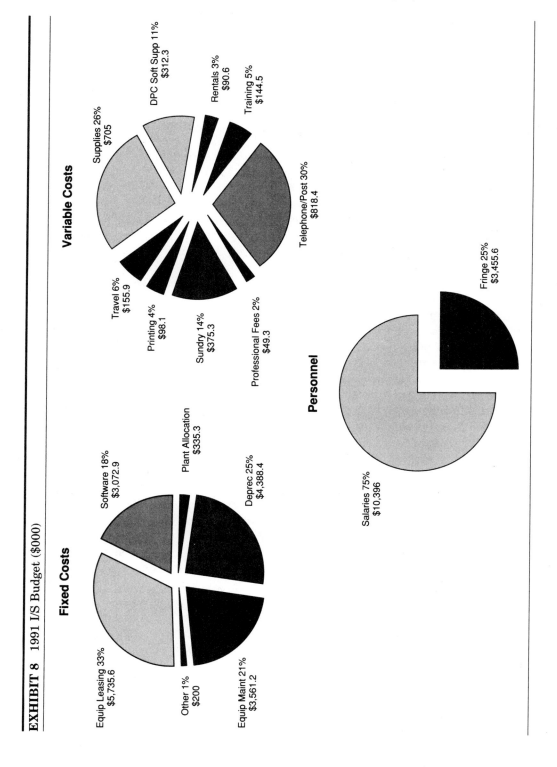

Variable Costs

DPC Soft Supp 11%
$312.3

Supplies 26%
$705

Rentals 3%
$90.6

Training 5%
$144.5

Telephone/Post 30%
$818.4

Travel 6%
$155.9

Printing 4%
$98.1

Sundry 14%
$375.3

Professional Fees 2%
$49.3

Fixed Costs

Software 18%
$3,072.9

Plant Allocation
$335.3

Deprec 25%
$4,388.4

Equip Leasing 33%
$5,735.6

Other 1%
$200

Equip Maint 21%
$3,561.2

Personnel

Fringe 25%
$3,455.6

Salaries 75%
$10,396

Savings were expected on the disk storage lease because second leases on equipment are normally cheaper than initial leases written when the equipment is up-to-date. The lease buy-outs would save money based on the same principle. Software available on both the DEC and the IBM mainframes would be reduced to one copy per function on either the DEC or the IBM. Users would have to key into the appropriate system to use the necessary functions rather than having duplicates available on both systems (less convenient due to switching between systems, but workable). Maintenance reductions would be made in the form of buying cheaper, lower-priority service contracts, and enduring longer downtimes while companies with higher priority service contracts received repairs first. Employees would have to be more careful with supplies because on-hand supplies (expensed at purchase during previous years) would be used for operations, and less would be purchased as replacements (this would only affect the 1992 budget). Longer downtimes would also have to be endured as spare parts were reduced (a one-time budget reduction, like supplies). Overtime would be cut, reducing the amount of work that could be finished and lengthening the time required to finish tasks. In addition, several fixed assets were to become fully depreciated in 1991. Their depreciation charges would, thus, be absent from the 1992 budget. Normal attrition would not be replaced, perhaps leaving some areas understaffed. The company would receive a credit from its parent corporation for running a sibling company's computer operations. In addition to cuts, ATMI's hardware, software, and other assets would have to be frozen, and new projects and ideas would be scrutinized extra-carefully to determine their degree of necessity.

To help explain why the I/S budget was so difficult to cut, Bob planned to show that I/S

services had increased dramatically over the previous several years. The number of PC LANs increased to 14 in 1991 from 3 in 1989. Workstation LANs increased to 13 in 1991 from 3 in 1989. I/S supported the new communication lines to the company's French affiliate (a $300,000/year budget item), EDI lines to customers (all airline customers had EDI), and communication lines to other ATMI buildings. In comparison with 1989's figures, I/S was supporting 155 percent more VUPS (DEC), 104 percent more students (trained in the Information Center), 64 percent more PCs, 59 percent more CRTs, 52 percent more disk storage, 49 percent more MIPS (IBM), and 45 percent more equipment moves (for employees changing location) with 21 percent fewer I/S employees.

In the future, Bob would be faced with additional budget pressures from ATMI's workstation strategy. The company had planned to replace many of its CADAM and CATIA stations (hardware only) with true workstations over the next three- to five-year period, spending $2–$3 million per year ($11 million total). CADAM and CATIA stations were the state-of-the-art technology when ATMI first acquired them in the late 1970s and early 1980s. However, workstations were later developed and could provide additional capabilities at a lower price (as little as $700/MIPS vs. the CADAM and CATIA IBM mainframe's $100,000/MIPS). Therefore, some computing would be moved to the workstations, at a cheaper price per unit of computing. Although the price difference was sizeable, workstations did not offer the data-storage, communications, capacity, and other capabilities of a mainframe (thus explaining the existence of such a vast price difference). Workstations would be purchased, rather than leased, and depreciation costs would be concentrated early in the five-year depreciable life of the machines.

During this cost-cutting time, the company would defer the replacement as long as necessary, but it would try to balance cost-cutting with the need to stay on the leading edge of technology.

Even though no projects were current targets for cuts, in order to reduce I/S as a percent of sales, future I/S budgets might have to be reduced further, thus forcing projects to be cut. (See the 1991 project portfolio, budgeted at $6,910,000 total in Exhibit 9). The projects generally resulted not from proposal and cost/benefit analysis of the individual projects, but rather from management directives to support the company's strategic projects such as focused facilities, quality improvement, and EDI. Extensive analyses of such strategic projects were made before the directives were given. In addition to the projects in Exhibit 9, several projects were waiting to begin (listed with worker-year estimates in Exhibit 10, at a total of 34 worker-years).

It was clear that the challenges facing the CIO and all of ATMI were stiff ones. Tough choices and incisive strategy were required to survive. The entire management team had resolved to implement the necessary business changes to regain ATMI's position as an industry leader.

EXHIBIT 9   1991 Project Portfolio

Title	Description	Benefit	Budget
Focused Facilities Systems	Establishment of a computer environment for two future focused facilities.	Necessary to realize the benefits of focused facilities themselves, creation of flexible, easy-to-use systems with a high degree of data accessibility.	$483,700
ATMI Support Services Systems	Development of a system to provide on-line inventory management, and establishment of the framework for a single, integrated system for customer service order processing.	Quick customer repairs via up-to-date component inventory data (currently, it takes several days to post and view data), and capability to manage by product line and provision inventory.	552,800
Financial Systems Upgrade	Upgrade and/or replacement of central accounting services and cost accounting systems over a five-year period. The replacement systems would be an integration of purchased and internally developed packages.	Government compliance, manual system automation, and improved information.	760,100
Optical Systems (OS) Integration	OS was a sibling company absorbed by ATMI. Its financial operations needed to be integrated into the ATMI financial system.	Necessary for the downsized OS to operate within ATMI.	207,300
Manufacturing Control Systems	Support of point-of-use inventory by allowing for the control of component inventories on the factory floor rather than in a central storeroom.	Cost reductions through reduction of inventories and cutting cycle times.	892,200
Mechanical Design and Drafting	Ongoing automation and improvement of the engineering design, analysis, and drafting of mechanical products.	Cycle-time reduction, reduction of mechanical product cost, and introduction of new products to the marketplace.	552,800
Project Planning and Tracking	Development of a cost and schedule performance measurement system, to evaluate and report program and functional performance vs. plan. The system would include the planning, budgeting and actual results of all job order activity.	Government compliance and significant improvements to internal operations.	276,400

EXHIBIT 9 *(continued)*

Title	Description		Benefit	Budget
Next-Generation Shop Floor Control	Development of a system that would work with new manufacturing procedures, such as repetitive manufacturing, cell-based manufacturing, and just-in-time concepts.		Simplified and improved manufacturing and management processes, and additional capabilities.	345,500
Maintenance/ Miscellaneous	Manufacturing	$639,180	Maintenance and upgrades.	2,902,200
	Purchasing	345,500		
	Central Finance	536,910		
	Engineering	230,100		
	Quality	357,930		
	Product Support	332,370		
	ATMI Support Systems	102,270		
	Space and Sea Systems	204,540		
	Miscellaneous	153,400		

EXHIBIT 10 Future I/S Projects

Title	Description	Benefit	Worker Year
Materials and Inventory Tracking System Enhancements	Development of an integrated system to manage overhauls, repairs, and modifications for the customer service center, from receipt of a request through shipment and invoicing. The system would provide repair instructions and status.	Better customer service (turnaround target = 30 days), streamlined service operations, replacement of a cumbersome and incomplete system.	6
J.D. Edwards Software Propagation	Long-term project to replace existing systems with packaged software (J.D. Edwards). The package would be introduced to Focused Facilities and some or all existing operations.	Cost reduction via staff reductions, increased flexibility and ease of use with a high degree of data accessibility.	3
Factory Execution System	Creation of an integrated factory flow environment including statistical process control, electronic work instructions, process planning, and configuration management. The system would collect, process, and integrate control data and will be introduced to focused facilities before other manufacturing operations.	Cost reductions and/or quality improvements via improved manufacturing control, improved data accessibility, and improved user friendliness.	3
Rules-Based (Expert System) Engineering	Creation of a prototype system to assist engineers in early design, including knowledge base and CATIA interface development.	Substantial cycle-time reduction for gear design, and support for the introduction of new technology into the company (i.e., rules-based engineering).	1
Blade Design System	Automation of tasks related to design, e.g., automatic finite element model generation, computer generation of engineering drawings, and blade design optimization.	Reduction of cycle time and cost, and facilitation of product cost and performance optimization (thus creating better products) via increased design iterations.	1
Process Control Database System	Creation of a database repository for all process information, thus standardizing shop floor input and consolidating system requirements for statistical process control. The database will be the basis for process characterization, feasibility analysis, and design-to-manufacture costing. It will also enable on-line viewing of operation sheets on the shop floor.	Process data had been collected via a variety of computer systems and manual methods, and much useful data was not collected at all. The system would standardize process data collection, yielding labor savings and allowing process improvements to reduce manufacturing costs.	3

EXHIBIT 10 (continued)

Title	Description	Benefit	Worker Year
Supplier Database	Redesign of the database structure to relational, and creation of a comprehensive database of supplier information.	Facilitation of corporate hierarchy tracking and document distribution tracking, as well as providing flexibility for future change.	3
Electronic Data Interchange (EDI)	Development of system interfaces with both customers and suppliers, and coordination of Electronic Data Interchange for business areas such as Purchasing, Accounts Payable, and Contracts.	EDI was seen by management as critical in acquiring future business, and it also would lead to improved inventory management.	1
Materials Management	Small- and medium-sized enhancements to existing manufacturing systems, including physical inventory, order policy maintenance, shop calendar maintenance, and materials requirements system improvements.	Systems support for the dynamic business/policy environment.	1
Tooling System Requests	Integration of tooling system controls, and establishment of portable bar coding for collection of gauge calibration data.	Reduced costs via data entry reduction and increased data accuracy.	2
Computer-Aided Logistics Support (CALS)	Definition of CALS impact on the company, recommendations for further action, and probable future implementation.	Compliance with U.S. government contractual requirements that specify CALS capabilities.	2
Hazardous Waste	Creation of tracking and reporting systems designed to help the company pro-actively comply with EPA guidelines and regulations.	Compliance with government tracking and reporting requirements.	1
Consolidated Corporate Payroll	Development of a corporatewide payroll and personnel system to process all salary and hourly payrolls.	Reduction in operating costs and significant information gains from a consolidated personnel database.	4
Program Management	Creation of a cost roll-up system designed to capture all charges across a work breakdown strucutre, both by program and function, focusing on the on-line, timely collection of charges.	Compliance with government reporting requirements and creation of a significantly more timely information base.	3

Chapter 10

A Portfolio Approach to IT Development

A large insurance company deactivates its old systems for a major affiliate on June 30 and implements a new one on July 1 on a new technology. Seven weeks pass before the firm can issue a policy, write a commission check, or send out a premium notice. Nearly 70 percent of the sales force resign in disgust during this period.

A large consumer products company budgets $100 million for a new computer-based order-entry and marketing information system to be ready in two years. Two years later $50 million has been spent, an estimated additional $100 million will be spent to complete the job, and the project completion time has been extended to five years. Both the project manager and the chief information officer have been replaced.

A mid-sized bank has spent $2 million on a new consumer loan system. Developed in complete isolation from the end users, its functions are judged so limited that its conversion is delayed eighteen months, and the system must be completely rewritten.

Nine months after it had installed a state-of-the-art office automation system at a cost of $900,000, a Midwest mail-order house found that 50 percent of the terminals were unused in spite of 90 percent of the work being simple word processing. Further, the communications system was incompatible with the main data processing, and system support was unobtainable. The firm returned the system to the vendor.

Stories from the Stage-1 and Stage-2 days of the late 1960s and early 1970s? Unfortunately not! These examples are from the late 1980s and early 1990s. Although it is embarrassing to admit, the day of the big disaster on a major information technology (IT) project has not passed.

Given business's more than 30 years of IT experience, the question is, Why? An analysis of these cases (all of them domestic companies; we could have selected equally dramatic examples from overseas) and firsthand acquaintance with a number of IT projects in the past 10 years suggest three serious deficiencies in practice that involve both general management and IT management: (1) failure to assess the individual project implementation risk at the time a project is funded; (2) failure to consider the aggregate implementation risk of the portfolio of projects; (3) lack of recognition that different projects require different managerial approaches.

These aspects of the IT project management and development process are so important that we address them in this separate chapter. Chapter 11 will discuss the influences of corporate culture and the technology's perceived strategic relevance on the balance of control between IT and the user over the various stages of the project management life cycle. Since many projects have multiyear life cycles, these project management issues must be dealt with separately from those of the management control system with its calendar-year focus, as discussed in Chapter 9.

PROJECT RISK

Elements of Project Implementation Risk

In discussing risk, we are assuming that the manager has brought appropriate methods and approaches to bear on the project— mismanagement is obviously another element of risk. Implementation risk, by definition here, is what remains after application of proper tools. Also, we are not implying that *risk* is *bad*. These words denote entirely different concepts, and the link between the two normally is simply that higher-risk projects must have potential for greater benefits.

The typical project feasibility study covers exhaustively such topics as financial benefits, qualitative benefits, implementation costs, target milestone and completion dates, and necessary staffing levels. In precise, crisp terms the developers of these estimates provide voluminous supporting documentation. Only rarely, however, do they deal frankly with the risks of slippage in time, cost overrun, technical shortfall, or outright failure. Rather, they deny the existence of such possibilities by ignoring them. They assume the appropriate human skills, controls, and so on, are in place to ensure success.

Consequences of Risk.   By risk we are suggesting exposure to such consequences as:

1. Failure to obtain all, or any, of the anticipated benefits because of implementation difficulties.
2. Implementation costs that are much higher than expected.
3. Implementation time that is much longer than expected.
4. Technical performance of resulting systems that is significantly below the estimate.
5. Incompatibility of the system with the selected hardware and software.

In practical situations, of course, these risks are not independent of each other; rather, they are closely related.

Project Dimensions that Influence Inherent Risk. At least three important project dimensions influence the inherent implementation risk:

Project Size. The larger the project in terms of dollar expense, staffing levels, elapsed time, and number of departments affected by the project, the greater is the risk. Multimillion-dollar projects obviously carry more risk than $50,000 projects and, usually, also affect the company more if the risk is realized. A related concern is the size of the project relative to the normal size of an IT development group's projects. A $1 million project in a department whose average undertaking costs $2 million to $3 million usually has lower implicit risk than a $250,000 project in a department that has never ventured a project costing more than $50,000.

Experience with the Technology. Because of the greater likelihood of unexpected technical problems, project risk increases as the project team's and organization's familiarity with the hardware, operating systems, database handler, and project application language decreases. Phase-1 and Phase-2 technology projects are intrinsically more risky for a company than Phase-3 and Phase-4 technology projects. A project that would pose a slight risk for a leading-edge, large-systems development group may be highly risky for a smaller, less technically advanced group. (The latter group can reduce its risk by purchasing outside skills for an undertaking involving technology that is in general commercial use. This rapidly growing market for outside skills is served by the major systems integrators such as Arthur Andersen, Computer Science Corporation, Electronic Data Services, and IBM.)

Project Structure. In some projects the nature of the task defines the outputs completely from the moment of conceptualization. Such schemes are classified as "highly structured." They carry much less risk than those whose outputs are more subject to the user-manager's judgment and hence are vulnerable to change. The outputs of a highly structured project are fixed and not subject to change during the life of the project.

An insurance company's automating the preparation of its agents' rate book is an example of a highly structured project. At the project's beginning, planners reached agreement on the product lines to be included, the layout of each page, and the process of generating each number. Throughout the life of the project there was no need to alter these decisions. Consequently the team organized to reach a stable, fixed output rather than to cope with a potentially mobile target.

Quite the opposite was true in the "low structure" order entry-marketing information project described at the beginning of the chapter. In that situation the users could not reach a consensus on what the outputs should be, and these decisions shifted almost weekly, crippling progress.

Project Categories and Degree of Risk

Figure 10–1 combines in a matrix the various dimensions influencing risk. It identifies eight distinct project categories with varying degrees of implementation risk. (Figure 10–2 gives examples of projects that fit this categorization.) Even at this grossly intuitive level, such a classification is useful to separate projects for different types of management review. IT organizations have used it successfully for understanding relative implementation risk and for communicating it to users and senior executives. The matrix helps to address the legitimate concern that all people viewing a project will have the same understanding of its risks.

Assessing Risk of Individual Projects

Figure 10–3 shows excerpts from a questionnaire developed by a company for assessing project implementation risk: a list of 42 questions that the project manager* answers about a project prior to senior management's approval of the proposal and then several times during project implementation. The company developed the questions after analyzing its experience with successful and unsuccessful projects. No analytic framework underlies the questions, and they may not be ap-

---

*Actually, both the project leader and the key user answer these questions, and then they reconcile differences in their answers; of course, the questionnaire data are no better than the quality of thinking that goes into the answers.

FIGURE 10–1 Effect of Degree of Structure, Company-Relative Technology, and Project Size on Project Implementation Risk

		Low Structure	High Structure
Low Company-Relative Technology	Large Project	Low risk (very susceptible to mismanagement)	Low risk
	Small Project	Very low risk (very susceptible to mismanagement)	Very low risk
High Company-Relative Technology	Large Project	Very high risk	Medium risk
	Small Project	High risk	Medium-low risk

FIGURE 10–2 Comparison of Project Implementation Risk by Degree of Structured and Company-Relative Technology—Examples

	Low Structure	High Structure
Low Company-Relative Technology	Spreadsheet support for budgeting	Inventory control of oil tank farms
High Company-Relative Technology	On-line graphic support for advertising copy	AI-driven bond trading

Size Risk Assessment

Risk Factor			Weight
1. Total development work-hours for system[a]			5
100 to 3,000	Low	1	
3,000 to 15,000	Medium	2	
15,000 to 30,000	Medium	3	
More than 30,000	High	4	
2. Estimated project implementation time			4
12 months or less	Low	1	
13 months to 24 months	Medium	2	
More than 24 months	High	3	
3. Number of departments (other than IT) involved with system			4
One	Low	1	
Two	Medium	2	
Three or more	High	3	

Structure Risk Assessment

Risk Factor			Weight
1. If replacement system is proposed, what percentage of existing functions are replaced on a one-to-one basis?			5
0% to 25%	High	3	
25% to 50%	Medium	2	
50% to 100%	Low	1	
2. What is severity of user-department procedural changes caused by proposed system?			5
Low		1	
Medium		2	
High		3	
3. What is degree of needed user-organization structural change to meet requirements of new system?			5
None		0	
Minimal	Low	1	
Somewhat	Medium	2	
Major	High	3	
4. What is general attitude of user?			5
Poor; against IT solution	High	3	
Fair; sometimes reluctant	Medium	2	
Good; understands value of IT solution		0	
5. How committed is upper-level user management to system?			5
Somewhat reluctant, or unknown	High	3	
Adequate	Medium	2	
Extremely enthusiastic	Low	1	
6. Has a joint IT–user team been established?			5
No	High	3	
Part-time user representative appointed	Low	1	
Full-time user representative appointed		0	

FIGURE 10–3   *(continued)*

Technology Risk Assessment

Risk Factor			Weight
1. Which of the hardware is new to the company?[b]			5
None		0	
CPU	High	3	
Peripheral and/or additional storage	High	3	
Terminals	High	3	
Mini or micro	High	3	
2. Is the system software (nonoperating system) new to IT project team?[b]			5
No		0	
Programming language	High	3	
Database	High	3	
Data communications	High	3	
Other (Please specify)	High	3	
3. How knowledgeable is user in area of IT?			5
First exposure	High	3	
Previous exposure but limited knowledge	Medium	2	
High degree of capability	Low	1	
4. How knowledgeable is user representative in proposed application area?			5
Limited	High	3	
Understands concept but has no experience	Medium	2	
Has been involved in prior implementation efforts	Low	1	
5. How knowledgeable is IT team in proposed application area?			5
Limited	High	3	
Understands concept but has no experience	Medium	2	
Has been involved in prior implementation efforts	Low	1	

Source: This questionnaire is adapted from the "Dallas Tire" case, No. 180-006 (Boston, Mass.: Harvard Business School Case Services, 1980).
Note: Since the questions vary in importance, the company assigned weights to them subjectively. The numerical answer to the questions is multiplied by the question weight to calculate the question's contribution to the project's risk. The numbers are then added to produce a risk score for the project. Projects with risk scores within 10 points of each other are indistinguishable in their relative risk but those separated by 100 points or more are very different in their implementation risk to even the casual observer.
[a]Time to develop includes systems design, programming, testing, and installation.
[b]This question is scored by multiplying the sum of the numbers attached to the positive responses by the weight.

propriate for all companies. Nonetheless, they provide a good starting point—and a number of other companies have used them as such in developing their own instruments for measuring implementation risk.

These questions not only highlight the implementation risks but also suggest alternative ways of conceiving of the project and managing it. If the initial aggregate risk score seems high, analysis of the answers may suggest ways of lessening the risk through reduced scope, lower-level technology, multiple phases, and so on. Thus managers should not consider risk as a static descriptor; rather, its presence should encourage better approaches to project management. Questions 5 and 6 in the "Structured Risk Assessment" section are particularly good examples of questions that could trigger changes.

The higher the assessment score, the greater is the need for corporate approval. Only the executive committee in this company approves very risky projects. Such an approach ensures that top managers are aware of significant hazards and are making appropriate trade-offs between risk and strategic benefits. Managers should ask questions such as these:

1. Are the benefits great enough to offset the risks?
2. Can the affected parts of the organization survive if the project fails?
3. Have the planners considered appropriate alternatives?

Periodically during the undertaking, the questionnaire is used again to reveal any major changes. If these assessments are positive, the risk continuously declines during implementation as the number and size of remaining tasks dwindle and familiarity with the technology grows.

The questionnaire data facilitate a common understanding among senior, IT, and user managers as to a project's relative implementation risk. The "fiascoes" commonly occur when senior managers believe a project has low implementation risk and IT managers know it has high implementation risk. In such cases IT managers may not admit their assessment because they fear that the senior executives will not tolerate this kind of uncertainty in information systems projects and will cancel a project of potential benefit to the organization.

PORTFOLIO RISK

In addition to determining relative risk for single projects, a company should develop a profile of aggregate implementation risk for its portfolio of systems and programming projects. While there is no such thing as a universally appropriate implementation risk profile for all firms, different types of companies and strategies suggest different risk profiles as being appropriate.

For example, in an industry where IT is strategic (such as banking and insurance), managers should be concerned if there are no high-risk projects. Such a cautious stance may be leaving a product or service gap for competition to step into. On the other hand, a portfolio loaded with high-risk projects would suggest that the company may be vulnerable to operational disruptions if projects are not completed as planned. In "support" companies, heavy investment in high-risk projects may not be

TABLE 10–1 Factors that Influence Implementation Risk Profile of Project Portfolio

Factor	Portfolio Risk Focus	
	Low	*High*
Stability of IT development group.	High	Low
Perceived quality of IT development group by insiders.	High	Low
IT critical to delivery of current corporate services.	No	Yes
IT important decision support aid.	No	Yes
Experienced IT systems development group.	Yes	No
Major IT fiascoes in last two years.	No	Yes
New IT management team.	No	Yes
IT perceived critical to delivery of future corporate services.	No	Yes
IT perceived critical to future decision support aids.	No	Yes
Company perceived as backward in use of IT.	No	Yes

appropriate. It is the wrong area for them to take strategic gambles. Often, however, even those companies should have some technologically exciting ventures in order to ensure familiarity with leading-edge technology and maintain staff morale and interest.

These examples suggest that the aggregate implementation risk profiles of the portfolios of two companies could legitimately differ. Table 10–1 lists the issues that influence toward or away from high-risk efforts. (The risk profile should include projects executed by outside software houses as well as those of the internal systems development group.) As the table shows, the aggregate impact of IT on corporate strategy is an important determinant of the appropriate amount of implementation risk to undertake.

Summary

In summary, it is both possible and useful to assess a project's implementation risk at the feasibility study stage. Discussion of risk is helpful to those working on the project and to the department as a whole. Not only can this systematic analysis reduce the number of failures, but equally important, its power as a communication link helps IT managers and senior executives reach agreement on the risks to be taken in relation to corporate goals.

PROJECT MANAGEMENT: A CONTINGENCY APPROACH

Much of the literature and conventional wisdom suggest that there is a single right approach to project management. A similar bias holds that managers should apply an appropriate cluster of tools, project management methods, and organizational linkages uniformly to all such ventures.

While there may indeed be a set of general-purpose tools, the contribution each device can make to planning and controlling the project varies widely according to the project's characteristics. Further, the means of involving the user—through steering committees, representation on the team, or as leader—should also vary by project type. In short there is no universally correct way to run all projects.

Management Tools

The general methods (tools) for managing projects are of four principal types:

- **External integration tools** include organizational and other communication devices that link the project team's work to users at both the managerial and the lower levels.
- **Internal integration devices** ensure that the team operates as an integrated unit. These include a variety of personnel controls.
- **Formal planning tools** help to structure the sequence of tasks in advance and to estimate the time, money, and technical resources the team will need for executing them.
- **Formal results-control mechanisms** help managers to evaluate progress and to spot potential discrepancies so that corrective action can be taken.

Results controls have been particularly effective in the following settings:[1]

1. Where clear knowledge of the desired results exists.
2. Where the desired result can be controlled (at least to some extent by the individuals whose actions are being influenced).
3. Where the controllable result areas can be measured effectively.

Highly structured projects that involve a low degree of technology satisfy these conditions very well. Formal results-control mechanisms

---

[1]Kenneth A. Merchant, *Control in Business Organizations* (Marshfield, Mass.: Pitman Publishing, 1985).

TABLE 10-2   Tools of Project Management

Integration Tools, External	*Integration Tools, Internal*
Selection of user as project manager.	Selection of experienced IT professional to lead team.
Creation of user steering committee.	
Frequent in-depth meetings of user steering committee.	Frequent team meetings.
	Regular preparation and distribution of minutes within team on key design evolution decisions.
User-managed change control process.	
Frequent and detailed distribution of project team minutes to key users.	
Selection of users as team members.	Regular technical status reviews.
Formal user specification approval process.	Managed low turnover of team members.
Progress reports prepared for corporate steering committee.	Selection of high percentage of team members with significant previous work relationships.
User responsibility for education and installation of system.	Participation of team members in goal setting and deadline establishment.
User management decision on key action dates.	Outside technical assistance.

Formal Planning Tools	*Formal Control Tools*
PERT, "critical path," etc.; networking.	Periodic formal status reports versus plan.
Milestone phases selection.	Change control disciplines.
Systems specification standards.	Regular milestone presentation meetings.
Feasibility study specifications.	Deviations from plan, reports.
Project approval processes.	
Project postaudit procedures.	

are very effective in those settings. For low-structured projects which involve a high degree of technology, none of the above conditions apply; consequently results control can make only a limited contribution. In those settings major contributions are derived from internal integration devices (personnel controls).

Table 10-2 gives examples of the types of integration and control tools that are commonly used by companies. The next paragraphs suggest how the degree of structure and the company-relative technology influence the selection of tools.

Influences on Tool Selection

High Structure–Low Technology Projects. Projects that are highly structured and that present familiar technical problems are not only the lower-risk projects but also the easiest to manage (see

Figure 10–1). They are also the least common. High structure implies that the outputs are very well defined by the nature of the task and that the possibility that the users will change their minds about the desired outputs is essentially nonexistent. The project leaders, therefore, do not have to develop extensive administrative processes in order to get a diverse group of users to agree to a design structure and then to stick to their decision. Such external integration devices as inclusion of analysts in user departments, heavy representation of users on the design team, formal approval of the design team by users, and formal approval of design specifications by users are cumbersome and unnecessary for this type of project. Other integrating devices, such as training users how to operate the system, remain important.

The system's concept and design stages, however, are stable. At the same time, since the technology involved is familiar to the company, the project can proceed with a high percentage of persons having only average technical backgrounds and experience. The leader does not need extraordinary IT skills. This type of project readily provides opportunities to the department's junior managers; it can give them experience that they can apply to more ambitious tasks in the future.

With their focus on defining tasks and budgeting resources against them, project life-cycle planning concepts—such as PERT (Program Evaluation and Review Technique) and "critical path"—force the team to develop a thorough and detailed plan (exposing areas of soft thinking in the process). Such projects are likely to meet the resulting milestone dates and keep within the target budget. Moreover, the usual results-control techniques for measuring progress against dates and budgets provide very reliable data for spotting discrepancies and building a desirable tension within the design team to work harder to avoid slippage.

An example of this type of highly structured project is the insurance agents' rate-book project mentioned earlier. A portfolio in which 90 percent of the projects are of this type should produce little unplanned excitement for senior and user managers. It also requires a much more limited set of skills for the IT organization than would be needed for portfolios with a different mixture of project types.

High Structure–High Technology Projects. Vastly more complex than the high structure–low technology projects, these projects involve some significant modifications of practices outlined in project management handbooks. A good example of this type of project is the conversion of one computer manufacturer's systems to those of another where all the code must be rewritten with no enhancements. Another example is the conversion of a set of manual procedures onto a minicomputer with the only objective being performance of the same functions more quickly.

The normal mechanisms for liaison with users are not crucial here; the outputs are so well defined by the nature of the undertaking that both the development of specifications with user inputs and the need to deal with systems changes from users are unimportant aspects of the project. Liaison with users is nevertheless important in two respects: (1) to ensure coordination on any changes in input/output or any other manual procedure changes necessary for project success, and (2) to deal with any systems restructuring that must follow from unexpected shortcomings in the project's technology.

In this kind of project it is common to discover during implementation that the technology is inadequate, which forces a long postponement while new technology is chosen or vital features modified to make the task fit the available technology. In one such situation an industrial products company had to convert some computerized order-entry procedures to a manual basis so that the rest of an integrated materials management system could be shifted to new hardware that had already been purchased.

Such technological shortcomings were the main difficulty faced by the insurance company described at the beginning of the chapter. In such a case, where system performance is much poorer than expected, user involvement is important both to prevent demoralization and to help implement either an alternative approach (less ambitious in selection of technology) or a mutual agreement to end the project.

The skills that lead to success in this type of project, however, are the same as those that make for effective administration of projects involving any kind of technical complexity. The leader needs a strong background in high technology projects (preferably, but not necessarily, in an IT environment) as well as administrative experience. The leader must also be effective in relating to technicians. By talking individually and collectively with the project team members at various times, the ideal manager will come to anticipate difficulties before the technicians understand that they have a problem. In dealing with larger projects in this category, the effective manager must establish and maintain teamwork through meetings, develop a record of all key design decisions, and facilitate subproject conferences as needed.

Project life-cycle planning methods identify tasks and suitable completion dates. Their predictive value is much less here than in the preceding category. The team will not understand key elements of the technology in advance, and consequently seemingly minor bugs in such projects have a curious way of becoming major financial drains.

Roughly once an hour an on-line banking system in one company generated "garbage" across the computer screen. Although simply hitting a release key erased this screen of zeroes and Xs, four months and more than $200,000 were spent eliminating the so-called ghost screen.

The solution lay in uncovering a complex interaction of hardware features, operating system functions, and application traffic patterns. Correction of the problem ultimately required the vendor to redesign several chips. Formal results-control mechanisms have limits in monitoring the progress of such projects, and personnel controls become more important.

In summary, technical leadership and internal integration are the keys in this type of project, and external integration plays a distinctly secondary role. Formal planning and control tools give projections which intrinsically may contain major inaccuracies, and the great danger is that neither IT managers nor high-level executives will recognize this. They may believe they have precise planning and close control when in fact they have neither.

Low Structure–Low Technology Projects. When low structure–low technology projects are intelligently managed they present low risk. Again and again, however, such projects fail because of inadequate direction. (In this respect they differ from the high structure–low technology project, where more ordinary managerial skills could ensure success.) The key to operating this kind of project lies in effective efforts to involve the users.

Developing substantial user support for *only one* of the thousands of design options and keeping the users committed to that design are critical. Essential aspects of this process include:

1. A user as either project leader or the number-two person on the team.
2. A user steering committee to evaluate the design.
3. Efforts to break the project into a sequence of very small, discrete subprojects.
4. Formal user review and approval on all key project specifications.
5. Distribution of minutes of all key design meetings to users.
6. Strong efforts to adhere to the key subproject time schedules. Low managerial and staff turnover in the user areas is vital in this respect, since a consensus on approach with the predecessor of a user manager is of dubious value.

The consumer-products company debacle described at the beginning of the chapter is an example of what can happen when this process does not take place. Soon after work started, under great time pressure, the project manager began reducing his liaison meetings with the key end users. He and his staff were geographically separate from the end users—their buildings were ten miles apart. The vice president of marketing was promoted to another division, being replaced by an individual from elsewhere in the company who had a very different background and different interests. Inadequately tuned into changes in priorities resulting from this move, the project team continued on a course that was inappropriate for the new direction of the company. The changing design made much of the programming obsolete. Tough, pragmatic user leadership throughout the design stages would have made a major difference in the outcome.

The importance of user leadership increases once the design is finalized. At that stage users almost inevitably will state some version of "I have been thinking . . ." Unless the alternatives they suggest are of critical strategic significance to the users (a judgment best made by a responsible, user-oriented project manager), the requests must be diverted and postponed until they can be considered in some formal change process. Unless this control is rigorous (a problem intensified by the near impossibility of distinguishing between the economies of a proposed alternative and those implicit in the original design), users may make change after change, with the project evolving rapidly to a state of permanent deferral, its completion forever six months in the future.

If the project is well integrated with the user departments, the formal planning tools will be very useful in structuring tasks and helping to remove any remaining uncertainty. The target completion dates will be firm as long as the systems target remains fixed. Similarly, the formal results-control devices afford clear insight into progress to date, flagging both advances and slippages. Personnel controls also are vital here. If integration with user departments is weak, for example, excessive reliance on these results controls will produce an entirely unwarranted feeling of confidence. By definition, the problems of technology management are usually less difficult in this type of project than in the high-technology ventures, and a staff with a normal mixture of technical backgrounds should be adequate.

In almost every respect, in fact, effective management of this type of project differs from that of the previous two. The key to success is close, aggressive management of external integration supplemented by formal planning and control tools. Leadership must flow from the user, rather than from the technical side.

Low Structure–High Technology Projects. Because these projects are complex and carry high risk, their leaders need technical experience as well as the ability to communicate with users. The same intensive effort toward external integration needed for low structure–low technology projects is necessary here. Total user commitment to a particular set of design specifications is critical; and again, they must agree to *one* out of the many thousands of options.

Unfortunately, however, an option desirable from the user's perspective may turn out to be infeasible in the selected hardware/software system. In the last several years such situations have occurred, particularly with network designs, and they commonly lead either to significant restructuring of the project or to its elimination. It is clear that users should be well represented at both the policy and the operations levels.

At the same time, technical considerations make strong technical leadership and internal project integration vital. This kind of effort requires the most experienced project leaders, and they need wholehearted support from the users. In approving such a project, managers must decide if it can and should be divided into a series of much smaller subprojects and/or if less innovative technology should be employed.

While formal planning and results-control tools can be useful here, at the early stages they contribute little to reducing overall uncertainty and to highlighting overall problems. The planning tools do allow the manager to structure the sequence of tasks. Unfortunately, in this type of project new tasks crop up with monotonous regularity, and tasks that appear simple and small can suddenly become complex and protracted. Further, unsuspected interdependencies between tasks often become apparent. Time, cost, and resulting technical performance are almost impossible to predict simultaneously. In the *Apollo* moon project, for example, technical performance achievement was key, and cost and time were secondary, which in the private sector is usually unacceptable.

Relative Contribution of Management Tools

Table 10–3 shows the relative contribution that each of the four groups of project management tools makes to maximizing the possibility of project success. It reveals that quite different management styles and

TABLE 10–3 Relative Contribution of Tools to Ensuring Project Success by Project Type

Project Type	Project Description	Contribution			
		External Integration	Internal Integration	Formal Planning	Formal Results Control
I	High structure–low technology, large	Low	Medium	High	High
II	High structure–low technology, small	Low	Low	Medium	High
III	High structure–high technology, large	Low	High	Medium	Medium
IV	High structure–high technology, small	Low	High	Low	Low
V	Low structure–low technology, large	High	Medium	High	High
VI	Low structure–low technology, small	High	Low	Medium	High
VII	Low structure–high technology, large	High	High	Low+	Low+
VIII	Low structure–high technology, small	High	High	Low	Low

approaches are needed for managing the different types of projects effectively. Although the framework could be made more complex by including more dimensions, it would only confirm this primary conclusion.

SUMMARY

The usual corporate handbook on project management, with its single-minded prescriptive approach, fails to deal with the realities of the tasks facing today's managers, particularly those dealing with information technology. The right approach for managing a project flows from the specific characteristics of the project.

Additionally, the need to deal with the corporate culture within which both IT and the project team operate further complicates the project management problem. Use of formal project planning and results-control tools is much more likely to produce successful results in highly formal environments than in ones where the prevailing culture is more personal and informal. Similarly, the selection and effective use of integrating mechanisms is very much a function of the corporate culture. (Too many former IT managers have made the fatal assumption that they were in an ideal position to reform corporate culture!)

The past decade has brought new challenges to IT project management and new insights into the management process. Our conclusions are threefold:

1. We will continue to experience major disappointments as we push into new application areas and technologies. Today, however, the dimensions of implementation risk can be identified in advance, and this information can be considered in the decision process. Inevitably, if all we implement are high-risk projects, we will sometimes fail.
2. The work of the IT development department in aggregate may be thought of as a portfolio in the same way that financial fund managers calculate and manage the risks within their portfolios. The aggregate implementation risk profile of that portfolio is a critical strategic decision.
3. Project management in the IT field is complex and multidimensional. Different types of projects require different clusters of management tools if they are to succeed.

Case 10–1

FRITO-LAY, INC.: A STRATEGIC TRANSITION (A)

In July 1986 a senior executive of Frito-Lay, Inc., explained the company's competitive picture:

> In the food industry, the retailers are slowly becoming more powerful than the manufacturers. As this plays out, it won't be enough just to know our business. We have to know theirs as well. We'll have to own the big brands and the key real estate in the store and generate the most profit for the store owners. The manufacturers who are important to the store will win.
>
> There is no single sustainable competitive advantage in this business. I can't think of a single thing that can't be duplicated. What we try to do is compete with class. We put a good mix of product on the shelves; we out-execute our competition; and we try to be "blue-chip" in every aspect of our business. There's a whole book to be written on the strategic advantage of execution. It's not a few big ideas; it's a whole series of little things that add up to superiority.

Frito-Lay, Inc., a major division of PepsiCo, Inc., posted $2.6 billion in sales in 1985 and earned $224 million in net operating profits. (Exhibit 1 shows financial statistics for PepsiCo's snack food segment.) Under the PepsiCo umbrella, Frito-Lay competed primarily in the salty snack segment of the U.S. snack food business, although it had entered the soft-cookie market with its acquisition of Grandma's Cookies in 1981. Foreign markets were served by PepsiCo's separate international snack division.

Frito-Lay's goal was to sustain real sales growth of 6 percent—twice the rate of the snack food market—and double-digit profit growth. As part of its growth program,

Frito-Lay was preparing to place computers literally in the hands of every salesperson. The company was putting the finishing touches on a data processing infrastructure which would allow it to implement a sales support system using hand-held computers throughout the nation. Charlie Feld, vice president of Management Services,[1] said:

> Beginning in 1987, our sales transactions will be captured by hand-held computers. The mountains of paper that we use today will be gone. There is so much that's positive in this project that everyone wants it. In fact, this will free up the sales force to do what they want to do, and that's *sell.*

Industry and Company Background

The $20 billion snack food market was divided into four main segments: salty snacks, sweet snacks, cookies, and crackers. Salty snacks represented about $3.7 billion in retail sales, and Frito-Lay claimed a 50 percent overall share in 1985. Frito-Lay "owned" the $1 billion corn chip market with a 90 percent share. It had only 28 percent of the $2.5 billion potato chip segment because of intense competition with regional

---

[1]Frito-Lay's information systems and telecommunications organization.

This case was prepared by Research Assistant Jane Linder under the supervision of Assistant Professor Melissa Mead as a basis for class discussion rather than to illustrate either effective or ineffective handling of an administrative problem.

EXHIBIT 1 Selected Financial Data ($ in thousands)

	1985	1984	1983	1982	1981
PepsiCo, Inc., and Subsidiaries					
Net sales	$8,056,662	$7,451,106	$6,899,884	$6,492,380	$6,025,261
Cost of sales and operating expense	7,316,600	6,738,432	6,359,372	5,881,603	5,454,352
Net interest expense	98,996	118,982	121,618	114,409	111,893
Operating income	638,066	593,692	418,894	496,368	459,016
Net income from continuing operations	420,081	275,015	278,292	203,501	268,870
Total assets	$5,861,160	$4,876,404	$4,421,079	$4,005,390	$3,883,057
Return on average shareholder equity (%)[a]	22.0%	18.5%	16.2%	17.6%	18.3%
Employees	150,000	150,000	154,000	133,000	120,000
Frito-Lay/PepsiCo Foods International					
Net sales	$2,847,100	$2,709,200	$2,430,100	$2,323,800	$2,177,900
Operating profit	401,000	393,900	347,700	326,400	298,500
Identifiable assets	$1,487,100	$1,254,500	$1,110,100	$949,500	$945,300

[a]Excluding the effect of unusual credits and charges.

and store brands. The other snack food segments were dominated by large consumer goods firms such as Procter & Gamble, Borden, Nabisco, and General Foods.

In the first half of the 20th century the U.S. snack market was fragmented, with many small, regional competitors. Entrepreneurs Elmer Doolin and Herman Lay started snack food firms in 1932. By the late 1950s, the two firms owned or distributed more than 18 regional brands, including Fritos corn chips, Lay's and Ruffles potato chips, Rold Gold pretzels, and Cheetos cheese snacks. After expanding their operations separately, they joined forces in 1961, set up headquarters in the Dallas, Texas, area, and stepped up their growth plans. By the time PepsiCo acquired the company in 1965, Frito-Lay boasted 46 U.S. plants, more than 150 domestic distribution centers, and a listing on the New York Stock Exchange.[2] In addition to its salty snack foods, the company marketed Mexican specialty foods and other lines of convenience foods. (Exhibit 2 shows a chronology of the brand introductions of Frito-Lay.)

Under PepsiCo's auspices, Frito-Lay continued its geographic expansion and leveraged Herman Lay's renowned store-door delivery system to achieve solid penetration in each new region. (Exhibit 3 explains the system.) The success of this approach was described in *In Search of Excellence:*

> What is striking about Frito is not its brand-management system, which is solid, nor its advertising program, which is well done. What is striking is Frito's nearly 10,000-person sales force and its "99.5 percent service level." In practical terms, what does this mean? It means that Frito will do some things that in the short run clearly are uneconomic. It will spend several hundred dol-

lars sending a truck to restock a store with a couple of $30 cartons of potato chips. . . . There are magic and symbolism about the service call that cannot be quantified. . . . The system succeeds because it supports the route salesman, believes in him, and makes him feel essential to its success. There are about 25,000 employees in the company. Those who are not selling live by the simple dictum, "Service to Sales."[3]

By 1980, six of Frito-Lay's potato and corn chip brands were counted among the top-selling 50 dry grocery brands, with more than $100 million in national retail sales.

Upheaval in 1981

In the fall of 1981, Frito-Lay saw its traditional growth options evaporating. Its geographic expansion had blanketed the nation with 10,000 salespeople. Frito-Lay products were sold in over 300,000 retail outlets across the United States, and there was little new territory to conquer. The company's attempts to introduce major new products had been marginally successful. During the 1970s Frito-Lay had become accustomed to passing inflation-induced cost increases along to customers. When inflation rates declined in 1981, the company found itself with less pricing freedom. While regional competitors had always been a factor, in the early 1980s national competitors began to make inroads in Frito-Lay's territory. Frito-Lay's sales growth slowed from the heady 15 percent to 20 percent of the 1970s to single-digit rates.

Jordan Takes Charge

The year 1983 brought some additional challenges for Frito-Lay. Unexpected manage-

[2]Frito-Lay, Inc., 1964 Annual Report.

[3]Thomas J. Peters and Robert Waterman, *In Search of Excellence* (Harper & Row, 1982), pp. 164–165.

EXHIBIT 2 Product Introduction Chronology

		Number of Route Salespeople
1932	Fritos corn chips (I)	
	Lay's potato chips (I)	
1948	Cheetos cheese snacks (I)	
1958	Ruffles potato chips (I)	
	Ta-Tos potato chips brand acquired by Frito Co.	
1961	Frito-Lay, Incorporated, formed.	2,800
	(Products include Fritos, Doritos, Lay's Potato Chips, Rold Gold Pretzels, Ruffles, Cheetos, and other regional brands.)	
1962	Round Fritos corn chips (I)	
	Consolidated all cheese puffs under Cheetos brand.	
	Consolidated all pretzels under Rold Gold brand.	
	Consolidated all bacon rind to Baken-Ets brand.	
1963	Round Fritos (N)	
1964	F-L acquired NuWay Foods (toppings, jams, desserts) and Belle Products (Towle and Sylvia brands of condiments).	
	Lay's dry-roasted peanuts (N)	
	Austex western-style beans with beef (T)	
	Fritos jalapeno cheese dip (T)	
	(also working on a nontobacco cigarette)	
1965	F-L acquired by PepsiCo in June.	3,200
1966	Doritos (N)	
1967	Fantastix puffed corn meal product with peanut butter and cheddar cheese centers (T)	
	Taco-flavored Doritos (T)	
	(Austex Foods division sold.)	
1968	Fandango corn chips: Buck Board pizza, and Galloping Green onion flavors (T)	
1969	Fandangos (N)	
	Funyons onion-flavored snack (T)	
	Munchos potato crisps (T)	
	Intermission popped corn chips (T)	
1971	Funyons (T)	
1972	Munchos (N)	
	Frenchips potato fries (T)	
	Bacon Nips imitation-bacon-flavored wheat chips (T)	
1973	Single-portion snacks: cheese and crackers, peanuts, beef sticks, beef jerky, oatmeal cookies, fudge brownies (I)	
	Sunchips premium potato chips (I)	
	Lay's sour cream and onion flavored chips (I)	
	Lay's enchilada dip (I)	
1974	Lay's sour cream and onion flavored chips (N)	
	Lay's enchilada dip (N)	
1975	Sunchips potato chips (T)	5,750
	Prontos crunchy grain chips (T)	
1976	Prontos crunchy grain snack (1/2 N)	6,000
	Ruffles barbecue-flavored chips (T)	
	Natural-style potato chips (no additives, foil pack) (T)	
	Natural-style corn chips (T)	

(I) = Introduced   (T) = Test-marketed   (N) = Distributed nationally

EXHIBIT 2 (continued)

		Number of Route Salespeople
1977	Natural-style potato chips (N)	7,000
	Tostitos corn chips (T)	
	Fantastix french-fry-shaped snack with green onion and cheese flavors (T)	
1978	Fantastix (I)	7,200
	Cheetos nacho cheese-flavored chips (N)	
	Doritos sour cream and onion flavored chips	
	Ruffles barbecue-flavored chips (N)	
	Tostitos (traditional and nacho cheese flavored) (T)	
1979	Cheetos as a ball (T)	8,000
	Frito Lights—a lighter, thinner Frito (T)	
	Zambinos—an Italian-style snack (T)	
1980	Tostitos (N)	8,700
	Biddles crispy rice chips (T)	
	Tiffles crispy corn chips (T)	
	(F-L acquired Grandma's Foods)	
1981	(F-L became PepsiCo's largest profit contributor)	>9,000
	Frito Lights (T)	
	Dorito crispy light tortilla chips (T)	
	Tiffles crispy corn chips (T)	
	Ta-Tos potato chips (T)	
	Grandma's single-serve cookies and snack bars (N)	
	New Small's sweet snack products (T)	
1982	Grandma's single-serve cookies (13% N)	
	Doritos Crispy Lights (N)	
	Fritos Lights (N)	
	Ta-Tos potato chips (expanded in Midwest only)	
1983	Grandma's single-serve cookies (1/3 N)	
	New Cheetos flavor	
	O'Grady's thick-cut potato chips (T)	
	Sabritas restaurant-style chips (T)	
	Sunchips corn chips (T)	
	Rich 'N Chewy brand packaged cookies (T)	
1984	O'Grady's potato chips (N)	
	Four new flavors of Frito brand cheese dips (I)	
	"More nacho cheese flavor" Doritos (I)	
	"King-size," crunchier Fritos (I)	
	Cheddar-flavored and sour-cream-flavored Ruffles (T)	
	Rich 'N Chewy brand packaged cookies (I)	
1985	Fritos chili cheese corn chips (I)	9,400
	Doritos Cool Ranch tortilla chips (I)	
	Lay's jalapeno and cheddar potato chips (I)	
	McCracken's apple chips (T)	
	Rumbles bite-sized granola snack nuggets (T)	
	Stuffers filled snacks (T)	
	Santitas restaurant-style tortilla chips (T)	
	Delta Gold premium potato dips (T)	
	Kincaids home-style potato chips (T)	

(I) = Introduced   (T) = Test-marketed   (N) = Distributed nationally

Source: Frito-Lay and PepsiCo Annual Reports.

EXHIBIT 3   Frito-Lay's Store-Door Delivery System

Frito-Lay's sales and distribution activities revolved around its "store-door" delivery system. In the early hours of the morning, salespeople loaded their trucks with snack food products and began their routes. Their job was to call on existing customers and to line up new accounts. They convinced customers to allocate shelf and end-cap space to Frito-Lay products, and they handled regular account maintenance by restocking shelves and removing stale products. They introduced new products to customers and they informed customers of promotions.

Most of the 10,000 salespeople worked from warehouses (that is, a warehouse manager ordered and received product from manufacturing). The salespeople stocked their trucks from the warehouse supply. About 4,000 salespeople operated from "bin locations." These individuals worked in rural areas where the routes were long and geographically dispersed. Rather than setting up warehouses, Frito-Lay shipped product directly to the salesperson's home or designated storage space.

Customers were divided into two types: supermarkets and so-called "up-and-down-the-street" accounts. The supermarkets were predominantly large chains. "Up-and-down-the-street" accounts were small, cash customers. These included everything from 7-Eleven franchises to bowling alleys and laundromats. Most of the 300,000 accounts were serviced twice weekly. Although the time for a sales call varied by the size of the account, a typical "up-and-down-the-street" call could be completed in about 45 minutes, not including transportation time. For small customers, the vast majority of the time was devoted to compiling the customer's order from the truck and placing product on the shelves. Supermarkets ordered in case lots; stocking shelves consumed most of the salesperson's time for these customers. For customers with especially strong sales, the salesperson asked to leave "back-stock." The store personnel would then be able to replenish the shelves between sales calls.

To make the stocking activity more routine and to enable substitute drivers to take over routes for vacation and sickness, the "national pattern" was used. It dictated the arrangement of products on the shelves, with a specific place for each product and package size.

The sales force was compensated with a base salary plus commission. In 1985, merchandisers received $800 per month base pay plus $.05 per bag sold. Route salespeople were paid the same base salary and 5% of the wholesale value of their sales. This compensation structure had been implemented in 1983, as part of the segmentation program. Prior to that, commission had been based on sales dollars regardless of customer type, and had been a larger proportion of the salesperson's total compensation.

---

ment changes at PepsiCo pulled Frito-Lay's president, D. Wayne Calloway, to the parent company's helm. Michael Jordan, then president of PepsiCo Foods International, was moved into the Frito-Lay presidency, and Bill Korn, senior vice president of sales and marketing, was named president of the Wilson Sporting Goods division of PepsiCo.

Feld described Jordan's 18-month tenure as a time of strategic introspection.

> When we saw that the sales growth had slowed, we were surprised. The "machine" that had churned out 18 percent growth year

after year had hiccoughed. We were doing the "right" things, but they weren't working. It didn't take us long to decide to do something about it, though. While Mike Jordan was president, we rethought our strategy and how we should be doing business. The aircraft carrier that we had built had to be refitted as a PT boat.

Although Jordan's tenure was a time of rethinking, he was responsible for two major initiatives: (1) the successful introduction of O'Grady's potato chips, and (2) a major reorganization of the sales force.

Jordan oversaw the introduction of O'Grady's potato chips—a new, $100 million brand. The test-market results for the product were overwhelmingly positive, and the sales force pushed the product into national distribution in a matter of weeks. This pace was uncharacteristic in a company that had traditionally held lengthy market tests for its new products; the O'Grady's introduction became a source of pride throughout the marketing and sales organizations.

Frito-Lay's store-door delivery system was showing some signs of strain, however. Each salesperson was responsible for serving all of the snack outlets on his or her route—both grocery stores and so-called "up-and-down-the-street" accounts. Because compensation was based on sales dollar volume, the salespeople had strong incentive to focus on the high-volume grocery outlets. One salesperson remarked that "some of the guys were making $40,000 or more in those days. There was a three-month waiting list to get a job at Frito-Lay back then."

Management decided to reorganize the sales force with a program called "segmentation." Under this plan, the sales force was divided into two groups: route and supermarket. The duties of both groups were similar, but the compensation plan differed. The route drivers' commissions continued to be based on sales dollar volume. The supermarket merchandisers, on the other hand, were paid 5¢ per bag sold, regardless of its unit price. Account managers were named to supervise the supermarket merchandisers and to deal at a professional level with supermarket purchasing staff. The account manager negotiated shelf space and promotional allowances, while the merchandiser delivered and shelved the product and removed stale packages. Management explained:

> This action allows one segment of the Frito-Lay sales force to focus as never before on supermarkets—the largest and fastest-growing distribution channel. Meanwhile,

other members of the route sales force can concentrate on more complete coverage of the smaller route customer channel.

The intent of the program was to focus attention on both kinds of distribution channels while establishing parity in the route salespeople's and merchandisers' compensation. As it was implemented, however, segmentation reduced the take-home pay of most of the sales force. To soften the impact, the company promised to "make up the difference" for a year and to give partial payments for two additional years.

The new supermarket routes had different appeal in different parts of the country. In the Southwest, where Frito-Lay held an 80 percent share of the salty snack market, experienced salespeople asked for the merchandiser positions. In regions where the company had to struggle for shelf space, drivers with seniority grabbed the convenience routes. In the words of one, "What I like about this job is the people. Why should I trade my route for a day full of bickering with supermarket receivers? They couldn't pay me enough to do that." Another route salesperson commented, "Segmentation was a disaster. When it first came out, they sent around a human relations guy to talk to us about it. He said he would hold meetings every quarter to help us work out the bugs. He got such an earful of problems at the first meeting, he never came back." A salesperson in another part of the country remarked, "Several guys walked off the job right then. I didn't because I couldn't match my pay anywhere else. If I could, I'd leave tomorrow." A supervisor added, "They talk about 'Service to Sales,' but a program like segmentation tells us what they really think of us."

Despite implementation difficulties, management persevered with the segmentation program. They used the sales force turnover as an opportunity to hire more college-educated salespeople and to fine-tune the route structure.

1985 — A New President

Just 18 months after Calloway's promotion, Jordan joined him as chief financial officer at PepsiCo, and Korn was called back from Wilson Sporting Goods[4] to assume the Frito-Lay presidency. In a speech to securities analysts, Korn articulated two goals for the company: (1) to sustain at least 6 percent real sales growth, and (2) to achieve double-digit profit growth. He outlined several key strategies for accomplishing this:

- Mount a marketing and sales offensive to build volume and share in the seven established brands that accounted for 80 percent of the current sales and profits.[5]
- Leverage the competitive strength of the store-door delivery system through segmentation.
- Improve productivity by pushing the technical limits of the production system and through research and development.
- Expand through new product development, both in flavor extensions of existing lines and in new snack categories.

Korn extended the segmentation concept up through the field sales organization to the level of the vice president of field sales (Exhibit 4). The program was also expanded to encompass more of the sales force. By 1986, 6,000 of the 10,000 salespeople were operating under segmentation. The remaining 4,000 worked in rural areas where segmentation was not feasible.

The company also moved ahead with an unprecedented stream of new product introductions. Dori Reap, director of planning, said, "New products are the biggest new news for Frito-Lay in 1986. With real growth in the salty snack market of only 3 percent to 4 percent, new products are a new avenue toward reaching our growth goals." The company had almost 100 products in 1985 and intended to expand its line to 400 items by 1990. Feld said, "We can't wait for only the $100 million brands to achieve our goals. We'll have to have the $20 million and $30 million brands in addition to make it." Management was especially interested in pursuing new snack categories that might bring opportunities for additional shelf space.

In addition to larger numbers of new products, management sought faster introductions. Bill Elston, vice president of manufacturing, remarked:

> I hear that Procter & Gamble sometimes takes 15 years to develop and test-market a product. A three- or four-year cycle has been normal for us. Management asked us to push "hat trick"[6] from the bench to full-scale production in fourteen months. We made a significant investment in manufacturing facilities before we had any firm test-market results.

The investment in new manufacturing facilities was consistent with the company's efforts to improve productivity. Out of 40 plants, 25 were "core mixing plants." These focused on the high-volume brands such as Doritos, Fritos, and all potato chips. Elston explained:

> The impact of product proliferation is that we could have more limited and single-focus facilities. Running new products into existing plants is disruptive. Frito-Lay has the kind of volumes that let us build single-focus plants; it's a competitive advantage for us.

---

[4]Wilson Sporting Goods, Inc., was divested in 1985.

[5]Ruffles, Lay's, O'Grady's, Fritos, Doritos, Tostitos, and Cheetos brands. These products were all among the top 50 grocery brands—each gaining more than $100 million in 1985 *retail* sales.

[6]The simultaneous introduction of three new products: Stuffers, Rumbles, and Toppels (the "hat trick" phrase refers to a single player scoring three goals in a single hockey game—a rare occurrence).

EXHIBIT 4　Organization Structure, 1986

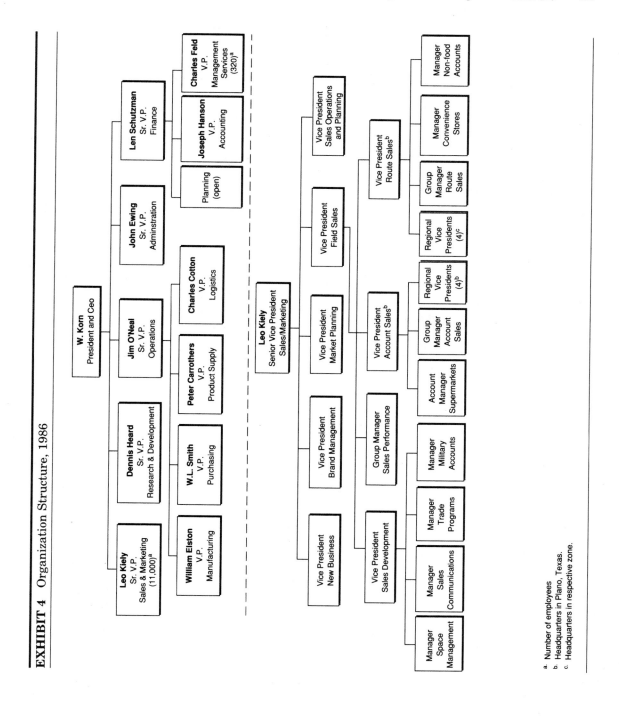

a. Number of employees
b. Headquarters in Plano, Texas.
c. Headquarters in respective zone.

Feld recapped the company's transition:

From 1968 through 1981, we enjoyed 15 percent to 20 percent annual revenue growth through geographic expansion, premium pricing, and major new products. We added two or three hundred new sales routes a year, and it was all incremental business. In those days, we were capacity-constrained; we just couldn't build plants quickly enough. By 1981, we had built manufacturing into an awesome machine, but all of a sudden the marketplace changed and we had excess capacity. We needed a new configuration of the company—not growth through pricing and geographic expansion but through higher-risk new products and sales productivity in our existing geography. The concept was certainly right, but the linkage between the strategies and the execution takes time. It's as if you had to get your championship football team to play basketball. You look around and find you have a lot of big guys still wearing helmets. Fortunately we're coming out of it now. Our spirit will carry us through.

The Hand-Held Computer Project

As part of the transition, one of management's major initiatives was the hand-held computer (HHC) project. This project involved giving each salesperson a computer to automate the sales process. The salesperson entered order information into the HHC; it automatically priced and printed the order and recorded the transaction for later sales reporting. At the end of the day, the salesperson plugged his or her HHC into a minicomputer in the warehouse. The day's transactions were transmitted automatically to headquarters for processing. (Exhibit 5 describes the salesperson's typical duties with and without the computer, and Exhibit 6 shows the computer itself.)

Monte Jones, director of sales systems development, described the birth of the project:

A few of us rallied around the concept of a "model division." We wanted to create the ideal sales organization. Our idea was to experiment—to change the sales organization, the compensation, and add in the hand-held computer—to see what could happen. Unfortunately, the organizational things became dissociated from the computer. Segmentation was implemented; compensation was changed; but no one really supported the hand-held computer. It was a whisper campaign in the beginning.

Korn remembered his early involvement: "I go way back with this idea—the project started in Sales in 1978. We were the first with the idea, but at the time, the technology just didn't exist." Frito-Lay found that the large computer companies were not interested in the hand-held computer business. To begin building their experience, the Frito-Lay people found a small supplier to work with them.

Korn continued: "I remember the infamous Balch Springs [Texas] shakedown test where we had to find out if we even had equipment that worked." The Frito-Lay sales environment was not especially hospitable. The HHC devices had to be dependable in spite of dust, spilled coffee, and extreme temperatures. The temperature inside the route trucks ranged from 120° F in the Texas summer to −30° F in the Minnesota winter.

A manager who was involved in the project described varying levels of executive support: "Calloway was not enthusiastic about the project originally. He wasn't sold. Jordan thought it was a good idea but that there was no pressing need. The project wasn't pushed, but it wasn't killed, either." To get some momentum, the project's supporters wanted to use an entire sales division as a proving ground for the benefits. A smaller pilot test was authorized. Despite general skepticism about quantifying the impact, they felt certain that a pilot would enable them to justify the expenditures. Korn recalled, "When I went off to Wilson

EXHIBIT 5   The Hand-Held Computer

The hand-held computer was designed to be easy to use. Its keypad was simple, with only numbers and large "yes" and "no" keys. For each product category—large bags of chips, small bags of chips, crackers, and cookies, etc.—the salesperson was led through a product list. He or she could enter a quantity, or simply press "no" to move on to the next item. As far as the salesperson was concerned, products and prices, including promotional discounts, were "inside the computer." (Changes were downloaded to the computers from Management Services during the third shift.) When not in use, the computer recharged in a cradle beside the printer in the truck. At the time national rollout began, the hand-held computers had 256K memory—the equivalent of that found in most standard personal computers. This was expected to increase to 512K, giving the hand-held greater capacity to support more sophisticated programs.

Servicing a Typical Small Account

Without Computer	*With Computer*
5:00 a.m. Warehouse:	
Salesperson checks route book for standard customer order quantities.	Same.
Picks product and loads truck.	Same.
Fills out consignment order form.	Enters consignment order into computer. At this time, price changes and new programs could be downloaded to the HHC from the DC minicomputer.
6:00 a.m. On the Route—For Each Store:	
Checks shelves and removes stales.	Same.
Fills out sales ticket (Exhibit 7).	Enters order quantity in computer.
Compiles order from stock on truck.	Printer prints pick list. Salesperson compiles order from stock on truck.
Checks in with store receiver.[a]	Same.
Enters stales as credits on sales tickets.	Enters stales in computer.
Puts product on shelves.	Same.
Calculates total order price, applying promotional prices where necessary.	"Confirms" order on the computer. Printer produces sales ticket (Exhibit 7).
Collects order price, usually in cash, from store manager.	Same.
4:00 p.m. At the Warehouse:	
Turns in sales tickets and fills out "end-of-day" report.	Uploads day's data to corporate computer.
Paperwork sent to sales administration for scanning.	
6:00 p.m. At Home:	
Reviews sales tickets to make sure calculations were correct.	

[a]The check-in process involved the salesperson counting all of the items in the order in front of the store receiver. This ensured that the salesperson had delivered exactly what was shown on the order.

445

EXHIBIT 6   On-Truck Equipment for Hand-Held Computer

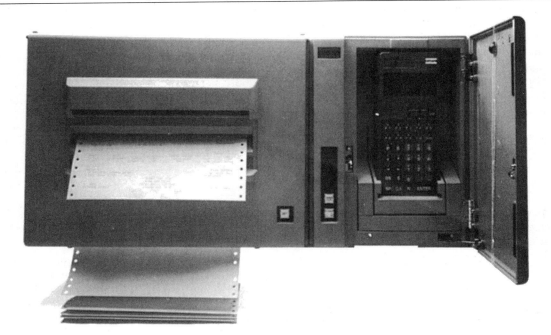

[Sporting Goods, Inc.], a small group of people were working on the project."

Korn continued:

> In the 18 months I was gone, the project lost some of its advocacy. No one believed we could sell it, and by the time I got back, the hand-held computer project was stalled. Within a week after that, I was meeting with sales and marketing people to try to light the fire again. It didn't take long, because it's a natural.
>
> What we're trying to do here is get rid of the things that keep the salespeople from doing their jobs. The people who like to sell aren't the same people who like to count. We have been asking our salespeople to spend one or two hours every day filling out forms and calculating numbers. It seems to me that we can provide some help for them. If we're not working on something that helps the field, we're not working on something important.

Project Costs and Benefits

In early 1985, a capital appropriation request (CAR) was prepared to secure funding for nationwide HHC implementation. In addition to savings from clerical headcount, forms, and postage, the CAR noted: "The effective use of the HHC is expected to result in 2½ hours per route per week of time saved pricing the tickets and completing end-of-day paperwork. Sales management is committed to using this time to drive an additional $20 million in annual sales to cover [the increase in] operating costs."

Jones summarized the project's cost/benefit justification:

> It costs us $12 million per year to run our current system. With the hand-held computer, the annual operating costs will increase by only $3 million. The differential is a small price to pay, considering the long-term strategic benefits we expect to achieve.

Jones described four areas in which benefits were anticipated:

- Information for trade development (detailed sales information for negotiating shelf-space allocation).
- Control accounting (solving the "over/short problem" with the sales force).
- Correct ordering (sales unit data for the 35,000 supermarket customers were available, but there was no unit information for the cash accounts).
- Promotion planning and analysis (determining which marketing tool drives volume best—advertising, coupons, or trade allowances).

One of the most compelling benefits of the project was that it replaced the existing sales transaction processing system. Because each of Frito-Lay's retail customers was serviced on an average of twice a week, the sales transaction volume was huge. With the product list growing, transactions were also becoming more and more complex. Each sales transaction for a charge customer now required two tickets reflecting approximately 200 line items, and these were in addition to end-of-day and ordering paperwork (see Exhibit 7). Further, the complexity increased geometrically when special promotions were applied (see Exhibit 8 for typical promotion program).

To capture the transactions, Frito-Lay had installed optical scanners in 1974. Feld estimated:

> It would take 1,200 or 1,300 keypunch operators to handle our current transaction volume. We do it with 5 scanners and 40 correction operators. The bad news is that IBM has stopped manufacturing the scanners. By 1988, we won't be able to get them repaired. We knew we needed an alternative, and the hand-held computer is it.

The scanners processed 1.7 million documents per 4-week period. This transaction volume included sales tickets for all charge customers, salespeople's orders, and daily

EXHIBIT 7 Sales Transaction Paperwork

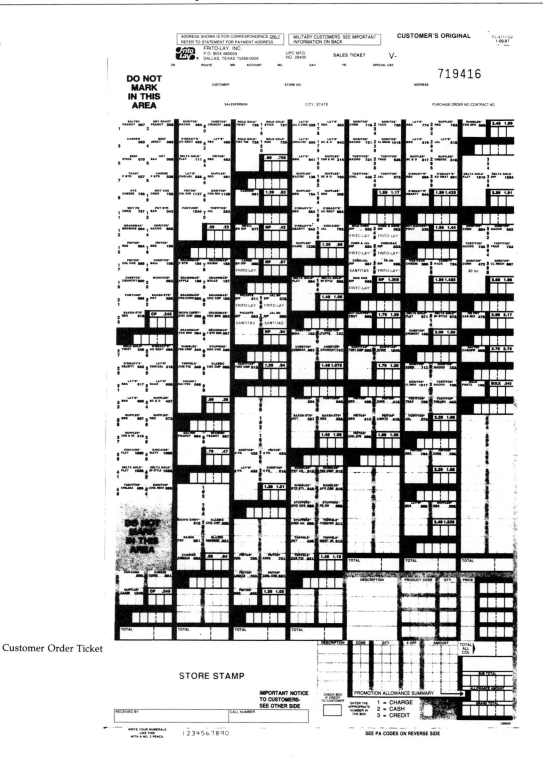

Customer Order Ticket

EXHIBIT 7 (continued)

841

841

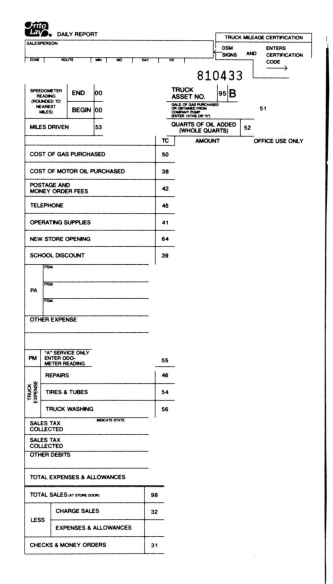

Daily Expense Report

EXHIBIT 8 Typical Frito-Lay Promotion Program, 1986

RETAILER PROMOTION PROGRAM
1986 WINTER TRADE EVENTS

○ KEY PAY PERIODS	1st PERIOD							2nd PERIOD							3rd PERIOD						
• HOLIDAY	NEW YEAR'S DAY							VALENTINE'S DAY							ST. PATRICK'S DAY						
• SUGGESTED RETAIL PRICE	S	M	T	W	T	F	S	S	M	T	W	T	F	S	S	M	T	W	T	F	S
	DEC. 29	30	31	①	2	3	4	JAN. 26	27	28	29	30	31	①	FEB. 23	24	25	26	27	28	①
	JAN. 5	6	7	8	9	10	11	FEB. 2	3	4	5	6	7	8	MAR. 2	3	4	5	6	7	8
	12	13	14	⑮	16	17	18	9	10	11	12	13	⑭	15	9	10	11	12	13	14	15
	19	20	21	22	23	24	25	16	17	18	19	20	21	22	16	17	18	19	20	21	22

PROMOTED PRODUCTS	PER UNIT DISPLAY ALLOWANCE ▼		TIMING
• .99¢ ROLD GOLD® Brand Pretzels—All Types	26¢		Two weeks from January 5 thru January 18, 1986.
• 1.59¢ DORITOS® Brand Tortilla Chips—All Types	12¢	OR	
• 2.19¢ DORITOS® Brand Tortilla Chips—All Types	16¢	OR	Two weeks from January 12 thru January 25, 1986.
• 2.59¢ DORITOS® Brand Tortilla Chips—Nacho	25¢		
N.P. FRITO-LAY'S® Brand Can Dips—9 oz. or larger—All Types	Non-Allowance Tie-in Promotion		
• 1.49¢ O'GRADYS™ Brand Potato Chips—All Types	14¢	OR	Any two consecutive weeks from January 26 thru February 22, 1986.
• 2.09¢ O'GRADYS® Brand Potato Chips—All Types	25¢		
• 1.39¢ FRITOS® Brand Corn Chips—All Types	10¢	OR	Any two consecutive weeks from January 26 thru February 22, 1986.
• 1.79¢ FRITOS® Brand Corn Chips—All Types	13¢		
• 1.39¢ LAY'S® Brand Potato Chips—All Types	13¢	OR	
• 2.49¢ LAY'S® Brand Potato Chips—Regular	25¢		
• 1.79¢ SANTITAS® Brand Restaurant Style Tortilla Chips	20¢		Two weeks from February 23 thru March 8, 1986.
• .99¢ ROLD GOLD® Brand Pretzels—All Types	10¢		Any two consecutive weeks from February 23 thru March 22, 1986.
• 1.39¢ RUFFLES® Brand Potato Chips—All Types	13¢	OR	
• 2.49¢ RUFFLES® Brand Potato Chips—Regular	22¢		

PERFORMANCE REQUIREMENTS FOR THE RETAILER PROMOTION PROGRAM

To qualify for the per unit display allowance, the retailer agrees to meet the following requirement:
SPECIAL DISPLAY: Maintain a secondary display of the promoted product(s), that is separate and apart from the primary Frito-Lay Section, for the duration of the promotion period. The per unit display allowance will be paid off-invoice on a store-by-store basis and only during the time that the special display is maintained — but not to exceed two consecutive weeks within the promotion time period. There are Merchandising and Advertising Program Options available for your use with details provided by your Frito-Lay Sales Representative.

1-86-21 • ACCOUNT SALES • NEW ENGLAND DIVISION • NEW YORK DIVISION and BOSTON DIVISION
ROUTE SALES • NEW YORK DIVISION and BOSTON DIVISION

PROMOTION OPTION PROGRAM
1986 WINTER TRADE EVENTS

NOTICE TO RETAILER:
Participation in the **PROMOTION OPTION PROGRAM** requires the following:
1. It is in lieu of the corresponding **Retailer Promotion Program** offer.
2. The retailer may participate in either program and may switch programs from one event to the next.

PROMOTED PRODUCTS	PER UNIT DISPLAY ALLOWANCE	TIMING
Event #1		
• 1.59¢ DORITOS® Brand Tortilla Chips—All Types		
OR		
• 2.19¢ DORITOS® Brand Tortilla Chips—All Types	10%	Any two consecutive weeks from January 5 thru January 25, 1986.
OR		
• 2.59¢ DORITOS® Brand Tortilla Chips—Nacho		
Event #2		
• 1.39¢ FRITOS® Brand Corn Chips—All Types		
OR		
• 2.19¢ FRITOS® Brand Corn Chips—All Types	10%	Any two consecutive weeks from January 26 thru February 22, 1986.
• 1.49¢ O'GRADYS™ Brand Potato Chips—All Types	10%	
Event #3		
• 1.59¢ DORITOS® Brand Tortilla Chips—All Types		
OR		
• 2.19¢ DORITOS® Brand Tortilla Chips—All Types	10%	Any two consecutive weeks from February 23 thru March 22, 1986.
OR		
• 2.59¢ DORITOS® Brand Tortilla Chips—Nacho		

PERFORMANCE REQUIREMENTS FOR THE PROMOTION OPTION PROGRAM

To qualify for the 10% off-invoice display allowance, the retailer agrees to meet the following requirement:
SPECIAL DISPLAY: Maintain a secondary display of the promoted product(s), that is separate and apart from the primary Frito-Lay Section, for the duration of the promotion period. The per unit display allowance will be paid off-invoice on a store-by-store basis and only during the time that the special display is maintained — but not to exceed two consecutive weeks within the promotion time period. There are Merchandising and Advertising Program Options available for your use with details provided by your Frito-Lay Sales Representative.

NOTICE TO OUR CUSTOMERS: Frito-Lay Inc. endeavors to offer varied promotion programs which are practical and useable by all retailers regardless of size in the programs described in this brochure are not practical or useable by you, please call or write Trade Promotions Calendar Manager Frito-Lay, Inc. P.O. Box 660634, Dallas, Texas 75266-0634, (214) 351-7000. If either party desires to bring action against the other party for any breach of a promotion, the time within which the action shall be commenced shall be one year after the delivery of merchandise under the promotion. These promotional offers are expressly limited to the retailer's acceptance of this reduced statute of limitations period.

450

activity reports. It did not include detailed sales information about the cash customers. Each salesperson summarized the cash transactions on one line of his or her daily report, as shown in Exhibit 7. (The cash-paying up-and-down-the-street customers—everything from "mom-and-pop" food stores to laundromats and bowling alleys—represented about 25 percent of Frito-Lay's revenue and about 80 percent of its accounts, according to Feld.)

A second major benefit of the project accrued to the salespeople. Through pilot efforts in Mesquite, Texas, and in Minneapolis, Management Services had documented efficiency improvements of at least a half hour per day for each driver. Furthermore, because each salesperson "bought" the contents of his or her truck each morning, accounting errors were charged directly to take-home pay. In 1985, out-of-balance was $4 million nationwide and growing. This was a source of extreme frustration for salespeople and sales management. It was not uncommon for a salesperson to be disputing up to $500 with the corporate sales service personnel. After implementation of the pilot, a salesperson in Mesquite, Texas, commented:

> The sales calls go faster, the end-of-day process is a snap, and my wife and I don't have to spend an hour every night going over the paperwork to make sure I did all the multiplication right. When we have problems with the hand-held computers, no one wants to tell headquarters, for fear they might take them away from us!

A third major benefit was anticipated in marketing effectiveness. Under the pressure of increased competition, the marketing organization had begun to talk about "micromarketing." During the heydays of geographic expansion, the sales force had relied on corporate headquarters to direct both trade- and consumer-level advertising and promotion. The so-called national pattern dictated the exact layout of products on the retailers' shelves. Under the micro-marketing concept, each store could conceivably be treated as a separate marketplace. The product line, promotional strategy, and even pricing arrangements could be tailored to optimize the relationship. Leo Kiely, senior vice president of sales and marketing, said:

> We're trying to move away from the rigid rules of the national pattern and the "must carry" lists. It is a sledgehammer approach. With regionalization and micro-marketing, we can increase sales by 10 percent to 15 percent without adding any new outlets. The hand-held computer is essential: it's the only way we will be able to get our hands around all the data.

Kiely was describing a new approach to trade development. Because of the high margins and turns in snack food, this product category was a very profitable use of shelf space for the store owner. One manager explained: "Adding four feet of shelf space in dog food gets you $500 a month in additional sales. In snack food, that number is $4,000 a month. Unfortunately, there's a limit to how much real estate a store can devote to snacks." With a dynamic or regionally optimized product mix, management believed it could move more product through its existing shelf space and make more money for both the customer and Frito-Lay. This concept hinged on having line item-level sales information by customer. Kiely described this as

> massive upgrading of our sales effectiveness. Forty percent of our sales calls—twenty-five percent of our dollar revenues—deal with cash accounts. We don't have any detailed information about these customers. Our assumption has been that the driver knows the best product mix for each store. With the hand-held computer, we'll change from an

implicit sales process to an explicit one. It's the only way we'll be able to get the most out of our expanding line of products. As we learn how to use the computer, we'll learn new ways to do business.

A senior executive said:

The hand-held computer is a shot in the arm for the sales organization. It's big and symbolic—they'll have the best tools in the industry. It lets them know that we're willing to support them to the hilt.

In addition, it gives us access to information that we've never had before. We'll be in a better position than the retailers to squeeze all the air out of our shelf space. It will allow us to "out-execute" our competitors. The value of the information is incalculable. It's as important as anything we're working on. If the lawyers would let me, I would trade patent protection for four or five projects like this one.

Implementation

The HHC implementation was divided into six related efforts. These were coordinated by Monte Jones and Charlie Feld.

1. **Fleet and facilities.** Trucks were wired and racks were installed to accept the HHC hardware. This was done in concert with normal truck maintenance. Minicomputers were installed in the major distribution centers (DCs). Local Sales Operations personnel managed these activities.
2. **Communications.** Communications networks and software were installed to link the DC minicomputer with the host computer in Dallas.
3. **Host software.** Accounting, sales, distribution, and HHC support software was developed or adapted from existing systems.
4. **HHC hardware/software.** An HHC vendor was selected and the HHC software was developed and field tested.
5. **New management processes.** Preparations were made to train field sales man-

agement to use the new reports that would be available.
6. **Training/field rollout.** The sales training function in Employee Relations was asked to prepare a training program to include field sales management, sales operations, merchandisers, and route salespeople. To accomplish the training, a "train-the-trainer" approach was planned. In addition, an HHC and a self-study program was to be made available to salespeople two weeks prior to the formal training.

In August 1986, the Management Services group was pressing to finish the "back-end" systems that would receive and process the data generated by the hand-held computers. Feld remarked:

The users went from "You're crazy!" to "It may be interesting," to "You're standing in my way!!!" as the business changed. We have one heck of a lot of work to do in the next few months to be ready to start the national roll-out. It's not just putting the computers out there; it's making sure all the systems back here tie together too. We've had to develop or revise 900 COBOL[7] programs. Out of 120 people working on systems development in the company, 45 are devoted to the hand-held project.

"This is only the 'core' layer of the project," Feld explained—"the things we absolutely have to do to make the hand-held work." Feld described three layers of development and enhancement work. The first "core" layer contained absolutely essential systems to support the hand-held computer. Layer two represented very important systems, such as sales compensation systems. Management Services planned to complete this

---

[7]COBOL is the language in which most mainframe, transaction-oriented applications are written. It tends to conserve machine resources, not necessarily programmer time.

development over the 10- to 14-month national rollout period. Layer three (a third layer of application systems) had been identified, but was not specifically planned or funded. Kiely explained that they intended to develop more detailed plans for level three systems the next year.

> We will put a couple of prime movers against the problem—full-time, director-level people. They'll ask themselves, "If I were regional marketing manager in Boston, what would I do differently?" and "If I were a district manager, how would I use the data?" Then they'll figure out the answers.

Building Infrastructure

Feld explained that he had few concerns about the ability of his systems development and technology support organizations to handle the project. "It's big for us. We may be a little late, but we'll pull it off." He was not as confident about his operations infrastructure:

> The data center[8] is still a question mark. But we have made great progress in preparation. Most of the sales guys don't understand the magnitude of the job we have to do in Management Services to pull this off—nor is it important that they do. We can't manhandle the volumes of data we're expecting; we have to put in a solid, reliable infrastructure.

Feld had invested $1.2 million to upgrade the data center facilities to prepare for the national rollout. Both processing and storage capacities were increased, and the telecommunications network was expanded significantly. One visible symbol of the change was an operations hub that some likened to the bridge of the starship *Enterprise*.[9]

---

[8]The corporate facility that housed the company's mainframe computers and telecommunications hub.

[9]The intergalactic vessel featured in the "Star Trek" television series and films.

Perhaps more important than the facilities changes was Feld's rebuilding of the staff, structure, and climate at the data center by personally managing that part of his organization for six months. Feld said:

> We now have programmer/analysts *asking* for positions in the data center. Last year, they would have considered that like moving to Siberia. The kind of upgrading we needed was a big deal, but we have put the right amount of muscle behind it.

Feld emphasized, however, that the project was not yet in hand:

> The hand-held project is like an airline reservation system. The day we go live will be the first real test of its soundness. The stakes are very high. If it doesn't work with precision, it could be a disaster.
>
> If everything goes well, we begin rolling out hundreds of hand-held computers per month beginning in February 1987. We still have to train all the warehouse operations managers; they will both train and support the route salespeople. Accounting systems will be integrated; the data will flow.

Looking to the Future

A senior executive assessed the company's interest in the project in terms of market power:

> Theoretically, the supermarkets have better information than we do. Through their scanners and direct product profitability programs, they should be able to tell exactly how much each product is earning for them. The truth is that they don't have this information yet, but it's only a matter of time. As they consolidate and get more sophisticated, they will learn how to make use of the scanner data. We don't want to be on the back end of that wave.

Reap indicated that Frito-Lay had been investing heavily in manufacturing and research activities for several years and that

PepsiCo expected the division to begin to capture the promised returns. Reap noted:

> We've been in the investment-spending mode for the past few years. At this point, productivity is at the top of our list of priorities. The hand-held computer project was based on sound economic criteria. The softer benefits were added-value.

Elson predicted that the long-term impact of the hand-held computer on manufacturing would be sizable:

> When we are running at capacity, we are clearly the least-cost producer. We have purchasing and manufacturing economies of scale, and we are working on automating our core plants even more fully. You have to understand our logistics to appreciate why this is important. Our plants work on a three-day cycle; we receive mix changes as little as 24 hours in advance. The warehouses keep only one and a half days in inventory because the products are perishable.[10] You have only 21 days to sell the product, so the longer it sits in our warehouse or in sales facilities, the more likely it is to become stale. Promotions make our scheduling problems even tougher. Sales orders for promoted items can blow up by 40 percent or 50 percent almost overnight. Anything that helps us schedule better or squeeze time out of our product flow means savings. We expect the hand-held computer to eventually give us more lead time in manufacturing so we can work toward longer runs and "just-in-time" logistics. We're already moving in this direction with experiments in

direct sales delivery. By shipping orders directly to supermarkets from the factory, we bypass two inventory locations and give the customer better service. We drop the product off at the store's dock, and our merchandiser takes over from there.

Frito-Lay was experiencing competitive pressure that was unprecedented in its history. Formidable marketing firms such as Procter & Gamble and Anheuser-Busch were making inroads into Frito-Lay's territory. As the company framed new offensives to achieve its growth goals, it focused on innovations. A senior executive highlighted the hand-held computer's contribution in this regard:

> If we put a statistical weighing machine on each chip line, we will get a 30 percent ROI, without question. But it doesn't *enable* anything. A hand-held computer in the salesperson's hands is entirely different. The future is wide open; it's a mosaic without boundaries. We can't even envision all the ways we will use the information that we're going to collect. All I know is that the closer we get to national rollout, the better the project looks.

Feld worried, however, that expectations around the hand-held computer project had risen to unrealistic levels.

> Some people think the hand-held will cure cancer and eliminate the national debt. I have had to sell it hard enough to make it happen, but I've tried not to create expectations beyond reality. This has been a difficult balancing act.

---

[10]Frito-Lay potato and corn chips contain no preservatives.

Case 10–2

H.E. BUTT GROCERY COMPANY

In May 1990, Gary Shipley had just completed a satellite investment proposal for a meeting with H.E. Butt Grocery Company's (H-E-B) Operating Committee. As manager of voice and data communications, he was requesting approval to develop a satellite network, which would replace virtually all dedicated and dial-up data lines in the company. The Operating Committee would need to commit $4 million to this project, which represented a new technology for the company and involved a greater degree of ownership and responsibility than previous communication systems.

Company Background

H-E-B began as a family-owned and -operated grocery store in 1905 and expanded to become the largest supermarket chain in south Texas by 1990. Headquartered in San Antonio, H-E-B had successfully resisted attempts by large national chains to capture a strong market position in the region during the 1970s and early 1980s. During price wars started by these new entrants, H-E-B reduced operating costs, matched their prices, and dramatically improved facilities by building new stores and remodeling older stores. As a result, H-E-B actually gained sales during the battle, and retained a leading position in its primary markets.

In the 1980s, expansion continued both geographically and in scope of product offerings. The scope of the stores increased with the introduction of Pharmacy, Photo, Video Rental, Deli, Bakery, and Specialty Meats departments within the supermarket. The size of the stores also increased as many new products were added to the shelves in response to manufacturer product line extensions and increasing customer sophistication. By 1990, H-E-B owned and operated 154 supermarkets, 29 stand-alone video rental stores, 14 Pantry Foods stores (a small, low-cost, narrow product-line store), and several H-E-B-brand food-processing facilities.

With a strong culture and a proven ability to compete effectively, H-E-B was looking for additional opportunities to reduce costs and improve margins. Margins were in the 1 percent to 3 percent range for after-tax return on sales, a range typical of the industry. Senior management, believing these margins could be increased without increasing prices, planned to increase activity in areas, such as information systems, that would reduce costs or increase market share.

Logistics and Information Systems

In the late 1970s, H-E-B installed a computerized warehouse management and inventory control system to reduce costs and improve delivery response times. With this automated system, store ordering to delivery time decreased from more than 24 hours to less than 12 hours, which in turn reduced store stockouts and allowed lower inventory levels in the store. Of course, with lower

Doctoral student Theodore H. Clark prepared this case under the supervision of Professor James L. McKenney as the basis for class discussion rather than to illustrate either effective or ineffective handling of an administrative situation.

costs of supply and storage came an increased dependence by the company on the information systems supporting the new process.

Expanding product offerings through the 1980s complicated the store supply problem and further increased demands on the logistics systems. The number of separate items, or SKUs, offered in an average H-E-B store increased from about 30,000 in 1980 to 55,000 in 1990. Also, average revenue per store tripled as store size increased dramatically during this decade. In spite of increasing SKUs and sales, the number of truck deliveries from the warehouse to the store increased only from about 18 per week in the early 1980s to 29 per week in 1990. During this time, costs of warehousing and transportation were reduced by more than 30 percent as a percent of sales. Although information systems were an important driver of this improvement, equally important was close attention to details and a culture obsessed with reducing costs.

Logistics systems at H-E-B in 1990 were believed to be among the best in the industry, but they still required significant manual labor and management judgment. This need was especially true for the store ordering process. There were two ways an order could be entered into the logistics systems for scheduled store deliveries. The first method replaced store shelf inventory as requested by each store; the second sent products to the stores at the initiative of the centralized marketing group.

Store-initiated orders were entered into a hard-held computer terminal by a store employee who walked the aisles looking for items on the shelves that needed to be replaced. He or she scanned the bar code of an item to be ordered and entered the quantity needed. After making sure that these items were not in the store's back room, the employee transmitted the order to the head-quarters mainframe computer using a modem and a dial-up line. The mainframe computer then "billed" the order and routed it to one or more of the seven H-E-B product warehouses for selection, loading, and delivery to their assigned stores. The headquarters computer also maintained a database of product inventory by store as well as historical sales by store and by product.

Marketing group-initiated orders ensured that promotional and seasonal merchandise reached the stores in sufficient quantity and in time to meet projected demand. These orders were combined with store-initiated orders in the mainframe "billing" (i.e., ordering) system, and were transmitted to the warehouse as a single order for the store.

H-E-B was planning a new store ordering system that would automate as much of the ordering process as possible. This new system, using point-of-sale (POS) data, could automate ordering for up to 80 percent of the case volume in the store. This would eliminate most of the manual terminal input and physical counting and would significantly reduce the time required for ordering, allowing managers more time to focus on exceptions to plan and overall store management. Using information on planned and actual sales over time, the company could also plan purchases further into the future. This move to a planned logistics and purchasing program would replace the existing ad hoc ordering process based on physical store counts and simple seasonal adjustments. This logistics and operations system was just one example of planned applications for integrating information systems across functional areas within H-E-B.

Operations and Information Systems

Information systems in operations were first used to automate clerical tasks, followed by automation of customer checkout with POS scanner systems in the late 1970s. Operational support then expanded with the introduction of automated time and attendance reporting, direct store delivery receiving and invoicing, and electronic mail (E-mail) systems in the late 1980s. Introduced in the MIS group, E-mail usage gradually expanded throughout the company, providing instantaneous on-line communications between stores, warehouses, and headquarters locations. By 1990, E-mail was considered a key operational system and accounted for as much traffic as all other on-line data systems combined.

With the introduction of POS scanners and the data they provided, information systems became an integral part of store operations. Early problems increased management awareness of dependence on these systems, which were initially justified by direct cost reduction based on improved speed and accuracy of checkout. However, they eventually became a competitive requirement as customers came to appreciate their increased convenience and accuracy. Reliability was a major concern because when the scanners were down, customers were delayed and the store lost sales. Dedicated minicomputer systems designed specifically for POS scanning provided acceptable reliability, but limited flexibility for integrating the systems with other applications.

H-E-B was in the process of installing in-store Unix-based minicomputers in all stores, a process that would be completed by mid-1992. Most host-based systems would migrate to this in-store processor, which would be linked to the headquarters mainframe and to all other systems within the store, including the POS scanners. This move would shift the dialogue between the stores and headquarters to a computer-to-computer link to support an ongoing exchange of information on sales, orders, and personnel. The new minicomputer in each store would be able to store information on

actual and planned sales at each location to facilitate automation of the ordering process.

Reorganization of Responsibilities

To implement a more focused strategy, H-E-B reorganized during 1989, forming two new line divisions: Prolistics and Retailing (See Exhibit 1.) Prolistics was formed by the merger of the procurement and logistics functions and was responsible for supplying merchandise to the stores at the lowest possible costs. Retailing, which combined the operations and marketing functions, was responsible for revenues and gross profits. Structurally, the reorganization was a fairly simple move of the procurement function from the operations group to the logistics group. The MIS group was part of the central staff that supported both Prolistics and Retailing.

Information Systems in Retail

In the late 1980s, H-E-B was one of the industry leaders in developing a system that used POS data to create useful customer information to improve marketing. Customers were invited to apply for a "Select Circle" card, which would provide discounts when used at checkout. The scanning system was programmed to discount certain items for these customers, and direct mailings announced monthly specials for them. By early 1990, only 28 stores in two cities offered this program, but a significant portion of H-E-B sales in these stores were to customers using these cards.

The Select Circle program allowed H-E-B to gather information about individual customers' purchases over time which could then be used in marketing and planning. The POS scanning systems went beyond their original cost-reduction role and became an important information-gathering tool. Early uses of customer purchase data

EXHIBIT 1 H.E.B. Organization in 1990

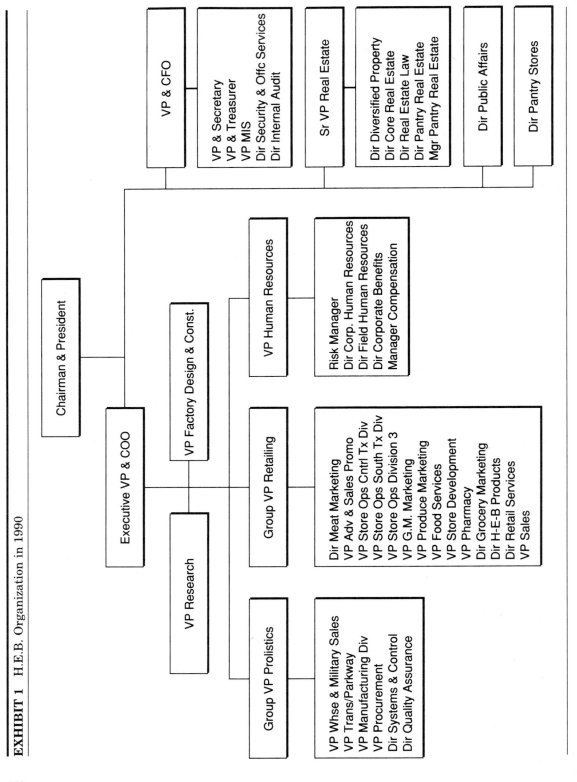

were simple but effective and indicated the strategic value of the information, if effectively harnessed. For example, after several weeks of remodeling in some of the stores, customer purchase records were analyzed to determine who had stopped shopping at H-E-B during the construction. Special mailers were sent to these customers, offering a special discount on their next visit to their local H-E-B store. Response was quite positive, and customer loyalty was quickly regained.

Managers at H-E-B believed that the potential of the Select Circle information available was only beginning to be understood. Information on family demographics combined with customer purchase data could enable Marketing to develop customized promotions. Targeted marketing could theoretically allow H-E-B to become the ideal grocery store for almost every family. This new organization was designed to strengthen the linkage between the stores and retailing and to shift the focus of the store manager from operations toward marketing.

Information Systems in Prolistics

The Prolistic group began testing an EDI program with suppliers in early 1990 to improve inventory management and supplier responsiveness. Electronic Data Interchange (EDI) connections linked vendor delivery systems directly with H-E-B actual sales data, enabling suppliers to schedule shipments to meet planned store inventory level objectives. In addition to reducing safety stock levels and increasing inventory turns for some products, EDI also was expected to assist H-E-B in negotiating more attractive and consistent pricing from manufacturers. An EDI and Rapid Response system had been successfully tested with one vendor, and H-E-B was actively recruiting other manufacturers for similar agreements.

Tight coordination between procurement and logistics as well as between stores and warehouses was needed to minimize inventory levels while avoiding stockouts. Using the integrated store and warehouse logistics systems, deliveries were timed to arrive at each store when shelf inventory was almost gone. This enabled the entire case of product ordered to be placed directly on the shelf and virtually eliminated back-room inventory within the store. Tight linkages between store and warehouse systems was necessary to plan and coordinate this just-in-time logistics system. With EDI, communications and coordination extended all the way from the store to the manufacturer, and excess inventory was eliminated throughout the entire logistics chain. Thus, maintaining tight and reliable linkages between geographically separated computer systems was becoming vital to store operations.

Communications at H-E-B

In late 1987, Gary Shipley was assigned the responsibility to bring together communications throughout the company into a single department to improve service and control costs. Several studies had increased management awareness regarding the benefits and opportunities of centrally managing communications. In 1983, as manager of MIS technical services (which included data communications) Gary became concerned about poor controls on overall communication costs. He conducted an audit of voice and data services throughout the company and discovered multiple billing errors and unnecessary facilities. Refunds of $200,000 from the telephone company and a reduction of $100,000 per year of ongoing expenses attracted senior management's attention on the potential savings from controlling communications costs. In 1986, internal auditing uncovered additional billing errors for services canceled but still being billed to the company. After this second study, the internal audit group recommended forming a dedicated department to coordinate communications services throughout the company. Gary was asked to manage the new department, reporting to the vice president of MIS.

As communications manager, one of the first questions Gary had to address was "what was communications?" or "what costs and services was he supposed to be managing?" Understanding total communications costs turned out to be more difficult than anyone expected when the communications department was first created, as many of the costs were embedded in functional or store operating budgets. Aggregating total communications costs identified a larger management opportunity than initially expected, with actual costs almost double previous estimates for communications expenses.

The SNA Network

In early 1986, Gary began investigating the possibility of installing a companywide SNA network as a means of linking the stores to headquarters in order to improve service and reduce costs. A limited point-to-point SNA network already existed between the warehouse and headquarters, but the stores were connected to headquarters through dial-up lines. New applications being developed for store automation and POS systems would increase data transmission dramatically over the next year or two, and an alternative to the existing dial-up connection was needed. The reliability and capacity of the proposed SNA network was attractive, but a strong tradition of cost control at H-E-B, particularly in the MIS area, made justification of the new network difficult without clear cost savings. Before his appointment as communications manager, Gary had been unable to find sufficient sav-

ings to cost-justify installing a companywide SNA network.

As communications manager, Gary was able to search more systematically for communication opportunities, and as a part of that search, Gary scheduled meetings with all department managers to better understand their communication costs and needs. During one of these meetings, Gary discovered that H-E-B was spending $300,000 per year on leased lines to connect the in-store ATM network. The ATMs were viewed as an unprofitable service provided for customer convenience, with communications as a major cost. After investigation, Gary found he could link the ATMs to servicing banks over the proposed SNA network and could save the entire cost of the leased ATM network. The total cost of the SNA network was only slightly more than $300,000 per year, and the proportional cost allocated to the ATM group was much lower than the prior expense of a separate network. Migrating to the SNA network changed the ATM business from an unprofitable to a profitable business. In addition, the SNA network increased data communications reliability and capacity for the rest of the company.

Usage of the SNA network expanded rapidly from 400 million bytes per week in 1988, the first year of operation, to more than 6.2 billion bytes per week in 1990. The SNA network initially carried mostly POS data from stores to the headquarters mainframe and began carrying E-mail traffic from a few users. By 1989, volume had increased sufficiently to force a redesign of the SNA system, which required $250,000 in nonrecurring costs. By 1990, E-mail had grown to more than 1 billion bytes of information per week and was used throughout the company. New applications such as time and attendance, on-line direct store delivery (DSD) ordering systems, and inventory and ordering information printouts added about

3.2 billion bytes of traffic per week. Finally, implementation of the Select Circle program in 28 stores increased POS data transmissions from 500 million bytes in early 1989 to 2.0 billion bytes per week in 1990. In total, the network carried more than 6.2 billion bytes of information per week by mid-1990, and new applications planned would probably double that requirement within the next two years. The network would have to be redesigned or replaced during 1991 because it was operating close to designed capacity.

The Communications Network in 1990

In addition to the SNA network, Gary had designed and implemented a managed voice system, which represented the dominant portion of the company's total communications expenses. The installed system provided better-quality service at a lower total cost to the company. The network consisted of PBX systems in headquarters and other corporate locations, connected by leased private lines between regional offices. The PBX systems significantly improved the quality and capabilities of H-E-B's phone services. Despite improved quality and increasing use, the total cost of basic voice communications had not risen, though new services and applications had increased nonvoice spending.

Network Description

By 1990, a companywide voice and data managed network linked all locations using a combination of dedicated and dial-up lines tied together with PBX systems. Several T1-lines (24 circuits at standard capacity) provided integrated voice and data services between regional hubs. Digital PBX systems in each large office location linked these T1-lines together. This network provided automatic least-cost routing to minimize cost without any inconvenience to users. Outbound and inbound (800 service) long-distance traffic was aggregated on the network over these T1 lines to increase leverage with long-distance vendors. The SNA data network consisted of single private lines at 9,600 bits per second (bps) linking each store and smaller location through one of the three T1 network hubs to the headquarters computing facility. (See Exhibit 2.) The T1 facilities were used for both voice and data, with voice services compressed to increase circuit capacity. Supplementing these leased-line networks were more than 500 local data dial-up facilities, and more than 3,500 local voice lines.

Long-Distance Vendor Negotiations

With voice traffic aggregated to a single point, H-E-B was able to offer long-distance vendors large traffic volumes and in turn obtain very attractive rates: for outbound long-distance service, 4.5 cents per minute for intraLATA calls (long-distance calls within a small calling area) and 8.5 cents per minute for other calls within the state of Texas (interLATA, intrastate calls). This outbound traffic was routed through Claydesta, a Texas-based long-distance carrier. Calls out-of-state cost about 17 cents per minute during the business day, a rate much lower than the company had been paying AT&T for unmanaged long-distance calls. H-E-B was able to offer competing vendors about 200,000 minutes of total traffic per month outbound from a single location, with a direct T1 connection to the vendor selected. In addition, the company was willing to switch vendors as often as necessary to keep negotiated prices low.

For inbound (800) calls, H-E-B was unable to negotiate as attractive rates because there were fewer competitors that could offer the capabilities it required. To be able to allocate costs of inbound calls (mostly from the stores to the regional or headquarters offices), H-E-B required the long-distance

EXHIBIT 2   The H.E.B. Communications Network in 1990

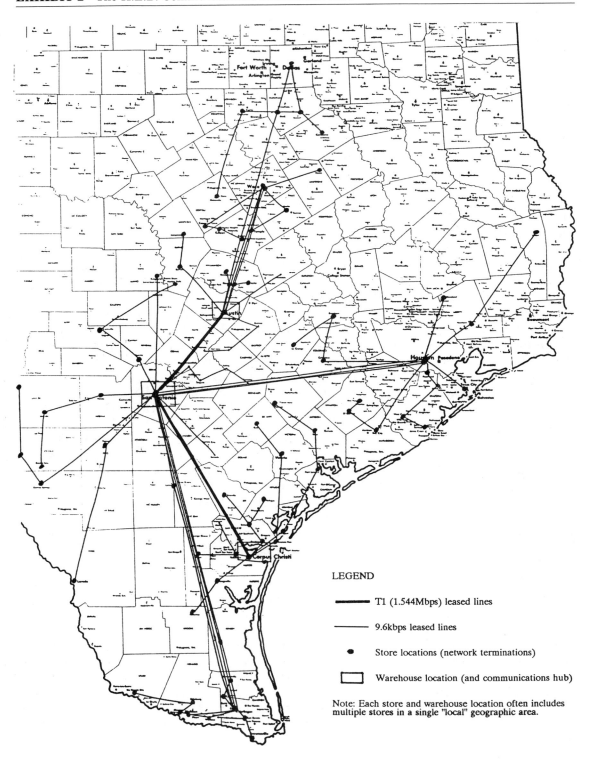

LEGEND

—————— T1 (1.544Mbps) leased lines

———— 9.6kbps leased lines

• Store locations (network terminations)

☐ Warehouse location (and communications hub)

Note: Each store and warehouse location often includes
multiple stores in a single "local" geographic area.

vendor to provide calling number identification on the bill. For calls from nonstore locations, a separate inbound number was used and caller ID codes were issued to users, enabling cost allocation by department for these calls as well. Total volume of 150,000 inbound minutes per month offered to vendors was enough to stimulate competitive bidding among ATT, MCI, and Sprint, the only carriers able to offer the required capabilities.

Billing Communications Costs

All of the costs of H-E-B communications for voice or data were charged to users with a simple but fair billing system. Although H-E-B has a single cost center for communications, no costs are retained in the Communications Department. Aggregating traffic and negotiating attractive volume deals with long-distance vendors reduced the cost of long-distance usage, but also created a large fixed-cost communications infrastructure. Viewed in isolation, many of the PBX and T1-line investments could not be cost-justified, but overall communications costs were reduced in total. Because all locations benefitted from the PBX and leased-line network that allowed traffic aggregation, all users of the system were billed for a portion of the fixed cost of the network. Gary's challenge was to develop a means of billing total communications costs which would be perceived as fair but would be simple to administer so that the costs of administration would not exceed the benefits provided by the charge-out system.

By 1990, the Communications Department had identified about a million dollars per year that was spent on data communications alone, with another $3 million spent on voice. These costs needed to be allocated among multiple departments and locations. SNA costs were divided equally among the number of connections to the network. Fixed costs of the voice network (including PBX costs) were lumped into a single fixed-cost account and divided by the total number of PBX extensions in the network, with each store location being charged for three extensions because they shared in the benefits of system even though they had no actual PBX extensions. Variable changes were identified by originating location or department and were charged proportional to usage, with no distinction based on call destination. Unidentified calls, a small portion of total traffic, were divided evenly among all extensions on the network. This billing system was felt to be reasonably fair, but it clearly benefitted some locations and departments more than others. However, a more complex cost-allocation system seemed to offer limited benefits relative to the additional costs potentially involved.

Communications Demands in 1990

Both voice and data service demands were increasing rapidly, but the growth in data service demand was the most pressing concern facing Gary in the coming decade. With the planned expansion of the Select Circle program from the 28-store trial to the entire chain, POS data transmission would increase from two billion bytes per week to more than 10 billion bytes. As the SNA network would be unable to handle this large an increase in demand without a major redesign, Gary decided to investigate alternatives to the existing system. As with the original SNA network proposal, justifying an alternative to the current system required uncovering additional costs for data services that could be replaced with a new network but were not on the current network.

After a complete review of total data services costs, Gary found that the SNA network accounted for only 51 percent of total data communications expenses. This low percentage was a surprise to many H-E-B managers, who had viewed data communications and the SNA network as being identical. Other data applications were primarily asynchronous dial-up applications, though one application, Ticketmaster, required asynchronous dedicated lines in a point-to-point network of 30 locations. Total communications costs by service are shown in Table A, with the majority of the non-SNA costs incurred for monthly rental fees for dial-up lines.

Gary estimated that voice traffic had increased at least 25 percent from 1987 to 1990. For calls on the leased-line network between H-E-B locations, growth appeared to have been much more rapid, because a 20-circuit capacity was full and often "busy" on a route that three years earlier had provided excess capacity with only eight circuits. Communications traffic had increased significantly, but measuring the actual benefits of increased voice communications usage was difficult.

The Satellite Network Proposal

Gary began investigating alternatives to expanding the existing SNA network in early 1989 and found that the satellite network was the best alternative for H-E-B's future data communication needs. A packet-switched network provided by the local telephone company was also considered, but was rejected because the satellite option offered greater capacity and flexibility at a similar cost. Senior management first became interested in satellites partly in recognition of increasing use of satellite networks by Walmart, K Mart, and other retail chains. Preliminary investigations indicated that a satellite network would cost about $7,000,000 and would realize only $500,000 per year in cost savings (the SNA network cost). However, during 1989, Gary and his staff had been able to significantly reduce the cost of the satellite option and to identify additional savings opportunities. A satellite network appeared to offer savings over total

TABLE A   Description of Data Communications Services at H-E-B

Data Service	% of Cost	Description of Service
SNA Network	51%	Leased line network between all stores and corporate locations
Ticketmaster	7	Leased asynchronous lines dedicated for remote concert ticket printing
SACA	5	Dial-up service for check authorization
Security	13	Two dial-up lines from each store for security systems
ENVOY	10	Pharmacy system for third-party payment authorization
Western Union Fax Service	4	Dial-up fax lines
Ordering	9	Dial-up lines for calling orders into headquarters mainframe
Other	1	Dial-up lines for energy management, etc.
Total	**100%**	

1990 data communications expenses and seemed better than any alternatives considered for meeting H-E-B's increasing communications demands. However, installing a satellite network was a major investment and represented a larger change in strategy than any previous network changes. Because of the importance of this decision, the COO and the Operating Committee had to approve the satellite proposal or recommend further evaluation of alternative options.

Satellite Economics

Total communications savings possible with a satellite network increased from the $500,000 initially projected (the cost of the SNA network) to more than $1,100,000 after a broadening of the definition of data communications. Most of this $1,100,000 savings would be in local monthly charges for dial-up business lines, not in long-distance private-line costs. The satellite network would be used to eliminate almost all non-voice facilities, and all communications outside the company would be aggregated at headquarters to use the discounted switched traffic rates negotiated with long-distance vendors. The voice network would be unchanged, though some T1 facilities might be replaced by lower-capacity fractional-T1 circuits.

While expanding the potential savings from a satellite system, Gary had also reduced the cost of the satellite alternative. Total cost under a five-year lease from GTE Spacenet would be $1,050,000 per year, with a two-year extension at half the initial annual rate. (See Exhibit 3.) GTE Spacenet was selected to provide the system because the terms and network design flexibility were the best offered by any vendor at that time. The system could also be purchased for about $4,100,000 with a monthly cost of $22,000 for the satellite space usage. This reduced cost of the satellite system was due partly to effective negotiations in a very competitive market and partly to redesigning the system to meet H-E-B's exact requirements. With lower costs and larger savings potential, the satellite network offered savings over current costs for data services. Expected growth in number of stores and growth in data transmission increased the potential savings of the satellite network.

Reliability and Redundancy

In evaluating the satellite network alternative, H-E-B management had to consider the level of redundancy necessary for the new network and the level of risk acceptable in installing the system. The satellite system would replace most local dial-up data lines and the entire SNA network, which would make the satellite link the only data link to some locations. The satellite vendor quoted very high reliability statistics and guaranteed four-hour on-site service, but some managers in the MIS area were worried about abandoning the existing SNA network and felt the satellite alternative should be tested for 6 to 12 months before signing a long-term commitment.

Installing local dial-up facilities to back up the satellite network in the event of failure was analyzed, but was rejected as an unnecessary expense. The cost of these facilities would increase the annual cost of the satellite network by about $170,000 per year ($70 per store per month for two dial-up lines), which would make it more expensive than the existing network. The SNA network had no backup systems and, after investigating experiences of other satellite customers, Gary was convinced that the proposed network would be at least as reliable as the existing one. Senior management decided that a downtime risk of three to four hours was acceptable to save $170,000 per year, because data would not be lost and could be retransmitted once the link was reestablished. This standard of reliability was

EXHIBIT 3 Comparison of Satellite Lease with Current Network Costs[a]

	Year 1	Year 2	Year 3	Year 4	Year 5	Year 6	Year 7
Satellite Lease Cost	$1,023,810	$1,023,810	$1,023,810	$1,023,810	$1,023,810	$ 511,905	$ 511,905
Current Network Cost	1,071,088	1,124,642	1,180,875	1,239,918	1,301,914	1,367,010	1,435,360
Savings from Satellite Network	47,278	100,832	157,065	216,108	278,104	855,105	923,455

[a]Assumes 200 VSATs with no growth in data transmission or number of locations. With growth in data or numbers of stores, savings increase.

considered acceptable for existing applications, and the backup lines could be installed later if needed for future applications.

Increased Flexibility and Capabilities

The satellite network would provide the company with increased flexibility and capabilities not possible with the existing network. For example, the Training Department planned to use the satellite network to broadcast training seminars to all locations. Training was important in H-E-B, because it helped strengthen company culture and improved employee effectiveness. Direct broadcast of training and presentations was expected to improve training effectiveness and reduce costs. This capability was cited as one of the benefits Walmart had gained from installing a satellite network. Potential uses of this satellite broadcast capability included CEO/COO "fireside chats," interactive companywide training sessions or meetings, distribution of training videos directly to all stores (recorded on VCR in the store for later training), regional meetings and conferences, and many other applications. Although this ability to train and use top executive talent and time more effectively was an important benefit of the satellite network, the company culture required the investment decision be based on cost savings or revenue enhancements. Business TV broadcasting was considered an attractive additional benefit once the satellite system was already justified on the basis of cost savings.

The satellite network also offered an easier and more flexible growth plan than the existing network. For example, an additional $800,000 investment plus an additional $22,000 per month would double its capacity. Already, the proposed satellite network would offer more than five times the capacity of the existing SNA network. Gary believed this increased capacity would be adequate for at least the next four to five years. For new applications, the satellite network offered the ability to experiment without large investments in supporting communications infrastructure. Thus, if an experiment failed, no large costs would be incurred.

Finally, the satellite network would provide H-E-B with an affordable means to connect with a disaster recovery center to back up the mainframe systems at headquarters. A dedicated backup system was too expensive, and the cost of leased lines to disaster recovery centers in Dallas or Phoenix was too high using terrestrial facilities. With a satellite system, GTE Spacenet (the vendor) was willing to provide a hub backup system in Houston, and a satellite dish could be installed at low cost at any disaster recovery center in the country. In addition, emergency backup for disaster at the store could be provided in a day or less, using a portable dish. This same portable dish could also be used to bring a new store location on line in one day, rather than waiting for up to six weeks for dedicated SNA lines to be installed by the local telephone company.

Alternatives Considered but Rejected

After evaluating several alternatives to expansion of the existing SNA network, Gary believed the satellite network was the most attractive for the company overall. The second best alternative was to replace the existing network with an X.25 packet-switched network. The total annualized cost of this alternative would be $980,000 per year, compared with $1,024,000 for a satellite lease. However, the potential savings of packet switching were more than offset by the additional benefits offered by the satellite network. In addition, the packet-switched service was a tariffed offering, and its costs were not guaranteed and could be increased. The cost of a satellite lease was fixed for the first five years.

The satellite network offered several advantages over the packet-switched alternative, such as greater capacity, reliability, and accountability. The packet-switched network would have about twice the capacity of the existing SNA network, compared with five times the existing capacity with the satellite network. The packet-switched network provided over local telephone company lines would not be as reliable as a satellite network, especially given the problems experienced with the leased-line SNA network. At least the satellite network would be provided entirely by a single vendor, whereas both the SNA and proposed packet-switched networks mixed leased lines from local telephone companies and interexchange carriers. Some H-E-B stores were serviced by small independent telephone companies with antiquated facilities and slow service responsiveness. Even Southwestern Bell provided slower service than the company often needed, especially for installation of lines into a new store location.

Timing and Other Considerations
Gary planned to start installing the satellite system by the end of 1990, to meet expected growth in demand, and a decision was needed soon to meet that deadline. Operationally, the installation needed to be carefully timed to prevent problems but mini-

mize redundant costs of dual networks. The H-E-B construction group committed to installing the entire satellite network on all 200 locations within six months for $200,000 less than the projected cost of vendor installation. With a decision soon, the network could be installed and operational by June 1991. This timing was important because the existing SNA network was becoming saturated and would need to be upgraded if a new network was not installed within the next year.

From a technology perspective, the satellite network was a short-term solution to the company's communications needs. With rapid advances in communications technology and continually declining costs, Gary believed that another technology or service offering would probably replace the satellite system within the next decade. In addition, the satellites would not last much longer than ten years before they would have to be abandoned or replaced by satellite vendors. Satellite economics were attractive in 1990 partly because the technology was mature and vendors were anxious to utilize excess capacity. This solution to H-E-B's communications needs would not have worked economically two years earlier because vendor prices were still too high, and it might not be the best solution if the same decision were made two years in the future. But for the next five years, Gary believed the satellite network was the best solution for H-E-B's data communications needs.

Chapter 11

Operations Management

A major investment banking firm operated all of its foreign exchange trading and other trading activities out of a large computing center containing $15 million worth of hardware, totally without backup. One Friday afternoon the water main that ran vertically through the building burst on the floor directly above the computing center. In a half hour the computing center floor was covered with three feet of water, and the entire $15 million worth of equipment was destroyed. The company went into the weekend with many of its key trading positions uncovered and, indeed, not even knowing what those positions were. Truly extraordinary efforts were made to replace all of the equipment in a 48-hour period in order to prevent massive balance-sheet erosion. Multiple sites, much tighter environmental measures, better controls, and new management were all parts of the solution.

As a result of software glitches in a new installation in January 1990, AT&T's long-distance phone system went down for 14 hours. One insurance company had to send home 500 people who were working on telephone follow-ups to direct mailings, losing a day's sales. The insurer now spreads its business over several carriers so as to avoid this type of vulnerability in the future.

The chief executive officer of an industrial products firm discovered that the delay in year-end financial closing was not due to reduced emphasis on close control of financial accounting, but to unexpected work and personnel problems in the IT department. Increased use (and associated problems) of an on-line query system to provide salespeople and customers with detailed delivery and cost information has absorbed all available system support personnel. Consequently, no time was left for revising the accounting system for mandatory changes in tax laws before year-end closing.

The IT director of a large aerospace firm is pondering whether to totally reorganize and consolidate the 10 operations centers in order to save more than $50 million. At present, each center is configured to provide total support to a business unit. Workloads are erratic, long response-time delays exist on some on-line systems, and the costs are high. A consolidated center offers the opportunity to address all three of those issues.

Unusual problems? Hardly! Historically, the "glamorous" part of the IT function has been the technology-oriented new systems development activity. Systems maintenance and day-to-day operations and delivery of service have been distinctly secondary. Failures in the operations function, however, increasingly jeopardize entire organizations. In this chapter the term *operations* is defined as the running of IT hardware and data input devices, equipment scheduling, and work forces associated with these activities. The chapter also deals with the movement toward outside-sourcing both software and development and operations, and the special challenges of security and privacy.

CHANGING OPERATIONS ENVIRONMENT

Both the management resources devoted to operations activities and the sophistication of management practices within the operations center have often been inadequate for the growth and change within companies' operations activities. Changing technology is now triggering major changes in the way these activities are managed.

Move to On-Line Systems and Networks.   Greatly increased on-line technology applications and increased sophistication in operating systems in the past decade have transformed a batch, job-shop environment with heavy human control into, first, a process-manufacturing shop, and now, a largely self-scheduled and -monitored 24-hour-a-day utility. This change in manufacturing work flow has precipitated a total rethinking of both what appropriate scheduling is and how adequate service levels are defined. These systems support thousands of internal devices and in many cases must provide "seamless" 24-hour-a-day service links to customers and suppliers around the globe. Any problems in this area immediately reflect unfavorably on the firm as a whole.

Diversity of Performance Measures.   There is no such thing as an ideal, standard IT operations management control system or an ideal measure of performance. Appropriate balancing of quality of service, response time of on-line systems, ability to handle unexpected jobs, costs, and ability to meet schedules on batch systems varies from one organization to another.

Efficiency–Effectiveness Balance.   Different IT operations environments must strike different balances between efficiency (low-cost production) and effectiveness in responding to unplanned, uneven flows of requests. IT operations cannot be *all things* simultaneously to *all people;* instead, they must operate with the priorities of trade-offs established by corporate strategy. Implementing these priorities has caused the reorganization of some large IT operations into series of focused, single-service groups, each of which can be managed to serve quite different user service objectives.

Changes in Staffing Needs.   Many formerly valuable employees are unsuited for new tasks, and their relatively simple jobs have been automated away. Such dilemmas have been complicated by the unionization of this function in many parts of the world. This is a relatively transitory problem in many settings where operations centers are becoming "lights-out factories."

Continued Change in Technology.   Evolving technology, while offering potential benefits of lower cost and new capabilities, poses significant problems of change and introduction of new operating procedures. It is an unusual IT operations center that has the same hardware/software configuration from one month to the next.

The Trend toward Outside Sourcing.   The major shift toward more outside sourcing for both IT processing and software development requires substantial changes in the procedures of the operations and development functions of a firm's IT department. Firms such as Eastman Kodak that have made this shift successfully have attracted widespread national attention to out sourcing.

These issues are similar to those involved in running a manufacturing facility characterized as utilizing *highly volatile technology* and *specialized labor,* serving *dynamic markets,* and operating within a *changing industry structure.* Consequently, much of the analysis in this chapter draws on work done in manufacturing management, particularly as it relates to efficiency–effectiveness trade-offs.

A Focused Service Organization Alternative—An Example

A key question stemming from this manufacturing analogy is how focused the department should be. Should it subdivide itself into sets of stand-alone services networked together as needed or be organized as a general-purpose IT service? The problem one company faced of either closing its books late or providing continuous on-line service for queries from the sales force stimulated the company to review the responsiveness of its operations to the demands of new services. They perceived that it was impossible for their single, monolithic unit to respond adequately to such very different user needs.

To address the problem, the IT development and maintenance group was reorganized into four independent systems groups, each operating independently of the others and reporting to the IT manager. One group supported the on-line query systems, with its goals being to provide 10-second response, one-day change implementation, and hourly refreshment of all data. This query system was moved to a stand-alone minicomputer in the corporate data center to keep its volatility of demand from disturbing the rest of the company's operations. The second group was devoted to the general ledger accounting system. Their goals were to keep the software up-to-date for month-end closing, to schedule work so as not to interfere with other systems, to ensure the quality and reliability of accounting data, and to close the books five days after the last working day of the month. This system ran on the data center's large mainframe computer. The third group was responsible for all material-management systems. Their objectives were to ensure that all desired changes to the system were made and that all production control persons were well trained in use of the system so as to reduce rerun time dramatically. The fourth group worked with the systems that supported new-product development. They were responsible for identifying system requirements of new products, maintaining the capacity simulator used in planning new-product development, establishing the data standards used to describe new products, and developing and performing analyses on new products as directed by the vice president of product development. Their systems also ran on the mainframe computer.

Each focused group included at least one user and two to three systems professionals, with the query group having their own computer as well. All worked full time on their respective services with the exception of the new-product group, which had spurts of work as new products hit the market and lulls after the market settled down. This structure has produced happier customers, significantly better perceptions of service, and increased employee morale.

Alternative Organizations

Historically, IT systems were developed to be run out of an integrated IT operations unit. As we have noted, some firms have reorganized IT development and operations in order to be more responsive to user needs. For example, many organizations have not only shifted application programmers to users, but have also allowed maintenance and operations to be decentralized around the local system. As IT's monopoly of system construction and make-or-buy decisions erodes to greater user control, the factory becomes fragmented into a series of focused services (for example, using a standard word processing system for customer mailings). For some users and applications this may be very effective. The services for other users, however, may be dependent upon an integrated set of data, in which case severe coordination problems are created by a focused factory concept. The challenge is to identify where focus in operations (either within the central unit or distributed to the user) is appropriate and where it is not. Implementation of this is discussed in the section on production planning and control later in the chapter.

These problems are further complicated by the fact that in all but the most decentralized corporations, central telecommunications networks have been developed for binding corporations' activities together. These include the capacity for electronic mail, document transfer, data file transfers, and so on. Including everything from local area networks to satellite links, many of the networks are both very large and highly sophisticated as they evolve links between fragmented services. For example, a large aerospace company recently initiated a total rearchitecturing of its network after a confidential E-mail message from the president to the financial vice president wound up on the desk of a production planner in another country.

To build on the manufacturing strategy theme and develop an appropriate range of make-or-buy plans, the operations management discussion in this chapter is organized around these topics:

- Development of an operations strategy.
- Technology planning.
- Measuring and managing capacity.
- Managing the IT operations work force.
- Production planning and control.
- Security.
- Privacy.

DEVELOPING AN OPERATIONS STRATEGY

As noted earlier, the management team of an IT operations activity is trying to stay on top of a utility that is radically changing its production system, customer base, and role within the company. Twenty years ago the manager and his staff could be described as monopolists running a job shop where the key issues were scheduling (with substantial human inputs), ensuring that telecommunications were adequate, managing a large blue-collar staff, and planning capacity and staffing levels for future workloads of similar characteristics. Today, on the other hand, they (1) operate an information utility that provides a 24-hour, 7-day-a-week service in support of thousands of terminals and PCs—perhaps located around the world—that must cope cost-effectively with uncertain short-term and long-term user demand; (2) manage a work force far more highly skilled, more professional, and much smaller in numbers; and (3) evaluate both internal and external competing services that in many cases offer the potential to solve problems more economically and more comprehensively. Key issues for the IT operations manager continue to include staff, capacity, and telecommunications. Prominent additions to this list, however, are appropriate assessment, assimilation, and integration of software and services emanating from outside the corporation.

Senior management must assess the quality of IT operations and—depending on how critical it is to the overall strategic mission of the corporation—must be involved in determining its structure and the standards for its quality of service. The central question for both senior management and IT management is whether the current IT operations organization effectively supports the firm.

In this context, an operations strategy must address four key issues:

1. Ensure that an architecture has been conceived and is being implemented.
2. Ensure that new systems are developed in ways that appropriately address their viability.
3. Ensure that internal/external sourcing decisions are carefully considered, both as to their outcome and as to who should determine operational characteristics of any outsourcing arrangement.
4. Determine the extent to which IT operations should be managed as a single entity or be broken into a series of perhaps more costly but more focused subunits that provide more customized user service than is possible with a single facility. (This topic is discussed in the Production Planning and Control section.)

The following paragraphs discuss these issues in more detail.

The Role of IT Architecture

In today's evolving technology, managing a firm's IT portfolio in order to gain a competitive advantage for the firm is akin to urban renewal. Great tensions are inherent in the need to meet today's needs while providing a platform that permits tomorrow's services to evolve. To balance these conflicting goals, many firms have attempted to develop an overall IT architecture. Architecture includes such technical items as the vision of an evolving network for linking the various parts of the corporation and the protocols for ensuring that wide-area networks and local-area networks can communicate seamlessly and cost-effectively. It includes data standards and dictionaries that ensure that files from different parts of the firm can be accessed and correlated appropriately and cost-effectively. It also includes standards for hardware/software vendors that ensure maintainability of uptime at a reasonable cost and easy interconnectivity between different parts of the organization. Standards on protocols like UNIX and Windows are crucial for the long-term growth and adaptability of the firm. This architecture (1) provides an operational vision, (2) is modified as an ongoing process, (3) allows concrete projects to be identified for the immediate future, (4) serves as a basis for establishing priorities and sequencing of IT projects, and (5) establishes a basis for organization change.

Vision.   The most celebrated operational vision was that of C. A. Smith (past CEO of American Airlines): the idea of a passenger name record for every reserved seat on American Airlines. Created in 1954, this idea drove the development of SABRE in the early 1960s and its subsequent modification. Such a vision encompasses the key business purpose of IT (examples: an active electronic link to every important customer for in-dustrial wholesalers; a complete product sales history and demographic profile for all financial service customers to facilitate crossmarketing). The practical implications of the vision—such as seat selection, boarding passes, frequent flier programs, and personal marketing—will evolve through ongoing discussion and implementation.

Ongoing Process.   Successful architectures are not bound in a book, but rather, are present in ongoing discussions among the key decision makers; they are architecture in action. As an illustration of this proc-ess, let us step into the strategy status room of a multinational bank. On one wall are posted descriptions of the key strategy and service objectives for each decision-making unit, retail branch, and overseas office and lists of new, electronic-based products for each major busi-ness. In 1990 these new products included the consolidation of branch banks acquired in a recent merger into a single operating system; the final phase of a combined purchasing incentive program between the firm, an oil company, and an airline; the introduction of a new credit card product; and an expert-system project. On another wall is a chart that lists all sites and the services provided and planned maintenance at each site. On the back wall is a list of all the hardware and the main software that provide these services. Senior management meets in this room once a month to review progress and deal with new issues.

Project Identification.   A working architecture permits and encour-ages the planning of sound projects that can be justified and initiated within the existing organizations. These projects originate from both business and IT staffs, stimulated by ongoing dialogue. For example, in a large chemical business the R&D group initiated an experimental local-area network (LAN) as a means to improve R&D productivity (an objective of their architecture). Over time the LAN grew into a network that supported corporate headquarters. It started in R&D and was phased into IT as it became perceived as a useful general service. In a publishing company, a group of editors formed a steering committee to explore how PCs could better support the entire editorial process. This was stimulated in part by an earlier series of architectural discussions on the role of work stations in supporting specific editorial tasks that had led to some very high payoff projects.

Priorities. A prime purpose of IT architecture is to facilitate the establishment of priorities for meeting today's needs while providing flexibility to grow to tomorrow's competitive challenge. The recent simultaneous explosion of PC use, expansion of communication services, and massive reorganization of data structures exemplify the contrast in needed time and resources for implementing interdependent services. A network development and implementation program may take years to accomplish, while new local-area-network terminal systems can be implemented in a matter of weeks. Without an architecture, short-term tactical moves can insidiously postpone long-term projects. Further implementation complications are caused by both the shift to buying (rather than developing) software and services and the shift of responsibility for these activities to line managers. Both of these must be managed carefully. Finally, an IT architecture imposes a global perspective on priorities for IT projects, because the pieces must fit together.

Organization Change

As we have noted in earlier chapters, IT identifies opportunities for restructuring work and fundamentally altering the way work is carried out in organizations. Architectural development provides these opportunities and fosters discussion of how they can be achieved. Technologies can open up opportunities for these changes but cannot guarantee that positive changes will occur.

System Design and Operations

Effective IT operations hinge heavily on ensuring that the first step of the systems life cycle, the design phase, is well executed. The key operations discussions for a system often occur early in the design phase. Both user and IT operational personnel should be intimately involved in the early design of significant processing systems. Strong IT operational input ensures that operational feasibility issues are given high priority from the beginning. It is easy for a development group to overlook such issues as appropriate restart points in case of hardware failures, adequate documentation and support for operational personnel when a program abnormally ends, and so on. They further need to ensure that inappropriate shortcuts are not taken during development and that the details of the conversion from the old to the new system have been conceived appropriately. These issues are particularly complex if an external package is sourced.

Externally Sourced Services—Pressures and Challenges

The shift from in-house software construction managed by IT staff to today's great reliance on purchased software and service is not surprising. While the supply and performance of inexpensive hardware have been growing dramatically, the human resources devoted to developing corresponding software have remained relatively constant. Neither user-oriented programming languages nor programmer "workbench" and other efficiency aids have fully addressed the problem of resource shortage. Consequently, salaries for skilled people have increased significantly.

In response to these two trends, a large market has developed for software developed by outside firms. These firms are able to provide reliable products at significantly lower user cost by spreading their costs over many users. The industry was born when software vendors developed complex technical software to support the operation of computers (operating systems, database handlers, inquiry languages, etc.). Vendor software, however, has now effectively moved "downstream" to products such as standard user-oriented software services including payroll and accounting packages, report writers, procedural language, computer-aided software engineering (CASE), and so on. Finally as noted earlier, the out sourcing of the entire IT operations function is being widely discussed as a way of allowing firms to concentrate their energies on things they believe will make a real difference.

Challenges. Purchased systems potentially generate special problems for IT operations management. These problems are particularly complex if the user has full authority to purchase and operate the new service while the IT operations department must maintain and operate other services and at the same time ensure their compatibility with the new service. Potential loss of sole control of operations poses four key challenges to IT operations management:

1. How to maintain existing services while building appropriate and necessary data bridges to the new ones in order to integrate them with existing services where needed.

2. How to evolve the IT operations organization from primarily an integrated data processing system to a series of services for the specific needs of various users and then to neutralize users' desire for independent operations in cases where it does not make sense.
3. How to educate the user about the real operational problems and issues associated with the systems under their control. (Early successful user independence has very often led to long-term operating problems.)
4. How to help users manage vendor relationships in order to protect the company against ill-advised changes to software that can hurt operations. (The 1986 announcement of the incompatibility of Lotus 1-2-3 Release 2.0 with the previous versions of Lotus 1-2-3 illustrates this type of problem.)

Individual skill levels and perspectives of IT operations managers further complicate these problems. Many of them are accustomed to exercising total control over operations while sharing control over selection and implementation of maintenance changes with users. They must now learn to share control of operations, and it has been very difficult for some. Evidence of this failure to adapt is provided by the many organizations that, because of senior management frustration over IT's unresponsiveness, have given users total authority for purchased services acquisition and operation.

External Facilities Management Firms.   Out sourcing the entire operations activity to facilities management firms is an important trend. Companies such as Electronic Data Systems (EDS) for Blue Cross/Blue Shield and state and local governments and Computer Science Corporation (CSC) for General Dynamics (a $3 billion–10-year contract) have created major market positions in the past decade. Companies such as Eastman Kodak have turned over major pieces of their operation to IBM and Digital Equipment Corporation (DEC). The key reasons for this movement include:

1. A desire to concentrate the company's energy around core missions or critical technologies (such as chemical engineering for a chemical company) and delegate responsibility for managing and staying abreast of other technologies to outsiders.
2. The need to both reduce costs and implement mechanisms for controlling cost growth. Many internal charge-out systems have associated with them a flavor of "funny money" that arm's-length contracts between independent firms do not have. For example, imagine that an internal user has a sudden systems desire and is told that it is feasible but will cost $50,000. This figure will be much more sobering if it comes from a third party.
3. The desire of professional staff for meaningful careers. Small and mid-sized firms, in particular, cannot provide the richness of job

positions that make for interesting careers and opportunities for self-renewal. Facilities management firms have this capability.

4. The salary caps particularly prevalent in civil service positions often make it impossible to attract and maintain the staff skill sets needed. Out sourcing allows an organization to sidestep this issue.

5. Out sourcing is an attractive way to "shake up" a troubled or frozen IT organization. Organizations have used intelligently planned out-sourcing approaches successfully to clean up and reprofessionalize their operation; after three to four years they have insourced.

6. Out sourcing can help a company work through a complex conversion scenario, where extraordinary skills are needed for a defined period of time.

Where these discussions are made in the corporation and the intensity of investigations brought to them depend critically on the strategic dependence on the technology and its future strategic impact. The chief information officer and the chief financial officer together can structure and approve the out sourcing for a predominantly "support" unit, as was done by a university for its back-office administrative activities. When a major bank recently out sourced a major piece of its operations activity, it was a matter of intense board-of-directors concern and CEO involvement. A critical part of the firm's daily operations and product innovation capability was being delegated to an outsider in the expectation that it could do a better job of controlling it.

Potential Problems. The potential problems with these arrangements are similar to those with a marriage. It is easier to enter the relationship than to exit it. The critical issues revolve around the following:

1. *Vendor viability* and its ability to renew itself. Financial failure of the vendor or deterioration of its service may cause deep problems, in some cases triggering large emergency investment in an operation the firm had no desire to invest in.

2. *Cost* that becomes more aggressive each year. The cost of moving out of the out sourcing arrangement can be so traumatic and expensive that there is a tendency to "ride along" for a while. Good initial contracting can alleviate this problem.

3. A *relationship* that becomes confrontational over time. With cash always passing hands between two profit-making entities, extraordinary efforts are required to ensure that a feeling of partnership develops and is maintained. If small incidents are not carefully managed, they can become cause célèbres. An understanding of the operational culture of the party providing the service is crucial in assessing whether it is likely to be successful. These are long-term relationships, usually ten years; three successful years do not guarantee seven more successful years.

4. *Dissolving* the relationship. This can take a long time. It is crucial that mutual obligations during this stage of the relationship be

carefully spelled out in advance, as this is where things can really go wrong. Realistically, however, with no anticipated future revenues, the service firm's professionalism and its concern for its reputation will be what you are depending on.

In short, out sourcing is not a panacea. While solving one set of problems, another potential set will surely come trailing in its wake.

TECHNOLOGY PLANNING

Technology planning for operations is a process of ongoing review of potential obsolescence and of opportunities. The scope and effort of this review should be determined by the nature of the business and the state of IT: for a bank it should be across many technologies and be very extensive; a mail-order business may concentrate on office support technology; a wholesale distributor may primarily focus on computing and telecommunications technologies. To be effective, the review must involve high-caliber, imaginative staff. (The role of the emerging technologies department was discussed in Chapter 8.) It should regard today's IT possibilities in the context of the potential available two or three years in the future. This potential must be based on technological forecasting.

If a company is trying to distinguish itself from the competition with its application of information technologies, the resources focused on technological planning should be quite extensive. If a firm is trying to just stay even with competitors and sees its IT activity primarily as "support," simple comparison with the operations of competitors or leaders in particular fields may be sufficient. Some firms periodically solicit bids from different vendors to help ensure that their IT department is fully up-to-date. For example, a large insurance company whose IT department is dominated by the technology of one vendor has annually asked a competitor of the vendor to bid an alternative system, even though they have not perceived a need for change. As a result of these bids, however, they recently switched to another vendor's minicomputers, and on another occasion they installed a large machine purchased from a different vendor. These moves have kept the annual bidding process honest.

The objective of the review is to determine—relative to available and announced systems—how cost-effective and adequate for growth the existing installed technologies are. The review should generate an updated priority list of technologies to be considered as replacements. Such lead time is critical; technology replacements or additions that are planned two years in advance cause a small fraction of the disruption that those planned only six months in advance do. (Realistically, of course, breakthrough announcements limit the precision of advance planning.) In order to better define the architecture of the future information service, the planning activity should include field trips to vendors, education sessions, and pilot studies as vehicles for obtaining an understanding of emerging technologies.

A useful approach to a technology review is to categorize the applications portfolio of operations systems by length of time since development or last total rewrite of each system. The finding that a significant percentage of the IT systems were designed a decade or more ago often indicates that a major redesign and rewrite will offer great opportunities for reduced maintenance and improved operational efficiency.[1] When a large international bank recently performed such a review, it discovered that 60 percent of its CPU utilization and 50 percent of its systems effort were devoted to maintaining and running transaction processing systems constructed in the second era (Figure 1–1).

The implementation of new technology may be transparent to the user if it involves hardware replacement or new systems that use existing hardware more effectively. Other replacement technology, however, affects users consciously by providing different or improved service—as do report writers for databases or new terminals. These technologies basically support users, rather than change their operations style. Still other replacement technologies impact user habits so dramatically that if success is to be achieved, user leadership must drive the implementation effort. Each implementation situation requires careful planning to ensure that service is not interrupted and that the affected individuals understand how to operate with the new service. Figure 11–1 summarizes the tensions and forces that must be managed in IT innovation.

FIGURE 11–1   Forces to Be Managed in IT Innovation

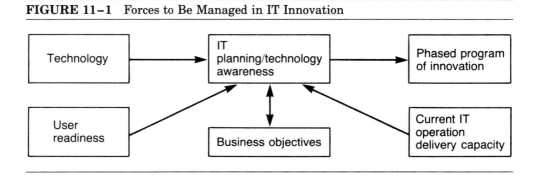

---

[1]Martin Buss, "Penny-Wise Approach to Data Processing," *Harvard Business Review,* July–August 1981.

Good technology planning includes an ongoing appraisal of user readiness, an inventory of the uses of existing technology, an awareness of where technology is going, and a program of appropriate pilot technology projects. A large consumer products company, for example, has an IT unit with a very strong emerging-technology group. As part of their activity they maintain for each division and function an updated log of services in use and an assessment of current problems. They are currently introducing a program of office support that includes a large portfolio of applications in a pilot division. Their detailed program for this division, scheduled over 24 months, includes benchmarks and reviews for evaluating benefits, operating problems, and progress. Such pilot testing stimulates broader organizational awareness of the opportunities and operational issues associated with new technology and permits better planning for full-scale implementation in the other divisions.

MEASURING AND MANAGING CAPACITY

The less one knows about computer hardware/software/networking technology, the more certain one tends to be in matters of capacity. In reality, the various hardware/software/network elements tend to interact in such a complex way that diagnosing bottlenecks and planning long-term capacity require a high degree of skill. To understand capacity and its key changeability, we must consider these factors:

1. Capacity comes in much smaller, less-expensive increments than it did a decade ago. In many organizations this has created an "asymmetric reward structure" for capacity excesses versus shortages; that is, a shortage of capacity in critical operating periods is very expensive, while the cost of extra capacity is very low. For these organizations, a decision to carry excess capacity is sound.

2. A capacity "crunch" develops with devastating suddenness. During one six-month period a mid-sized sign manufacturer operated with few difficulties with a 77 percent load on the central processing unit (CPU) during peak demand. Senior management refused to listen to IT management's warning that they were on the edge of a crisis and would not permit IT management to order additional equipment. During the next six months the introduction of two new minor systems and the acquisition of a major contract brought the CPU load during the first shift to 85 percent. This created a dramatic erosion in on-line systems response time and a steady stream of missed schedules on the batch systems. Working through weekends and holidays failed to alleviate the situation. To the untutored eye, the transition from a satisfactory to a thoroughly unsatisfactory situation occurs suddenly and dramatically.

3. There has been an explosion of diagnostic tools, such as hardware and software monitors, that assist in identifying systems' capacity problems. These tools are analytical devices and thus are no better than the ability of the analyst using them and the quality of the forecasts of future demands to be placed on the systems. In firms where operations play a vital role, these tools and their contributions have led to significant growth in both the number and quality of technical analysts in the IT operations group.

4. A dramatic increase has occurred in the number of suppliers of computer peripherals. This has sharply reduced the number of firms that are totally committed to a single vendor's equipment. Additional features, coupled with attractive prices of specialist manufacturers, have pushed many firms in the direction of IT vendor proliferation. Combined with the integration of telecommunications and office support, this phenomenon makes the task of capacity planning more complex and increases the need to referee vendor disputes when the firm's network fails.

5. Complex trade-offs must be made between innovation and conservatism. Companies in which IT offers *significant* (in terms of overall company profitability) cost reductions or the possibility of significant strategic competitive advantage should push innovation much harder than other firms. Similarly, firms that are very dependent on smooth minute-to-minute operation of existing systems must be more careful about introducing new technology into a network than other firms. Unanticipated interaction with existing systems could jeopardize reliable operation of key parts of the organization. (That was at the root of the AT&T network collapse noted at the beginning of the chapter. Inadequately tested switching software at one AT&T node interacted in an unexpected way with the rest of the network's software.)

6. The cost and disruption caused by change may outweigh the specific advantages associated with a particular technology. Therefore, skipping a generation of change is desirable in some circumstances. This must be examined carefully from two perspectives:

   a. The system design practices of the 1960s and early 1970s were quite different from those of today. Some firms, anxious to postpone investment, have stayed too long with the older systems and have exposed themselves to great operational risk when they have tried to implement massive change in impossibly short periods of time. In many cases the results have been disastrous. (These time pressures were triggered either by external vendor decommitment of key components of an operating hardware/software configuration *or* an urgent need to modify software drastically to meet new competitive needs.) Software, like a building, depreciates. Because industry accounting practices, except for those of software companies, do not recognize this, it is very easy for general managers to overlook the problems of this aging asset. Fundamentally, too many operating managers mistakenly think of IT development as an *annual* operating expense as opposed to a capital investment or asset maintenance activity.

    b. Certain changes in the hardware/software configuration are critical if the firm is to be competitive; other changes cannot legitimately be considered essential. Investments in this latter category clearly can be postponed.

7. As investments in the products of small software and hardware vendors increases, the issues of vendor viability and product maintainability become important. The mortality rate among these small suppliers has been high since the early 1970s. In evaluating hardware vendors the issues are, If they go under, is there an acceptable, easily convertible alternative; Is it easy to keep existing systems going in both the short term and the long term; and, What are the likely costs of these alternatives? In evaluating software vendors the question is, Does the contract provide for access to source programs and documentation if the vendor goes out of business? An additional area of complexity is the vendor's posture toward program maintenance. This includes error correction and systems enhancements. How will these changes be charged? As noted earlier, experienced IT operations thinking is critical in these negotiations. Very unhappy outcomes have all too often ensued when either the user or the systems and programming department purchased software without understanding the long-term operating implications.

8. Finally, a hidden set of capacity decisions focuses on appropriate infrastructure backup—such as power, height above the flood plain, and adequate building strength for the weight of the equipment. The importance of the reliability of these items is often underassessed. For example, the temperature in a large metropolitan data center rose from 78 degrees to 90 degrees in a two-hour period, shutting down the entire operation. A frantic investigation finally found that three floors down a plumber had mistakenly cut off a valve essential to the cooling system room.

    These points clearly show that capacity planning is a very complex subject that requires as much administrative thinking as technical thinking. Few organizations in the 1990s are building a new "factory" but, rather, they are implementing a continuous program of renovation and modernization on the factory floor while maintaining full production on the assembly line. This is a formidable and, unfortunately, often seriously underestimated task.

MANAGING THE IT OPERATIONS WORK FORCE

The personnel issues in the operations function have changed significantly in the past few years. Most dramatic has been the major reduction, and in *many* cases elimination, of the data input and preparation departments. The introduction of on-line data entry has not only changed the type of tasks to be done (keypunching, key verification, job-logging procedures, etc.), but has permitted much of this work to be transferred to the department that originates the transaction. Indeed the work is often transferred to the person who initiates the transaction or it is a by-product of another activity (such as cash register sales of bar-coded items). This is a desirable trend because it locates control firmly with the person most directly involved and it reduces costs. In some settings, however, it has been exceptionally difficult to implement, with users proving to be less enthusiastic than anticipated about taking over this accountability. In general, however, the large centralized data entry departments have faded into history.

At the same time, the jobs in the computer operations section are being altered significantly. For example,

1. Database-handling jobs are steadily being automated. The mounting of tapes and disks is automated and reduced. Many firms have successfully automated the entire tape library function. Further, as cathode-ray tubes (CRTs) have exploded in popularity, the amount of paper handling at the IT operations center has been reduced. It is likely that image processing will further impact this. The "lights-out factory" is becoming reality. (The wide use of facsimile machines and desktop printers is contributing to the good health of the paper industry.)
2. The formerly manual functions of expediting and scheduling have been built into the computer's basic operating system, eliminating a class of jobs.
3. Consolidation of data centers allows significant staff reductions as well as reductions in software site rentals. A recent consolidation of 10 large data centers reduced staff from 720 to 380.
4. The establishment of work performance standards in this environment has become less feasible and less useful. As the data input function disappears and the machine schedules itself rather than being paced by the operator's performance, the time-and-motion performance standards of the 1960s and 1970s have become largely irrelevant. Inevitably, evaluating the performance of the remaining highly technical individuals has become more subjective. These people are either trouble-shooting problems or executing complex operating systems and facilities changes.

As these factors indicate, the composition of the operations work force has changed dramatically. The blue-collar component has been significantly reduced, while the technical and professional components have been increased significantly. In an environment of continuous technological change, the skills of these staff must continually be upgraded if they are to remain relevant.

Career Paths.   In this environment, career path planning is a particular challenge. At present, three major avenues are available for professionals. Those with technical aptitude tend to move to positions in either technical support or systems development. A common exit point for console operators is as maintenance programmers. As a result of operations experience, they have developed a keen sensitivity to the need for thorough testing of systems changes. The second avenue is a position as a manager in operations, particularly in large shops where management positions ranging from shift supervisors to operations managers are filled mostly through internal promotions. (The number of these jobs, however, is steadily decreasing.) Finally, in banks and insurance companies in particular there have been a number of promotions out of IT operations into other user positions in the firm. In the manufacturing sector this avenue of opportunity is especially rare. Any of these promotion paths, if given the proper attention, can make the operations environment an attractive, dynamic place to work.

Unionization.   Although the trade union movement has been relatively inactive in the U.S. IT environment, it has been quite active in Europe and portions of western Canada. Organizing this department gives the union great leverage in many settings, because a strike by a small number of individuals can virtually paralyze an organization. For example, strikes of small numbers of computer operations staff in the United Kingdom's Inland Revenue Service have caused enormous disruptions in its day-to-day operations in the past. Changes in the skill mix that favor highly professional and technical staff suggest that this concern will be less important in the future.

In thinking about the potential impact of unionization, these points are important:

1. The number of blue-collar jobs susceptible to unionization has dropped dramatically. IT shops were more vulnerable to being organized in the technology of the past generation than in the current or future generations.
2. The creation of multiple data centers in diverse locations tends to reduce a firm's vulnerability to a strike in one location. The networks of the future will reduce the risk even further. This has been a factor, although generally not the dominant one, in some moves toward distributed processing.

3. The inflexibilities that accompany unionization can pose enormous problems in this type of manufacturing organization given the frequency and unpredictability of operating problems and the need for high-technology skills. Further, the dynamics of technical change continuously transform IT operating functions and jobs. If the technology were ever to stabilize, the inflexibilities presented by organized labor would be of less concern.

Selection Factors for Operations Manager and Staff

Selecting the appropriate IT operations manager and key staff is crucial. Several factors generate the need for particular skills in different environments.

Scope of Activities. As scope widens from on-line satellite to knowledge-based systems, the IT activity demands greater diversity of staff, and the complexity of management increases dramatically. Significantly more sophisticated managerial skills are required.

Criticality of IT Operations Unit. Firms that are heavily dependent on IT operations ("factory" and "strategic") are forced to devote higher-caliber professional staff resources to this area. Uneven quality of support is very expensive for such companies.

Technical Sophistication of the Shop. A shop that is heavily devoted to batch-type operations (there are still some around) with a relatively predictable workload and a nondynamic hardware/software configuration requires less investment in leading-edge management than does a shop with a rapidly changing workload in a volatile technical environment. The latter type of shop requires staff who can effectively lead such efforts as upgrading operating systems.

These factors suggest the impossibility of describing a general-purpose IT operations manager. Not only do different environments require different skills, but over time the requirements within an individual unit shift. The overall trend of the last decade is toward demand for an even higher quality of manager. The tape handler or console operator of the early 1970s has often proven inadequate for the job.

Human Issues in Managing the Work Force

A series of long-term human issues must be dealt with in managing the work force effectively.

1. The problem of staff availability and quality is a long-term challenge for IT operations. In an environment where small numbers of highly skilled workers are needed, intensified efforts are needed to attract quality individuals to the IT operations group. Career paths and salary levels require continuous reappraisal. In "factory" and "strategic" companies, IT operations must not be treated as an unwanted "stepchild" of the development group.

2. IT operations must develop appropriate links to both the users and the development group. The linkage to development is needed for ensuring that standards are in place so that both new systems and enhancements to existing ones are operable (without the development staff being present or on call every time the system is run) and that no unintended interactions with other programs and data files occur. Establishing a formal IT operations quality assurance function is a common way to deal with this. No system is allowed to run on the network until it has been certified by the IT operations unit as meeting the company's standards. The user linkage is critical for ensuring that when an operating problem occurs the user knows who in the IT operations unit can solve it—and for avoiding endless rounds of finger pointing.

3. A long-term IT operations staff development plan that includes specific attention to training needs needs to be generated.

4. Issues concerning the quality of work life must be addressed continuously. These include such items as flexible time, three- or four-day workweeks, shift rotation, and so on.

No single ideal policy or procedure can address these issues. Rather, a continuous reassessment must occur to ensure that the best of current practice is being examined and that the unit does not inadvertently become frozen in obsolete work practices.

PRODUCTION PLANNING AND CONTROL

Setting Goals

Operations production planning is complicated by the multitude of goals an IT operations function may have. Among the most common goals are these:

- To ensure a high-quality, zero-defect operation. All transactions will be handled correctly, no reports will be lost or missent, and so forth.
- To meet all long-term job schedules (or to meet them within some standard).
- To be able to handle unanticipated, unscheduled jobs, processing them within x minutes or hours of receipt provided they do not consume more than 1 percent of the CPU resource.
- To provide an average response time on terminals for key applications during the first shift of x seconds. No more than 1 percent of transactions will require more than y seconds.

- To limit day-to-day operating costs to specified given levels. Capital expenditure for IT equipment will not exceed the budgeted levels.

Establishing Priorities

By and large IT operations goals are mutually conflicting, in that all of them cannot be optimized simultaneously. For companies where IT operations support is critical to achieving corporate missions ("factory" and "strategic"), establishment of priorities requires senior management guidance. In environments where it is less critical, these goals can be prioritized at a lower level. Failure to set priorities in a manner that makes for widespread concurrence and understanding of the trade-offs to be made has been a primary cause of the poor regard in which some operations units have been held. When their goals were not prioritized, their task has been impossible.

A firm's priorities give insight into how the firm should address two other items, organization of the capacity and ensuring consistent operating policies.

Organization of Capacity. Whether to have a single, integrated computer configuration or a series of modular units either within a single data center or in multiple data centers is an important strategic decision—assuming the nature of the workload allows a choice. Setting up modular units ("plants within a plant," at some cost) allows specialized delivery of service for different applications and users. These multiple factories also allow for simpler operating systems and for quite different types of performance measures and management styles to be implemented for each. This focused factory concept has been too often overlooked in IT operations.

Consistent Operating Policies. Uncoordinated management specialists, each trying to optimize his or her own function, may create a thoroughly inconsistent and ineffective environment. For example, in a large insurance company the following policies were simultaneously operational:

- An operator wage and incentive system based on meeting all long-term schedules and minimizing job setup time.
- A production control system that gave priority to quick-turnaround, small-batch jobs that met certain technical characteristics.
- A quality control system that focused on zero defects, ensuring that no reruns would have to take place.
- A management control system that rewarded both low operating budgets and low variances from the operating budgets. Among other things, this control incentive had pushed the company toward a very constrained facilities layout as a means of minimizing costs.

While each of the policies could have made sense individually, collectively they were totally inconsistent and created tension and friction within the IT operations group. Not surprisingly, the key users' perceptions of service varied widely.

Strategic Impact of IT Operations

The management focus brought to IT operations depends on the IT function's role in the firm. IT operations in the "support" and "turnaround" categories can appropriately be oriented toward cost-efficiency. Deadlines, while important to meet, are not absolutely critical to these organizations' success. Quality control, while important on the error dimension, can be dealt with in a more relaxed way. It is appropriate to take more risks on the capacity dimension for both job-shop and process-type IT operations in order to reduce the firm's financial investment. Less formal, less expensive backup arrangements are also appropriate. Finally, corners can safely be cut in user-complaint response mechanisms.

The "factory" type of operation poses very different challenges, because IT is integrally woven into the ongoing fabric of the company's operations. Zero-defect accuracy, fast response time, and prompt schedule meeting are absolutely critical. Capacity to meet various contingencies is critical, because severe competitive damage may occur otherwise. Consequently, the issue of capacity needs to be managed more carefully and more reserve capacity for contingencies usually needs to be acquired. New operating systems and hardware enhancements must be very carefully evaluated and managed to avoid the danger and financial damage of downtime. These factors cause a company to make any necessary cost-reduction decisions more carefully than in organizations less dependent on IT service.

The "strategic" operation faces all the issues of the "factory" operation plus several others. Capacity planning is more complicated because it involves major new services, not simply extrapolating figures for old services with new volume forecasts. A stronger liaison must be maintained with users in order to deal with the potential service disruptions associated with adding new technology and new families of applications. These factors suggest the need for more slack in both capacity and budget to protect vital corporate interests.

Implementing Production Control and Measurement

The issues raised in the previous section show why only an evolutionary, adaptive control and reporting structure will work. The indexes, standards, and controls that fit one organization at a particular time will not meet their own or other organizations' needs over an extended period of time as both the technology and the organization evolve more toward on-line systems.

Within the appropriate goals for the operations department, there is a critical need to establish both performance indexes and performance standards. This allows actual data to be compared against standards. Performance indexes should include items in the following areas:

- Cost performance, both aggregate performance and the performance for different IT services.
- Staff turnover rates.
- Average and worst 5 percent response times for different services.
- Quality of service indicators, such as amount of system downtime, by service.
- Number of user complaints, by service.
- Number of misrouted reports and incorrect outputs.
- Usage of services—such as word processing, electronic mail, and computer utilization—and peak hours.
- Surveys of user satisfaction with service.

While the data generated may be quite voluminous, the data (including trends) should be summarizable in a one- to two-page report each week or month. Such quantitative data provide a framework for making qualitative assessments of performance against the standards that reflect the department's goals.

SECURITY

One of the emotional topics related to IT operations is how much security is needed for protecting the site and how much actually exists. This complex subject is discussed only briefly here in order to call attention to the nature and importance of security. Exhaustively covered in other sources, the breadth of the issue is defined by the following points:

1. Perfect security is unattainable at any price. The key need is to determine the point of diminishing returns for an organization's particular mission and geography. Different units in the organization and different systems may have distinctly different security requirements.
2. Smaller organizations for which the IT activity is critical have found it desirable to go to something like the SUNGUARD solution, by which consortium of firms has funded the construction and equipping of an empty data center. If a member firm incurs a major disaster, this site is available for use.
3. Large organizations for which IT activity is fundamental to their functioning and existence appropriately will think about this dif-

ferently. Such firms will be strongly motivated to establish multiple remote centers (to avoid the investment bank's experience explained in the first example at the beginning of the chapter). Duplicate data files, extra telecommunications expense, and duplicate staff and office space all make this an expensive (although necessary) security measure. These firms have come to the conclusion that if they do not back themselves up, no one else will. The architecture of these networks is extraordinarily complex to design in an efficient yet responsive fashion.

4. For organizations in which the IT operation is less critical, appropriate steps may include arranging backup with another organization. (This sounds simpler in theory than it is in reality.) Another alternative is to prepare a warehouse site with appropriate wiring, telephone lines, air conditioning, and so on. (In a real emergency, locating and installing the computer is the easiest thing to do. Locating and installing all the other items consumes much more time.) Backing up the network is much more complex than just data centers. The insurance company in the example at the beginning of the chapter now has two entirely separate networks with two carriers and carefully allocates work between them in order to reduce their operational vulnerability. Reuters news service has processing nodes around the world with multiple paths out of each node. If one path fails, the network is unimpacted; if a node fails, the network degrades but does not fail in all respects.

5. Within a single site, a number of steps can be taken to improve security. Listed here are some of the most common, each of which has a different cost associated with it.

    a. Limiting physical access to the computer room. Methods from simple buzzers to isolated "diving chamber" entrances can be used.

    b. Complex access codes that serve to deny file and system entry to unauthorized personnel. External Hackers have successfully penetrated a large number of organizations who have not paid attention to this item.

    c. Surrounding the data center with chain-link fences, automatic alarms, and dogs. Monitoring access to inner areas by guards using remote TV cameras.

    d. Ensuring an uninterrupted power supply, including banks of batteries and stand-alone generators.

    e. Storing a significant number of files off-site and updating them with a high level of frequency.

    f. Use of a Halon inert gas system to protect the installation in case of fire.

    g. Systematic rotation of people through jobs, enforcement of mandatory vacations (with no entry to building allowed during vacation time), and physical separation of IT development and operations staff.

This is merely an illustrative list and in no sense is intended to be comprehensive. Sadly, it is extremely difficult to fully secure files in a world of PCs, viruses, and floppy disks that go home at night.

PRIVACY

An explosive issue that cuts across the IT applications world of the 1990s is that of the increasingly intrusive role of IT on individual privacy. This issue transcends all aspects of the field of information technology and is included in this chapter only as a matter of organizational convenience. Consider the following examples.

- A consumer foods company uses information from redeemed coupons and rebate forms to create a database for targeted marketing. It is assailed in a national consumer-advocacy publication with the headline "Smile—You're on Corporate Camera!"
- An entrepreneur realizes that he can easily tie together several credit-bureau databases and some other sources of information (such as motor vehicle records) about individuals. When he begins to market this service to small businesses for credit checking and pre-employment screening, the state assembly passes a bill that would significantly regulate his activities.
- Many credit bureaus offer services in which mailing lists are "pre-screened" according to a customer's stated criteria. In addition, some credit bureaus transfer selected information from their credit files to marketing databases, from which mailing lists are sold for targeted marketing. These policies became major topics of discussion in a House of Representatives subcommittee hearing, where there were many calls for additional federal legislation.

These examples—all of which occurred in 1990—demonstrate an increasing challenge to managers for the 1990s. Societal concerns about information privacy—the belief that limits are needed on access to information about individuals—are increasing, and these concerns could erupt in the next decade with considerable force. Unless proactive steps are taken, firms will find themselves grappling with these societal anxieties in two forms: public-opinion backlash against various computerized processes, and a tightened legal environment with additional governmental control.

The Roots of the Privacy Issue

Two forces are behind this focus on privacy in the 1990s: the new technology capabilities that allow these new applications and the vacuum surrounding the distinction between "right and wrong."

Technological Capabilities. Much more information is in computer-processable form today. Information that was previously stored in handwritten or typed paper files is now digitally encoded and electronically accessible from thousands of miles away.

Owing to less-expensive storage devices, faster processors, and the development of relational database techniques and structured query languages, it has become both more feasible and vastly more economical to cross-classify information. Likewise, passing and correlating information between organizations is now relatively inexpensive and easy to accomplish. As networks become commonplace, new strategic applications pool data from different sources.

In addition to the problem of potential intrusiveness of this pooling, there is also the almost unsolvable issue of correcting errors in information. In many cases, it is virtually impossible to stop the trickle of errors as data pass from firm to firm.

Not only have the speed and cost of computing undergone phenomenal improvements in the last decade, but the trend is accelerating. Thus, in the future it will be even easier and more economical to search for information and store it. As personal computers and local-area networks proliferate across organizations in the hands of nonsystems personnel, people will propagate uncontrolled databases (on personal hard disks and file servers), and the number of people accessing networks will increase.

Add to this the growing use of artificial intelligence. As more decision rules are automated in expert systems, perceptions of these problems may be amplified as mistakes are inexorably carried to their logical conclusion in a documented form.

Taken together, these technological trends could easily and inexpensively lead to applications that would create unacceptable intrusions into people's privacy.

Ethical Concerns. The technological forces operate in a large vacuum regarding right and wrong. Situations have been created for which the rules of behavior that worked well in earlier decades do not offer meaningful guidance. We are confronting a new set of policy decisions. While it is true that individuals and organizations may be inappropriately harmed by certain applications and activities, the degree of the impact is uneven. Some practices can be deeply damaging to people, while many others lie in the category of "merely inconvenient." Some inconvenient results of increased information gathering—such as mailbox clutter—are accepted by many as the "cost of progress," but society will eventually draw a line to protect against other applications that are recognized as more damaging.

For example, tenant-screening services, which allow landlords to exchange information about problems with former tenants, can lead to the unjust refusal of an individual's rental application if incorrect information is in the database or if mistaken identification occurs.[2] More often than not, however, such services protect landlords from losses incurred in renting to tenants who have already proven to be bad risks, and they thereby facilitate lower rents. Will society demand that such screening services be restrained?

The Implications

Questions for Organizations.   Firms must anticipate potential privacy problems as they make decisions and take action to avoid negative public opinion and extreme legislative responses to inflammatory charges. Good planning may help your firm avoid the cost of adapting to new rules. Some critical questions regarding privacy issues are discussed here.

Storage of Information.   Is there any information in the organization's files that should not be there? If it were brought to light that such information was being collected and stored, would there be a public backlash? For example, several insurance firms have recently struggled with this issue as it applies to AIDS test results, and where and how this information should be disseminated. Some advocates became outraged when they learned that individuals' files contained notations about positive test results. Lawsuits and numerous pieces of legislation (mostly at a state level) followed quickly.

Use of Information.   Is information being used for the purposes individuals believed it was being collected to serve? Many individuals who provide information for what they believe is one purpose become angry when they learn it has been used for a different purpose. For example, a credit-card issuer came under legal scrutiny when it installed a computer system that could evaluate cardholders' purchasing histories for the purpose of enclosing targeted advertising material with their monthly statements. In another example, a car dealership installed an interactive computer system that asked potential customers to answer questions about their personalities and attitudes. The computer printed a "recommended car profile" for each customer. It *also* printed—with a different printer, in a back room—suggested sales strategy for the salesperson based on the customer's answers. Had the potential customers known about this back-room printer, they might never have entered the dealer's showroom.

Sharing of Information.   Are pieces of information about individuals being shared electronically with other organizations? If so, would

---

[2]Some of the examples used here are adapted from *The Privacy Journal,* an independent monthly newsletter based in Washington, D.C.

individuals approve of this sharing if they knew about it? Certainly, extraordinary opportunities for gaining strategic advantage have come through such sharing activities (micromarketing strategies). However, some individuals object when a company with which they do business sells their names and addresses, purchasing histories, and other demographic details to other companies. If the shared information is highly sensitive—if, for example, it concerns individuals' medical or financial histories—the reaction to having it shared—sold even—is dramatically exacerbated.

Human Judgment. *Are decisions that require human judgment being made within appropriate processes?* Individuals legitimately become upset and request governmental protection when decisions that they feel require human judgment are being made without it. For example, an insurance company's decisions on whether to accept or reject new applicants—made within prescribed formulas and without direct human involvement—caused considerable difficulties when blindly applied in extraordinary situations that had not been contemplated when the rules were formulated.

Combining Information. *Are pieces of personal information from different sources combined into larger files?* The concerns of individuals and lawmakers are heightened when disparate pieces of information—even if innocuous in themselves—are pulled together. The possibility of creating a single profile of an individual's life is, to many, a threatening prospect. The entrepreneur who tied together several databases in order to provide "one-stop shopping" for several types of information through one vehicle faced this perception.

Error Detection and Correction. *Are appropriate procedures in place for preventing and correcting errors?* At issue here are both deliberate and inadvertent errors. Deliberate errors, which include unauthorized intrusions into databases, are often subject to audit controls. Inadvertent errors, on the other hand, are much more subtle and stubborn. They include misclassifications, data-entry errors, and the sorts of errors that arise when information is not updated as circumstances in people's lives change. It is impossible to achieve 100 percent error-free operation, but observers may reasonably ask whether the trade-offs a company makes for assuring accuracy are reasonable. *If your organization were examined by lawmakers or consumer advocates, would you appear to be making the "correct" trade-offs?*

An example from the public sector centers on the National Crime Information Center, a nationwide computer system that is linked to many state criminal-justice information systems. Outstanding warrants, parole violations, and other criminal data are often entered into local systems and are later "uploaded" to the national system. Law-enforcement agencies can then query the system to learn if individuals are wanted in other areas. Unfortunately, for a long period of time, problems with inaccurate data and mistaken identities were not uncommon. These problems led to improper arrests and incarcerations, and a number of lawsuits were filed.

Other Issues. An audit of the questions we have enumerated often reveals several items for action in the organization. Additional issues to be considered by firms include the following:

Long Term versus Short Term. Line management should carefully think through each new use of information before they embrace it. In some cases, a "quick hit" for short-term profitability can yield disastrous results later. For example, an insurance company sold a list of its policyholders to a direct-marketing firm, earning a healthy fee. However, many policyholders determined that the company had done this—because of unique spellings of their names and other peculiarities—and were unhappy about it. The company received an avalanche of mail complaining about this use of their names and addresses, as well as a nontrivial number of policy cancellations, which brought the CEO to vow "never again." The short-term gain was not worth the long-term fallout.

Education. Problems can be avoided through appropriate education initiatives. An organization's clients (customers or other individuals about whom information is stored) should be informed regarding the corporation's use of information about them when it strays from the narrow purpose for which it was collected. Clients should be told (1) the type of information about them that is permanently stored in the corporation's files, (2) what is done with the information they provide, and (3) whether additional information from external sources is added to their files. This education process can take place in several forums, including inserts with monthly statements, special letters, and press releases. Corporations in particularly sensitive industries might provide toll-free telephone lines for clients' questions about information use.

Organizational Mechanism. Through both an initial audit and on a continuing basis, the internal and external uses and distribution of data should be given close scrutiny—especially if the firm is in an industry where such data sharing is likely to occur, such as consumer marketing or financial services. In very sensitive situations, a standing "Data Distribution Committee" can provide a forum for evaluating these issues. Such a committee should have high visibility and comprise senior executives. It could also be augmented by outside advisers (such as corporate directors) to ensure that objective viewpoints are provided and that problems are approached with sufficient breadth.

As laws and public opinion change in the next decade, it will be necessary to check current and planned applications against evolving policies and attitudes. Data files should be organized in ways that facilitate such ad hoc evaluations. For example, one might be called upon to list all data elements that are exchanged between internal organizational entities and with external entities. Could your organization construct this list in a quick and credible way?

Conclusions.   Our discussion of these issues indicates the complexity of the privacy concerns growing up around IT use. Chief information officers and other members of senior management should brace themselves for intense scrutiny of their activities by both legislators and privacy advocates. No doubt, there will be more focus on commercial IT activities than on governmental ones in the 1990s. The tension between the effective functioning of commerce and individuals' rights to privacy will certainly become more pronounced. It is far better for the business community to be taking a voluntary, proactive stance now than to have to adopt a reactive posture later.

SUMMARY

IT operations management is a complex, evolutionary field. This is partly due to a changing technology that continually makes obsolete existing IT service delivery processes and controls, partly due to the continuing questions related to in-house versus out sourcing of the service, and partly due to the changing profile of the IT work force. Major insights for dealing with these issues come from applying the understandings gained in managing technological change and manufacturing to this very special type of high-technology endeavor. Most large firms now know how to schedule and control multiprocessing batch computer systems working on numerical data from decentralized input stations. Building upon this base to include word processing, electronic mail, CAD, image processing, links to outside customers and suppliers, and a host of more decentralized IT activities is an extraordinarily challenging task. Underlying this, the most critical need for operations success is for recruiting, training, and retaining knowledgeable people to operate, maintain, and develop IT services. Finally of course, is the issue of privacy, what forms of Data Files should be kept, what forms of cross correlation are acceptable and who should have access to them.

Case 11–1

SEARS, ROEBUCK AND CO.: OUTSOURCING WITHIN THE COMPANY (A)

It was early 1988; chief information officer Charles Moran was reviewing the evolution of communications and data processing activities at Sears, Roebuck and Co. (Sears). Recognition of communications network consolidation opportunities across its diverse and highly autonomous business groups in the early 1980s had led the company to form the successful Sears Communication Network (SCN) in 1983. During the next five years, the network contributed to lowered unit costs, improved service, reliable and expandable capability, and timely development of new applications without causing major disruptions in the business groups' activities. Now Moran, with Charles Carlson, vice president of information systems and data processing for the Merchandising Group, Selby Shaver, general manager and president of SCN, Inc., and Gary Weis, vice president of data communications and software services for SCN, Inc., was contemplating data processing consolidation opportunities across the business groups.

Many of Sears' information systems executives were becoming increasingly alarmed by the rising costs of data processing operations, and were looking both inside and outside the company for answers. Moran and his colleagues wondered if an internally managed central utility could provide many, if not all, of the same services to the business groups at a lower cost to the corporation. The key question was whether the business groups would agree to a centrally managed utility and concentrate their information technology (IT) efforts on business applications development activities. Was the concept of a corporate utility even feasible given Sears' culture of autonomy across the various business groups, and would the savings be real? Moran recalled a meeting with Edward A. Brennan, chairman and CEO of Sears. After hearing the arguments for and against the corporate utility concept in September 1987, Brennan had remarked: "Everyone needed to make this happen is in this room. Decide and move forward."

Company Background

"We are in the merchandising business . . . the insurance business . . . the lending business . . . the asset management business . . . and the real estate business. We view our efforts as building on several longstanding Sears strengths by developing new products and new channels—within and across our businesses."[1] This was how chairman, president and CEO Brennan had described Sears' family of companies—Sears Merchandise Group, Allstate Insurance Group, Dean Witter Financial Services Group, and Coldwell Banker Real Estate Group (see Appendix). The Sears Merchandising Group, with 1987 sales of $28.09 billion on assets of

---

[1]Sears, Roebuck and Co. 1989 Annual Report.

Professor Nancy S. Balaguer prepared this case as the basis for class discussion rather than to illustrate either effective or ineffective handling of an administrative situation.

EXHIBIT 1   Consolidated Financial Highlights (millions, except per common share data)

	1987	1986	1985	1984	1983
Revenues	$45,904	$42,303	$39,349	$37,898	$35,883
Net income	1,633	1,339	1,294	1,452	1,342
Common share dividends	756	648	639	631	537
Per common share					
Net income	4.30	3.58	3.51	4.00	3.80
Dividends	2.00	1.76	1.76	1.76	1.52
Investments	25,120	22,183	19,249	17,203	15,434
Total assets	75,014	66,009	66,426	57,073	46,176
Shareholders' equity	13,541	13,017	11,776	10,903	9,787

$23.82 billion, was the largest marketer of merchandise in the world. Allstate Insurance, with 1987 revenues of $15.56 billion on assets of $24.50 billion, was ranked second (5.5 percent) in the insurance market. Dean Witter Financial Services Group generated revenues of $4.0 billion on $24.57 billion in assets; and the Coldwell Banker Real Estate Group had continued to expand, (Coldwell Banker Residential had garnered approximately 10 percent of the residential market), generating revenues of $1.24 billion, up 8 percent from 1986. (Exhibit 1 presents Sears' financial performance for the five years ending in 1987; Exhibit 2 contains financial highlights for the four business groups.)

The following company strengths were believed to constitute Sears' principal advantages in the marketplace: a business relationship with 70 percent of America's households, coupled with a strong reputation for trust and service; multiple consumer product and service distribution channels, with some 328,000 employees in *direct daily contact* with customers through more than 12,000 selling units from coast to coast; one of the nation's most sophisticated information processing and telecommunications networks linking its four businesses; and a solid

financial base, anchored in sales of $48.44 billion and assets of $75 billion.[2]

Founded in 1886, Sears was exclusively a mail-order business until 1928 when Robert E. Wood, upon becoming chairman, initiated the move into retailing and established the Sears' vision. This vision centered on reliability, trust, and providing value to the customer. Throughout the company's long history, the people who worked for Sears had viewed themselves primarily as merchandisers. Even after Wood founded Allstate Insurance as a wholly owned subsidiary in 1931, the merchandising culture remained central. Sears maintained a very small corporate staff. Overarching was a norm of decentralization; store managers ran the store and each division ran its own business. Wood opposed centralization, believing that store problems were best solved on the spot.

In 1982, Sears was basically two very large enterprises—Sears Merchandising and Allstate Insurance—with two newly acquired companies, Coldwell Banker and Dean Witter. The decision to acquire these companies had been a part of a strategy to

---

[2]Sears, Roebuck and Co. 1987 and 1989 Annual Reports.

EXHIBIT 2   Five-Year Summary of Business Group and Segment Financial Data (millions)

Revenues	1987	1986	1985	1984	1983
Sears Merchandise Group					
Merchandising	$22,894	$22,092	$21,549	$21,671	$20,439
Credit	2,011	2,068	2,098	1,894	1,404
International	3,180	2,914	2,905	2,943	3,246
Sears Merchandise Group total	$28,085	$27,074	$26,552	$26,508	$25,089
Allstate Insurance Group					
Property-liability insurance	$11,487	$ 9,698	$ 8,244	$ 7,551	$ 7,004
Life-health insurance	4,005	2,884	2,089	1,404	1,079
Noninsurance	64	56	46	34	41
Allstate Insurance Group total	$15,556	$12,638	$10,379	$ 8,989	$ 8,124
Dean Witter Financial Services Group					
Securities-related	$ 2,747	$ 2,563	$ 2,031	$ 1,845	$ 1,544
Consumer banking	$ 1,248	$ 852	$ 826	$ 651	$ 564
Dean Witter Financial Services Group total	$ 3,995	$ 3,415	$ 2,857	$ 2,496	$ 2,108
Coldwell Banker Real Estate Group	$ 1,244	$ 1,152	$ 949	$ 826	$ 704
Corporate and other	$ 176	$ 489	$ 424	$ 359	$ 196
Intergroup transactions	$ (616)	$ (487)	$ (446)	$ (350)	$ (338)
Total	$48,440	$44,281	$40,715	$38,828	$35,883

Income Before Income Taxes, Equity in Net Income of Unconsolidated Companies and Minority Interest					
Sears Merchandise Group					
Merchandising	$ 807	$ 885	$ 738	$ 1,196	$ 1,182
Credit	463	502	582	483	285
International	132	98	94	16	(27)
Sears Merchandise Group total	$ 1,402	$ 1,485	$ 1,414	$ 1,695	$ 1,440
Allstate Insurance Group					
Property-liability insurance	$ 702	$ 441	$ 261	$ 363	$ 373
Life-health insurance	14	177	164	124	96
Noninsurance	(1)	3	(1)	(1)	6
Allstate Insurance Group total	$ 715	$ 621	$ 424	$ 488	$ 475
Dean Witter Financial Services Group					
Securities-related	$ 148	$ 154	$ (3)	$ (94)	$ 138
Consumer banking	$ (115)	$ (212)	$ 21	$ 24	$ 52
Dean Witter Financial Services Group total	$ 33	$ (58)	$ 18	$ (70)	$ 190
Coldwell Banker Real Estate Group	$ 132	$ 151	$ 130	$ 121	$ 76
Corporate and other	$ (352)	$ (374)	$ (332)	$ (332)	$ (289)
Total	$ 1,930	$ 1,825	$ 1,654	$ 1,902	$ 1,892

EXHIBIT 2   (continued)

Net Income	1987	1986	1985	1984	1983
Sears Merchandise Group					
Merchandising	$ 488	$ 458	$ 447	$ 656	$ 654
Credit	263	253	294	243	144
International	36	25	25	6	(17)
Sears Merchandise Group total	$ 787	$ 736	$ 766	$ 905	$ 781
Allstate Insurance Group					
Property-liability insurance	$ 928	$ 631	490	505	$ 469
Life-health insurance	35	117	114	155	83
Noninsurance	'-	2	1	1	3
Allstate Insurance Group total	$ 963	$ 750	$ 605	$ 661	$ 555
Dean Witter Financial Services Group					
Securities-related	$ 76	$ 80	$ -	$ (45)	$ 69
Consumer banking	$ (75)	$ (117)	13	$ 12	$ 31
Dean Witter Financial Services Group total	$ 1	$ (37)	$ 13	$ (33)	$ 100
Coldwell Banker Real Estate Group	$ 93	$ 94	$ 86	$ 76	$ 48
Corporate and other	$ (195)	$ (192)	$ (167)	$ (154)	$ (142)
Total	$ 1,649	$ 1,351	$ 1,303	$ 1,455	$ 1,342

Assets					
Sears Merchandise Group					
Merchandising	$ 8,272	$ 8,233	$ 8,240	$ 8,332	$ 6,771
Credit	13,291	12,070	11,887	11,825	10,312
International	2,257	2,068	1,917	1,881	2,064
Sears Merchandise Group total	$23,820	$22,371	$22,044	$22,038	$19,147
Allstate Insurance Group					
Property-liability insurance	$17,217	$15,442	$13,372	$11,913	$11,140
Life-health insurance	7,211	4,834	3,520	2,591	2,154
Noninsurance	69	66	53	49	61
Allstate Insurance Group total	$24,497	$20,342	$16,945	$14,553	$13,355
Dean Witter Financial Services Group					
Securities-related	$13,952	$12,600	$18,720	$12,760	$ 7,282
Consumer banking	$10,622	$ 8,639	$ 7,253	$ 6,408	$ 5,155
Dean Witter Financial Services Group total	$24,574	$21,239	$25,973	$19,168	$12,437
Coldwell Banker Real Estate Group	$ 1,852	$ 2,124	$ 1,451	$ 1,236	$ 1,045
Corporate and other	$ 1,907	$ 2,300	$ 1,981	$ 1,627	$ 1,552
Intergroup eliminations and reclassifications	$ (1,659)	$ (2,381)	$ (1,977)	$ (1,549)	$ (1,360)
Total	$74,991	$65,995	$66,417	$57,073	$46,176

diversify into businesses that fit the following criteria: large, national presence; consumer-oriented; low barriers to entry; and a reputation compatible with the trust with which the American public regarded Sears. Businesses in the financial services industry had surfaced as viable options and, during the week of October 8, 1981, Sears announced the purchase of Dean Witter Reynolds and Coldwell Banker. Ed Telling, then chairman and CEO of Sears, observed:

> the real genius behind Allstate was not the decision to go into the insurance business. . . . All we want to do with our new diversification strategy is take what we did with Allstate and do it again in the area of financial services. Nothing more, nothing less.[3]

Information Technology Environment

With the exception of communications, the information technology function at Sears was independently carried out by each Business Group. Applications systems planning and development, data center operations, technical support and planning, technical training, and acquisition and financial management were performed on a decentralized basis. (Exhibit 3 describes each of these functions.) The specific form of the organization and pattern of execution varied across the business groups that managed these activities. The data processing environments of the business groups prior to 1988 are described below and in Exhibit 4.

Sears Merchandise Group

By April 1988, after several years of consolidation, all retail and catalog field applications and headquarters applications were processed by six data centers within the

Merchandise Group. All equipment was procured by a headquarters staff in Chicago, and technical support was provided centrally all under Carlson's leadership. A common training staff provided all technical training for applications systems development. Of 705 IT support function personnel,[4] 451 were involved with data center operations.

Allstate

The Home Office's Corporate Information Processing organization provided technical support and planning and acquisition and financial management for all Allstate business units. Data center operations were not centralized; each business unit's data center reported directly to its business unit's management. Technical training was centrally located at Home Office and served the needs of all applications development groups. Some 259 IT professionals out of a total of 806 IT support function personnel maintained Allstate's decentralized data centers.

Dean Witter Financial Services Group (DWFSG)

In 1986 a comprehensive study of Dean Witter's information technology requirements had been conducted by Dean Witter internal staff, a consulting company, and Sears' business group technical staffs. They concluded that IT support functions were utility functions that could be provided to Dean Witter's diverse business units by a common organization. The study further concluded that Dean Witter needed to focus on applying new technology within its businesses to obtain a strategic advantage over its competi-

[3]Sears, Roebuck & Company and the Retail Financial Services Industry (B), HBS Case No. 387-182.

[4]The "IT support function" includes the following functions: data center operations; technical support and planning; technical training; and acquisition and financial management services.

EXHIBIT 3   Definitions for Information Technology Functions[a]

Definition of application requirements and coordination with functional users, typically referred to as *applications systems planning,* included development cost estimation, negotiation of development schedules with the users, and arbitration of conflicts and priorities among users.

Programming and testing of applications systems, or *applications systems development,* began with the delivery of systems specifications from the Application Systems Planning function and concluded with delivery of a tested production system.

Management of data center hardware and software, or *data center operations,* consisted of the installation and daily operation of applications systems. Because operating efficiencies dictated the sharing of the hardware resource among various applications, this activity was established within each business group as a generic function independent of individual application requirements. Negotiated standards ensured independence.

Development and support of the technically complex software required to operate the shared data center computers, or *technical support and planning,* was provided by the hardware vendor, tailored to the specific hardware environment. This group usually performed problem determination and managed the resolution of complex problems within data centers. Most business units chose to plan and manage the introduction of new technology through this function.

Training and development of application system designers and programmers, or *technical training,* was typically responsible for recruiting, as well. Some smaller business units did not organizationally separate this function, and others used outside resources to accomplish training.

Procurement and charge-out of data processing expense, or *acquisition and financial management,* included contract negotiation, equipment and software evaluation, purchasing, invoice payment, and other procurement-related activities.

[a]Based on Sears' definitions of the basic information technology functions. See "Managing Information Technology: Organization and Leadership," HBS Case No. 189-133, for a more detailed description of each of these functions.

---

tion and that this technology focus should be directed by a common organization for all Dean Witter businesses, a finding supported by the role IT played in the successful introduction of the Discover Card in 1985. As of April 1988, Dean Witter was supported by 222 IT professionals maintaining three data centers and an additional 193 IT support personnel responsible for technical support and acquisition and financial management.

Coldwell Banker Commercial and Residential (CBC and CBR)

Though CBC and CBR had chosen common hardware and software platforms, management decided not to attempt to coordinate or consolidate any of the IT support functions because the diversity of businesses was a deterrent to exploiting operational synergies between companies. As of April 1988, 22 IT support function professionals were responsible for three data centers; the remaining IT personnel were involved in non-data center functions.

Corporate IT Steering Committee

The Corporate Synergy Committee (CSC) was established in the early 1980s to exploit opportunities for reducing expenses through activities such as coordinated volume purchase agreements, exchange of technical information, and sharing of resources. Information technology and general managers

EXHIBIT 4

Sears Data Processing Resources[a]
(by Business Group; 2nd Quarter 1988)

	SMG	Allstate	Dean Witter	Coldwell Banker	SCN	Total
Number of Data Centers[b]	7	20	3	3	1	34
Processing Power (MIPs)	458[c]	957	234	27	132	1,808
Disk Storage Space (billions of characters)	1,610	3,534	648	83	190	6,065
Print Capacity (thousands of pages/hour)	456	480	360	12	15	1,323

Sears IT Support Function Headcount
(by Business Group; 2nd Quarter 1988)

	SMG	Allstate	Dean Witter	Coldwell Banker	SCN	Total
Technical Support	101	73	65	7	4	250
Data Center	451	259	222	22	16	970
Non-Data Center	153	474	128	0	50	805
Total	705	806	415	29	70	2,025

Sears IT Support Function Expenditures
(in thousands of $; 1988 budget)

	SMG	Allstate	Dean Witter	Coldwell Banker	SCN	Total
Personnel	$ 25,981	$ 24,942	$15,810	$1,982	$ 2,580	$ 71,295
Occupancy Expense	7,644	5,357	7,801	2,300	856	23,958
Data Center Operations	79,168	118,851	40,150	3,717	8,371	250,257
Other	2,619	1,541	4,547	177	395	9,279
Total	$115,412	$150,691	$68,308	$8,176	$12,202	$354,789

[a]Data Center staffing, as of May 1988, was divided into three main categories: Technical Systems Support; Data Center Operations; and Non-Data Functions. The definitions of each follows:

Technical Systems Support. Personnel in this category are directly responsible for supporting the operating system and all technical software tools used to support the Data Centers. Examples of functions in this group would be systems programmers, technical consultants, managers of technical systems, CICS system consultants, etc.

Data Center Operations. Personnel in this category are directly related to the operation of the Data Center. Examples of functions in this group would be tape librarians, computer operators, production managers, IPF administration personnel, operations specialists, etc.

Non-Data Center Functions. Personnel in this category are related to Data Center activities but not supportive of only one Data Center. Examples of functions in this group would be Data Security, Network Control, Data Entry operators, financial analysts, equipment purchasing, support of application developers and end users, etc.

[b]These Data Centers vary greatly in size. For example, one of Coldwell Banker's Data Centers had less than one MIP; some of Allstate's Regional Office Data Centers range from 20 to 60 MIPs and Sears Merchandise Group had several Data Centers with over 100 MIPs.

[c]In addition to data center MIPs, Sears Merchandise Group had over 2,500 Series 1 MIPs distributed in non-Data Center locations.

from the various business groups participated on the committee on a voluntary basis. CSC-sponsored projects—mainly corporate-wide volume purchase agreements but also including exchange of technical information, sharing of resources, purchase of office equipment and supplies—had generated gross savings of more than $200 million during the ensuing years.

The IT Steering Committee, a CSC subcommittee, was responsible for reviewing several IT and communications activities. It was believed that a corporate information technology utility could extend these savings by providing a number of immediate and "positioning" advantages, for example, by: minimizing equipment purchase and data center operations and software expenses; improving staffing efficiencies; assuring corporate information assets; and promoting efficient, consistent, and secure access to information. Less quantifiable synergistic benefits also were expected to be derived from the formation of a corporate information technology and data processing organization.

Moran, Carlson, and other members of the subcommittee believed there was a great deal of evidence that IT support functions could be better managed as a common resource for all business units *within* a business group. Although there was no universal IT organization structure common to all business groups, Carlson surmised that an IT support function, serving all of the business groups, would be viable and more effective than separate IT support functions for each business group.

Concept of a Corporate Information Technology Utility

The IT Steering Committee knew that developing and selling the concept of a utility to business group management—senior, general, and IT managers—would be a major task. They knew that differing technical, functional, and corporate cultures would create variations in possible definitions of a corporate information technology function. They also were acutely aware of the wide variations in how such a function could be implemented.

Carlson and a small group of colleagues reviewed the basic information technology-related functions performed by the business groups within the Sears context. Their intent was to partition that environment into two distinct parts: that which was generic and common across all business groups; and that which was unique and distinct to each business group. Of the basic data processing functions, two—applications system planning and applications systems development—were unique to each Business Group. The remaining four—data center operations, technical planning and support, technical training, and acquisition and financial management—being focused on the data processing technology used rather than application content, had much in common among the business groups. Fortuitously, all Sears' business groups had similar hardware, software, and technical strategies, as well as a common primary vendor, and this commonality provided the basis for consideration of a common corporate information technology function.

Applications systems planning and development activities had been intentionally omitted from inclusion in the corporate utility concept. It was agreed that the independence of each business group had to be maintained with respect to the planning, development, programming, implementation, maintenance, and administration of application systems used in the conduct of their business. Each business group was best equipped to develop its own business systems. Planners, systems analysts, and programmers had large amounts of practical and basic knowledge about their specific business group, industry, and system. This expertise generally was not transferable, nor was there any point in consolidating the various knowledge bases as it would not lead to any benefit such as greater specialization or expertise. Consolidation of these activities would not yield economies of scale, and it was generally agreed that the applications development efforts were appropriately sized and worked effectively independently of one another.

Clearly, it was the common technical functions and operations, which were nearly identical across business groups, that promised to benefit most from consolidation. Carlson offered the following analogy for the corporate utility concept.

> The situation might be compared to a residential development. The potential residents might have differing requirements in terms of style, space, density, and function of a residence, just as each business group requires systems that address their own particular needs. Likewise, potential residents could construct their homes using their own building codes, conforming to their own zoning codes, and providing their own private water wells, generators for power, police and fire protection, and waste disposal. Obviously this approach is more expensive and less effective, just as separate implementations of similar technologies and data processing operations are more expensive and less effective.
>
> What is needed is an organization that would provide community planning and zoning, a unified building code, and common services for the various distinct and individual residences. Just as these residents would not be concerned with the technicalities of how fuel, water, electricity, telephone, fire, and police protection were provided, application systems developers would be able to take the technological infrastructure for granted, knowing that it was already there—part of a shared, less costly organization that allows them to concentrate on the business application system, not the supporting technology. Of course, business groups must accept the requirement to conform to certain standards not totally of their own making.

Rationale for Establishing a Corporate Information Technology Function

A corporate information technology entity was not a new idea at Sears. The concept had been discussed shortly after the acquisitions of Dean Witter and Coldwell Banker in 1982. "After these acquisitions," Moran recalled, "we began examining ways to develop and exploit new product and distribution channels. The natural question that surfaced was 'Would it be easier to develop and share products across business groups if a centrally coordinated technology group were established?' "

Considerable evidence supported the belief that consolidating IT technical support functions and viewing data centers as utilities for multi-business group data processing constituted an advantageous Corporate strategy. Specifically, two examples of business group utility functions, created to service independent business units within a business group, were cited.

Data Center Consolidation Experiences —Merchandising and Dean Witter

Over a period of several years, the Merchandise Group had consolidated its more than 20 data center operations and organization into a single, centralized entity that operated independently of geography and business unit structures. The economies and efficiencies achieved by this consolidation were reflected in cost/performance ratios; equipment availability and improved transmission capabilities, for example, enabled more work to be done with fewer locations, with attendant reductions in payroll.

A maverick territorial data processing manager named Chuck McDougall had planted the seeds for the consolidation effort in the early 1970s, when he decided to close his data center in Haywood, California, and run the Seattle catalog plant's data processing operations out of his Los Angeles data processing center. This was radical thinking at the time. The result of McDougall's independent actions was not lost on the Merchandise Group's management; these actions set off a series of consolidation efforts and prompted the eventual consolidation of data processing activities into four territories and headquarters. During the mid-1980s, McDougall's "new way of thinking" bore fruit. Economies of scale already were being realized from the resulting four data processing operations centers. Asked what would happen if all territories were to close? Carlson, then vice president of data processing at the Merchandise Group, responded: "Nothing— we've already taken that step; they (the data centers) are already reporting to me."

In addition, Moran recalled Dean Witter's efforts regarding consolidation which began under his direction when he was chief operations officer of Dean Witter. Dean Witter developed and implemented a data center/ technical support utility concept in 1987 and early 1988. The Dean Witter utility organization was responsible for defining architectural direction, technical support and training, equipment resource planning and allocation, data center management, communications support, and security policies. Business units within Dean Witter were responsible for their own systems development, including the selection and prioritization process, programming, quality assurance, systems implementation, and long-term systems plans and budgets. The goals and challenges Dean Witter faced were viewed as a microcosm of those at the Sears corporate level.

Sears Communications Network Experience

The Sears Communications Network (SCN) also had demonstrated the benefits of a corporate-level technical services utility. The SCN project had begun in 1983. A safe, conservative approach was taken to ensure a smooth transition of responsibility from the business groups to the newly formed Sears Communications Network, Inc. A five-year time frame was allocated for a three phased implementation approach (planning, building of network base, and migration of business group networks). Installation of the corporate backbone network began in 1984, and the migration was completed in 1986. Business groups were insulated from start-up costs, which were projected in 1984 to be $2.6 million. Given actual savings in 1985 and 1986, of $2.4 and $11.4 million, respectively, the initial objective of containing communications expense through corporate-wide optimization of communications facilities was clearly realized.

SCN also added greatly to connectivity and network functionality, which did not show up as savings. The network was considered absolutely essential to the timely, cost-effective launching of the Discover Card, and continued to be an important part of the support infrastructure as Discover grew rapidly. Bill Martin, senior vice-president of operations for Discover Card Services, explained:

> Our transaction costs run about a nickel below the industry average, and we spend about $40 per year to service each of our accounts, which is about $10 below what most of our competitors pay. What makes all of this possible is the attractive pricing from the SCN network. If we'd had to build this thing ourselves from scratch, the whole project might have been totally cost-ineffective.[5]

The SCN organization was assembled from portions of existing business group organizations, principally the Merchandise Group and Allstate Insurance. Despite ini-

---

[5]"The Competitive Edge," *Network World,* December 18, 1989.

tial reservations, the result had been an effective communications service utility that functioned well without seriously impacting the independence of the participating businesses. "Quite the contrary," remarked Weis,

> SCN has resulted in the provision of significantly enhanced data communications facilities that individual business groups would not have been able to justify based on their own requirements. For example, early in the game we needed a way to provide credit card authorization transactions at a low cost for Discover's merchants. One alternative was to put our own equipment in each LATA and hook-up with Feature Group B Service.[6] A more traditional and less capital-intensive alternative would have been to use an "800" service. The latter would have been less expensive in terms of equipment expense, but it was two to three times as expensive as the *unit* cost of the Feature Group B Service option.
>
> Discover had enough critical mass to undertake the first alternative. It was a good business decision and it helped other business groups in Sears. For example, Sears Payment Systems (SPS) is now in a competitive position to offer products outside of Sears using the existing infrastructure. SPS would not have been able to afford to put the necessary equipment node in each local office.
>
> Basically, it's a fundamental idea. One business group establishes a critical mass that enables other business groups to use the same service for different applications at decreasing unit costs as each new application comes on line.

Shaver provided another example of the leverage business groups could extract from the shared network from a voice perspective.

Less than 15 percent of Sears' voice traffic involved point-to-point lines. Given this, the only way to cost-justify a private line network was to combine all locations from all of the business groups. Although there was some initial resistance, primarily based on turf issues, the performance and price of the dedicated voice network proved successful.

According to John O'Loughlin, senior vice-president and chief planning officer for Allstate, Allstate executives regularly use SCN's 43 two-way videoconferencing rooms to hold meetings, interview prospective employees, and train workers.[7] He offered that the videoconferencing had enabled Allstate headquarters staff to stay in close contact with managers in the field, which is especially important given Allstate's reduction of about 600 management and support personnel.

Shaver explained:

> Rather than have each business group lease their own full-time satellite circuits and have them under-utilized, an SCN-managed videoconferencing service can lease fewer circuits, which all of the business groups can use, with better utilization. However, unlike the voice network example, what we're primarily leveraging is SCN staff expertise, vendor contacts, and volume purchasing.

Weis commented on the SCN experience from the business group perspective.

> The basic transparency of telecommunications services was an important enabling factor. Each user and each business group operates as if they still have their own network or, in the case of voice communications, as if they were still using the public switched network. The fact that network functions are performed remotely and on distributed leased

---

[6]A Bell Operating Company's offering that can provide a nationwide seven-digit number for use within each LATA. Feature Group B service is billed on a per-second basis rather than in minimum blocks of seconds (e.g., 30-second or 10-second blocks).

[7]"The Competitive Edge," *Network World,* December 18, 1989.

facilities, out of sight, if you will, helped to produce the transparency effect, but the underlying reason is that the multiplexing methods used in telecommunications allow resources to be shared without any operational or application system coordination between business groups. In short, the businesses are not aware that others are sharing the network, although this clearly affects the physical network topology and network planning.

"SCN has shown," Weis added,

that it is possible to extract and centrally manage a common shared service when the operations are properly standardized and the interfaces are adequately defined. SCN has been able to act as a sort of synergy liaison between business groups in a few instances, perhaps hastening the joint use of such new functionality. In the future, it may be possible to present new or "take-off" technologies to the business group system planners in an effort to coordinate their introduction into the network on a joint application basis.

SCN had been in place for nearly five years, and its good track record was widely acknowledged. SCN had successfully consolidated and centralized all technical and communications activities, both voice and data; it had gained the respect of information technology vendors, information processing and telecommunications industry publications, and even competitors;[8] and it was viewed as a tremendous corporate asset, virtually unmatched in size, scope, and diversity of services.

The SCN journey was not without issues and problems. Perhaps most difficult was defining and agreeing on the boundaries between the business groups and the corporate telecommunications utility. To some extent, the separation of the telecommunications

---

[8]Ibid.

functions from data processing technical services and data center operations was not a natural one because the telecommunications host functions in VTAM had to operate in close cooperation with host-based program products such as CICS, IMS, DB2, and the operating system. The fact that these software products, the operating system, and VTAM, had to share resources in the host became an issue when they were to be controlled by different organizations.

"SCN has shown that the shared utility concept can be successful if all business groups can be served well without unduly changing their business processes," Carlson observed.

Sharing of corporate facilities can even lead to application synergies. The economics of sharing and central management are real. In the telecommunications area, the economies of scale have been particularly significant and are growing. The concentration of expertise and greater specialization can contribute to gains in overall effectiveness and avoid duplication of function. Service transparency to users was important to implementability; most users only care about availability, chargeback costs, and responsiveness to problems.

The interface between corporate utility units and the business units can result in some difficulties, but none that could not be overcome with understanding and patience. The bottom line, for both Sears and the business groups, is a savings in telecommunications expenditures of more than $80 million since the inception of SCN through 1988 accompanied by an uncommon level of innovation and service.

Business Group Perceptions

Responses to the central data processing utility proposal varied widely. Many business group managers were concerned that the "over-engineering" required to accommodate specific business groups would be reflected in higher costs (chargebacks) than more locally optimized solutions. "The effects of deregulation in the communications industry, which have contributed to the success of SCN, have no parallels in the computer industry," one observed. Other managers voiced concern about the lack of influence. "We are a very small business group," said one. "Our voice will never be heard. It's not because they're less interested in our needs, rather it's a case of the natural requirement to be more responsive to your largest customer." Another manager was concerned about the fit of this idea with the Sears corporate culture. "Going back to our initial objectives for operation of our company," he said, "we strongly believe in decentralized and autonomous business groups. It's not clear to me that this proposal is consistent with that philosophy and our current culture."

Finally, one manager warned of using the consolidation of data centers *within* business groups to justify data center consolidation *across* business groups. He expressed his opinion that, "you cannot effectively segregate operations from systems development. The natural synergies lie within business groups—not across them. I've never seen a

company actually realize savings in this context. The cost of coordination and communication offset the expected savings."

Pursuing the Corporate Information Technology Function

Moran sought perspective on the Corporate Information Technology function proposal. An anticipated initial investment of $10 million over the first two years of the consolidation was expected to yield a total savings potential of $170 million over an eight-year period (including the two start-up years).

Everything appeared to be in order, but major questions still remained unanswered. Did it make sense to build this capability in-house? Was this where Sears should be concentrating its efforts, or should it focus on applications development? Would outsourcing of the data processing operations be a better alternative? Would the business groups recognize the potential synergies and advantages? Would they buy into the corporate utility concept? What objections might they raise? Was the SCN experience relevant, and how would Moran and his colleagues address their concerns?

APPENDIX   Description of Business Groups

Merchandising
Offers merchandise
and merchandise-
related services
through retail stores
and catalogs

Credit
The largest single
provider of consumer
credit in the
United States

*Specialty
Retailing*
Meeting today's
consumer needs
through innovative
marketing at
specialty retail stores

*Personal
Insurance*
Provides personal
auto and
homeowners
insurance and
related products and
services

*Life/Health
Insurance*
Markets individual
and group life, health,
annuity and pension
products and
services

*Business
Insurance*
Offers commercial
property/liability
insurance and
reinsurance services

DEAN WITTER

*Consumer
Markets*
Provides individual
clients with a full
range of financial
services and
products

*Capital
Markets*
Offers sales, trading,
research, and
investment banking
services to
institutional clients

*Consumer
Banking
Division*
Is comprised of
credit-card related
operations and
mortgage and
consumer-lending
businesses

COLDWELL
BANKER

*Residential
Group*
Offers complete
range of residential
real estate services

*Commercial
Group*
The largest full-
service commercial
brokerage and real
estate services
organization in
North America

*Homart
Development
Co.*
One of the nation's
leading developers of
retail, office and
multi-use properties

APPENDIX (continued)

Sears Merchandise Group

Sears Merchandise Group offered approximately 630 product lines and a wide range of services. Established as a watch and jewelry mail order company in 1886, the Merchandise Group had more than 800 stores and 2,300 catalog sales outlets. Three-fourths of all American households visited a Sears store every year, and Sears catalogs served a core customer group of 22 million. Most Sears customers (a base of 43 million accounts) had SearsCharge credit cards.

Merchandising sold a wide range of products and services through its stores and catalogs. Generally, buying activities were divided among six categories: home appliances and home electronics; home fashions; women's apparel, accessories, shoes, and luggage; men's and children's wearing apparel; home improvements; and automotive and recreation. Merchandising also provided a variety of services to consumers, including installation of home improvement products and automotive and product repair, the latter supported by more than 800 repair centers nationwide.

The Credit operation initiated and maintained customer credit accounts generated by Merchandising. The Specialty Merchandising Division, formed early in 1987, consisted of Eye Care Centers of America (optical superstores) and Pinstripes Petites, Inc. (for women's apparel in petite sizes).

Allstate Insurance Group

Founded by Sears in 1931, Allstate first sold only automobile insurance exclusively through direct mail and the Sears catalog. By 1987, the Allstate Insurance Group was engaged in the property, life, and health insurance businesses. Allstate serviced the personal insurance market through 28 regional marketing offices and 13 regional processing centers throughout the United States.

Allstate marketed an assortment of products to meet the property-liability insurance needs of businesses and the reinsurance needs of other businesses. Its Business Insurance division maintained, in addition to two claims processing centers, 26 marketing/underwriting locations throughout the country.

Through Allstate Life Insurance Company and Allstate Life Insurance Company of Canada—wholly-owned subsidiaries of Allstate Insurance Company—Allstate offered a wide range of personal and group life, health, annuity, and pension products.

APPENDIX   (continued)

Dean Witter Financial Services Group

Dean Witter Financial Services Group provided a broad range of securities-related and consumer banking services, including securities and futures brokerage and securities principal trading, investment management for mutual, pension, and other funds, investment and merchant banking, consumer credit, deposit-taking and lending, and mortgage banking for individuals and institutions. It offered its products and services through three business divisions: the Consumer Markets Division, which historically accounted for the greatest revenue and income, served the investment needs of nearly two million client households; the Capital Markets Division offered a full range of financial products and services to corporate and institutional clients; the Consumer Banking Division comprised Discover Card operations, mortgage and consumer lending activities, and Sears Payment Systems Inc. (a provider of third-party payment processing to merchants).

Coldwell Banker Real Estate Group

Coldwell Banker Real Estate Group brokered residential and commercial real estate, invested in, developed, and managed commercial real estate, provided mortgage and investment opportunities, and offered other real estate related services in selected markets throughout the United States. Collectively, the three operating units of Coldwell Banker—Coldwell Banker Commercial Group, Coldwell Banker Residential Group, and Homart Development Co.—served every major real estate market in the United States.

Coldwell Banker Commercial (CBC) Group in 1987 was the largest full-service commercial real estate organization in the United States; CBC provided commercial brokerage and investment properties management and capital markets and capital management services to real estate users, developers, and investors. Coldwell Banker Residential (CBR) Group, which provided brokerage, mortgage, and other services related to home sales, was the nation's largest company-owned residential real estate operation. Homart Development Co., one of the largest development firms in the nation, served commercial real estate needs in growing communities and metropolitan areas throughout the United States. Homart had developed 61 regional malls, 19 office buildings, and five multipurpose projects in the nation's 25 top suburban commercial real estate markets since its founding in 1959.

Case 11–2

EASTMAN KODAK CO.: MANAGING INFORMATION SYSTEMS THROUGH STRATEGIC ALLIANCES

Katherine Hudson, vice-president, Corporate Information Systems (CIS) at Eastman Kodak Co. (Kodak), surveyed the reports that detailed the performance of her organization over the past year. She was pleased with the progress that had been made but knew that there was much more to be done to achieve her goals of delivering both high-quality and cost-effective information technology (IT) services to Kodak businesses.

When Kodak CEO Colby Chandler created the CIS unit in January 1988 and appointed Hudson head, she became at once the first head of IT and first woman corporate vice-president in the company. Hudson was directed to overhaul the existing IT organization to promote the use of IT to improve the competitive position of Kodak businesses while dramatically lowering costs. Despite a lack of IT management experience, Hudson was no stranger to organizational challenges. Her previous job at Kodak had been to dismantle the $239 million instant camera business subsequent to the company's loss of a costly lawsuit with Polaroid.

Upon assuming her position, Hudson reviewed the results of an outside vendor's studies of Kodak's IT services. She supplemented these findings with other internal and external studies. "Every study said we needed help," Hudson recalled, explaining that throughout the organization separate entities were managing diverse, redundant technology platforms established under different operating standards. "The right hand," she remarked, "had no idea what the left was doing!"

"The results of the studies," Hudson observed

generated new questions. For example, should Kodak invest millions of dollars fixing the in-place IT infrastructure or use that money to support our core businesses of imaging, photography, health, and chemicals? We knew that IT was critical to the business but had never stopped to consider which IT functions and services were "core" and which were support. Throughout the company, we were moving toward selling off non-core businesses and services. Why shouldn't we apply that same logic to our IT services?

Throughout 1989, Hudson inaugurated a series of organizational initiatives that not only would dramatically change the IT function within Kodak but would rock the industry. She outsourced data center operations, telecommunications services, and personal computer (PC) support to IBM, Digital Equipment Corporation (DEC), and BusinessLand, respectively. In doing so, she effectively challenged the cultural inertia of the 109-year-old manufacturing company,

Professor Lynda M. Applegate and Research Associate Ramiro Montealegre prepared this case as the basis for class discussion rather than to illustrate either effective or ineffective handling of an administrative situation.

forced rival IT vendors to collaborate openly before the international press, transformed job descriptions and work environments for more than 2,000 people, and created a new wave of interest in outsourcing that forced IT managers around the world to seriously evaluate its potential for their organizations.

In June 1991, over one year after the last of the strategic alliance contracts had been signed, Hudson surveyed the results of her efforts. While many of the original objectives had been achieved, new challenges in managing the alliances required significant attention. The recent announcement by BusinessLand of its decision to merge, be acquired, or declare Chapter 11 drove home the point: clearly, the honeymoon was over.

Company Background

The Eastman Kodak Company was founded in 1880 by inventor-entrepreneur-philanthropist George Eastman, a young bank clerk. Since his development of the first snapshot camera in 1888, Kodak had celebrated many creative milestones.

In 1904, Eastman had articulated the company's competitive philosophy: "Nothing is more important than the value of our name and the quality it stands for. We must make quality our fighting argument."[1] Its commitment to highest quality products and services led Kodak to adopt a high level of vertical integration. Kodak operated its own laundry service to ensure that the cloth used by personnel in the manufacture of film possessed the requisite softness and was free of detergent residue. The company also ran its own fire department, blacksmith, bank, and cafeteria among many other services. Most

---

[1]"Focus on the Future: A Guide to Kodak's Business Units and Products," Eastman Kodak, 1988.

of these services were still being run by Kodak as the company entered the 1980s.

Kodak's organization structure also reflected the company's early roots. Although it had become a very large, diversified corporation, Kodak was still organized as a classical hierarchy, with the CEO presiding over a single monolithic, functional structure. "That works fine in a small company or if you have a single product serving a cohesive market," observed Chandler, "but Kodak is no longer operating in that kind of environment."

The solution, undertaken in 1984, was to reorganize the company into 29 separate business units grouped into four lines of business: (Photography (PPG), Commercial Imaging Group (CIG), Chemicals (EEC), and Health (HG)), and three international segments (Latin America, Europe, and Asia/Pacific). See Exhibit 1. Each business unit operated as a profit center under a general manager. Centralized corporate functional units downsized considerably as business units assumed control of the functions needed to produce their products, including marketing, manufacturing, and research and development, among others. Chandler, calling this "a much more decisive structure," observed that "our development time to bring out new products is less than half what it was."

In 1986, as the company faced significant cost pressures secondary to stiff competition and the Polaroid lawsuit, a second, painful organizational change was made. Kodak downsized its core businesses. Employees were cut by 10 percent and the operating budget by 5 percent. Simultaneously, Kodak diversified into new businesses including office equipment and biotechnology, through more than 20 acquisitions and joint ventures. Despite these moves, second-quarter profits plunged 85 percent in 1989, prompt-

EXHIBIT 1 Eastman Kodak Co. Organization — 1991

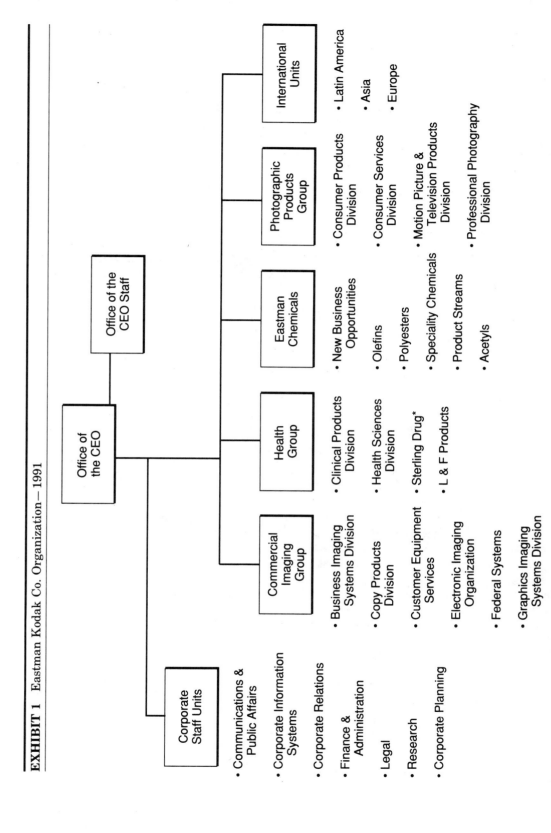

*Sterling Drugs, Inc. Was acquired in 1987.

ing a second round of cost cutting. More than 4,500 additional jobs were eliminated as unprofitable businesses were consolidated or eliminated. Between 1982 and 1989 revenues per employee rose from $79.52 to $133.32, but sales per employee of $140,000 in 1989 were still well below the $380,000 per employee of Kodak's arch-rival, Fuji Photo Film Company.[2] A financial summary is provided in Exhibit 2.

Information Technology at Kodak

While Kodak fought to regain its competitive position, the Information Systems Division (ISD), a centralized functional unit that managed information and communications technology services for Kodak businesses, also began to restructure in line with the new organization. In 1985, responsibility for development of business applications and management of small scale computer and network operations (e.g., minicomputers, personal computers, and local area networks) was shifted to each of the 29 business units. ISD remained responsible for management of the large data centers and voice and data communications.

Directed by the CEO to increase efficiency and decrease costs, ISD between 1986 and 1987 began a process of consolidating and standardizing data center and telecommunications operations. (A 1987, *Information Week* study ranked Kodak number 15 among the 100 largest information systems installations.) The creation of the Corporate Information Systems unit in 1988 and appointment of Hudson as head marked the beginning of a more aggressive approach to

---

[2]Ansberry, C. and Hymovitz, C., "Kodak Chief is Trying for the Fourth Time to Trim Firm's Costs," *Wall Street Journal*, 9/19/89.

restructuring the IT organization. Exhibit 3 presents an organization chart for CIS. Hudson described the challenges she faced upon assuming her new position.

When we launched CIS at the beginning of 1988, the entire IS management team knew that we had our work cut out for us. I wanted to analyze the IT function using the same criteria that Kodak was using to analyze our other businesses. In the businesses we had used portfolio analysis to answer the questions: Is there value here? and Is this a core function of the company? If the answer was yes, we kept it; if no, we outsourced or eliminated it. I commissioned a number of internal and external studies to help us assess the IT function and provide an overview of our current strengths and weaknesses. [See Exhibit 4 for a summary of the IT areas identified as core and non-core.] Based on these studies we made the decision to outsource non-core IT services, recognizing that, in the case of IT, non-core IT services would remain inextricably intertwined with core services. Outsourcing IT services, unlike outsourcing laundry services, could not be handled by a simple, contractual hand-off—the equivalent of throwing the functions over the wall to an outside vendor. Instead, we would have to craft a set of strategic alliances that would allow the relationships to grow and evolve as our needs and our partners' needs changed. We adopted the slogan the Partnership in Innovation Process (PIP) to capture the philosophy we wanted to communicate as we began implementing the outsourcing decision.

Initially, the strategic alliance agreements were to cover only non-core services in the Photography (PPG) and Commercial Imaging Group (CIG) areas. Kodak's chemical (ECC), health (HG), and international (IG) businesses were to continue to operate their own computing and telecommunications services as they had in the past.

EXHIBIT 2 Eastman Kodak Financial Summary

	1990	1989	1988	1986	1984	1982	1980
Sales	$ 18,908	$ 18,398	$ 17,034	$ 11,550	$ 10,600	$ 10,815	$ 9,734
Earnings from operations	2,844	1,591[b]	2,812	724[c]	1,547	1,860	1,896
Earnings before income taxes	1,257[a]	925	2,236	598	1,624	1,872	1,963
Net Earnings	703[a]	529[b]	1,397	374[c]	923	1,162	1,154
Earnings and Dividends							
Net Earnings-percent sales	3.7%	2.9%	8.2%	3.2%	8.7%	10.7%	11.9%
-percent return on average shareowners' equity[1,2]	10.5%	7.9%	21.8%	5.8%	12.6%	16.2%	20.2%
-per common share[1,2]	2.17	1.63	4.31	1.10	2.54	3.17%	3.18
Cash dividends declared-on common shares	649	649	616	551	578	581	517
-per common share[2]	2.00	2.00	1.90	1.63	1.60	1.58	1.42
Common shares outstanding at close of year	324.6	324.4	324.2	338.7	350.0	372.5	363.1
Shareowners at close of year	168,935	171,954	174,110	172,713	189,972	203,788	234,008
Balance Sheet Data							
Current Assets	$ 8,608	$ 8,591	$ 8,684	$ 5,857	$ 5,131	$ 5,289	$ 5,246
Properties at cost	17,648	16,774	15,667	12,919	10,775	9,344	6,861
Accumulated depreciation	8,670	8,146	7,654	6,643	5,386	4,286	3,426
Total assets	24,125	23,652	22,964	12,994	10,778	10,622	8,754
Current liabilities	7,163	6,573	5,850	3,811	2,306	2,146	2,247
Long-term obligations	6,989	7,376	7,779	981	409	350	79
Total net assets (shareowner's equity)	6,737	6,642	6,780	6,388	7,137	7,541	6,028

EXHIBIT 2 (continued)

	1990	1989	1988	1986	1984	1982	1980
Supplemental Information							
Sales-Imaging	$ 7,128	$ 6,998	$ 6,642	$ 8,352	$ 8,380	$ 8,935	$ 7,904
-Chemicals	3,588	3,522	3,123	2,378	2,464	2,151	2,070
-Health	4,349	4,009	3,597	1,056			
-Information	4,140	4,200	3,937				
Research and development expenditures	1,329	1,253	1,147	1,059	838	710	520
Depreciation	1,168	1,181	1,057	956	758	575	339
Taxes (excludes payroll, sales, and excise taxes)	719	551	973	329	793	801	881
Wages, salaries, and employee benefits	5,783	5,877	5,469	4,912	4,148	4,446	3,643
Employees at close of year-in the United States	80,350	82,850	87,900	83,600	85,600	93,300	84,400
-worldwide	134,450	137,750	145,300	121,450	123,900	136,500	129,500
Subsidiary Companies Outside the U.S.							
Sales	$ 8,668	$ 8,391	$ 7,748	$ 4,387	$ 3,367	$ 4,279	$ 4,125
Earnings from operations	1,150	771	997	400	113	302	446
Eastman Kodak Company equity in net earnings (loss)			661	167	25	72	254

[1]Based on average number of shares outstanding.

[2]Data for 1986 have been restated to give effect to the 3-for-2 partial stock split in 1987.

[a]After deducting $888 million for the litigation judgment including post-judgment interest which reduced net earnings by $564 million.

[b]After deducting restructuring costs of $875 million which reduced net earnings by $549 million.

[c]After deducting unusual charges of $520 million and certain other special charges of $134 million which in total reduced earnings from operations by $654 million. Net earnings were reduced by the $373 million after-tax effect of special charges and an additional $50 million from the retroactive repeal of the U.S. investment tax credit as a result of the 1986 tax law change.

[d]After deducting unusual charges of $563 million which reduced net earnings by $302 million and net earnings per share by $.89. Net earnings were reduced by $373 million because of all special charges and an additional $50 million from the retroactive repeal of the U.S. investment tax credit as a result of the 1986 tax law change.

EXHIBIT 3 Corporate Information Systems— 1989

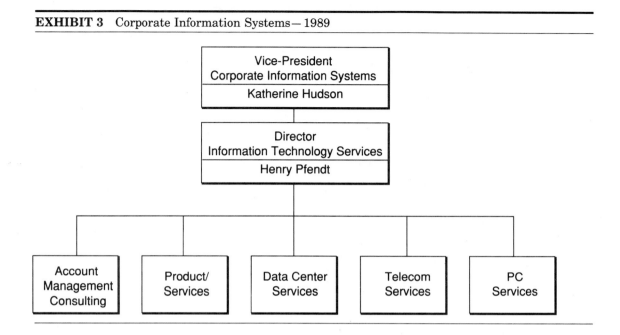

The Partnership in Innovation Process

Defining the Change Management Organization

Hudson's first priority was to develop the organization structure and identify key players needed to implement the organization change. She recognized that she would need to provide executive leadership and recruit the assistance of a strong manager who combined both technical and business savvy and was well-known and respected by IT and business unit employees. Hudson chose Henry Pfendt for this key position. During his 32-year tenure with Kodak, Pfendt had worked in a number of key technical and business positions throughout the organization. In 1986, he had been appointed to head a small team of IT professionals charged with defining the IT organization of the future. It was this group that had led the consolidation efforts of 1986–1988.

Two levels of cross-functional teams were created to implement the Partnership in In-novation Process. At the executive level a steering committee, comprising some 25 executives from business units and corporate staff functions, was formed to provide overall business leadership and direction. Douglas Mabon, head of the Financial Planning Department and a member of the steering committee, described its role. "The members of the steering committee were selected," he explained,

> because of their special expertise related to business and functional issues that would need to be defined in the outsourcing agreements. For the most part, we were not IT experts. Our job was to take the broad vision defined by Kathy and to translate it into the business initiatives that would be needed to make it happen. Our role was to communicate the vision and oversee its implementation, but not to implement it directly.

Implementation of the vision rested with the three Partnership in Innovation Process (PIP) teams associated with each major outsourcing initiative. Each team had adopted

EXHIBIT 4 Corporate Information Systems: Guidelines for Strategic Alliance Decisions

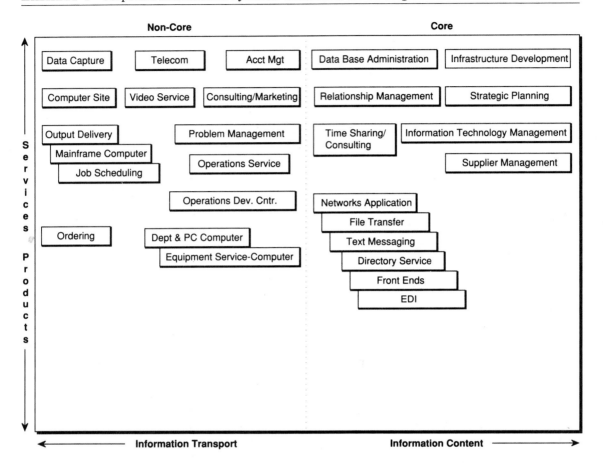

a code name for its project: data center (BlueStar); telecommunications (TelStar); and personal computer services (MicroBuddy). The PIP teams were to define the specific details and manage the implementation of each outsourcing agreement. PIP teams comprised 8 to 10 Kodak employees, including project and technical leaders, and representatives from the financial, marketing/customer service, business planning, human resources, and legal areas. "All three of the PIP teams reported directly to Kathy and Henry," Mabon explained. "The steering committee provided guidance but had no formal authority over the PIP teams."

Early on, Hudson and Pfendt recognized that defining and managing the outsourcing partnerships was primarily a "relationship" process. Conflict Management Inc. (CMI), a consulting firm that advised organizations and individuals on the management of critical internal and external relationships and the development of an effective negotiation process, was hired jointly by Kodak and the respective partner organizations to assist with the development of the alliance relationships. CMI's brochure described its philosophy in working with organizations.

> Increasingly, organizations have come to realize that *how* they approach problems, disagreements, and opportunities has an impact on the substantive outcome. Where one must rely on persuasion and influence, the *process* by which a negotiated agreement is reached affects both the quality and durability of the result, as well as any subsequent relationship between the parties. The ability to negotiate, build, and sustain effective and durable *working* relationships becomes more critical to "success" in a world that requires agility, innovation, interdependence, and quality decision-making.

CMI President and CEO Elizabeth Gray and two CMI professionals, Mark Smith and Jeff Weiss, worked jointly with Kodak and the respective partner organizations (IBM, DEC, and BusinessLand). They trained team members in effective negotiation and relationship management skills and helped them develop the processes through which the alliance partnerships would be forged and maintained.

Establishing the Process
Hudson stated four overarching interests to guide the steering committee and PIP teams in the development of outsourcing alliances: improve shareholder value; create quantum improvements in the quality and productivity of services delivered; maintain or improve the quality of employees' worklife; and position Kodak for the IT developments and business challenges of the future. These were translated into specific issues that each vendor was to address in its proposals. Each

potential partner was required to identify how it would improve or maintain:

* the transition and development opportunities for employees.
* service quality.
* the cost structure.
* the identification and assimilation of emerging technologies.
* support systems and management processes.

The PIP teams then developed a five-step process that defined the methodology to be used to identify, select, negotiate, and implement the outsourcing alliances. See Exhibit 5.

Identification and Selection
Each PIP team began the process with a "preferred partner." Hudson had initially intended to choose vendors for outsourced services based on their reputation in the industry and experience managing similar outsourcing arrangements. Of the three vendors chosen, however, only one, BusinessLand, made it to the contract stage.

Roy Hartwell, a financial analyst working on the BlueStar PIP team, explained:

> The preferred partner had extensive experience in managing data center operations for other *Fortune* 500 firms, and they rapidly developed a proposal that spelled out the relationship in extreme detail. The vendor seemed intent on finding ways to fit us into established practices, resisting many requests to tailor the proposal to meet our requirements. We became very concerned that the detailed proposal would become a detailed contract, and that the inevitable problems that would surely arise would lead to an endless stream of contract renegotiations and additional service charges. The vendor's drive for immediate decisions also conflicted with our focus on developing a relationship, creating considerable tension between the two organizations.

EXHIBIT 5 Partnership in Innovation Process

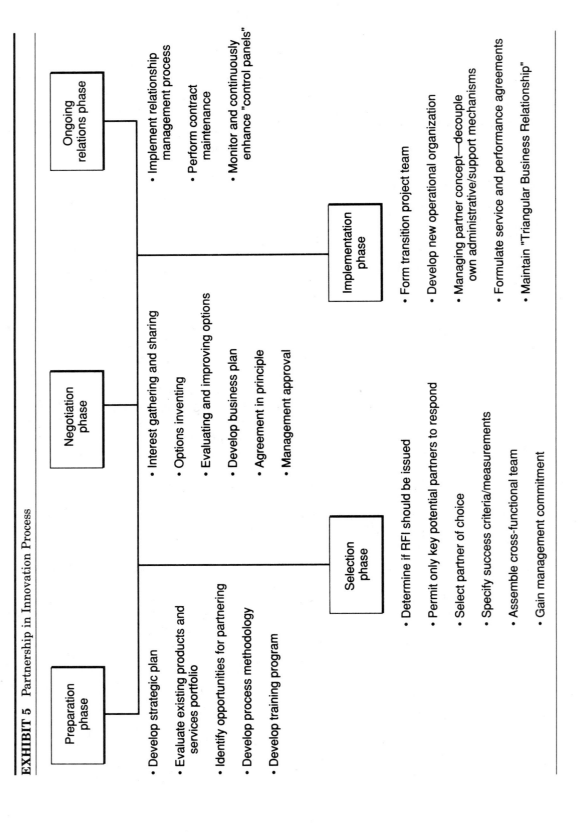

Preparation phase

- Develop strategic plan
- Evaluate existing products and services portfolio
- Identify opportunities for partnering
- Develop process methodology
- Develop training program

Selection phase

- Determine if RFI should be issued
- Permit only key potential partners to respond
- Select partner of choice
- Specify success criteria/measurements
- Assemble cross-functional team
- Gain management commitment

Negotiation phase

- Interest gathering and sharing
- Options inventing
- Evaluating and improving options
- Develop business plan
- Agreement in principle
- Management approval

Implementation phase

- Form transition project team
- Develop new operational organization
- Managing partner concept—decouple own administrative/support mechanisms
- Formulate service and performance agreements
- Maintain "Triangular Business Relationship"

Ongoing relations phase

- Implement relationship management process
- Perform contract maintenance
- Monitor and continuously enhance "control panels"

An internal Kodak team had also been commissioned to present the economics of consolidating Kodak's data centers within the company. "Most of the economies of scale that stood to be realized from consolidating our data centers and running them in-house," Hartwell explained, "could be achieved by creating a data center that operated in the range of 300 to 400 MIPS. As our consolidated data center would operate at about 600 MIPS, we knew economies of scale could be gained through internal consolidation."

Pfendt elaborated.

> We estimated that to offer these services in-house we would need to spend approximately $30 million for new facilities in the Rochester area alone and $15–20 million for new systems. And that was just the initial estimate! We questioned whether this was the most appropriate place for Kodak to spend its scarce resources. In the end it was not the economies of scale but the *economics* that drove our decision. By re-engineering the IS value chain, we became convinced that commodity-type IS services could best be procured through alliances and partnerships with world-class service providers, thus allowing the internal resources to be focused on high value-adding IS activities.

Exhibit 6 presents a summary of the key selection criteria used in the final choice of the three alliance partners.

Negotiation

The negotiation process was formalized in an alliance contract, in the case of IBM and DEC, and in a business plan in the case of BusinessLand. (BusinessLand's agreement had a much smaller dollar value than the other two, and BusinessLand did not have a lawyer on its negotiating team.) Exhibit 7 provides an overview of the categories of agreements covered in the contracts.

It became clear in the course of negotiations that the concept of the contract needed

EXHIBIT 6 Key Selection Criteria for Choice of Strategic Partners

- Strong technical expertise in the service area but past experience managing the service for outside customers was not required.
- Excellent reputation within the industry and strong image as a quality leader.
- Solid financial performance.
- Reputation as a "good" employer with high quality of worklife for employees.
- Ability to work together to solve problems; atmosphere of trust and cooperation.
- Willing to work together on development of a relationship management process.
- Management style and culture similar to Kodak.

to be re-evaluated. The contract needed to support "fluid" and "collaborative" relationships among all alliance partners. No one could specify those relationships in a detailed way in advance. Ideally, the contract would provide a framework for a relationship and the process by which it would be negotiated. Michael Pearlman, a lawyer on the BlueStar team, contrasted two of the contracts developed with alliance partners. "The contract with IBM," he observed,

> really fits the company's style. IBM wanted to develop a framework for its future outsourcing business. The contract that resulted is very compact and in plain English. It includes such topics as termination conditions, pricing, personnel, liabilities, warranties, responsibilities of the parties, and the transition process and incorporates in an Appendix detailed schedules, time tables, equipment, and software. The DEC contract is much more detailed. The parties found it necessary to attempt to specify issues more rigidly. As we began operations, we found that many of the details just didn't fit with the way things worked.

EXHIBIT 7 Kodak Outsourcing Alliances: Sample Contract

Table of Contents

1.0 Introduction

2.0 Executive Overview

- 2.1 Introduction
- 2.2 Finance
- 2.3 Human Resources
- 2.4 Products and Services
- 2.5 Future Positioning
- 2.6 Proposal Benefits

3.0 Business Plan

- 3.1 Financial
- 3.2 Personnel Plan
  - 3.2.1 Personnel Philosophy
  - 3.2.2 Affected Personnel
  - 3.2.3 Transition
  - 3.2.4 Compensation and Benefits
    - 3.2.4.1 Medical
    - 3.2.4.2 Holidays/Vacation
    - 3.2.4.3 Pension/Retirement
    - 3.2.4.4 Other
- 3.3 Products and Services
  - 3.3.1 Organizational Structure
  - 3.3.2 Technical Plan
    - 3.3.2.1 Planning/Engineering
      - 3.3.2.1.1 Investment
      - 3.3.2.1.2 Technology
      - 3.3.2.1.3 Physical and Logical Architecture
      - 3.3.2.1.4 Inventories
      - 3.3.2.1.5 Capacity
    - 3.3.2.2 Operation/System Management Controls
      - 3.3.2.2.1 Operations
      - 3.3.2.2.2 Problem Management
      - 3.3.2.2.3 Configuration Management
      - 3.3.2.2.4 Performance and Availability Management
      - 3.3.2.2.5 Disaster Recovery Management
      - 3.3.2.2.6 Capacity Management
      - 3.3.2.2.7 Change Management
      - 3.3.2.2.8 Security
      - 3.3.2.2.9 Product Evaluation

EXHIBIT 7   *(continued)*

Table of Contents

CMI, according to Pearlman, had suggested a valuable negotiation tool to support contract development. "Before the contract drafting process," he explained,

> both parties would sit down and discuss in detail the specific business concerns to be covered in the contract. From this a single, joint document was prepared and revised as necessary to clarify mistaken assumptions and areas of conflict. This proved to be a very valuable way to ensure that all parties were operating on a common understanding.

Implementation

Contracts were signed with vendors in July 1989 (IBM), September 1989 (Business-Land), and February 1990 (DEC). Work subsequently began on building the necessary interorganizational structures, work systems, and management processes. But in the end, explained Robert Kordish, Personnel Relations Manager, Kodak and its partners recognized that success in forging the new alliances rested with people. Kordish explained, "Outsourcing is a people process."

> Transferring our human assets was in many ways more difficult than transferring our physical assets. We knew from the beginning that our success was dependent on how well we managed the transition of the 600+ Kodak employees who would be transferring to the alliance partner organizations. We could not afford to lose their knowledge of Kodak's IT systems and how they influenced Kodak's business operations. In each alliance agreement we worked out a human relations package that would provide the employees a quality of worklife that was comparable to their current one. The average length of service for the outsourced employees was approximately 18 years. In many cases, their spouses and other family members were also Kodak employees. They did not want to leave Kodak nor move from Rochester.

Recognizing that the transition of employees would best be supported by open and honest communication, various members of management met with them approximately every four to six weeks to provide an update on the current status and developments. In addition, a daily electronic news bulletin (questions and answers) was maintained throughout the project. Talks were held on all three shifts to ensure that everyone could attend. For the two largest outsourcing projects there were two major meetings associated with the specific strategic alliance: one when the alliance partner was selected and one before the contract was signed. Kordish recalled DEC's selection.

> We had a meeting in the auditorium with all of the Kodak employees who would be moving to DEC. Various DEC vice-presidents and employees, and Kathy Hudson and I explained the proposal. There was plenty of time to ask questions and discuss concerns. Then we had an informal social hour in which coffee and cake were served so that everyone could get acquainted.

Another auditorium meeting was held when the contract with DEC was ready to be signed. At the end of the meeting, DEC management welcomed the Kodak employees to DEC.

Each employee received a manual containing a job description, compensation details, and a comparison of the new benefits package with the previous Kodak benefits package. Generous signing bonuses and guaranteed raises were offered by IBM, DEC, and BusinessLand. Personnel were offered three options: accept and sign the agreement within 60 days; personally find another position within Kodak; retire or resign from Kodak. "Most people made their decision within two weeks," recalled Kordish, adding that, "of the 600 people affected, 586 accepted the strategic alliance offer."

Managing the Ongoing Relationships

An alliance organization was defined and managed on two levels; specific alliance organizations were formed for each alliance partner while cross-alliance organizations governed the actions of all three alliance partners with Kodak. Exhibit 8 presents an overview of Kodak's IS organization in 1991. The new organization represented a blending of three distinct organizational entities: Kodak's Corporate IS organization; Kodak's Business Group/Business Unit IS organizations; and the alliance organizations. It also represented a complex intermingling of team-based and hierarchical structures. (Team-based structures are represented by circles, and hierarchical structures by boxes in Exhibit 8.) Exhibit 9 summarizes the responsibilities of the three organizations.

Organization Structure

The hierarchical organization included Kodak's Corporate IS unit and Business Group/Business Unit IS organizations and the alliance organizations within Kodak and its three alliance partners. Corporate IS, headed by Hudson, included Information Technology Management (a 20-person unit responsible for technology transfer into the company, standards, and supplier management), Human Resources (a five-person unit), and Administrative Services (a 20-person organization). Kodak Data Center, PC Services, and Telecommunications Services organizations supported Kodak end-users of CIS systems and services that were not outsourced.

The alliance organization structure, described as a "networked" organization, was composed of a collection of teams and hierarchical organizational units that helped manage the complex service delivery processes among alliance partners and between the alliances and Kodak end-users. Four types of teams were defined: the Information Systems Policy Board; the Information Systems Executive Council; Relationship Management Boards; and Alliance Advisory Councils.

The *Information Systems Policy Board* functions were performed by the management council of the company chaired by Whitmire. It included Hudson and the heads of each of the business groups and senior functional representatives, such as the CFO. This committee met monthly on a variety of corporate topics. During the outsourcing decision process, significant agenda time was devoted to discussing IS issues and outsourcing in particular. The Policy Board was responsible for setting broad policy guidelines for the use of IT within the company.

The *Information Systems Executive Council* was chaired by Hudson, and included the business group IS Directors. The committee met five times per year and was responsible for translating the broad IT policy statements into specific IT strategic initiatives needed to support business strategies, and for monitoring Kodak's progress in meeting its corporate-wide IT/Business goals. They relied heavily on input from the IT planning and strategy groups within the Information Technology Management organization.

Policy, strategic direction, and management were provided to each alliance through a *Relationship Management Board*. Hudson sat on all boards with the respective alliance managers from Kodak and the partner organizations. The Relationship Management Boards met quarterly. Cross-alliance Relationship Management Boards met monthly to define and implement interalliance policy, strategy, and management.

Alliance Advisory Councils, composed of technical professionals from Kodak and the alliance partner organizations, met monthly to define technical standards, plan the evolution of technological platforms, and manage the prioritization and funding of services.

Each Kodak alliance manager was responsible for a hierarchical organization composed of Kodak employees who worked closely with their counterparts in the partner organization to provide data center, tele-

EXHIBIT 8 Eastman Kodak IS Organization—1991

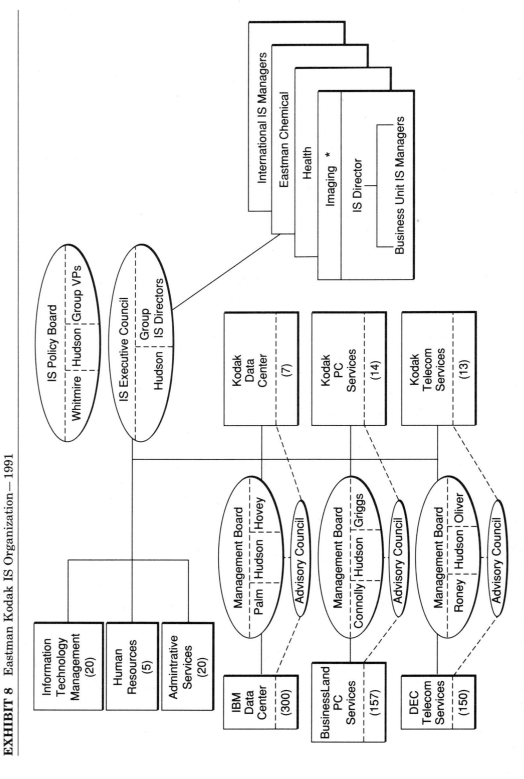

The numbers in parenthesis represent head counts.

*The Commercial Imaging and Photographic Products groups were combined to form the Imaging Group.

EXHIBIT 9 Eastman Kodak IT Roles and Responsibilities—1991

	Photography/Commercial-Imaging	Eastman Chemical	Health	International
Information Technology Services (Data Center | Personal Computers | Telecommunications)	CIS*/Alliances	BG/BU**	BG/BU	Region/Country
Integrated Corporate Applications	CIS	CIS	CIS	CIS
Manufacturing/Business Applications	BG/BU	BG/BU	BG/BU	Plant Site
Corporate Architecture/Strategies Standards/Infrastructure	CIS	CIS	CIS	CIS

*CIS = Corporate Information Systems
**BG/BU = Business Group/Business Unit

communications, and personal computer services. Seven Kodak employees coordinated and controlled the integration of services across alliance partner organizations. Alliance partners provided the outsourced services specified in the alliance contracts, through hierarchical organizations within their companies.

Service Delivery Process

One of the first tasks to occupy the alliance partners was the redesign of the service delivery process. Alliance partners recognized early that this process involved more than each partner working with Kodak independently; all three vendors needed to define the interalliance service delivery processes. For example, a Kodak end user acquiring a personal computer from BusinessLand had to contact not only BusinessLand, but also IBM to establish a mainframe account and DEC to install network connections. See Exhibit 10 for a summary of the complex, interorganizational process of fulfilling a PC order. In 1991, BusinessLand was in the process of developing an automated system to streamline order fulfillment so that a Kodak user could order a personal computer and the mainframe account and networking via a single, on-line request.

Frank Palm, BlueStar Alliance manager at IBM, explained the complexity of these interorganizational relationships in terms of his organization's relationship with DEC. "One of my managers," he explained,

> meets weekly, and sometimes daily, with his DEC counterpart to define the evolving nature of our integrated services. In addition, we have a formal process, called a document of understanding, to define complex problems involving the intersection of our services. So far these mechanisms have worked so well that all problems have been solved through discussions at that level. It has been quite a culture change on the part of DEC and IBM to think of each other as partners rather than

competitors. We have taken steps to help promote that collaborative culture. For example, the IBM alliance organization hosted a welcome party for the DEC alliance organization when they won the contract. The most powerful force for helping to forge the collaborative culture, however, has been the background of the IBM and DEC employees working in the alliance organizations. Because they were all former Kodak employees who had lived and worked in Rochester for many years, the conditions for collaboration were already present. As managers, it was up to us to nurture it.

Management Control

Long-range planning and development of policy and strategic direction were handled by the appropriate Kodak and alliance level management boards. Operational planning was the responsibility of the management of each alliance and varied for each alliance partner. Interalliance planning was handled at the cross alliance management boards' joint monthly meetings.

Service planning and control systems were implemented to support fulfillment of the contracted service level agreements. Both IBM and DEC followed the same basic procedure for planning and managing service delivery. Annual negotiations with Kodak defined an agreed-upon service level, which could be renegotiated at mid-year and year end. IBM and DEC would then bill CIS monthly for actual charges. CIS, in turn, billed Kodak end users.

Planning was still based on customer demand and each alliance organization had evolved its own unique management style. All three alliance partners recognized that they had operated and continued to operate primarily in a "project-oriented" or, in some cases, "crisis-driven" manner. Because formal control systems were still in the process of being developed, customer surveys and request backlogs were used to assess service quality.

EXHIBIT 10   Process for Acquiring a Personal Computer

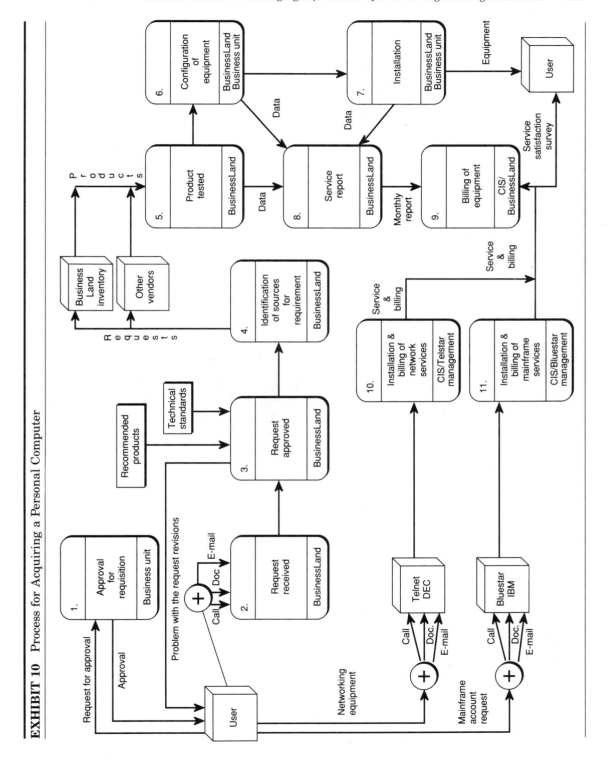

The need for a more formal process was addressed in spring 1991, when the interalliance management boards developed a framework, called the Relationship Management Planning and Control Cycle, to guide the development of interalliance planning and control systems. See Exhibit 11 for the management systems and support tools (many of them automated) that were in the process of being developed.

Under this framework, alliance and interalliance mission and strategies would be defined through the creation of a business plan that would be revised yearly based on contractual and service level agreements, past and future strategies and plans, and the results of the previous year's operations. The business plan would be used to define goals and specify new projects and service level agreements, and would provide a basis for defining alliance activities. An automated system, called the CIS Document Manager, was being developed to help track project progress and problem resolution and develop a historical record of alliance and interalliance activities.

The business plan would also be used to define a set of process and customer service performance measures that would enable alliance managers to control the interalliance service delivery process consistently throughout the year. Formal approaches to measuring the value of IT services were being developed to ensure continuous improvement of the service delivery process, and an automated tool called the Control Panel was being developed to help support the interalliance management control process. See Exhibit 12.

Where to Next?

Surveying the performance reports for the past year, Hudson reflected on the significant progress that had been made since 1988. She believed the decision to outsource data center, telecommunications, and personal computer services had been a good one. Cost savings of 15 percent had been realized with one outsourcing function and 3 percent with another. The third partner had experienced some difficulty meeting its cost objectives, but she believed the appropriate service delivery and management processes had been put in place to remedy this situation by the end of the year. Despite initial periods of adjustment, service quality was at least equal, and in some cases was superior to previous levels, and valuable lessons had been learned along the way. See Exhibit 13.

But Hudson realized that much more needed to be done. She was comfortable with the networked alliance organization structure, despite its complexity, but recognized that interalliance service delivery processes and planning and control systems needed more attention. Cost, quality, and speed of implementation were critical measures of process performance that needed to be specified in greater detail to fully implement the "Control Panel" approach to management control, and automated management support systems would be needed to manage the complexity. Although great care had been taken to define a compensation and benefits package that would be beneficial to the former Kodak employees, Hudson knew that new incentive systems and performance evaluation mechanisms that reflected the complexity of the interalliance partnerships would be needed. Career development issues, she knew, would also have to be addressed. Moreover, the same human resource management issues would also have to be addressed within Kodak. Hudson was also planning to reduce each Kodak alliance unit to 2 or 3 employees within the next year. Finally, managing the interalliance relationships would continue to require considerable time and attention as the various alliance partners faced significant internal and external challenges that were prompting them to undertake their own corporate-wide organizational transformations.

EXHIBIT 11 Proposed Planning and Control Framework

1. The Planning Cycle

Mission	Strategies	Projects	Implement	Measure

2. The Interaction of Process and Tools

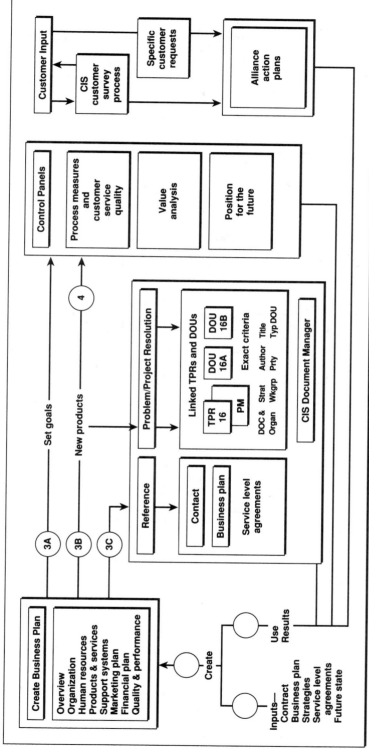

TPR = Tactical project record
DOU = Document of understanding

EXHIBIT 12 Proposed Management Control System

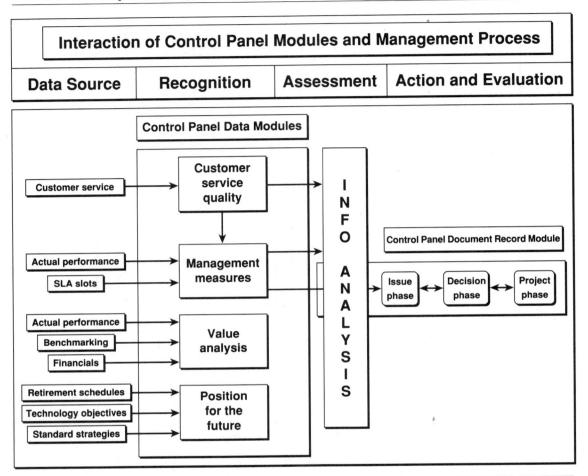

EXHIBIT 13   Lessons Learned

The Outsourcing Decision
- Non-core services (Information Transport), not core services (Information Context) are candidates for outsourcing.
- Non-core services are inextricably intertwined with core services.
- Outsourcing IT is a strategic alliance, not a simple "hand-off."
- Previous problems will still remain problems.

Selecting a Partner
- Ability to work together over long term is critical.
- Begin relationship management process early.
- Be sure negotiation team will still be involved in long term management.
- Understand how partner will make money on the deal.

Contract Negotiation
- The contract should serve as a framework for the relationship. Don't try to specify everything in detail.
- Define ownership of current & *future* assets (e.g., software, information).
- Both sides should write down what they think the contract says and compare understandings before signing.

Long-Term Management
- There is significant overhead in coordination and control.
- Service delivery and management control processes must be redesigned to incorporate interorganizational nature of alliance.
- Both organizations are undergoing significant organization changes. Partners must work together to manage change.

Case 11-3

AGRICO, INC.—A SOFTWARE DILEMMA

George P. Burdelle, vice president of information systems at Agrico, Inc., walked into the computer room with his systems and programming manager, Louise Alvaredo, at 6:30 P.M. on Wednesday, May 27, 1987. Alvaredo typed a few keystrokes on a systems computer console and turned to Burdelle. "So, as you can see, Jane Seymour [the software engineer for Agrico's new AMR system] left the source code on our computer when she left for dinner." She paused, and then asked, "Should I copy it to tape and ship it to our off-site storage facility?"

Agrico's $500 million portfolio of farm management properties was set for conversion to the new computer system over the upcoming weekend. AMR, a vendor of farm management software, had been selected to provide the software for the new system. The previous summer AMR had agreed to supply the object code for the system but had been quite reluctant to release the source code to Agrico.[1] The software purchase agreement between Agrico and AMR provided that the source code be placed in escrow to provide protection in case of a natural disaster or in the event of AMR's bankruptcy or inability to provide adequate support for the software. But, despite repeated attempts, Burdelle had been unable to reach an acceptable arrangement with the software company regarding the escrow of the source code.

Burdelle and Alvaredo knew that Agrico would have certain access to the most recent version of the source code should they choose to copy it now and secure it. Given his experience with AMR over the past year, Burdelle was not confident that AMR's proposed arrangements to escrow the source code were adequate. And if Agrico's $500 million portfolio were converted to the new computer system and something happened to the existing object code, the possibility existed that the object code could not be reproduced.

Furthermore, Burdelle had an operational concern. He wanted to be sure that any future modifications to the software were made using the most recent version of the source code, which included all previous modifications. Otherwise, there was a risk that the portfolio data could be altered—or, corrupted—without anyone's knowledge.

---

[1]*Source code* contained a computer program's statements written by programmers in high-level programming languages like BASIC, COBOL, FORTRAN, PL/I, C, etc. It could be printed out on paper or shown on a display terminal and read much like text. A compiler (a special computer program) translated the source code into *object code,* which was in a binary format executed by the computer. Usually, object code could not be read by programmers or easily modified. To make changes to an existing program, programmers usually changed the source code and then recompiled the program, thus creating a new version of the object code. (Most computer software packages purchased by consumers, e.g., LOTUS 1-2-3, contained only the object code. The source code was seldom distributed in such packages.)

Research Associate H. Jeff Smith prepared this case under the supervision of Professor F. Warren McFarlan as the basis for class discussion rather than to illustrate either effective or ineffective handling of an administrative situation. All identities have been disguised.

He recalled the words of Agrico's attorney from a discussion held earlier that week:

> What if you *could* get a copy of their source code through some means? The contract states we cannot have a copy of the software without AMR's written permission. On the other hand, the agreement clearly calls for an escrow agreement that is acceptable to both AMR and to Agrico. If it ever got to court that we took their source code, the judge or jury could well side with us, especially when we explained the trouble we have had with AMR and their unsatisfactory response to our concerns. Still, a lawsuit would be bad publicity and would consume a lot of everyone's time, even if we won. If we lost, it is not clear what the impact might be.

Now, because of an AMR employee's oversight, Burdelle had access to the source code.

"When do you need a decision?" Burdelle asked his systems manager. "Jane said she'd be back from dinner by eight o'clock," Alvaredo replied, "so I need to know in an hour or so."

"I'll give you an answer at 7:30," responded Burdelle, as he walked to his office.

Agrico—Company Background

Agrico, Inc., started by two farmers in Des Moines, Iowa, in 1949, provided farm and ranch management services for 691,000 acres of land in several midwestern states. With market value of its portfolio at $500 million by 1987, Agrico ranked as one of the nation's larger agricultural management firms. Maintaining four regional offices housing an average of five farm managers each, Agrico was able to provide cost-effective management services for more than 350 farms and ranches. The company, acting as an agent, bought equity interests in farms and ranches for their clients (usually pension funds) and managed them to provide operating cash flow and capital appreciation.

Agrico had three different arrangements for the properties. Under crop-share lease arrangements, which represented 47 percent of their portfolio, tenant farmers would agree to farm land managed by Agrico in return for a portion of each year's crops, which Agrico would ultimately sell in commodity markets. Under cash-rent leases (51 percent of the portfolio), farmers made cash payments for use of the land. Agrico also directly managed a few properties (about 2 percent of its total). (See Exhibit 1 for selected data on Agrico and Exhibit 2 for an organizational chart of the company.)

Agrico's New Computer System[2]

During their 1985 business planning process, Agrico's executives decided that their existing arrangement for computer services—an agreement with a nearby commercial real estate concern that provided all services for a yearly fee—was not adequate for their present or future needs. The same year they also identified a need for office automation to improve productivity. Their local contract for computer services expired on September 30, 1987, and as summers were traditionally slow (buying, selling, and leasing of farms took place in the winter and spring and supervising of crop harvests in the fall), June 1, 1987, was set as the target conversion date.

Since Agrico had no internal computer systems staff, they contracted with a large computer consulting firm for recommendations on their computing needs and responsibility for them. The consulting firm assigned several of its employees to the project, including a project manager—George P. Burdelle, a mid-1970s graduate of Georgia Tech who had received his MBA from the Harvard Business School shortly thereafter. The results of the systems plan-

---

[2]See Exhibit 3 for a summary of Agrico's experience with its new computer system.

EXHIBIT 1 Agrico, Inc.—A Software Dilemma

Selected Company Data
(for 1987 unless otherwise noted)

Acres under management	691,000	
Market value of properties	$500 million (approx.)	
Number of farms	250	
Number of ranches	130	
Number of employees	83	
Number of clients	170	
Tenants:		
Crop-share lease	175	
Cash-rent lease	197	
Total Tenant Leases	372	

Other data:	*1986*	*1985*
Revenues	$5,272,000	$5,157,000
Net income	487,000	436,000
Total assets	3,027,000	2,691,000

---

ning project indicated that Agrico should do in-house data processing. But as they had little expertise, and to minimize cost and installation lead time, it was recommended that they use a software package rather than attempt to develop a custom-coded system. Thus, a software selection and systems design project was begun in March 1986.

Functional requirements for the system were very complex, since it was expected that a single software package would be used for all three property arrangements under Agrico management. The cash-rent leases offered few problems—that accounting was fairly straightforward. The directly managed properties, though few in number, required a different focus—"all the logistics of running a farm or ranch," according to Burdelle. As for the crop-share leases, since Agrico not only shared all expenses and revenues from these farms, but also often received part of the crops for payment, it was

heavily involved in farm commodity markets. So, in addition to the program requirements needed to manage the receiving, selling, and delivering of its portion of the crops, the software had to accommodate the commodity market information.

Agrico insisted that these software requirements be met by a single vendor offering an integrated package. From an initial list of more than 40 potential vendors, only two were identified; each was asked to submit a bid in a "request for proposal" (RFP) process. Agrico selected AMR for their software. As Burdelle later explained:

When you came down to it, it was a relatively straightforward decision for Agrico. AMR had 12 clients up and running, and they had excellent references. We visited 2 clients and saw demonstrations of features we knew we needed. The software ran on a minicomputer that also provided excellent office automation capabilities. The only major

EXHIBIT 2   Agrico, Inc.—Organization Chart

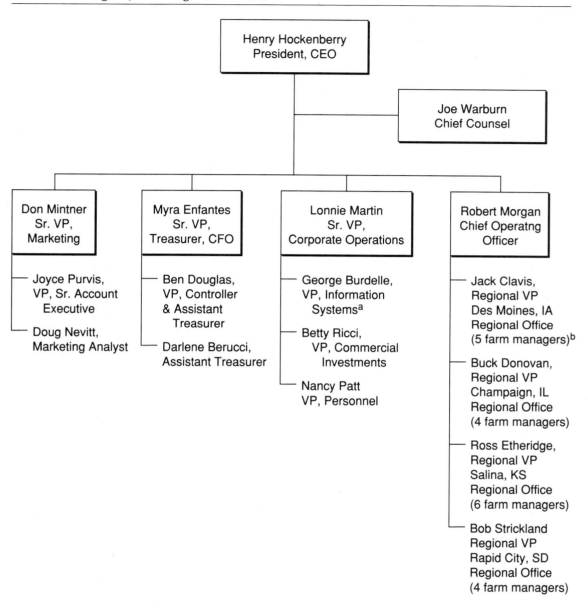

[a]One systems and programming manager, two programmers, and two computer operators reported to Burdelle.
[b]In addition, for directly managed properties, other employees were often included in reporting through the farm managers.

EXHIBIT 3　Agrico, Inc.—Experience With New Computer System—Major Events

Date	Event
1985—Business Planning Process	Executives set June 1, 1987, as target conversion date.
March 1986	Software selection and systems design project started; consulting team in place (including Burdelle).
July 1986	Work on system installation project begun. Burdelle accepts job at Agrico; resigns from consulting firm. AMR agreement signed.
September 1986	New computer hardware delivered; systems staff on board.
October 1986	AMR delivers object code.
October 1986—January 1987	Software acceptance testing; Agrico team (staff and consultants) work at AMR's Omaha offices.
March 1987	Significant software flaws corrected. Jane Seymour (AMR's software engineer) begins work on Agrico's computer in Des Moines.
May 26, 1987	Burdelle speaks with Agrico attorney.
May 27, 1987	Seymour leaves source code on computer.

risk we saw was the fact that AMR was a small company.

Our second-choice vendor—a mid-sized software house with about 120 employees—sold software that met most of our functional requirements, but they had only sold three copies, none of which were in production yet. Their software ran on a mainframe, with heavy systems support and operations expertise requirements. In addition, the mainframe had very limited ability to support office automation.

A number of modification and enhancement requirements were identified for the AMR software during the selection process, and the cost and completion schedule were included in the RFP response from the vendor. Work on the system installation project began in July 1986.

Throughout this period Agrico was impressed with Burdelle's grasp of its complex system needs; they offered him the position of vice president of information systems, and Burdelle accepted on July 11, 1986. He said:

> Agrico had a need for someone to build a systems department, and I enjoyed working with the company personnel. The June 1, 1987, conversion target date allowed us adequate time for the installation, and we had the ability to run parallel with the old system before cutting over.

The AMR Relationship

AMR, a small software outfit headquartered in Omaha, Nebraska, had been founded in 1977 by A. M. Rogers. It sold only one software package—a system for managing farm and ranch portfolios. With 12 clients in nine states, AMR appeared to hold the solution for Agrico. Burdelle described them:

> They were a small company with 10 employees, including Rogers himself. We called ev-

ery one of their customers and got the same story: positive experiences. Rogers was the core of AMR and had his hand in everything, from marketing to software design and programming. The other employees were systems people, but they were more "carpenters" than "architects."

In July, Agrico and AMR signed an agreement stating that AMR would provide software consistent with Agrico's needs; AMR would be required to make modifications to its software package. The total purchase price for the software, including modifications, was approximately $200,000. Agrico would also pay 1 percent of this amount monthly as a maintenance fee. The modified object code was to be delivered to Agrico no later than October 1, 1986; the agreement stated that Agrico's access to the source code was limited to "viewing listings reasonably necessary to test the sys-

tem." Only AMR was allowed to make modifications to the code. Commented Burdelle:

> We realized that a good percentage of Rogers's revenue came from modifying the software to meet unique client requirements, so we offered to pay more to buy the source code. We acknowledged that if we modified his source he would not be responsible for retrofitting our changes to his new software releases. However, he apparently was afraid that someone would steal a copy of his software. We offered to sign nondisclosure agreements, whatever, but Rogers was really irrational about keeping the source code.

The software purchase agreement required AMR to maintain the software in escrow with a third party to insure adequate backups. (See Exhibit 4 for excerpts from the agreement, which was prepared primarily by Agrico's attorney.)

EXHIBIT 4 Excerpts From AMR Agreement

Agreement made and entered into this 10th day of July 1986, between AMR Software Company, Inc. ("AMR"), a Nebraska corporation with its principal place of business in Omaha, Nebraska, and Agrico, Inc. ("Agrico"), an Iowa corporation with its principal place of business in Des Moines, Iowa.

[Specifics of the sales agreement followed in items 1–14. Included was an agreement that Agrico could examine the source code listings "reasonably necessary to test the system." Item 15 described the monthly maintenance fee—1 percent of the purchase price—and defined the support services to be provided.]

16. AMR PROPRIETARY MATERIAL:

  a) The software may not be copied or reprinted in whole or in part without the prior written permission of AMR.
  b) Agrico shall not allow anyone other than Agrico or AMR personnel to copy any code or documentation manuals. Agrico shall not give, sell, or allow access to any person not employed by Agrico or to any other company a copy or listing of any of the programs contained in the software, except to *bona fide* consultants of Agrico who, prior to such access, execute with AMR a nondisclosure agreement.
  c) The software, including the programs therein and the documentation manuals, is proprietary information of AMR and Agrico shall not disclose any of this proprietary information to any other parties except as otherwise provided in 16.b above.
  d) The source code listings shall not be copied or duplicated.
  e) Agrico or Agrico's consultants shall not disclose the fact that AMR has provided the source code listings to Agrico hereunder.
  f) The source code listings shall not be removed from Agrico's premises.

EXHIBIT 4   (continued)

[Items 17–22 referred to responsibilities of the parties.]

23. ESCROW OF SOURCE CODE: AMR shall place a copy of the source code for programs comprising the software in the custody of a third party (in escrow) that is satisfactory to both Agrico and AMR. AMR warrants and represents that it will update the source code in the possession of the custodian on an annual basis at no cost to Agrico. AMR shall charge Agrico for the cost of escrowing the source code.

AMR warrants that in the event AMR commences a voluntary case or other proceeding seeking liquidation, reorganization or other relief with respect to itself or its debts under any bankruptcy, insolvency, or other similar law now or hereafter in effect or seeks the appointment of a trustee, receiver, liquidator, custodian or other similar official for AMR or a substantial part of AMR's property; or an involuntary case or other proceeding shall be commenced against AMR seeking liquidation, reorganization or other relief with respect to AMR or its debts under any bankruptcy, insolvency, or other similar law now or hereafter in effect or seeking the appointment of a trustee, receiver, liquidator, custodian or other similar official for AMR or any substantial part of its property, and such involuntary case or other proceeding shall remain undismissed and unstayed for a period of 60 days; or an order for relief shall be entered against AMR under the federal bankruptcy laws as now or hereafter in effect; or AMR discontinues marketing or support of the software, and upon Agrico's reasonable belief that AMR is no longer able to provide maintenance of the software, after demand has been sent to AMR at their current address by registered mail, the custodian shall deliver to Agrico the source code and all technical documentation.

Agrico reserves the right to test the escrow disk pack at AMR's office to insure the software is an exact duplicate of the current version of the Agrico software.

24. WARRANTY: AMR hereby represents and warrants to Agrico, such representation and warranty to be in effect as of the date hereof and for so long thereafter as Agrico pays the monthly fee described in item 15 hereof, that the software delivered hereunder is free from defects in manufacture or materials and will continue to meet the specifications and requirements as described in the proposal, the RFP and this agreement after installation, and AMR will, without charge to Agrico, correct any such defects and make such additions, modifications, and adjustments to the software as may be necessary to keep the system in good operating order and performing in accordance with the foregoing representations and warranties. In addition, AMR warrants that all modifications made to the software meet the business objective of the modification, will be fully unit tested, system tested, documented, and will not adversely affect the system.

[Item 25 detailed several general clauses regarding payment agreements and official addresses.]

IN WITNESS WHEREOF, the parties hereto have executed this agreement under seal in duplicate originals as of the date first written above.

[Signatures followed.]

The Software Experience

AMR delivered the object code, as promised, by October. It was installed on Agrico's new computer, which had been delivered in late September. During this same time, Burdelle completed the hiring of his systems staff, which included a systems and programming manager, two programmers, and two operators.

The software acceptance test followed. Both the new Agrico staff and the consultants were involved in the testing. Burdelle related the experience:

We quickly discovered that all was not right. There was no standard software, as AMR had installed 12 versions—one for each of its clients—around the country. No two were the same—the AMR programmers added or deleted code based upon the needs of each client. We wanted to use practically all of their options, and apparently none of their clients had used them all together. While the individual options worked, they did not always work correctly when combined. We also found out that a number of functions had never been thoroughly tested anywhere.

As it turned out, AMR usually installed and converted the software and then fixed bugs when they were discovered by the client. We were not willing to live with that approach.

Given this situation, we rearranged our schedule to provide more time for software acceptance testing. Our purchase contract required us to pay 20 percent of the software price upon contract signing, 60 percent of it 30 days after completion of software acceptance testing, and the remaining balance 90 days after system conversion. We had AMR's attention, because they did not get most of their money until the software passed our acceptance test. I was not going to jeopardize our clients' assets with bug-filled software. Furthermore, I began to see that the escrow of our software was very important, since a standard version literally did not exist.

From October through January, the Agrico team worked at the AMR offices in Omaha. Significant flaws were identified in the software, but AMR had successfully corrected them by March, and Jane Seymour from AMR had begun working on Agrico's computer in Des Moines. But this testing and repair process had exacted its toll on the relationship between Rogers and Burdelle. A contentious tone had crept into their correspondence, which was frequent. On one occasion Rogers complained about the Agrico project team's "tiger testing" of the software, and Burdelle noted, "I instructed the team to be ruthless in identifying bugs. I refused to sign off on the acceptance test until the software was perfect. It was not a pleasant experience."

Off-Site Escrow

During this same period, Burdelle began lengthy discussions with Rogers to define the specific arrangements for the escrow of the object and source code. Burdelle explained:

> When we realized that every one of AMR's installations was unique, we understood just how important it was to have copies of the unique source code for our system stored for backup purposes. Without source code, there was potential for our being forever locked into the existing system with no chance for enhancements or modifications. It was possible we would have to go through the detailed software acceptance testing process again if any changes were made. Given our experience with AMR to date, I was not willing to take it on faith that our source code was adequately protected.
>
> Rogers claimed that we should be satisfied with his backup plan, in which he occasionally took tapes to his bank's vault in Omaha. However, we had no independent way to verify that the source code AMR stated was our escrow copy was in fact the source code that generated our object code. There are companies that store computer tapes in special facilities, like the one we employed in Des Moines for our data tapes, and we wanted that kind of security. Plus, we wanted an independent third party to insure that the latest version was available. The easiest way: escrow the source in the off-site facility we already used.
>
> But Rogers was afraid that we'd modify or sell his source code if it was in the same off-site facility we use, and he was paranoid about keeping control. We talked and talked with him, but our discussions came up empty. He said he thought our concerns about backup procedures were overblown.

Concerned that the June 1 conversion date was fast approaching with backup procedures for code storage still unclear, Burdelle discussed the situation with Agrico's attorney on Tuesday, May 26:

> The attorney said that we had a classic problem of ambiguity. The contract did require AMR to provide us with access to the source code so that we could understand it, but only AMR had the right to copy and store it. Yet, AMR was supposed to store it in a "satisfactory" manner; apparently, we each defined "satisfactory" differently. The attorney felt that if we could get access to the source code we might have a good court argument for storing it ourselves. But technically getting and storing the code did violate the contract.

Burdelle had also considered other solutions, such as discontinuing the relationship with AMR and looking for other vendors. He said:

> Many times along the way, I thought about telling AMR "thanks but no thanks." I realized that the expenses we had incurred were really sunk costs: things like our consultants' bills for debugging the software, which by then had accumulated to $75,000. The biggest problem was that there were few other options: we already knew there was only one other vendor that had even a remotely similar software package, and it used different hardware.
>
> Time was of the essence; any delays in converting to the new system would cost Agrico dearly. We did not want to start over and develop a custom system; that would have been a monumental project. I was confident that the software now worked as it should, but I was concerned about future modifications.
>
> We had also created much ill will with Rogers, and he was becoming even more irrational as the days went by.

In contrast to the deteriorating relationship with Rogers, Agrico had developed great rapport with Jane Seymour. On Wednesday, May 27, Alvaredo said, in fact, that she believed Seymour may have "looked the other way" in leaving the source code on the computer when she went to dinner. "I think Jane knows the bind we are in with Rogers," she told Burdelle.

Burdelle's Decision

Burdelle, alone in his office, pulled the AMR contract from his file cabinet and read again the words concerning access to source code. He thought once more about the attorney's advice, and he quickly reviewed the ramifications of the potential need for modifications to the software. "While we've had more than our share of disagreements, I have always been honest with Rogers, and I've tried to prove that he had no reason to distrust us," Burdelle mused. "I want to abide by the terms of the contract, but I don't want to jeopardize Agrico's clients' assets."

At 7:30 P.M., Burdelle walked to the computer room to give Alvaredo his decision.

Chapter 12

Transnational IT Issues

The head of Management Information Systems (MIS) of a major European research company suddenly discovered that three of its largest foreign subsidiaries had recently ordered medium-sized computers and were planning to move their work from the corporate IT department to installations in their respective countries. This would reduce the workload in the corporate data center by 45 percent. The reasons cited for the decision were that it would provide better control over day-to-day operations, offer more responsive service, and reduce costs. Located in a country with a small, high-cost labor pool, the MIS head was unsure of how to assess the risks this change posed to his operation and to the company as a whole.

A large pharmaceutical company's head of corporate IT recently held a three-day meeting of the IT heads of the company's 15 largest foreign subsidiaries. A major unresolved issue discussed at the meeting was the appropriate relationship of corporate IT to the more than 50 smaller foreign subsidiaries that also have computing equipment. Historically, the department has responded to requests for assistance (five to eight requests per year) but has not gone beyond that. The head of corporate IT is increasingly doubtful that this level of involvement is appropriate.

These stories are representative of a major, largely unreported, unstudied IT story; namely, that management of transnational IT support for any company is very complex and that its issues go well beyond legislation relating to transborder information flows. These issues have become more significant in the past decade as the post–World War II explosion of transnationals, in both numbers and scope, has continued. This growth has sparked the need for development and expansion of management systems that permit appropriate coordination of geographically distant business activities.

In the past, investigation of these issues has been neglected by two schools of thought. On the one hand, the area has seemed too specialized and technical to the scholars of international business. On the other hand, the scholars of information technology management have been highly national in their orientation, and so they, too, have tended to avoid transnational IT issues.

Transnational IT management is a major challenge today, and the need to resolve its issues is likely to grow rapidly in the coming years. Managing the forces (described as six "trends" in Chapter 2) driving transition in IT is complicated in the international arena by the wide diversity in national infrastructures (for example, those of Germany versus those of Sri Lanka), corporate manufacturing and distribution technologies, and scope and sophistication of IT applications. Building on the concepts of strategic relevance, culture, contingent planning, and managing diffusion of technology, this chapter focuses on aspects of transnational business that influence IT.

IT support coordination issues for international operations are vastly more complex than purely domestic ones, because they involve all the issues of domestic operations plus many additional difficulties. During the coming decade, IT will continue to be challenged by the opening of Eastern Europe to private enterprise, the need to share technologies within a firm for common problems around the world, and the continued evolution of transnational firms in both products and structure. The cross-border flows of goods and materials are accelerating, requiring new and complex information infrastructures. Financial and human resources for global operations require extremely coordinated management. Many firms have growing pools of staff that require extensive global coordination and development and their electronic support. Finally, technology skills, expertise, and intelligence all require much tighter coordination in the multinational realm. Information technology is central to accomplishing this.

Additional complexity is provided by the wide differences in culture, labor/technology costs, products, and need/viability of IT support in different areas of the world. A subsidiary in India, for example, with its cheap labor and marginal telecommunications, realistically poses fundamentally different integration issues than one in Singapore with its high-cost labor, high-quality telecommunications, and small geography. Additionally, recent technology advances that have impacted firms' overall organization structures now permit moving tasks around the globe while maintaining tighter control and facilitate new ways of defining and doing work.

The first section of this chapter describes the impact of IT on transnational firms. The second section deals with national characteristics that determine what type of IT support is both possible and appropriate for a firm's operations in a country. The third section explains IT environmental issues that influence how a firm can develop IT support in another country. The fourth section discusses company-specific issues that can help corporations develop and coordinate IT activity internationally. The final part describes some IT policies that firms have adopted and discusses the factors of their appropriateness in particular settings.

INFORMATION TECHNOLOGY IMPACT ON TRANSNATIONAL FIRMS

The new technologies of the past decade have affected the ways and places where firms do work in many ways, and their impact will be even greater in the coming decade, as the technologies evolve and firms gain experience in implementing the changes enabled by the technologies. Organization structures, control procedures, and tasks are being altered, albeit with great effort and expense.

Geographic Transfer of Work

The new technologies have facilitated the physical movement of work from areas with high-cost labor pools to areas where labor pools are both high quality and low cost. A domestic U.S. example of this is Citibank's move of its credit card operation from high-cost New York City to Sioux Falls, South Dakota. (Citibank achieved enormous savings.) In the same vein, American Airlines has moved a significant amount of its data entry work out of Dallas. Documents are now keyed in Barbados. The resulting outputs are transmitted electronically back to Dallas. Several years ago a U.S. insurance company developed a significant systems development and programming unit in Ireland. This allowed them to access the much less expensive, high-quality Irish labor pool, effecting important savings. An added bonus was that the firm was able to use the third shift of the domestic computer operations for debugging because of the five-hour time difference between Ireland and the United States. Similarly, a number of programming organizations have developed in the "free trade" zones of India that compete cost-effectively with Western Europe and American systems development activities, particularly for highly structured tasks.

In a world where the economy is increasingly service-oriented and where telecommunications costs continue to drop, these trends will accelerate. In this new transportable business world local tax authorities must avoid becoming too greedy lest big pieces of the economy will disappear overnight. Clerical and knowledge-based work is movable; office buildings and factories are not.

Global Networking and Expertise Sharing

Firms like IBM and Digital Equipment Corporation (DEC) have developed very sophisticated international electronic mail and conferencing procedures. Tens of thousands of professional support staff around the world now have direct electronic access to each other. Global sources of knowledge can be quickly tapped, the barriers of time zones swept away, and the overall response time to problems sharply altered. (Recall the example cited in an earlier chapter of a marketing representative assembling documentation from around the world and preparing a 200-page, multimillion-dollar project proposal in 48 hours.) As overseas markets, manufacturing facilities, and research facilities proliferate, these coordinating mechanisms become vitally important in a world where competition is time-based. Inexpensive, broad-band, global communication provides important opportunities for sharing and managing designs, manufacturing schedules, and text. Identifying expertise and then sharing it globally will allow some transnational firms to distinguish themselves in the 1990s. The new capabilities made possible by optical fiber will only accelerate this.

Global Service Levels

The standards of what constitutes world-class service are sharply increasing. For example, several years ago a major U.S. trucking company could tell you where every one of their trucks was and what was on it. That is, it could tell you a truck had just left the depot in Kansas City and that it should arrive in San Francisco in 36 hours. The truck's location at the moment was unknown, and there was no way to direct the driver to cities in between for emergency pickups. (This was as good as any of its competitors could do.) Today, on top of each of the company's trucks is a small satellite dish with a computer in it. The firm now knows exactly where each truck is (within a city) and at any time can send instructions to drivers to alter their routes as customer needs emerge and change. In the overseas transportation business, global information links have allowed U.S. carriers such as American President Lines to survive in a world dominated by low-cost competitors. Since the 1970s they have used IT to provide a highly customized and differentiated electronic-based service for their customers around the world. In so doing they have neutralized the significant labor cost advantage of their competitors by providing a highly valuable customer service. This service includes up-to-the-minute cargo locations, reliable delivery promises, and flexibility in handling emergencies. Such advantages, of course, do not endure forever, and there is constant pressure to innovate to maintain this edge.

Time-Based Competition

The required response time in the global community is dramatically shrinking. Automobile manufacturers and large construction firms, for example, have been able to shave months and years off the design cycle as local computer-assisted-design equipment is linked internationally to CAD equipment owned by them, their suppliers, or their customers. In financial services, the question repeatedly arises, "Is two-second response time enough, or are we at a significant competitive disadvantage?" A speaker at a telecommunication conference recently noted that within a week after the opening of the new London stock exchange, which allows automatic electronic tracking, firms using satellites had shifted to optical fiber because the 50-millisecond delay put them at a distinct competitive disadvantage. In between these extremes, of course, are situations where we talk about taking weeks off order entry, order confirmation, and manufacturing cycles. A U.K. chemical company's $30 million investment in manufacturing and information technology recently transformed what had been a ten-week order entry and manufacturing cycle to one or two days. Needless to say, this changed the rules of competition in the industry and put unbearable pressure on some competitors. In the words of one of our colleagues, "competing on the basis of time may be done not just by speeding up the mess, but by enabling the construction of very different infrastructures that challenge every aspect of the firm's procedures." Global time-based competition will be a major item for world business in the next decade.

Cost Reduction

The much tighter information links between overseas operations, customers, and suppliers allows a firm to eliminate significant slack from their manufacturing systems. This results in significant reductions in buffer inventories and staffing levels and a general acceleration in asset utilization. At the extreme, it enables the creation of "hollow" global corporations such as Benetton, which owns virtually nothing but a sophisticated global information system that links the activities of its franchises with its suppliers.

The sum of these observations is that IT has transformed the very structures of transnational organizations, the type of work they do, and where they do the work. More importantly, the new technologies assure continued evolution in this impact. The dark side of this, of course, is a huge increase in the operational dependence of firms on their networks, central processors, and so on. This has forced them to build high levels of redundancy into their networks, creating alternative paths for information flow to back up their computing centers and so on. As noted earlier, Reuters, for example, provides more than a dozen electronic information paths from one part of the world to others. For a number of firms, these issues are so fundamental and of such potential impact that the IT activity is positioned near the top of the firm and is intimately involved in all strategic planning activities in order to ensure a fit between IT and the firm's plans.

DIVERSITY OF COUNTRIES

A number of factors inherent in a country's culture, government, and economy determine which IT applications are feasible in that country, how they should be implemented, and how they should be directed by a corporate IT function located in another country. The most important of these factors are discussed here.

Sociopolitical

A country's industrial maturity and form of government are particularly important factors when considering the use of information technology. Developing countries with high birth rates have views and opportunities far different from those of mature industrialized nations with their shrinking labor populations. Mature industrial societies have well-established bureaucracies that provide the necessary stability for development of communication systems. In some countries investments in technical infrastructure are made at the expense of such other national priorities as food and medical care.

Language

A common language facilitates technical communication and the sharing of relevant documentation. When this is lacking, the potential for errors, mishaps, or the like is greatly increased. Frequently senior managers of international subsidiaries are fluent in the language of the parent company, but lower-level managers and staff technicians are not. N.V. Philips, the large Dutch electronics company, has made a major effort to develop English as the companywide language, but realistically full fluency lies only at the senior management and staff levels.

Local Constraints

A multitude of local cultural traditions can inhibit the development of coordinated systems and orderly technology transfer between countries. Differing union agreements, holidays, tax regulations, and customs procedures all force major modifications of software for applications such as accounting and personnel. Further, differences in holidays, working hours, and so on, complicate coordination of reporting and data gathering.

Also important are issues relating to geography and demographics. For example, a large phonograph record company has centralized its order-entry and warehouse management functions for France in Paris, because it fits the structure of that country's distribution system. In Germany, however, the company had to establish multiple factories and distribution points and a quite different order-entry system for serving the German market, because that structure reflects the realities of German geography and prevailing distribution patterns. Unfortunately, as a result the software and procedures used in the French subsidiary are inappropriate for German operations.

Economic

A mature industrial economy normally has an available pool of well-trained, procedurally oriented individuals who are well paid relative to world standards. Further, the economic incentive to replace clerical people with IT systems is complemented by the limited availability of well trained clerical staff. It is a sensible economic decision. In countries with low wage rates, many of them dependent on one or two main raw-material exports for currency, there is typically a lack of both talent and economic incentive toward IT. (In many such countries this is changing fast, however.) They need to develop a reliable source of available information—a noneconomic decision. Implementing this new system, however, may move against both economic and cultural norms in the country. Trying to serve the interests of different national cultures in a transnational IT organization often means developing different solutions for each country.

Currency

The operation of international data centers is complicated by currency restrictions and the volatility in exchange rates. A change in exchange rates may make a location that was cost-effective for providing service to neighboring countries suddenly quite cost-ineffective. This happened with several Swiss data centers between the early 1970s and the late 1970s as a result of the heavy appreciation of the Swiss franc against other currencies.

Autonomy

Also important are the universal drive for autonomy and feelings of nationalism. The normal drive for autonomy in units within a country is intensified by differences in language and culture as one deals with international subsidiaries. In general, more integration effort is needed for coordinating foreign subsidiaries than for domestic ones. Coordination difficulties increase with the subsidiary's distance from corporate headquarters, as its relative economic importance to the corporation decreases, and with different spoken languages.

National Infrastructure

The cost and availability of utilities, particularly telecommunications utilities, and a transportation system can place important constraints on feasible alternatives. On the other hand, their absence can serve as an opportunity to experiment with certain emerging technologies. For example, to overcome one country's unpredictable transportation and communication systems, a South American distributor developed a private microwave tower network to link the records of a remote satellite depot with the central warehouses. Direct ground links to satellites promise to by-pass the need for expensive ground line installation in some developing areas.

Summary

All of these factors make coordination of international IT activities more complicated than coordination of domestic IT activities. As noted above, the factors leading to these complications are so complex and deep-rooted as to provide enduring challenges. Consequently, some companies have found it necessary to develop special staff and organizational approaches for handling these issues.

NATIONAL IT ENVIRONMENT ISSUES

In addition to the many differences between countries, some specific IT issues make coordinating and transferring information technology from one country to another particularly challenging. These are due in part to the long lead times necessary for building effective systems and in part to the changing nature of the technology. The most important of these issues are discussed in this section.

Availability of IT Professional Staff

Inadequate availability of systems and programming resources, a worldwide problem, is more severe in some settings than others. Further, as soon as people in some English-speaking countries develop these skills, they become targets for recruiters from more industrialized countries where salaries are higher. This is a particular problem in the Philippines, for example.

This personnel shortage has led to the growth of India-based software companies, which take advantage of India's high skill levels and very low wage rates to bid effectively on overseas programming jobs. Obviously, geographic distances limit the types of work these companies can bid on. Highly structured applications are much easier to develop in these ways than ones that have less structure and thus require much closer interaction between end user and developer.

When an attempt is made to supplement local staff with individuals from headquarters, the results may not be totally satisfactory. There is usually an initial outburst of productivity by the expatriates and an effective transfer of technology. Later, however, this may result in resentment by the local staff (whose salaries and benefits are usually much lower) and broken career paths for the expatriates, who find they have become both technically and managerially obsolete when they return to corporate headquarters. Management of IT expatriates' re-entry has generally been quite inadequate.

Central Telecommunications

The price and quality of telecommunications support vary widely from one country to another. On both dimensions the United States sets the standard. In many European countries the tariffs on these services are an order-of-magnitude higher than those in the United States. Also, lead times to get extra land lines, terminals, and so forth, can stretch to years instead of weeks in many countries—if they are available at any price. Finally, communication quality, availability, and cost differ widely among countries. Varying line capacity, costs, and uptime performance can make profitable home-country on-line applications cost-ineffective, inadequate, or unreliable in other countries.

National IT Strategy

In some countries development of a local computer manufacturing and software industry is a key national priority. This is true of France, Germany, Singapore, and the United Kingdom, for example. In these situations subsidiaries of foreign companies often view buying the products of the local manufacturer as good citizenship and as an opportunity to build credit for later dealings with the government. This creates a legitimate need for local deviation from corporate hardware/software standards.

Some countries, such as India and Nigeria, require that computer vendors sell a majority share of their local subsidiary to local shareholders in order to do business in the country. IBM and some other vendors have preferred to withdraw from a market rather than to enter into such an arrangement. Complying with such a requirement also may force a deviation from corporate-mandated IT standards. In the 1990s, however, both computer vendors and manufacturers are proving to be more adaptable and flexible in working around this difficulty.

Finally, concern may exist about whether the country exporting the hardware will continue to be a reliable supplier in a world of turbulent national politics and shifting foreign policies. A number of South African companies, for example, unsure of their ability to get a sustained flow of products from any one country, moved to prevent potential disruptions of equipment delivery by dealing with vendors of several countries. In making this move they committed themselves to significant additional costs.

General Level of IT Sophistication

The speed and ease with which companies can implement or develop an IT activity in another country are linked to the general level of IT activity in the country. A firm located in a country with a substantial base of installed electronic-based information systems and well-trained, mobile labor can develop its IT capabilities more rapidly and effectively than if none of these conditions exist. Countries with limited installed electronic-based information systems require substantially more expatriate labor to implement IT work, as well as great effort and time to educate users in the idiosyncrasies of IT and how best to interface with it. Careful investigation of the staff mobility factor is particularly important, because bonding arrangements and cultural norms may place considerable rigidity on what appears to be a satisfactory labor supply.

Size of Local Market

The size of the local market influences the number of vendors who compete for service in it. Thus in small markets a company's preferred international supplier may not have a presence. Further, the quality of service support often varies widely from one setting to another; vendors who provide good support in one country may give inadequate support in another. Another important issue is the availability and quality of local software and consulting companies (or subsidiaries of large international ones). A thriving, competent local IT industry can do much to offset other differences in local support and availability of staff.

Data Export Control

A topic receiving significant publicity since the mid-1980s is legislation that would dramatically reduce the amount of information relating to people and finances that may be transmitted electronically across national boundaries. This is driven both by concerns about individual privacy and the often weak security and low quality controls over these data.

A relatively benign topic in the 1980s, it will rear its head much more vigorously in the 1990s. The use of personal data generates a wide range of sensitivities in different societies. In general, it is of most concern in Western Europe today, particularly in the Scandinavian countries, and is of less concern in the United States. Existing legislation and practice varies widely among countries, as do criteria for evaluating and resolving these issues. The current apparent lack of interest in these issues in many countries should not be misread by the business community. The issues are deep and emotional, and the spotlight will surely make this a burning issue in the 1990s. What is seen in one environment as a sharp consumer micromarketing implementation may be seen as deeply intrusive and immoral in another. The word *Orwellian* is increasingly being used in describing some new IT applications that use personal data. (See the material on privacy in Chapter 11.)

Technological Awareness

Awareness of contemporary technology spreads very rapidly around the globe because IT magazines and journals are distributed internationally. This awareness poses problems in terms of orderly development of applications in less IT-sophisticated countries, because it leads subsidiaries to promote technologies that they neither understand nor need and that they are incapable of managing. Conversely, starting with a high degree of IT awareness has advantages, because distinctly different paths may be implemented for exploiting information technology in the subsidiaries than are used in home offices.

Border Opportunities

In periods of fluctuating exchange rates, significant discontinuities often appear in vendor prices for the same equipment in different countries. In 1980, for example, there was a period when a 15 to 20 percent savings could be achieved by buying equipment in Italy for use across the border in Switzerland, as opposed to buying it in Switzerland.

Summary

For the transnational firm the practical implication of these factors is severe restraint of the degree to which standard policies and controls can be placed on diverse international activities. Rigid policy on many of these issues cannot be dictated effectively from corporate headquarters, often located a vast distance from the subsidiary's operating management. There are many legitimate reasons for diversity, and considerable *local* know-how must be brought to the decisions.

CORPORATE FACTORS AFFECTING IT REQUIREMENTS

Within the context of the different national cultures and the current state of the IT profession in different countries, a number of factors inside a company influence how far it can move to manage the transfer of information technology and how centralized its control of international IT activity should be. Because of the many factors discussed in the previous sections, more control must be delegated in an international environment than in a domestic one. However, important opportunities exist for technology transfer, and potentially important limitations in service will occur if these opportunities are not managed. The more important company-specific factors are discussed here.

Nature of Firm's Business

Some firms' businesses demand that key data files be managed centrally so that they are accessible, immediately or on a short delayed-access basis, to all units of the firm around the world. Airline reservation files for international air carriers require such access. A United Airlines agent in Boston confirming a flight segment from Tokyo to Hong Kong needs up-to-the-minute access to the flight's loading to make a valid commitment, while other agents around the globe need to know that seat is no longer available for sale. Failure to have this information poses risks of significant loss of market share as customers perceive the firm to be both unreliable and uncompetitive.

American President Lines, an international shipping company, maintains a file, updated every 24 hours, as to the location of each of its containers, its status, and its availability for future commitment by regional officers in 20 countries. Without this data the firm would most likely make unfulfillable commitments, which would present an unreliable image to present and potential customers. In another example, the standards of international banking have evolved to where the leaders provide customers with an instantaneous worldwide picture of clearances, and so on, thus opening the door for more sophisticated cash management—for which the banks charge significant fees. Those firms not providing such services find themselves increasingly at a competitive disadvantage.

Other firms require integration and on-line updating of only some of their files. A European electronics firm attempts to provide its European managers with up-to-date, on-line access to various key operational files on items such as production schedules, order status, and so forth. This is done for its network of 20-plus factories in order to manage an integrated logistics system. No such integration, however, is attempted for their key marketing or accounting data, which essentially are processed on a batch basis and organized by country. While developing such integration is technically possible, at present the firm sees no operational or marketing advantage in doing so.

Still other firms require essentially no integration of data, and each country can be managed on a stand-alone basis. A U.S. conglomerate, for example, manages each division on a stand-alone basis. Eight of its divisions have operations in the United Kingdom, and by corporate policy they have no formal interaction with each other in IT or any other operational matters. (A single tax specialist who files a joint tax return for them is the sole linking specialist.) The company's staff generally perceives that this is an appropriate way to operate and that nothing of significance is being lost. These examples suggest the impossibility of generalizing about how transnational IT activities should be organized.

Strategic Impact of IT

If IT activity is strategic to the company, tighter corporate overview is needed to ensure that new technology (with its accompanying new ways of operating) is rapidly and efficiently introduced to outlying areas. One of the United States' largest international banks, for example, has a staff of more than 100 at corporate headquarters to develop software for their international branches and to coordinate its orderly dissemination to them. The bank feels the successful use of IT is too critical to the firm's ultimate success to be managed without technical coordination and senior management perspective. At the other extreme is a reasonably large manufacturer of chemicals that sees IT as playing an important but clearly a *support* role. At least twice a year the head of the European IT unit and the head of corporate IT exchange visits and share perceptions with each other. The general consensus is that there is not enough potential payoff to warrant further coordination.

Corporate Organization

As its international activity grows, a firm adopts different structures, each of which requires quite different levels of international IT support and coordination. In the earliest phase of an export division there are only limited numbers of overseas staff, who require little if any local IT processing and support. As the activity grows in size it tends to be reorganized as an *international* division with an increasing number of marketing, accounting, and manufacturing staff located abroad. At this stage an increasing need may arise for local IT support. A full-blown level of international activity may involve regional headquarters (in Europe, the Far East, and Latin America, for example) to coordinate the activities of the diverse countries.

Coordinating such a structure is very complex, because not only are there vertical relationships between corporate IT and the national IT activities, but cross-border marketing and manufacturing integration requirements create the need for relationships between individual countries' IT units. Appropriate forms of this coordination, of course, vary widely among organizations. A multibillion dollar pharmaceutical firm was discovered to have very close links between corporate IT and its major national IT units (defined by the firm as those with budgets in excess of $5 million). None of the IT unit managers, however, knew the names of their contemporaries or had visited any of the other units. Since there was little cross-border product flow and none was planned for the near future, this did not appear to present a significant problem.

At the most complex, firms are organized in a matrix fashion—with corporate IT activity, divisional IT activities (which may or may not be located at corporate headquarters), and national IT activities. Here, balancing relationships is a major challenge. Divisions that have substantial vertical supplier relationships with each other and substantial integration of activities across national borders have even more complicated relationships. In such cases the policies that work for the international divisions are too simplistic.

Company Technical and Control Characteristics

Level of Functional Control. An important factor in effective IT control structures is the corporation's general level of functional control. Companies with a strong tradition of central control find it both appropriate and relatively easy to implement line IT control worldwide. A major manufacturer of farm equipment, for example, has for years implemented very strong management and operational control over its worldwide manufacturing and marketing functions. Consequently it found considerable acceptance of similar controls for the IT organization. Most of the software that runs their overseas plants has been developed and is maintained by the corporate IT headquarters group.

At the other extreme is a 30-division, multibillion-dollar conglomerate with a corporate staff of approximately 100 people who are involved mostly in financial and legal work associated with acquisitions and divestitures. This company has totally decentralized operating decisions to the divisions, and the number of corporate staff is deliberately controlled as a means of preventing meddling. At present a two-person corporate IT "group" works on only very broad policy and consulting issues. Effective execution of even this limited role is very challenging, and its expansion is very difficult to visualize.

Technology Base. Another element of significance is the technology base of the company. High-technology companies with traditions of spearheading technical change from a central research and engineering laboratory and disseminating it around the world have successfully used a similar approach with IT. Their transnational managers are used to corporately initiated technical change. Firms without this experience have had more difficulty assimilating information technology in general as well as more problems in transplanting IT developed in one location to other settings.

Corporate Size. Finally, corporate size is also relevant. Smaller organizations, because of the limited and specialized nature of their application, find transfer of IT packages and expertise to be particularly complex. As the scope of the operation increases, finding common applications and facilitating transfer of technology becomes easier, perhaps because the stakes are higher.

Other Considerations

Other factors also influence IT coordination policies. Is there substantial rotation of staff between international locations? If so, is it desirable to have common reporting systems and operating procedures in place in each subsidiary to ease the assimilation of the transfers? Do the firm's operating and financial requirements essentially demand up-to-the-week reporting of overseas financial results? If not, consolidation of smaller overseas operations on a one-month, delayed-time basis is attractive.

TRANSNATIONAL IT POLICY ISSUES

As the preceding sections explain, great diversity exists in the policies for coordinating and managing international IT activities. This section identifies the most common types of policies and relationships and briefly focuses on key issues associated with the selection and implementation of each. The scope of these policies and the amount of effort needed to implement them are influenced by the degree of needed central control, corporate culture and policies, strategic importance of information technologies, and other factors.

Guidance on Architecture

The most important central IT role is to facilitate the development and implementation of a view on appropriate telecommunications architecture and database standards. The firm must pragmatically move to ensure that these standards are installed in all of its operations. There are no substitutes in this task for travel, pragmatism, and the ability to listen. Ideas that make perfect sense in Detroit often need selective fine tuning in Thailand, if indeed they are even viable there.

The opportunity to transmit data electronically between countries for file updating and processing purposes has created the need for a corporate international data dictionary. Too often this need is not addressed, leading to clumsy systems designs and incorrect outputs. Where data should be stored, the form in which it should be stored, and how it should be updated are all considerations that require centrally managed policy—operating, of course, within the framework of what is legally permissible.

Similarly, central guidance and coordination in the acquisition of communication technology are needed. At present, communication flexibility and cost vary widely from country to country and they are shifting rapidly.

Effective anticipation of these cost and flexibility changes requires a corporate view and broad design of telecommunications needs for meeting the demands of growth and changing business needs over the coming decade. It must be specific in terms of service levels that will be needed and the technologies to be utilized. Such a plan requires capable technical inputs and careful management review. An important by-product of the plan is guidance for corporate negotiation and lobbying efforts on relevant items of national legislation and policies regarding the form, availability, and cost of telecommunication.

Central Hardware/Software Concurrence or Approval

The objectives of a central policy for acquiring hardware and software are to ensure that obvious mistakes in vendor viability are avoided and that economies of scale are achieved in purchasing decisions. Other benefits include the bargaining leverage a company achieves by being perceived as an important customer, the reduction of potential interface problems between national systems, and the enhancement of applications software transferability between countries. Practical factors that require sensitive interpretation and execution of central policy include the following:

- Degree of awareness at corporate headquarters of the vendor's support and servicing problems in the local country.
- Desire of the local subsidiary to exercise its autonomy and control of its operations in a timely way. The Korean subsidiary of a large bank wanted to buy a $25,000 word-processing system. Its request for approval took six months to pass through three locations and involved one senior vice president and two executive vice presidents. Whatever benefits standardization might have achieved for the bank in this situation seemed to be more than offset by the cost and time of the approval process.
- Need to maintain good relationships with local governments. This may involve patronizing local vendors, agreeing not to eliminate certain types of staff, and using the government-controlled IT network.
- Level and skill of corporate headquarters people who set the technical and managerial policies. A technically weak corporate staff dealing with large, well-managed foreign subsidiaries must operate quite differently from a technically gifted central staff dealing with small, unsophisticated subsidiaries.

Central Approval of Software Standards and Feasibility Studies

Central control of software standards can ensure that software is written in a maintainable secure way so that the company's long-term operational position is not jeopardized. Control of feasibility studies can ensure that potential applications are evaluated in a consistent and professional fashion. Practical problems with this policy of central approval revolve around both the level of effort required and the potential erosion of corporate culture.

Implementation of such standards can be expensive and time-consuming in relation to the potential benefits. The art is to be flexible with small investments and to review more closely the investments that involve real operational exposure. Unfortunately, this approach requires more sensitivity than many staffs possess.

Further, directly counter to central control may be a decentralized company's prevailing management control system and the location of other operating decisions. The significance of this conflict depends on the size and strategic importance of the investment. Relatively small, distinctly "support" investments in decentralized organizations should clearly be resolved in the local country. Large, strategic investments, however, should be subject to central review in these organizations, even if time delays and cost overruns result.

Central Software Development

In the name of efficiency, reduced costs, and standard operating procedures worldwide, some firms have attempted to develop software centrally, or at a designated subsidiary, for installation in subsidiaries in other countries. The success of this approach has definitely been mixed. Most companies that have succeeded with this have well-established patterns of technology transfer, strong functional control over their subsidiaries, substantial numbers of expatriates working in the overseas subsidiaries, and some homogeneity in their manufacturing, accounting, and distribution practices. Success has also been fostered when the IT unit assigned responsibility for the package's development and installation has carried out very intensive marketing and liaison activities.

When these preconditions have not been present, however, installation has often been troubled. The reasons most commonly cited by IT managers for the failure include:

• The developers of the system did not understand local needs well enough. Major functions were left out, and the package required extensive and expensive enhancements.

- The package was adequate, but the efforts needed to train people to input data and handle outputs properly were significantly underestimated (or mishandled). This was complicated by extensive language difficulties and insensitivity to existing local procedures.
- The system evolution and maintenance involved a dependence on central staff that was not sustainable in the long run. Flexibility and timeliness of response were problems.
- Costs were significantly underestimated. The overrun on the basic package was bad enough, but the fat was really in the fire when the installation costs were added.

These statements seem to reflect the importance of organizational and cultural factors. In reality, an outside software house, with its marketing orientation and its existence outside the corporate family, often does a better job of selling standard software than an in-house IT unit in a decentralized transnational environment. Finally, in many settings the sheer desire on both sides for success is the best guarantee of that success occurring.

IT Communications

Although they are expensive, investments in improving communications between the various national IT units have paid big benefits. Several devices have proven useful:

Regular Interunit Meetings.   An annual or biannual conference of the IT directors and the key staff of the major international subsidiaries. For organizations in the "turnaround" or "strategic" categories, these meetings ought to take place at least as frequently as meetings of international controllers. Small subsidiaries (IT budgets under $1 million) probably do not generate enough profitable opportunities to warrant inclusion in this conference or to have a separate one.

The agenda of the conference should combine planned formal activities—such as technical briefings, application briefings, and company directives—with substantial blocks of unplanned time. The informal exchange of ideas, initiation of joint projects, and sharing of mutual problems are among the most important activities of a successful conference.

Corporate–Subsidiary Exchange Visits.   Regular visits of corporate IT personnel to the national organizations, as well as of national IT personnel to corporate IT headquarters. These visits should take place at planned intervals, rather than only when there is an operational crisis or technical problem. Less contact is needed with the smaller units than with the larger ones.

Newsletters.   Preparation and circulation of a monthly or bimonthly newsletter to communicate staffing shifts, new technical insights, major project completions, experience with software packages and vendors, and so forth.

Education.   Organization of joint education programs where possible. This may involve the creation and/or acquisition of audiovisual materials to be distributed around the world. A large oil company recently supplemented written communications about a radically different IT organization structure with the preparation of a special film, complete with sound track in five languages.

One of the largest U.K. chemical companies has literally a one-person corporate IT department. The individual continuously travels the world, helping to facilitate education and training sessions and identifying appropriate topics and sources of expertise for IT staff in far-flung places. This individual is a member of the most senior general management of the firm and clearly adds substantial value. General-management and middle-management staff awareness programs remain a central 1990's challenge for this leader.

A fundamental need is for developing stronger psychological links between the national IT units. These links can be as important as the formal ties between the national IT units and the parent company's IT unit.

Facilitating the development of centers of systems expertise in many parts of the world is another important need. It is not obvious that a single-system unit in the parent company's home country is the best way to operate. Many jobs can usefully be split over three or four development centers. One of the large entertainment companies recently assigned large portions of its financial systems, marketing systems, and production systems to its U.K., German, and French development units, respectively. While each unit was enthusiastic about leading their part of the effort, they also knew that if they did not cooperate with the other units, they would not receive the cooperation necessary to assure that their unit's output would be successful. This approach tapped new sources of expertise and was successful because of the *shared* interdependencies of *leadership* and innovation.

Staff Rotation

An important way of addressing the issue of communications is by rotating staff between national IT units and corporate IT.

Advantages.   Key advantages that stem from this include:

- Better corporate IT awareness of the problems and issues in the overseas IT units. As a corollary, the local IT units have a much better perspective on the goals and thinking at corporate headquarters because one of their members has spent a tour of duty there.

- More flexibility in managing career paths and matching positions with individual development needs. Particularly to someone working in a crowded corporate IT department, an overseas assignment could seem very attractive.
- Efficient dispersion of technical know-how throughout the organization.

Disadvantages. On the negative side of staff rotation, practical problems can occur:

- As pointed out earlier, people can jeopardize their career paths by moving from corporate headquarters to less-IT-developed parts of the world. The individuals bring leading-edge expertise to the overseas installation and have a major positive impact for several years. When they return to corporate headquarters they may find themselves completely out of touch with the contemporary technologies being used. Also, some of these people have been dropped out of the normal progression stream through oversight.
- Assignment of individuals overseas is not only expensive in terms of moving allowances and cost-of-living differentials, but it also raises a myriad of potential personal problems. These problems, normally of a family nature, make the success of an international transfer more speculative than a domestic one.
- Transfers from corporate to smaller overseas locations may cause substantial resentment and feelings of nationalism in the overseas location: "Why aren't our people good enough?" Such problems can be tempered with appropriate language skills and efforts on the part of the transferred executive, corporate control over the number of transfers, local promotions, and clearly visible opportunities for local staff to be transferred to corporate.

Appropriately managed within reasonable limits, the advantages far outweigh the disadvantages.

Consulting Services

Major benefits can come from a central IT group providing foreign subsidiaries with consulting services on both technical and managerial matters. In many cases corporate headquarters is not only located in a technically sophisticated country, but its IT activities are bigger in scope than those of individual foreign installations. Among other things, this means that:

1. Corporate IT is more aware of leading-edge hardware/software technology and has had firsthand experience with its potential strengths and weaknesses.

2. Corporate IT is more likely to have experience with large project management systems and other management methods.

In both cases the communication must be done with sensitivity in order to move the company forward at an appropriate pace. All too often the corporate group pushes too fast in a culturally insensitive fashion, creating substantial problems. Movement through the phases of technology assimilation can be speeded up and smoothed, but no phase should be skipped.

As an organization becomes more IT intensive, effective IT auditing becomes increasingly important for shielding the organization from excessive and unnecessary risks. As mentioned earlier, IT auditing is a rapidly evolving profession that faces a serious staff shortage. The shortage is more severe outside the United States and Europe. Thus the corporate audit group of a transnational frequently must take responsibility for conducting international IT audits and for helping to develop national IT audit staffs and capabilities.

Central IT Processing Support

Whether IT should be pushed toward a central hub or a linked international network depends on the firm's type of industry and the dimensions along which it chooses to compete. At one extreme is the airline industry, where it is a significant competitive disadvantage to be unable to confirm seats on a global basis. Originally, international airlines were driven to centralize as an offensive weapon; now it is a defensive one. At the other extreme is a company that has a network of operations for converting paper (a commodity). Transportation costs severely limit how far away from a plant orders can profitably be shipped. Thus the company handles order entry and factory management on a strictly national basis, and there is little interchange of data between countries.

Technology Appraisal Program—An Example

An international appraisal can provide perspective that allows greater coordination of overseas IT efforts. A U.S.-based transnational company with a long history of European operations discovered that their operations in the Far East and South America were posing increasingly complicated information problems. General management initiated a three-year program for bringing the overseas operation under control. The first step was to appraise the condition of each national IT unit and its potential business. This appraisal was conducted by a three-person IT team with multilingual abilities. It was followed by a formulation of policies and appropriate action programs at the annual meeting of company executives.

Originally planned as a one-time assessment of only 11 national IT units, the effort was considered so successful that it was reorganized as an established audit function. The team learned to appraise locally available technology and to guide local management's attention to judging its potential. This required at least one week and often two weeks in the field, typically in two trips. The first visit appraised existing services and raised general concerns that could be pursued effectively by the local management. The second visit assessed problems of:

1. Government restrictions.
2. Quality and quantity of available human skills.
3. Present and planned communications services.

Alternatives to the present means of service were examined further, and economic analyses of at least three standard alternatives were prepared. The three standard alternatives were:

1. Expansion of present system.
2. Transfer of all or portions of IT work to a neighboring country.
3. Transfer of all or portions of IT work to regional headquarters.

The enthusiasm of local managers for this review was not universal, and in several countries long delays occurred between the first and second visits. However, in 7 of the original 11 units the appraisals succeeded in generating appropriate change by bringing better understanding of the potential impact of uncertainties—such as changing import duties, planned market introduction of new technologies by U.S. suppliers, and a new satellite communications alternative. This organized appraisal significantly increased senior management's awareness and comfort concerning IT. The activity became an ongoing effort for the company, and several persons were added to the appraisal team.

SUMMARY

Coordinating international IT is extraordinarily complex. Corporate IT management may have maximum responsibility but only limited authority over distant staff and technologies. Leadership demands persuasion and cajoling plus being well informed on new technologies, the corporate culture, and the wide diversity that exists in the world. The job requires very high visibility and a sound reporting structure inside the firm. This is particularly important because of the need to lead through *relationships*. The IT leadership must be represented at the very top of the firm, where acquisition, divestiture, and other components of changing corporate strategy are developed. The IT department's effectiveness crucially depends on being heard in this forum. Further, the function varies widely by industry, global reach, and size of firm. For example, the nature of the international airline business requires a large central hub. The IT leadership role in this industry consequently has a very strong line management component. The earlier described chemical company's operations, on the other hand, are contained within individual, autonomous national units. Hence an entirely different structure of central IT is appropriate for that company, and IT leadership involves little line responsibility but high-placed coordination.

International IT development must be managed actively in order to avert major, long-term difficulties within and between national IT activities. This is complicated, because assimilation of information technology in other countries is often more heavily influenced by local conditions than by the current state of the technology. Overcoming obstacles presented by the local conditions demands much more than simply keeping abreast of technology. Thus a long view is required to succeed.

Case 12–1

FINNPAP/FINNBOARD (A)

In the London office of Finnpap in December 1985, Reginald Smith looked at his computer terminal screen and commented, "At least the invoices arrived so we can get the rolls through customs. It's very strange that ships are faster than computer systems." The previous Thursday a shipment of paper rolls had left the Finnish loading port of Helsinki, arriving Monday at Purfleet docks, east of London on the River Thames. The shipping documents caught up with the shipment on Tuesday, one day later. "The present system must be changed," mumbled Smith, as he returned to his task of processing the customs declaration.

The Paper and Paperboard Marketing Associations

The paper and paperboard mills of Finland sold their products to the world through jointly owned marketing associations. The Finnish Paper Mills' Association—Finnpap—established in 1918, and the Finnish Board Mills' Association—Finnboard—established in 1942, together represented 45 mills. Headquartered in Helsinki, Finland, the associations shared nearly 100 sales offices, agents, and warehousing/distributing organizations throughout the world. Because the mills had the option of using other marketing channels, the associations' success depended on their being able to offer the best marketing alternative to their owners. At present, 90 percent of the Finnish sales went through the associations. The Helsinki offices housed approximately 550 administrative employees, while the sales staff of nearly 600 was located in 50 countries, with only a small number remaining in Helsinki (Exhibit 1 gives recent financial data for Finnpap and Finnboard.)

In the early days of the Finnish paper and paperboard industry, the mills primarily produced bulk products such as newsprint and liner board. Marketing consisted of obtaining annual contracts with customers for standard-grade products. The associations' task was to negotiate with the customers and then allocate the orders among the mills. By the 1980s, the mills had developed their own specialized products and brand names, making the allocation task secondary to an increasingly sophisticated marketing effort. To meet the new marketing challenge, the associations decentralized their marketing efforts and initiated training programs for their salespeople to foster a commitment to customer service.

The associations' primary markets were located in Central Europe and the United Kingdom, although significant sales were made to the United States, the Soviet Union, Denmark, Australia, and Japan. (See Exhibit 2 for sales volumes by export market.)

Responsibilities connected with the sales effort included order handling and invoicing, accounting, distributing orders to the mills, export financing, handling complaints, warehousing products in domestic and foreign ports, handling deliveries from

Associate Professor Tapio Reponen and Research Assistant Duncan Copeland prepared this case under the supervision of Professor F. Warren McFarlan as the basis for class discussion rather than to illustrate either effective or ineffective handling of an administrative situation.

EXHIBIT 1   Finnpap and Finnboard Financial Data

Income Statement, December 31, 1984 (Finnish mark, in thousands)

	1984		1983	
	Finnpap	*Finnboard*	*Finnpap*	*Finnboard*
Turnover (commission income)	409,136	59,139	376,876	54,666
Expenses				
Salaries	43,305	15,119	38,056	14,163
Social Security contribution	11,999	4,327	9,769	4,407
Rents	9,027	1,580	8,757	1,351
Other	62,039	22,951	52,743	20,896
Operation margin	282,766	15,162	267,551	13,849
Depreciation and amortization				
Machinery and equipment	3,866	1,255	3,458	964
Other fixed assets	407	401	255	287
Net earnings from operations	278,493	13,506	263,838	12,598
Other income				
Interest received	67,002	7,088	35,809	6,238
Dividends received	148	—	217	—
	345,643	20,594	299,864	18,836
Increases in reserves				
Reserve for bad debts	8,500	1,300	5,600	1,438
Interest expenses	337,207	19,343	294,313	17,396
Taxes	9,016	1,251	6,041	1,438
Loss for the period	9,080	1,300	6,090	1,436

Note: Exchange Rate: 1984 — U.S. dollar = Finnish mark 6.0
1983 — U.S. dollar = Finnish mark 5.5

stocks in foreign ports to customers, and information processing to support the marketing and transportation functions. The associations charged the companies for the services they offered, depending on the number of orders and on sales values.

Finland's mills mainly belong to privately owned, independent companies that are responsible for the manufacture of paper and paperboard products and for ground transportation of the product to the loading ports. No mill's market share exceeded 20 percent of Finnish production. Together, the mills and the associations determined the produc-

tion schedules for each product. The method of payment to the mills differed slightly for the two associations. Although both charged the mills a fee for each item sold, Finnpap paid the mills when the products left Finnish ports, thus financing sea transportation and foreign warehousing, while Finnboard made payment only upon delivery of the product to the customer.

To control transportation costs, the paper and paperboard industry owned Transfennica, a company responsible for all sea transportation from Finnish loading ports to the destination ports in foreign markets.

EXHIBIT 1   (continued)

Balance Sheet, December 31, 1984 (Finnish mark, in thousands)

	1984		1983	
	Finnpap	*Finnboard*	*Finnpap*	*Finnboard*
Assets				
Current assets				
Cash and bank deposits	601,932	114,351	242,193	113,373
Accounts receivable	3,648,630	418,575	2,982,497	337,529
Other current assets	197,122	8,205	70,819	6,039
Total current assets	4,447,684	541,131	3,295,509	456,941
Fixed assets				
Machinery and equipment	18,309	6,586	16,026	5,184
Securities	20,389	5,261	12,428	4,741
Other fixed assets	2,656	2,463	1,809	2,042
Total fixed assets	41,354	14,310	30,263	11,967
Loss				
Loss from previous years	23,746	3,628	17,656	2,189
Loss from financial year	9,080	1,300	6,090	1,438
Total losses	32,826	4,928	23,746	3,627
Total assets	4,521,864	560,369	3,349,518	472,535
Liabilities				
Current liabilities				
Bank loans	3,265,650	108,832	2,615,608	73,880
Accounts payable	349,886	7,963	272,568	97,663
Other current liabilities	624,905	389,483	223,572	253,828
Total current liabilities	4,240,441	506,278	3,111,748	425,371
Long-term debt				
Loans from pension institutions	28,809	8,939	26,175	7,944
Reserves				
Reserve for bad debts	27,606	3,250	19,106	1,950
Member companies loan equity	225,008	41,902	192,489	37,270
Total liabilities	4,521,864	560,369	3,349,518	472,535
Guarantees/other liabilities	269,592	28,657	275,216	30,062

Note: Exchange Rate: 1984 —U.S. dollar = Finnish mark 6.0
1983 —U.S. dollar = Finnish mark 5.5

The mills handled the delivery of cargo, usually by rail, to the loading ports. The sales offices and agents, or their service companies, were in charge of foreign distribution. Transfennica coordinated the transportation schedules along the entire distribution chain. In addition, the company arranged transport for Finnish forest products other than paper and paperboard. Transfennica employed about 100 people in 1985.

Optimizing the transportation costs of domestic and foreign overland routes, as well

EXHIBIT 2   Deliveries Per Country, 1984 (in tons)

Country	Finnpap	Finnboard	Total
Austria	48,054	5,357	53,411
Iceland	2,132	1,427	3,559
Norway	43,756	5,853	49,609
Portugal	19,465	343	19,808
Sweden	46,360	10,940	57,300
Switzerland	58,668	11,891	70,559
	218,435	35,811	254,246
Belgium and Luxembourg	87,851	29,507	117,358
Denmark	167,743	38,834	206,577
France	248,352	89,517	337,869
West Germany	522,888	121,517	644,405
Greece	43,777	13,600	57,377
Ireland	40,240	16,108	56,348
Italy and Vatican City	61,005	18,877	79,882
Netherlands	151,436	77,007	228,443
United Kingdom	1,061,915	181,630	1,243,545
European Economic Community	2,385,207	586,597	2,971,804
Bulgaria	2,409	1,423	3,832
Czechoslovakia	329	–	329
East Germany	1,003	2,814	3,817
Hungary	13,680	5,640	19,320
Poland	3,038	150	3,188
USSR	354,912	142,144	497,056
	375,371	152,171	527,542
Madeira	137	–	137
Malta	1,155	81	1,236
Spain	74,321	15,127	89,448
Turkey	3,393	–	3,393
Yugoslavia	3,174	–	3,174
Other Europe	82,180	15,208	97,387
Europe[a]	3,061,193	789,787	3,850,979
Canada	29,231	3,645	32,876
United States	386,440	6,562	393,002
Canada and United States	415,671	10,207	425,878
Argentina	12,547	1	12,548
Barbados	34	235	269
Belize	77	–	77

Note: The exhibit excludes mills' direct deliveries and free deliveries.

[a]Excluding Finland

EXHIBIT 2   (continued)

Country	Finnpap	Finnboard	Total
Bolivia	–	57	57
Brazil	36,438	–	36,438
Chile	2,689	–	2,689
Colombia	15,207	5,563	20,770
Costa Rica	451	20	471
Cuba	–	702	702
Dominican Republic	10	1	11
Ecuador	551	–	551
El Salvador	587	–	587
Guatemala	43	–	43
Guyana	9	–	9
Honduras	35	–	35
Jamaica	1,198	–	1,198
Mexico	17,453	158	17,611
Nicaragua	803	–	803
Panama	156	–	156
Peru	1,328	–	1,328
Surinam	2	–	2
Trinidad and Tobago	223	–	223
Uruguay	1,399	–	1,399
Venezuela	24,869	–	24,869
Latin America	116,109	6,737	122,846
Afghanistan	14	–	14
Bahrain	1,101	–	1,101
Burma	107	–	107
China, People's Republic	11,077	14,179	25,256
Cyprus	552	2,260	2,812
Hong Kong	4,887	5,088	9,975
India	20,945	–	20,945
Indonesia	10,901	11,282	22,183
Iran	46,997	11,674	58,671
Iraq	21,406	879	22,285
Israel	10,404	7,269	17,673
Japan	132,496	491	132,987
Jordan	9,880	970	10,850
South Korea	860	572	1,432
Kuwait	4,971	278	5,249
Lebanon	11,869	2,460	14,329
Malaysia	9,409	5,119	14,528
Mongolia	34	45	79
Nepal	295	–	295
Oman	796	–	796
Pakistan	1,296	112	1,408
Philippines	2,627	2,359	4,986
Saudi Arabia	40,485	7,444	47,929
Singapore	11,022	2,027	13,049

EXHIBIT 2   (continued)

Country	Finnpap	Finnboard	Total
Sri Lanka	57	–	57
Syria	4,375	1,418	5,793
Thailand	9,201	1,344	10,545
Taiwan	6,732	114	6,846
United Arab Emirates	2,328	1,438	3,766
North Yemen	956	–	956
South Yemen	97	–	97
Asia	378,177	78,822	456,999
Algeria	3,013	–	3,013
Cameroun	142	2,164	2,306
Egypt, Arab Republic	33,084	5,892	38,976
Ethiopia	632	–	632
Ghana	2,094	419	2,513
Ivory Coast	–	5,521	5,521
Kenya	953	2,359	3,312
Liberia	13	–	13
Libya	1,247	2,758	4,005
Malawi	10	–	10
Mauritius	20	–	20
Morocco	7,721	7,415	15,136
Mozambique	293	–	293
Nigeria	11,272	7,582	18,854
Senegal	1,642	945	2,587
Somalia	9	–	9
South Africa, Republic	63,907	–	63,907
Sudan	89	915	1,004
Tanzania	83	–	83
Tunisia	–	4,949	4,949
Zaire	–	6,463	6,463
Zambia	9	10	19
Zimbabwe	24	–	24
Others	–	64	64
Africa	126,257	47,456	173,713
Australia	151,959	2,387	154,346
New Zealand	3,171	21	3,192
Oceania	155,130	2,408	157,538
Export Deliveries	4,252,537	935,417	5,187,953
Finland	448,812	150,859	599,671
Total Deliveries	4,701,349	1,086,276	5,787,624

as many alternative sea routes, made for a highly complex task. Exhibit 3 gives some statistics on the scope of the Finnish paper industry; for purposes of comparison, the sales of leading U.S. paper companies are also provided. Exhibit 4 illustrates the information network for paper and paperboard export. Exhibit 5 describes the order-information flow through the distribution chain.

The Forest Products Industry

The history of paper begins in 105 A.D. in the Imperial Court of China, where paper was first produced by combining mulberry fibers, fish nets, old rags, and hemp waste. The art of papermaking slowly drifted westward, and by the 14th century there were a number of European paper mills, particularly in Spain, Italy, France, and Germany.

With the invention of printing in the 1450s, the demand for paper greatly increased. The papermaking process remained essentially unchanged until a shortage of linen and cloth rags fueled a drive to devise a papermaking process that utilized more abundant raw materials.

In the early 1800s, practical methods were developed for manufacturing paper from wood pulp and other vegetable pulps. Several major pulping processes, principally chemical and mechanical methods, were gradually developed. Now the industry was no longer dependent on cotton and linen

---

EXHIBIT 3 Scope of Finnish Paper Industry

Finnpap and Finnboard are owned by 19 companies, which have 30 paper mills, 50 pulp mills, 16 paperboard mills, and 300 sawmills.
Some important operational statistics on the Finnish paper industry:

    24 sales offices
    50 agents
    5,600 customers
    110,000 invoices a year
    8 million rolls/pallets a year
    2.6 billion dollars a year in sales
    5.7 million tons a year
    26 loading ports
    290 destination ports

For purposes of comparison, the sales of leading U.S. paper companies are listed below ($ millions):

	1984		1983	
	Paper and Allied Products	*Total*	*Paper and Allied Products*	*Total*
International Paper Company	$3,773	$4,716	$3,504	$4,357
Kimberly-Clark Corp.	3,435	3,616	3,100	3,274
Champion International, Inc.	3,297	5,121	2,534	4,264
Scott Paper Company	2,770	2,847	2,496	2,708
Crown Zellerbach Corp.	2,741	3,095	2,406	2,670

Source: Lockwood's Directory of the Paper and Allied Trades.

EXHIBIT 4   Information Network for Paper Export

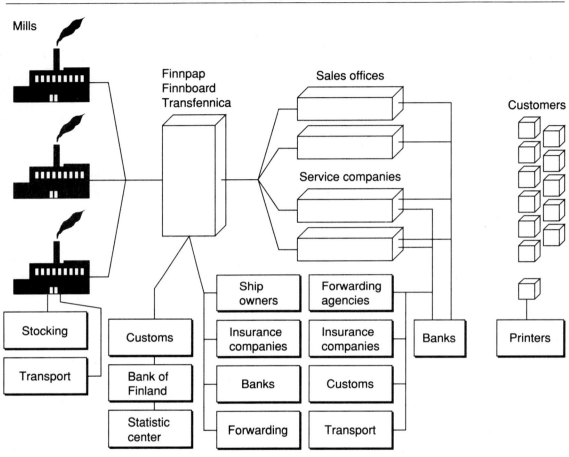

rags, and modern large-scale production became possible.

In 1983, world production of paper and paperboard products totaled 177.3 million metric tons (Exhibit 6). Paper products divide into four categories, according to their end use:

- *Newsprint* includes standard, thin, telcut (for telephone directories), and special grades.
- *Magazine* includes coated and uncoated grades.
- *Fine* includes writing paper and office-quality stationery.

- *Specialty* includes wallpaper, sack paper, envelopes, tissue, flexible packaging (for example, soft-sided cigarette packs), and grocery bags.

Paperboard products come in two categories:

- *Carton boards* are used in a variety of retail packaging applications. They also have some graphic end uses like greeting cards, book covers, and record sleeves.
- *Container boards* are used as liner and corrugating medium in corrugated cases.

EXHIBIT 5   Order Information Flow

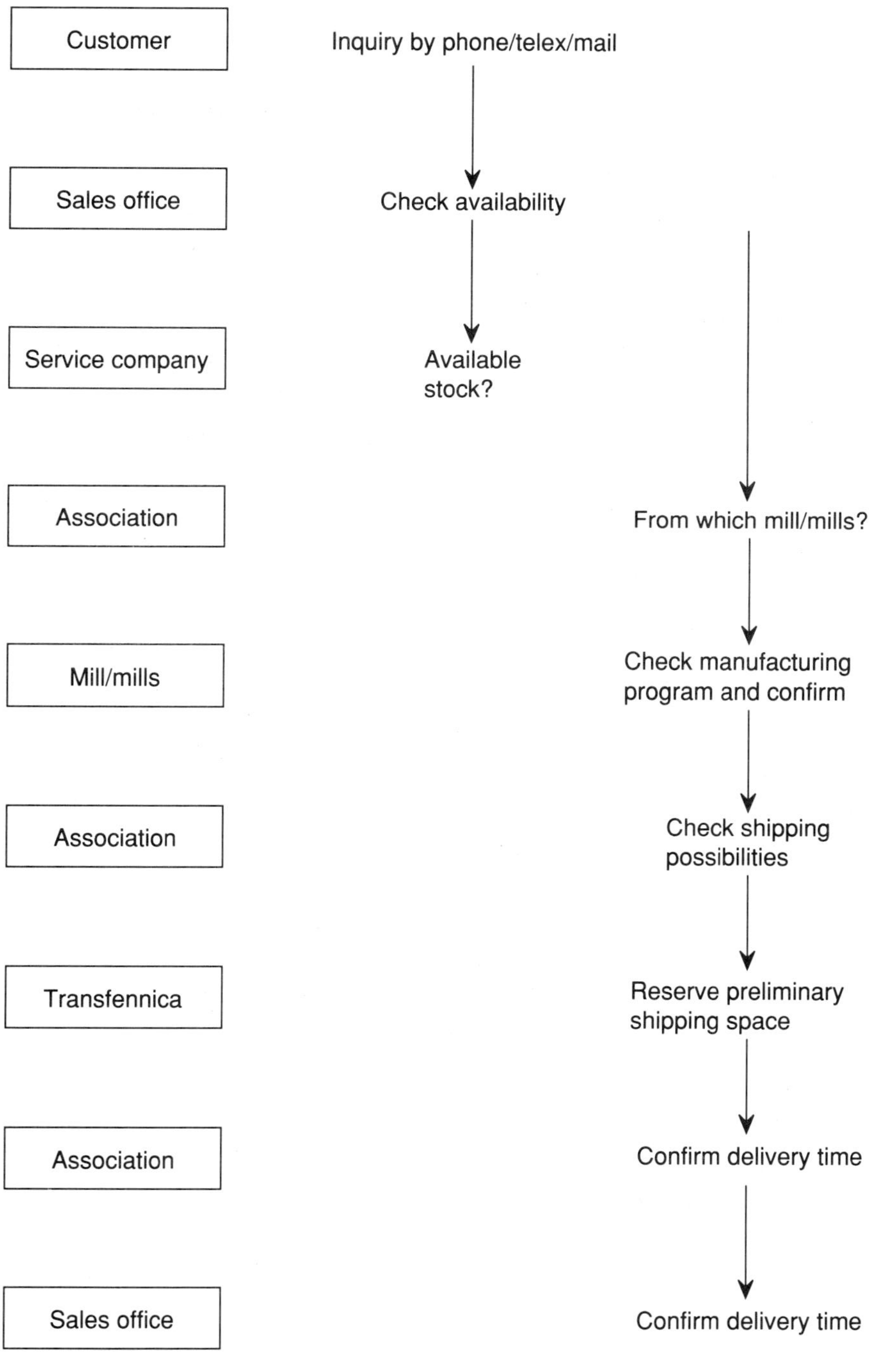

Customer	Inquiry by phone/telex/mail
Sales office	Check availability
Service company	Available stock?
Association	From which mill/mills?
Mill/mills	Check manufacturing program and confirm
Association	Check shipping possibilities
Transfennica	Reserve preliminary shipping space
Association	Confirm delivery time
Sales office	Confirm delivery time

EXHIBIT 5 (continued)

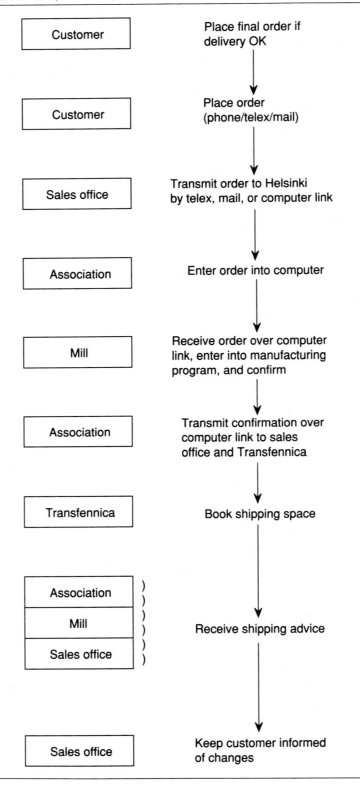

EXHIBIT 5   (continued)

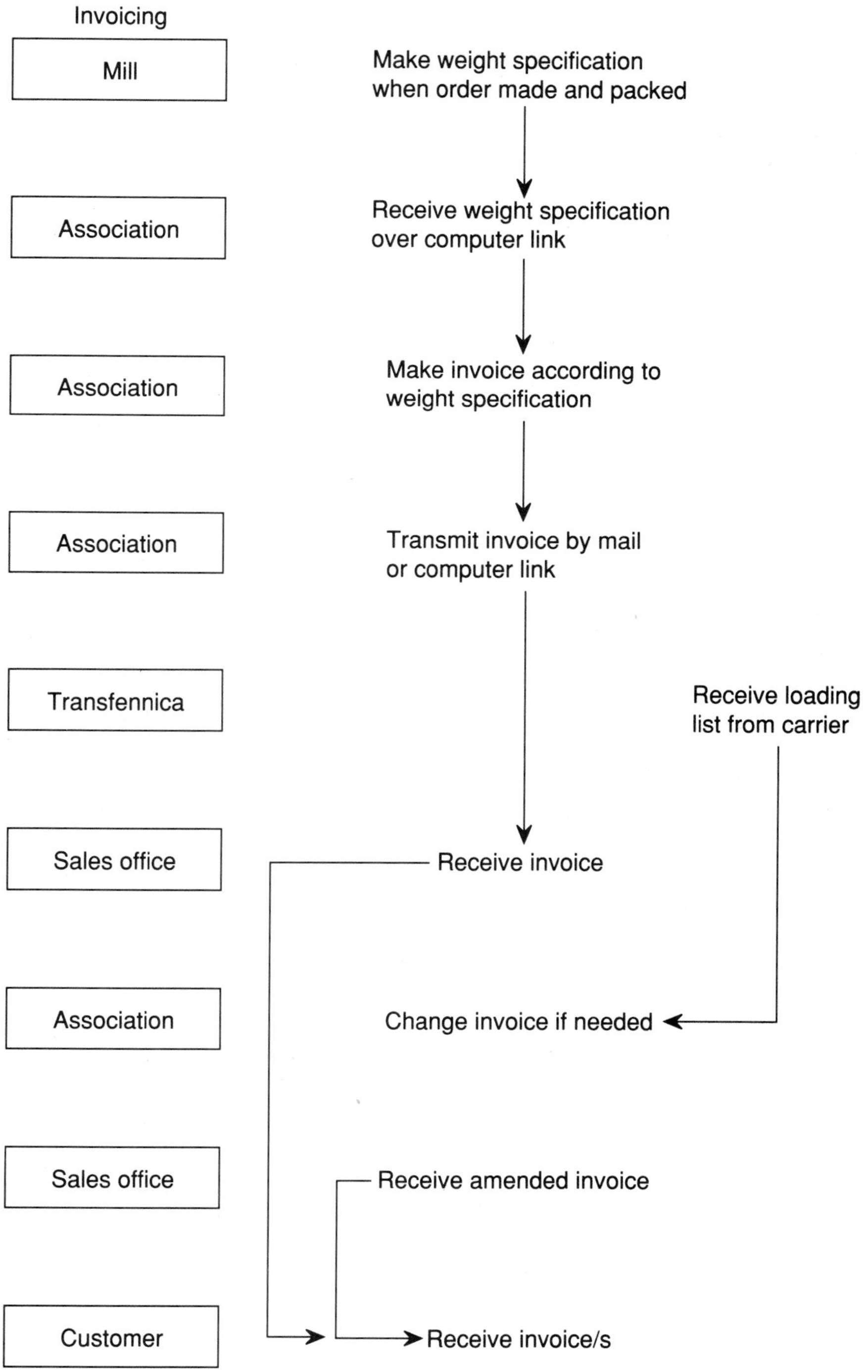

Invoicing

Mill	Make weight specification when order made and packed
Association	Receive weight specification over computer link
Association	Make invoice according to weight specification
Association	Transmit invoice by mail or computer link
Transfennica	Receive loading list from carrier
Sales office	Receive invoice
Association	Change invoice if needed
Sales office	Receive amended invoice
Customer	Receive invoice/s

EXHIBIT 6 The 12 Biggest Producers of Paper and Paperboard in the World, 1983 (million metric tons)

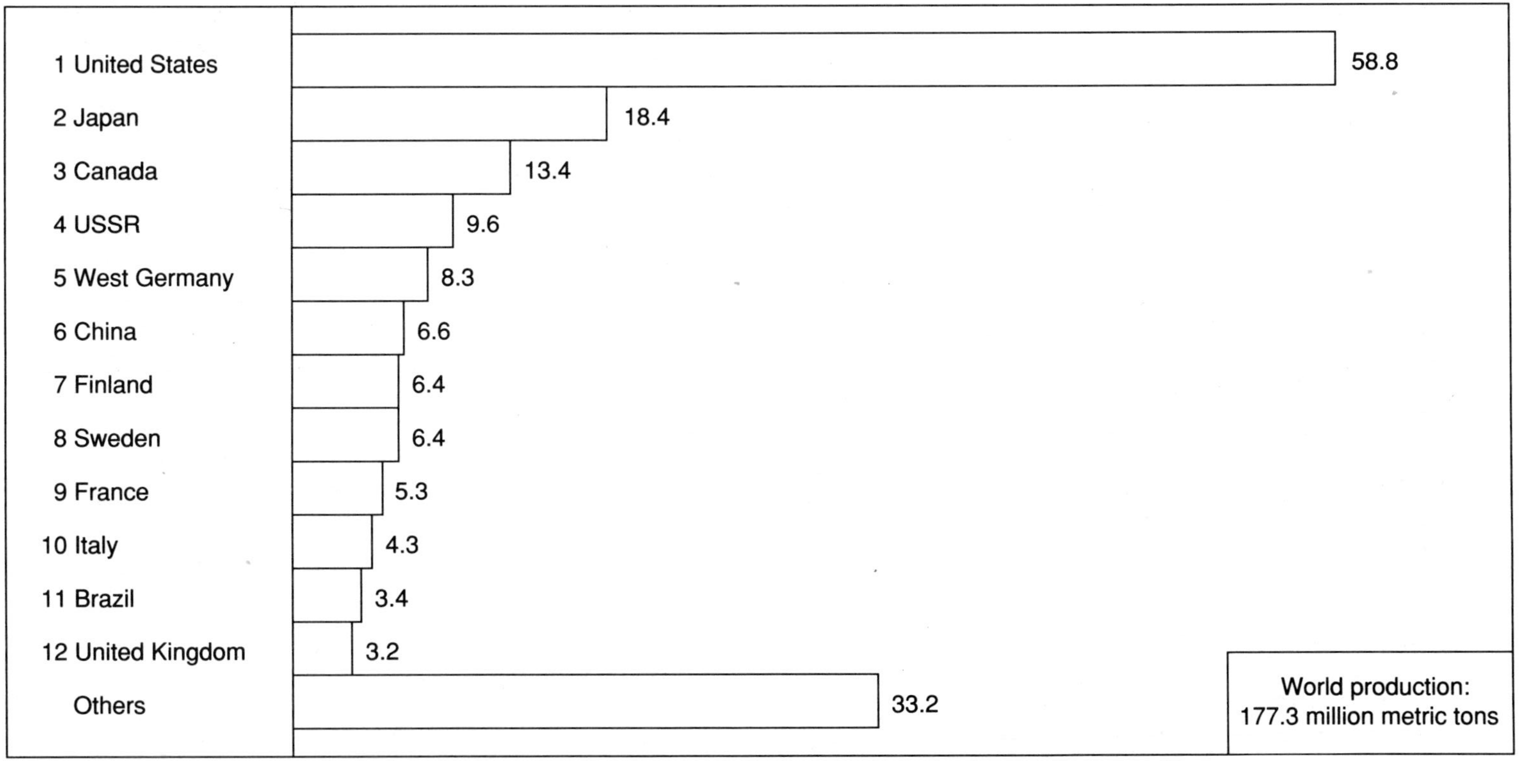

Rank	Country	Production
1	United States	58.8
2	Japan	18.4
3	Canada	13.4
4	USSR	9.6
5	West Germany	8.3
6	China	6.6
7	Finland	6.4
8	Sweden	6.4
9	France	5.3
10	Italy	4.3
11	Brazil	3.4
12	United Kingdom	3.2
	Others	33.2

World production: 177.3 million metric tons

Finland covers approximately 337,000 square kilometers, making it the fifth-largest country in Europe; two-thirds of Finland is forested. Not surprisingly, wood processing is the country's largest industry and the backbone of the Finnish economy, accounting for more than 30 percent of manufacturing input in the gross domestic product (Exhibit 7). In 1983, Finland was the seventh-largest producer of paper and paperboard in the world and the second-largest in Western Europe. Finland's share of total world production in 1983 was 4 percent, yet it accounted for 15 percent of the world's exports (Exhibit 8).

Finland's paper and paperboard industry had been completely rebuilt since 1960. Beginning as a bulk producer of grades like newsprint and liner board, the industry grew to become a versatile supplier of multiple grades to satisfy increasingly sophisticated market demands. During this restructuring, strategic guidelines concentrated on adding value throughout the production process, improving profitability, and developing the paper production mix to be responsive to the changing requirements of the market. As a result of the large capital investments in the past decade, by 1985 Finland's paper industry was one of the most modern and efficient in the world. Exhibit 9 contains mill capacity data for Finland and several of its competitors.

One major disadvantage faced by Finland was price competitiveness. Prices for raw materials and wages were about the same as those of their main European competitors. The Finnish currency (FIM) had been strong for many years; thus the relative costs were high. Because of Finland's remote location, transportation of products to other countries proved costly and required a lead time of seven to ten days for direct shipments from mill to customer. The principal competitors of Finnish paper goods were products produced by mills indigenous to Finland's export markets. These local companies faced neither transportation costs nor delays. They enjoyed the additional advantages of direct mill/customer contact, reduced paperwork, and no language or cultural barriers.

Information Technology at Finnpap/Finnboard

Electronic data processing (EDP) began at the associations in the late 1960s, when two consultants developed a long-range information plan for Finnpap. The first applications for order handling and invoicing were run on a service company's computer, until Finnpap purchased its own hardware in 1973.

The basic features of the current systems were planned and designed in 1974. At the time, the marketing associations took less responsibility for product delivery than they did by 1985; their job ended at the receiving port. As an example of the degree of change, at the end of the 1960s Finland's paper industry maintained negligible stocks abroad. By 1985, 40 percent of finished goods were stored in foreign warehouses, permitting salespeople to be more responsive to customers' demands. The existing systems were meant to address the business needs of 1974, and as such, focused on accounting applications in an effort to reduce the clerical work load. The systems' designers could not foresee the competitive and technological climates of 1985; thus the programs were coded for batch processing and required significant effort to be modernized. In 1980, the information technology (IT) resources of Finnboard were merged with those of Finnpap. Finnboard employed Univac 90/40 hardware, and the EDP department stressed user requirements over technology. At the time of the merger, this relatively small group was starting to consider forward IT integration issues. Finnpap, on the other hand, utilized

EXHIBIT 7 Forest-based Industry's Share of Total Manufacturing Input in Gross Domestic Product, 1983

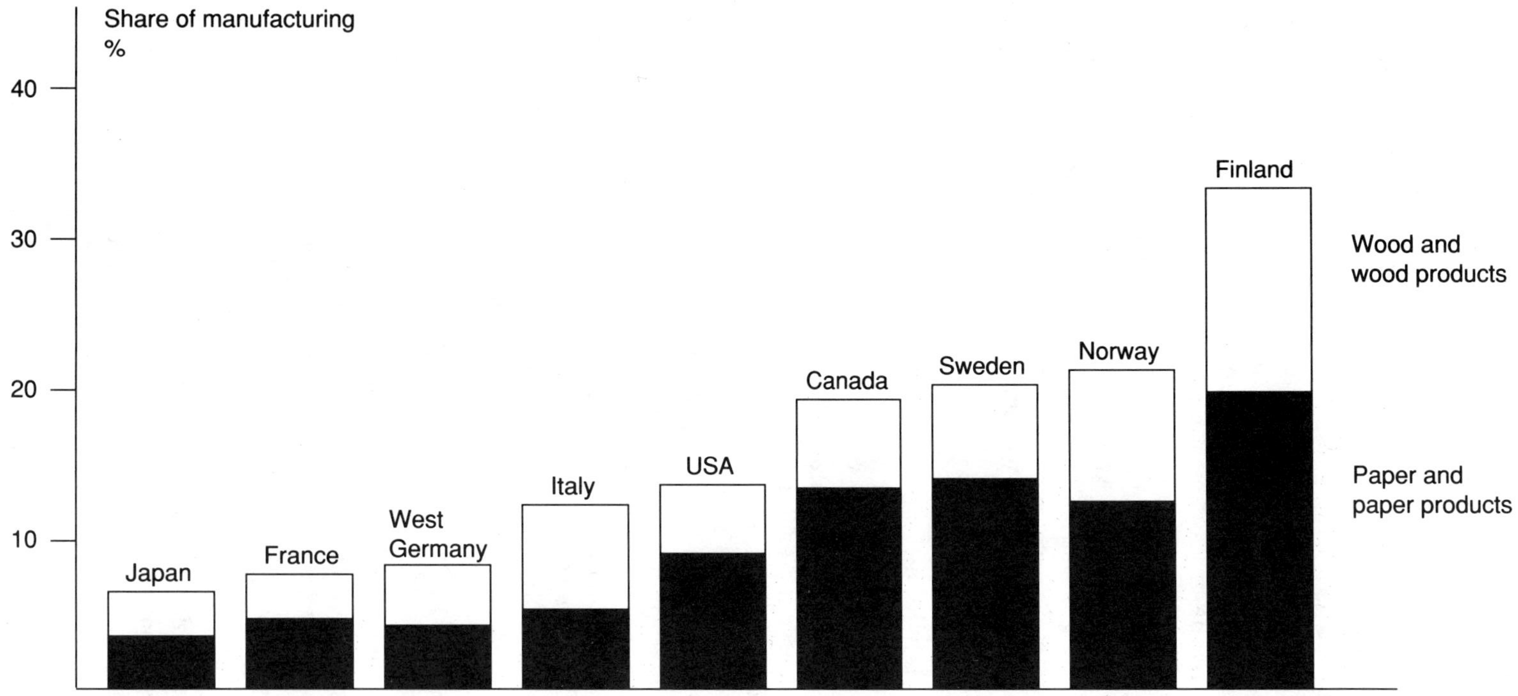

EXHIBIT 8 Exports of Paper and Paperboard, 1983 (million metric tons)

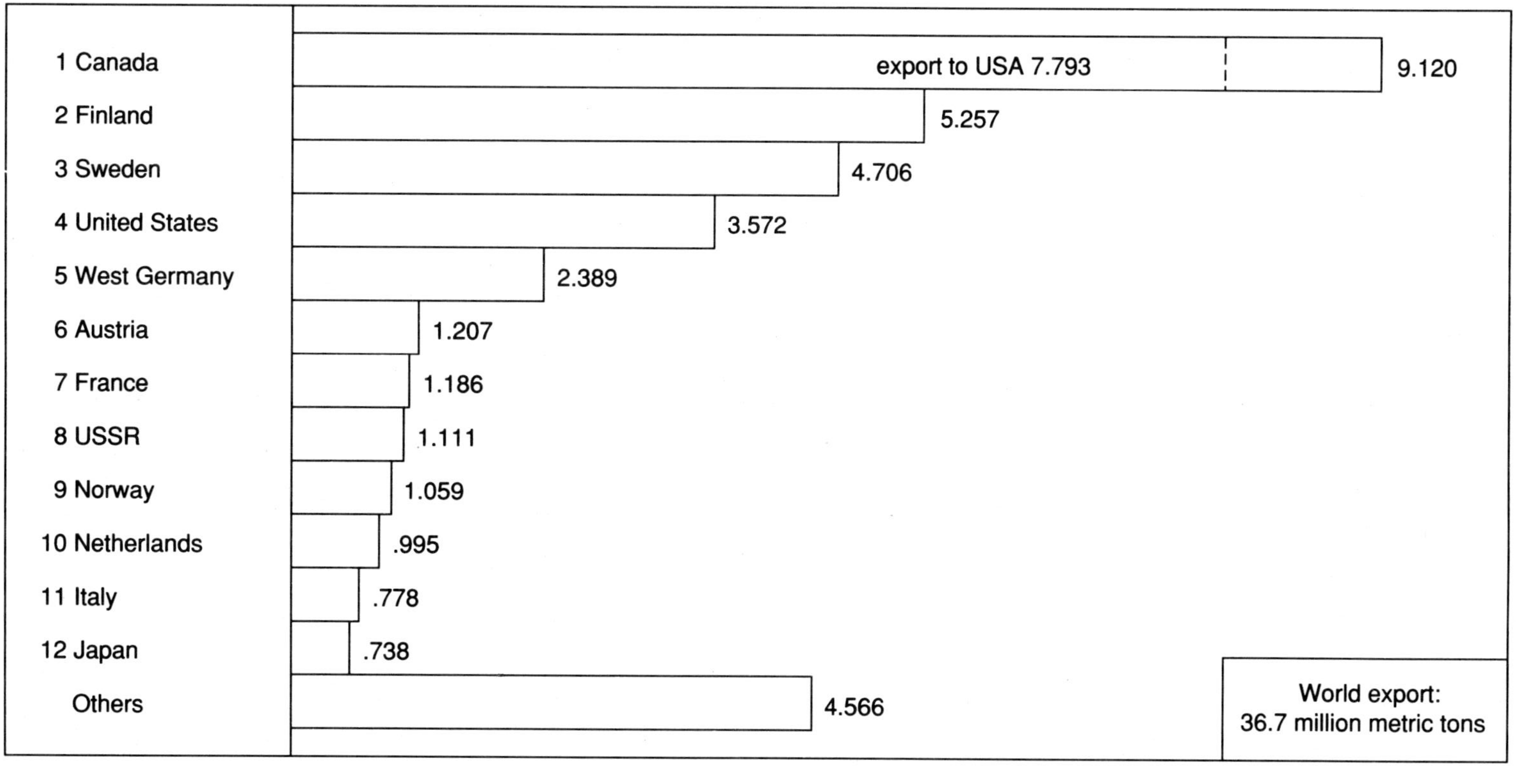

1 Canada	9.120 (export to USA 7.793)
2 Finland	5.257
3 Sweden	4.706
4 United States	3.572
5 West Germany	2.389
6 Austria	1.207
7 France	1.186
8 USSR	1.111
9 Norway	1.059
10 Netherlands	.995
11 Italy	.778
12 Japan	.738
Others	4.566

World export: 36.7 million metric tons

EXHIBIT 9   Paper and Paperboard Capacity Per Mill, 1983

Capacity tons/year	USA	Canada	West Germany	France	Finland	Sweden
1–50,000	268	18	167	138	12	25
50,001–100,000	110	16	18	15	11	11
100,001–200,000	91	24	13	10	6	5
200,001 +	112	34	8	2	17	15
Total number of mills	581	92	206	165	46	56

IBM equipment, with the EDP department setting its own direction, emphasizing technology. Of approximately 15 Finnboard IT staff persons who moved to Finnpap, all but the computer operators had left the company by 1985. The Finnpap data center also sold information-processing services to Transfennica and two other Finnish marketing associations, Converta and Finncell.

In 1985, the systems had grown to include nearly 8,500 programs and were supported by an EDP department with an annual budget of $3 million and a staff of more than 75 people. Personnel were divided among the computer center (30), applications development (34), planning and liaison (6), and the information center (5). The applications development department had 24 systems analysts or programmers.

Qualified systems professionals were in short supply in Finland, especially in Helsinki, where the demand was greatest. This had led to high salaries relative to other functional departments as well as competition among employers. Turnover for EDP professionals in 1984 neared 20 percent; among systems analysts and programmers the figure was much higher.

The mainframe computer was an IBM 3083-B24, with 32MB, 16CH, 6.2MIPS. The predominant software consisted of VM/SP, VM/SP-HPO, MVS/SP, DFP, ACF/VTAM, ACF/NCP, CICS/VS, EASYTRIEVE, AS, COBOL, and APL. Increases in central processing unit capacity were planned for the near future. An IBM Series/1 was used for telex-host connection. Exhibit 10 describes the evolution of computing resources. The network consisted of 870 remote terminals. Used for order entry and message switching, these terminals linked headquarters with the mills, loading ports, and sales offices. Exhibit 11 describes the distribution of terminals. Exhibit 12 illustrates the communication network. In the United Kingdom, there were two IBM S/38 computers and one IBM 8100. In Germany, there was one IBM S/38.

The main applications included

- Order handling and invoicing for Finnpap, Finnboard, and Converta.
- Accounting for Finnpap, Finnboard, Converta, and Transfennica.
- Sales budgeting for Finnpap and Finnboard.
- Stock control in Germany and Denmark for Finnpap and in the United Kingdom for Finnboard.
- Sales office reporting.
- Communication links to mills for transmitting orders and weight specifications.
- Communication links to ports and sales agents for transmitting shipping documents.
- Communication links to banks, insurance companies, and customs offices.
- Loading lists for Transfennica.

EXHIBIT 10   Evolution of Computer Resources

Year	Central Processing Unit	Central Memory (millions of bytes)	Efficiency (million instructions per second)	Disk Space (gigabytes)
1973	IBM S/1130			
1974	IBM S/370-135			
1975	IBM S/370-135	0.5	0.2	0.2
1976	IBM S/370-135	0.7	0.2	0.6
1977	IBM S/370-148	2.0	0.4	2.5
1978	IBM S/370-148	3.0	0.4	3
1979	IBM S/370-148 NAS 3000	9.0	1.3	4
1980	IBM S/370-148 NAS 3000	9.0	1.3	7
1981	IBM 4341-1 NAS 3000 UNIVAC 90/40	14.6	2.3	10
1982	IBM 4341-2 IBM 4341-2 UNIVAC 90/40	24.6	3.0	12
1983	IBM 3083-B24 UNIVAC 90/40	24.6	6.2	20
1984	IBM 3083-B24 UNIVAC 90/40	24.6	6.2	35
1985	IBM 3081-K48	48.0	15.0	80

Maintenance of these applications demanded considerable resources, which led to an expanding backlog of user requests for new development projects. In EDP, 12 people had worked on the conversion to IBM COBOL for more than two years; these 12 made up half of the systems development staff. Two contract analyst programmers had also been working on the same conversion for two years. Systems development activity in the United Kingdom and Germany was devoted to stock control, sales ledger, order handling, and invoicing.

Errors and delays in the systems resulted from one or more of the following problems:

• The planned mill shipping date was entered in the system at the time an order was confirmed, then not updated for subsequent changes.

• Invoices were prepared based on the mills' weight specifications. But when transportation damaged rolls and pallets, the customer received less product than invoiced, causing correction invoicing.

• Data-entry delays occurred at the ports.

• Some shipping documents were still sent by mail.

The communication network used leased lines to send orders from sales offices to the associations and then on to the mills, and to transmit transportation data from the mills to the associations, Transfennica, and the ports. The network had reduced the volume

EXHIBIT 11 EDP Center Customers

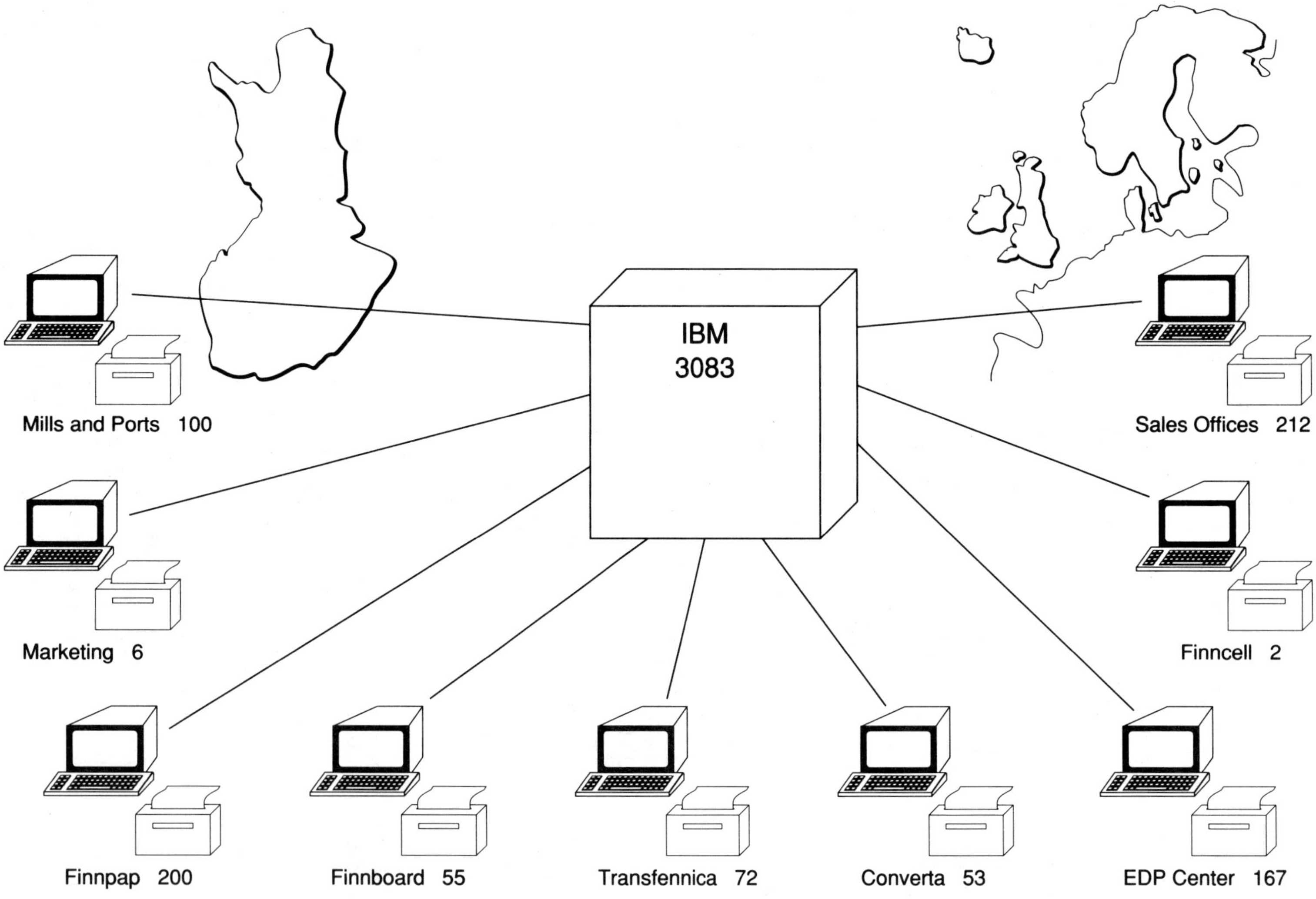

EXHIBIT 12 Agency Communications Network

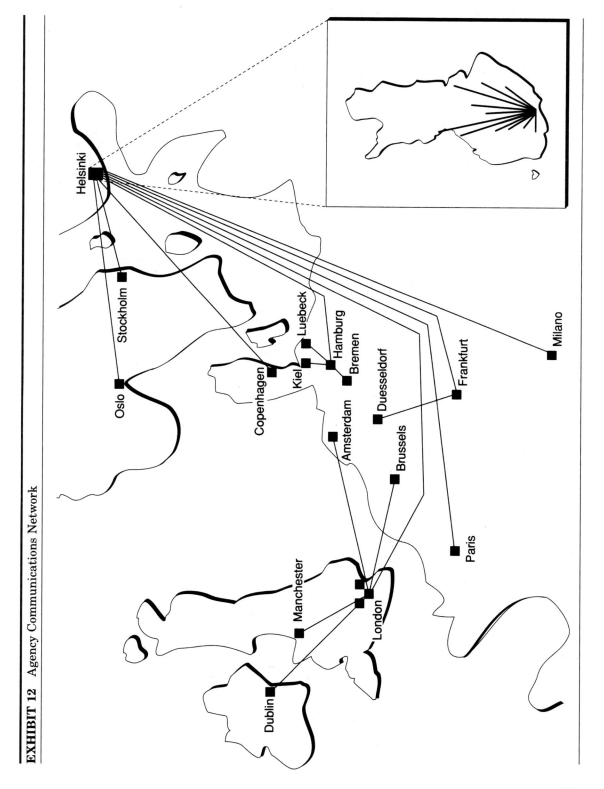

of shipping documents that traveled by mail, but information flow problems remained. These were due mostly to tasks that still required manual intervention.

Although the use of microcomputers was increasing in 1985, the EDP managers thought these would not solve the main data-processing problems of the organization. Finnboard used a small number of micros for word processing, and Finnpap had installed one in each department for word processing, statistical analysis, and budgeting. Some sales offices were beginning to work with micro-based electronic spreadsheets. For small sales offices, the EDP department had developed a stand-alone order-handling and stock-control package for micros. There were also plans to slowly replace the 870 existing mainframe terminals with microcomputers.

Because of the difficult competitive position of the Finnish forest industry, information processing played an essential role in operations. The strategy of the mills was increased product differentiation with strict cost control. Differentiation meant shifting from bulk operations to a service orientation with more specialized marketing and transportation needs. Just-in-time deliveries were required, and demands were increasing for quality control and production records data with each paper roll. The successful management of this complex environment called for accurate, timely information at each phase of the marketing chain.

The managing directors of Finnpap and Finnboard, Thomas Nysten and Jarl Kohler, agreed that improved information technology was needed to strengthen their competitive position. In Nysten's words:

> We have created a marketing network that enables us to gather information on markets and anticipate their future development. We are able to build a marketing database which would support our sales activities, keeping in mind that our owners, the mills, are partially competitors with one another, so data secu-

rity is a strict requirement. Strategy formulation depends on collecting different signals from abroad, like end-user trends, new packaging and publishing/printing problems, prices of competing materials and packaging systems, competitor moves, customer needs, development of printing and packaging technology. Our salespeople are in a position to perform this function, but we must do it more systematically. We already have a lot of useful data in our systems, but it is virtually inaccessible.

> If our information systems are to be used as a competitive weapon, we must develop a new generation of programs, which may include such applications as customer-initiated order entry and reporting formats tailored to customers' unique needs. It will require heavy investments in both hardware and software. Since the needs of our different users vary, we need a long-range plan to prioritize this development work. We should strive to achieve an image as a modern user of information technology in our operations. We conduct business in a unique environment, however, and our plans must take this into consideration.

Information Technology and the Marketing Associations

The Helsinki headquarters housed both marketing and administrative employees. Almost all the information flowing between customers, sales offices, and mills passed through Helsinki. Headquarters personnel negotiated annual sales budgets with the mills, prepared marketing plans, divided orders among the mills, and generally coordinated all operations. Managing information was a key component of their work.

The marketing people were not satisfied with the output from the present systems. The lack of adequate information forced them to spend much of their time using the telephone to track down needed data. Their greatest need was for information on order status. They needed to know when an order was scheduled for manufacture (ex-mill date), when it would be transported to a loading port, when it left the loading port, when it arrived in the destination port, and when it was transported to the customer. The mills, transportation companies, and sales offices also wanted this information.

Tuula Virolainen, assistant sales director at Finnboard, discussed this need for information:

> In the carton board grades there are an increasing number of special orders, while average order size is decreasing. The customers aim for just-in-time purchasing. The number of orders has doubled in the last two years, and the many different grades and special features make each order more complex. Correct and quick information is a must in this kind of environment. However, at present even the order and invoicing system does not work very well. There are often errors, and it takes a lot of time to correct them. Routine work has increased for us because of these errors as well as new tasks, such as responding to inquiries from the mills, which are much more cost-sensitive than before.
>
> Getting special reports out of the existing systems is not easy. It is often faster to make manual calculations. I have a feeling that there is a lot of data in our system, but we can't get at it. This lack of flexibility has given computers a bad name in the marketing departments. I think it will be difficult to introduce any new systems without strong evidence of their usefulness. I sometimes wonder whether our needs here at Finnboard receive a low priority now that EDP has been consolidated within Finnpap.

Marketing personnel in both associations considered the order status and a good customer file to be high priorities. The existing files contained a customer's name and address but not much more. Desired customer information included a short history of supplies, prices, competitors' supplies, inventories, order stock, and machinery. Maintaining such a file would require input from salespeople, mills, Transfennica, and the associations.

Raija Tuukkanen, assistant sales manager at Finnpap, expressed her dissatisfaction with present circumstances:

> The EDP department doesn't have any clear long-range plan, and consequently all the schedules are delayed. And there are multiple applications for the same function, like stock control. Their way of thinking must change. To be fair, though, the conversion of Finnboard's programs to our IBM standard has required a lot of work and could explain some of the delays.

Claes Ehrnrooth, Finnboard's assistant director in charge of planning and marketing research, also worried about the service he was receiving:

> We have been waiting a long time for certain customer information lists. I've developed a few of them myself using AS, our application generator language, but they are only designed for my purposes. The program structure may not be the best possible, but the reports will satisfy our urgent needs. In my experience, end-user computing is the only way to develop the needed programs quickly enough. The EDP department is so large and the models they want to build are so comprehensive that their work will never end.
>
> Now Finnpap and Finnboard have a common EDP organization. Sometimes I think my own computer would be a better solution. We have also been thinking about the urgency of our information needs, and we have concluded that the need for on-line transmission is quite low as far as the management information is concerned. It is possible to reduce costs with batch transmission of data and satisfy our requirements at the same time.

Information Technology and the Sales Offices

Lamco Paper Sales Ltd., the London marketing company owned by Finnpap, sold 1.5 million tons of paper in 1984, mainly newsprint and magazine papers. For these two products, Lamco's share of the U.K. market was 30 percent and 55 percent, respectively. The associations faced a marketing challenge in the United Kingdom because customers were knowledgeable about price levels, faced great profitability pressures, and could easily turn to alternative suppliers. Customer service was therefore critical in the British market.

Lamco sold from stock in the United Kingdom and provided customers with a weekly listing of its inventory levels. Lamco was the first supplier to offer this service, forcing other suppliers to provide similar information. Lamco had recently begun to explore the possibility of installing its terminals at some customer sites; customers were enthusiastic about the idea.

Berndt Brunow, a director of Lamco, was skeptical of the central computer system's ability to satisfy his company's needs:

> For many years we have waited for a solution to our problems, but we have been disappointed. We never get all the needed information. There are continually errors in the reports, the shipment documents come late, etc. Because of our poor experiences with the central systems, we would like to develop our own system capabilities here. We have a System 38 and qualified programmers who know our local problems and working methods. At Lamco there are nine DP professionals (a DP manager, a system analyst, three programmers, three operators, and a user coordinator) and three contract programmers. Actually, there is very little we need from the Finnpap system. We are of course willing to supply Finnpap with any information they need, but they'll have to transform it for their own purposes.
>
> Local systems suit us best. We currently have links to the U.K. ports from our system. Ports here have very simple systems, and we cannot influence their methods of operation. We have to be able to adapt to their choices. The central systems just are not responsive enough, and I'm not confident about the communications link to Finland.

In general, the reasons for the lack of confidence in Finnpap's system were these:

- Breaks in the international communication links.
- Downtimes in computer equipment.
- Mistakes in programs and operating.
- Delays in maintenance and repairs caused by distance and time differences.

Lamco, with 200 employees, was the associations' largest marketing company. Many smaller sales offices in a number of countries also had disappointing experiences with the central systems. Although too small to acquire their own computing power, they were increasingly vocal in requesting local solutions for enhanced flexibility and uninterrupted operations.

Varma Services Ltd., a London service company that handled ground transportation in the United Kingdom, had recently bought an IBM S/38 for many of the same reasons expressed by Brunow. Kauko Pekkanen, a manager at Varma, had lately been working on the transportation process. He said:

> At present we are working on reducing the number of documents required for each shipment. Some of the Finnish ports already receive loading lists from mills through our network. We've also been able to eliminate the bill of lading for some destination ports. By reducing the amount of necessary paper, we're able to save a lot of money.
>
> Another important area is the roll identification. The volumes are very large, and it is extremely time consuming to manually identify the packages in each phase of the transportation chain. One possible solution is the bar code system. Some of the mills are using them internally, and some of our customers have asked for them, but there are no international standards for codes. Because some of the mills have already invested in a certain system, it is difficult to make changes. Even if we could agree on a standard we would still have the problem of identifying the great

number of codes in ports and warehouses. How could we read the codes from each roll or pallet? The technology does not seem safe enough at present.

Information Technology and Transportation

The coordinating function performed by Transfennica was more complicated than the transportation requirements that faced most of Finland's competitors. The quantities handled by Transfennica were larger, however, so their unit costs tended to be lower. These large quantities, combined with the increasingly specialized nature of the orders, created the need for an excellent information system.

Tuure Lahermaa, managing director of Transfennica, maintained a positive attitude toward information systems development. He commented:

A smoothly operating information system would clearly be one source of competitive advantage. Finnish industry is not a giant—even in aggregate. Its markets are very dispersed. Only through a common solution is it possible to maintain strengths because then the volumes are large enough for economies of scale. Common transportation is possible only when combined with common marketing.

The Swedes have tried both—transportation and marketing cooperation—but they failed because of disagreements. Success also requires a good computer system; failure there means total disaster. Information is needed for decisions concerning manufacturing, transportation, and warehousing. It is currently possible to lose track of rolls or pallets for long periods of time.

We in Transfennica receive many inquiries concerning transportation. A great number of working hours have been wasted responding to these questions. Mills are interested in transportation routes and order status. That information should be available to them on their terminals, but now the mills have no means to control their marketing and trans-

portation costs. We need an open and responsible reporting system to restore everyone's trust in our operations.

Transportation costs are about 15 percent to 25 percent of the sale price. These costs can be reduced with better information systems, but the investment must be in line with the benefits. There are several opportunities for reducing costs in the operating chain, but we must be able to clearly define the spheres of responsibility in this chain.

Arto Jantunen, a Transfennica transportation manager responsible for the United Kingdom and Ireland, described very clear demands for an information system:

We need real-time information to follow up on the financial aspect of transports. Each year we should make a transportation budget based on sales budget. That exercise should include discussions on the service level we offer to our customers. Based on that decision we can make budgets on the transportation capacity needed and sea freights. All these budgets must be in our computer system.

For everyday operations we need real-time data on ex-mill date, loading date, date of arrival, and the cost of transportation. For making effective transportation decisions, I need information on alternative routes and their budgeted costs, the actual costs of transportation, and the profitability of that route. Our present systems don't come close to these objectives. We must have one total system with linkages between subsystems. All parties now have their own systems, resulting in a great deal of redundancy.

The associations and Transfennica must work together to develop the needed systems. At present our requirements have a very low priority because transportation costs are hidden by the existing systems, and if there are some mistakes in operations, the reasons should be clearly identified.

Transfennica's cargo included Finnish products other than paper and paperboard. Some producers of these other cargoes had let it be known that they could benefit from access to the associations' communications network.

Information Technology and the Mills

Although information technology in the mills varied, in general, process control systems were very up to date, while the quality of administrative systems varied greatly. Approximately 30 mills were connected to the associations' network, and that number was increasing. The mills had either Finn-pap terminals or facilities for batch processing communication with the central system. In 1984, there were no CPU-to-CPU links between Finnpap and any mill system.

Some of the mills received customer orders through their terminals and then entered their weight specifications into the Finnpap system. The weight specifications included data on the manufactured products, which were used by Transfennica and agents in loading ports. In addition to this computer communication, there were numerous telephone calls between the mills and sales offices, Transfennica, and the associations. These calls concerned, among other things, negotiations, confirmations, inquiries, and complaints.

Because the mills were parts of independent companies, they had made their own decisions regarding computer hardware and software, which resulted in incompatible architectures. The mills were interested in receiving better information regarding order status, customers, and costs for transportation and marketing. As already noted, because the mills competed with one another, they stressed confidentiality.

Bjorn Rajalin, mill manager of A. Ahlstrom Co. Ltd., represented a high-quality producer. He said:

> The ordering process should be automated as much as possible, perhaps from customer to mill. The order should include the same data as the invoices; that way, we could rational-

ize the order-invoicing process. There is currently duplication of effort between the mills and the associations. We have to reduce the amount of paper in these processes, and to do that we need computerized data transmission.

> It's very important to have close contact between the customer and the mill. We have special products with little or no warehousing. We are now developing our own EDP systems. The associations have a couple of years to show us that they are capable of designing and installing useful systems; otherwise we'll have to do it all ourselves.

> We need to be able to control the operation of Transfennica and the associations. The mills must have alternative ways of operating if those organizations become too bureaucratic. We are prepared to supply them with more information, but we want to control that data. We cannot have a totally open computer system. Our research work is our competitive strength, and we must protect our proprietary advantages.

This research and development work involved product development aimed at new or improved paper grades to satisfy the changing needs of the customers.

Pehr-Eric Patt was mill manager of Metsaliitto, a magazine paper manufacturer. He expressed views similar to Rajalin's. However, since warehousing was extremely important for magazine grades, Patt was concerned about inventory control:

> We should first get the existing programs in good shape. Only then will we be able to improve customer relations with customer terminals. We also have to think very carefully about the costs of our systems. Is it even possible to cover the development costs with the price we get from the market? The other problem is how to divide the development costs fairly between the different users. The value of information is very different to different people.

In general, the IT managers at the various mills would have preferred to be more informed about the central system projects. They managed their own development backlogs and did not want to devote resources to redundant projects.

Information Technology and the EDP Department

Jussi Berlin had been the manager of Finnpap's EDP department for only a few months, although he had been with the unit since 1975. Addressing the situation, Berlin had these comments:

> We definitely favor a centralized solution around a database concept. We must of course ensure that local operations can continue in the event of serious problems with the network. But distribution of computer centers is not practical now, for the following reasons:
>
> 1. Maintaining current, consistent data in multiple locations dramatically increases programming complexity.
> 2. We would need software for handling mistakes and for recovery.
> 3. When all the data are not stored in every location, production of summary reports is much more difficult.
> 4. Multiple computer centers increase installation, operating, and maintenance costs.
> 5. Extra costs, in both time and money, would be incurred for duplicate development tools.
> 6. Building a common database is very difficult.
> 7. We would lose flexibility in the use of our systems people.
>
> In five years, it will be possible to implement distributed processing without significant extra work. Now we must focus on reducing the problems we have with the centralized solution. Our main problems are a lack of system reliability and an old-fashioned architecture. Given the present technology, if we want to serve all users online, the only realistic alternative is centralized processing. The users have legitimate

> problems with our systems, but the real difficulty is our shortage of resources. There is tremendous competition for qualified people in Helsinki, but despite this we have built about 8,500 programs here. We have to admit that because of their age they are batch-oriented programs, but we have plans for improving them.
>
> We have been accused in the past of not listening to the needs of end users. This attitude has changed. For example, we have a schedule to build a new order and invoice handling system that will satisfy their needs for order status information. But it is a very large system and will take two years to develop. Different users have different priorities for systems development work. We would like to have a clear decision on these priorities; then we will be able to request the appropriate machine capacity and personnel. My staff is now kept busy maintaining the existing systems.

The Decision

Finnpap's managing director, Thomas Nysten, had now listened to all parties concerned. He knew he must resolve the intertwined issues of distributed processing, the need for new hardware, the large investments necessary to satisfy user demand, and the prioritization of that demand. Nysten also recognized that IT strategy should support overall business goals, but he was unsure of the best way to achieve this.

At the beginning of April 1985, Nysten asked Jussi Olkinuora, director of the Specialty Paper Department, to prepare a position paper on information strategy by the end of the year. At Specialty Papers, there were already many marketing development activities that demanded Olkinuora's attention, but he promised to spend the coming weekend organizing an approach to his new assignment.

Case 12-2

FINNPAP/FINNBOARD (B)
FIN-PROJECT

In February 1988, Pentti Kallio, newly appointed executive vice president of administration, member of the board of management, and the man responsible for information systems oversight, was reviewing the progress of the Finnpap/Finnboard IT organization. Over two and a half years had passed since Jussi Olkinuora (now responsible for specialty papers, NOM [New Operating Model], and chief financial officer) had presented to Thomas Nysten, president, his new information strategy for Finnpap and Finnboard, Finland's two paper-products sales associations. This strategy was adopted, and a new information technology (IT) organization to implement it was in place. Implementation of a full suite of new application software for the central system and for a network of distributed processors was proceeding at full speed. Pilot field operation of the first sales office had recently commenced.

However, in mid-1987, Kallio had noted that sales-company software work was behind schedule. The decision on chargeback principles had been reopened, a data networking decision loomed, and a spinoff proposal for IT had surfaced. Kallio was considering what, if any, changes he should make in information technology directions for 1988.

Significant Business Developments

Major changes had taken place since 1985 in the business environment. These changes involved the marketing associations, the associations' member companies and their mills, and the global marketplace.

Paper, paperboard, and forest products were still vital components of Finland's economy, in 1986 representing 36 percent of the nation's total exports. The Finnish companies' primary competitive strength continued to be their ability to produce top-quality product across several important product categories. However, competition in overseas markets continued to intensify.

Although up considerably in absolute tonnage, by 1987 Finnish paper output had dropped from a 1983 figure of 4 percent of world production to 3.7 percent, with its share of the world export market falling from 15 percent to 13.9 percent. Total invoiced deliveries in 1987 of Finnish paper were up 0.6 percent in tonnage and up 2.7 percent in revenue as compared to 1986. Total 1987 Finnpap export tonnage was up 1.0 percent from 1986.

Structural changes had occurred in the Finnish paper industry. Enso-Gutzeit Oy had resigned its membership as of December 31, 1986. Finnpap management noted that the mainly government-owned Enso had, in one sense, never been a "full" member in the first place. Selling only its newsprint through Finnpap, unlike any other member, Enso had always maintained its own marketing channels through which it

Information Systems Fellow Richard G. Mills prepared this case under the supervision of Professors Tapio Reponen of Turku School of Business, and F. Warren McFarlan, as the basis of class discussion rather than to illustrate either effective or ineffective handling of an administrative situation.

had handled independently its large output of other paper, pulp, and board products.

One senior manager remarked that "capacity in other mills has increased more than the capacity lost," and several others noted that the change did not signal other defections or a weakening of the commitment to a common approach, through the associations, to international marketing and distribution. Nevertheless, the Enso departure and that of another, relatively tiny mill, together with a flurry of mergers and mill-ownership realignments affecting other members, had resulted in a net reduction in the share of total Finnish paper exports marketed internationally through Finnpap/Finnboard from its 1986 level of about 90 percent to nearer 75 percent at year-end 1987 (no member of Finnpap contributed more than 20 percent of its volume).

Information Technology Strategy Formulation

In April 1985, Jussi Olkinuora had presented to Thomas Nysten, Finnpap managing director, a five-year information systems planning proposal for Finnpap and Finnboard.

The Olkinuora strategy-development proposal specified the staffing and organization for a strategic planning team and laid out the team's initial work program. It noted:

> The decision to exploit information technology to gain marketplace advantage creates major changes affecting all existing and future information systems. To implement such a major change requires the full support of every business entity touched by the changes. This support will only be forthcoming if member companies, field sale companies, and head-office people work together to develop jointly the new IT strategy.
>
> To facilitate this joint work project, teams of key players must be established. The chairmen of the five teams will make up a "Project Group" responsible for pulling together the final strategy (Exhibit 1, IT Strategy Planning Team Organization Chart). Each company will nominate representatives to this team.
>
> The project group must develop a credible, five-year plan for using information technology to improve the competitiveness of the

EXHIBIT 1   Finnpap/Finnboard (B) Fin-Project: The Strategic Planning Team Organization

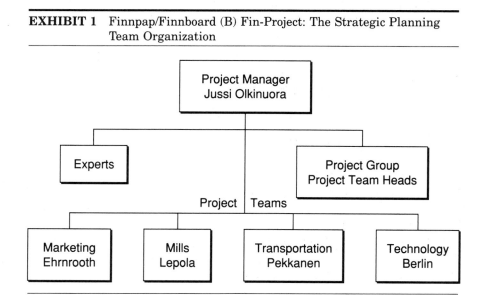

Finnish paper and board industry. The challenge is to ensure that information technology becomes a contributing element in the marketing of our products.

By June 1985, the Olkinuora proposal had been approved by the Finnpap supervisory board and the Finnboard board of directors. The project was staffed, and the detailed development work begun.

In fall 1985, the project group prepared a preliminary report that included:

- A list of Critical Success Factors for marketing paper and board.
- A list of the critical information requirements implied by the Critical Success Factors.
- An overview of the users' needs for information.
- Priorities for applications development.
- A network architecture.
- A plan for on-line customer connections via the network.
- A new organization for the Information Technology Department.
- Preliminary cost/benefit analyses for the required investments.

Two difficult problems surfaced in this strategy development work: (1) how to distribute computing power and (2) how to estimate the total level of investment for processing capacity, networks, and software.

Both mill and sales office team members insisted on distributing computing capacity from its current concentration in Finnpap to the mills and sales offices. In a meeting of the mills team, Ismo Lepola, director of United Paper Mills, said,

> We need a flexible and simple system. We don't know for sure what is going to happen in our business in the future, and our systems must be extremely responsive to unanticipated change. Building a giant central facility would take too long, and once in place it would be hard to redirect and evolve.

> We should build a network of minicomputers located in the mills and sales offices, not a large, centralized system. Of course, we will continue to need reports that summarize data across all mills and all sales companies, but that doesn't require much computer capacity in Helsinki. We must have direct links between the mills and the sales offices; the present system of funneling everything through Helsinki is too slow.

Thomas Nysten's comments were similar and reflected his developing view of a new overall business strategy. Mr. Nysten noted,

> The sales offices need more independence in their decision making. Many functions currently performed in Helsinki must be transferred to the sales offices or mills. Our information systems strategy must support this change.

This shift of decision authority and business functions from Helsinki upstream to the mills and downstream to the sales offices was considered attractive by both mill and sales office staff. In Finnpap, however, the systems professionals were concerned. They believed it would be impossible to distribute order handling and invoicing because of the "impossibility" of distributing the databases upon which these systems depended heavily.

After a considerable discussion, the conflict was resolved in favor of the decentralists. All possible operations would be dispersed to the sales offices (Exhibit 2 shows the future information network; and Exhibit 3 gives more detail on the central-system software; Exhibit 4 gives more detail on the sales-company software).

Estimating the five-year financial investment was difficult. Each team within the project group developed an estimate of future business and transaction-volume growth, which were converted into numbers of terminals and likely data volumes foreach. Then figures were consolidated across all groups producing an estimate with

EXHIBIT 2   Future Information Network

Future Information Network

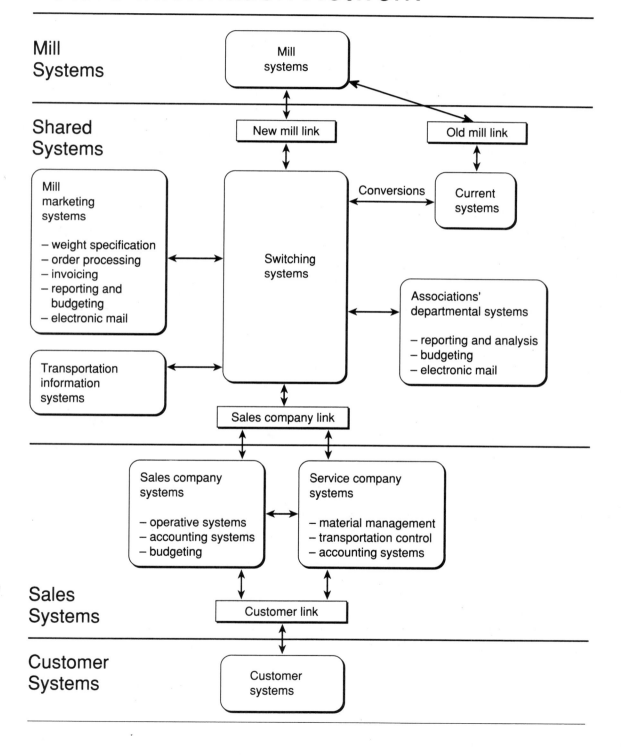

EXHIBIT 3   Central System Software

Development in Two Phases

The development of the centralized applications in the FIN-project has been divided into the following phases:
• Integration of the existing mill connections and the existing central applications to the new sales company system
• Developing the kernel of the new central applications and the mill connections. The new system is called "Mill connection system."

Finnpap's existing applications were developed in the beginning of the 1970s, which means that they are exceptionally old. It is expected that there will be mills using the existing connections for several years. That is why these old applications will be maintained until all mills have been switched to the new system.

Finnboard's existing applications are fairly new because they were built in the beginning of the 1980s. They will also be supported until all Finnboard's data processing can be moved to the new mill connection system.

The ongoing development Phase 1 is meant to support the existing applications. The new sales company system will be connected to the mills by using the existing terminal sessions and the existing mill link application. The outside connections and the existing applications will be used by converting the new format orders to the old format orders.

Development Phase 2 will build the kernel of the new mill connections systems which will replace the existing centralized system in the future. The first version will be limited but it will give basic order processing and invoicing services to the mills that will start to use it. More sophisticated versions will be developed in consecutive phases after that.

---

a large uncertainty range. For example, the number of terminals for 1990 might range from 2,000 to 5,000, compared to the 900 in use in 1985.

The various computer vendors expressed particular concern about the consequences of estimating too low, producing horror stories of situations in which actual future growth could not be accommodated because the architecture had been based on too conservative a forecast. The project group, however, set a maximum limit of 2,000 terminals on the system in 1990, believing this growth rate would provide the Association with enough capacity to meet its goals within bounds of financial prudence.

With terminal and transaction-volume estimates in hand, the project group requested that the computer vendors estimate required hardware capacities and the investment needed to provide them, recognizing the roughness of the resulting estimates.

The figures provided by the vendors were considered by the mill representatives to be extremely high (complicated by the fact that many of the mill representatives lacked firsthand experience with information processing costs).

The Strategy

The project group then prepared an information systems strategy with the following elements:

• A coordinated distribution of computing power. Basic data processing systems

EXHIBIT 3   (continued)

Development Phase 1

The result of the first development phase is an addendum to the existing central system. It contains links to the present applications and to the sales companies, and the following applications:

The *weight specification application* contains damage and short shipment details from domestic ports through Transfennica and terminal connections to the mill. The application is tested by the member mills of Finnpap and implementation has started.

The *switching application* manages all data transmission services between the centralized applications, the sales companies, the mills, Transfennica, and outside systems. It will allow computer systems to communicate directly with each other. It is based on a modern and standard data transmission architecture but it also supports the traditional batch transmission method.

The *reference data application* will be used to maintain the integrated basic data for all applications.

The *conversion application* changes order records, invoices, NFOB-records and codes to a form which is suitable for the existing applications.

Separate conversions have to be made to Finnpap and Finnboard because they have different systems.

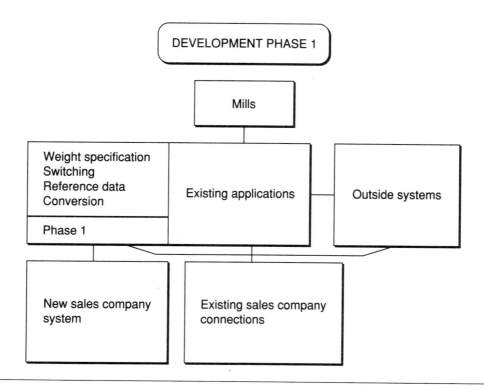

EXHIBIT 3   (continued)

Development Phase 2

Development Phase 2 will build the first limited version of the new mill connections system. The target system which now will be only partly implemented is roughly presented below.

The first version of the mill connections system has the following features:

The *basic order processing system* contains a directory to search orders for different purposes. As a result a new order sheet or an order note can be printed. A proposed prime route will be picked to the order from Transfennica's applications. Change management will be supported. Order confirmation contains possibilities to give ex-mill date, freezing date, voyage number and references. If the application has not received confirmation of a prespecified date a request will be sent to the mill. The application also contains record transmission to mill systems.

The *weight specification application* will be further developed to suit Finnboard's applications. Also direct weight specification entry and record format transmission will be added.

```
                    ┌──────────────────────────────┐
                    │   MILL CONNECTIONS SYSTEM    │
                    └──────────────────────────────┘

  S    ┌─────────────────────────────┐    ┌─────────────────────────────┐
  w    │ Order Processing            │    │ Production Information       │
  i    │ New orders, changes,        │    │                             │
  t    │  cancellations              │    │ Sales plans                 │
  c    │ Order confirmation,         │    │ Production plans            │
  h    │  e-mail entry               │    │ Processing programs         │
  i    │ New order sheet             │    │ Actuals                     │
  n    │ Price and cost information  │    └─────────────────────────────┘
  g    │ Shipping advice, prebooking │
       │ Order directory             │    ┌ ─ ─ ─ ─ ─ ─ ─ ─ ─ ─ ─ ─ ─ ─┐
  s    │ Alarms                      │      Data base
  y    │ Record formal order for     │    │                             │
  s    │  mail systems               │      New integrated data base
  t    └─────────────────────────────┘    │ Two way connections to old ????│
  e                                         ┌─────────────────────────┐ │
  m    ┌─────────────────────────────┐    │ │ Free reporting by generator │
       │ Invoicing                   │      │ Query system            │ │
       │                             │    │ └─────────────────────────┘
       │ Based on weight             │    └ ─ ─ ─ ─ ─ ─ ─ ─ ─ ─ ─ ─ ─ ─┘
       │  specification              │
       │ Port confirmation activates │    ┌─────────────────────────────┐
       │ Invoices, credit and        │    │ Port connections            │
       │  additional invoices        │    │ Vehicle lists to port       │
       │ Change information to ????  │    │ Weight specification        │
       │ Direct mill invoices        │    │  maintenance                │
       │ Connection to accounts      │    │ Port confirmation           │
       │  receivable                 │    │ Port invoices               │
       │ Connection to sales office  │    └─────────────────────────────┘
       │ Other distributions         │
       │ Statistics                  │
       └─────────────────────────────┘
```

EXHIBIT 3   (continued)

The *mill invoicing application* will make automatic invoicing possible by using weight specification information. Invoicing order and invoice data will be converted to the existing systems for reporting and outside connections.

Conversions from existing application will be added in order to fill the data base with data from sales organizations which are not yet using the new sales company system.

The first version has only limited functions. It is in a way the skeleton of the applications which will be added with more features in the next version. Phase 2 will be partly developed on a fixed contract basis by a software bureau.

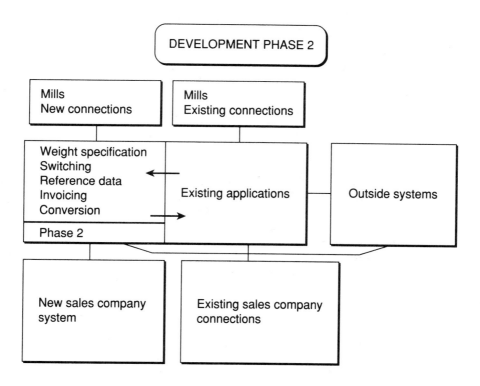

would reside in the Helsinki mainframe, but the local programs and decision support would be distributed.
- The present leased data transmission lines to Europe would be kept, but the development of value-added networks would be pursued.
- Electronic customer connections would be tested with a few pilot customers. Only af-

ter the systems had stabilized and customer-connection experience had been gained, would other customers be connected (perhaps as many as 200–300).
- The information systems department would be restructured to emphasize new software development.
- Application development would proceed according to the original five-year plan.

EXHIBIT 4   Distributed Software

The Sales Company Operative System Project

The project has been divided into the following subprojects:
- The **sales application** has functions which cover customer inquiry and order processing, feasibility evaluation, order confirmation and status follow up, delivery ordering and reporting.
- The **stock administration** covers landing processing, stock maintenance, consignment note processing, stock monitoring, delivery order processing and reporting.
- The **invoicing application** has invoice processing, debit and credit notes, special invoicing, acceptance, transfer to other systems and reporting.
- The **purchasing application** has conversion processing, mill orders, weight specification processing, voyage advice, customs clearance, shipping and purchase price calculation functions.
- The **damage handling application** covers claims, damages, returns, inspection and disposal processings and reporting.
- The **conversion application** has conversion orders, converted goods recording and conversion order control functions.

The Budgeting Project

The project is responsible for making new applications and for taking care of budgeting for the year 1988.
The parties involved have been divided into three groups:
- the pilot sales companies, Finpaka, Wiemeyer and Finapar and Lamco's fine dept.
- sales departments on FP/Hki (FB/Hki)
- three pilot mills—Veitsiluoto, Kangas and Jämsänkoski.
   The system includes applications as follows:
- The **annual budgeting** contains sales, costs, stock and purchase budgets for the sales companies and consolidation on the association level.
- The rotating short term and three-year **sales forecasts** are included in the system.
- The **monthly follow-up** reporting will serve all three groups: the pilot sales companies, associations and the pilot mills.

The Sales Company Accounting System Project

The system will be implemented by a standard application package. It contains following applications:
- The **accounts receivable application** covers customer records, credit control and dunning, cash entry, financial forecasting, payments processing, customer notes and reporting.
- The **accounts payable application** includes payment planning and control, payment handling, documents processing and reporting functions.
- The **bookkeeping application** is integrated with other applications. It covers legal accounting, administrative budgeting and cost control.

EXHIBIT 4 (continued)

The Cost Handling System Project

The project is responsible for creating an internal cost accounting system for the sales companies. The applications are
- The **precalculation application** is meant to support the estimation of costs on a mill order level and the definition of a purchase price from a mill.
- The **cost collection application** will collect and form invoices from various sources, calculate and check tonnages and values on them and register them on the mill order level.
- The **postcalculation application** will compare the precalculated estimates and the actual costs on desired calculation levels and form a basis for reconciliation of the possible profit/loss to a mill.

The Switching System Project

Because only a small fraction of the business transactions are processed by the new system the switching system will not reach its final form in the first implementation phase. It is an addendum to the existing central system. A lot of work is needed to integrate the present applications, to the mills and to the sales companies.
- The **weight specification subproject** makes an addendum to the present system. It contains damage and short shipment details from domestic ports through Transfennica and connection to the mill invoicing.
- The **mill invoicing subproject** will make improvements to the present system by making automatic invoicing possible.
- The **order switching application** will transmit data between sales companies, mills and Transfennica. It contains order storage and conversions to the present systems. It offers data transmission services also to the other systems.
- The **extended link application** offers possibility to transmit new data and it contains conversions to the present systems.
- The **reference data application** will be used to maintain the joint basic data.
  The order switching and the extended link applications form a kernel for the new switching system which will allow other systems to communicate directly.

The Operative Transportation Network Project

The operative transportation network facilitates order handling and cost handling applications, maintaining up-to-date information on routes available (especially the prime route, i.e., the most suitable route for each order) and cost standards involved. The cost standards are divided into three cost classes:
1) Transportation from mill to port of loading.
2) Sea freight.
3) Delivery costs from port of discharge to the consumer's destination (incl. handling costs and rental).

The application produces lists of all possible route alternatives. It also allows the user to cost simulate arbitrary chosen routes from the mill to the consumer or/and destination.

For the order handling, the operative transportation network application provides for each order a prime route. The route suggested by this application can naturally be changed as required by other circumstances.

Once the given route has been accepted, the operative transportation network offers all the cost standards involved for the precalculation application.

EXHIBIT 5 FIN-Project Staffing and Financial Actuals Versus Original 1985 Plan (numbers in millions of dollars)

	Staffing				
	1986	*1987*	*1988*	*1989*	*1990*
1985 Plan For:					
Total IT staff	100	115	125	135	140
Actual IT staff	94	94[a]			
Current plan DP staff			105[a]	105[a]	105[a]

	Financials ($ millions)					
	1986	*1987*	*1988*	*1989*	*1990*	*Total*
Original Plan						
Hardware	13.9	4.5	13.6	4.9	6.2	43.1
Staff	1.2	1.6	2.1	2.2	2.2	9.3
Total	15.1	6.1	15.7	7.1	8.4	52.4
Actual & Revised Plan						
International staff	0.4	0.5	1.1	1.2	1.3	4.5
Consultants	0.1	3.1	2.8	3.8	3.8	13.8
Hardware	3.8	5.5	7.0	5.4	4.0	25.7
Total	4.3	9.1	10.9	10.4	9.1	43.8
Variance	+10.8	(3.0)	+4.8	(3.3)	(0.7)	+8.6

[a]In addition, 20 outsiders from two software companies and Digital Equipment are assigned full-time to the project and totally integrated into the team. Paid more than double regular employees, they were viewed as temporary help.

The project group believed that the investments required during the next five years would total $50 million. (Exhibit 5 shows the initial plan and results through 1987.) The project group found no cost differences among the centralized or distributed alternatives.

Approval of the Strategy

The strategy proposal was presented to the Supervisory Board in November 1985, but after an active discussion the board wanted more details before approving the proposal. They had expected the benefits of the system would be quantified and that the degree of distribution would be specified. The board asked the project group to address these elements at the January 1986 board meeting.

In January the board focused particularly on how the investments to be made in information systems would be recovered. The project group prepared additional evaluations of the significance of the new system for paper and board marketing. They presented figures showing reductions in cost per order over the preceding 10 years and estimates of possible further savings (Exhibit 6 summarizes costs and estimated savings).

The project group was aware that making quantitative estimates was both difficult and risky. The members would have preferred to emphasize the importance to the associations of the exploitation of information technology in support of marketing and to gain competitive advantage. These benefits were impossible to quantify, however, and mill executives were not satisfied with them as the sole justification for so large a program.

During the board meeting the discussions were very lively, addressing particularly the magnitude of the required investment and the extent to which processing and information resources would be distributed outside of the Helsinki data center.

The investment discussion was complicated by the need to consider a data processing investment program covering a several-year period. Previously, IT had been funded on a year-by-year basis.

The mills repeatedly raised the question of the extent to which processing power and responsibility would be distributed. Based

---

EXHIBIT 6   Cost Summaries

	Finnpap		Finnboard	
	1974	*1984*	*1974*	*1984*
Sales (1,000 tons)	2,695	4,701	829	967
Number invoices	47,730	72,300	13,800	33,000
Tons/invoices	62.1	65	60.1	29.3
Costs ($ millions)				
Salaries	10.9	10.7	4.7	5.1
IT	2.4	4.6	0.3	1.2
Mail, phone, telex	1.3	2.5	0.5	0.5
Total Cost	14.6	17.8	5.5	6.8
Cost/invoice	306	246	400	207
Cost/ton	5.1	3.6	6.7	7.0
Number personnel	450	440	170	150

	Savings Estimates	*Value*
		($ millions/year)
Personnel (Finnpap and Finnboard)	10 percent	1.9
Shorter inventory times	1–2 weeks	8.2
Lower transport costs	3–5 percent	18.7
Faster invoicing and collection	3–6 weeks	0.8
Overall added value	0.5–3 percent	25.0
Total Estimated Value Savings/Year		54.6

on their positive experiences with minicomputers, the mill representatives believed distributed capacity should be maximized and the central system reduced to a minimum.

The Supervisory Board granted conceptual approval to the new strategy at the January 1986 meeting. The board also stated its expectation that IT costs would be fully allocated to users on a usage basis. Supervisory Board Chairman Juhani Ahava noted in the meeting minutes:

> Every IT investment must be clearly justifiable on a strict business basis. The mills do not make investments that are not clearly justifiable, and our IT investment decisions must follow these same principles. Every large investment must be brought to the Supervisory Board for a decision.
>
> As to the allocation of IT costs, we must move to the causality principle. Full usage-based charging for all IT costs should be in place by January 1987.

Implementation of the Strategy

IT Developments During 1986 and 1987
Implementation of the newly approved strategy began in February 1986. This first year of operation under the new strategy was a critical period of reshuffling and direction-setting. The first months saw extensive organizational and general decision-making activity.

Reorganization of the IT Function. The existing IT unit was significantly restructured to deliver on the enormous commitment to build a new generation of software. In the reorganization, IT was divided into two units, Information Systems Development (ISD), which housed the new development work, and Data Processing (DP), which ran the data center and telecom operations (Exhibit 7).

The mission of ISD was to coordinate the design and programming of the new systems and to develop the links to the mills. DP was charged with operating the Helsinki data center, maintaining current systems, and providing data communications and user support.

An IT steering committee was appointed. The membership consisted of mill, association, and sales-company representatives; an outside consultant served as chairperson.

As one of its first actions the steering committee developed a skills profile for the new position of Information Technology Director. This person had to have business management experience as well as familiarity with the associations' operational environment. Pentti Kallio, a 10-year Finnpap employee was selected for this position based on his experience in designing Finnpap's transportation network and his knowledge of the whole marketing/transportation chain.

Some of the software development functions that previously reported to DP manager Jussi Berlin were split off and transferred to Pentti Kallio. This partitioning of the organization divided a formerly integrated staff into two camps, and some friction developed. As part of a team-building effort a series of meetings of the two groups was held to discuss the new strategy. At one meeting Systems Designer Pentti Myllari, noted:

> The staff should be kept better informed about what's happening. For instance, what is going to happen to the central IBM mainframe? What does "distribution" really mean? For what computers will the software be developed? Too much uncertainty about the future is going to cost us some good people. . . .
>
> The new system, after all, will be based on the current one. There are a few people here who effectively maintain and evolve the current system. Their contribution to the new system will be critical. . . . We just need better internal communication in general.

These team-building efforts resulted in staff turnover in 1986 and 1987 being noticeably lower than in previous years (4 percent in 1986 and 15 percent in 1987; well be-

EXHIBIT 7 Finnpap/Finnboard Information Technology Organization

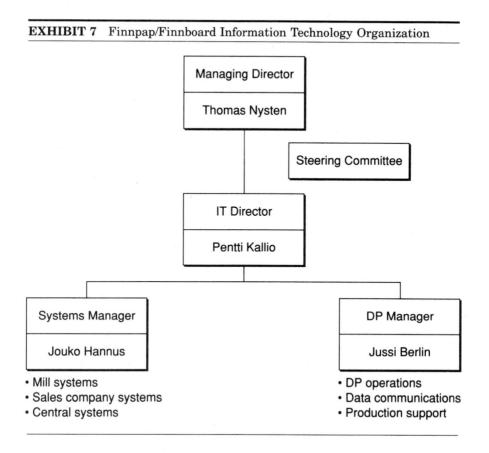

low prevailing Helsinki company standards). These figures were particularly impressive in the tight Helsinki IT labor market.

Hammering Out the Details

Pentti Kallio as Information Technology director bore the brunt of the project start-up. His first priority was to initiate the actual design of the new software. Other immediate tasks were (1) vendor selection for the sales-company departmental computers and (2) the hiring of new data communications staff for the IT organization.

Hardware Selection and Installation

Choosing the machine for the sales offices and mills was a critical 1986 project. Digital Equipment's VAX computer was ultimately selected. Software development tools were selected at the same time, including ADA-BAS and NATURAL, which support both the IBM and the VAX environments.

During 1986 the central mainframe capacity became saturated, and response times soared. The decision to move to a distributed concept offered potential relief by 1988. However, the ultimate load distribution between the central and the departmental machines was unclear, making it very difficult to estimate accurately the central-machine capacity requirement. Clearly, however, additional central-system capacity was necessary, and a larger IBM machine was scheduled for installation at the beginning of

1987. The selected machine was a used IBM 3084 (enabling significant cost savings over the initial plan). A data processing center relocation at the end of 1986 was coordinated carefully with the arrival of the larger machine. Although it was one of the biggest computer center moves in Europe, this combined relocation and upgrade went very smoothly.

New Software Development
Distributed-System Software. New software was required both for the central and the distributed (sales company) systems. The development of sales-company software was set up as a separate project. A top-notch project manager was recruited from outside to run it.

The sales company software project, called the "FIN-Project," was to be ultimately staffed by 40 people (including outside programmers from three companies). The project had its own control group to monitor progress and keep work on schedule.

FIN-project, with its apparent "elite" status, created some friction between the project team and other IT staff. These internal frictions cost the project some time.

Central-System Software. The main central-system software project for early 1986 was documentation of existing software. Its initial high-pressure development had omitted documentation, making subsequent enhancements exceptionally difficult. Various general software changes and improvements were also delivered for the central system, the most conspicuous being the long-sought Order Status Report.

An IT budgeting system was also written during 1986, and the 1987 operating budget was prepared using it. Although a major expenditure, the budgeting system had been a priority item of the Supervisory Board.

At the end of an extremely busy two years, Pentti Kallio reported to Thomas Nysten that his IT projects were mainly on track, with only a few tasks requiring rescheduling. The first set of new distributed-processing concepts had been tested in a German sales company using modified existing software. It was anticipated that the new sales-company software would be ready for test in the Amsterdam sales company in early 1988.

Changes in Finnpap Operations

The "New Operating Model"
During 1986, Finnpap senior management recognized that other, fundamental alterations to established business practices and relationships were required if the Finnish paper industry was to remain competitive in global markets. A re-examination of current Finnpap operating practices produced what was referred to as the "New Operating Model" (NOM) for this association. The term "operating model" referred to the basic roles of, and relationships among, the various interworking components—mills, sales offices, head-office support units, and other business entities—that were involved at one stage or another of the process of selling and delivering paper and paperboard products (Exhibit 8).

The operations review results were consistent with the information systems move toward distribution of data processing. Following a strategy of "coordinated decentralization," the main benefits from the new operating model were closer coupling between the mills and their markets and customers and increased independence and "bottom-line consciousness" of the sales companies. For example, sales companies were required to assume full legal ownership of the product when it reached them.

The NOM meant that much operational activity in association headquarters in Helsinki would be pushed out to the sales companies. Division of responsibilities among

EXHIBIT 8 News Release

June 17, 1987
Juhani Ahava, Chairman of the Board of Directors, Finnpap

New Operating Model for the International Marketing of Paper

The Finnish Paper Mills' Association—Finnpap's board of directors, has approved details of the new operating model at its meeting in June. The objective of the change is to improve the mills' profitability by increasing the effectiveness of customer service. The model's main principle is to bring the mills closer to Finnpap's sales network and markets, to clarify the division of responsibilities, and to create opportunities to better cost allocation.

The new operating model puts Finnpap's member companies' strategic goals into effect by providing the paper mills with direct connections to the markets and to the customers. The mills receive direct feedback from the markets which improves their readiness to develop products and service. Eliminating overlapping functions brings cost savings, and information exchange with the computer links will be easier and faster.

The operational work concerned with paper orders and deliveries will shift to being between Finnpap's sales companies and the member companies' mills. Formerly, all ordering and invoicing was done by Finnpap's Helsinki office. The introduction of the new models involves nearly 200 million marks of investments in building and modernizing the communications network and software over the years 1986–1990.

The model will be put into practice in phases. By the end of the next year, Finnpap's sales companies which operate in the largest market areas will move to direct links with the mills. All parties—the member companies and their mills, Finnpap Helsinki and the sales and services companies, as well as Transfennica—have had a hand in developing the model. The functioning of the model has already been tested in the West German market and in the framework of specialty papers.

"Coordinated Decentralization" as the Strategy of Change

The objective has been the efficient distribution of costs which will safeguard the just and fair treatment of Finnpap's member companies and mills.

The model does not change Finnpap's rules. Even though division of responsibility will be clarified with responsibility divided between the different mills, the only object is the improvement of the mills' profitability. Finnpap-Helsinki and its sales companies receive commission to cover their expenditure. The member companies can evaluate the results of the marketing organization better than before on the merits of its developed information and accounting systems.

Financing and responsibility will be taken on the one hand by the mills, and on the other by Finnpap's sales companies.

The competitiveness of the transportation will be improved. Furthermore, the mills will take care of sea transportation directly with Transfennica.

Exhibit 8 *(continued)*

Changes in Jobs of Finnpap Helsinki

The benefits of the cooperative marketing will, naturally, be retained. Strategic planning and decisionmaking is done in Finnpap's governing body. Finnpap Helsinki will coordinate and control the sales companies' operation. Other special functions of the head office of the international company such as market research and development work, administration and reporting, development of DP functions, training, and communication, will also be taken care of in Helsinki.

Marketing in the USSR and other CMEA countries, in Finland and in the overseas countries other than the United States, Canada, Australia, and Japan, will stay in Helsinki. The business units set up markets will operate in the same ways as independent sales companies in the other markets.

Building the Communications Network and Programs

Direct computer links between sales companies and the mills are being built for the new operating model. In addition to the sizeable equipment and network investments, a large amount of DP software and application work is being done in cooperation with Finnboard. The first area computer center has been set up in Antwerp for some of the western European sales companies. The next area computer center is planned for West Germany to service central Europe.

The work which is currently being done and partly already completed, has been described as the largest DP project in Finland at this time. The project consists of numerous different software applications, some needing to be created as their own independent developments and part to be connected to the different mills' and sales companies' existing programs.

Old Operating Model

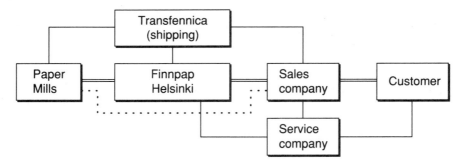

New Operating Model

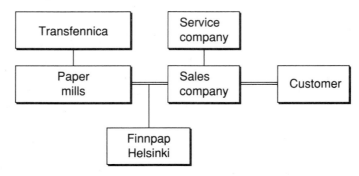

the entities along the mill-to-customer chain was formalized. For each entity the degree of autonomy and responsibility for its own operating results would be sharply increased. The "principle of causality" was to guide cost-allocation decisions. At the same time it was strongly emphasized by the board that the mills would be the only profit centers in the financial structure.

In mid-1986 it was confirmed that the emerging IT strategy was consistent with NOM and would create the necessary information systems capability to support it. It became clear that NOM could only be put into effect after prerequisite systems were in place. For example, the sales companies could successfully implement NOM only if (1) their electronic links to the mills were functioning and (2) their departmental processing systems were operational.

The IT Strategy and the New Operating Model

In late 1987 Thomas Nysten again stressed the significance of information systems in relation to the New Operating Model:

> Implementation of the NOM requires a strong data processing capability, since the model needs both direct links between the mills and the sales companies and decentralized invoicing. I must have a firm software availability schedule. I can't determine a NOM implementation schedule without it.

Implementation of the NOM was also discussed in Finnboard, but it was not considered to be a rush project. Indeed, Finnboard was concerned that the tight schedule for NOM would drive system-development costs significantly higher. Claes Ehrnrooth, Finnboard's planning director, noted:

> Much of the programming work we are paying for stems from Finnpap's decision to implement its New Operating Model. NOM is not critical for Finnboard, as our needs and markets are quite different.

Our software priorities are being hurt by these Finnpap-driven projects. For instance our order invoicing software doesn't function like it did before conversion from the Univac. We need resources to put this right, or else we need cost relief.

ALTERNATIVES FOR 1988

In early 1987, Pentti Kallio had identified a number of substantive questions that would require fast resolution. Some involved substantial redirection of the associations' IT plans and a possible major restructuring.

The Separate Company Issue

The idea of restructuring the associations' IT function as a separate corporate entity came up in connection with the general planning for an evolving information technology functional unit. Alternatives included:

- Form a separate company wholly owned by Finnpap/Finnboard.
- Form a separate company owned jointly by Finnpap/Finnboard and an IT company.
- Sell, in effect, the Finnpap/Finnboard IT department to some outside information technology company.
- Restructure Finnpap/Finnboard to establish the IT department as a profit center.
- Continue as now, with IT operating as a cost center.

Jussi Olkinuora noted:

> In my mind if an IT company is to be set up it should be done as quickly as possible. A reliable, cooperative partner must be found.
>
> The proposed separate-company approach has clear advantages: speeding up application development, improving the staff's marketing orientation, emphasizing results-oriented thinking, making possible more flexible staff compensation arrangements, controlling costs better, and so forth. For a separate IT company to work it is vital that we first get our

chargeback system into operation, and then the changeover should be made as quickly as possible.

Pentti Kallio supported the idea of the change, but was concerned about its impact on FIN-project:

It makes sense to form the company, but only when the FIN-project software is working. To do it now will certainly slow application development for several years. Setting up a company involves time-consuming work and the inevitable start-up problems. Our most important task now is to develop and install the new software, and only after that's done—in 1989 at the earliest—can we make large structural changes.

DP Manager Jussi Berlin also supported the separate-company idea but noted:

It wouldn't be useful to form a separate entity unless the new firm has skills and capabilities that extend our present ones. We would need additional business-management know-how, for example, to help us manage it.

How, exactly, would the move actually be done? How would Finnpap's ownership transfer to the company? What is involved in actually setting up the joint venture, and which parts of IT would be moved into it? The new company must clearly have products it could live on in reserve during the start-up period. Also, it couldn't be just a computer center; it would need a system design capability.

The IT Steering Committee chairman noted:

We can only make this kind of change after the associations are in stable, reliable operation. An effective chargeback system must be in place, and the IT company must have good products. It's too risky unless all these conditions steps are met.

Cooperation with an outside firm only makes sense if the partner has something substantive to contribute. We should test the relationship in a joint project before making a final commitment.

The mills were neutral. If spinning off IT produced cost improvements or other tangible benefits they would support the idea. Finnpap's administration director, Mats Weckstrom, shared this view.

The associations had met with several potential partner firms, and all had indicated interest. However, all wanted a strong hand in the associations' data processing.

FIN-Project Progress

Pentti Kallio had reported earlier that the FIN-project was slightly behind schedule, citing a longer than planned specification phase as the reason. On-time completion of sales-company systems was important because of the dependence on them of the New Operating Model. A shortage in the project of staff who knew in detail the association's systems meant that the only practical way to make up the lost time was to postpone other tasks. Adding additional contractors was an unattractive solution because there was already a high percentage of contract staff. Hiring lead times and the burden on experienced staff of the necessary training ruled out solving the problem by adding full-time staff. Concern also existed as to what to do with new staff when FIN-project was completed.

Pekka Makela agreed that the specifications had taken a little longer than anticipated, but he considered this to be an indication of careful work. Makela thought the resulting better specifications would pay off in the implementation phase, and he found no particular reason to be concerned about the slippage.

Pentti Kallio's plan called for postponement to year-end of all maintenance and enhancement work on the current invoicing systems. The postponed jobs would then be done in the sequence in which they had been requested. He further proposed to delay the development of the conversion programs needed for "bridging" between the old and the new versions of the order-processing and invoicing systems. The released resources would be used to finish the new software.

The postponed conversion programs would have to be written as soon as possible to make the parallel operation of old and new invoicing transparent to the mills. It appeared that parallel operation might go on for as long as two years. During the parallel, and until the conversion programs could be written, the mills would be carrying an extra workload. Kallio said it was impossible, with his limited resources, to do everything at once.

A further problem for the sales office software had appeared in the form of a language requirement. This distributed, multicountry system would have to accommodate the different language of the various countries. Training would be required in each language. Pentti Kallio was asked to develop an initial proposal to further specify the problem.

The Networking Decision

The possibility of using value-added carriers and public networks instead of private leased circuits for data communications had been under consideration for some time. However, the issues surrounding the selection of a telecommunications architecture were very difficult to resolve, and no final architectural decisions had yet been made. The problems associated with interfacing the network to the various differing computer types in use at the mills and in customer offices seemed especially difficult.

A DECNET network would make it easy in the future to interconnect the sales offices' VAX computers. An IBM SNA decision would harmonize well with the existing SNA links to the mills. A third alternative involved the possibilities of blending any or all of DECNET, SNA, value-added packet services, and normal leased and dial-up public network services. At this stage, detailed cost analysis work had not been done. Three network configurations were under consideration. They were basically SNA, DEC-NET, and a blended approach (Exhibit 9).

Chargeback—Principles Under Review

The Supervisory Board had expected IT to develop and install a full chargeback system during 1986. Staffing problems and unexpected complexities intervened, however, and the topic was only addressed in depth in 1987.

Chargeback

Prior to 1986 all EDP costs had been allocated to the mills based on their percentages of total Finnpap/Finnboard revenues. A simple calculation, in the pre-FIN-project days when IT expenses were very small, its simplicity was felt to outweigh any of the distortion of allocation between the member firms. As it became clear that the IT expenditures were going to be a much bigger part of total Finnpap/Finnboard operating expenses and that the several companies were placing quite different demands on the resource, it was increasingly felt that these distortions would become unacceptable and changes would have to be made.

In 1987, a task force developed a new algorithm to more fairly allocate computer resources and maintenance expenses among the users. Each month the mill would receive a bill based on seven items.

1. Number of orders processed for mill.
2. Number of invoices processed for the mill.
3. Number of file inquiries by the mill.
4. Number of electronic mail messages.
5. Number of accounting transactions.

EXHIBIT 9 Networks

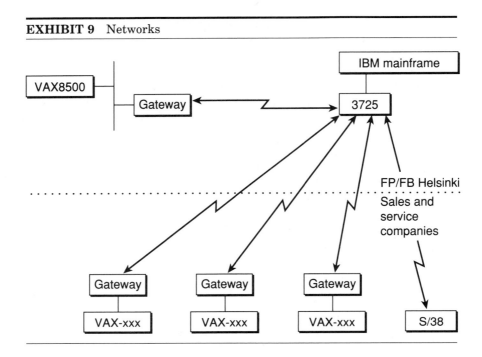

---

6. Volume of dedicated-line data communications.
7. Special software work.

A standard charge was derived for each of the items; it would be reviewed three times a year to ensure costs were being appropriately recovered. It was expected that costs would be neither over nor under resources. During the trial period, about 10 percent of IT costs (exclusive of FIN-Project) were directly charged to the mill (the remainder were split between Finnpap and Finnboard for ultimate assignment to the mills on a percent of revenue).

It was felt that this system would have to be rethought and refined during 1988 particularly in the light of the probability of setting up IT as a profit center. Issues of concern were:

• In addition to monthly usage charges, should the mills be charged a fee for being a member of Finnpap's IT? This would not only reflect the real fixed costs associated with a new member but also reduce variable charges.
• Should an attempt be made to associate specific charges on FIN-project and maintenance with specific mills? Should these charges be done at a standard estimated charge or at actual out-of-pocket expense?
• How should new companies joining the system be charged? At just a daily usage rate, or should they contribute to the capital investment associated with the software?
• How much of a premium should be charged to the nonmill sponsors using the network?

EXHIBIT 9   (cont.)

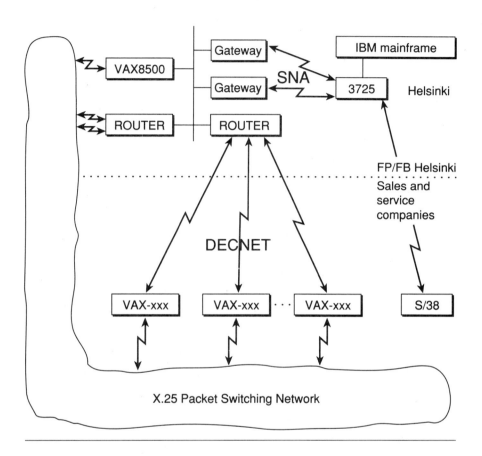

DECNET Network

Jukka Narinen, designer of the existing charging principles, noted:

> The user absolutely has to see in detail where his charges come from. Usage measurement must therefore be very precise, and we must be able to substantiate the charges in great detail. The literature has quite clearly stated that simple calculations lead to waste of resources due to wrong usage decisions.

Kauko Pekkanen, business manager and Transfennica's representative on the DP Committee, again stated his opinion:

> Charges must be understandable to the users and must be based on transaction volumes—for example, on the number of invoices processed. Nobody can be bothered with investigating complicated chargeback calculations, and they leave users wondering about whether the charge was really "causality

---

EXHIBIT 9   (cont.)

Combined Network

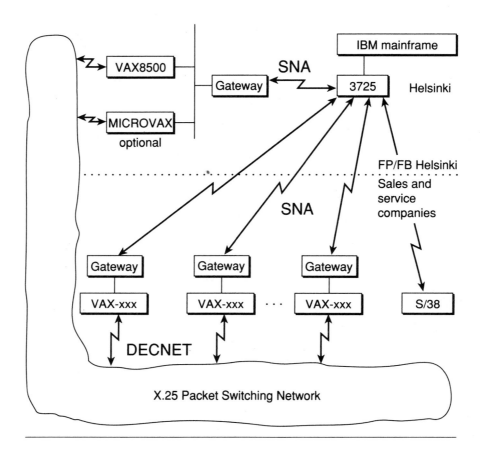

---

based." Cost measurements can and should be precise, but the chargeback principles should still be kept very simple. An audit, perhaps annually, can confirm that charges are tracking closely enough with actual usage.

Chapter 13

IT Planning:
A Contingent Focus

A manufacturing company has just eliminated its five-person IT planning staff, reassigning three persons to other jobs in the IT organization and letting two go. In commenting on this the vice president of finance states, "We just didn't seem to be getting a payoff from it. After three years of trying we thought we could find a better place to spend our money."

A financial institution's executive vice president of operations is overheard speaking of a recently completed business systems planning effort. She says, "This has given us a whole new picture of how much we need to devote to IT expenditure and where we should spend it over the next five years. We would be lost without it."

The head of IT planning for a major financial services organization is discussing his disillusionment with planning. He notes, "When we started IT planning two years ago we were very enthusiastic about its potential for invigorating the company. It worked for a while, but now it seems to have gone flat."

These comments are typical. Organizations launch IT planning efforts with great hope and often positive early results. Subsequently, however, many of the these efforts run into difficulty. This chapter explores key managerial issues surrounding IT planning and provides guidelines that can help to assure success.

As information technology applications have grown in size and complexity over the past two decades, the development of a strategy for assimilating these resources into firms' operations has grown steadily more important. A key vehicle for strategy development is a sensitively architected planning process. To be effective, such a planning process must deal simultaneously with the realities of the firm's organizational culture, corporate planning culture, various technologies, and the importance of IT activities to the corporate goals.

Many studies have shown a positive correlation between user *perception* that IT activities are effective and a focused, articulated, appropriate planning process.[1] However, since good standards do not exist for measuring the overall effectiveness of the IT activity, the evidence linking its effectiveness with planning processes is necessarily diffuse and fragmentary.

This chapter is organized around four topics:

1. External and internal pressures that generate the need for an articulated IT planning process.
2. Pressures that limit the value that can be derived from IT planning.
3. The relationship between IT planning and corporate strategy formulation.
4. Corporate factors that influence the effectiveness of IT planning—tailoring the IT planning process to a specific firm.

PRESSURES TOWARD IT PLANNING

External (Corporate) Pressures

A variety of external pressures define the need for IT planning. The more important ones are discussed here.

Rapid Changes in Technology.   Hardware and software continue to evolve rapidly, providing substantially different and potentially profitable IT applications from year to year. This requires continual interaction between IT staff and management groups to ensure that they have properly identified the technology changes that are significant to the company and have developed appropriate plans and pilot projects. IT staff must make potential users, such as office managers and analytical staffs, aware of the implications (including the potential problems) of these new technologies so that they can identify potential new applications in their areas of responsibility that the IT staff might not recognize.

As the technology changes, planning becomes increasingly important in order to avoid the problems of incompatible systems and inaccessible data files. The networked organization is becoming reality, and developing network linkages frequently requires implementation schedules of up to four years.

---

[1]Philip Pyburn, "Information Systems Planning—a Contingency Perspective," DBA thesis, Harvard Business School, 1981.

For example, an insurance company has instituted a two- to three-year program for placing a portable PC with expert financial counseling software in it into the hands of each of its more than 5,000 agents. A detailed plan was absolutely critical to maintaining senior management's confidence in the integrity of the program and the sales force's effectiveness and good morale during the implementation.

Personnel Scarcity.   The scarcity of trained, perceptive analysts and programmers, coupled with their long training cycles, continues to restrain IT development and to demand that planning priorities be established. As discussed earlier, these appear to be long-term difficulties rather than cyclical problems. This is forcing increasing amounts of software and electronic data to be sourced from outside the firm and necessitating tough internal resource allocation decisions. Indeed despite the proliferation of IT productivity tools and software tools for distributing work to users, an increasing number of U.S. firms are looking overseas for English-speaking technical personnel to meet staff shortages at attractive U.S. salaries. Firms have also outsourced portions of software development to such countries as India and Ireland, where the labor costs for comparable skills are dramatically lower.

Scarcity of Other Corporate Resources.   Limited availability of financial and managerial resources is another planning pressure. IT is only one of many strategic investment opportunities for a company, and the potential financial returns of investments in it must be weighed against those of alternative investments. This problem is intensified by the financial accounting practice in most U.S. companies of charging IT expenditures against the current year's earnings even though much of it is actually a capital expenditure. Review of the effectiveness and the efficiency of these expenditures is of great importance, as resource availability is a critical limiting factor for new projects—particularly in companies that are under profit or cost pressures.

Scarcity of IT middle-management personnel, particularly in the area of systems development, is also a significant constraint. The inability of some companies to train sufficient project leaders and supervisors has significantly restrained those firms' IT development. This has forced significant reductions in their systems development applications portfolios and the undertaking of projects that pose very high risk solely because of inadequate human resources.

Trend to Database Design and Integrated Systems.   An increasing and significant proportion of the applications portfolio involves the design of relational data architecture for supporting sophisticated applications that link different parts of the firm as well as its customers and suppliers. A long-term view of the evolution of applications is critical in order to appropriately select database contents, the methods for interrelating them, and the protocols for updating them.

Validation of Corporate Plan.   In many organizations new marketing programs, new-product design, and introduction and implementation of organizational strategies depend on the development of IT support programs. Understanding these points of dependency is critical. If the corporate strategy is infeasible due to IT limitations, that message needs to be highlighted for corporate management, because the problem must be faced and resolved while alternatives are still available.

As we have pointed out many times, in organizations where IT products and processes are integral to elements of the corporate strategy, this linkage is very important. A large paper company, for example, was forced to abandon its planned new billing discount promotions—a key part of its marketing strategy—because its IT function was unable to translate the very complex ideas into the existing computer programs with the present level of staff skills. Advance coordination between IT and marketing management would have identified the problem much earlier and permitted satisfactory solutions to be identified.

Internal (IT Process) Pressures

At various points in the evolution of an information technology the balance between pressures shifts and planning serves substantially different purposes. Reflecting upon the advent and growth of business data processing, databases, distributed systems, fiber optics, image processing, and other new technologies (as noted in earlier chapters) one can identify four distinct phases of technology assimilation, each of which poses different pressures.

Phase 1: Technology Identification and Investment.   The basic focus of planning in the initial phase of a new technology is oriented toward both technology identification and the need for new human resource skills. Key IT planning problems include identifying the appropriate technologies for study, preparing the site, developing staff skills, identifying potential product champions, and managing development of the first pilot applications of the technology.

In this phase short-term technical problem resolution is so critical and experience is so limited that effective long-term strategic thinking about the implications of the technology is often precluded. This is not bad, since those involved usually do not yet have a strong enough background in the technology to think long term about its implications for the company. As the organization gains experience with the technology through pilot projects, selecting appropriate new applications for the technology becomes a topic of interest. This signals the evolution to the second phase. (As noted earlier, in some IT organizations, "Emerging Technologies" departments have been established to ensure that appropriate technologies are identified and streamed through Phases 1 and 2.)

Phase 2: Technological Learning and Adaptation. The basic thrust of planning in this phase is to develop potential users' consciousness of the new technology's existence and to communicate the ways it can be useful to them. Sequencing projects and ensuring that there is good coordination between team members is also important as the company continues to master the technology's nuances. The initiation of a series of user-supported pilot projects is a measure of the effectiveness of the planning.

As a secondary output, the planning process for technologies in this phase focuses on identifying the number of staff and the skills that must be acquired. The direction that comes out of Phase-2 planning is not necessarily an accurate indicator of the pace of future events. This is because individuals are still learning and do not yet have sufficient insight to be concise and accurate about the real implications of the technology in their operations and about how hard it will be to achieve the desired results.

Since technology will continue to evolve for the foreseeable future, there will normally be a Phase-2 flavor to some part of a company's IT development portfolio. Our observations of successful planning in this phase suggest clearly that:

1. A new technology is best introduced by starting with a pilot test to generate both IT staff and user learning, rather than by spending years on advance introspection and design without any practical hands-on experience.
2. Attracting the interest of potential users on *their* terms and stimulating their understanding about what the technology can do for them is critical to success. Success here leads to later requests for service, and the pilot users are your most important allies.
3. Planning during this phase (and Phase 1 as well) involves a program of planned technological innovations, encouraging users to build upon their past experience, and organizational receptivity to change. There is a desirable "softness" in specificity of the tangible and intangible benefits associated with these projects.

Phase-2 planning has a heavy strategic focus. However, as is true of companies that are in a rapid growth phase in new industry sectors, precision of the plan is limited by user's and developer's lack of familiarity with the technology and its implications. Therefore, planning for technologies at this phase does not have the same predictive value as planning for technology in the later phases. What the technical developer initially envisions as the implications of a new technology are often quite different from the ultimate actual applications.

Phase 3: Rationalization/Management Control.   Effective planning for technologies in this phase has a strong efficiency focus; the emphasis shifts to get the results of the successful pilot projects implemented cost-efficiently. Whereas planning for technological learning and adaptation (Phase 2) has a long-range (though not terribly accurate) perspective, planning for Phase-3 technologies has a short-term—one- to two-year—efficiency focus. This includes getting applications identified and completed, upgrading staff to acceptable knowledge levels with the new technology, reorganizing to develop and implement further projects using the technology, and efficiently utilizing the technology. For technologies in this phase, planning's objective is to set appropriate limits on the types of applications that make sense and to ensure they are implemented cost-efficiently. In terms of Robert Anthony's framework,[2] effective planning for Phase-3 technologies has a much stronger management and operational control flavor and a weaker strategic planning thrust.

Phase 4: Maturity/Widespread Technology Transfer.   The final phase is one of managed evolution in which the technology is transferred to a wider spectrum of applications within the organization. With organizational learning essentially complete and a technology base that has appropriate controls in place, it is appropriate to look seriously into the future and to plot longer-term trends in exploitation of the technology. If one is not careful, such planning—based on the business and technology as they are now understood—can be too rigid. Unexpected quirks in the business and evolution of technology may invalidate what has been done during Phase-4 planning as the technology is superseded by a still better one.

Given the current dynamic state of information technology, technologies in all four planning phases are normally present simultaneously in a typical firm. Planning for business batch data processing for most companies in 1991, for example, was in Phase 4, while electronic mail was in Phase 3, and image processing was somewhere between Phases 1 and 2. This suggests that uniformity and consistency in IT planning

---

[2]Robert Anthony, *Planning and Control Systems: A Framework for Analysis* (Boston: Division of Research, Harvard University Graduate School of Business Administration, 1965).

protocols throughout the firm are inappropriate, because the organization is dealing with a portfolio of technologies, each of which poses a different planning challenge.

For example, one manufacturing company studied was in Phase 4 in terms of its ability to conceptualize and deal with enhancements to its on-line MRP-II production scheduling system. At the same time, it was in Phase 3 in terms of driving its new CAD system across the entire engineering and product development functions. Finally, the company had just made an investment in several local-area word-processing networks as well as in two quite different approaches to the graphic user interface. It was clearly in Phase 1 with respect to these technologies. The firm's plans for the MRP-II system were detailed and crisp, whereas the local-area network was essentially a research project, and no coherent view existed as to where it was going.

In summary, "planned clutter" (as opposed to consistency) is desirable in a firm's approach to IT planning. Similarly, the approach to IT planning for different organizational units within a company should vary, since each often has quite different familiarity with specific technologies.

LIMITATIONS ON IT PLANNING RESULTS

As new products appear, as the competitive environment shifts, as laws and corporate strategies change, and as mergers and spin-offs take place, the priorities a company assigns to its various applications appropriately evolve. Some previous low-priority or unconceived applications may become critically important, while others that were once seen as vital will diminish in significance. This volatility places a real premium on building a flexible management framework that permits orderly and consistent change to meet evolving business requirements.

In a similar vein, every IT planning process must make some very specific assumptions about the nature and role of technological evolution. If this evolution occurs at a different rate from the one forecasted (as is often the case), then major segments of the plan may have to be reworked in terms of both scope and thrust. Suppose, for example, the present speed of access to a one-billion-character file were suddenly increased in the coming year by an order of magnitude beyond current expectations with no change in cost. Many organizations' plans would require careful reexamination, not just of the priority of applications but, more important, of their very structure as completely new application areas would become possible. Some individuals have used this as a reason not to plan but, rather, to "remain creatively opportunistic" on a year-to-year basis. On balance, we have found the evidence supporting this viewpoint to be unconvincing.

Planning as a Resource Drain

Every person and every dollar assigned to IT planning represent resources that are diverted away from such activities as new systems development. The extent to which human and financial resources should be devoted to planning is always in question. Just as the style of planning changes over time as parts of the organization pass through different phases with different technologies, the commitment of resources to planning also should change. This too suggests that the instability in an IT planning process relates positively to its role of stimulating a creative view of the future. If not carefully managed, IT planning can evolve into a mind-numbing, noncreative process of routinely changing the numbers, as opposed to a sensitive focus on the company's real opportunities and problems.

Fit to Corporate Culture

An important aspect of IT planning is implementation within the realities of the corporate culture. For example, in organizations with a very formal corporate planning process that is actively supported by senior management, the internal user–management climate typically supports formal approaches to IT planning. In middle management's eyes, IT planning is a legitimate activity, and devoting time to it is an appropriate thing to do. Other organizations, however, have quite different cultures and approaches to corporate planning. These factors significantly alter both the form and the degree of commitment that can be expected from users to an IT planning process. This is discussed further later in the chapter.

Strategic Impact of IT Activities

As discussed in earlier chapters, for some organizations IT activities are an area of great strategic importance, while for other organizations they play (and appropriately will continue to play) a cost-effective, useful, but distinctly supportive role. It is inappropriate for organizations in which IT plays a distinctly support role to expect the same amount of senior management thinking to be devoted to IT items as in organizations of the former type. Making the issue more complicated, the IT function that in the past did not have strategic importance may, because of its new-technology-enabled applications portfolio, have great significance in the future. Thus, IT planning may become very important to the firm at some time, and in the process it must face and surmount the challenge of breaking the habits and molds of the past.

In an environment of management turmoil, high turnover, and reassessment, it is unlikely that there can be the same intensity and commitment to IT planning that is possible in a stable environment in which individuals have a strong emotional attachment to the organization. Although such negative factors limit the benefits of planning and make the process more complex, they do not eliminate the *need* for it. Rather, they increase the multidimensional complexity of the planning task and they diminish reasonable expectations of the output's quality.

For other organizations, the opposite is true. While IT now plays an important operational role, future applications may not offer great payoff or significance. In that event, a less intensive focus on IT strategic planning will be in order, and different people will be involved than in the past when it was more significant.

These ideas (discussed first in Chapter 2) are illustrated here within four quite different IT environments. (Also see Figure 13–1.)

Strategic. "Strategic" companies are critically dependent on the smooth functioning of the IT activity. Appropriately managed, such firms require considerable IT planning, and IT planning is closely integrated with corporate planning in a two-way dialogue because IT can open new operational capabilities for the firms. Not only does IT need the guidance of corporate goals, but the achievement of corporate goals can be severely impacted by IT performance and capabilities or lack thereof. In short, the impact of IT on the firm's performance requires significant general management involvement in IT planning.

Comments by the chief executive officer of a large financial institution to his senior staff captured this perspective:

> Most of our customer services and much of our office support for those services involve some kind of systematic information processing. Without the computer hardware and software supporting these processing efforts, we would undoubtedly drown in a sea of paper—unless we were first eliminated from the market because our costs were so high and our services so inefficient that we had no customers to generate the paper. Either way, it is abundantly clear that information systems are critical to our survival and our success.
>
> In our businesses, the critical resources that ultimately determine our marketing and our operating performance are people and systems.

Turnaround. Similarly to "strategic" companies, "turnaround" firms also need a substantial IT planning effort, and it is closely linked to corporate planning. Corporate long-term performance can be severely impacted by shortfalls in IT performance and capabilities, with crucial initiatives being missed. Here also, the impact of IT on the firm's future is such that significant general management involvement in IT planning is appropriate.

FIGURE 13–1 Information Technology Strategic Grid

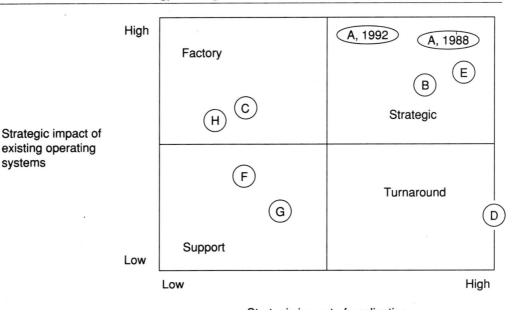

Key:

A. Major Bank 1988-1992
B. Major Insurance Company
C. Medium-size Grocery Chain
D. $100 Million Distributor
E. Major Airline
F. Major Chemical Company
G. Major Process Industry Manufacturers
H. Insurance Broker

These firms may receive considerable amounts of IT operational support, but the company is not absolutely dependent on the uninterrupted cost-effective functioning of this support for achieving its short-term or long-term objectives. Successful implementation of the applications under development, however, are absolutely vital for the firm's reaching its strategic objectives.

A good example of this was a rapidly growing manufacturing firm. The IT embedded in its factories and accounting processes, although important, did not require instantaneous reliability for the firm to operate effectively. However, the rapid growth of the firm's domestic and international installations—in number of products, number of sites, number of staff, and so forth—had severely strained its management control systems. This had made improving its global IT systems strategically important. The company enhanced the IT leadership, gave IT new organizational placement, and increased its commitment to IT planning in order to resolve the situation. As this example illustrates, improved IT planning is very frequently only one of the changes that must be implemented to enhance senior management's overview of IT in a "turnaround" company.

Factory. Strategic goal setting for IT and linkage to long-term corporate strategy are not nearly as critical for "factory" firms. Whereas good IT planning requires appropriate guidance regarding the corporation's direction, only limited feedback about IT constraints and capabilities need to be fed into corporate planning. Senior management involvement in IT planning appropriately is much less in this environment, but detailed year-to-year operational IT planning is absolutely critical. The 1987 flood in the computer room of a major New York investment bank (described earlier) with its massive dislocation of operating procedures, gives vivid testimony to what can happen when management fails to focus appropriately on operational issues when they really matter.

Support. For companies in the "support" quadrant strategic goal setting for IT and its linkage to long-term corporate strategy is not nearly as important as it is in "turnaround" and "strategic" environments. IT constraints are not critical to corporate success, and overachievement or underachievement of IT departmental performance do not significantly impact the firm's performance. Senior management involvement in the IT planning process can be much less here. The key danger, however, is that new opportunities may arise in the world of evolving technology, and the firm will be so "stuck" in "support" procedures that it will completely miss the opportunities.

Mismatches: Using the Strategic Grid

Selecting the appropriate planning approach is further complicated when a mismatch exists between where an organization is on the grid (see Figure 13–1) and where senior management believes it *should* be. In such a case more planning is needed for energizing the firm to make appropriate adjustments. An example illustrates the complexity of this problem.

A large financial institution's senior management was very comfortable with the company's IT performance, although it appeared on their agenda only infrequently. The IT management team, however, was deeply concerned that their senior IT managers lacked a thorough understanding of the firm's goals, what its products would be four to five years hence, and the types of organization structures and controls that would be needed. IT management knew that senior IT managers needed this input so that IT could provide the necessary support for achieving the firm's goals.

The institution was a large international one with a very sophisticated but closely held corporate planning activity. Appropriately in a world of major shifts in what financial institutions can and should do, there was great concern at the top about the confidentiality of this information, and only a handful of individuals (four or five) knew the full scope of this direction. Since neither the IT manager nor his boss was among this handful, IT was substantially in the dark about the plans of the organization and could only crudely assess it by trying to guess why some projects were funded and others were not.

The company had a full-time IT planning manager, who had three assistants and reported to the IT manager. For the last two years the IT planners had worked closely with middle-management users and the information technologists to develop strategies and applications portfolios that were seen by both sides as relevant to their needs. Because there was little formal or informal linkage between the IT planning activity and the corporate planning department (repeatedly corporate planning had communicated, "Don't call us, we'll call you"), the IT staff had two overriding concerns:

1. The plans and strategies developed for IT might be technically sound and might meet the needs of user management as they understand them today, but they may be unproductive or indeed counterproductive if they do not support the corporate thrust.
2. Corporate plans are developed "at the top" by four or five executives who are completely isolated from IT and its issues. This could unwittingly place onerous or unworkable support requests on IT in the future.

At this stage senior management perceived IT as a "factory," believed it was being staffed and managed appropriately, and had no concerns about the IT planning process. IT saw itself as "strategic" but could not sell the concept to anyone.

This frustration was resolved when an outside review of the institution's overall strategy (initiated by the chairman) noted in its conclusions that IT, a strategic force in similar firms, was not being treated as such in this firm and was moving in an unproductive direction. The outside reviewer's credibility was such that senior management readily accepted that they had misunderstood the role of IT and that IT should indeed be treated as strategic. Unfortunately, they perceived IT management as inadequate for this newly defined (newly *recognized*) challenge, and many senior IT staff did not survive the transition.

On the surface, when one read the written plan, IT planning had looked good. In fact, it had failed to come to grips with the realities of the corporate environment. Consequently, an organization for which IT activities were of significant strategic importance had been left in a state of potential unpreparedness and risk. This was fatal for the IT planners when IT activities were belatedly recognized as critical to the organization's achievement of its product and productivity goals, because they were unfairly held accountable for this state of affairs.

FIGURE 13–2 Portfolio Analysis Questionnaire

	Percentage of Development Budget	*Strategic Weight*[a]
1. Projects involved in research impact of new technologies or anticipated new applications where generation of expertise, insight, and knowledge is the main benefit.	0–5	1
	5–15	2
	Over 15	3
2. Projects involved in cost-displacement or cost-avoidance productivity improvement.	Over 70	3
	40–70	2
	Under 40	1
3. Do estimated aggregate improvements of these projects exceed 10% of firm's after-tax profits or 1% of sales?	Yes	2
	No	0
4. Projects focused on routine maintenance to meet evolving business needs (processing new union contract payroll data) or new regulatory or legal requirements.	Over 70	1
	40–70	2
	Under 40	3
5. Projects focused on existing system enhancements that do not have identifiable hard benefits.	Under 10	3
	10–40	2
	Over 40	1
6. Projects whose primary benefit is new decision support information to top three levels of management. No tangible identifiable benefits.	0–5	0
	5–15	2
	Over 15	4
7. Projects whose primary benefit is new decision support information to middle management or clerical staff.	0–5	0
	5–15	1
	Over 15	2
8. Projects that allow the firm to develop and offer new products or services for sale or that	Over 20	4
	10–20	3

[a]Larger numbers denote greater strategic importance.

Assessing the extent to which IT is strategic is useful for the company as a whole and for the individual business units and functions. IT's impact typically varies widely by unit and function, and thus the IT planning process must be adapted to deal with these differences. Those units where IT is of high impact require much more intense IT planning than those units for which it is of low impact, of course. This makes the planning more complex, but it also makes it more useful.

Figure 13–2 presents the questionnaire one firm uses to analyze the strategic thrust of the development portfolio for each of its organizational units. The questions were designed to uncover whether, on balance, the developmental work being done is critical to the firm's future competitive posture, or whether it is useful but not strategic to competitive success. Similarly, Figure 13–3 presents the questionnaire the

---

FIGURE 13–2   *(continued)*

	Percentage of Development Budget	*Strategic Weight[a]*
enable additional significant new features to be added to existing product line.	5–10	2
	Under 5	1
9. Projects that enable development of new administrative control and planning processes. No tangible benefit.	Over 20	4
	10–20	3
	5–10	2
	0–5	1
10. Projects that offer significant tangible benefits through improved operational efficiencies (reduce inventory, direct reduction in operating costs, improved credit collection, etc.).	Over 20	4
	10–20	3
	5–10	2
	0–5	1
11. Do tangible benefits amount to 10% of after-tax profit or 1% of gross sales?	Yes	2
	No	1
12. Projects that appear to offer new ways for the company to compete (faster delivery, higher quality, broader array of support services).	Over 20	4
	10–20	3
	5–10	2
	Under 5	1
13. Size of development budget as a percent of value added.	Over 4	3
	3–4	2
	2–3	1
	2	0

[a]Larger numbers denote greater strategic importance.

---

firm uses to analyze how critical the existing systems are to an organizational unit's achieving its basic operating objectives. The firm uses these questionnaires as rough diagnostic tools.

Table 13–1 suggests that a firm's position on the strategic grid not only influences its IT planning needs, but has numerous other implications, including the role of the executive steering committee, the placement of IT in the organization, the appropriate IT management control system, and so on. Further, since organizational units within a company may be in different quadrants of the grid, the planning, organization, and control approaches suitable for one unit may be inappropriate for another. Finally, an IT planning approach that is suitable at one time may be totally wrong if the firm's position on the grid changes.

IT PLANNING AND CORPORATE STRATEGY

As noted in earlier chapters, IT has been a very sharp competitive weapon for a number of organizations and has significantly altered the firms' competitive postures. The extent to which it can be used competitively

FIGURE 13–3 Operational Dependence Questionnaire[a]

1. Impact of a one-hour shutdown at main center
   Major operational disruption in customer service, plant shutdown, groups of staff totally idle.
   Inconvenient, but core business activities continue unimpaired.
   Essentially negligible.
2. Impact of two-to three-week total shutdown at main center
   Almost fatal; no ready source of backup.
   Major external visibility; major revenue shortfall or additional costs.
   Expensive; core processes can be preserved at some cost and at reduced quality levels.
   Minimal; fully acceptable tested backup procedures exist; incremental costs manageable; transition costs acceptable.
3. Costs of IT as percent of total corporate costs
   Over 10%.
   2%–10%.
   Under 2%.
4. Operating systems
   Operating system software totally customized and maintained internally.
   Major reliance on vendor-supplied software but significant internal enhancements.
   Almost total reliance on standard vendor package.
5. Labor
   Data center work force organized; history of strikes.
   Nonunionized work force; either inexperienced and/or low morale.
   Unorganized work force; high morale.
6. Quality control—criticalness of processing errors
   Major external exposure.
   Modest external exposure.
   Irritating; modest consequence.
7. Number of operationally critical on-line systems or batch systems
   10 or more.
   3–5.
   0–2.
8. Dispersion of critical systems
   One location.
   Two to three installations.
   Run by multiple departments; geographic dispersion of processing.
9. Ease of recovery after six-hour failure
   Three to four days; heavy workload, critical system.
   12–24 hours; critical systems.
   Negligible; almost instantaneous.
10. Recovery after quality control failure
    Time-consuming, expensive; many interrelated systems.
    Some disruption and expense.
    Relatively quick; damage well contained.
11. Feasibility of coping manually, 80%–20% basis (i.e., handling 20% of the transactions that have 80% of the value)
    Impossible.
    Somewhat possible.
    Relatively easy.

[a]First answer to each question indicates great operational vulnerability; last answer indicates low operational vulnerability.

TABLE 13–1 Managerial Strategies for "Support" and "Strategic" Companies

Factor	"Support" Company	"Strategic" Company
Steering committee	Middle-level management membership. Existence of committee is less critical.	Active senior management involvement. Committee is key.
Planning	Less urgent. Mistakes in resource allocation not fatal.	Critical. Must link to corporate strategy. Careful attention to resource allocation is vital.
Project portfolio risk profile	Avoid high-risk projects because of constrained benefits. A poor place for corporate strategic gambles.	Some high-risk, high-potential-benefit projects are appropriate if possibility exists to gain strategic advantage.
IT capacity management	Can be managed in a looser way. Operational headaches are less severe.	Critical to manage. Must leave slack.
IT management reporting level	Can be low.	Should be very high.
Technical innovation	A conservative posture one to two years behind state of art is appropriate.	Critical to stay current and fund R&D. Competitor can gain advantage.
User involvement and control over system	Lower priority. Less heated debate.	Very high priority. Often emotional.
Charge-out system	Managed cost center is viable. Charge-out is less critical and less emotional.	Critical that it be sensitively designed.
Expense control	System modernization and development expenses are postponable in time of crisis.	Effectiveness is key. Must keep applications up to date; save money other places.
Uneven performance of IT management	Time is available to resolve it.	Serious and immediately actionable.

influences how a firm should think about and plan IT. Of particular importance is the firm's *underlying basis of competitive strength*.

Generic Competitive Strategies and IT Role

Michael Porter's book *Competitive Strategy*[3] provides a framework for thinking about this. Porter suggests that there are three generic strategies a firm can adopt. We mentioned them briefly in Chapter 3 and

---

[3] Michael Porter, *Competitive Strategy: Techniques for Analyzing Industries and Competitors* (New York: Free Press, 1985).

describe them here in more detail as they relate to IT as a component of corporate strategy.

Strategy 1: Be the Low-Cost Producer. This strategy is appropriate for a standardized product. Significant profit and market-share increases come from driving operating costs significantly below those of the competition. IT offers strategic value in this environment *if* it can:

1. Permit reductions in production and clerical staffs. This will reduce the cost per unit by lowering labor costs.
2. Permit fuller utilization of manufacturing facilities by better scheduling and other means. Less fixed-asset expense will be attached to the cost per unit.
3. Allow significant reductions in inventory, accounts receivable, and so forth. That is, reduce interest costs and facilities costs.
4. Provide better utilization of materials and lower overall costs by reducing waste. Use of lower-grade materials is possible in settings where quality degradation is not an issue.
5. Permit customer-perceived value-added differentiation along one or more aspects of the value chain, thus changing the rules of competition.

If the firm's manufacturing and distribution technologies do not permit these types of savings or offer the opportunity to create the customer-perceived value-added differentiation that can transform the rules of competition, IT is probably not of strategic importance to the firm's long-term competitive posture. Consequently, close, sustained linkage between the IT and corporate planning processes would not be essential. However, in this world of fast-moving technology an intense study should be undertaken every four to five years to revalidate this.

Strategy 2: Produce a Unique, Differentiated Product. This differentiation can occur along a number of dimensions such as quality, special design features, availability, and special services that offer end-consumer value. IT offers strategic value to this corporate environment *if* it:

1. Is a significant component of either the product or key aspects of the firm's value chain—hence an important, distinguishable feature. Banks, brokerage houses, and credit card operations all compete on IT-based service differentiation; operations, inbound logistics, outbound logistics, and after-sales service each have strong IT components.
2. Can significantly reduce the lead time for product development, customization, and delivery. In many industries today computer-aided design/computer-aided manufacturing (CAD/CAM) provides this advantage.

3. Can permit customization of a product to the customer's specific needs in a way not possible before. This is seen in the use of CAD/CAM in producing such made-to-order specialized-textile items as men's suits.
4. Can provide a visibly higher and unique level of customer service and need satisfaction that can be built into the end price. An example of this is special-order inquiry status for key items.

If IT cannot produce unique features for firms and business units competing in this way (or deliver such massive cost reductions as to change the rules of competition), it is unlikely to have strategic impact on the firm's ability to achieve long-term competitive position. Accordingly, a close linkage between IT planning and corporate planning will not be essential on an ongoing basis. Again, a study should be undertaken every several years to validate this.

Strategy 3: Identify and Fill the Needs of Specialized Markets. Such a market might be a geographic region or a cluster of very specialized end-user needs. IT plays a strategic role for this type of firm *if:*

1. IT permits better identification of special areas of customer need and unevenness in the market through collection and analyses of company or industry sales databases to spot unusual trends. Micro-marketing in a variety of industries such as food, credit cards, and clothing has enabled firms to gain significant advantage by tailoring product performance and mix features to very specific submarkets with great success. Firms that have not reacted have felt considerable pain.
2. The firm's outputs are IT-intensive products or products whose end features can be modified by IT customization to specialized needs.

Again, this analysis gives important insight into how close the link between corporate planning and IT should be.

Summary.   These paragraphs suggest that:

1. The competitive position of a business unit and its generic business strategy profoundly influence how intensely the firm should engage in planning for potential IT investments. Key inputs to the strategic/turnaround/factory/support categorizations flow from analysis of the firm's competitive position and underlying bases of advantage.
2. The business units within a firm may have very different competitive positions in their sector and thus have quite different generic competitive strategies. Consequently, no single approach is likely to be appropriate for planning IT's contribution and role in each business unit.
3. Since competitive position, competitive strategy, and technology all change over time, a long-term approach to IT planning that does not vary in response to such changes is almost always inappropriate.

Corporate Environmental Factors that Influence Planning

Research has identified four corporate environmental factors that influence how IT planning must be structured in order to improve the likelihood of success.[4]

Perceived Importance and Status of the Systems Manager.   The IT manager's status must align with the role that IT plays, or *should* play, in the overall operation and strategy-formulating process of the company. In an environment where IT has strategic or turnaround importance, a low-status IT manager (low status in reporting level and/or compensation) has difficulty getting the necessary information from general management in the planning process. If the corporate communication culture (style) at the top is informal, this low status can be fatal, as the IT manager will be outside the key communication loop. If the corporate culture is more formal, development and management of appropriate committees and other formal processes can significantly alleviate this potential problem.

In a company where IT is and should be serving a support function, lower status is appropriate for the IT director, and less effort needs to be made to assure alignment of IT and corporate strategy. A lower level of investment (in dollars and type of staff) in IT planning is also appropriate for such situations. These factors are apparent in the comments of a director of strategic planning for a large process-manufacturing company: "We relate to IT by giving them insight on the corporate goals and the elements and forms of a good planning system. Because of their role in the company, we do not solicit feedback from them as to 'the art of the possible.' The nature of their operation is such that they can provide no useful input to decisions of corporate strategy."

Physical Proximity of the Systems Group and the General Management Team.   In an organization where many important decisions are made informally in ad hoc sessions and where IT has strategic or turnaround importance, key IT management staff should be physically close to the senior line manager. (Their offices should be nearby.) Regardless of the systems manager's status, being an active member of the team in this type of organization is difficult when one is geographically distant from the other members of the team. According to a manager in one such company, "The people who are around when a problem surfaces are the ones who solve it. We don't wait to round up the missing bodies." When the prevailing management culture is more formal, physical proximity is less important. In these situations formal

---

[4]Pyburn, "Information Systems Planning" (see footnote 1).

written communications and scheduled formal meetings largely replace the informal give-and-take.

In informal organizations in which IT is "strategic" or "turnaround," it is critical that the IT managers, and preferably a small staff, be at corporate headquarters, even if their systems development groups must be located many miles away. For "support" and "factory" organizations with informal cultures, location at corporate headquarters is much less critical.

Corporate Culture and Management Style. In an organization where the management culture is characterized as "low key and informal" and the relationship between the IT manager and senior management is informal and personal, formal IT planning procedures do not appear to be critical to effective planning. Development of this relationship is typically assisted by geographic proximity and the IT manager's status. As an organization becomes more formal, however, disciplined IT planning becomes more significant, even in a systems environment that is not highly strategic.

Organizational Size and Complexity. As organizations increase in size and complexity and as IT applications grow larger and more complex, formal planning processes help to ensure the kind of broad-based dialogue that is essential to the development of an integrated vision of IT. This relates to the previous comments concerning management culture and style, because greater size and complexity typically necessitate more formal practices. If the business unit size is small and relatively simple, formal planning approaches are less critical, irrespective of other factors. Similarly, for a smaller business unit where the systems environment is primarily "support," IT planning can safely be more informal. However, as the portfolio of work increases in size and integration across user areas, planning must be more disciplined and formal.

In aggregate these corporate environmental items explain why recommendations on how to do IT planning "in general" almost always are too inflexible for a specific firm. Even within a firm, these issues often force considerable diversity of practice between organization units.

An Example. Here is an example that illustrates how these issues have shaped the planning process in a billion-dollar manufacturing organization.

Key aspects of the corporate IT environment include:

1. The company has a medium-sized corporate IT facility and stand-alone IT facilities of some significant size in its six U.S. divisions. The divisional IT facilities report "straight-line" to their respective divisions

and "dotted-line" to the corporate IT function. The corporate IT group is part of a cluster of corporate staff activities, and considerable power has traditionally been located at the corporate level.

2. The corporate planning activity reports to the vice president of corporate IT. In addition, this officer has enjoyed a long personal and professional relationship with both the chairman of the board and the CEO, and the management culture of the company is informal. Responsibility for IT was initially given to him because the number of operational and developmental problems had reached crisis proportions. Under normal circumstances IT has had a "support" role, but these difficulties had pushed the firm into the "turnaround" category.

3. The closeness of relationships between the division general managers and their IT managers varies widely. The size of the divisions' application portfolios in relation to their overall size also varies considerably, with IT activities playing a more significant role in some divisions than in others.

IT planning at the divisional level begins when the corporate IT group gives them some rather loose guidelines concerning technological direction. It culminates in the preparation of a division IT plan. The planning processes and dialogues vary widely from division to division in terms of line manager involvement. In some divisions the line managers are intimately involved in the process of developing the plan, and the division general manager invests considerable time in final review and modification. In other divisions the relationship is not so close. IT plans are developed almost entirely by the IT organization, and review by general management is very limited. These differences seem to reflect the respective contributions of IT to the strategic functioning of the individual divisions.

Critical to the IT planning process is an annual three-day meeting of the vice president of corporate IT and his key staff, where the divisional IT managers present their plans. The vice president of corporate IT plays a major role in these sessions, as he critiques and suggests modifications to the plans to ensure their fit with corporate objectives. His thorough understanding of the corporation's plans, the thinking of the divisional general managers, and the thinking of the chairman and president enable him to immediately spot shortfalls in IT plans, especially in those of divisions with weak IT–line management relationships.

As a result, IT plans emerge that fit the real business needs of the organization, and the IT activity is well regarded. A set of planning processes that might lead to disaster in other settings has worked well here because of the special qualities of the vice president of corporate IT and style of communication between him and general management that is appropriate for this firm's culture.

SUMMARY

Research evidence continues to show a correlation between effective IT planning and user perception of effective IT activity. Effective execution of IT planning, however, has been found to be far more subtle and complex than envisioned by earlier authors. In addition to generating new ideas, a major role of the IT planning process is to stimulate discussion and exchange of insights between the specialists and the users. Effectively managed, it is an important element in averting potential conflicts in the firm.

The absence of this planning process can lead to enormous communication problems. A financial institution that we studied, for example, attempted at least four different approaches to IT planning over a six-year period. Each was started with great fanfare and with different staffs and organizations, and each limped to a halt. However, when the firm abandoned its planning efforts, deep and ultimately irreconcilable differences arose between IT and the user organization. Communicating viewpoints and discussing problems and potential opportunities may be as important as selecting appropriate projects.

In this context we conclude that:

1. Organizations in which IT activity is integral to corporate strategy implementation have a special need to build links between IT and the corporate strategy formulation process. Complex to implement, this requires dialogue and resolution along many dimensions. Key aspects of the dialogue are
   :a. Testing elements of corporate strategy to ensure that they are possible within the existing IT resource constraints and capabilities. On some occasions the resources needed are obtainable; in other settings resources are unavailable, and painful readjustments must be made. Conversely, it is important that the potentials of new technologies are well understood by the formulators of corporate strategy, because they may suggest new ways of operating.
   b. Transfer of planning and strategy-formulation skills to the IT function.
   c. Ensuring long-term availability of appropriate IT resources.

   In "support" and "factory" settings such linkage is less critical. Over time the nature of this linkage may appropriately change as the firm's strategic IT mission evolves.
2. As an organization grows in size, systems complexity, and formality, IT planning must be directly assigned to someone in order to retain focus and avoid the risk of significant pieces "dropping between the cracks." The job is subtle and complex. A strong set of enabling and communication skills is critical if the planner is to relate to all

individuals and units affected by this technology and cope with their differing familiarity with it. Ensuring the involvement of IT staff and users for both inputs and conclusions is key. The great danger is that planners will define the task with more of a *doing* orientation than an *enabling* one and inappropriately interpose their own priorities and understandings. To overcome this problem, many organizations define this job as a transitional one, rather than a career one.

3. "Planned clutter" in the planning approach is appropriate, because the company's applications portfolio should contain *technologies* in different *phases* with different *strategic payouts* to different *units* of the firm at different *times*. While it may seem superficially attractive and orderly to plan all technologies for all business units at the same level of detail and schedule, in reality this would be inappropriate.

4. IT planning must be tailored to the realities of the organization's environment. Importance and status of the IT manager, physical placement of senior IT staff in relation to general management, corporate culture and management style, and organization size and complexity all influence how IT planning should be carried out.

5. The planning process must incorporate and integrate a broad range of technologies—internal and external electronic communications, data processing, image processing, personal computers, ...

Case 13–1

CHILD WORLD, INC.: INFORMATION TECHNOLOGY PLANNING

A profitable 1986 Christmas season marked the end of the chronic stockout problems that had plagued Child World's 134-store network of "toy supermarkets." Child World's success followed the chain's strategic evolution from a closely held group of children's furniture stores to a finely tuned "retail machine" after its acquisition by Cole National in early 1981.

Child World President Gilbert Wachsman felt that, as relative latecomers to the use of computers, Child World was able to move more quickly to specific targets. "Merchandising is the heart and soul of a retail company, demanding accurate product selection and rapid and decisive response to the market. For these activities to exist, Child World needs information systems," he asserted. Wachsman pointed to new systems for automated product replenishment and dynamic postreceipt allocation of inventory to stores. An electronic mail system linked the company's six distribution centers with headquarters in Avon, Massachusetts, about 20 miles south of Boston. In Child World's newly created Marketing Services Department, computer-aided design technology was used for store layouts and merchandise presentation diagrams, and data for competitive analysis were being retrieved from an advanced database management system installed on a powerful microcomputer. Bob Antall, Child World's vice president of MIS, felt that their portfolio of large-scale, high-volume computer systems was carefully aligned with the firm's strategic goals, and saw new opportunities for an information

technology-based preemptive strike. A study with AT&T had identified, among other communications-based opportunities, "nonstore shopping" (consumer access via catalog, telephone, etc.) as a potential strategic application. A proponent of nonstore shopping, Antall was ready to provide leadership.[1]

The Era of the Toy Supermarket

The toy industry was becoming more dynamic in response to changes in consumption patterns. Once, virtually all operating income had been generated in the fourth (Christmas) quarter, but toy supermarkets such as Child World were becoming profitable year round via aggressive merchandising and marketing of basic products and predicting and acquiring "hot" products for the Christmas season. In the spring of 1987, market observers noted that "hot products for Christmas 1987 will surface later than in the past. There is no consensus at the moment over which product and/or category will drive the business." Toy industry sales increased 50 percent from 1981 to 1986, while Child World sales increased 250 percent. By Christmas of 1986, the leading four toy supermarkets had about 22 percent of

---

[1]See *Child World, Inc.* case 9-582-053, for industry background and Child World history to 1981.

This case was prepared as the basis for class discussion rather than to illustrate either effective or ineffective handling of an administrative situation.

that year's $14 billion toy market, and increased their share to 27 percent of $15 billion the following year (see Tables 1 and 2). Analysts expected the supermarket share of the toy market to reach 35 percent by 1988. The market losers were catalogers, department stores (such as Bloomingdale's, which closed its toy department in 1983 in response to falling margins), and the weaker of the full-line discounters.

Toys "R" Us, which originated the toy supermarket concept, dominated toy retailing with sales larger than the combined sales of the next 10 toy supermarket chains. Child World's Chairman Dennis H. Barron once commented about Toys "R" Us, "They're not really our competitors, they're our idols." In recent years, Child World had homed in on an everyday low-price strategy, selling popular products such as Ohio Art's *Animator* (a state-of-the-art version of *Etch-A-Sketch*) at $49.99 when the product was priced between $54.99 and $80.00 in other stores.

Industry surveys indicated that consumers increasingly preferred discount outlets and toy supermarkets as sources for toys, and purchases of multiple items were becoming the normal pattern. Toy prices were increasing sharply: the maximum toy price of $9.99 was outdated, and the new upper limit was $25 or more for conventional toys.

In 1976, Atari and others had moved high-technology toys into the elite market niche formerly occupied by toy trains. By 1987, "interactive" toys in the $50 to $250 range had expanded this niche.

Sophisticated media marketing was used to precisely shape the tastes of the decision makers: "Saturday morning television and the consumer's children are transforming the toy business from a staple to a fashion industry similar to apparel, in which 'Mr. T' roller skates won't make money after the show goes off the air, even though they are great for skating," said Child World Executive Vice President and Chief Financial Officer Dick Ryan. Ryan also felt that "trends toward celebrity licensing and peer networking make goods more vulnerable to obsolescence, thus increasing risk."

These changes had a powerful impact on marketing, merchandising, and distribution management systems in the industry. Logistics was a particularly difficult problem because the unit price of the average toy left little margin for error. Typically, the combined capacities of stores and distribution centers were only a fraction of Christmas-quarter sales volumes, and "controlling the cube" (the volume of goods at each step from initiation of the purchase order through placing goods on the shelves) was a critical

TABLE 1 Comparing Toy Supermarkets—Year End, 1987

Chain	Sales (millions)		Number of Stores	Total Sales Area (millions of square feet)
	1986	*1987*		
Toys "R" Us	$1,976	$2,434	338	6,725
Child World	513	629	134	3,025
Kay-Bee	401	505	636	2,044
Lionel Leisure	246	272	68	1,624

Source: *Discount Store News.*

TABLE 2   Child World Performance 1981–87 ($ × 1,000)

Data:	1981	1982	1983	1984	1985	1986	1987 (budget)
Net Sales	$178,220	$220,347	$283,161	$360,001	$435,470	$513,148	$628,834
Gross Margin	51,663	70,226	85,334	108,640	135,773	157,612	189,888
Income Before Taxes	567	10,605	13,303	19,375	19,058	20,802	26,012
Number of Stores (End)	68	71	79	90	104	121	134
Market Share	1.8%	2.0%	2.4%	2.8%	3.3%	3.7%	4.2%

success factor. If warehouse capacity was not managed well, either excess warehouse space or supply bottlenecks could result.

Child World Since 1981

Management Changes
From the time of its founding in 1956, Child World's style had been opportunistic. The company built stores on cheaply acquired real estate, gave buyers wide latitude to exercise individual business philosophies, and did not develop strong management or control systems.

After Cole National's 1981 purchase, management strengthened the financial staff, installed new financial planning and control disciplines, redesigned and increased the number of stores, then focused on accurately stocking them in response to consumer tastes and to meet seasonal demand. Cole itself was purchased in a management leveraged buy-out in September 1984. In August 1985, Child World sold publicly 18.5 percent of its common stock, some 2.125 million shares, at $16.75 per share, and earmarked the proceeds for inventory, store expansion, and remodeling.

Store Operations
Distinctive castle towers crowned newer Child World units to assure easy recognition of the 36,000-square-foot "racetrack" stores, usually located near a major enclosed shopping mall. (All Child World stores were east of the Mississippi River. Those in the Midwest were operated under the "Children's Palace" marque.) The term "racetrack" referred to an extra-wide aisle within the brightly colored 25,000-square-foot selling space that was designed to help consumers navigate the mixed merchandise groupings. Products were arranged on 18-foot-tall shelves by type (e.g., bicycles, books); by age (e.g., baby, preschool); and by manufacturer (e.g., Fisher-Price, Kenner). The four racetrack corners were anchored by baby furniture, bikes, books, and seasonal products such as swimming pools. A computer and electronics section was located near the registers and information desk at the front of the store. The cash registers were linked to Child World headquarters via a point-of-sale (POS) network.

Toys formed the bulk of the merchandise, with a small sports department. Child World did not sell children's apparel. Product price tags jutted prominently from the shelves, and many rows of each item were stacked side by side, with featured products on the ends of the broad aisles. New stores tended to open at or above company average sales volume.

Marketing
In 1986, Child World strengthened marketing and hired a new vice president, Linda Goodman, who articulated Child World's promotional strategy:

We are instilling a sense of immediacy through circulars, our primary advertising vehicle, while we aggressively promote an everyday low-price image via TV and newspapers. When I first arrived, Bob Antall and I spent a lot of time together figuring out what we needed and customizing reports. Marketing is now heavily automated, and has the ability to retrieve quality information and take instant action.

Assortment planning and store layout are moving more and more to the Plan-O-Gram, a microcomputer-based software tool that models merchandise presentation and helps optimize space utilization. Next to people and inventory, real estate is our most precious commodity.

Merchandising

The 1985 Christmas season was difficult for most retailers, and holdover inventory was a problem throughout the toy industry. The sharp fall in Cabbage Patch doll business, coupled with declines in sales of home computer hardware and entertainment software, left Child World with a serious inventory problem.

Using computerized tools, the firm embarked on an aggressive program to reshape inventory resources during 1986. Raw sales data were acquired via Child World's point-of-sale network and fed to IBM's INFOREM (a tool used for sales analysis) to help spot trends. Buyers could then get wanted products before they became in short supply. It would also increase profits on basic items and allow Child World to work down unwanted inventory. "Our buyers evolved from skeptics to believers as predictions started to come true," reported Merchandising Vice President Stanley Walsh.

Toy supplies were dominated by 10 vendors, and popular items could be obtained only by buying (and thus warehousing) early in the cycle, or by close cooperation between suppliers and retailers. Increased confidence in Child World's performance translated directly into profit potential because toy manufacturers, ever wary of unsold merchandise, were reluctant to commit to produce and ship the quantities of goods needed to meet ambitious sales targets. According to one major vendor, in 1986, Child World had been the first to identify key merchandise trends.

The 1987 Toy Fair also marked an important step toward putting in place strategic linkages with key suppliers. Fisher-Price, a conservative supplier with a major share of the quality toy market, indicated its willingness to link Child World to their well-developed systems to provide Child World with current production data. This data sharing was a key component in a broader cooperative agreement involving pricing, advertising, and access to up-to-date Child World sales information.

Distribution

Child World added three distribution centers between 1981 and 1986 to keep pace with the growth in retail outlets. Toys "R" Us had distribution centers serving an average of 10 stores each, versus 25 for Child World.

"The peak sales period for toys is short, and toy packaging is bulky relative to product value. The transportation network between our vendors and the store must have high peak throughput capacity, with low unit costs for handling, warehousing, and transportation," reported Ronald Hidalgo, manager of Child World's Avon distribution center. ["Throughput" is a measure of flow; the physical and systems capacity to receive products from the manufacturers, hold them until needed by the stores, and ship them to the correct retail outlet.] Because the total distribution center capacity was less than half of store needs for the Christmas season, product logistics were critical.

Distribution used a fleet of leased trucks for delivery to the stores. The Avon distribution center had five receiving docks for goods arriving by rail, and 25 docks that could be allocated to trucks carrying incoming or outgoing goods. Vendors packed products to Child World specifications, and drivers delivering to Avon unloaded goods according to instructions provided on arrival. Modified forklifts and custom pallets were used for some products.

Batch computer reports allowed a "cross-docking" dispatcher to compare received products to store needs: needed goods were shipped to stores overnight. A more dynamic inventory allocation system to support same-day shipping was in the design stages. Computer systems were used to validate receipt and shipping transactions, communicate between process steps, and monitor space utilization, inventory shrinkage, and employee productivity.

Management Information Systems

By early 1987, Child World MIS executives felt they were becoming independent of the day-to-day support that characterized the early period of the Cole takeover. In 1984, systems were late, computer operations were unable to provide an adequate level of service, and communications with functional areas were in disarray. New leadership, increased resources and reorganization had turned MIS around. Bob Antall's predecessor had laid some of the groundwork for recovery, but was soon promoted by Cole and joined the parent company.

Having left a Midwestern drug chain to join Child World, Antall had moved quickly to establish needed service level and project management disciplines, and to stabilize hardware and software architectures to provide a sound base for the firm's growth to a billion dollar company. In 1984, he informed management of the urgent need to upgrade MIS support systems by adding a more powerful operating system to improve on-line applications availability and resource utilization, and a database management system for the firm's growing data resources.

By Christmas of 1986, some departments had microcomputers linked to the central computer, and easy-to-use mainframe tools for inquiries, analyses, and reports were installed. Antall established a support unit to help solve technical problems and to facilitate end-user access to data. Office automation was introduced. Avon headquarters acquired a network of word processing units, and electronic mail linked headquarters departments with regional distribution centers. New applications to improve merchandising and distribution performance had been implemented, based on sales transaction data captured at the point of sale (POS). These new functions were established with a budget limited to slightly less than 1 percent of sales in 1984, and growing at a slightly lower rate.

As Child World's maturing strategic planning process became linked with tactical and operational planning, information technology (IT) was tied into critical issues and action plans. IT planning matured from a 1982 "wish list" to the 48-page 1986 plan detailing MIS links with corporate strategy and establishing the technology and personnel and financial resources needs over time.

Planning at Child World

Corporate Strategy

Child World's annual planning process produced four baseline plans: the two half-year operating plans (spring and fall) demanded by the seasonal business cycle; a one-year capital budget (with projections for the second year) to support operating plans; and an annual strategic plan to address long-term issues. Functional plans, such as the MIS Strategic Systems Plan, were linked to the baseline plans. Most planning was performed by line managers invited to Executive Committee meetings, rather than by staff.

The 15-page 1986 strategic plan defined the company's mission, highlighted strengths, weaknesses, opportunities, and threats (SWOT), and identified three "critical issues": increase sales per store; increase the number of stores to increase leverage from overhead and support expenses; and convert more sales dollars to profit. Information systems applications were explicitly identified in support of the latter issue only. These issues were refined into two or three strategic targets for each issue, supported by about 30 clearly defined tactics for integration into the two operating plans and the capital budget.

Linking I/S Plans

Strategies were refined and tactics developed in planning meetings called "Vision Discussions" among the executive committee. CFO Ryan explained: "One of our visions was that 'merchandise will be restocked by an invisible hand as the customer takes it off the shelf.' The resulting discussion characterized the physical and information flows that would be required to do this, and this appeared in Antall's MIS plan as an application to dynamically reallocate product arriving at the distribution center to stores on the same day."

The IT Planning Process

In January of 1985, Bob Antall attended an AT&T-sponsored seminar in Boston that described Information Technology Management (ITM), a methodology to identify and evaluate strategic IT opportunities. The nine-step ITM process combined industry and competitive analysis, based largely on frameworks developed by Michael Porter of the Harvard Business School, with a structured search for IT applications that would achieve competitive advantage. ITM also included SIX + ^{SM}, a Strategic Information Exchange Planning Service that used an AT&T proprietary computer model to match infor-

mation technologies with business information flows. Although some of the individual techniques used in the ITM process were not new, their combination by AT&T into a single connected process was unique.

After the ITM seminar, Antall asked Lisa Radomsky, the AT&T sales representative to Child World, to work with him to implement ITM. Radomsky called Patsy O'Grady, a consultant at AT&T's Regional Technical Center in White Plains, New York, and together the two developed a plan for an ITM study at Child World. In June, Radomsky began gathering data through interviews and library research. As she completed each phase of the ITM process, Radomsky reported the results to O'Grady, who analyzed the information and prepared capsule summaries.

The first phase was a description of Child World's business and an industry analysis. The latter used Porter's "five forces" model and attempted to quantify the impact of each force. A strategic analysis came next, leading to summary statements of Child World's strategy and competitive scope. Individual elements of the strategic environment—target markets, product policy, cost position, etc.—were analyzed in more detail. The third phase included an analysis of Child World's value system and value chain, again using frameworks of Michael Porter.

With this environmental and strategic profile, Radomsky and O'Grady moved into phase four of ITM—identify and prioritize strategic opportunities for information technology. The first step identified internal and external linkages of activities outlined in the value chain that could have strategic potential for Child World. Next, the opportunities associated with these linkages were described in detail and their probable impact assessed. For example, Radomsky wrote:

Opportunity: Catalog Shopping. Create a new sales channel for Child World, providing access to consumers who do not live near a Child World store, thus creating additional opportunities to sell Child World merchandise.

Impact: First and foremost, increased sales would result, etc.

O'Grady and Radomsky prepared an interim report for Child World management. "By this time," O'Grady said later, "Child World management was up to speed on IT and clearly understood the work we had done so far. From AT&T's point of view, we had increased our visibility and rapport by tailoring our sales process to customer needs. We needed to make sure that the linkages were truly strategic—a judgment call that requires input from top management." O'Grady presented the results to top management in October and Child World management agreed to pursue the recommendations.

During this time, the company sponsored an additional study by AT&T. AT&T's SIX+ Planning Service was a tool to help clients exploit new technology opportunities for effective information exchange. The SIX+ Planning Service began with a series of workshops over a period of two days that identified about 300 information flows within various functions at Child World. Each flow was profiled in terms of over 100 qualitative and quantitative information-exchange requirements. This was fed into a computer model. In addition to assessing the support quality of current technologies used for these information flows, the computer model matched the flows with new and emerging support technologies that presented potential new opportunities to enhance the company's external and internal information exchange. For Child World, electronic mail with document-exchange capabilities, voice mail and messaging, packet switching, and a centralized inbound/outbound communications center were recommended. Actual technology proposals that fit these applications

were the responsibility of Brian McGillicuddy, Radomsky's successor as the AT&T account executive to Child World.

Laying New Track for the Retail Machine

In preparation for the first 1987 Vision Discussion, Bob Antall reviewed the AT&T recommendations. Five strategic opportunities for the application of information technology had been identified:

Market Intelligence: Capture of detailed customer information, development of a database linking attributes of the consumer, purchases and stores over time, and providing access to this information to suppliers.

Electronic Data Interchange: Transmission of purchase order and verification information to increase leverage with suppliers.

Nonstore Shopping: Creation of a new sales channel to provide access to consumers who do not live in a Child World store area.

Electronic Shopping Aid: Provision of an automated in-store shopping directory to suggest selections based on attributes of the child.

Vendor Ticketing: Have vendors attach Child World price tickets to merchandise, saving labor and paving the way for a transition to Universal Product Codes.

Antall wondered how to gain management support for a project to explore nonstore shopping as a new market channel. He believed that the other Child World executives would agree that the continued growth of the firm rested on its ability to make long-term changes in the way operating departments worked, but nonstore shopping was an entirely new business. While he knew the firm's lack of experience in this arena increased the risk of failure, he felt the basic concept was sound if the risks could be contained.

Another risk factor that affected every proposal was the relatively small size of Child World's MIS staff and the scarcity of good technical people in the Boston area. Recruiting sufficient technical resources to convert to the planned operating system had recently been a problem, and the firm's migration to database technology would absorb all slack MIS resources over the next year or so. Child World did not yet have the MIS technical infrastructure required to succeed in a strategic development effort based on the new technologies identified in the study. Antall was confident that this risk was manageable, but he knew he would have to convince the Executive Committee.

The more he thought about the study, the more risks he saw. Marketing people had no prior experience with the electronic shopping aid, the nonstore shopping opportunity, or the market intelligence application, nor was he sure that he could convince Goodman to pull any of her top people off to support the development process. Without support from both Marketing and Merchandising, Antall didn't think these applications would generate enough added sales to cover their costs.

Although Antall thought the proposed electronic linkage between Child World and the suppliers was a great concept and had strongly supported it, one aspect of the project bothered him. Could Child World prevent sensitive sales information from finding its way, in a conveniently machine-readable format, to Child World's competitors? On a broader scale, how would competitors react to each of Child World's new electronic initiatives, and how could the Executive Committee best evaluate these risks against those of not taking action?

EXHIBIT 1   Child World Organization, 1987

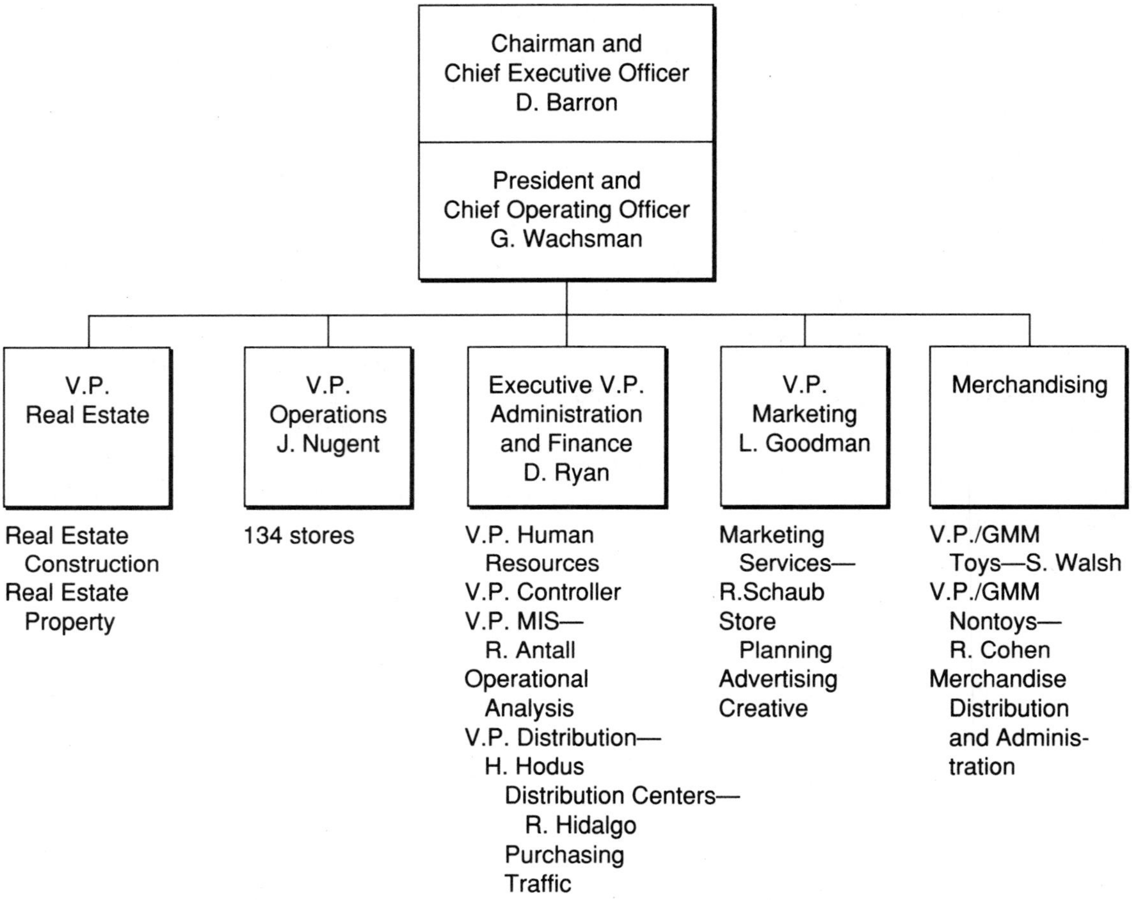

```
                        ┌─────────────────────────┐
                        │  Chairman and           │
                        │  Chief Executive Officer │
                        │  D. Barron              │
                        ├─────────────────────────┤
                        │  President and          │
                        │  Chief Operating Officer │
                        │  G. Wachsman            │
                        └─────────────────────────┘
```

V.P. Real Estate	V.P. Operations J. Nugent	Executive V.P. Administration and Finance D. Ryan	V.P. Marketing L. Goodman	Merchandising

Real Estate
  Construction
Real Estate
  Property
	134 stores	V.P. Human
		  Resources
		V.P. Controller
		V.P. MIS—
		  R. Antall
		Operational
		  Analysis
		V.P. Distribution—
		  H. Hodus
		    Distribution Centers—
		    R. Hidalgo
		  Purchasing
		  Traffic
			Marketing
			  Services—
			R.Schaub
			Store
			  Planning
			Advertising
			Creative
				V.P./GMM
				  Toys—S. Walsh
				V.P./GMM
				  Nontoys—
				  R. Cohen
				Merchandise
				  Distribution
				  and Adminis-
				  tration

EXHIBIT 2   Consolidated Balance Sheets

	January 31, 1987	February 1, 1986
Assets		
Current Assets:		
Cash and temporary cash investments	$ 43,467	$ 22,325
Accounts receivable	1,685	2,086
Inventories	178,837	141,183
Prepaid expenses and other	4,626	3,899
Total Current Assets	228,615	169,493
Property and Equipment, at cost:		
Land and buildings	5,600	5,838
Furniture, fixtures and equipment	35,968	26,449
Leasehold improvements	17,058	13,089
	58,626	45,376
Less—accumulated depreciation and amortization	(12,668)	(6,563)
Total Property and Equipment, net	45,958	38,813
Leased Property Under Capital Leases, net	28,875	31,993
Other Assets	543	578
Cost in Excess of Net Assets of Purchased Business, net of accumulated amortization of $4,713 and $2,693, respectively	76,087	78,107
Total Assets	$380,078	$318,984
Liabilities and Stockholders' Equity		
Current Liabilities:		
Current portion of long-term debt	$ 400	$ 100
Current portion of capital lease obligations	1,935	1,769
Accounts payable	129,440	87,536
Accrued liabilities	28,069	20,672
Accrued income taxes	6,992	5,185
Total Current Liabilities	166,836	115,262
Long-Term Debt, less current portion	5,500	5,900
Capital Lease Obligations, less current portion	24,245	26,180
Deferred Income Taxes	1,689	783
Stockholders' Equity:		
Preferred stock—par value $1.00 per share, authorized 5,000,000 shares; no shares issued	—	—
Common stock—par value $.10 per share, authorized 25,000,000 shares; issued and outstanding 11,500,000 shares at January 31, 1987 and February 1, 1986	1,150	1,150
Capital surplus	158,781	158,781
Retained earnings	21,877	10,928
Total Stockholders' Equity	181,808	170,859
Total Liabilities and Stockholders' Equity	$380,078	$318,984

The accompanying notes to consolidated financial statements are an integral part of these balance sheets.

EXHIBIT 3 Selected Financial Data

	The Company			The Predecessor Company (1)	
	52 Weeks Ended Jan. 31, 1987	52 Weeks Ended Feb. 1, 1986	Pro Forma (2) 53 Weeks Ended Feb. 2, 1985	52 Weeks Ended Jan. 28, 1984	Jan. 29, 1983
Income Statement Data:					
Net Sales	$628,834	$513,148	$435,470	$360,001	$283,161
Costs and Expenses:					
Cost of goods sold	438,946	355,536	299,697	251,361	197,827
Operating expenses	148,282	119,862	103,161	81,133	63,717
Depreciation and amortization	11,355	10,177	9,251	5,335	4,925
Total Operating Expenses	598,583	485,575	412,109	337,829	266,469
Income from Operations	30,251	27,573	23,361	22,172	16,692
Interest Expense, net	4,239	6,771	4,303	2,797	3,389
Income Before Income Taxes	26,012	20,802	19,058	19,375	13,303
Provision for Income Taxes	15,063	11,434	10,656	9,377	6,464
Net Income	$ 10,949	$ 9,368	$ 8,402	$ 9,998	$ 6,839
Earnings per Share	$ .95	$ .91	$ .73		
Weighted Average Number of Shares, in thousands	11,500	10,286	11,500		
Dividend Per Share (3)					

EXHIBIT 3 (continued)

| | The Company | | | The Predecessor Company (1) | |
	52 Weeks Ended Jan. 31, 1987	52 Weeks Ended Feb. 1, 1986	Pro Forma (2) 53 Weeks Ended Feb. 2, 1985	52 Weeks Ended Jan. 28, 1984	52 Weeks Ended Jan. 29, 1983
Balance Sheet (at period end):					
Total Assets	$ 380,078	$ 318,984	$ 296,366	$ 181,495	$ 134,547
Long-Term Debt, Including Current Portion	5,900	6,000	6,000	6,000	600
Non-Current Portion of Capital Lease Obligations	24,245	26,180	25,998	26,180	30,198
Stockholders' Equity	181,808	170,859	168,696	59,917	49,395
Other Data:					
Selling Square Footage	3,269,000	2,851,000	2,463,000	2,094,000	1,803,000
Number of Stores	134	119	104	90	79

(1) In September, 1984, CNC Holding Corporation acquired Cole National Corporation (Cole), then the Company's parent. The term "Predecessor Company" refers to the Company, for accounting purposes, prior to the acquisition, which for financial reporting purposes, has been treated as a purchase effective September 22, 1984.

(2) Gives effect to the acquisition, as discussed in Note 1 above, and the sale of common stock in August, 1985 as if they had occurred on January 29, 1984, the beginning of the fiscal year.

(3) In 1985, the Company made a one-time distribution of $40 million to Cole in the form of a dividend, which distribution approximated the accumulated retained earnings of the Company since its acquisition by Cole in fiscal 1980.

EXHIBIT 4   Nonstore Shopping

Nonstore shopping has established roots: rural Americans of another generation cherished the Montgomery Ward and Sears' catalogs (as today's urban generation reviews Sharper Images) for access to new apparel styles, to magazine subscriptions, home accessories, and home and office tools and equipment. Research indicated that home shoppers tended to be female, to have larger than average families and above-average household income.

As communications technology shifted from printed catalogs to electronic media, several new television-based shopping channels emerged, offering close-out merchandise at deeply discounted prices, financial services, and other goods. By mid-1986, one channel, Florida-based Home Shopping Network (HSN), was seen in 8.5 million homes, had 349,000 paid subscribers, and was studying establishing a 24-hour national distribution network.

EXHIBIT 5   MIS Resource Plans

	MIS Personnel Resources: (from 1986 plan)				
Year Ending Feb:	1985*	1986*	1987*	1988	1989
MIS Management	4	4	4	5	5
MIS Support Staff	2	2	3	4	4
Computer Operation	9	10	12	14	16
Production Control	7	7	8	9	10
Technical Support	2	2	3	4	5
Retail Systems	3	3	4	4	4
Telecommunications	0	3	4	5	6
Information Center	15	1	2	3	5
Systems Development	0	7	3	2	0
Data Entry	8	18	18	20	25
Total MIS personnel	50	57	61	70	80
MIS Financial Plan:	$4,152	$4,647	$5,515	$6,549	$7,520
% of Sales	0.9%	0.9%	0.9%	0.8%	0.8%

*Actual Staff Positions

Child World Hardware and Software Tools: 1986

Description	Product	Vendor
Hardware		
Personal computers	PC/XT or AT	IBM
Remote access	leased lines	AT&T
Mainframe	4381	IBM
Minicomputers	S/36	IBM
POS network	9020/9100/751/2152	NCR
Mainframe Systems Software		
Database/dictionary	Datacom/DB-DD	ADR
Query language	Dataquery	ADR
Report generator	Easytrieve Plus	Pansophic
Application generator	IDEAL	ADR
Program librarian	VOLLIE/Librarian	ADR
PC-mainframe link	Omnilink	Online
Operating system	DOS-VSE(MVS/VM planned)	IBM
Mainframe network	VTAM-NCP-SDLC (SNA)	IBM
POS network	nonstandard bisynch	NCR
PC Software		
Spreadsheet	1,2,3	Lotus
Business graphics	1,2,3	Lotus
Word processing	Multimate	Multimate
Database	D-Base III	Ashton-Tate
	R-Base 5000	MicroRim

EXHIBIT 6   Systems Development Priorities, early 1986:

---

1. Merchandise/Distribution Systems
   a. Migration from files to database technology
   b. Sales Forecasting
   c. Shipping Manifest
   d. Warehousing Systems
   e. On-line Receiving
   f. Physical Inventory
   g. Stock Status
   h. Purchase Order Management
   i. Pricing
   j. Assortment Planning
   k. Expansion of Warehouse Network
2. Store Information Systems
   a. In-store Processor
   b. Layaway
   c. Electronic Mail
   d. Payroll/Time Attendance
   e. Labor Scheduling
   f. Check Guarantee
   g. Receiving
3. Financial Systems
   a. Accounts Payable
   b. Invoice Matching
   c. Purchasing Planning
   d. Merchandising Planning
   e. Marketing Information Systems
4. MIS Infrastructure Systems
   a. IDEAL
   b. Job Accounting
   c. VSE to MVS operating systems conversion
   d. VM Operating System

Source: 1986 MIS Strategic Plan.

EXHIBIT 7 Application Projects Priorities, Early 1986

MIS established seven criteria to prioritize applications projects:
1. Consistency with division strategy plan
2. MIS objectives defined by CEO
3. Availability of user/MIS resources
4. ROI/tangible benefits
5. Corporate requirements
6. Intangible requirements
7. Dependencies to other projects/requirements

EXHIBIT 8 Miscellaneous Financial Data

Data	Year:	1981	1982	1983	1984	1985	1986	1987
($ × 1,000)								
Net Sales		$178,220	$220,347	$283,161	$360,001	$435,470	$513,148	$628,834
Gross Margin		51,663	70,226	85,334	108,640	135,773	157,612	189,888
Income Before Tax		567	10,605	13,303	19,375	19,058	20,802	26,018
# of Stores (End)		68	71	79	90	104	121	134
Sales/Store (End)		$2,621	$3,103	$3,584	$4,000	$4,187	$4,241	$4,694
Selling Sq. Footage		1,525,639	1,602,000	1,803,384	2,093,663	2,462,888	2,851,000	3,269,000
Sales/1,000 Sq. Ft.		$117	$138	$157	$172	$177	$180	$192
# Distribution Ctrs		3	3	3	3	4	6	6
Return on Sales (PR)		0.32%	4.81%	4.70%	5.38%	4.38%	4.05%	4.4%

Chapter 14

The IT Business

Previous chapters have presented frameworks for viewing the information technology activity and the functions of IT management. Taken together, the chapters of this book specify in detail how to conduct an IT management audit. This final chapter concludes the book by highlighting the impact of its six major themes:

- Information technology has different strategic importance to different organizations.
- The merging of the computing, telecommunication, and office support technologies into a single whole.
- The importance of organization learning to technology assimilation.
- The shift of make-or-buy decisions toward greater reliance on external sources of software and computing support.
- The continuing validity of the systems life cycle concept.
- The need to balance continuously the pressures of the three constituencies: IT management, user management, and general management.

"THE IT BUSINESS" ANALOGY

We have chosen to view an organization's IT activity as a stand-alone "business within a business" and, in particular, to apply the concepts of marketing-mix analysis. This permits us to develop a synthesis of the concepts of organization, planning, control, and strategy formulation for IT. Within this analogy we will speak of the business's strategy formulation as its "marketing mix," its steering committee as "the board of directors," and its IT director as "the chief executive officer." These items are particularly relevant to the interface between the IT business and its host, or parent, organization—the firm.[1] We will not explain the details of operating strategy, since the general aspects of IT operations management are covered in Chapter 11. Nor do we discuss here the issues of internal accounting and control within the IT organization, as they do not impact directly on the interface between the two businesses. For similar reasons we discuss only those IT organizational issues that deal with external relations of the IT business.

IT is a high-technology, fast-changing industry. A particular "IT business" in this industry may be growing rapidly, remaining more or less steady, or declining. Its "territory" encompasses the development, maintenance, and operation of all information technologies within a firm, regardless of where they are located and to whom they report.

The scope of technologies to be coordinated by the IT business has expanded tremendously as computers, telecommunications, and office support have merged, and its product offerings are exploding into such new consumer areas as electronic mail, editing, and computer-aided design/computer-aided manufacturing. The complexity of implementing projects, the magnitude of work to be done, and the scarcity of human resources have forced it to change from a business that primarily *produced* things to one that *distributes* things; a significant percentage of its work now involves coordinating the acquisition of outside services for use by its customers. This shift has forced major changes in its approach to planning and controls in order to deal effectively with these new products and new sources of supply.

Implicit in this view of the IT business is that, at least at a *policy* level, the overwhelming majority of firms require an integrated perspective and approach to IT. The IT activities include not just the corporate IT center and its directly linked networks, but also standalone PCs, distributed systems development activities, outside software company contracts, computer service bureaus, and so on. Many users of IT services—its customers—possess options to buy services from providers other than the central IT organization—the business within the business.

We believe this analogy is useful for applying management principles and theories to the IT function in a way that generates important insights. Similarly we believe that the analogy we draw between general management and a board of directors is useful in conceptualizing a realistic role for an executive steering committee.

Like all analogies, this one can be pushed too far, and some caution is in order. For example, the financing of the IT business is not analogous to the corporate capital markets, since its capital support comes

---

[1]Throughout this chapter the term *firm* refers to the parent holding company of the IT business.

directly from the firm (with no debt analogy), and its revenues—exclusively in many cases—also come directly from the firm. In many respects, the customer bases of the IT business and the firm are dependent on common files, et cetera, so the customers cannot be treated as entirely independent. Similarly, the IT business is free from many of the legal and governmental constraints on the firm. Other legal and governmental constraints—such as the Equal Employment Opportunity Commission (EEOC), for instance—are placed on it in the context of the firm's total corporate posture, and there is little possibility or need for the IT business to strike an independent posture.

The rest of this chapter is devoted to three topics related to managing the IT business:

- The IT marketing mix.
- The role of the IT board of directors.
- The role of the IT chief executive officer.

THE IT MARKETING MIX

The Products

The IT product line is continuously evolving. Table 14–1 summarizes the key aspects of change. Some of the dynamism of the product line is due to the enormous proliferation of opportunities afforded by the economics of new technology. Other dynamic elements are changing customer needs as a result of ordinary shifts in business and new insights (Phase-2 learning) into how technology can be applied to specific operations.

IT products range in size from very small to enormous in terms of development time and complexity to operate. A large product can have such a lengthy development period that significant uncertainty exists whether it will meet the current customers' needs when it is completed. (Four years—the time needed to rebuild some automobile manufacturing processes—is not uncommon.) The introduction of some products can be delayed with only limited damage. If delays of any magnitude occur in the development of other products, severe damage to consumers (users) will occur. In terms of day-to-day operations, the importance of cost, good response time, quality control, and so on, varies widely.

Product Obsolescence. Product obsolescence is a major headache in the IT business. Products eventually become clumsy, and introducing the necessary enhancements—styling changes—to keep them relevant is increasingly expensive. Eventually major factory retooling is

TABLE 14–1   Changes in IT Product Line

Factor	Focus	
	The Past	*The Future*
Product obsolescence	Developing new products.	Heavy maintenance of old products to meet challenges of obsolescence.
Source	Most products manufactured inside.	Significant percent sourced from outside.
Dominant economic constraint	Capital intensive (hardware; economy of scale).	Personnel intensive (economy of skill).
Product mix	Many large, few medium, many small products.	Some large, many medium, thousands of small products.
Profits/benefits	Good return on investment.	Many projects have intangible benefits.
New-product technologies	New technologies.	New technologies and re-groupings of old ones.
Services	Structured, such as auto-mated accounting and in-ventory control.	Unstructured, such as execu-tive decision support sys-tems and query systems.

necessary. Consumer needs (which can be satisfied by new technologies) and new manufacturing technologies offer significant opportunities for systems enhancements.

Sources, Marketplace Climate.   The method of delivering IT products is shifting as the IT customer makes sourcing decisions. An increasing percentage of IT development expenditures are going to software houses and time-sharing vendors, while production expenditures are being devoted to stand-alone minicomputers and personal computers. Formerly IT was primarily a *developer* and *manufacturer* of products; now it is becoming a significant *distributor* of products manufactured by others, including being a complete distributor in outsourcing situations, such as, the previously mentioned Eastman Kodak and General Dynamics cases. The distributor role involves identifying and evaluating products and professionally evaluating those identified by customers.

IT products run the gamut from those for which the need is clearly, correctly understood by customers (such as point-of-sale terminals) to those for which there is no perceived need and considerable, extended sales efforts must precede a sale. They range from those that are absolutely essential and critical to the customer (inventory control systems, for instance) to those that are desirable but whose purchase is essentially postponable (such as standard databases for spreadsheet files). Obviously, products at the two extremes require quite different sales approaches.

Sourcing decisions are complicated by differences in maturity of IT suppliers. For example, a relatively stable competitive pattern exists among suppliers of large mainframe computers. Conversely, there is much turbulence in the personal computer and office support markets. In fact, there is considerable uncertainty as to which companies will survive and what form their products will have five years from now. A competitive pattern is emerging here, but the AT&T divestiture and cellular innovations will confound the nature of competition for the foreseeable future in telecommunications.

Further, in the past, monopoly control over product delivery gave IT businesses considerable discretion in timing their introductions of new products. The changed climate of competition among suppliers means that IT has lost control over the marketing of new products in many organizations.

Profits/Benefits.   In terms of benefits the products range from those that can be crisply summarized in a return-on-investment (ROI) framework for the customer to those whose benefits are more qualitative and intangible in nature. Again, products at the ends of the spectrum require different marketing approaches. Some products are absolutely structured (certain types of accounting data), while others are tailored to individual tastes and preferences. Further, in many instances a product's complexity and inherent factors that influence quality are not easily comprehended by purchasers. Finally, some products require tailoring during installation. These products need specific field support and distribution staffs.

Implications for Marketing.   This description of IT product characteristics points to the complexity of the IT marketing task by showing that the IT business distributes evolving products distinguished by a wide range of characteristics. In other businesses a strong effort is often made to streamline the product line in order to facilitate economy and efficiency in manufacturing and distribution. The inability to accomplish this in many IT businesses has contributed to turbulence in their management. Too often they are trying to deliver too many products from their traditional monopoly-supplier position with weak promotion, surly sales, and fixation on manufacturing—as opposed to distributing. What works for one set of products may not work for another. Recognizing the need for and implementing a differentiated marketing approach is very difficult, particularly for a medium-sized IT business.

The IT Consumer

Description of the Consumer.   The IT consumer is changing in terms of needs and sophistication. Table 14–2 summarizes important aspects of these changes. After 20 years of working with mature technologies, older consumers have developed a sensitivity to the problems of working within constraints. Many of them are quite unaware of the newer technologies and the enormous behavioral modifications they must make in order to use them properly. They bring their old purchasing habits to the new environment without understanding that it is new. Younger consumers, on the other hand, have close familiarity with personal computing and tend to be intolerant when they are unable to get immediate access to it. They also tend to be naive about the problems of designing and maintaining IT systems that must run on a regular basis. In general, both classes of consumers have major educational needs if they are to become responsible consumers.

The new user-friendly technologies have made the problem more complicated, because many consumers see the opportunity to withdraw from reliance on the IT business and set up their own small business. They are often propelled in this direction by their own entrepreneurs

TABLE 14–2   Changes in IT Consumer Profile

| | Consumers | |
Factor	Older	Younger
Experience with older technologies	Experienced.	Inexperienced.
Attitude toward newer technologies	Leery.	Enthusiastic and unsophisticated (but they do not recognize their lack of sophistication).
Visibility	Identifiable as consumers.	Often unidentifiable as consumers; numerous at all levels in organizations.
Attitude toward IT unit	Willing to accept IT staff as experts.	Many are hostile because they want to develop their own solutions.
Self-confidence	Low confidence in their own abilities (often cautious because of cost).	High confidence in their abilities and judgment (often unwarranted).
Turnover rate	High.	High.

or purchasing agents (that is, decentralized systems analysts) who are long on optimism and short on practical, firsthand expertise and realistic risk assessment.

In this environment, the IT marketing force needs to target new consumers and reach them before they make independent decisions. New application clusters and groups of consumers keep surfacing. The ever changing composition of consumer groups sustains the need for a field sales force. An effective job of educating people does no good if they move on to other assignments and are replaced by people who are unaware of current technologies and the sequence of decisions that led to the present status of the organization.

Firsthand personal computing experience and a barrage of advertising have substantially raised consumers' expectations and their general level of self-confidence in making IT decisions. Unfortunately, this confidence is often misplaced; there seems to be a lack of appreciation for subtle but important nuances and for the IT control practices necessary for a significant probability of success. This also increases the need for sustained direct sales and follow-up.

In today's environment there is an explosion in the number of service alternatives for customers, some of them with very low prices. It is confusing to the end consumers when products essentially similar to those available in-house appear to be available at much lower prices out of house. Great consumer sophistication is needed to identify a *real* IT bargain.

Implications for Marketing.   These factors have substantially complicated the IT marketing effort. An unstable group of consumers with diversified, rapidly changing needs requires a far higher level of direct-selling effort than do consumers without this cluster of characteristics. The need to spend promotion money on a difficult group has been intensified by a low regard for corporate IT in many settings. Consumers who are hostile about the quality of IT support welcome solutions that will carry them as far away as possible from reliance on the central IT business unit. Trained to respond correctly to many of yesterday's technologies, they are inappropriately trained for today's. Underinvestment in the marketing that is necessary for dealing with these realities has been a major cause of dissatisfaction among users.

Costs

Cost Factors.   From a marketing viewpoint, significant changes are occurring in the costs of producing and delivering systems. Table 14–3 identifies some of these changes. On the one hand, the cost of many elements of IT hardware has decreased dramatically and is likely to

---

TABLE 14–3   Changes in Consumer Costs

	Cost to the Consumer	
Cost Factor	*The Past*	*The Future*
Hardware	Very expensive.	Very expensive.
Economies of scale	Major in large systems; user stand-alones not feasible in most cases.	Limited in large systems; user stand-alones very attractive.
Software systems development	Expensive.	Less expensive in some cases.
Software acquisitions	Limited cost-effective outside opportunities.	Attractive cost-effective opportunites.
Development and production	Hard to estimate.	Hard to estimate.
Maintenance	Underestimated.	Soaring.

---

continue to drop significantly. On the other hand, progress in reducing the cost of software development is likely to continue to be slow for some time. On top of this, the ability to accurately estimate the development, production, and maintenance costs for large, high-technology, low-structure systems continues to be disappointing.

A critical component of cost explosion has been the steady increase in the cost of maintaining installed software. These expenses are usually not factored in carefully at the time of purchase, and they tend to grow exponentially as the business grows and changes over the years. In the short term these costs can be deferred with apparently little damage. In the long term, however, neglecting them can cause a virtual collapse of the product.

The proliferation of software houses and packages and the cost changes have accelerated the movement of the IT business into the distributor role. It is now cost-effective to purchase specialized databases and software that are useful to many users and that would be utterly uneconomic if developed by single users for their own purposes. Not all efforts in developing shared software have been successful, however. For example, a consortium of 25 regional banks funded a joint $13 million software development project (in areas such as demand deposit accounting and savings accounts). The consortium's inability to manage the project doomed it to failure. Another change is the growing number of users who have their own computer capacity. At some business schools 100 percent of the students and over 90 percent of the faculty own personal computers. The schools no longer own this equipment but facilitate its acquisition by the students and faculty.

As will be discussed in the section on pricing, it is difficult to identify potential or actual total costs for a particular product or service. In part this is because a particular data or software development may support multiple products and consumers. This generates concern as to whether costs should be treated as joint costs or by-product costs. Another complicating issue is the extent to which previously spent R&D costs (to get to today's skill levels) should be treated as part of a product's cost.

While cost management and control are a critical component of the IT business strategy, how they are executed varies significantly among IT settings. In high-growth, product-competitive environments there is less emphasis on IT efficiency and cost control than in environments where the IT products are more stable and competition is cost-based.

Implications for Marketing.   In summary, the changing cost structure of IT *products* has forced the IT *business* to reconsider its sourcing decisions and has pushed it to assume a much stronger distribution role. The relative emphases an IT business places on cost control, product-line growth, quality, and service depend on its business strategy. Thus wide variances exist.

Channels of Distribution

As described in Chapters 2, 7, and 8, the number of channels of distribution (to users) and their relative importance have been shifting rapidly. Table 14–4 shows some of the important changes in this domain. Historically, the major channel for both manufacturing and delivering the IT product has been the IT business itself; in most firms it has had a complete monopoly. Changing cost factors and shifts in user preferences have placed great pressure on this channel and have caused deep concern inside the IT business as it has tried to adapt to the new challenges of a competitive market—which it cannot totally serve in a cost-effective fashion from its manufacturing facility. Adapting to a new mission, the IT business is now *not* the sole channel but, rather, one of many sources of manufacturing, and it has assumed the major new role of identifying products in other channels and assessing their cost, quality, and other aspects. Adapting to this new role has made many IT businesses very uncomfortable psychologically as they have struggled with such incorrect notions of loss of power.

Risks in Using New Channels.   Successful, rapid adaptation by the IT business is critical to the health of its present and future consumers. The new channels, while offering very attractive products and cost structures, introduce sizable risks in many cases. The most important of these risks include:

TABLE 14–4   Changes in the IT Channels of Distribution

Distribution Factor	The Past	The Future
Development by central IT	Heavy.	Significant but smaller percent of total.
Direct purchase of hardware/software by user	Limited.	Major.
Service source for individual user	Limited to service from large, shared system.	Can obtain powerful independent system.
Service bureaus	Sell time.	Sell products and time bundled together.
Use of external databases via time-sharing	Limited.	Major.
Number of software and processing services	A few; crude.	Many.
Software development by users	Limited.	Major (facilitated by packages and user-friendly languages).
Reliance on external contract analysts/programmers	Very significant.	More significant; full outsourcing is a real alternative.

1. Misassessment of the real development and operations costs of the products in the channel. Important short-term and, more important, long-term cost factors may be completely overlooked.
2. Consumer vulnerability to abuse of data by failure to control access, install documentation procedures, and implement data disciplines.
3. Financial vulnerability of the supplier. If there is a possibility of failure, the consumer's fundamental interests need to be protected in some way.
4. Obsolescence of products. If the supplier is not likely to keep the products modernized (at some suitable cost) for the consumer over the years, alternatives (if they are important) should be available. (Obviously, a financial-transaction processing system may be more vulnerable to obsolescence than a decision support model.)

Considerable marketing and internal adjustment of perspectives are needed by the IT business if its consumers are to feel that they can rely on the IT staff to evaluate alternate channels objectively—instead of pushing their own manufacturing facility at every opportunity. A long-term solution will develop knowledgeable consumers. Failure to execute this mission will ultimately cripple the IT business's effectiveness in servicing its customers' needs. This will occur through fragmentation of data needed by many consumers, redundant development efforts, and an increase in poorly conceived and managed local factories.

Competition

The IT-marketing-mix analogy is weakest in describing administrative practice and problems in the area of competition. The IT business faces two principal competitive obstacles:

1. Potential consumers independently seeking solutions without engaging the IT business in either its manufacturing or its distribution capacity.
2. Potential consumers failing to recognize that they have problems or opportunities that can be addressed by IT.

In the first case, competition arises because of poor performance of the IT business. Its inability to formulate and implement sensible, useful guidelines to assist consumers in their purchase decisions is a failure of IT to adapt its product line to meet the needs of the changing times. For the broad purposes of the firm it may be useful to run this aspect of the IT business as a loss leader. Loss of manufacturing business to other channels in a planned or managed way should not be seen as a competitive loss to the IT business, but simply as a restructuring of its product line to meet changing consumer needs. One of the most successful IT businesses the authors have seen has recently halved its central IT manufacturing capacity. It has created in its place a series of small manufacturing centers near major clusters of users (at divisional headquarters). These systems include an explosion of stand-alone office support systems with all phases of the systems life cycle except the construction phase under user control.

With regard to the second case, competition—really the cost of delayed market opportunity—arises as a result of ineffective management of price, product, or distribution policies and results in consumers in an imperfect market allocating funds to projects that may have less payoff than IT products. The IT business has a monopoly responsibility: sometimes it produces a product; other times it stimulates consumer awareness of appropriate external sources of supply. The notion of aggressive external competition hurting the IT business through pricing, product innovation, and creative distribution is not appropriate in this setting.

Promotion

The rapid changes in information technology and the turnover in consumers make promotion one of the most important elements of the marketing mix to manage. This is because, unlike the previously discussed elements, it is largely within the control of IT management. Phase-2 learning by consumers is at the core of a successful IT business. Even as today's mature technologies are being delivered to consumers, a strong need exists to cultivate tomorrow's consumers by exposing them to tomorrow's products. Price discounts (introductory offers), branch offices (decentralized analysts), and a central IT sales force are key to making this happen.

A multinational electronics company, for example, has a 400-person central IT manufacturing facility near its corporate headquarters. Included in this staff are five international marketing representatives who constantly promote new IT products and services. Their job consists of preparing promotional material, organizing educational seminars, and making frequent trips to overseas units so as to develop and maintain close professional relationships with IT consumers. These relationships permit them to effectively disseminate services and to acquire insight into the performance of the existing products and the need for new products. This level of effort is regarded as absolutely essential to the IT business.

In large part the need to adapt is due to the recent shift in the industry. From the beginning of the industry to the late 1970s, the large information systems suppliers sold primarily to the IT managers. Most vendors that initially had a strong industrial marketing approach have now added a retail marketing one. Office-support and computer suppliers have not only opened retail stores; they also now sell directly to end users. This has forced the IT business to promote the validity of its guidelines within the firm to protect its firm's users from disasters.

A number of IT businesses have organized both their development and production control activities around market structure, as opposed to manufacturing technology. In other words, rather than a traditional development group, a programming group, and a maintenance group, they have assigned development staffs to specific clusters of consumers. This structure promotes close, long-term relationships and better understanding and action on operation problems as they arise.

The extreme of this approach was McGraw-Hill's 1984 corporate reorganization away from a media-oriented structure (newspaper, television, etc.) toward an end-customer structure, each unit of which can be served by a mix of media. Within these market units it is appropriate to fund specific integrating and liaison positions, as opposed to purely technical positions. This approach is critical, since as a result of past performance and poor marketing, the IT business may be in a weak competitive position compared to outside software companies with large marketing staffs. This large investment in promotion is often among the IT unit's most important expenditures and should be the last to be cut back.

IT newsletters containing announcements of new services and products—that is, advertising and promotional material—should be sent to key present and potential business consumers regularly. Similarly, IT can conduct a program of consumer educational seminars or classes and publicize appropriate external educational programs to assist the marketing effort. Complemented by appropriate sales calls, this can accelerate Phase-2 learning.

The ideal mix of these promotional tools varies widely by organizational setting. Just as industrial and consumer companies have very different promotion programs, so also should different IT units. The strategic relevance of products to consumers and the consumers' sophistication level and geographic location are some factors that affect appropriate promotion.

Price

The setting of IT prices—an emotional and rapidly changing process, as noted in Chapter 9—is a very important element in establishing a businesslike, professional relationship between the IT business and its consumers. Indeed, aggressive, marketing-oriented pricing policies legitimize the concept of the stand-alone IT business. Issues that make pricing complicated are discussed here.

Inefficient Market. Establishing rational, competitive criteria is complicated by several factors:

1. Product quality is largely hidden and is very elusive to all but the most sophisticated and meticulous consumer. Prices that on the surface appear to be widely disparate may actually be quite comparable.
2. Vendors differ in their goals, product mixes, and stability. A small vendor that is trying to buy into a market may offer a very attractive price in order to defuse questions about its financial viability.
3. Vendors may price a service as a by-product of some other necessary business. This can produce a more attractive price than a pricing system that attempts to charge each user a proportionate share of the full cost of the manufacturing operation. This explains the bargains available when in-house operations try to dispose of excess capacity in return for some "financial contribution." Long-term sta-

bility should be a concern to the consumer. (What if my output were to become the main product and the other consumer's output the by-product?)

4. Excess-capacity considerations may allow attractive short-term marginal prices. A variant of this is a bargain entry-level price to attract the consumer. Once captured, the customer is subjected to significantly higher prices. This pricing practice is particularly prevalent for large, internally developed telecommunications systems.

Introductory Offers.   To stimulate Phase-2 learning and long-term demand, deep discounts on early business are often appropriate. This can generate access to long-term profits at quite different price or cost structures.

Monopoly Issues.   Review and regulation of pricing decisions by senior management is sometimes needed because of IT's de facto monopoly position. Highly confidential data and databases needed by multiple users in geographically remote locations are examples of IT products that cannot be supplied by providers other than the firm's IT business. It is important that the prices of these services be appropriately regulated to prevent abuses.

"Unbundling."   The pricing strategy should incorporate two practices that are not widely used. The first is "unbundling" development, maintenance, operations, and special turnaround requirements into separate packages, each with its own price. Establishing these prices "at arm's length" in advance is critical in maintaining a professional relationship with the consumers. The IT business must negotiate the prices with as much care as outside software companies exercise in their negotiations with these consumers. This negotiation can be useful in educating users on the true costs of service.

The second desirable practice is making prices understandable to the consumers. This is accomplished by stating prices in *consumer* units such as price per number of report pages, per number of customer records, per invoice, and so on, rather than as utilization of such IT-resource units as CPU cycles and MIPS. The added risk (if any) of shocking a potential consumer with the facts of economic life tends to be more than offset by much better communication between the IT business and the consumer.

Profit.   A final pricing issue, which also strains the independent-business analogy, is the amount of emphasis that should be placed on showing a profit. In the short term (in some cases even for the long term), *should* an IT business make a profit, or even break even in some settings? IT businesses in firms where consumers need a lot of education and where much Phase-1 and -2 experimentation is needed may appropriately run at a deficit for a long time. This issue must be resolved before the pricing policy is established.

Establishing an appropriate IT pricing policy is one of the most complex pricing decisions made in industry. An appropriate resolution, critical to a healthy relationship with the IT consumer, weaves a course between monopolistic and genuine competitive issues, deals with imperfect markets, and resolves ambiguities concerning the role of profits.

THE ROLE OF THE BOARD OF DIRECTORS

A subject of general interest that first surfaced in Chapter 1 is the appropriate relationship of the firm's general management to the IT business. We find it useful to think of it as similar to the role of a board of directors in any business. (Many firms give this de facto recognition by creating an executive steering committee.) Viewing its role in this way, the key tasks of general management can be summarized as follows:

1. Appoint and continually assess the performance of the IT chief executive officer (normally a function of the nominating committee).
2. Assure that appropriate standards are in place and being adhered to. This includes the receipt and review of detailed reports on the subject from the IT auditor and a more cursory review by the firm's external auditors (normally a function of the audit committee).
3. Ensure that the board is constructed to provide overall guidance to the IT business from its various constituencies. Unlike the board of a publicly held firm, the IT board does not need a representation of lawyers, bankers, investment bankers, and so forth. It does need senior user managers who can and are willing to provide user perspective. (As the strategic importance of the IT business to the firm decreases, the level of these managers should also decrease.) At the same time, people from R&D and technology planning and production (people who have IT development and operations backgrounds) need to be present to ensure feasibility of suggestions.
4. Provide broad guidance for the strategic direction of the IT business, ensuring that comprehensive planning processes are present within the IT business and that the outputs of the planning processes fit the firm's strategic direction. Practically, the board will carry out this surveillance through a combination of:
   a. IT management presentations on market development, product planning, and financial plans.
   b. Review of summary documentation of overall direction.
   c. Formal and informal briefings by selected board members on how the IT business is supporting the firm's business needs.
   d. Request for and receipt of internal and external reviews of these issues as appropriate.

This definition of the board's role addresses the realities of the members' backgrounds and available time for this kind of work. Focusing on operational or technical detail is unlikely to be suitable or effective. In many settings periodic (every one to two years) education sessions for the board members have been useful for making them more comfortable in their responsibilities and for bringing them up to date on trends within the particular IT business and the IT industry in general.

THE ROLE OF THE IT CHIEF EXECUTIVE OFFICER

Historically a high-turnover job, the IT chief executive position is difficult and demanding, requiring a steadily shifting mix of skills over time. It is critical that the IT CEO:

1. Maintain board relationships personally. This includes keeping the board appropriately informed about major policy issues and problems and being fully responsive to their needs and concerns. A need for a strong link between the board and the customers exists that is not present in many other settings.

2. Ensure that the strategy-formulation processes evolves adequately and that appropriate detailed action programs are developed. As in any high-technology business, high-quality technical review of potential new technologies is absolutely essential. Its interpretation is crucial and may well lead to major changes in organization, product mix, and marketing strategy. Without aggressive CEO leadership, the forces of cultural inertia may cause the IT business to delay far too long.

3. Pay close attention to salary, personnel practices, and employee quality-of-life issues. The IT work force is far more mobile and difficult to replace than the firm's other employees.

4. Give high priority to manufacturing security, which is more important in an IT business than in most other businesses. A single, disgruntled employee can do a vast amount of damage that may go undetected for a long time.

5. Assure an appropriate management balance between the marketing, manufacturing, and control parts of the IT business. Of the three, marketing—in its broadest sense—is the one most often neglected. CEOs who have begun their careers in manufacturing and dealt with operating difficulties tend to be most sensitive to manufacturing issues. However, since their manufacturing experience was at a particular time with a particular mix of technology assimilation problems and a particular set of control responses, even their perspectives in these areas may not be appropriate for today's manufacturing challenges.

6. Develop an IT esprit de corps. A key factor of success in the IT business is the belief in IT's value to the firm. Senior IT managers must develop team spirit and lead their organizations into new ventures with enthusiasm. At the same time, they must earn the confidence of the board by exhibiting good judgment—not only taking risks but also making wise decisions on how to limit the market and when to forgo a useful technology. They must balance keeping abreast with reading the market's receptiveness accurately.

SUMMARY

This chapter has discussed several important complicating aspects of the IT business. Complex and shifting products, changing consumers, new channels of distribution, and evolving cost structures have forced a major reanalysis and redirection of IT's product offerings and marketing efforts. The changed marketing environment has forced significant changes in IT manufacturing, organization, control systems, and most fundamentally, in its perception of its strategic mission.

Ted Levitt's classic article, "Marketing Myopia"[2] best captures this idea. Levitt noted that the great growth industry of the 19th century—the railroads—languished because the owners and managers saw themselves in the *railroad* business, rather than the *transportation* business. The point here is that IT is not in the electronic-based computer, telecommunications, and office support business. Rather, it is in *the business of bringing a sustained stream of innovation in information technology to companies' operations and*, in many cases, *products*. Far too many people in the IT business myopically believe they are running a computer center! Failure to perceive and act on their broader role can lead to a collapse of their operations, loss of jobs, and great disservice to the customer base.

When IT is defined in this way, the dynamic, successful marketing mix for the 1990s suddenly snaps into focus. To rely on an existing product structure and attempt to devise more efficient ways to deliver the old technology within old organizational structures will certainly lead to dissolution of the IT business. The IT organization has been an agent of change for its customers for 30 years. The change agent itself also must change if it is to remain relevant.

---

[2]Theodore Levitt, "Marketing Myopia," *Harvard Business Review*, September–October 1975.

Annotated Bibliography

GENERAL MANAGEMENT LIBRARY FOR THE IT MANAGER

Ackoff, Russell L. *Creating the Corporate Future: Plan or Be Planned For.* New York: John Wiley & Sons, 1981.

An important book that provides a broad context for IT planning.

Anthony, Robert N. *The Management Control Function.* Boston, Mass.: Harvard Business School Press, 1988.

This book introduces the framework of operational control, management control, and strategic planning and has been a major contributor to thinking about the different areas of IT application and their different management problems.

Badaracco, Joseph L. Jr., *The Knowledge Link.* Boston, Mass.: Harvard Business School Press, 1991.

How firms cooperate to exchange information in order to capitalize on each other's knowledge.

Barabba, Vincent P., and Gerald Zaltman. *Hearing the Voice of the Market.* Boston, Mass.: Harvard Business School Press, 1991.

How to develop an inquisitive market program that develops competence in utilizing information.

Bartlett, Christopher A., and Sumantra Ghoshal. *Managing Across Borders: The Transnational Solution.* Boston, Mass.: Harvard Business School Press, 1991.

A succinct and mind-expanding discussion of the impact, true costs, and strategic value of computer systems and their notable future influence.

Bower, Joseph L. *Managing the Resource Allocation Process:—A Study of Corporate Planning and Investment.* Boston, Mass.: Division of Research, Harvard Business School Classics, 1986.

This in-depth analysis of corporate planning and capital budgeting provides critical insights relevant to both the role of steering committees and how IT planning can be done effectively.

Buzzell, Robert D., ed. *Marketing in an Electronic Age*. Boston, Mass.: Harvard Business School Press, 1985.

A series of essays on how information technology will impact the marketing function.

Clark, Kim B., and Takahiro Fujimoto. *Product Development Performance*. Boston, Mass.: Harvard Business School Press, 1991.

A descriptive analysis of European, Japanese, and U.S. automobile manufacturing to demonstrate the salient aspects of quality and timely manufacturing management.

Foulkes, Fred K. *Executive Compensation*. Boston, Mass.: Harvard Business School Press, 1991.

Thirty leading compensation consultants advise on effective programs.

Heskett, James L. *Managing in the Service Economy*. Boston, Mass.: Harvard Business School Press, 1986.

Practical advice on the issues in managing a service organization. Much of this advice translates directly to the IT resource.

Kimberly Miles and Associates. *The Organizational Life Cycle*. San Francisco: Jossey-Bass, 1981.

Reports, findings, and analyses of key issues concerning the creation, transformation, and decline of organizations.

Lawrence, Paul R., and Jay W. Lorsch. *Organization and Environment: Managing Integration and Differentiation*. Boston, Mass.: Harvard Business School Classics, 1986.

This classic presents the underlying thinking of the need for specialized departments and how they should interface with the rest of the organization. It is relevant for all IT organizational decisions.

Merchant, Kenneth A. *Control in Business Organizations*. Marshfield, Mass.: Pitman Publishing, 1986.

An excellent framework for thinking about contemporary management control issues.

Porter, Michael E. *Competitive Advantage: Creating and Sustaining Superior Performance*. New York: Free Press, 1985.

The comprehensive text on how to identify and achieve competitive advantage.

Porter, Michael E., ed. *Competition in Global Industries*. Boston, Mass.: Harvard Business School Press, 1986.

A series of articles relating to competitive issues in the international environment.

Schein, Edgar H. *Organizational Psychology,* 3rd ed. Englewood Cliffs, N.J.: Prentice-Hall, 1980.

This classic book on the field focuses on how to manage the tension between the individual and the organization.

IT LIBRARY FOR THE GENERAL MANAGER

Anderla, Georges, and Anthony Dunning. *Computer Strategies: 1990–1999: Technologies Costs Market.* New York: John Wiley & Sons, 1987.

A description of the Japanese chip-maker strategy and the economic implications of chip development, and the true "costs" of computing in the 1990s.

Bradley, Stephen P., and Jerry A. Hausman., eds. *Future Competition in Telecommunications.* Boston, Mass.: Harvard Business School Press, 1989.

A symposium of industry suppliers, customers, and regulators discussing the future impacts of deregulation.

Heskett, James L. *Managing in the Service Economy.* Boston, Mass.: Harvard Business School Press, 1986.

An analysis and set of examples of leading service companies from hospitals to transportation firms.

Itami, Hiroyuki, with Thomas W. Roehl. *Mobilizing Invisible Assets.* Cambridge, Mass.: Harvard University Press, 1987.

A description of how the Japanese organization brings experience and analysis to bear in developing and implementing strategy.

Keen, Peter G.W. *Every Manager's Guide to Information Technology.* Boston, Mass.: Harvard Business School Press, 1991.

A glossary of key terms and concepts of computer and planning procedures.

Keen, Peter G.W. *Shaping the Future: Business Design through Information Technology.* Boston, Mass.: Harvard Business School Press, 1991.

A succinct and mind-expanding discussion of the impact, true costs, and strategic value of computer systems and their notable future influence.

Leebaert, Derek, ed. *Technology 2001: The Future of Computing and Communications.* Cambridge, Mass.: MIT Press, 1991.

A set of articles by research scientists from every major player in the business, e.g., IBM, DEC, Cray, Apple, etc. A sound view of the future.

Rochester, Jack B., and John Gantz. *The Naked Computer.* New York: William Morrow and Company, Inc., 1983.

An interesting and broad compendium of computer lore that has shaped the myths and realities of developing and using computer systems.

Walton, Richard E. *Technology and the Organization.* Boston, Mass.: Harvard Business School Press, 1989.

A thoughtful perspective on how to develop and maintain congruence between the organization and systems in the implementation of an IT-based strategy by a leading organizational scholar/consultant.

Zuboff, Shoshana. *In the Age of the Smart Machine.* New York: Basic Books, 1988.

An insightful integration of the dual nature of the influence of computer-based systems on a working group and discussion of how best to manage to create a learning organization.

Index of Cases

Index

A